Penal Systems
A Comparative Approach

Michael Cavadino and James Dignan

With Don Anspach, Robert Cario, Frieder Dünkel,
Raimo Lahti, Tadashi Moriyama, Vania Patané, John Pratt,
Wim Valkenburg, Dirk van Zyl Smit, Hanns von Hofer
and Andrew McLean Williams

SAGE Publications
London ● Thousand Oaks ● New Delhi

First published 2006
Reprinted 2006 (twice)

SAGE Publications Ltd
1 Oliver's Yard
55 City Road
London EC1Y 1SP

SAGE Publications Inc.
2455 Teller Road
Thousand Oaks, California 91320

SAGE Publications India Pvt Ltd
B-42, Panchsheel Enclave
Post Box 4109
New Delhi 110 017

British Library Cataloguing in Publication data

A catalogue record for this book is available
from the British Library

ISBN-10: 0-7619-5202-0   ISBN-13: 978-0-7619-5202-2
ISBN-10: 0-7619-5203-9   ISBN-13: 978-0-7619-5203-9 (pbk)

Library of Congress Control Number available

Typeset by C&M Digitals (P) Ltd., Chennai, India
Printed on paper from sustainable resources
Printed and bound in Great Britain by Athenaeum Press, Gateshead

Contents

List of associate authors

Australia – Andrew McLean Williams (formerly Griffith University, Queensland)
Finland – Raimo Lahti (University of Helsinki) (assisted by Perttu Puro)
France – Robert Cario (Université de Pau et des Pays de l'Adour)
Germany – Frieder Dünkel (Ernst-Moritz-Arndt-Universität, Greifswald)
Italy – Vania Patané (Universität degli Studi di Catania)
Japan – Tadashi Moriyama (University of Takushoku)
Netherlands – Wim Valkenburg (Universität van Tilburg)
New Zealand – John Pratt (Victoria University of Wellington)
South Africa – Dirk van Zyl Smit (University of Nottingham and University of Cape Town)
Sweden – Hanns von Hofer (Stockholms Universitet)
USA – Don Anspach (University of Southern Maine)

Foreword

by David Downes

The comparative study of crime and punishment, which languished for much of the past century, underwent a marked revival over the past two decades. The case for comparative method is overwhelmingly strong. Robust, commonsensical beliefs, such as that capital punishment 'obviously' deters people from murder, can only be tested and, in this case, found to be hugely misconceived, by painstaking contrasts over time and between different societies. But the pitfalls facing comparative study are immense, and help to account for its relative rarity. Gathering data about different societies, with their varying languages, cultures, and institutional structures, is far more complex than focusing on one society alone, difficult as that may be. It is all too easy for comparative projects to run into the sand, gathering mountains of data with no clear basis for their analysis, or falling prey to 'criminological tourism', a resort to superficial indicators of what is going on in crime and punishment terms in a range of societies. And some 'comparative' studies do not really compare but merely collect together singular and largely unrelated studies of crime and punishment in different societies. These may be valuable in their own right, but they do not add up to more than the sum of their parts. This is precisely what the present authors *have* achieved. In surmounting these pitfalls, they demonstrate how the promise of comparative penology can be fulfilled.

Mick Cavadino and James Dignan deal successfully with these pitfalls by several key methods. They have evolved from the work of their predecessors, not least Rusche and Kirchheimer (1939), a broad theory of the likely links between criminal justice policies and penal systems, on the one hand, and the nature of a society's political economy, on the other. They weigh this perspective against a selected range of societies, at least one from each continent, avoiding ethnocentrism by working with colleagues who are leading experts in the field in the societies concerned. They thus maintain a common authorial voice, allow for diverse opinions about the interpretation of key developments, but do not 'lose the plot'. They also gain greatly from the inter-disciplinary character of their work. Their typology of political economy is highly informed by recent work in comparative social policy. Overall, the book is knitted together, despite the wealth of meticulous detail, by a style which conveys complex ideas and analysis with fluency and apparent ease.

All in all, this is a major, and should prove a seminal book, providing a template for the analysis of penal policy and political economy, which in future could be fruitfully extended both to other societies and to changes in those studied here. It could hardly be more timely, as penal policy in the USA at least is now a factor in international relations. The 2000 presidential election pivoted on the results in Florida, which were crucially influenced for Bush and against Gore by the huge numbers of pro-Democrat black and hispanic constituents denied the chance to vote by penal and felon disenfranchisement.

For the first time since the transportation of prisoners came to an end, penal policy is no longer a purely domestic affair, but a field that has ramifications for world politics. It is also now so big a factor that domestically it has become a force for changing the political economy rather than simply being a peripheral outcome. The relation has become a two-way, interactive process, as the authors stress, with the prison budget severely denting those for health and education in states such as California.

It would be all too easy, given this scale of penal increase in the world's most powerful nation, to end on an apocalyptic note. And it is indeed a key question as to whether the USA is a harbinger or an outlier in terms of penal futures for societies which have traditionally embraced far more sparing penal policies, practices and regimes. Cavadino and Dignan resist that lure. They are rightly measured and judicious in their predictions, all too aware of the dangers of mass imprisonment but also of the scope for resistance and reform. Some societies, Sweden, Finland and Japan, for example, despite recent increases in their prison population, and despite their chapter on Japan being an eye-opener for those who thought its low crime and imprisonment rate stemmed from 'reintegrative shaming', present a very different set of possibilities. It is for its attention to the peculiar character of each country's penal culture, which is replete with fascinating variations, as well as for its analysis of over-arching trends, that this book should command a close reading and a wide readership.

David Downes
Mannheim Centre for Criminology and Criminal Justice
London School of Economics

January 2005

Preface

The nature of this book

Most comparative penology books to date have fallen into one of two categories. Some (for example, Muncie and Sparks, 1991; Vagg, 1994) cover a relatively limited subject such as imprisonment. Others contain separate chapters from different authors in a range of countries, with the result that (to caricature somewhat) a chapter on parole in Poland might be followed by one on imprisonment in Indonesia or community service in Colombia. In less common vein, van Kalmthout and Tak (1988) is a valuable but relatively atheoretical reference work on the details of different European criminal justice systems, while Downes (1988) is a comparison between just two systems (English and Dutch). Van Zyl Smit and Dünkel (2001) contains individually-authored reports from 26 countries plus a number of chapters by different authors on comparative aspects of imprisonment while Hamai et al. (1995) contains individually authored reports on probation in various countries. This book differs from all of these others. We present and analyse information from a wide variety of countries representing Western Europe (England and Wales, France, Germany, Italy, the Netherlands, Sweden and Finland), the non-European English-speaking world (USA, Australia and New Zealand), the fascinating but rather special case of South Africa, and a single representative of East Asia in the shape of Japan. We hope this width of coverage leads to some interesting comparisons without over-stretching the book hopelessly. However, apart from Japan, these are all broadly speaking 'Western' countries, and although we hope we have in places raised some interesting questions about the relationships between punishment in the 'West' and what happens in the varied areas of the 'East' we can only hope to scratch the surface of some of these broader issues.

Rather than having separate chapters relating to different countries by different authors, we have organized the book more thematically. Parts 1 and 4 attempt an overview of all the countries studied, while Part 3 contains five chapters about two specific aspects of penal theory and practice: youth justice and prison privatization. In these three parts, the comparisons between countries are drawn within each chapter, giving the reader a more synoptic and genuinely comparative vision of penality in different jurisdictions. Part 2 does admittedly contain nine chapters about the individual countries and the historical trends in their penality, but even this part is organized around the concept of 'penal crisis', with the aim of comparing the different countries' tendency to this prevalent malady.

The chapters have all been written by the two principal (English) authors (Cavadino and Dignan), our analysis being based on information supplied by our eleven associates in the other countries. The intended result is a work combining a certain level of theoretical depth with a degree of overall coherence which could be easily lost in a book with several authorial voices. (We have found to our gratification that our associates usually agree with our analyses and general outlook, but entire unanimity of viewpoint – let alone prose style – would be too much to hope for, unless we were all members of some disciplined international Marxist organization. Which, we hasten to add, we are not.) So we have included the occasional note of dissent from our associates where appropriate.

Most of the information was gathered by sending a series of questionnaires (six in total) to each associate, asking them all the same detailed questions about the penal systems with which they were familiar. Where necessary, the principal authors followed up subsequently with requests for further or more detailed information from individual countries or accessed information directly from internet sources. Preliminary analyses and drafts were submitted for comment to associates, and this book is the result. The principal authors are of course extremely grateful to all our associates for the wealth of fascinating information they submitted, only a fraction of which is directly used in this book. (Where information about a penal system is unattributed, it was as likely as not provided by one of our contributors. Unless it's wrong, in which case we probably just imagined it.) Cavadino and Dignan take responsibility for the facts, interpretations and values expressed in this book.

This book is designed to complement our textbook on the penal system of England and Wales (Cavadino and Dignan, 2002); we have tried to minimize the degree of repetition between the two volumes while cross-referring to the other as appropriate.

Some words of explanation, and an explanation of some words

There are various words and concepts which we will be applying repeatedly throughout this book, and it seems helpful to explain some of them here. Not, however, the vital distinction between different types of modern state – *neo-liberal, conservative corporatist, social democratic* and *oriental corporatist,* for whose definitions the reader must wait until Chapter 1.

Penal philosophies and penal aims

Penal philosophies, or philosophies of punishment, are ideas about what might morally justify practices of punishment. Typically such philosophies also indicate the *aims* that a morally justified practice of punishment should pursue (and perhaps, should actually achieve if the punishment is to be justified.) (See Cavadino and Dignan, 2002: Chapter 2 for an introduction to penal philosophy.) Such aims include the prevention or reduction of crime through deterrence of offenders and potential offenders and the 'incapacitation' of offenders by physically preventing their reoffending through such means as imprisonment. Punishment can also seek to reduce crime by denouncing the offence and sending out moral messages as to the wrongfulness of the offence, and by reforming or (a near-synonym) rehabilitating the offender. We shall at times be distinguishing between *reform* and *resocialization* – both of these if successful should lead to an offender ceasing to offend, but the latter is conceived of as a more social process, in which society as a whole plays an important part. (The terms 'welfare model' and 'penal welfarism' also refer to this rehabilitationist approach.) On the other hand, the *retributivist* philosophy of punishment seeks not to reduce crime so much as to ensure that offenders receive their 'just deserts' in terms of suffering in return for the wrong they have done. One important school of retributivist thought is the *'justice model'* with its emphasis on due process and the need for proportionality in punishment, which has influenced penal thinking since the early 1970s. Finally, the approach known as *restorative justice* seeks to ensure that offenders perform reparation to their victims and to the community, that relations are restored and that offenders are reintegrated into the community.

The word *'positivism'* refers to the theory that criminal behaviour is determined by forces (such as genetic predisposition, upbringing and social situation) beyond the control and responsibility of the individual offender, whose crimes are not therefore seen as resulting from an exercise of free will. Consequently, offenders should not be blamed or given their supposed 'just deserts' but given treatment that will reform them, while if necessary incapacitating them from committing crimes for the time being. The contrary approach, *classicism*, holds the opposite: that offenders are and may be held responsible for their crimes and visited with retributive and/or deterrent punishments.

Penal strategies and approaches

The penal *strategies* that governments and policymakers might pursue are related to these penal philosophies, but not as neatly as one might suppose (see Cavadino and Dignan, 2002: 53–4). With Iain Crow, we have developed a threefold typology of penal strategies (Cavadino et al., 1999). *Strategy A* is an extremely harsh and punitive approach influenced by 'law and order ideology' (Cavadino and Dignan, 1997) or 'populist punitiveness' (Bottoms, 1995), which involves punishing offenders as severely as possible. *Strategy B* represents the application of modern *managerialism* to punishment to attempt to make the criminal justice system as effective, efficient and economical as possible. *Strategy C* seeks to protect and uphold the *human rights* of individuals, including offenders, victims and potential victims of crime. This approach has several variants, since there has been (and remains) a wide range of views and schools of thought about what it should mean to respect human rights and to be humane in the penal context. Some proponents of Strategy C favour measures to reform and resocialize offenders; others favour restorative justice; still others propound the retributivist 'justice model' approach as the best way to safeguard human rights.

A slightly different but related typology of approaches to punishment (or 'models') is one which we shall make particular use of in Chapters 12 to 15. This distinguishes between the *welfare, justice, minimum intervention, restorative justice* and *neo-correctionalist* models. The justice and restorative justice models have already been briefly explained, and we shall expand on the minimum intervention model (and indeed, all the others) in Chapter 12 in the context of youth justice. The 'welfare model' is a version of 'positivism' (see above), which stresses the importance of taking action which will be for the benefit of offenders and which will ensure their reform or resocialization.

'*Neo-correctionalism*' is a broad term, which we use to characterize an approach that has been increasingly adopted in many countries in recent decades; sometimes almost to the exclusion of others. This approach embodies the uncompromising punitiveness of Strategy A (see above), and is put forward, in particular by increasingly influential right-wing commentators and politicians, as the real answer to problems of law and order. Sometimes the harshness of Strategy A is relatively unalloyed by any other approach – simple harshness, and in particular a growing reliance on the sanction of imprisonment, is seen as the answer to crime. Sometimes this 'toughness' is combined with the managerialism of Strategy B, to produce an approach we have called 'punitive managerialism' (Cavadino et al., 1999: 54).

We should also indicate and explain a general dimension that encapsulates many of the detailed differences between philosophies, strategies and approaches. '*Exclusive*' or '*exclusionary*' approaches deal with offenders by rejecting them as members of the community and shutting them out of mainstream society by measures such as imprisonment or by stigmatizing them. The exclusionary approach favours punishments such as imprisonment (or even the extreme exclusion of the death penalty), and is allied to Strategy A and to notions of deterrence, incapacitation and an illiberal version of retributivism. The '*inclusive*' or '*inclusionary*' approach, on the other hand, seeks to maintain offenders within the community and reintegrate them into mainstream society. It can be found embodied in notions and practices of reform, resocialization, restorative justice and more liberal versions of retributivism (such as the 'justice model'). (See further Cavadino et al., 1999: 48–50; see also Sanders, 2002).

Penality: harsh and lenient

We use the word *'penality'*, in accordance with established academic usage, to refer not only to the practice of punishment but also to *ideas* and discourse about punishment.

Finally, a word of explanation prompted by the horrified reaction of our Swedish associate Hanns von Hofer when we suggested entitling the section on Sweden and Finland 'Nordic Social Democratic Leniency'. When we use words like *'harsh'* and *'lenient'* in relation to punishment we mean them relatively and neutrally. That is, what we call a 'harsh' or 'lenient' punishment is one which is *more* harsh or lenient than what is usually found, and does not necessarily mean that we approve or disapprove. Our general opinion, however – as those who know us are well aware – is that a great deal less 'harshness' and a great deal more 'leniency' would not go amiss in any of the countries we study in this book, for reasons we have explained elsewhere (Cavadino and Dignan, 2002: Chapter 2; Cavadino et al., 1999: Chapter 2).

Acknowledgements

As well as our associate authors, thanks are also due to Anton van Kalmthout (Netherlands) and David Moore (Australia), who helped get our research on their countries off the ground, to Yasu Watanabe, who provided additional feedback in relation to Japan, and to David Downes, David Greenberg, Julian Roberts and Tony Bottoms.

And, of course and as ever, to Lucille Cavadino and Angela Dignan for their love and support.

Part 1

ABOUT COMPARATIVE PENOLOGY

1

Introducing
Comparative Penology

This book was largely prompted by the uneasy feeling that understanding the international dimensions of punishment is on the one hand increasingly vital for the student of penology, and on the other hand inherently problematic.

It is increasingly vital for a number of reasons. Firstly, because developments in penal ideas and practices are flitting ever faster around the globe like epidemics of Asian (or more often American) influenza. Whatever one takes to be the nature of 'globalization', this is partly because of the accelerating international velocity of both information and people in the late modern age, and partly because of the increasing activity of multinational agencies such as intergovernmental bodies and large capitalist corporations. We need to understand all this if we are to comprehend the directions in which punishment in any country has been developing and is likely to go in the future. And this is the case whether we approve of these trends or not. Comparative study can serve to elucidate which trends are likely to spread pretty well inexorably, because they are linked to other economic and social developments common to many countries, and which ones might fail to catch on, or be successfully resisted. In Part 2, for example, we investigate the apparent absence of a penal crisis centred on a drastically high prison population in countries such as Finland and Japan, contrary to the general picture which has been developing in English-speaking countries and much of the rest of Europe. We need to understand both *commonalities and discontinuities* between countries, and the reasons for them, if we are to make sense of penality generally, analyse it and engage with it.

Comparative knowledge is not only a requisite in academic discourse, but also in the realm of penal political debate. It is, of course, one of the commonest tricks in the book when advocating or criticizing any social policy to declare (whether accurately or otherwise, but usually in the hope that one's opponents are insufficiently knowledgeable to contradict you) that they do things so much better/worse in Ruritania. But it remains of real importance to know how they do things elsewhere and what effects different policies do have, even if only for the purpose of participating in arguments about whether 'three strikes and you're out' penalties are efficient in reducing crime in the USA[1] or whether Sweden's experiences with electronic tagging should encourage us to follow their example. Indeed, the realm of political discourse is more vital than ever. As icy trade winds of punitive law and order ideology seemingly sweep the globe, we need to hold fast to the recognition that things can be done differently to the dictates of the current gurus of penal fashion.

Is comparative penology possible?

But all this is inherently problematic. Is it possible to compare different penal systems at all? How do we begin to think about and explain the differences and similarities which are apparent between penal systems in countries with widely differing cultures, traditions, political and economic systems, histories and crime patterns? Is there even such a thing as a single entity of 'punishment' or 'penality' that exists in all societies, and if so how is it to be conceptualized? Can any of the existing theoretical frameworks cope with the diversity of penal systems in a wide range of societies?

We discuss some of these deep theoretical issues in due course. But at a less profound level, there are also pervasively knotty methodological problems involved in international comparison-making. Even when dealing with supposedly 'hard' statistical data, how sure can we be (for instance) that the meaning of a category such as 'property offender' or 'remand in custody' is even roughly consistent between countries; let alone that the number of people in each category is computed in a similar manner in different systems? Knowing as we do that practices of recording of crimes and clear-ups can vary alarmingly between adjacent police stations in a single country, the only honest answer is that we can never be at all sure. In many, perhaps most cases we can on the contrary be fairly certain that supposedly comparative figures never really comparing like with like. To some extent these problems are intractable, so that any such statistics in this book must be taken with at least a pinch of low-sodium salt. Nevertheless, if we do not attempt to use too fine a brush, we still think it is valid to point to, for example, the 2002 difference between Finland's 70 prisoners per 100,000 population with the USA's 701 (Walmsley, 2003b) as demonstrating some significant discontinuity between penal practices in these two countries.

One particular issue here concerns the standard measure of 'punitiveness' that we employed in the previous paragraph. This is the 'imprisonment rate' of a country, by which is meant the number of prisoners in a country expressed as a proportion of its total population (usually the number of prisoners per 100,000 general population). It has been argued, most strenuously and cogently by Ken Pease (1991, 1992, 1994), that it is a cardinal error to use this 'imprisonment rate' as a general index of how harshly each country punishes offenders. Such a crude measure, Pease argues, ignores vital factors such as differing crime and conviction rates and may severely distort the ways in which countries respond to crime in relation to each other.

We fully accept that 'imprisonment rate' is a highly imperfect and in many ways unsatisfactory statistic to use. Unfortunately, it is often the best available. And this is not only because it is the one most commonly and easily calculated and promulgated on a comparative basis. Alternative measures – such as numbers in prison as a proportion of crimes officially recorded, or prison population per number of criminal convictions – might in theory seem preferable, but suffer from their own drawbacks. The official recording of crimes reported to the police is notoriously unreliable and variable even within the same jurisdiction,[2] let alone across national frontiers; and even before that there is every reason to believe that the proportion of crimes that are reported to the police in the first place is also likely to vary widely. Concentrating on criminal convictions will distort matters because it leads us to ignore the differing ways in which minor offenders in particular are dealt with from country to country. In some countries, police or prosecutors may discontinue cases or in effect levy a fine as a functional equivalent to what elsewhere would result in prosecution, conviction and a lesser court sentence. If so, a 'prisoners per conviction' statistic would be likely to make such a country appear much more punitive than it really is, since a much higher proportion of court convictions would lead to prison rather than a minor disposal such as a fine, these lesser cases having been kept out of the court's caseload in the first place.

Ideally, when we are assessing a country's relative punitiveness we should try to compare the penalties it inflicts (and the other penal-related and procedural decisions it makes) upon similar offenders at similar stages of the criminal and penal process. Strangely enough, when this has been attempted at the crucial stage of sentencing of offenders convicted of similar offences, the rank ordering of countries' punitiveness tends to come out looking very much like the ordering produced by the crude 'imprisonment rate' statistic (NACRO, 1999; Pease, 1992; cf. Cavadino and Dignan, 2002: 110–11). This suggests – fortunately for our purposes – that with all the caveats issued above, it may be valid to use the imprisonment rate as at least a rough and initial measure with which to compare the punitiveness of countries, or to trace trends in punitiveness in individual jurisdictions over time.

Theorizing comparative penology

Both common sense and rational theorizing suggest that comparative penology is actually possible – although, as we have already indicated, we need to take care when doing it. To begin with, we *can* validly speak of an entity of 'punishment' in any society. It is not necessary to be a thoroughgoing functionalist in social theory to hold that in any human society it must be the case – almost by definition – that there will be deviant actions and that any society will require some system for responding to and sanctioning at least certain kinds of deviance. And this will be the case whether the society is simple or complex, early capitalist or late modern, Western or Eastern, or whatever.[3] This is a fairly minimal proposition. It does not mean, for example, that every society needs formal, official punishment institutions regulated by law; so it allows for the existence of non-legal punishment in simple societies and even for possibilities such as the stateless communist society ultimately envisaged by Lenin (1965) in which anti-social acts are prevented by spontaneous informal action by the community. But it does mean that every society needs punishment – or at the very least some functional equivalent – if it is to survive as a society. Societies organized along different lines will diverge to some extent in the social rules that are vital to maintain their diverse social orders, as well as in the precise methods of social control employed. But, as famously argued by H.L.A. Hart (1961: Chapter IX), in any society there must be a 'minimum content of natural law', with at least some effective rules governing the use of violence on the one hand and of scarce resources on the other.

We can go further than this. In general, we might expect societies which are similar in other ways – in their economies, cultures, languages and politics – also to resemble each other in penality, although we should perhaps be prepared for a few surprises and anomalies. Thus, for example, we have developed a typology of late-modern capitalist societies (based on that of Esping-Andersen, 1990) to distinguish between the countries in our study and to relate these differences in political economy to penal differences. And we have found in general – to give away and summarize what is perhaps our main finding in this research – that countries with a similar profile in terms of this typology do indeed tend to resemble each other in the penal realm.

In some important respects, all the societies discussed in this book – with the notable exception of Japan – are extremely similar. They are all 'Western', developed, industrial democracies (albeit that universal suffrage has of course only just arrived in South Africa, and the Eastern part of Germany only recently joined the club of Western democracy) at the beginning of the twenty-first century. All of them seem to be societies that can be analysed in terms of the 'radical pluralist' theory of society, which we sketch out both below and elsewhere (Cavadino and Dignan, 2002: Chapter 3). So it will not be surprising to discover a high level of commonality in punishment among these countries compared with societies of more widely varying types. We should expect this commonality to be pre-existing even before any convergence was brought about by the 'globalization' that is generally reckoned to be a special characteristic of the late twentieth and early twenty-first centuries.

This is certainly borne out in respect of the role of the 'rule of law' in penality. One unifying dimension of Western democracies is, in the words of our Australian contributor Andrew McLean Williams, 'the broad acceptance of the law as a mechanism for social ordering and dispute resolution. This applies in both the common law legal tradition, and in countries that have embraced the continental or Roman tradition'.[4] (Again, the South African case can be seen as something of an exception among our countries, given its extremely partial application of the rule of law doctrine in the apartheid era.) Associated with the rule of law is the still-evolving notion of human rights. It is implausible to see this as a mere accident of juristic or political culture; rather, the rule of law is an inherently desirable quality of the state in developed industrial human societies, necessary for providing a basic level of predictability and efficiency as well as legitimacy. It is a central component in the 'legal authority' that Weber (1968) saw as being, for good reasons, the characteristic form of authority in modern Western societies. One might add that much of the juristic and political cogence of individual 'human rights' can be seen as deriving from the individualization of culture associated with contemporary consumer capitalism.

Following these considerations further, we should expect the following pattern to be followed – barring the unlikely event of the state ultimately withering away as envisaged by Lenin, or of a Brave New World in which deviance is extirpated by total technological manipulation of the population. All developed societies in the late modern age and hereafter will not only have highly developed legalized systems of punishment, but ones which become increasingly complex, sophisticated and regulated. This would be in line with Weber's analysis, which suggests that the further development of bureaucracy and legal authority is concomitant with economic change and social modernization. Such changes are likely to happen in the same general direction (if not at an equally even pace) in more or less all the countries under scrutiny. Thus, to take just one example, we find that – unevenly, but pretty well unidirectionally – there is a growing tendency towards *managerialism* in criminal justice (Cavadino et al., 1999: 41–5, 212–13).

Our conceptualization of this process differs from that of one currently popular school of thought – notably propounded by Jonathan Simon (1993; Feeley and Simon, 1992; Simon and Feeley, 1995), but also by others including our New Zealand contributor John Pratt (2000a). This is the notion that some recent trends in penality (dubbed 'the new penology' by Feeley and Simon [1992]) indicate a transition from the 'modern' age of punishment into a coming era which some call 'postmodern' penality. Features of this new postmodern penology are said to include a burgeoning technocratic managerialism, abandonment of the 'modernist' project of diagnosing, treating and rehabilitating individual offenders ('the collapse of the rehabilitative ideal' or of 'penal welfarism'), a shift towards managing and controlling aggregate categories of deviants rather than individuals, a retreat from notions of individual rights, and the adoption of a diverse range of penal techniques both novel (such as electronic tagging) and 'premodern' (including informal and restorative justice). And, perhaps more salient than any other recent trend, *rising levels of imprisonment* in most countries.

While all these trends can indeed be discerned, we think that it adds little coherence to the picture simply to label them all 'postmodern' or 'new'. Along with David Garland (1995, 2001), we think all these developments are more comprehensibly conceptualized as facets of *a continuing process of modernization*, in line with the Weberian analysis already mentioned. We would prefer to talk, therefore, not of postmodern penality but of a penality of 'late' or 'high' modernity (Giddens, 1990) – or perhaps even (to borrow a term from an avant-garde school of chess players of the 1920s) *hypermodern penality*. Increased managerialism clearly fits this analysis; as does the deployment of new technology in the penal realm. More complex, however, is the relationship of modernization to harsher phenomena such as rising levels of punishment, the apparent decline of human rights discourse in the penal realm[5] and the resurgence of interest in 'premodern' modes of punishment.

Relevant here is the typology of 'penal strategies' we explained in the Preface: the harshly punitive Strategy A, the managerialist Strategy B and the human rights approach we call Strategy C. As already noted in the Preface, Strategy C has several variants, since there has been (and remains) a wide range of views and schools of thought about what it should mean to respect human rights and to be humane in the penal context. For much of the twentieth century it was assumed that humanitarianism necessitated pursuing the reform and rehabilitation of individual offenders: the 'welfare' or 'individualized treatment model'. From the 1970s onwards, by contrast, proponents of the 'justice model' school argued – on the contrary, and reverting to early Enlightenment thinking on the subject – that the treatment model violated human rights, which would be better served by giving offenders their 'just deserts' in the form of punishment proportionate to the severity of the crime. Yet another school advocates 'restorative justice', whereby positive measures (such as reparation) are taken to repair the relationships between offenders, victims and their communities.

The undeniable onward march of 'Strategy B' managerialism – perhaps the most powerful of all penal trends in the late twentieth century – is clearly a 'modernizing' one. The decline of individualized rehabilitation – and hence the near-demise of one version of Strategy C in such countries as the USA and the UK[6] – has been seen by some as a sign of 'postmodernism'. However, it can also be seen as a combination of, on the one hand, a development within modern human rights discourse (replacing one interpretation of human rights with others), and, on the other hand, a result of the *rationalizing* tendency of modernism. Rational research and auditing of penal techniques seemed to show that attempts to 'treat' offenders were in reality ineffective, inefficient and arbitrary – because it seemed that 'nothing worked' to reform criminals – while the attempt to do so by leaving them in the hands of supposed experts who had vast discretion over their treatment led to unacceptable disparity and waste of resources.[7] Tellingly, now that since the 1990s it has become the received managerialist wisdom in the UK that some things *do* work to some extent to reduce reconviction rates for the right kind of offender there has been a revival of official interest in rehabilitation as one strand within managerialist strategy. (Postmodernists might have difficulty explaining such an apparent lapse back into modernism.)

The rise of the harsh punitiveness of Strategy A since the early 1970s in many (but not all[8]) countries can also be seen as representing the eclipse of modernism in favour of postmodernism and/or 'regression to a stone-age morality' (as Stuart Hall (1980: 3) once put it – nicely, if without total historical accuracy). Conversely, it can be seen as another consequence of late modernity. In modern societies, traditional authority and traditional deference thereto crumble and need to be replaced by new legitimations for authority, which accord with the understandings of modern citizens. We have seen a general decline in public trust in and deference to their social 'betters', including politicians, judges and supposed experts in crime and punishment. One result has been a rise in 'the popularization of crime politics' (Simon and Feeley, 1995: 168), whereby politicians appeal over the heads of the experts and criminal justice practitioners to Ordinary Joe voters at the level of common sense rather than rely on knowledge imparted by experts. Since at present most people's common sense (falsely) tells them that a strategy of harsh punishments is likely to be effective in reducing crime rates – or at any rate this is what politicians believe most people think[9] – this is what politicians have been increasingly promising and delivering. (This could be conceptualized as a mechanism whereby the collective punitive sentiments of the populace are translated and expressed into punitive practices, as classically postulated by Émile Durkheim – see Cavadino and Dignan [2002: 71–4] – although we shall later be casting some doubt upon this.) The irrationalism of this development, with its appeals to emotion rather than to intellect, pulls strongly against the general rationalizing tendency of modernity. But it is nevertheless also a product of the same modernization of society; both ultimately spring from the decline of traditional authority and the search for new methods of legitimating authority in a modern age.

Something similar can be said about the reintroduction of elements of informal and restorative justice into penality. Paradoxically, one possible consequence of late modernity's quest for greater efficiency may be to recognize the limitations that are inherent in the bureaucratizing process, which fails to satisfy the personal needs of people for less formal relationships and interactions. Moreover, the intransigent fact remains that any social system (so far) is always held in being to a much greater extent by informal than by formal processes of social control. This leads, for example, to official interest (albeit often intermittent and uncomprehending) in *informal justice* – including forms of 'restorative justice', discussed further in Chapter 12 – which may be granted a licensed role within or alongside the formal criminal justice system.

Another prominent characteristic of late modern society is of course globalization. ('Modernity is inherently globalising' – Giddens [1990: 63].) If, as we suggest, it is true that the more societies resemble each other in other respects the more similar they will be in penality, does this mean that globalization is likely to bring about *penal convergence*, or even a homogenization of punishment across the world? To some extent this depends on what view is taken of globalization, the subject of the next section.

Globalization and penal convergence

A poll of Russian schoolchildren in the mid-1980s (presumably employing multiple choice questions) found that the majority of them believed Madonna to be the owner of the world's largest chain of burger restaurants. This illustrates at least four points about globalization[10] – its extent, its limitations, its overwhelmingly capitalist and commercial nature (linked to the transnationalization of capital) and the cultural and economic predominance of the USA.

To begin with, we need to bear in mind that 'globalization' has several different meanings and aspects that are not always synchronized. Firstly, and undeniably, there has been and continues to be a massive increase in the international flow of information, and also of people and products of all kinds. This has been associated with a burgeoning of international commerce and a world-wide onward march of free market ideology and practice, although we would not see such an association as an inevitable one. Aspects of culture – especially of politically and economically dominant cultures, pre-eminently the USA – have also been exported around the globe. But the progress of all of these 'globalizations' has been uneven, and in particular non-American cultures have remained in many ways stubbornly, even sometimes defiantly, non-American. For although globalization enables people to gain a greater awareness of others, how people choose to use such information will be influenced by their own local cultures. To put it simply, if banally, hardly anywhere is untouched by the ever more rapid movement of ideas, culture, products and people around the world, yet localities remain distinct and different. Not everyone in the world eats Disney-sponsored Big Macs while listening to Britney Spears on their iPods; and even for those who do, it is certainly possible to buy some of the products without buying the whole culture and philosophy they may be seen as representing. (Indeed, if anything sums up the supposedly postmodern consumer it could be this very pick-and-mix superficial eclecticism.)

This is as true in the realm of penality as it is true of globalization generally. There has certainly been an enormous increase in the international traffic of information about punishment, and much greater readiness to import ideas and practices from elsewhere. For example, even as recently as the 1970s it took several years before an American school of thought as influential as the 'justice model' started making much impact in England (Bottomley, 1980), whereas in the 1990s concepts such as 'three strikes and you're out' and 'zero tolerance' have made the same Atlantic crossing with considerably greater speed. And the same is true of practices such as electronic monitoring or tagging. But this increased swiftness of transit has hardly equalized US and English imprisonment rates (see Table 1.2 later in this chapter, and Chapters 3 and 4), let alone led to the reintroduction of capital punishment in Western Europe. Indeed, if the USA races ahead of the rest of the world as it so often does, this could well mean that the distance between them actually *increases* as other nations are pulled along in the American slipstream but with less velocity. We are still different countries. Moreover, in some countries national pride can provide incentives to *differentiate* oneself from the USA in certain respects rather than slavishly imitating in all things. It should follow, to answer the question posed at the end of the previous section, that while we are likely to see an acceleration of *penal convergence*, we are still a long way from global *homogenization of punishment*, which may never occur.

To the extent that 'penal globalization' does exist, its process and effects are uneven, but the influence of the USA undoubtedly retains predominance. For example, Andrew McLean Williams reports that 'Australian correctional practice closely parallels (particularly) American trends, to the extent that often unique aspects of the local system seem to be replaced with a generic product. Convergence may not even be the correct form of imagery (which suggests some kind of hybridized blending). Given the presence now in Australia of large American correctional companies, what we are seeing is more a kind of *correctional imperialism* than convergence, as American-style prison facilities are becoming the new uniform standard. At the same time, the politicization of correctional policy is following an American lead (i.e. "truth in sentencing"; "boot camps", "three strikes" legislation, and so on).'[11] Important players in this process are not only policy makers in government and lobbying governments, but increasingly, as McLean Williams indicates, commercial concerns (often American-based multinationals) who have a vested interest in the export sale of their penal products, giving rise to what has been nicely called 'a corrections-commercial complex' (Lilly and Knepper, 1992) between private corporations, government agencies and professional organizations. The economic power of American capitalism allies with American cultural dominance to ensure that the USA has a substantial balance of payments surplus in penal ideas and practices. As we shall see. But we shall also see countries taking a lead from nations other than the USA, especially from politicians who are viewed as successful. Thus, centre-left politicians in the Netherlands, Germany, Sweden, Australia and New Zealand have all to some extent copied the 'tough on crime, tough on the causes of crime' approach of Tony Blair and New Labour in the UK.

Finally we should mention the role of intergovernmental organizations and cooperation in fostering both globalization and indeed a degree of penal convergence (see Sim et al., 1995: 3–8). Although we detect as yet relatively little sign of such deliberate 'harmonization' between countries in the penal field, there are already some notable examples. Perhaps the most remarkable single instance has been the discontinuance of capital punishment in Russia brought about by Russia's desire to join the Council of Europe (which she did in 1996)[12] – interesting for several reasons, not the least being that this took Russia in a penal direction *opposite* to that of the USA. Similarly, the operation of the European Convention on Human Rights, to which Council of Europe countries must subscribe, has played a role in improving and harmonizing the rights of prisoners in European countries. Again this is interesting, partly because this development can be seen as an aspect of increasing modernization (not postmodernization) – being the application of an extrapolation of the modernist ideology of the rule of law – and partly because it in some respects runs counter to other international trends towards excluding offenders from the normal realms of citizenship. Conversely, we will also see examples where such harmonization and modernization threatens to flow in the opposite direction, such as the ending of the 'waiting list' system for Dutch prisons and the feared threats to Finland's lenient penality from the international harmonization of criminal justice policies (see Chapters 8 and 10). Clearly, the relationships between internationalization of penality and the actual directions that punishment may take as a result are by no means simple.

A radical pluralist analytical framework

We contend that, at least in the countries studied in this book, all this can be adequately conceptualized within the framework of what we call a 'radical pluralist' theory of society, which seeks to synthesize aspects of the Marxist, Durkhemian and Weberian traditions in sociology (Cavadino and Dignan, 2002: 76–9). Radical pluralism conceives of societies as containing a plurality of interest groups which contend to have power exerted in their favour. These interest groups *include* economic classes: it is in no way our intention to write class conflict out of the equation. Class (and race – and increasingly nationality – and gender) relations are critical to any adequate social analysis. The state[13] mediates this contest between groups, but not in an impartial manner, being inherently biased towards groups that already possess wealth, established power and status. The social world in which this all occurs, like any social realm (including penality), has material, cultural and ideological[14] components, which interact reciprocally. Whereas Marxism traditionally sees economics as the 'base' of society that ultimately determines the 'superstructure' containing the realms of ideology, politics and law, we do not believe that any one realm is 'basic': neither economics, culture nor ideology are the ultimate fundamental determinant of social reality.[15] However, the precise nature of the relationships between politics and economics, ideological and material

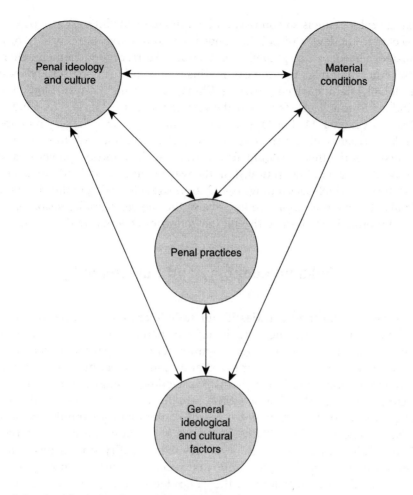

Figure 1.1 *A radical pluralist analytical framework*

factors, and the interplay between them, is likely to vary within different kinds of societies. A society's *penal* ideology and culture will be greatly shaped by (and to some extent will also shape) the more general ideology and culture of the society, as well as by its material conditions. Finally, penal practices will be influenced by both general and penal ideology and the culture and the material realm in which they operate, and will also have some reciprocal effect on these forces and factors. (This is presented diagrammatically – in greatly simplified form[16] – in Figure 1.1.)

We do not claim that the radical pluralist model as outlined above is an adequate framework for analysing all present-day human societies, let alone any societies that have been or might be. For example, the model clearly does not fit simple stateless societies. It is also unlikely that it could be made to fit totalitarian or colonized countries.[17] And there may well be large and important societies in which the ruling elite is so compact and dominant or the interest groups with any real access to the levers of political power are so few that the plurality of power postulated here does not prevail – and so on. We reserve judgement, therefore, over whether (and if so, to what extent) this framework can be usefully applied to such globally significant countries as China, the former Eastern bloc countries, and indeed to much of Africa and the rest of the Third World. (And indeed we shall see in Chapter 11 that Japan, where political power is largely monopolized by a relatively small elite, can be seen as a partial exception.) We think that a modified version of the theory should also work for such countries; power relations in these societies may not be 'pluralist' in the way we have described, but a similarly 'plural' theory, which sees a range of different and interacting realms in operation, could also be made to apply. In any event, the radical pluralist vision of society does seem broadly to characterize all the countries covered by this book.[18]

Political economy and punishment

Not, of course, that the countries in our sample are all the same. In particular, the relationship between the state, its citizens and interest groups differs significantly across these countries. Several attempts have been made to analyse the main differences in terms of their social and economic organization between different contemporary 'welfare capitalist'[19] societies (Esping-Andersen, 1990; Lash and Urry, 1987, 1994; Mishra, 1999). We have utilized these reflections to develop profiles of four different types of contemporary capitalist society (see also Dignan and Cavadino, 2003). These are depicted in the form of a typology in Table 1.1. The main aim of the typology is to identify similarities – in terms of their form of economic organization and social structure – that appear to characterize societies which belong to the same 'family grouping', and at the same time distinguish them from those belonging to different groupings. One of the central themes we will be exploring in this book is the expectation that societies which share the same type of social and economic organization (and cultural and ideological predilections) will also tend to resemble one another to some extent in terms of their penality. (It is perhaps not giving away too much of the plot at this stage to say that we do find this expectation satisfied.) We will also be examining the extent to which these material, cultural and ideological factors may help to explain differences in the forms of penality that are encountered in societies belonging to different 'family models'.[20]

The neo-liberal state

One ideal type of modern state (on the political right) is the *neo-liberal* state exemplified by the USA. We must immediately make it clear that the concept of

Table 1.1 *Typology of political economies and their penal tendencies*

Socio-economic and penal indices	Regime types			
	Neo-liberalism	Conservative corporatism	Social democratic corporatism	Oriental corporatism
Economic and social policy organization	Free market, minimalist or residual welfare state	Status-related, moderately generous welfare state	Universalistic, generous welfare state	Private sector based 'welfare corporatism'; bureaucratic, paternalistic
Income differentials	Extreme	Pronounced but not extreme	Relatively limited	Very limited
Status differentials	Formally egalitarian	Moderately hierarchical, based on traditional occupational rankings	Broadly egalitarian, only limited occupational status differentials	Markedly hierarchical, based on traditional patriarchal ranking
Citizen–state relations	Individualized, atomized, limited social rights	Conditional and moderate social rights	Relatively unconditional and generous social rights	Quasi-feudal corporatism; strong sense of duty
Social inclusivity/exclusivity	Pronounced tendency towards social exclusion, ghetto-formation, etc.	Some exclusion in form of limited participation in civil society for some	Very limited tendency towards 'social exclusion'	Alienation of 'outsiders', but otherwise little social exclusion
Political orientation	Right-wing	Centrist	Left-wing	Centre-right
Dominant penal ideology	'Law and order'	Rehabilitation	Rights-based	Apology-based restoration and rehabilitation
Mode of punishment	Exclusionary	Mixed	Inclusionary	Inclusionary
Imprisonment rate	High	Medium	Low	Low
Receptiveness to prison privatization	High	Moderate	Low	Low
Archetypal examples	USA	Germany	Sweden	Japan
Other examples	England and Wales, Australia, New Zealand, South Africa	France, Italy, the Netherlands	Finland	

'neo-liberalism' means something very different from – in fact, almost the opposite of – the standard meaning of the word 'liberal' when applied to American politics. 'Neo-liberalism' refers to the (politically conservative) late twentieth-century revival of the nineteenth-century approach of *economic* liberalism, based on free-market capitalism. Typically – though by no means universally – those who favour such arrangements tend to be politically less 'liberal' in other senses. Those usually thought of as 'political liberals' tend to favour greater social and personal liberty, but also a *greater* degree of government regulation of the economy including tax and welfare arrangements designed to minimize inequality and poverty. 'Liberals' such as these favour relatively high taxation, high levels of public spending, less material inequality and more regulated markets. 'Neo-liberalism', however, is the other way around: under economic neo-liberalism the welfare state is minimalist and residual. It is founded chiefly on the principle of means-tested welfare benefits, and any universalistic benefits that may have evolved – for example non-means tested pensions, health or unemployment benefits – are limited in scope and tend to be supplemented (by those who can afford them) by private pensions and health care insurance. Moreover, entitlement to benefit is often heavily stigmatized. Consequently, in comparison with the other groupings of states we will be examining, the status and economic well-being of citizens tends to be much more heavily dependent on the market in this type of society.

Although social relationships in neo-liberal societies are formally egalitarian, the strong commitment to market forces, which are only marginally attenuated by welfare payments, results in extremely marked (and currently still widening) income differentials. This material inequality – combined with a certain lack of social entitlements afforded to individuals as of right – results in the *social exclusion* of those who find themselves marginalized by the markets, particularly the labour market and the housing market (Lash and Urry, 1994: 156ff.). The term 'social exclusion' is not merely a synonym for poverty, but is used to refer to the denial of full and effective rights of citizenship in civil, political and social life.

There is a marked tendency in neo-liberal states for whole communities to experience the effects of social exclusion, one symptom of which is a withdrawal from the area of a variety of institutions, ranging from commodity markets (in the form of neighbourhood shops), employment markets (in the form of job opportunities), welfare state institutions and trade unions. To the extent that these institutions may have had a regulatory effect (whether in economic or social terms) their disappearance is likely to leave a normative vacuum. Moreover, the one remaining institution that has traditionally fulfilled an important informal social control function – the family – has itself been severely dislocated as a result of the economic and social changes brought about by the unmitigated effects of deindustrialization. In the USA, the phenomenon of social exclusion is most often discussed in terms of an emerging 'underclass', and is frequently associated with 'ghettos' of acute economic deprivation. It is also much more likely to be depicted as a racial and black phenomenon than is the case elsewhere, even in those parts of the world (for example, the UK) that have experienced a combination of relatively high levels of immigration by ethnically different peoples together with a comparable process of deindustrialization and concomitant increased levels of deprivation.

Among the countries that are featured in this book, the USA is the archetypal example of a neo-liberal society. The other 'Anglo-Saxon' nations (the UK, Australia and New Zealand) also feature in this group because – at least since the 1980s – the attenuated nature of the social rights that are conceded to their citizens also makes them highly dependent on the market for their status and well-being, and these countries have seen marked increases in material inequality with the introduction of free-market economic policies. However, as we shall see in Part 2, none of these countries can be regarded as *prime* examples of neo-liberalism, due to their having moved significantly in the direction of social democracy prior to the 1980s. South Africa can also be seen to be a non-archetypal example of neo-liberalism, although as we shall see its particular historical legacy has led to a very idiosyncratic and interesting amalgam of neo-liberal and social democratic corporatist elements (see Chapter 6).

The conservative corporatist welfare state

A second ideal type of modern society (in the political centre) is the conservative version of '*corporatism*' whose standard case is the Federal Republic of Germany. Under corporatism, in contrast to neo-liberalism, important national interest groups (notably and pre-eminently, organizations representing employers and workers) are integrated with the national state and granted a degree of control over those they represent on condition that this control is exercised in line with a consensual 'national interest'. In return, members of those national interest groups enjoy welfare benefits that are more generous than those associated with neo-liberal states. And perhaps more importantly, these benefits are enjoyed as *a social right* of a kind not recognized in the neo-liberal system. The overall philosophy and ethos of conservative corporatism is a *communitarian* one, which seeks to include and integrate all citizens within the nation, with individuals' membership of interest groups and other social groupings providing a vital link between the individual and the nation state.

The conservative corporatist model tends to generate significantly less inequality than does neo-liberalism; but it is not egalitarian since its welfare state enshrines and perpetuates traditional class and status divisions between different groups of citizens.[21] The system is based on a hierarchical ordering of occupational groups (with civil servants at the apex) whose members are subject to different regimes of social insurance. In comparison with neo-liberal states, conservative corporatist states offer their citizens somewhat greater protection against the vagaries of unbridled market forces; but the social rights they are willing to concede are nevertheless conditional on beneficiaries' observance of the reciprocal obligations (particularly with respect to employment and family) that are placed upon them.

Another typical feature of the conservative corporatist state is its strong support for, and reliance upon, other traditional institutions such as churches.[22] In Europe, the typical form of conservative corporatism has been 'Christian Democracy', based upon Christian moral values (including the Christian obligations to feed the hungry and take care of the sick), and predicated upon the assumed existence of a Christian community, and a Christian moral consensus, in the nation as a whole. In some countries (such as Italy) this has been founded upon a single church to which the great majority of the population traditionally belong, while in others (such as Germany, Belgium and the Netherlands) Christian Democracy has embraced more than one denomination.

Corporatism also relies heavily upon the traditional institution of the family, including expecting the family to discharge some of the welfare functions that might otherwise be undertaken by the state itself. One consequence has been the retention of a more traditional pattern of employment, which assumes a single (relatively highly paid) wage earner and a relatively low rate of participation by women in the labour force. Conversely, family benefits tend to encourage motherhood, and the state assumes a residual role in providing welfare support, which only comes into operation where the family is unable to cope.

Possibly as a result of these factors, conservative corporatist states appear to experience a rather different form of social exclusion from that associated with neo-liberal states. While the formation of ghettos and the development of a distinct 'underclass' appear to have been mostly avoided – although strains are now showing, as traditional ties between individuals, social groups and the state have been weakened – this may have been achieved at the expense of full participation in the labour market (and consequently in other aspects of civil, political and social life also) by women and many minority groups.

Although the Federal Republic of Germany is correctly acknowledged as the prime exemplar of the conservative corporatist approach, its position is nevertheless complicated by the strains imposed by the unification of West Germany with its previously Communist Eastern neighbour in 1990. Other countries featured in this book that have also experienced conservative social policies, particularly during the postwar period, include France and Italy. The Netherlands is more difficult to place within the typology, as we discuss at greater length in Chapter 8. Although we see the Netherlands as an essentially Christian Democratic country, in social policy terms (and in terms of punishment) it has for a long time had more in common with the Nordic social democratic model, which we describe next, although more recently it has moved with some swiftness in the direction of neo-liberalism (and of harsher penal policies).

Social democratic corporatism

A third arrangement (on the political left) is the 'social democratic'[23] version of corporatism – both more egalitarian and more secular than Christian

Democracy. The prime example is Sweden. Here, the wellsprings of social policy were lubricated by a powerful and unified trade union movement committed to the principle of 'universalism' and a willingness on the part of employers to accept high levels of investment in return for wage restraint by the unions. For its part, the state undertook a commitment to promote full employment, the pursuit of profit, the funding of generous welfare reforms, and an active labour market programme, which would seek to minimize the disruptive effects of deindustrialization and changes in economic conditions (for example by absorbing, retraining and moving redundant workers).

In terms of social policy, the approach has sought to combine corporatism with an egalitarian ethos and generous universalistic welfare benefits. Thus, all citizens are covered by the one universal insurance programme. Benefit levels are substantial, rather than being pegged at minimum rates, as elsewhere, though they are graduated according to accustomed earnings. This model goes furthest in acknowledging unrestricted rights of social citizenship, and also in assuming direct responsibility for the care of the very young, the elderly and the infirm. It appears to offer a high level of emancipation for all sectors of the community, but at the same time requires all who are capable to assume responsibility for themselves by working, since the cost to the state would otherwise be prohibitive. This is reflected in the much higher rate of female participation in the Swedish labour force (over 75 per cent of non-student females between the ages 16–64) compared with Germany (39 per cent, Lash and Urry, 1994: 182; see also Esping-Andersen, 1990: 208ff.).

The cluster of social democratic corporatist countries is comparatively small. Among the countries that are featured in this book, only Sweden and Finland qualify (although we shall see elements of social democracy in some other countries, such as the UK, Australia and New Zealand). In both Sweden and Finland, the adoption of relatively generous social security and income protections systems appear to have largely avoided any serious 'social exclusion' problems, despite a substantial increase in the number of people who are unemployed in recent decades.

The oriental corporatist state

The fourth and final ideal type is yet another variant of the corporatist approach – the oriental corporatist society found in Japan. (There may be no other countries which fit this model; certainly we know of no country quite like Japan.) While in many respects Japan appears to come within the family cluster of corporate welfare states, the social and political context in which this operates is so distinctive as to place it in a separate hybrid category that combines elements of a corporatist approach with those found in neo-liberal systems.

Japanese capitalism has been described (Hill, 1981) as a form of bureaucratized corporate paternalism, which embodies a number of distinctive features. These include a high degree of occupational security (sometimes characterized as 'employment for life') and a hierarchical but progressive career structure. The latter ensures that wages and a wide range of other occupational benefits (such as company housing and medical, educational and leisure facilities) are related to an employee's age and increasing social responsibilities (including family commitments) rather than their productivity or the market value of their skills. For their part employees are both dependent on and loyal to their employers.

This employment structure is by no means universal in Japan, since it is mainly associated with the 'core' labour force employed by the larger private sector corporations. It thus excludes many women, temporary workers and employees of subcontractors as well as those working for small- and medium-sized firms.[24] Other groups in Japanese society – notably the elderly and non-working members of extended families – also lost out as the rapid economic growth which Japan experienced after the period of postwar reconstruction placed increasing strains on more traditional family or community based systems of mutual support.

Japan's initial response to these economic changes and their associated effect on the country's social structure was to lay the foundations for a comprehensive welfare state along Western European (corporatist) lines (Tabata, 1990). Thus, by 1973 wholesale improvements had been made in the coverage of Japanese health insurance and pension schemes (Yamasaki and Hosaka, 1995), and further improvements followed during the 1970s, which included the introduction of children's allowances and the socialization of medical expenses for the elderly. Although the scale of social security expenditure still looked relatively modest in comparison with that of most European countries,[25] it appeared to be changing. In 1994 the Ministry of Health and Welfare estimated that by 2025 expenditure on social security payments would represent 28.5–32.5 per cent of national income, which is comparable to the current levels for Germany and France.

From the late 1970s, however, Japan's economy entered a low-growth phase and this, together with the escalating costs of its social security spending, has prompted a radical reassessment of its social welfare policies. This has resulted in an explicit renunciation of the erstwhile goal of creating a Western European style 'welfare state', and the adoption in its place of a 'Japanese-type welfare society' (Tabata, 1990: 2). Although this is portrayed as a an indigenous adaptation that is more in keeping with Japan's own distinctive traditions and circumstances, the reality is that this change of approach is just as heavily influenced by a 'foreign model' as its predecessor was. But this time, the model owes more to the neo-liberal strategies that were being adopted during the early 1980s by the USA and UK. The result has been a drastic scaling-back in the level of a wide range of benefits,[26] in an attempt to keep welfare spending under control, and an increasing reliance on the operation of the market within a reinvigorated private-sector economy.

Although the long-term effect of these changes may well be to push Japan increasingly in the direction of a 'market-oriented society which is qualitatively different from the West-European-type welfare states' (Tabata, 1990: 24), it also differs significantly in many respects from other neo-liberal states. We will comment briefly on differences in income and status differentials and also in the way Japanese citizens and institutions relate to one another.

In terms of income differentials, Japan has a much less unequal income distribution than the USA, and in this respect at least resembles much more closely the pattern found in such European welfare states as the Netherlands, Sweden and Norway (Currie, 1985). At the same time Japan is a much more hierarchical society than any of the others we have been describing, and is much more highly 'relational' in the sense that people are likely to belong to a relatively complex, dense and inter-locking set of relationships whether at home or in work and social settings. Moreover, Japanese institutions of all kinds appear to be much more 'inclusive' in seeking to foster and maintain such relationships where possible. 'Authoritarian communitarianism' sums it up well.

Following the latest social policy changes in Japan, the notion of 'social rights' may appear to be just as attenuated there as in the neo-liberal model. However, compared with their neo-liberal counterparts, Japanese citizens seem to be imbued with a much more highly developed sense of 'social duties', with respect to their families, teachers, class and workmates, friends and social superiors. These sharp contrasts between the oriental corporatist and neo-liberal models would appear to render the former much less vulnerable than the latter to the more extreme forms of 'social exclusion' and their attendant symptoms of alienation, despite the fact that sections of Japanese society do also experience an increasingly high degree of economic, social and cultural deprivation.

Welfare state types and penality

Is there a significant association between these different types of welfare state and penality? There certainly seems to be if you look at the twelve countries in our sample and their imprisonment rates as set out in Table 1.2. At the beginning of the twenty-first century there are clear dividing lines between the different types of political economy as regards imprisonment rates. All the neo-liberal countries have higher rates than all the conservative corporatist countries; next come the social democracies, with our single oriental corporatist country (Japan) having the lowest imprisonment rate of all. Admittedly, this particularly neat result will not necessarily hold 100 per cent true if one compares a greater range of countries, or even some of the same countries at different points in history. (For example, as we shall see in Chapter 10, in the 1970s social democratic Finland had a very high imprisonment rate by contemporary Western European standards. And conversely, as we shall see in Chapter 8, in the 1970s and 1980s the conservative corporatist Netherlands had a rate of imprisonment lower than the Nordic social democracies.) But it is striking nonetheless.

Table 1.2 *Political economy and imprisonment rates*

	Imprisonment rate (per 100,000 population)	Year
Neo-liberal countries		
USA	701	2002
South Africa	402	2003
New Zealand	155	2002
England and Wales	141	2003
Australia	115	2002
Conservative corporatist countries		
Italy	100	2002
Germany	98	2003
The Netherlands	100	2002
France	93	2003
Social democracies		
Sweden	73	2002
Finland	70	2002
Oriental corporatism		
Japan	53	2002

Source: Walmsley (2003b)

Thus, at least on this measure, it is the neo-liberal states who are the most punitive out of the range of countries covered in this book. And it is the USA – the archetypal and increasingly neo-liberal polity – that has in many ways been a world leader in escalating harshness of punishment in recent years. The USA not only imprisons a higher proportion of its population than any other country in the world but also resorts to the death penalty on a scale that is again unrivalled in any other late capitalist country (see Chapter 3). But why should there be this relationship between neo-liberalism and harsh punishment?

One likely factor in any explanation concerns the balance between different methods of social control in different types of society, including the balance between formal and informal social control. We have already noted that the kind of social and economic policies that are associated with neo-liberal societies are highly exclusionary – socially marginalizing – in their impact on some individuals and indeed whole communities. This is likely to have *criminogenic* consequences, which in turn will tend to influence the balance between different types of social control. Failure to provide adequately for those who are adversely affected by the vagaries of the market place (and stigmatizing those in receipt of whatever residual benefits *are* available) is itself likely to result in more crime being committed. This will be particularly likely if the society as a whole remains relatively affluent, giving rise to gross material inequalities, relative deprivation, and that staple element of criminology known as *anomie*: the 'strain' between people's socially-induced aspirations to material prosperity and the practical unlikelihood for many of achieving such material rewards by legal means. Moreover, free market social and economic policies are also likely to disrupt existing communities and thereby undermine the informal social controls that might otherwise have been exerted by family, friends, colleagues or neighbours. As Paul Ormerod (1977: 88) has noted, societies with relatively low crime rates tend to be those with strong community relationships which 'both foster a sense of belonging and provide ... the setting in which informal social sanctions against aggression and crime can operate effectively'.[27] An aggressively individualistic society, of course, provides the opposite kind of setting. It will also tend to inhibit the development of possible alternative, welfare-based methods of social control such as subsist within other advanced welfare capitalist societies. To put it bluntly (while misquoting Bob Dylan), when you've got nothing – and the welfare state won't give you anything – you have relatively little to lose by misbehaving. Except, of course, that you may be punished.

So it is perhaps not surprising that in neo-liberal societies the level of public demand for, and recourse to, formal methods of social control based on the prosecution and punishment of offenders appears to be far greater than in other advanced welfare capitalist countries. For example, as we shall see in Chapter 15, the age of criminal responsibility tends to be far lower in most neo-liberal societies than in any other type of state. Moreover, the penal sanctions that are imposed also tend to be highly '*exclusionary*' – notably in the extensive use of imprisonment, which excludes the offender from mainstream society in the most literal, physical manner as well as symbolically by the stigmatization which imprisonment confers.

But it is certainly not simply – and perhaps hardly at all – the fact that neo-liberalism may be criminogenic that leads to high levels of formal punishment. For this to be so, there would have to be a strong association between the level of crime and the amount of punishment meted out by the state – and (perhaps strange to say), there is not very much good evidence of any such strong association.[28] It is more to do with the cultural attitudes towards our deviant and marginalized fellow citizens as embodied (and embedded) in the political economy. The neo-liberal exclusion both of those who fail in the economic marketplace and of those who fail to abide by the law is no coincidence, as several commentators have suggested (Currie, 1996; Dignan, 1999a; Faulkner, 1996; Greenberg, 1999). Both are associated with a highly individualistic social ethos. The individualistic ethos leads a society to adopt a neo-liberal economy in the first place, but conversely the existence of such an economy in return fosters the social belief that individuals are solely responsible for looking after themselves, thus reproducing the individualistic culture. In neo-liberal society, economic failure is seen as being the fault of the atomized, free-willed individual, not any responsibility of society – hence the minimal, safety-net welfare state. Crime is likewise seen as entirely the responsibility of the offending individual. The social soil is fertile ground for a harsh 'law and order ideology'. And as neo-liberal societies have become even more neo-liberal in recent decades, so have they become more punitive. Speaking of the USA, Greenberg (1999: 306) refers to the toughening of criminal justice and penal policies during the Reagan and Bush (senior) presidencies, which accompanied a systematic reversal of various 'incorporative' social policy initiatives in other spheres. These included the weakening or dismantling of regulatory regimes that had been set up to protect employees, consumers and the environment. (See further Chapter 3.) A similar observation could be made in respect of parallel penal and social policy developments during the Conservative governments led by Prime Ministers Thatcher and Major in the UK during the same period. There, too, the adoption of a variety of exclusionary social policies in the spheres of housing, employment, and welfare benefits accompanied the pursuit of an increasingly harsh and punitive penal policy – as we shall discuss further in Chapter 4.

Conversely, corporatist societies such as Germany – and to an even greater extent, social democratic ones like Sweden – have traditionally had a different culture and a different attitude. These other late capitalist countries differ greatly from neo-liberal states both in the balance between formal and informal methods of social control and in the attitude towards the failing or deviant citizen. As we have already noted, corporatist and social democratic states tend to pursue more inclusionary economic and social policies that offer their citizens a far greater degree of protection against the vicissitudes of unfettered market forces, binding citizens to the state via national interest groups and ensuring the provision of welfare benefits and care of various kinds to ensure that all citizens are looked after. The communitarian ethos, which gives rise to these policies (and which is in return shaped by them), also finds expression in a less individualistic and less rejecting attitude towards the offender, who is regarded not as an isolated culpable individual but as a social being in need of *resocialization*, which is the responsibility of the community as a whole. The corporate citizen, unlike the neo-liberal, is much more his brother's keeper – even if he has done wrong – with a stronger sense that 'there but for the grace of God go I' – in terms of both economic failure and criminal activity. A more developed welfare state goes along with a less punitive penal culture.

Such a culture typically, although not invariably[29] and never in a pure form, takes the form of a *penal welfarism* (Garland, 1985, 2001) which seeks to respond to crime with measures aimed at improving the lot of the offender and thereby effecting his or her reformation and reintegration into society. Thus 'welfare' is the response to the offender as well as the economically disadvantaged citizen. Of course, the two categories in any event overlap to a significant extent, and providing welfare to impoverished non-offenders can also be seen as a way of trying to prevent them from becoming offenders. As Greenberg (2001: 81) puts it, 'locking people up or giving them money might be considered alternative ways of handling marginal poor populations – repressive in one case, generous in the other'.

In *conservative corporatist* states, the protection and maintenance of traditional informal social control institutions, such as the family and religion, are major social policy objectives in their own right. As such, they have not only shaped the content of other social welfare policies but are also likely to act as a 'brake' that will tend to increase resistance towards some of the more exclusionary economic and social policies that are associated with neo-liberal countries. With regard to those who break the law, there is a greater emphasis on rehabilitation and resocialization than on punishment, and a more welfare-based approach towards young offenders in particular, than is found in most neo-liberal states. Compared with the latter, conservative corporatist states also tend to have a higher age of criminal responsibility, show a greater willingness to divert young offenders from prosecution and, conversely, a greater reluctance to routinely transfer young offenders to the adult jurisdiction (see Part 3). All these tendencies are consistent with a tendency to place less reliance on formal social control methods, particularly where they are related to the use of exclusionary sanctions.

Social democracies are also 'inclusionary', in the sense that they have developed a relatively egalitarian concept of citizenship that affords extensive protection against a variety of economic, social and also biological and physical misfortunes. In contrast with conservative corporatist countries and Japan's oriental corporatist variant, however – which tend to delegate responsibility for citizens' welfare to non-state institutions such as the family, church, employers and voluntary organisations (Hallett and Hazel, 1998) – in social democracies the state itself is likely to assume a much more active role in providing this protection. This is likely to have mixed implications for the balance between formal and informal methods of social control.

On the one hand, the fact that the state is less likely to espouse the protection and maintenance of traditional social institutions such as the family and organized religion as overriding policy objectives in their own right could result in a weakening of their informal social control potential. Indeed, Bottoms (1983: 194) has suggested that a decline in the provision of 'lay care' by such institutions in welfare-capitalist societies could be linked to an increase in both the actual volume of crime (presumably because of the weakening of informal social controls); and also in its *apparent* volume. The latter seems plausible since people may be more likely to call in an official agency (the police) to deal with a crime – which will increase its likelihood of being recorded – instead of handling it themselves within the informal community networks that are likely to have flourished more successfully in the past. The decline in the effectiveness of such informal social control methods (whether real or apparent) is likely to increase the pressure for a more formal (and potentially more exclusionary) response to those crimes that are committed.

On the other hand, however, the social democratic state's commitment to full employment and broadly redistributive social and economic policies, if successful, might be expected to reduce the amount of crime that can be attributed to economic misfortune and relative disadvantage. Moreover, Bottoms (1983) and others have also suggested that the development of more extensive state welfare provisions could *increase* the scope for different forms of social control to be exercised within the informal structures of society without having to rely so heavily on formal penal measures. If this were to happen, then it could offset (in whole or in part) the reduction in the effectiveness of other, more traditional kinds of informal social control. And this in turn could reduce the (perceived) need for, and dependence on, formal externally imposed social controls that are linked to the application of 'exclusionary' sanctions on those who have offended.

As might be expected, social democratic corporatist states also appear to have a rather distinctive type of penality, notably with regard to the overall level of punishment, which appears to be remarkably low; even in comparison with conservative corporatist states. It is not entirely clear why this might be, though it could be linked to the very strong emphasis on inclusiveness, the feeling that everyone is a part of the same society. Perhaps it is also associated with the principle of egalitarianism, since most forms of exclusionary punishment will tend to make offenders worse off than the rest of society, which is inconsistent with this ideal. The social democratic society is the one which 'cares' the most about those at the bottom of the heap. It is also possible that in a social democratic culture people are not so ruthlessly held responsible for the offences they have committed, which are less likely to be attributed to the free will of the individual offender. Without necessarily going so far as to say that 'society is to blame' for all crime, there could nevertheless be a greater willingness to assume a degree of collective responsibility for the fact that an offence has been committed.

Social democracies tend to have the highest age of criminal responsibility of any states that we have been considering. Moreover, in other respects also they appear to be far more reluctant to invoke formal social control measures against young offenders, many more of whom are either diverted from the criminal justice system altogether, or else are dealt with by social welfare authorities. This tendency is also consistent with the analysis above.

The *oriental corporatist* state found in Japan is of particular interest with regard to the variable balance between formal and informal methods of social control. As we have seen, although it lacks the generous levels of welfare spending associated with most European corporatist and social democratic states, its pattern of income distribution nevertheless closely resembles that of the Netherlands and Nordic countries, such as Sweden and Norway. Moreover, it appears to have retained a much more traditional hierarchical social structure, which Western observers are apt to associate with 'quasi-feudal' societies rather than late capitalist ones. This is particularly true of the reciprocal obligations that traditionally defined the relationships between large private sector corporations and their employees, but a similar pattern of mutual expectations also characterizes many other relationships within a wide variety of social settings.

Japan has been described (Masters, 1998: 326ff.; Sato, 1996: 119) as a highly 'relational' or group-oriented society in the sense that the Japanese sense of personal identity is closely bound up with their membership of various informal social groupings, all of which have a legitimate claim on their social and personal obligations. The relatively weak sense of personal individuality, and the reciprocal desire to remain as part of the group, and not to be excluded from it, may also help to account for the significant role of the apology (Wagatsuma and Rosett, 1986: 472–8), both within Japanese society at large, and also as a major influence on decision-making within the Japanese criminal justice system.

The apparent willingness of Japanese wrongdoers to confess and voluntarily apologize for what they have done may be seen not only as a desire to maintain or restore positive relations with the person who has been harmed directly by their actions; but also because the maintenance of harmonious relations within the other social groups to which the wrongdoer belongs requires such obligations to be respected. A willingness to apologize and make restitution to the victim is thus likely to be interpreted by others – including criminal justice officials such as the public prosecutor and sentencing judge – as evidence of the wrongdoer's capacity for resocialization, based on their commitment to the preservation or restoration of harmonious relationships with those around them. Apology makes it possible for no formal action to be taken, even in the case of relatively serious wrongdoing. (The extent to which Japan relies on informal rather than formal methods of social control when dealing with offenders is highlighted by the fact that as many as 99 per cent of all juvenile offenders under the age of 20 are diverted from formal prosecution.) Conversely, as we shall see in Chapter 11, where an apology is not forthcoming or where persistent wrongdoing casts doubt on its likely sincerity or effectiveness, extremely harsh measures may be taken – but only against those who are deemed to have incorrigibly rejected the authoritarian norms of Japanese society.

The Japanese example represents a striking obverse to the linkage we remarked on previously between the pursuit of exclusionary penal policies and exclusionary social policies in countries that are characterized by relatively weak informal social control mechanisms. The overall impression is that Japan shows a marked preference for inclusionary social and penal policies that are linked with what appears to be a remarkably effective regime of informal social controls. There are notable exceptions, including the exceptionally harsh treatment that is meted out to a minority of convicted persistent offenders, and also Japan's continuing failure to observe internationally supported procedural standards and safeguards relating to the detention and interrogation of suspects. But there is still a remarkable contrast between Japan's broadly 'inclusionary' approach to criminal justice and social policies and the predominantly 'exclusionary' approach that is associated with neo-liberal countries in general, and the USA in particular. The result, as can be seen from Table 1.2, is an imprisonment rate which even undercuts those of social-democratic countries such as Sweden and Finland.

Our analysis so far broadly concurs with that of David Greenberg (1999),[30] who also suggests that corporatist and especially social democratic countries tend to be both relatively lenient in terms of their penality as well as being relatively generous and supportive in other aspects of their social policies, both of these being 'manifestations of a high degree of empathic identification and concern for the well-being of others (1999: 297). Greenberg also goes further, however, proposing that it is possible to demonstrate statistically a significant inverse correlation between a country's level of punishment and a single unidimensional factor, namely the country's degree of 'corporatism': in other words that 'the more corporatist societies are less punitive.' We are not so sure about this. Greenberg uses a complex quantitative measure of 'corporatism' derived from the work of Pampel et al. (1990), one limitation of which is that it does not distinguish national characteristics that we would identify as social-democratic from those we would call corporatist. In particular, the measure places a very heavy emphasis on state-funded public retirement benefits – the more generous, the more 'corporatist' the country is taken to be. Consequently, countries that we would typify as both social democratic *and* corporatist (such as Sweden) find themselves rated highest on this scale of 'corporatism'; though it certainly is interesting to note that these *are* among the least punitive of our four main groupings of late capitalist countries. (We would say that both corporatism and social democracy tend to lessen rates of punishment, and the Nordic combination of the two leads to particularly low rates.) In contrast, Japan appears to have a relatively low ranking on Pampel et al.'s 'corporatist score', at tenth place out of eighteen countries surveyed. This is almost certainly because the emphasis on state-funded public retirement benefits means that the measure fails to capture the highly distinctive contribution made by Japanese corporate enterprises in providing some of the redistributive benefits (such as pension expenditure) that in other countries (and particularly in social democracies) are considered to be primarily the responsibility of the state. France and Italy (see Chapter 9) also rank lower than they should on this score, appearing to be less 'corporatist' than New Zealand and Australia, a result which overemphasizes the financial quantum of state provision rather than national ethos as the touchstone of corporatism. We would speculate that a better measure than 'corporatism' for differentiating 'low punishment' from 'high punishment' societies would be one based on an index of 'social inclusiveness', were it possible to operationalize such a measure.

Both our analysis and our specific findings also have much in common with the work of Beckett and Western (2001) and Downes and Hansen (2003).

Downes and Hansen (forthcoming) found that countries with relatively high welfare spending as a proportion of gross domestic product (GDP) had relatively low imprisonment rates (although Japan was a major exception); Beckett and Western found something very similar when comparing different US states. Intriguingly, both studies found that this statistical relationship has become much stronger in recent years (and specifically since the 1990s).[31] Again, these facts fit our theory. More corporatist countries, and especially social democracies, generally have higher welfare spending and lower punishment levels. Japan, however, has low state welfare expenditure and lesser punishment – because the important factor is not state welfare as such but the inclusiveness of the society's culture towards its members. The reason for the inverse welfare–punishment ratio becoming stronger over time is perhaps because the differences between different countries and different states in both these respects were not so marked in the past: for example, the USA was not at all a consistently low spender on all aspects of public welfare in previous decades (Downes, 2001: 72). The worlds of welfare and of penality are in many respects actually becoming more polarized, not globally homogenized, making the relationship between the two more marked.

Another empirical finding, which fits well with our analysis, is that, as a general rule, economic inequality is related to penal severity: the greater the inequality in a society the higher the overall level of punishment (Beckett and Western, 2001: 50; Wilkins and Pease, 1987; Young and Brown, 1993: 41–3). (Interestingly, Japan with its relatively low inequality of income but low expenditure on state welfare fits this pattern although not fitting into the welfare–punishment pattern discussed in the last paragraph.) One theory is that punishment is a sort of 'negative reward': societies which are prepared to reward 'success' with higher incomes and greater social status are also more willing to punish failure with both poverty and formal sanctions. Or one could say, as we would, that a more egalitarian society is both more inclusive and less willing to consign offenders to an even more unequally low level of existence. In any event, as we have seen, our typology of nations will also yield this general association between inequality and punishment.

One would expect, following this analysis, to find that public attitudes towards those who break the law would be significantly different in countries which fall within these different clusters of nations. Some empirical evidence is available here thanks to the International Crime Victim Survey (ICVS), which has conducted surveys in 58 countries from around the world in 1989, 1993, 1996 and 2000. Drawing on a recent analysis by Mayhew and van Kesteren (2002),[32] Table 1.3 shows how attitudes towards punishment vary in each of the countries in the current study (excepting Germany, which has not been covered by the ICVS since 1989). The table also shows how these attitudes relate to each country's imprisonment rate.

The ICVS measures attitudes towards punishment by using a standardized exercise in which respondents are asked what sentence they would recommend for a recidivist burglar. The 'punitiveness score' used in Column A of Table 1.3 takes

Table 1.3 *Political economy and attitudes to punishment*

	A Punitiveness score	B Average score for cluster	C Imprisonment rate 2002/3	D Ranking for A	E Ranking for C
Neo-liberal countries		13.6			
South Africa	31		402	1	2
USA	16		701	2	1
England and Wales	12		141	3	4
Australia	5		115	7	5
New Zealand	4		155	8	3
Conservative corporatist countries		4.7			
Italy	6		100	5=	6=
The Netherlands	6		100	5=	6=
France	2		93	10	8
Social democracies		2			
Sweden	3		73	9	9
Finland	1		70	11	10
Oriental Corporatism		10			
Japan	10		53	4	11

Sources: Mayhew and van Kesteren (2002: 87–9; data from the latest ICVS sweep in each country are used in the table); Walmsley (2003b)

into account both what proportion of respondents favoured a prison sentence and the lengths of sentence recommended by those who did so.[33] As can be seen from Table 1.3, public attitudes towards punishment are broadly (but not precisely) in line with expectations with regard to the different types of political economy. Thus, the average score for each cluster (Column B) shows clear differences in the expected direction, with the interesting and notable exception of Japan, though the comparatively low scores of New Zealand, Australia and France are also noteworthy. One factor that might account for the higher than expected punitiveness score for Japan is that the 'offender' in question was a recidivist and, consequently, may have been viewed as someone with a reduced capacity for resocialization and therefore less deserving of leniency. As for the lower than expected punitiveness scores for Australia and New Zealand, it may be worth reiterating our earlier observation that prior to the 1980s these were countries with pronounced social democratic tendencies. So it could be that these are still reflected to some extent in people's attitudes towards punishment, even though their politics and economies may subsequently have moved in a neo-liberal direction.

Table 1.3 also demonstrates that a country's ranking in terms of its imprisonment rate is by no means totally determined by the 'punitiveness score' of its people. If it were, we would expect Australia, New Zealand and France to have lower imprisonment rates than they have, and Japan's to be much higher.[34] And in general, while research to date has occasionally shown some correspondence between a country's imprisonment rate and the punitiveness of its public as measured by such surveys, the association does not always show up strongly (Mayhew and van Dijk, 1997; Mayhew and van Kesteren, 2002: 72–4). Consequently, imprisonment rates cannot be a simple Durkheimian reflection of the common sentiments of ordinary people; nor – it would appear – are these public attitudes entirely conditioned by the political economies of their countries. Hanns von Hofer (2003b) has referred recently to the extent to which punishment is 'a political construct' shaped by the policy choices of politicians and state functionaries – members of what we term a country's 'penal elite', comprising the group of people who have particular power to determine a nation's penality. (We would add that political economies are also largely political constructs in this sense, and that, for example, neo-liberal politicians can play a part in making the economy more neo-liberal and penality more neo-punitive than one would expect when measuring the views of the public.) (We shall return to this issue in our concluding chapter.) (The interplays between public opinion, the political realm, public policy and penal practice are complex. But they are always conditioned by the type of society in which they occur.[35])

For example, within neo-liberal societies, not only are public attitudes towards law-breakers likely to be more punitive and intolerant, as we have seen, they are also more likely to be shaped and reinforced by privately-owned and market-oriented media, and by increasingly competitive, market-oriented and populist politicians. In some neo-liberal societies such as the USA, political parties are relatively weak in terms of the 'platform' they espouse, with the result that contenders for political office may feel the need to reflect and promote populist issues that are felt likely to resonate with the electorate. Where key criminal justice officials (including judges and public prosecutors) are themselves either elected or nominated and confirmed by political (and sometimes highly politicized) processes, as is also the case in many US jurisdictions, significant shifts in public opinion towards more hard-line 'law and order' approaches are more likely to result in dramatic increases in the rate of imprisonment. Again, however, this is not simply a transmission of punitiveness from public to politicians. Katherine Beckett (1997) has demonstrated how politicians and the media can *lead* public opinion in a more punitive direction, which politicians can then exploit for electoral purposes.

In other countries that show marked neo-liberal tendencies, there are likely to be similar pressures to adopt a more punitive response towards offenders. However their influence may be less profound, particularly where criminal justice officials are more likely to be appointed to tenured positions by means of less heavily politicized processes, as in most of the other neo-liberal jurisdictions within this study. Moreover, political parties tend to be stronger outside the USA, and tend to run for office on the basis of more comprehensive platforms, in which 'law and order' issues will not necessarily be given the prominence that they have been in recent US elections.[36] In circumstances such as these, the effect which even increasingly punitive attitudes might have on penal policy is likely to be much more moderate.

In more collectively-oriented countries, not only are public attitudes likely in general to be considerably less punitive to begin with, but the institutional context in which penal policy is shaped is also markedly different from the American position. The ownership, control and role of the media, for example, are very different in countries with a more corporatist and bureaucratic power structure, such as Germany. Major portions of the German news media (including all radio and television stations, but not newspapers and magazines) were until recently publicly organized and controlled (Savelsberg, 1999: 929). Because the broadcasting media are largely controlled by governing boards, which include representatives from a range of corporatist institutions including the main political parties, churches, unions and employers' organizations, they are far less market-oriented, and likely to be much less populist, than their counterparts in the USA.

Also in contrast to the USA, German politicians are more likely to subscribe to well-defined and comprehensive party platforms, and are thus more likely to act and legislate in accordance with their party mandates than in direct response to public pressure. And because German criminal justice officials such as judges and prosecutors are appointed as tenured civil servants rather than being directly elected or nominated by politicians, they are likewise much more insulated from public and political pressures than their US counterparts. These marked differences in the institutional context within which political ideologies are shaped and find expression may be just as significant as the ideological differences themselves in helping to account for the relative leniency in punishment levels in many corporatist countries compared with neo-liberal nations.

We should like to be able to account, not only for differences in the apparent levels of punitiveness between different countries, but also for *changes* in these countries' punishment levels over time. One obvious line of explanation – and one from which we shall be getting plenty of mileage – is, as one might expect, also to do with our typology of modern states and developments in relation to it. Thus, for example, one might well find (as we often have) that as a society moves in the direction of neo-liberalism, its punishment will tend to become harsher. Conversely, a move in the direction of corporatism or social democracy (not that many countries have experienced strong developments like this recently) might make punishment more lenient or at least mitigate trends towards greater harshness.

But this is not the whole story. For it is also important to be able to account for the relative *stability or instability* of punishment levels over time, as depicted in Figures 1.2–1.5. We find that punishment levels are relatively stable in the majority of conservative corporatist countries (with the notable exception of the Netherlands); relatively upwardly volatile in countries with marked neo-liberal

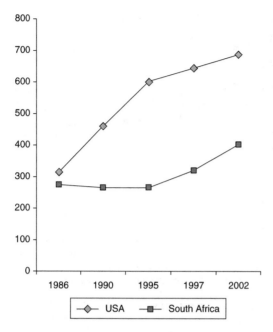

Figure 1.2 *Imprisonment rates for the United States and South Africa*

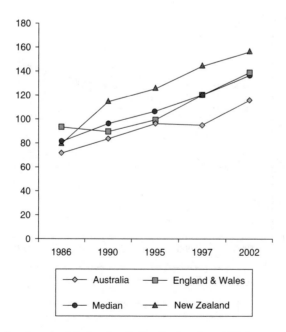

Figure 1.3 *Imprisonment rates for Australia, England and Wales, and New Zealand*

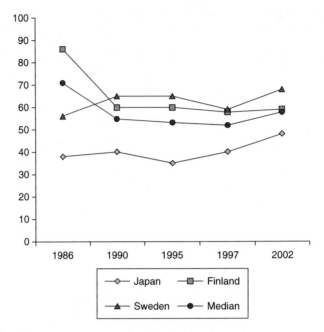

Figure 1.4 *Imprisonment rates for Sweden, Finland and Japan*

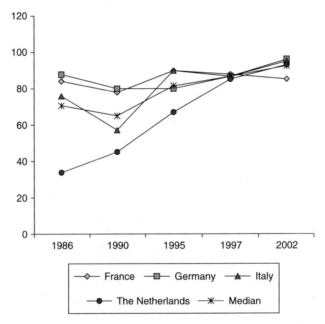

Figure 1.5 *Imprisonment rates for France, Germany, Italy and the Netherlands*

tendencies; and usually much less likely to increase rapidly in the social democracies – although Sweden may currently be proving something of an exception (see Chapter 10) – and in Japan (again, at least until very recently). Among the social democracies, the significant *reduction* in the national rate of imprisonment in Finland from 1976 to 1999 is of particular interest because it bucked the otherwise generally upward, or at best static, trends that characterize every other country in the study.

One cogent factor may well be the variable interrelationships that exist in different kinds of countries between ideological factors and attitudes on the one hand, and the institutional contexts within which these attitudes may be shaped, influenced and expressed, on the other. Changes in punishment levels – or indeed lack of change – may again be largely explicable in terms of the interplay between rival sets of influences. The first set of influences consists of pressure from public opinion, the influence of the media, and the degree of populism with regard to law and order issues on the part of rival political parties. Particularly in countries where they act in concert, such influences are capable of powerfully shaping the direction of criminal justice and penal policies. A second set of influences comprises the opinions and values of sections of the country's 'penal elite' namely senior public servants, including criminal justice professionals themselves. In other countries these appear to have been the predominant forces that have shaped the direction of penal policy. The institutional differences, which (as we saw above) typically exist between corporatist and neo-liberal countries and which generally make for a tendency to greater *leniency*, also tend to make for greater penal *stability* by partially insulating the penal elite and penal practitioners – and hence the penal system – from the effects of populist punitiveness.

With regard to the exceptional *decline* in the rate of imprisonment in Finland between 1976 and 1999 – in marked contrast to the trend seen in most other European, Commonwealth and North American jurisdictions – this has also been attributed by Patrik Törnudd to the more bureaucratic power structure that operates in Finland. Within this much more bureaucratic structure, senior civil servants and the penal experts who are regularly consulted by them are particularly powerful members of the penal elite, and their views have had a much greater impact on the direction of penal policy than public sentiment. Consequently, when this influential professional elite was persuaded during the early 1970s that Finland's rate of imprisonment was both unacceptably and needlessly high, it mobilized a consensus for reform on the part of key civil servants, the judiciary and prison authorities. This attitudinal shift on the part of a key professional elite was felt by Törnudd to have been a far more potent factor than any structural or demographic changes, and more important even than the precise mechanisms used to effect the change. A remarkably similar constellation of factors and circumstances has also been credited with the even more dramatic reduction in the early postwar rate of imprisonment in the Netherlands. (See further Chapters 8 and 10.)

Much of this can be summarized in Joachim Savelsberg's (1999) suggestion that two general dimensions of political arrangements are important when explaining the stability or instability of a country's punishment levels. One is the degree of *centralization* of political power within the state (seen at its extreme in totalitarian countries); another is the degree to which a country's politics are *bureaucratized* (with powerful political parties and civil services and a high degree of regulation of decision-making) or *'personalized'*, with a higher reliance on individual political and legal decision-makers.[37] He postulates that the decentralized but bureaucratic nature of the Federal Republic of Germany helps to explain its relative penal stability over time, in contrast to the highly centralized bureaucracies of East Germany and Poland, where punishment levels have varied dramatically over very short time periods in response to political edicts from the apices of power. Whereas in the USA – decentralized and personalized – he finds relative stability on punishment levels from one year to another, but dramatic changes over longer periods (decreases in the 1960s followed by very large increases from 1972 to the present day), as changing ideologies and populist politics make their way into penal practices. We shall be saying more about Savelsberg's thesis in Chapters 7, 8 and 10, and suggesting some modifications to it.[38]

All of these explanatory factors can, we think, be of use in explaining how countries compare in their penality, and can also be assimilated successfully into the broad church of our general radical pluralist explanatory framework. We need to stress that our approach is not a reductionist one. We cannot explain all variations in punishment and penality by reference to the differences in political economies and cultures we have mentioned. There are other factors as well. We have already mentioned, for example, the influence of penal ideologies from other countries and the operations of commercial interests in encouraging certain penal policies at the expense of others. However many factors we incorporate into our theory, it will still not give us the whole story. Individual nations can be just as quirky and esoteric as individual human beings. People sometimes talk about the 'exceptionalism' of France or the USA; but it is not going too far to say that we have found all of the 'countries in this study to be exceptional in at least some respect. Consequently, penality remains irreducibly *relatively autonomous* from any particular factor or combination of factors, however powerful. Particularities of geography, history, and even highly specific political circumstances, can all play their part, as we shall see. All of which makes life, punishment – and, hopefully, this book – more interesting.

Notes

1 They aren't, incidentally. See for example Stolzenberg and D'Alessio (1997) or Zimring et al. (2001).

2 For example in England, government studies have found that fewer than half the crimes suffered by victims are reported to the police, and that furthermore up to a half

of crimes which are reported to the police may not be recorded by them, and hence fail to make their way into the official figures (Simmons and Dodd, 2003: 29, 32).

Another reason for not attempting to relate imprisonment rates to crime rates is that – perhaps remarkably – most research studies have discovered little evidence of any statistical relationship between the two (although it may be that rates of *violent* crime have a stronger association with imprisonment rates than rates for all crimes). See, for example, Rutherford (1986: esp. 43–4); Young (1986: 126–7); Young and Brown (1993: 23–33); Zimring and Hawkins (1991); Halliday (2001: 99); Beckett and Western (2001: 49–50); Greenberg (2001: 82) and works cited therein.

3 This is analogous to the 'law-jobs' theory of the jurist Karl Llewellyn (1940), which postulates that for any human group to survive it requires social processes which have the function of performing certain 'jobs' concerned with the avoidance and settlement of disputes between members of the group.

4 Andrew McLean Williams, response to questionnaire.

5 In fact, this decline is only partial, and in some respects (and in some countries) the reverse has been happening. For example, the operation of the European Convention on Human Rights has contributed to a greater recognition of the formal legal rights of prisoners in many European countries, including several of those within our sample.

6 Not in all countries however, as we shall see (especially in Parts 2 and 3). As a generalization, the 'collapse of the rehabilitative ideal' can be said to have occurred in both the English-speaking 'neo-liberal' states (the USA, UK, Australia and New Zealand) and in the Nordic social democracies, but not in 'conservative corporatist' European states such as Germany, where belief in the 'resocialization' of the offender has remained strong.

7 Another (partial) explanation of this development concerns the role of penal subjects (especially prisoners in the USA) who struggled against the arbitrary injustices meted out to them under the guise of reformative treatment. See below, Chapter 3, Note 6.

8 Finland is the obvious example within our sample of countries; but there have also recently been reductions in prison populations in some African and Eastern European countries. Various other countries have had relatively stable prison populations in recent years.

9 There is evidence to the contrary, at least in some countries. For example, a recent British study (Hough and Roberts, 1998: Chapter 4) found only 20 per cent of a representative national sample believing that the most effective way to prevent crime was to make sentences tougher (increasing discipline in the home and reducing unemployment were more popular strategies), while most respondents would rather develop community penalties than build more prisons at the taxpayer's expense, an option favoured by only 18 per cent. Such findings are particularly interesting in the light of other studies showing British public opinion as relatively punitive compared with other countries (excepting the USA): see van Dijk and Mayhew (1992: 46); Mayhew (1994: 5); Mayhew and van Kesteren (2002).

10 Not only does globalization itself gather pace, so does the quantity of literature theorizing about it. See for example Giddens (1990), Lash and Urry (1994). See also Mishra (1999), who has written specifically about the impact of globalization on the welfare state. We are grateful to Tony Bottoms for drawing this particular source of theorizing to our attention. Although we only encountered it a relatively late stage in our inquiry, we were gratified to discover that Mishra's general thesis with regard to globalization's impact on social policy in general is broadly congruent with our own.

11 Andrew McLean Williams, questionnaire response.

12 A similar point could be made in respect of Turkey, which also abolished capital punishment in 2003 for a similar reason.

13 Especially in more 'corporatist' countries, it is not only the state which performs this mediating operation: see Note 18 below.

14 A couple of definitions. By 'ideology' we mean the entire realm of ideas, including philosophies, which may affect people's attitudes and practices. This is wider than the classic Marxist concept, which sees 'ideologies' as ideas which function socially in the interests of particular classes. Within 'culture' we include both ideology and what Émile Durkheim called 'collective sentiments' – socially determined feelings, emotions and attitudes.

15 In this respect radical pluralism can be seen as 'Weberian': see Cavadino and Dignan (2002: 74–8).

16 One omission from Figure 1.1 is the realm of political practice. Like penal practice, politics has reciprocally influential relationships with the ideology, culture and material conditions of society, and is likely to impinge directly on penal practice as the result of political initiatives in the area of 'law and order'.

17 Though it may apply (with suitable modifications) to some countries that have recently made the transition to democracy (for example South Africa) or which have been conquered in the recent past (such as postwar Japan).

18 There is an important sense in which 'neo-liberal' states such as the USA are more 'pluralist' than other types of state within our sample. In these 'neo-liberal' countries, differing interest groups operate within something more like a 'free market' of political policy. In more 'corporatist' countries, policies tend to be determined by institutionalized elites containing representatives of different blocs of interests, who mediate their competing claims. Nevertheless, we still have a plurality of competing interests (and therefore the broad 'radical pluralist' framework fits); it is just that their competition is structured and mediated differently.

19 Lash and Urry (1987, 1994) see contemporary Western societies as having recently entered a realm of 'disorganised capitalism'.

20 One row in Table 1.1 refers to the receptivity of different types of state to privatization of punishment. We deal with this aspect of penality at length in Chapter 16, but will say no more about it here.

21 Mishra (1999: 83) describes the German welfare state as a 'status-maintaining system, helping to reinforce rather than mitigate market differentials'.

22 An exception here is France – generally conservative corporatist in other respects – with its strong republican tradition of 'anti-clericalism'. See Chapter 9.

23 For our use of this term, see Chapter 10, Note 1.

24 For this reason Japan is often referred to as having a 'dual labour market'.

25 According to Mishra (1999: 93), Japan's spending on social protection initiatives was only 11.57 per cent of GDP in 1990, compared with an OECD average of 21.6 per cent.

26 But see Peng (2000: 100–2), who has pointed to evidence of a swing back towards state provision in the 1990s, due partly to the declining role of corporate welfare. One example he cites is the introduction of the Chronic Care Insurance programme for the elderly.

27 See for example Tham (1998). As Tham demonstrates, both the UK and Sweden saw increases in both economic inequality (and hence in the number of socially marginalized people) and crime in the 1980s. However, the more marked increase in inequality in the UK was accompanied by a greater increase in crime than that witnessed by Sweden.

28 See above, Note 2.

29 An exception is the (far from unalloyed) acceptance of the 'justice model' rather than a rehabilitative approach in Sweden and Finland (see Chapter 10).

30 Greenberg situates his account within a Durkheimian explanatory paradigm (see Cavadino and Dignan, 2002: Chapter 3). Following the sociological tradition of Émile Durkheim, Greenberg seeks the explanation for differing punishment levels and their association with different types of welfare state in societal culture, which is seen as explaining both the society's type of state and its penality. Our radical pluralist account is subtly different from this. We would see the configuration of a country's welfare state as both largely *determined by* the national culture and also as contributing towards *determining* that culture and the mindset of its citizens, including their attitudes towards their less fortunate and less well-behaved fellow citizens and towards the responsibilities of the state vis-à-vis these citizens. Although, as we shall see shortly, public opinion is only part of the picture.

31 Similarly, Downes (1988: 78), when trying to explain the relative leniency of the Netherlands in the 1980s, failed to find any correlation between the proportion of GDP spent on welfare by different Western European countries and their imprisonment rates at the time.

32 We are grateful to Julian Roberts for drawing this study to our attention.

33 This is one of three measures used by Mayhew and van Kesteren (2002). Another is based on a simple percentage of those choosing imprisonment. The third is based on the mean number of months in prison recommended *by those who opted for imprisonment* as a punishment (referred to as the 'sentence length measure').

34 South Africa's 'punitiveness score' is also extraordinarily high. Mayhew and van Kesteren found high punitiveness scores in Africa generally.

35 Recent analyses by Törnudd (1993) and Savelsberg (1999) have helped to inform this account.

36 In the UK, for example, law and order issues played relatively little part in the 1992 General Election campaign, or in party politics generally over the preceding five years. This was, however, in sharp contrast to the 1979 British General Election campaign, and again during the five years culminating in the 1997 General Election (see Cavadino and Dignan, 2002: 334–8).

37 Clearly this factor is not independent of our 'neo-liberal/corporatist/social democratic' dimension, as corporatist countries (whether social democratic or not) will inevitably be relatively bureaucratic – although the converse is not necessarily true.

38 In particular, we shall be suggesting – in the light of the Finnish and Dutch historical experiences – that bureaucratized democracies are not necessarily as stable in their penality as Savelsberg suggests.

Part 2

PENAL SYSTEMS IN CRISIS?

2

Globalized Penal Crisis?

In some Western countries we have become accustomed to what could almost be called institutionalized penal crisis. Prisons are continually reported to be over-populated, overcrowded, squalid and insecure, inhabited on the one hand by staff who are demoralized, disaffected and restless, and on the other by inmates simmering on the point of riot and rebellion. There is a general *crisis of penal resources* as places in prison and other facilities are stretched to deal with ever-increasing numbers. The whole criminal justice system – not just the penal system – suffers from a chronic *crisis of legitimacy*, being generally viewed as simultaneously ineffective in controlling crime, inefficient and often inhumane. And none of this is new: the situation has been prevailing for decades – although it may appear to be constantly deteriorating – to such an extent that the 'crisis' has become institutionalized as part of our routinized expectations of the social scene.

It may consequently come as a surprise to some that penal crisis is not a universal and inevitable feature of life at the beginning of the twenty-first century. As we shall see, some countries – such as the USA and England and Wales[1] – can be fairly said to suffer from penal crises of the kind we have described – although even in these countries not all the supposed characteristics of a crisis may be currently present. Other countries, however – such as Finland and Germany – cannot be said to have penal crises. In Chapters 3 to 11 we shall deal with each of the countries in our sample in turn and detail the ways in which the features of a stereotypical penal crisis are and are not exhibited by each countries' penal systems and discuss the reasons for both the similarities and differences which exist. Before we do so, however, we shall discuss some of the characteristics of 'penal crisis' in more general terms.

The first of these, and in many ways the most notable and crucial characteristic of penal crisis, concerns the sheer number of people imprisoned. There is a very widespread international trend as regards numbers of prison[2] inmates. Numbers – both absolute and in proportion to general populations – are at historically very high or even all-time record levels; there has been dramatic growth in recent years; and the current trend is still sharply upwards. But, though this may be *generally* true, it is not true of all countries, as we shall see.

Table 2.1 *Total prison populations in selected countries, 1986, 1995, 1997/8 and 2002/3*

	Total prison population			
Country	**1986**	**1995**	**1998**	**2002/3**
USA***	744,208	1,585,589	1,725,842	2,033,331
South Africa	110,481**	112,572	142,410	180,952
New Zealand	2,654	4,375	5,236	5,881
England and Wales	46,581	51,265	65,906	74,452
Australia	10,815	15,327	17,661	22,492
The Netherlands	4,906	10,200	13,618	16,239
Italy	43,685	49,642	49,477	56,574
(West) Germany	53,619	66,146	74,317	81,176
France	47,628	53,178	53,259	55,382
Sweden	4,649	5,767	5,221	6,506
Finland	4,219	3,018	2,798	3,617
Japan	++	45,057	49,414	67,255

Sources: Council of Europe, Prison Information Bulletin, June 1986 and January 1987; *Prison Statistics England and Wales* 1995, 1996; Walker et al. (1990); Törnudd (1993); Walmsley (1999, 2003b); contributors' questionnaire responses. Figures are for 1 September wherever possible.

**1989 figures
***Includes prisons and local jails
++Data not available

The USA, where there has been a massive 400 per cent increase in the prison population between the mid-1970s and the present day, is the most prominent and dramatic current example of (hyperincarceration.) Other countries, as in so many other respects, tend to trail along behind the USA in this regard, but the general direction is the same. For example, the English prison population has risen from under 40,000 in 1975 to 46,581 in 1986 and 66,300 in 2001, exceeding 75,000 in 2004. New Zealand has seen its prison population rise even more sharply, from 2,654 in 1986 to 7,327 in August 2004, while in next-door Australia the numbers of those imprisoned went from 10,815 in 1986 to 22,492 in 2002.

Tables 2.1 and 2.2 present comparative figures for the countries in this study for the years 1986, 1995, 1997/8 and 2002/3. Table 2.1 provides actual numbers of people incarcerated; Table 2.2, more helpfully, presents imprisonment *rates*: numbers imprisoned per 100,000 of the population. They demonstrate an overall increase in the prison populations in eleven out of our twelve countries between 1986 and 2002/3. Contrasting with large increases in countries such as the USA, the Netherlands and New Zealand, Finland is the only country out of the twelve which has *reduced* her imprisonment rate over this time period. However, it should be noted that several countries – South Africa, West Germany, France, Italy, Sweden and England have all seen reductions in their prison populations *at times* during the 1986–2003 period.[3]

Table 2.2 *Imprisonment rates in selected countries, 1986, 1995, 1997/8 and 2002/3*

| Country | No. of prisoners per 100,000 population | | | |
	1986	1995	1997/8	2002/3
USA***	313	601	645	701
South Africa	373**	273	321	402
New Zealand	75*	120*	145	155
England and Wales	93	99	125	141
Australia	70	90*	95	115
The Netherlands	34	67	87	100
Italy	76	90*	86	100
(West) Germany	88	80*	90	98
France	84	91	91	93
Sweden	56	65	59	73
Finland	86	60	55	70
Japan	++	35	39	53

Sources: Council of Europe, Prison Information Bulletin, June 1986 and January 1987; *Prison Statistics England and Wales* 1995, 1996; Walker et al. (1990); Törnudd (1993); Walmsley (1999, 2003b); contributors' questionnaire responses. Figures are for 1 September wherever possible.
*Rounded to nearest 5
**1989 figures
***Includes prisons and local jails
++Data not available

It may come as no great surprise to learn that, as a general rule, high and fast-rising prison populations tend to be associated with the other indices of crisis mentioned at the start of this chapter.[4] The more inmates a system has to accommodate, the more stretched resources are likely to be, leading to prison overcrowding, low morale among correctional staff and the likelihood of disturbances and incidents and practices that decrease the legitimacy of the penal system. Abstractly, one might imagine that one could avoid a 'crisis of resources' and its effects by increasing spending on prisons in line with the increase in prison population, but in practice this is near-impossible even for the richest of nations, as the USA has found. Given such rising trends, even a determined attempt to increase resources is likely to lag woefully behind the upwards spiral of incarceration. Put bluntly, it is generally found that in such times, prisons fill up faster than you can build them.

Before we proceed to explore whether and to what extent punishment and crisis levels have risen in our individual countries, we shall discuss briefly some of the reasons why there might have been this *general* (if not universal) increase in apparent punitiveness.

First of all, is it really only an increase in *apparent* punitiveness? Is it simply that there is more crime and more criminals leading to more prisoners, or perhaps, are more criminals being caught and ultimately incarcerated? The short answer is no. It is true that the general trend is for crime to rise, but studies have not found any consistent relationship between crime rates and imprisonment rates.[5] Countries such as the USA, and England have been seeing *declining* crime rates recently (after 1980 in the USA and from the mid-1990s in England) – but their imprisonment rates have gone on rising apace. Nor can their imprisonment rates be attributed to more offenders, or more serious offenders, coming before the courts for sentencing (see, for example, Halliday, 2001: 79–80). Rather, what is generally found is that – to use one of our own soundbites – *sentencing is the crux of the crisis* (Cavadino and Dignan, 2002: Chapter 3). This is not to say that other factors, such as the operation of laws on pre-trial detention and the early release of prisoners cannot have important effects on prison populations. But as a general rule the most salient factor in imprisonment rates and changes in those rates is the sentencing practice of the courts when dealing with offenders.

Such sentencing practice can in turn be affected by many external factors, such as (obviously) the legal framework within which sentencing operates – introducing new minimum sentences such as 'three strikes and you're out' provisions are indeed likely to have a measurable effect, as can 'sentencing guidelines' which steer rather than fetter the court's discretion in sentencing. Above all, perhaps, sentencing is affected by the penal mood and temper of the times, as expressed in political and media discourse about crime and punishment (and indeed this mood and temper will also obviously shape any legislation which affects the legal sentencing framework). Thus ultimately – and in line with our general thesis – it will often be a country's *penal culture and ideology* which is largely responsible for bringing about a particular rate of imprisonment rather than any material truths about the amount of crime or the number of criminals.

This is not necessarily to say, however, that the long term postwar increase in crime has had no effect at all on imprisonment rates – but the effects could be mostly indirect. David Garland (2001) propounds a theory about the development of a punitive 'culture of control' in late modern societies, in which the growth of crime plays an important part. However, it is not that more crime means more criminals which means more prisoners. Rather, it is that more crime means less tolerance of crime in general, which leads to harsher punishment and consequently more prisoners. In particular, Garland suggests that the politically influential professional middle classes – previously largely isolated from the everyday effects of crime – now feel more threatened by crime and less inclined to favour policies aimed at the rehabilitation of offenders rather than excluding them and making them suffer. This seems plausible, and has been supported by some empirical research (Cesaroni and Doob, 2003).

We should also add that such shifts in attitude are what might be expected in societies which have *all* – even the most social-democratic of societies such as Sweden – moved in the direction of neo-liberalism in recent decades. As we mentioned in Chapter 1, other developments which have been associated with this move towards neo-liberalism include a more populist politics and more competitive and sensationalist mass media representations of crime, which we can also reasonably assume have played their part in shaping public attitudes and official policies regarding punishment. These factors all combine and conspire over time. The march of globalization, free market forces and other rapid changes in technology, economics and culture – not least the fragmentation and destruction of traditional communities and traditional lifelong jobs – has led to both an increase in crime and to deep-seated feelings of insecurity in the psyche of the late modern individual. This in turn has fed a tendency to fear and hate 'outsiders' such as criminals – what Garland (2001) calls 'the criminology of the other'[6] – and consequently to reward politicians who offer a punitive, exclusionary fix for crime. At the same time, modern politicians have increasingly tended to orientate their policies and pronouncements in line with opinion polls and focus groups, with the result that they are more and more likely to adopt policies which are (superficially) attractive to these more punitive voters (Cavadino et al., 1999: 215). By such means, politicians hope to garner votes despite a long-term decline in the public's confidence in governments, a lack of legitimacy fuelled by governments' apparent inability to satisfy their citizens in a number of areas, including keeping them safe from crime.

One factor which deserves a special mention is increased levels of migration towards the end of the twentieth century and at the commencement of the twenty-first. Developments such as economic decline in Eastern Europe and wars in various parts of the world have caused mass movements of refugees and would-be economic migrants, leading to people in Western nations increasingly feeling under siege from a tidal wave of foreigners who are seen as a threat to well-being and way of life. All of these dislocations can also be seen as products of the 'globalization' that has brought about the fall of the Iron Curtain, brought the ravages of free market capitalism to Eastern Europe, widened the global gap between rich and poor, and simultaneously in various ways encouraged and facilitated the movement of displaced, impoverished and persecuted people from one place to another. This has come at a time when many in the West have, as we have seen, felt pretty dislocated and insecure themselves. And, to put it glibly, during the Cold War there may have been the threat of nuclear war, but short of that eventuality you knew where you were and who the enemy was, and at least the Iron Curtain and other barriers kept them more or less safely away from you. Now there is a growing perception of seemingly strange and scary foreigners and outsiders flooding in – a feeling hardly likely to be alleviated by terrorist acts such as the attack on the World Trade Center on 11 September 2001. Both geographical and psychological boundaries and barriers feel under threat. One result has been increased levels of support for right-wing anti-immigration parties in many countries, and perhaps more importantly an adoption of harder policies on immigration and asylum by mainstream politicians.

Xenophobia, racism and harsh attitudes on law and order have always been in close alliance.[7] 'The Other' is feared as a generally dangerous entity, and fear of crime melds with fear of the outsider: the arrival of outsiders is feared for the crime it may bring in, and when they have arrived crime is blamed on them (despite a general paucity of evidence that asylum seekers and immigrants are any worse behaved than the indigenous population). It is a commonplace observation that in the political realm harsh rhetoric and policies on 'law and order', asylum and immigration can be used and perceived as code for racist attitudes. As Joe Sim et al. (1995: 9) put it, 'Since 1990, the shifting social arrangements in Europe in general, and the attempt to construct a new hegemonic order in Western Europe in particular, have intensified the targeting of not only traditional but also new folk-devils whose presence has been not simply understood in terms of the crimes they may or may not engage in but more symbolically read in terms of the politics of internal infestation, a threat to these new shifting social arrangements.' Thus they seem to see the demonization of the foreigner and refugee as to an important extent politically engineered in a conscious attempt to create a new social order. Whether or not it is right to take such a 'conspiratorial' view of these phenomena,[8] there can be no doubting the powerful nature of the demonization that is occurring.

Western politicians and governments have for many years been largely trying to 'pull up the drawbridge' and create, for example, 'Fortress (Western) Europe'. Many of the methods for dealing with incoming asylum seekers are essentially the same as or similar to those used for offenders – detention (including in some countries detention in prisons along with criminal offenders) and various methods of supervision and control in the community (which typically resemble bail conditions.) At the same time, disproportionately high proportions of the 'ordinary' prison populations in many countries are composed of non-nationals and ethnic minorities.[9] Garland's (2001: 137) encompassing phrase 'the criminology of the other' is indeed apt: the outsider, whether perceived as criminal, foreign or both, is seen as 'the threatening outcast, the fearsome stranger, the excluded and embittered'.

Whether such developments are inevitable and bound to continue is a question to which we will briefly return in our final chapter. But we hope the answer is no – and we hope that some seeds of that answer can be found here and there in this part of this book.

Notes

1 England and Wales share a single legal and criminal justice system. (Scotland and Northern Ireland, which also form part of the United Kingdom, each have a separate system.) In this book, England and Wales are treated as a single country, often referred to for convenience simply as 'England' or 'English'.

2 In this book we usually use the term 'prison' widely, to cover incarcerative penal institutions which may go under a variety of other names. In particular, there is a distinction in the USA between federal and state 'prisons' and local 'jails'. Unless otherwise indicated, we use the word 'prison' (and 'imprisonment') for all such institutions.

3 England's reduction in imprisonment – from a peak of 49,949 in 1988 to 44,565 in 1993 (a decline of 10 per cent) does not show up in Tables 2.1 and 2.2 because of the years selected for comparison; by 1995 England's prison population was already on a step upward trend. See further Chapter 4 and Cavadino and Dignan (2002). For the fluctuations in the prison population of the other countries mentioned, see Chapters 6, 7, 9 and 10.

4 For a 'radical pluralist' account of one country's penal crisis, see Cavadino and Dignan (2002: 28–31).

5 See Chapter 1, Note 2.

6 At the same time, paradoxically, there has been developing what Garland calls a 'criminology of the self'. This is the attempt to represent crime as a normal phenomenon which can be controlled by rational measures of crime prevention. This latter 'criminology' is one we are unable to focus upon in this book.

7 This is true at the level of individual psychology as well as the social level: strong correlations exist between racially prejudiced ideas and the belief that criminals should be harshly punished (Eysenck, 1954: 130; 1958: 286–7).

8 A less conspiratorial view would be that politicians are on the one hand responding to public concerns (of varying degrees of rationality), partly in the hope of electoral reward, partly to defuse the threat of right-wing parties, and partly because they share the same feelings themselves, while on the other hand trying to manage the economic and other problems caused by mass migrations.

9 This may have little to do with the propensity of different national or ethnic groups to commit crime. For example, the over-representation of ethnic minority groups in England's prison population is in part a product of the imprisonment of large numbers of foreign nationals from poor third world countries who are convicted of drug smuggling offences.

3

The United States Of America: Law and Order Ideology, Hyperincarceration and Looming Crisis

In some respects the USA is a paradigm case of penal crisis.[1] Its prison and jail[2] populations have rocketed skywards faster than that of almost any other country; it has significant problems with overcrowding and prison conditions and other signs of stretched penal resources; and the system lacks legitimacy for many both inside and outside its perimeters. However, as we shall see, the USA still does not fully fit a stereotyped image of a generalized penal crisis where every aspect of the penal system is in a dangerously critical state.

The USA currently leads the world in punishment in more ways than one. Not only does it have the highest imprisonment rate of the countries covered in this book (see Table 2.2 in Chapter 2), it also tops the world league tables in this respect. But it has also been leading in the sense of moving in directions that others follow, not only in its penal practices but also in the ideology of how countries should respond to crime. In particular, it has adopted and exported what we call 'law and order ideology'. We have previously defined this term – a concept effectively synonymous with Tony Bottoms' (1995) phrase 'populist punitiveness' – as 'a complex if naive set of attitudes, including the belief that human beings have free will, that they must be strictly disciplined by restrictive rules, and that they should be harshly punished if they break the rules or fail to respect authority' (Cavadino and Dignan, 2002: 27). It is this ideology which informs what we have called Strategy A: the attempt by governments to manage the problem of crime by means of ever harsher punishments (Cavadino et al., 1999; see also the Preface to this book), and also, more widely, what we have called 'neo-correctionalism' (see the Preface).

These ideas have become pervasively popular in recent years – arguably gathering force ever since the early 1970s in most countries, most dramatically in the

USA but with significant if lesser impact elsewhere. Many people have become convinced – if indeed they ever needed convincing – that punishments have been unwontedly soft and that the answer to crime is more harshness directed against offenders (Currie, 1998: 4–5). To a great extent, its rise can be traced in the increases in prison populations we have already discussed, for – generally speaking[3] – the more a population and a polity endorses this ideology the higher its imprisonment rate will tend to be. It even seems that a mere heightening of law and order *rhetoric* in the political realm – without any accompanying legislative or administrative changes – can have significantly noticeable effects on levels of imprisonment simply by influencing judges to sentence more harshly (Cavadino and Dignan, 2002: 26).

Why has the USA led the way in this alteration in ideological fortunes? There is much about the USA in the last three decades which may have made it fertile soil for law and order ideology. To begin with, the ideology's conjunction of beliefs in free market capitalism and in the free will of the individual expresses a very American rugged individualism,[4] which may help to explain the particularly strong burgeoning of punitive politics and its popular appeal in the USA. The neo-liberalism of American society is predicated upon individual responsibility in a way highly consonant with the law and order attitude. The American Dream is one in which every good individual has the opportunity to succeed whatever their initial disadvantages – a recurrent theme of feel-good Hollywood films with happy endings including *Pretty Woman*, *Working Girl*, *Forrest Gump* and even that supposed critique of 1980s capitalism, *Wall Street*. Consequently, economic failure is seen as normally being the fault of the individual and no responsibility of society (hence the minimal, safety-net welfare state) – and so is crime. As we said in Chapter 1, corporatist and social democratic societies have a different culture and a different, less individualistic and more sympathetic attitude towards both the economic failure and the criminal.

An obvious objection to this analysis comes from America's earlier espousal of *penological positivism*, which peaked in the 1960s (a time, incidentally, when the American prison population was reduced). Positivism is the school of thought – central to 'penal welfarism' – which holds that individual free will does not exist, that criminal behaviour is the inevitable result of prior causes such as biological endowment and environment, and that consequently offenders should be 'treated' rather than 'punished' (Cavadino and Dignan, 2002: 49–50; see also the Preface). If America is so innately and ruggedly individualistic and this philosophy has so much influence on penality, how could the USA have gone so far in the direction of positivism? We need to understand, however, that positivism was never fully incorporated into the common sense of the American public despite the attractions it held for many officials in penal administration between the 1950s and early 1970s. For a long time those who were its adherents tended towards what in everyday American language is called political 'liberalism', which is of course far removed from individualistic 'neo-liberalism'. (In our terms, an American 'liberal' is likely to favour greater 'corporatism' in societal arrangements.) It is also the case that the version of positivism which gained popularity in the USA was one which has been rightly termed 'the *individualized treatment model'* (American Friends Service Committee, 1971) – a paradigm which seeks to locate the causes of crime in physical and psychological defects within the individual deviant (rather than within society) and to respond to crime by imposing quasi-medical but compulsory treatment upon that individual. (This contrasts subtly with the concept of 'resocialization' of the offender, which retains a degree of popularity in corporatist countries.) This model also chimed in with America's optimistic beliefs – even stronger prior to the 1970s than currently – in its own benevolent progressiveness: treatment rather than punishment was seen as the scientific wave of the future, and the USA was leading the way.[5]

Broadly speaking, the USA today can be characterized as an exemplar of a neo-liberal society, but previously it had moved significantly in the direction of corporatism after World War Two (and indeed before it, at least from the time of Franklin D. Roosevelt's New Deal in the 1930s). The high point of US corporatism (such as it was) can in retrospect be located, with enormous political irony, during the presidency of Richard Nixon (1969–74), and for most of the time up to that point the theory and practice of punishment in the USA became progressively more positivistic. But then, for a brief but significant moment in the early 1970s, positivism came under powerful attack from the penological 'left' in the shape of the *'justice model'* (see the Preface; also Cavadino and Dignan, 2002: 51–2).

The justice model school represented the concerns of liberal (in the US sense) penologists and penal administrators as well as owing much to revolts by prisoners themselves protesting against the repressive excesses of positivism in practice,[6] and to research results which were portrayed and perceived as showing that 'nothing works' to reform offenders (Cavadino and Dignan, 2002: 37–8). Positivism favoured punishments (or 'treatments') designed to rehabilitate the individual offender, with no necessary relationship between the severity of the sanction and the seriousness of the offence, and with an important place for indeterminate sentences where the release date was determined on the basis of experts' assessments of the inmate's progress in terms of rehabilitation. The justice model condemned this package as a repressive charade, leading to untrammelled executive discretionary power, systematic discrimination against poor and black offenders, and an unjust lack of proportion between offence seriousness and sanction. Its adherents called for a return to 'just deserts' in the form of punishments whose severity was consistently proportionate to the gravity of the offence. The justice model dealt a severe blow to the dominance of positivistic ideology and 'penal welfarism', doubtless weakening its defences against the coming law and order onslaught. But overall, and despite some significant but limited successes in influencing penal developments in a wide variety of jurisdictions both within and outside the USA, the justice model's fate was to be partially co-opted and thoroughly overwhelmed by the rise in law and order ideology which accompanied the swing back towards 'neo-liberalism' in the USA and other Western societies since the mid-1970s. (The justice model did, however, have a deeper and more lasting impact in some other countries, notably Sweden and Finland, as we shall see in Chapter 10).

The beginnings of the rise of law and order ideology can be traced back at least as far as the right-wing presidential campaigns of Barry Goldwater in 1964 and of Richard Nixon and George Wallace in 1968 (when, significantly, the phrase 'law and order' was used and seen by many as code for a white backlash against the civil rights movement of the 1960s). However, it is the period since the mid-1970s which has seen this ideology's steady advance in company with the swelling prison population. One manifestation of this development has been the effective reintroduction and subsequent increasing use of and support for the death penalty. This is not so much because execution is used in a high proportion of cases – it has been estimated that only around one in a thousand of those charged with culpable homicide in the USA is ultimately executed (Hood, 1996: 184) – but because the death penalty is a highly visible symbol, symptom and spur to punitive attitudes and policies in general.

By the early 1960s, few US states were carrying out executions. A total moratorium in 1967 was followed by the 1972 Supreme Court decision in *Furman* v. *Georgia*,[7] which effectively ruled all existing death penalty statutes unconstitutional. However, later judgments in *Gregg* v. *Georgia*[8] and other cases upheld redrafted state laws as constitutional, and executions recommenced with the death by firing squad of Gary Gilmore in Utah in January 1977. By 1 July 2003 there had been 859 executions. Currently 38 states and the federal jurisdiction have death penalty statutes, and 3,374 people were on death row at the end of 2003 (although numbers have been declining since 2000).

This doubtless both reflects and reinforces a palpable swing in public opinion on the subject: whereas in 1965 only four out of ten Americans supported capital punishment, by 1991 the figure was seven out of ten and in 1994 eight out of ten (Garland, 2001: 276; Hood, 1996: 48). Despite a more recent relative decline in support for the death penalty,[9] abolitionism is seen as a cause which is both hopeless and professional suicide for any serious American politician to espouse. The fact that the USA is now the only major Western country to retain capital punishment both *de jure* and *de facto*, and the only country covered in this book apart from Japan to do so, explains why we do not discuss it at length; but it is also a dramatic manifestation of the extent to which the USA has been a standard bearer in espousing law and order ideology and putting it into practice.

It is, however, other concomitants of law and order ideology which have had a more direct result on indices such as numbers in prison. In particular, it has been changes rendering more severe the law and practice of *sentencing* which have primarily fuelled the increase in incarceration. (As we saw in Chapter 2, it is certainly not rising crime which has created the rise: while the prison and jail population increased by 400 per cent between the mid-1970s and the present day, crime rates have been dropping since the early 1980s.) One particular component has been the so-called 'War on Drugs' which was initiated during Ronald Reagan's presidency (1981–9), escalated during George H.W. Bush (1989–93) and continued under Bill Clinton (1993–2000) and George W. Bush (2001-present), and which has ensured that convicted drug offenders receive enormously long sentences in the USA compared with many other countries. In 1995, 60 per cent of federal prisoners and 23 per cent of state inmates were drug offenders. For other types of crime, too, both mandatory sentences – such as California's much-copied 'three strikes and you're out' law,[10] adopted in 1994 – and harsh sentencing guidelines have been introduced in state and federal jurisdictions alike over this period. Similarly, so-called 'truth in sentencing laws', which severely restrict the possibility of early release, have been widely introduced (not least because federal funding to states was made dependent on their introduction). Along with a general hardening of the penal culture making sentencing harsher generally, this has all given rise to the current record levels of incarceration. It is necessary to bear in mind, however, that some states have deviated from this general picture. (This state-by-state variation is one reason why this chapter is relatively short and we have restricted ourselves to drawing a broad picture of American developments.)

Both the movement towards neo-liberalism and that towards a harsh neo-correctionalism in criminal justice continue to this day, not only in the USA but more generally. This is despite – one could almost say because of – the coming to power in several countries of left-of-centre governments exemplified by Bill Clinton's Democratic presidency in the USA (1993–2001) and Tony Blair's New Labour Government in the UK (first elected in 1997). Such governments represent the so-called 'Third Way' in politics, whereby parties of the left seek to gain power by accepting and adopting much of the free-market neo-liberalism of their right-wing predecessors in the 1980s. One common feature of such 'Third Way' parties and governments has been a determined effort to shed their erstwhile images as being 'soft on crime'. Again, Clinton and Blair are exemplars. The unsuccessful 1988 Democratic presidential contender Michael Dukakis had suffered in his campaign against George Bush (senior) from the case of Willie Horton, a black convicted murderer who committed rape while on temporary release in Massachusetts while Dukakis was Governor of the state. By contrast, Clinton travelled back to his own state of Arkansas from the 1992 campaign trail especially to approve the execution of another black (and mentally handicapped) killer by the name of Ricky Ray Rector. Tony Blair, less dramatically but equally successfully, revamped the British Labour Party's profile as a 'party of law and order', with the slogan 'tough on crime, tough on the causes of crime' (Cavadino et al., 1999: Chapter 2). Both the Clinton and Blair governments continued and extended at least some of the Strategy A policies of their conservative predecessors. In the USA, of course, conservatism returned with a vengeance in the person of George W. Bush, who became President in 2001 following his incumbency as governor of Texas, the state which at the time carried out more executions than any other. The Bush administration has witnessed further increases in economic inequality, while its first-term Attorney General John Ashcroft took a variety of measures to discourage what he saw as (still) excessively lenient sentencing and prosecuting practices.[11]

Where the USA leads; others often follow. Yet despite US cultural influence and the 'correctional imperialism' we mentioned in Chapter 1, none of our other countries have embraced law and order ideology or imprisoned people to anything like the extent of the USA. This 'American exceptionalism' (Downes, 2001) may perhaps be partially attributed to the more general American tendency to take things to extremes, as well as to its archetypal neo-liberalism, its ruggedly individualistic cultural tradition, and its politics. On the one hand, US politics is subject to the potent 'culture of contentment'[12] so trenchantly described by John Galbraith (1993), which leads to the voting public feeling no need to vote for changes to improve the lot of their impoverished but effectively disenfranchised fellow citizens. On the other hand, there is the USA's location within Joachim Savelsberg's (1999) political typology (see Chapter 1). The politics of the USA is 'decentralized', being democratic and federal, which makes *very rapid* shifts in penality or penal direction unlikely. However – as we saw in Chapter 1 – American public life is also highly 'personalized' rather than 'bureaucratized', depending greatly on individual political and legal decision-makers rather than political parties and civil services. This facilitates a populism which in turn has translated increasingly punitive public attitudes into dramatically harsher punishment over the longer term. This translation is greatly assisted by the fact that judges and district attorneys are directly elected in many places. Add to this the influence of almost unrivalled populist tabloid media fanning fear of crime and hatred of the criminal, and the results are the signs of looming penal crisis which we shall now detail.

Prison numbers: although the USA only contains 5 per cent of the population of the planet, it accounts for nearly a quarter of its prisoners. Its imprisonment rate of 701 prisoners per 100,000 general population in 2002 outstrips any other country in the world.[13] In February 2000, the number of people incarcerated in American prisons exceeded 2 million for the first time. On 31 December 2002, 2,033,331 people were incarcerated in US prisons and jails (Walmsley, 2003b), representing 0.7 per cent of the population of the USA. This represents a 400 per cent increase in numbers incarcerated since the early 1970s,[14] in contrast to the fifty-year period from the early 1920s to the early 1970s, when inmate numbers remained relatively stable. (Indeed, there was a reduction in the American imprisonment rate during the 1960s, at the height of penal welfarism [Savelsberg, 1999: 51–2].) To these figures must be added the much larger number of persons under other forms of correctional supervision (probation and parole), which has quadrupled since 1980, standing at 4.7 million adults at the end of 2002. Currently, a grand total of 6.7 million Americans, over 3 per cent of the adult population, are under some form of punitive confinement or supervision.

The penal scene in the USA is by no means homogeneous, and these overall figures disguise some significant variations between the fifty states, the federal jurisdiction and local counties. Beckett and Western (2001) – in a statistical analysis which fits our general theses well – have demonstrated that states which spend relatively little on welfare are likely to have higher imprisonment rates (as also are those with larger poor and African-American populations and Republican-dominated legislatures). States with large prisoner populations include Texas, Florida, California, Illinois, Michigan, New York, New Jersey, Ohio and Pennsylvania. In 2002 Louisiana had the highest overall incarceration rate (with 794 sentenced inmates per 100,000 inhabitants), while Maine and Minnesota had the lowest (at 141).[15] Even Maine and Minnesota, however, had an imprisonment rate higher than eight of our twelve countries at around the same time (see Table 2.2 in Chapter 2).

Not that the USA's imprisonment rate was ever low in general terms. At almost its *lowest* point since World War Two, the rate was an estimated 188 inmates per 100,000 general population in 1972 (Cahalan, 1979: 12), already higher than any of our other countries (except South Africa) have reached in the early 2000s. To some extent these high imprisonment rates could be attributed to a high rate of crime, especially serious violent crime, in the USA – but only to some extent (see Currie, 1998: Chapter 1). The USA still suffers disproportionately from violence even following the decreases in crime since 1980, albeit to a lesser extent; however, the general risk of being a crime victim in the USA is now not uncommonly high compared to other Western countries (Mayhew and White, 1997).

Overcrowding: one result of these high numbers and large increases is that – despite what has turned into the largest prison construction programme in American history – penal institutions have become more overcrowded. At the beginning of 1995, prisons in the USA were on average operating with 15 per cent more inmates than their rated capacity.[16] By 2002 this figure had increased to 33 per cent above rated capacity across the system as a whole (which includes minimum security facilities). However the degree of overcrowding was significantly higher in secure facilities (at 42 per cent, 58 per cent and 41 per cent in low-, medium- and high-security facilities respectively) (USDOJ, 2002).[17] This state of affairs is unconstitutional as well as deplorable: in 1995, thirty-nine of the fifty states were under federal court orders because of unconstitutional crowding conditions at one or more of its facilities (Wood, 1996: 52). While overcrowding is the most common condition for which such court orders are granted, other factors contribute to what can rightly be termed a general *crisis of conditions* within the American prison system: in 1995, 378 state facilities and 113 federal facilities (41 per cent of a total of 1,196 confinement facilities) were under court decrees to change conditions of confinement, limit the numbers of inmates or correct their policies or procedures (Beck et al., 1997: v). The sheer number of such orders in existence at one time suggests that these prisons are slow to rectify matters.

Again, however, we must make the point that penality in the USA is far from homogeneous between different jurisdictions. Generally speaking, those states which have large prison populations also suffer from major problems of over-crowding: for example, at the end of 1995, the high-imprisonment states of Ohio and New Jersey were operating at 171 and 164 per cent of their maximum inmate capacities respectively.

Another factor contributing to the general crisis of conditions within US prisons (not least because of its potential impact on inmate disorder) relates to the way inmates are dealt with by prison staff. In 2000, the United Nations Committee against Torture expressed public concern with regard to the brutal treatment of inmates in some USA penal institutions, citing the use of elec-troshock belts and chairs as a means of restraint. Concern was also expressed about the excessively harsh regimes in so-called super-maximum prisons, includ-ing the practice of putting inmates in chain gangs, especially in public (Reuters, 15 May 2000).

Staff unrest and *inmate disorder* can perhaps best be described as constant but low-profile realities in US prisons and jails. The numbers of staff in federal and state prisons more than doubled in the decade between 1984 and 1994 while local jail personnel also increased by 38 per cent; this increased number of staff may have kept pace with the construction of new prisons, but not with the num-bers of extra prisoners over this period. Serious industrial action is rare in American prisons and jails, but so is a high level of staff morale. Something sim-ilar could be said of inmate disorder. Major riots are not common at present. There has been no recent repetition of events such as the inmates' strike at California's Folsom Prison in 1970 and the rebellion at Attica State Prison in New York in 1971, but disturbances occur at lower and less publicized levels, and in 1995 a string of disturbances in federal institutions in various states led to a national lockdown in the federal prison system (Fleisher, 2001: 689). At the level of the individual prisoner, one rather unsatisfactory index of disorder and control problems is the number of recorded prison rule violations. (These range from smoking contrary to regulations to serious offences such as assault, rioting and murder; while the relationship between violations committed and those recorded is of course necessarily somewhat obscure). A national survey of state prisons in 1986 (Stephan, 1989) found that 53 per cent of inmates had been charged with at least one violation during their present stay in prison; of these 90 per cent were found guilty, and they committed an average of three violations each per year.

Escapes have not been a salient problem in the US penal system in recent years. For example, in 1994 there were 8,543 reported escapes from state prisons and 655 from federal prisons, including 259 from maximum- and medium-secure facilities. However, 80 per cent of escapes consisted of prisoners walking away from community-based programmes, and 72 per cent of escapers were returned.[18]

Does the US penal system suffer from a general *crisis of resources*? Perhaps it is more of a looming than a present crisis. Certainly there are stretched resources within the prisons and jails, giving rise to overcrowding and the other problems we have noted. But so far, despite occasional expressions of concern (see for example *USA Today*, 2003), politicians have been prepared to devote an ever-rising share of public finances to incarceration while American voters have seemed willing to support such policies. It is questionable whether this wasteful spiral can continue indefinitely, with its inevitable knock-on effects on the general economy and budgets for other public services. As Elliot Currie (1996: 7) points out, 'between 1980 and 1993 total federal spending on employment and training programmes was cut nearly in half. Federal spending on correctional activities meanwhile increased by 521%.' Already in California expenditure on prisons has increased from 2 to 10 per cent of the state budget, now exceeding the amount spent on higher education (*The Guardian,* 25 June 1996). A study for the Rand Corporation in 1995 estimated that in order to finance the 'three strikes and you're out' sentencing law implemented by California in March 1994, total state spending for higher education and various other services would have to fall by more than 40 per cent over the next eight years (Greenwood et al., 1995).

David Downes (1997, 2001; see also Western and Beckett, 1999) has made the intriguing suggestion that – in some respects, and over a relatively short time period – US-style hyperincarceration can actually be functional to the economy. The 2 million incarcerated Americans together with around 1.5 million prison staff add up to about 4 per cent of the male labour force; this reduces the unemployment rate significantly and has contributed towards the strong performance of the US economy in the recent past. In a perverse variation of Keynes's hypothetical cure for recession – get the state to hire large numbers of people to dig holes and then fill them in again – the USA has hired one lot of people to keep another lot locked up. But this analysis suggests that you cannot spend your way out of penal crisis indefinitely – and not only because the direct financial costs are so much greater than just providing people with wages and spades. The strategy – if it can be dignified with such a name – 'relies on an increasing rate of incarceration, whose long-term effects damage employability ... and which therefore tend to increase crime to a disproportionate extent ... The US is now locked into a penal economy which both relies on imprisonment to conceal the true extent of unemployment and on increasing incarceration to staunch its own criminogenic effects.' This 'may hold the line for the time being, but the mixture is highly volatile' (Downes, 1997). Perhaps US voters will continue to vote happily for ever more 'law and order' as long as they remain 'contented' – as long as the economy prospers and crime rates fall (for reasons mostly unconnected with criminal justice and punishment: see Cavadino et al., 1999: Chapter 2; Currie, 1996) – but the trick may not go on working when these benign trends go into reverse, as they inevitably must at some point. Indeed, as we write we may already have seen the beginnings of this reverse, with US growth rates declining at the start of the twenty-first century along with growing federal and state budget deficits and the costs of the 2003 war on (and subsequent occupation of) Iraq mounting up. Many states are now trying to limit the use of prison in response to budgetary pressures, in some cases abolishing certain mandatory sentences (Carter, 2003: 10).

So at some stage the tide may turn against law and order ideology, and indeed, as we shall discuss further shortly, there may be some signs of this already. All this has implications for the question of whether the USA suffers from a *crisis of penal legitimacy*. It does not, in the sense that the general public is not scandalized by the harshness and inhumanity of its penal system. But if this is the test, then few countries – certainly, few democracies – could ever be described as having such a crisis. At a much lower level, various excrescences of the system provide material to prick at least selected consciences. Investigations in the late 1990s into allegations of mass brutality including murders of inmates by guards in California's maximum security Corcoran state prison provide one such scandal. The largest single running sore in the legitimacy of American penality is unquestionably the issue of race. African-Americans make up only 13 per cent of the US population, but they account for around half of those in jail or prison. Various other telling statistics are regularly highlighted: 29 per cent of black American males born today will end up in prison at some stage (Bonczar and Beck, 1997); one in three young black males are already in prison or on parole or probation (Downes, 2001: 72); over 3 per cent of all black American males are currently incarcerated; black American males are eight times more likely to find themselves in prison or jail than whites. There has also been a massive increase in the number of Hispanic prisoners, which has quintupled since 1980 (Currie, 1998: 14). Conversely, however, the majority of probationers are non-Hispanic whites (Bonczar, 1997: 3), indicating that different processes operate within the criminal justice system upon white and non-white offenders. Most gruesomely of all, around 42 per cent of those on death row at the end of 2003 were black, and around 12 per cent Hispanic (Bureau of Justice statistics). Opinions differ as to the exact role played by racism within the institutions of criminal justice in producing figures such as these,[19] but they convey an unmistakeable whiff of racial injustice. This detracts from the legitimacy of the system in the minds of many citizens; where those citizens are either employees or subjects of the penal system, their disaffection contributes to the rumbling staff and inmate discontents mentioned earlier.

Overall then, American penality can be loosely described as in a state of present and looming 'crisis'. Not in the sense that all the stereotypical components of penal crisis are present or threateningly acute; nor is it likely that the whole system will collapse or explode in the near future (cf. Cavadino and Dignan, 2002: 10). But it is in a critical state.

Perhaps the vital question is whether the USA can and will draw back from the brink of crisis. Some think it may already be doing so. Michael Tonry (2004; and see Cavadino, 2005) judges that the USA is coming to the end of a particular 'cycle of intolerance' in its penal 'sensibilities', having been through similar cycles of intolerance with regard to drug use. Signs of a slight softening of penal sensibilities include judicial weakening of three-strikes laws (which have also been the object of popular protests in California, although a proposition to amend the law was defeated by popular vote in November 2004), the appearance of a more lenient approach to drug offenders and the growth of restorative justice programmes. Punitive attitudes as displayed in surveys of US public opinion, including a decline in support for the death penalty, have also shown signs of softening in recent years.[20] But it is too soon to say that a cycle of intolerance is coming to an end, rather than perhaps just taking a slight downturn in some respects before spiralling upwards again. It is tempting to say we can believe it when the US prison population shows a significant and lasting decrease – of which there is as yet no sign. Perhaps the best hope is that, as we have suggested, America will one day decide that hyperincarceration is simply too expensive.

Notes

1 See Cullen et al. (1996: 21–2) for a selection of references to commentators who have described American penality as in a state of 'crisis'.

2 Incarcerative penal institutions in the USA comprise federal and state 'prisons' and local 'jails'. In general in this book we use the word 'prison' (and 'imprisonment') for all such institutions, but in this chapter we need to make the distinction occasionally.

3 We shall be qualifying this generalization in Chapter 17.

4 David Downes (personal communication) suggests that what distinguishes the USA is that as a nation of immigrants it had to absorb more myriad cultures, in a shorter period of time, than any other society. Combined (we would add) with its 'frontier' tradition, this has led to a highly resilient culture placing enormous emphasis on individual freedom and responsibility.

5 It is also worth mentioning that another recurrent happy ending in American fiction concerns the flawed person who repents and becomes good (*Groundhog Day*, *Doc Hollywood*). This redemptive theme (by no means uniquely American, of course: witness the 'lost sheep' and 'prodigal son' parables of Jesus and Dickens's *A Christmas Carol*) is echoed, albeit in a non-voluntaristic mode, in positivism's promise to reform bad people and make them good.

6 The role of prisoners' protests in the rise of the justice model is often overlooked. But no major literary or academic expression of the justice model was published prior to the American Friends Service Committee's *Struggle for Justice* in 1971. This was preceded by the strike at Folsom Prison, California, in November 1970. The strikers' demands – in sharp contrast to those put forward in American prison riots in the 1950s – were anti-positivist in both tone and content, calling *inter alia* for an end to the indeterminate sentences characteristic of positivism (Fitzgerald, 1977: Chapter 12).

7 (1972) 408 US 238.

8 (1976) 428 US 153.

9 A significant event was the moratorium on executions announced by the governor of Illinois in January 2000 in response to concerns about miscarriages of justice in capital cases. Following this, polls found support for the death penalty declining to 66 per cent (Garland, 2001: 276). The number of executions per year declined from a peak of 98 in 1999 to 65 in 2003 (Bureau of Justice statistics).

10 California's version of this law mandates a sentence of '25 years to life' for an offender's third felony conviction, provided that the first two were for 'serious *or* violent' felonies (including crimes such as attempted burglary.

11 One example was a policy directive limiting federal prosecutors' use of plea bargaining (*The Guardian*, 24 September 2003).

12 Not that Americans are necessarily actually *contented* – arguably, modern society creates more and more frustrations and dissatisfactions – but they increasingly see little point in voting to assist those less advantaged than themselves.

13 Its nearest rival currently is Russia, which as recently as 1999 had an imprisonment rate of 730; but by 2003 this had been reduced to 606 (Walmsley, 2003b).

14 In 1972 there were approximately 391,500 inmates in state and federal prisons and local jails in the USA (calculated from Cahalan, 1979: 12). In 1974 there were an estimated 218,205 prisoners in prisons (see above, Note 2) (Murray, 1997), to which must be added around 150–200,000 inmates in local jails.

15 *Sourcebook of Criminal Justice Statistics*: Table 6.24 (available online at: http://www.albany.edu/sourcebook).

16 'Rated capacity' refers to the number of places in a prison certified as acceptable for that institution by a rating official.

17 In marked contrast, local jails in the United States were operating at 93 per cent of the rated capacity at midyear 2002 (Bureau of Justice Statistics, available online at: http://www.ojp.usdoj.gov/bjs/jails.htm, accessed at 13 November 2003).

18 *1995 Sourcebook of Criminal Justice Statistics*, BJS, Washington DC.

19 See for example Wilbanks (1987). However, there are several studies indicating strongly that race is a telling factor influencing sentencing, including the decision as to which murderers receive the death penalty (see for example Spohn et al., 1981–2; Baldus et al., 1989, Lambie, 2002; *The Guardian,* 25 April 2003). It is also convincingly argued that the 'War on Drugs' has been inherently biased against black offenders, targeting the toughest sentences on drug offences in which black people are most likely to be involved. Most notably, federal laws introduced in 1986 penalize crack cocaine offences as harshly as offences involving quantities of powder cocaine 100 times larger (Tonry, 2004: 15, 218).

20 Some of these are detailed by Greenberg (2001: 88). See also Note 9 above.

4

England and Wales: Stop-go and the upwards Zig-zag

You say stop, and I say go, go, go!

The Beatles

'Stop-go policy' is a phrase sometimes used by commentators to describe (and insult) the economic policies of governments. It means that a variety of fiscal and other measures are employed to encourage growth in the national economy when it is felt to be expanding too slowly, and then the brakes are slammed on when it starts threatening to grow too fast. For all its faults, this is a policy that has a certain rational basis: the government has a fairly clear, fairly consistent idea of what amount of growth is desirable, safe and sustainable and it tries to fine-tune the economy accordingly. English[1] penal policy in recent times has also been a matter of 'stop' and 'go', but without the underlying rationality and consistency. The national government has repeatedly changed its mind about whether the prison population should be reduced, contained or expanded, and about how these goals should be achieved. The result has been a tortuous and at times violent penal policy zig-zag as levels of punishment have fluctuated erratically as seen in Table 4.1. Usually imprisonment levels have moved upwards, but this upwards movement has varied from the gradual to the dizzying; occasionally there has been downwards movement, but the general long-term trend points sharply upwards, with the sharpness becoming razor-like in the years since 1993.

Already in the 1970s the size of the English prison population was giving rise to concern. In 1975 it stood at just under 40,000 (81 per 100,000 of the general population). The Home Secretary[2] of the time then said that should it rise to 42,000 'conditions in the system would approach the intolerable and drastic action to relieve the position would be inescapable' (quoted in Stern, 1987: 38). Yet by 1979 the 'daily average population'[3] of the prisons was 42,220.

The response to this by both Conservative and Labour governments in the 1970s was predominantly *pragmatic*. Efforts were made to restrain the prison

Table 4.1   *Prison population of England and Wales 1975–2004*

1975	39,820
1976	41,443
1977	41,570
1978	41,796
1979	42,220
1980	43,109
1981	43,346
1982	43,754
1983	43,773
1984	43,349
1985	46,278
1986	46,889
1987	48,963
1988	49,949
1989	48,610
1990	45,636
1991	45,897
1992	45,817
1993	44,566
1994	48,794
1995	51,047
1996	55,281
1997	61,114
1998	65,298
1999	64,770
2000	64,602
2001	66,301
2002	70,861
2003 (30 June)	73,657
2004 (30 June)	74,488

Source: Home Office statistics.
1975–2002 figures are daily average populations.

population – to keep the brakes on – by exhorting sentencers to use custody less extensively and for shorter periods, while providing them with a greater variety of non-custodial penalties to use as alternatives. (We call this the *strategy of encouragement* [Cavadino and Dignan, 2002: 101–2, 122–3], since it relies on *encouraging* sentencers to use non-custodial penalties rather than limiting their powers to pass sentences of imprisonment.) At the same time, an increased number of prisoners were released on parole. The overall strategy for the prison population was to attempt to achieve a *standstill*. As Rutherford says, this 'amounted to an effort to hold the line on prison population size but did not include a concerted strategy to effect substantial reductions ... By the end of the 1970s standstill policy was near to collapse' (Rutherford, 1986: 56).

Abandonment of standstill, 1979–1987

It was at this stage, in 1979, that the Conservative government of Margaret Thatcher came to power. The Conservative Party has normally portrayed itself as being 'tougher on crime' than its Labour opponents, and for a long time this stance met with the approval of the general public. However, 'law and order' had never been such a prominent election campaign theme as it was in 1979, when the Conservatives committed themselves to increase the resources of the criminal justice system (especially the police), to introduce a tougher regime – known as the 'short sharp shock' – into detention centres for young offenders, and to increase the sentencing powers of the courts. In March 1982, Home Secretary William Whitelaw effectively announced the end of the 'standstill policy' by telling Parliament: 'We are determined to ensure that there will be room in the prison system for every person whom the judges and magistrates decide should go there, and we will continue to do whatever is necessary for that purpose' (HC Deb, 25 March 1982; Rutherford, 1986: 56–7). This heralded the birth of England's most extensive programme of prison building in the twentieth century. The signal had turned to 'go'.

This did not, however, mean that the Thatcher government's penal policies in the early 1980s were entirely determined by law and order ideology. One material factor was that, since the process of building prisons is a slow one, the continuing rise in the prison population was almost inevitably bound to outstrip the provision of new places for some time. So pragmatic considerations still encouraged the government to make some attempt to limit the rise in the prison population by (relatively discreetly) continuing to encourage diversion from court and custody and shorter sentences for many 'run-of-the-mill' offenders. Thus, for example, the same White Paper (Home Office, 1980) that introduced the 'short sharp shock' detention centre also approved the practice of cautioning juvenile offenders, an approval later extended to older less serious offenders. The government also lent support to the use of 'alternatives to custody' such as community service orders and intermediate treatment for juvenile offenders.

But these measures were to apply only to supposedly 'less serious offenders'. There was a general policy of 'bifurcation', with less harsh measures being advocated for petty offenders while the full force of 'law and order' rhetoric and treatment was focused on the more serious 'violent criminals and thugs' (as the 1979 Conservative Manifesto called them).

Overall, it could hardly be claimed that the penal strategy of the early 1980s proved an outstanding success. The prison population continued to rise for most of the 1980s (from 42,220 in 1979 to a peak of 49,949 in 1988, with a record leap of almost 3,000 in the year of 1985), while outbreaks of riots and disorder within prisons continued to be a regular occurrence. The 'short, sharp shock' had proved a disappointment. Recorded crime had risen in every calendar year of the decade except for a 1 per cent drop in 1983, and Britain's inner cities were hit by serious rioting in the summers of 1981 and 1985. The magazine *Punch* once memorably said of the Thatcher government that her bark might be dogmatic but her bite was pragmatic, and so it proved now. In the second half of the 1980s, the Conservative government tried to change the signals back from 'go' to 'stop'.

'The Hurd approach' 1987–1992

A profound change in the government's approach to criminal justice took place following the Conservative victory in the General Election of 1987. The shift occurred first under Douglas Hurd, who was Home Secretary from 1985 to 1989, but the new policies continued to be pursued under his successors until 1992. The resulting new approach, which has been dubbed 'the Hurd approach', represented a shift towards eclectic pragmatism and to a great extent away from domination by the ethic of 'law and order'. It meant that the volume of 'law and order' rhetoric emanating from government was significantly toned down, and was combined with other themes and approaches to crime and punishment such as voluntarization, privatization, crime prevention and a new emphasis on the role of the 'community' in schemes such as neighbourhood watch. Prominent in this new pragmatic mix was the theme of *managerialism*, which included a continued favouring of a 'systems management' approach to criminal justice, and in particular the expanded use of cautioning for adult offenders as well as juveniles. Justice for prisoners also received attention: following Lord Woolf's report (published in 1991) on the causes of the serious riots in Strangeways and other prisons in 1990, various reforms were put under way to improve conditions and regimes within prisons. Above all, there was the package of reforms contained in the Criminal Justice Act of 1991, which were designed to rationalize the process of sentencing and punishment in a way which would reduce the prison population.

The 1991 Act was preceded by a Green Paper (consultative document) in 1988 and a White Paper in 1990 which showed distinct signs of a fresh approach by the government, even being described by one Home Office minister as aiming 'to change the way we think about criminals and punishments'. The Green Paper stated categorically that 'imprisonment is not the most effective punishment for most crime. Custody should be reserved for very serious offences, especially when the offender is violent and a continuing risk to the public' (Home Office, 1988: para. 1.8). Both Green and White Papers contained a procession of negative statements about imprisonment, exemplified by the White Paper's much-quoted phrase that prison 'can be an expensive way of making bad people worse' (Home Office, 1990: para. 2.7). They advocated dealing with many more offenders than hitherto by means of community penalties rather than custody – the policy of *'punishment in the community'*. However, this was still a *bifurcatory* policy, for the thrust was not only to divert less serious offenders from custody, but simultaneously to treat violent and sexual offenders more harshly. Moreover, this was what we call *punitive bifurcation* – meaning that it was punitive not only towards the more serious offenders, but also towards the less serious. True, the intention was to deal with them in the community rather than in custody; but the influence of `law and order' ideology lingered on in the explicit insistence that the non-custodial measures were to take the form of *punishment*. They were intended primarily to punish offenders rather than to rehabilitate them or to make them perform reparation for victims.

The 1991 Act combined this theme of punishment in the community with another policy strand, that of 'just deserts' (the watchword of the 'justice model', mentioned in the Preface and discussed further in Chapters 3 and 10). Punishment was not only to be punitive (whether inflicted by imprisonment or in the community), its punitiveness was to be of the level that the offender deserved by having committed the offence – the punishment should fit the crime. The Act consequently included provisions requiring that punishments should be 'commensurate with' (i.e. proportionate to) 'the seriousness of the offence' (sections 2(2)(a) and 6(2)(b)). Again – and in the interests of diverting as many lesser offenders as possible towards community punishments rather than prison – sentencers were instructed not to pass custodial sentences unless the offence was 'so serious that only such a sentence can be justified' (section 1(2)(a)). In both cases, the Act allowed 'bifurcatory' exceptions for violent and sexual offences where sentences more severe than those 'deserved' by the seriousness of the offence were deemed necessary to protect the public (sections 1(2)(b) and 2(2)(b)). At the same time, various measures were put in place to 'toughen up' non-custodial penalties, to ensure that punishment in the community was genuinely punitive and to encourage sentencers to use these options instead of prison.

Although the 1991 Act introduced for the first time a fairly coherent framework for sentencing in England, including the 'seriousness' criteria for custody and length of sentence, its provisions were framed with sufficient vagueness to leave the interpretation and implementation of the policy of punishment in the community in the hands of the sentencers. At first, there was some evidence that this strategy was being at least partially effective. In the first months following the implementation of the Criminal Justice Act 1991 in October 1992, the proportion of custodial sentences passed dropped significantly, from 16 per cent in the period January–September 1992 to 12 per cent in the last quarter of 1992. The prison population also fell, from 45,835 in September to 40,606 in December 1992. But it was not to last.

'Prison works', 1992–1997

Perhaps coincidentally, or more probably not (see Cavadino and Dignan, 1997: 296–7), the government reached for the 'law and order card' at a time when it was in deep political trouble, jettisoning 'the Hurd approach' and replacing it with more harshly punitive policies which it presumably hoped would bring electoral benefits. The Conservative government of John Major (who had replaced Mrs Thatcher as Prime Minister in November 1990) had won a General Election in April 1992 but on 16 September ('Black Wednesday') had hit the political and economic rocks as the UK was forced to leave the European Exchange Rate Mechanism and devalue the pound. On the criminal justice front, there was a backlash from sections of the media and the judiciary against what was perceived as the 'softness' of the Criminal Justice Act 1991, combined with public horror over the murder of a 2-year-old boy, James Bulger, at the hands of two 10-year-olds in Liverpool. Instead of defending the policy package, which had been so painstakingly put together over a period of five years by successive Conservative Home Secretaries, the government moved more and more into the remarkable role of critic of its own policies and legislation. Key components of its strategy, most notably the attempt to reduce the prison population by means of the 1991 legislation, were abandoned, and certain important provisions within the Act (although not perhaps the most important) were hurriedly repealed in 1993.

The government's strategy included the appointment as Home Secretary in May 1993 of Michael Howard, a right-winger with a profound attachment to the rhetoric and ideology of law and order, who was put in charge of implementing a 'crusade against crime' by pursuing a punitive approach. At the Conservative Party conference of October 1993, Michael Howard announced a twenty-seven-point programme to toughen up the criminal justice system. The twenty-seven points included restrictions on bail and cautioning, the building of six new private prisons, compulsory testing of prisoners for drugs, and new rules to make community service orders more punitive. It was made clear that the government had abandoned the objective of reducing the prison population when Howard proclaimed that 'prison works' to deter crime and protect the public and said this of his package of proposals: 'This may mean that more people will go to prison. I do not flinch from that. We shall no longer judge the success of our system of justice by a fall in the prison population.' Howard subsequently introduced further measures designed to make sentences and punishments harsher, including (in the Crime (Sentences) Act 1997) provisions for American-style 'three strikes and you're out' sentences for certain categories of repeat offenders. (This type of mandatory minimum sentence has been copied only in Britain and in two Australian jurisdictions.) In what was, remarkably, the Conservatives' third different penal policy since 1979, the signals were changed yet again, this time from 'stop' to 'go, go, go!'

We did not have to wait for the implementation of all Howard's proposals to see effects of the Conservatives' 'crusade against crime' on sentencing and on the prison population. Sometimes the mere use of law and order rhetoric by government ministers can be potent on its own. Sentencers responded to the encouragement of the Prime Minister and his home secretaries, both implicit and at times explicit, to make more punitive decisions. Although the 1991 Act – including the 'seriousness' criteria for custody and sentence length – remained mostly intact, the vagueness of its wording provided plenty of leeway for sentencers to take a more punitive tack when invited to do so by the government. The numbers of people sentenced to custody rose from 58,000 in 1992 to 69,200 in 1994. The prison population rose from 40,600 in December 1992 to 43,600 by May 1993 and continued to rise thereafter. Every year from 1995 to 1998 it broke all previous records, reaching a daily average population of 65,300 in 1998 – a spectacular 61 per cent rise from the December 1992 figure. This rise was not due to any increase in the number of offenders before the courts – their number had actually declined since 1992 – but because the courts imposed more, and longer, prison sentences on those before them (White and Powar, 1998: 3; Penal Affairs Consortium, 1999; and see Halliday, 2001: 99).

Tough on crime and tough on the causes of crime: New Labour, 1997 onwards

In May 1997 the Conservative Party was ejected from power as Labour, led by Tony Blair, enjoyed a landslide victory. Tony Blair, following a 'Third Way' approach not unlike that of Bill Clinton in the USA, had striven with great success to reform and 'rebrand' the Labour Party as 'New Labour', and nowhere was this more apparent than in the field of criminal justice policy. While Shadow Home Secretary between 1992 and 1994 (when he assumed the party leadership) and thereafter, Mr Blair sought to alter Labour's public image from that of a party 'soft on crime' to one that was – in his constantly reiterated slogan – 'tough on crime and tough on the causes of crime'. Although the phrase 'tough on the causes of crime' indicated that the Labour Party was still concerned with what it traditionally saw as the social roots of crime such as unemployment, the whole slogan (and Labour's general rhetoric from 1992 onwards) was clearly calculated to appeal to populist sentiments by fostering an impression that Labour wants to deal severely with offenders. This did not mean that the Labour Party went along with all the Conservatives' law and order policies, but it did mean that on occasions it judiciously avoided opposing them. At times, indeed, Labour while in opposition sought to outdo the Conservatives in apparent 'toughness', for example by repeatedly if vaguely proposing tougher penalties for crimes of violence. One effect of this was to encourage the Conservative government to pursue harsher and harsher law and order policies in an effort to 'put clear blue water' between themselves and Labour and come across as even tougher. By the time Labour took power in 1997, the whole centre of gravity of penal politics had shifted significantly in the direction of 'toughness', a lasting legacy of the Conservatives' law and order policies in the 1980s and 1990s.

Following May 1997 the New Labour government introduced a flurry of new proposals and policies relating to punishment. Unlike the period 1993-7, when almost every initiative of the Conservative government was geared to increasing 'toughness', the New Labour policies were a mixed bag. There was a notable shift back towards a more *managerial* approach to criminal justice (reminiscent of the 'Hurd era'), with a strong emphasis on cost-effectiveness and 'evidence-based' policies. Labour Home Secretary Jack Straw (1997-2001) declared that, unlike Michael Howard, he had 'no interest in chanting a simplistic mantra that prison works'.[4] But the mantra of 'tough on crime and tough on the causes of crime' was much in evidence, as for a time was 'zero tolerance' (a conceptual import from the USA: see Cavadino et al., 1999: 28-30). The 'three strikes and you're out' legislation placed on the statute book by Michael Howard was brought into effect, although his plan to practically abolish the system of early release from sentences of imprisonment was jettisoned. Some of the most energetic new policy-making concerned young offenders. Here there was a mixture of a firm 'zero tolerance' approach – with young offenders being restricted to one police reprimand and one 'final warning' before being taken to court – and the more liberal notion of 'restorative justice', with new powers given to courts and to 'youth offending teams' and 'youth offender panels' to arrange or order that young offenders make reparation to their victims or to the community.[5]

As regards imprisonment, the Labour government stepped back from Michael Howard's drive to make prison conditions more austere – for example, his dogmatic blanket ban on the introduction of in-cell televisions was removed. But resource limitations inevitably make regimes difficult to improve unless prisoner numbers are reduced – so what of these? Although the New Labour government occasionally expressed a desire to reduce prison numbers and have more offenders dealt with by community penalties, the main plan for achieving this was – initially at least – a re-run of the old combination of the 'strategy of encouragement' and 'punishment in the community' – trying to ensure that community punishments have a tough enough image so that sentencers will use them more often in preference to custody – which has failed so miserably in the past. Nor has there been any sign of it working under New Labour. The daily average prison population continued to rise at much the same rate in 1997 and 1998 (see Table 4.1), despite a slight decline in the passing of custodial sentences after mid-1997 (Penal Affairs Consortium, 1999). There were slight reductions in 1999 and 2000. This was due to Labour's one major innovation to restrain prison numbers – one that formed a marked contrast to the Conservatives' plans to all but end early release – in the form of 'home detention curfew' (Crime and Disorder Act 1998, section 99).

Under this provision, implemented in 1999 and extended in 2002, prisoners serving sentences of less than four years can be released up to three months early (in addition to any existing entitlement to early release) provided they are assessed as low risk and are subject to a home curfew enforced by electronic tagging. By 19 September 2003 3,669 prisoners were on home detention curfew. But the reduction in 1999–2000 was just another small downturn in the upwards zig-zag. As Table 4.1 shows, the English prison population has continued to rise to all-time record levels, standing in mid-2004 at a rate of 141 per 100,000. In April 2004, a record prison population of 75,544 exceeded the system's theoretical absolute maximum ('usable operational capacity'), requiring a frantic 'game of musical cells' in which prisoners were bussed around the country in search of vacant cells (*The Guardian*, 7 April 2004).

This is despite the dramatic falling-off in hyper-tough talk from the government since the days of Michael Howard and more mixed messages being put across by ministers. However, the preponderance of rhetoric from the government and its highest-profile policies have continued to be on the 'tough on crime' side of the policy equation, with Home Secretaries Jack Straw (1997–2001) and David Blunkett (2001–4) stressing the need to control crime with firm measures and (in the case of David Blunkett) attacking judges for allegedly being soft and out of touch with ordinary people's concerns about crime. In particular, both these Home Secretaries pressed for the imposition of harsher sentences for repeat offenders, effectively abandoning the 'just deserts' approach of the 1991 legislation which sought to relate punishments to the seriousness of the current offence rather than the offender's previous record. In 2003 the government introduced a new minimum sentence of five years' imprisonment for unlawfully carrying a firearm and new statutory criteria designed to significantly increase the sentences served by those convicted of murder.[6] Such rhetoric and policies, as is usually the way, have had their effect on sentencing practice and on prison numbers.

If the prison population were really to be reduced on an enduring basis, it is prisoners' entry through the front door via sentencing which would need to be tackled, rather than slipping a few of them out of the back door via early release. And it is over this crucial issue of sentencing that the most vital question mark currently hangs. Sentencing is to be more closely regulated in future under a new legislative framework provided by the Criminal Justice Act 2003. Although the Act pays lip service to the notions that imprisonment should be a sentence of last resort and that sentences should be proportionate to the seriousness of the offence, other provisions allow for the indeterminate detention of offenders deemed dangerous and require repeat offenders to be sentenced more severely. Sentencing is to be regulated in future by a comprehensive system of guidelines to be promulgated by a Sentencing Guidelines Council assisted by a Sentencing Advisory Panel. This represents a shift from a mere 'strategy of encouragement' towards a more directive approach to sentencing. But it remains to be seen whether the sentencing guidelines which ensue, and the way in which they are implemented by the courts, will have any effect on imprisonment levels – in either direction.

Most recently, the government has shown signs of wishing – for managerial reasons, and using managerial techniques – to restrain the growth in prison numbers, but of having no ambition to reduce them. Home Secretary David Blunkett has welcomed guidance to sentencers from the Lord Chief Justice to replace short prison sentences with 'rigorous' community penalties.[7] The Carter Report (a government-commissioned review of correctional services – Carter, 2003) was warmly received by the government (Blunkett, 2004). This review, heavily managerial in tone, concluded that sentencing had become much more severe in recent years, with the result that penal resources such as prison places and the probation service were being misapplied, overstretched and wasted. The proposed solutions included a new 'National Offender Management Service' combining the prison and probation services, and more 'targeted and rigorous sentences', with greater use of police cautions (with conditions attached), restorative justice measures, fines related to the means of offenders, an extension of electronic monitoring, and custody being reserved for serious, dangerous and highly persistent offenders. Prison numbers, which had been projected to rise to 93,000 by 2009, could be limited to 80,000 (still a substantial rise) by such means. Carter's 'targeting' approach (intended to ratchet down the harshness of sentencing from its present levels) is likely to influence the new directions to sentencers produced by the Sentencing Guidelines Council. However, the temptation for government politicians to continue to talk tough and to use the mechanisms provided by the legislation to influence the Council in the direction of populist harshness seems unlikely to be resisted, especially in the face of a Conservative opposition – currently led by none other than Michael Howard – which is demanding a return to the even harsher policies of 1993–7.

In summary, then, levels of punishment in England have been severely ratcheted upwards in recent years, thanks largely to the revving of the accelerator applied by the Conservative government from 1993. New Labour may have taken its foot off the accelerator, but it has not so far applied the brake. Unless and until it does, the long term upward trend looks likely to continue – although it may zig-zag slightly at times.

Penal crisis in England and Wales

With levels of imprisonment rising as fast as shown in Table 4.1, it would be surprising if the English penal system did not suffer from problems that could be described in terms of a 'crisis'; even bearing in mind the controversies and reservations which may surround the use of a word which is simultaneously so dramatic and such a cliché (Cavadino and Dignan, 2002: 9–10). In terms of our indices of penal crisis, England scores highly on almost all counts, and has done for some time. (We shall merely give brief details here: for a fuller account see Cavadino and Dignan, 2002: Chapter 1.) The high and rapidly rising prison population (together with the overloading of the probation service noted by Carter) means that there are general crises of penal resources, of prison conditions, of control over prisoners, and of staff unrest. Prison overcrowding is a chronic problem. Whereas in 1992 only 7,251 prisoners were sleeping two to a cell designed for one inmate, by February 2003 this figure had risen to 17,000 despite a massive expansion in prison capacity from 46,239 in June 1992 to 66,654 on 19 September 2003. In May of that year ninety of England's 138 prisons were overcrowded. Within prisons, prisoners have been spending more time locked in their cells and less time in purposeful activity, and especially in education (Penal Affairs Consortium, 1999). While there has been no recent repeat of major incidents such as the Strangeways riot of 1990 or the mass industrial action of 1986, there remains serious unrest among prison staff and severe feelings of injustice among inmates. Although English prisons have never in fact had a bad record for security (in the sense of preventing escapes from custody), the system is still feeling the effects of the notorious escapes from the high-security Whitemoor and Parkhurst prisons in 1994 and 1995. The measures taken to tighten security following these breakouts served to divert resources and worsen regimes at a time when the Conservative government was cutting the overall funds allocated to prisons. More recently, the New Labour government has provided substantial additional funding for prisons, in order to provide additional capacity, carry out urgent repairs and increase 'purposeful activity' by inmates. It remains to be seen how far such extra resources will go in the context of a still-rising prison population.

Above all, it cannot be said that the English penal system has emerged from its vital 'crisis of legitimacy' (Cavadino and Dignan, 2002: 22–4). On the one hand, disturbing official reports of conditions in prisons such as Brixton and Feltham Young Offender Institution, rising numbers of inmate suicides and the jailing in 2000 and 2001 of prison officers at Wormwood Scrubs for crimes of brutality trouble the liberal conscience, and many informed observers, practitioners and subjects of the system are convinced that the system is unfair and unjustly harsh. As elsewhere, there is a racial aspect to the system's legitimacy problems, with ethnic minorities comprising 23 per cent of the prison population compared with 9 per cent of the general population in June 2002 (Home Office, 2004a; see more generally Cavadino and Dignan, 2002: Chapter 10). (Britain is also one of those countries in which the influx of asylum seekers has recently been a contentious and inflammatory issue.) On the other hand, the perception of the general public – encouraged by sections of the media and the political profession – is still that of a criminal justice system which is ineffectively weak against offenders. A good example of penal crisis, and a situation which remains perilously close to a full-blown crisis which could erupt at any time.

Political culture and penality in England

The history we have just sketched does not fit totally neatly into our schema of neo-liberal, conservative corporatist, social democratic and oriental corporatist political economies with penalities ranging from the harshest to the relatively most lenient. This does not mean that this schema is incorrect, merely that there are other factors at work as well. We have (appropriately, we think) placed England and Wales in our group of neo-liberal countries, and at the present time it has a level of punishment commensurate to what one would expect of such a nation. However, England is not an archetypal neo-liberal country like the USA; moreover the 'stops' and 'gos' in her penality do not fully correspond with moves towards and away from neo-liberalism. Up to and including the 1970s, the UK – which includes Scotland and Northern Ireland as well as England and Wales – could be described as a broadly social-democratic nation. (Much the same was true of Australia and New Zealand.) In the UK the acceptance of the Beveridge Report by all major political parties in the 1940s had marked a water-shed in social policy. The ensuing reforms enacted by the Labour Government of 1945–51 embodied a clear commitment to the notion of universal social rights of citizenship and a concomitant weakening of people's dependence on unal-loyed market forces. However, this was always far removed from Nordic-style social democracy. On the one hand, the British welfare state was never so gen-erous and universalistic as that in Sweden (despite a National Health Service that in some ways remains a model of socialized medicine), nor were taxation levels as high. On the other hand, trade unions and other interest groups were not integrated into decision-making institutions in the way they were in both Christian Democracies and Nordic social democracies – partly because British trade unions resisted the attenuation of their independence and the wage restraint inherent in such incorporation and insisted instead on retaining 'free collective bargaining'. The overall picture was one of *social democracy without corporatism*.[8]

Arguably, this absence of corporatist institutions left British social democracy vulnerable when the winds of the neo-liberal revival began blowing strongly in the late twentieth century. A state in which a variety of powerful interest groups were strongly entrenched within policy-making processes might have offered more effective resistance to the tide of free market ideology which was chan-nelled into public policy by the Conservative governments of Margaret Thatcher and John Major in the period 1979–97. Social democratic elements of the polit-ical economy and culture were by no means obliterated during this time, but they were severely eroded. Nor were they restored thereafter: the 'New Labour' government of Tony Blair which took power in 1997 was committed (like that of Bill Clinton in the USA) to a 'Third Way' in politics which retains a great deal of Thatcher/Reagan free market ideology and policy.

This has been reflected in English penality. Before 1979 – indeed, one could say until 1993 – British governments generally attempted to pursue relatively lenient penal policies, keeping a lid on the penal population and favouring the rehabilitation of offenders by humane and reformative measures. There were already some signs of toughening criminal justice policies under the Labour government of 1974–79 as the economy slid into trouble, economic policy became tinged with monetarism and neo-liberalism and the Conservative opposition began to assert a confident campaign on law and order issues (Hall et al., 1978; Hall, 1979). Perhaps the greatest historical anomaly as regards the usual neo-liberalism/punitive penality correlation, however, is the following. One might imagine that the Conservative government of Margaret Thatcher (1979–90) would have been the apotheosis of penal harshness, given Mrs Thatcher's iconic status as both a personal believer in strict Strategy A law and order policies and as a world pioneer in introducing neo-liberalism to the late twentieth century. This was not, however, the case. Her government began by pursuing some very high-profile policies of the expected type – such as the 'short, sharp shock' detention centre, although even here the new detention centre regimes were by no means as harsh as they might have been, and the policy was combined, as we have seen, with a push to divert more young offenders away from prosecution altogether. As time went on, however – and especially from 1987 onwards – her government took a much more pragmatic stand aimed at containing and even reducing the prison population.

Doubtless factors such as the personalities and histories of individual politicians and senior civil servants played an important part: Mrs Thatcher seemed to take only an intermittent personal interest in criminal justice issues during her later years in office, while ministers such as Douglas Hurd developed their own very non-Thatcherite policies. Drawing back from personalities, the development of the relatively liberal 'Hurd approach' during the late Thatcher years can be seen as embodying a conflicting historical tendency to the onrush of neo-liberal economy and culture: *the rise of managerialism*. This long-term development (see Preface and Chapter 1) tends to favour more rational, more cost-effective policies which seek to install smoothly running, efficient systems. The concern of managerial-minded ministers and civil servants was that the escalating prison population would prove not only too expensive to run but too difficult to control: deteriorating prison conditions could lead to riots and disorder – leading, of course, to yet more expense and political embarrassment.

It was under Mrs Thatcher's blander-imaged Conservative successor John Major that penal policy took its harshest turn in living memory. Even taking care to recall that the Major government of 1990–7 took the UK much further down the neo-liberal road than Mrs Thatcher had ever managed in various other respects as well, such a volte-face can hardly be entirely explained as a mere concomitant of generally conservative attitudes. Partly it was a result of a particular political conjuncture, where a ruling party found itself in desperate trouble and sought what it saw as a trusty vote-winner in populist law and order approach. In making this judgement, it was undoubtedly highly influenced by recent American political history and the way in which American politicians (such as George H.W. Bush in the presidential contest against Michael Dukakis in 1988) had reaped significant benefits by promising heavier punishments for criminals.

New Labour's mixed bag of penal policies and philosophies fits reasonably well with its general approach. This is to accept a great deal of the neo-liberalism which has gone before, and indeed in some respects to increase the sphere of free markets and private provision, not generally seeking either to turn the clock back or to go forward to a new social democracy (save for certain policies such as the introduction of a minimum wage). Similarly, no attempt seems likely to reduce rates of imprisonment to a pre-Thatcherite (or even Thatcherite) level. But if New Labour is anything, it is 'modern': managerialism is very much to the fore. The government is interested in achieving value for money, in ascertaining 'what works' to contain and reduce crime, and wants policy to be 'evidence-based'. It accepts that the evidence does *not* show that 'prison works'. And the communitarian moral instincts of politicians such as Tony Blair, Jack Straw and David Blunkett – although arguably at odds with their acceptance of a predominantly neo-liberal economy – combined with their enthusiasm for things 'modern', leads them to display interest in ideas such as restorative justice. All the time, however, New Labour is concerned with providing a voter-friendly package and image which will keep the Labour Party in power, and above all, perhaps, it will beware of being seen as 'soft on crime'. We must be tough; we must be modern; we must get value for money; we must be re-elected. It is this combination of attitudes and desires which are currently shaping the penal scene in England.

Notes

1 England and Wales – two countries within the UK of England, Wales, Scotland and Northern Ireland – have a single integrated penal (and legal) system. 'England' and 'English', here and elsewhere in this book, mean 'England and Wales' or 'English and Welsh'.

2 The Home Secretary is the British senior government minister whose responsibilities include the criminal justice system.

3 This statistic refers to the average population of the prisons on an average day in the year.

4 Quoted in *Prison Report* No. 41, Winter 1997, p. 3.

5 These developments are explained in greater detail in Chapter 12.

6 Criminal Justice Act 2003, s. 287, Part 12 Chapter 7 and Schedule 21.

7 *The Guardian*, 6 March 2002; Lord Chancellor's Department Press Notice, 14 June 2002.

8 A looser form of 'corporatism' did make some headway in Britain for a time, embodied in 'tripartite' arrangements (bringing together government and both sides of industry) in bodies such as the National Economic Development Council. (The NEDC was created in 1962, had its role much reduced by Conservative governments in the 1980s, and was abolished in 1992.) This attenuated corporatism may be seen as having reached its highest point during the 'social contract' between the Labour government and the trade unions in the mid-1970s.

5

Australia and New Zealand: Neo-Liberal Punitiveness Down Under

Australia and New Zealand are two English-speaking countries, neighbours in the southern hemisphere, with similar and interlocked histories, cultures and political systems. New Zealand has the smallest population of all our sample of nations (around 4 million souls at present) while Australia's current population of around 20 million[1] is fifth smallest out of our eleven countries. Both countries have been becoming distinctly more punitive in recent years, especially New Zealand.[2] Australia's overall imprisonment rate increased from seventy prisoners per 100,000 population in 1986 to 116 in 2001 (115 in 2002), overtaking Italy, France, Germany and Finland in this time. New Zealand began with a higher imprisonment rate of 82 in 1986, which has climbed even faster to a level of 157 in 2001 (155 in 2002) – higher than anywhere in Western Europe, including England. In 2004 New Zealand's rate had reached 179.[3]

This general picture of increasing harshness of punishment is well in line with our basic thesis linking penality with forms of (and developments in) political economies and cultures. Like the UK, both Australia and New Zealand were best categorized as 'social democracies' in the late 1970s, having a relatively egalitarian ethos and generous universal welfare benefits. But (also as in the UK) in neither country was this welfarism embedded into the body politic by powerful corporatist institutional arrangements such as exist in the European Christian Democracies and Scandinavian social democracies. One factor in this was the traditional fear on the part of trade unions in all three countries of losing their independence and freedom of action by becoming locked inextricably in the grip of the state. Arguably, this lack of corporatist entrenchment left all three English-speaking social democracies with less protection against the rise of neo-liberalism – the anti-welfarist, free-market ideology of the 1980s and after, personified most memorably by Margaret Thatcher in the UK and by Ronald Reagan in the USA. In the Antipodes, however, the first major steps in the neo-liberal direction were taken not by conservative politicians but by the Labor governments of Bob Hawke in Australia (1983–91) and David Lange in New Zealand (1984–9). Hawke and Lange could therefore be said to have anticipated the 'New Labour' Party of Tony Blair in Britain[4] by over a decade in that their traditionally and nominally social democratic parties adopted a large measure of neo-liberal ideology and policies appropriated from conservative parties and governments (notably, again, those of Reagan and Thatcher).

Since the mid-1980s successive governments in both Australia and New Zealand of both political complexions have been winding back the welfare state, a process which in Australia has occurred at both Federal and State level. The change has been particularly dramatic in New Zealand, which from being one of the world's most highly regulated social democracies has become a highly deregulated (and much more unequal) economy. The process may now have stalled somewhat following the election in 1999 of a Labor-led minority coalition government – partly dependent upon Green Party parliamentary support – under Helen Clark, who could fairly be described as generally 'Blairite' both generally and in the field of law and order policy. However, both Australia and New Zealand can now be said to fall within the 'neo-liberal' category of political economy. And, as we generally find, neo-liberalism brings with it 'authoritarian populism' (Hall, 1988) including what we term 'law and order ideology' and a 'Strategy A' or 'neo-correctionalist' approach to penal policy (see Preface), which in turn brings more penal harshness and (as one of its symptoms) a rapidly increasing penal population.

The imprisonment rate of both countries in 1986 was around the West European average (see Table 2.2 in Chapter 2) – higher, for example, than that of Sweden, but lower than England and West Germany at that time. But by the late 1990s, New Zealand's rate was higher than any of our West European countries, while Australia's rate was exceeded only by England among our West European countries (and only by Scotland, Spain and Portugal outside our sample) – a situation that persists. Thus it was in general the countries who were the most neo-liberal by the start of the twenty-first century that exhibited the highest imprisonment rates, with the countries that had moved from social democracy to neo-liberalism (New Zealand, Australia and England) showing large increases.

More generally, penal policies in both Australia and New Zealand – like their political ideologies – have, both historically and in the present day, normally been imported either from the old colonial motherland or in addition (more recently) from the USA. Both Australia and New Zealand were of course originally British colonies, although from a penological point of view they started off as opposites. Australia was primarily a land of penal settlements to whom Britain transported her convicts from 1787 to 1867, while New Zealand never received Britain's convicts (indeed, in the nineteenth century she transported a few of her own to Tasmania). But in terms of their penal philosophies and practices, they have generally followed Britain (see, for example, Pratt, 1992). This is still largely the case in both countries, as instanced by the New Zealand Labor Party's Blairite approach to criminal justice policy and the adoption of Tony Blair's 'tough on crime and tough on the causes of crime' slogan by politicians such as Peter Beattie (Labor Premier of Queensland since 1998). Other policies and developments, such as the introduction of 'truth in sentencing' in New South Wales in 1989, 'three strikes and you're out' sentences in Western Australia and the Northern Territory in the 1990s,[5] and prison privatization (see Chapter 16) owe more to American influences.

However, one important exception to this pattern of importation of penal policies from other Anglophone nations concerns restorative justice measures for young offenders, which both Australia and New Zealand have played a pioneering role in developing and in exporting back to the motherland and even (in the case of 'police-led restorative conferencing') to the USA. We shall deal with these restorative processes in Chapter 1. For the moment, however, we will merely note that, as in England, the philosophy and practice of restorative justice has so far only been applied to any great extent to juvenile offenders in both Australia and New Zealand, with adults being largely left to the mercy of a more traditional, and increasingly harsh, penality.[6]

Australia

Three particularly notable features about the Australian penal scene are the wide variations in punishment between different states, the over-representation of Aboriginal people in prison (Brown, 1998), and the remarkable progress of prison privatization in Australia. (This third feature will be dealt with in detail in Chapter 16, and will not be discussed further in this chapter.)

Australian culture contains a strong element of (good-natured) rugged individualism, epitomized by the hero of the popular 1986 comedy film *Crocodile Dundee*. The stereotypical image of Australians – certainly the male ones, and some would say the women as well – is of people who are tough, macho, aggressively classless and unaffected, plain-speaking, matey yet pugnacious, proudly independent yet with a sentimental streak and a sense of fair play (or giving everyone a 'fair go'). In fact, rather like Bob Hawke, the popular Labor Prime Minister (1983–91) who did much to introduce neo-liberalism to Australia. The contradictions inherent in this cultural image – which is as much used by Australians to define themselves as by non-Australians – and the mindset that it represents means that it can work itself out in terms of penality in some sharply varying ways, as indeed it has at different historical times, and in the different jurisdictions (which may be an academic way of saying, or avoiding saying, that it is not easy to detect exactly what effect the Australian national character actually has on punishment). Thus, Australia's social democratic and less punitive period could be seen as having brought out the Australian sense of fair play and senti-mentality, while its more recent neo-liberalism and harsher punishment may reflect the country's more macho side.

Historically, Australia has had its periods of relatively lenient punishment lev-els. In the mid-1980s its imprisonment rate was lower than those of England and several other West European countries (including Italy, France, West Germany and Finland). (This reflected a decline in the early 1980s, following on from a slow increase throughout the 1970s: Freiberg, 1997b: 157.) A comparison between Australia and England at that time (Walker et al., 1990) found – as such com-parisons commonly do find – that the difference was not due to varying rates in the commission or detection of crime, but in different patterns in the decisions made by courts (cf. Cavadino and Dignan, 2002: Chapter 4). The relevant deci-sions were not only those concerning the sentencing of convicted offenders, although it was indeed the case that that English courts sent a higher number of offenders to prison. (Differences in the 'prison-or-not?' sentencing decision loomed larger in Walker's comparison than decisions as to the *length* of sentence of those sent to prison.) But of equal importance were decisions as to whether untried defendants should be granted bail or be remanded in custody and thus contribute to the numbers of remand prisoners in the system. Since then, imprisonment rates have risen in both countries – and, if our analysis is right, for much the same rea-sons in both countries – but Australia has remained behind England in the pun-ishment stakes while overtaking several corporatist European countries along with social democratic Finland.

Australia today scores highly on certain of our indices of whether or not a coun-try suffers from a 'penal crisis'. Prisoner numbers are high both historically and in relation to areas such as Western Europe (although not compared to the USA, South Africa or Russia), and the general trend is still strongly upwards. Prison overcrowding is a potent reality in almost all Australian jurisdictions, despite sub-stantial prison building programmes in recent years (Brown, 1998: 376–8). This necessarily has an adverse effect on the conditions within prisons, although in general physical conditions within Australian prisons (many of which are of rela-tively modern design) are not as bad as one might expect. Prison escapes, riots and industrial unrest are not major problems, although there were some serious prison disturbances in the 1970s and there are still occasional incidents such as the riot at Woodford prison near Brisbane (Queensland) in January 1997.[7]

Accommodating the rising prison population is of course an expensive busi-ness, not necessarily alleviated by the introduction of a substantial privatized sector into the prison systems of several jurisdictions (see Chapter 16). Perhaps, though, this does not as yet amount to a generalized 'crisis of penological resources'. The most critical problems of current Australian penality are undoubt-edly those of legitimacy. On the one hand, there is a common feeling such as is found in many countries today – and one which some Australian politicians have been eager to try to exploit – that the criminal justice system is excessively lenient on offenders. On the other hand, there are the specific legitimacy problems created by the system's treatment of Aboriginal people.

Australia's Aborigines have been called 'the most imprisoned race in the world' (Brown, 1998: 376).[8] People of Aboriginal or Torres Strait Island descent make up about 2 per cent of the overall Australian population, but around one-fifth of its prison population, and even higher in some jurisdictions (Freiberg, 2001: 50–1). Seventy cent of the Northern Territory's (proportionately massive) prison population is Aboriginal (compared with 20 per cent of the NT general population), although over-representation of Aborigines in prison is actually higher in several other states. Overall, Aborigines are over-represented in Australia's prisons by a factor of 10. (This compares with an over-representation factor of around 3 to 3.5 for black prisoners in countries such as England, the USA, South Africa and New Zealand.) There has been particular concern surrounding the disproportionate number of Aborigines who commit suicide or otherwise die in prison and in police custody, which led to the setting up of a Royal Commission into Aboriginal Deaths in Custody (1991). More recent developments in the direction of 'Strategy A' law and order policies have further exacerbated the Australian penal system's problem of racial illegitimacy, as they have borne with particular harshness on Aborigines. In July 2000 the United Nations Human Rights Committee singled out the mandatory sentencing laws enacted by Western Australia and the Northern Territory[9] (and subsequently abandoned in the latter) in this respect in criticizing Australia's treatment of Aborigines.

All this, of course, is in the historical context of a multiply dispossessed indigenous people who were ruthlessly expropriated, exploited, disenfranchized and discounted by the white settlers and their descendants, in a nation which simultaneously for over a century pursued the notorious, overtly racist 'White Australia' immigration policy (largely abandoned in 1966, but completely abolished only in 1973). So far, 'Fortress Australia' is the only Western country that detains all incoming asylum seekers. Australia's inhospitable stance in this respect was dramatized in August 2001 when its government refused entry to 433 mainly Afghan refugees who had been rescued by the Tampa, a Norwegian freighter, from a sinking ferry off Indonesia (a highly popular stance which was credited with winning the November 2001 General Election for John Howard's conservative coalition). Some have put this attitude down to the fragile ego of a country with a relatively small population, one quarter of it already of immigrant origin, which consequently readily feels under threat from the outside. If so, this is an attitude which could well spill over against 'the outsider within' – the Aborigine – with the result that Aborigines are socially excluded to an even greater extent, and harshly punished when they break the law as a result.

Responses to the increasing problems of the penal system have taken forms in Australia which are in general similar to those observed elsewhere. Brown

(1998: 386) speaks of 'a period of upheaval and reform in the 1970s, and a period of reaction and increased punitiveness in the 1980s and 1990s'. The 1970s saw some serious prison disturbances and militancy among prisoners (mirroring developments in other countries such as England and the USA). Rising prison populations and inquiries such as the highly critical Nagle Royal Commission into prisons in New South Wales (Nagle, 1978) motivated some liberal prison reforms and the creation of new non-custodial sentences such as community service. In the 1980s, loss of faith in the rehabilitative worth of punishments gave rise to a growing influence of the notion of 'just deserts' with its corollaries of 'truth in sentencing' (abolition or restriction of early release from prison sentences) and moves to create a more regularized system of punishments proportionate to the offence. But, also commencing in the 1980s, these developments have been largely overtaken by a populist 'law and order' tide favouring harsher measures such as mandatory sentences (notably in Western Australia and the Northern Territory).[10] Australian politicians from all parties – like those in the USA and the UK – have in recent years tended to compete with each other as to who can come across to the electorate as 'toughest on crime', and the differences between parties over penal policies – like their differences in political philosophies and policies generally – have become increasingly blurred.[11]

In every one of these developments, Australia could be said to have followed in the footsteps of the USA – partly because similar developments were occurring in the two countries, but importantly also because penal ideas were imported from the USA. Australia perhaps more than many other countries has a propensity to copy international trends, for behind its often bluff vaunting of its own national identity, many have discerned an inferiority complex vis-à-vis (in particular) both the old mother country and the United States, leading to a 'cultural cringe' (a phrase minted by former Labor Prime Minister Paul Keating) which facilitates the kind of 'correctional imperialism' which recurs so often in this book.

Other developments equally familiar from other countries have also been apparent in Australia. *Bifurcation* – the strategy whereby lesser punishments are sought for less serious offenders whereas simultaneously new extra-long sentences are targeted on a sub-group of supposedly especially dangerous or serious offenders – has also made its mark, with legislation allowing for the indeterminate detention of particular categories of offender having been introduced in several states. And, as elsewhere, the move to increase sentences for the 'dangerous' has been more effective than the attempt to reduce punishments at the lower end. *Managerialism* has also been much in evidence, with attempts to manage penal systems by objectives and performance indicators. The managerial approach is typified by the 'corporatization' of Queensland's prisons under the Queensland Corrective Services Commission (following the Kennedy Report of 1988), and the creation (by the Criminal Justice Act 1989) of

Queensland's Criminal Justice Commission, with the remit to monitor the performance and resources of the state's criminal justice system. The remarkable progress of private prisons in Australia (see Chapter 16) can also be seen as one manifestation of the 'managerial' approach to punishment.

Geographically, there are huge variations of punishment levels within Australia. The country has eight penal jurisdictions in total – six states (New South Wales [NSW], Queensland, Victoria, South Australia, Western Australia and Tasmania) and the two Territories, Northern Territory, (not strictly an autonomous state) and the small Australian Capital Territory (ACT) surrounding Canberra. Unlike the USA, there is no federal penal system, although the Australian parliament can create federal criminal offences, which may be subject to federal sentencing legislation. This geographical division means that it is possible for different penal cultures to develop even in locales that are not only part of the same nation state and physically close to each other, but which are in many other relevant respects similar. (In like manner, there are also significant inter-state differences in the USA and Germany – see Chapters 3 and 7 – and in Canada: see Gaucher and Lowman, 1998.) The situation is analogous to that whereby neighbouring courts in countries like England can – sometimes for no apparent reason – have very disparate 'sentencing cultures' whose differences can persist over long periods of time. The 'penal elite' of Australia – unlike that of New Zealand – is divided between the jurisdictions; one could even say that Australia has not one but eight penal elites and eight different criminal justice systems. Imprisonment rates vary greatly between jurisdictions: the Northern Territory has an extremely high rate, while Western Australia, Queensland and New South Wales also have high rates compared with the other states and the ACT.[12]

A rough correlation may be observed between imprisonment rates and the political ideology of the government at both state and federal level, with more conservative and neo-liberal governments tending to preside over higher prison populations (Walker, 1994). Given the convergence between political parties we noted earlier and their recent tendencies to try to outbid each other in penal harshness, this by no means always neatly follows party lines. But, for example, New South Wales's prison population increased significantly under the Conservative government which held power from 1988 to 1995, an increase which made a substantial contribution to the rise in the national prison numbers (NSW being the most populous state in Australia). A major and high-profile player in *New South Wales* at this time was the populist Minister for Corrective Services Michael Yabsley, who described liberal penal views as 'hogwash' and introduced a wide range of harsh, Strategy A-type measures (Brown, 1991; 1998: 387–8). One such was the Sentencing Act 1988 which introduced a measure of 'truth in sentencing' – a notion with appeal both to advocates of 'just deserts' and 'law and order ideology'. The abolition of remission and severe restriction on the availability of parole, introduced without any serious concomitant attempt to reduce the length of prison sentences passed by the courts, had the predictable effect of contributing to an explosion of the NSW prison population by increasing average time in custody by an estimated 20 per cent (Gorta, 1997: 153). At the same time, liberal reforms of prison regimes were reversed, sparking off major disturbances in prisons throughout the state (Brown, 1991).

In *Queensland* (the third most populous state) prison populations declined following the election of Labor governments in 1989 and 1998, but there were sharp increases in the 1990s, commencing under a Labor government and continuing under a conservative coalition. The Penalties and Sentences Act 1992 directed judges to use the sentence of imprisonment as a last resort, but amendments introduced under the conservative administration watered down this principle substantially and created a new category of 'serious violent offences' attracting mandatory minimum sentences of fifteen years' imprisonment, with predictable results. The more recent reduction in Queensland's prison population since Labor's election in 1998 is perhaps notable for coming despite the 'tough on crime' rhetoric and policies emanating from all political parties. Despite this reduction – which resulted in the state's prisons operating below capacity in 2000 – Queensland's imprisonment rate remains well above the Australian national average (Criminal Justice Commission, 2001), similar to that of New South Wales.

Victoria is different from both these two. Although also a populous state (second to NSW) on the eastern seaboard, bordering NSW and with a similar history and culture, it has for a long time had little more than half NSW's imprisonment rate (Brown, 1998: 372). The official government and legislative policy that imprisonment should be used as a punishment of last resort seems to have been more effective than in some neighbouring states. The reasons for this difference are not altogether obvious, although one possible factor is race. Australian jurisdictions with relatively high proportions of Aborigines in their population tend to have high imprisonment rates[13] (though by no means necessarily higher crime rates), and Victoria has a much smaller proportionate Aboriginal population than either NSW or Queensland.[14] It seems that the *mechanisms* which produce the differential are again largely the decisions made by courts when sentencing convicted offenders (Brown, 1998: 373). One particular often-quoted factor is the availability of an extended range of non-custodial sentences, which are popular with the courts (Freiberg, 1997b; Randla, 1995). But experience elsewhere (including England and France) suggests that the mere provision of various non-custodial alternatives can often make little or no difference to custody rates, since the non-custodial options are merely used as alternatives to each other rather than instead of custody. So what needs to be explained is why this 'strategy of encouragement' (Cavadino and Dignan, 2002: Chapters 4 and 5) has worked in Victoria when it has failed elsewhere. And here it has been suggested that (as in the Netherlands, at least until recently) the answer lies with the culture and ideology prevailing among the sentencers. In Victoria, as in the Netherlands, the judiciary 'has generally taken a view that imprisonment is ultimately unproductive, has undesirable side effects, and should be used as a sanction of last resort' (Ministry of Justice, 1998: Appendix 2). Sentencers have also resisted the introduction of sentencing guidelines and presumptive and mandatory sentences, preferring to sentence according to their own relatively lenient lights.

Despite its low imprisonment rate, some very similar trends and developments can be detected in Victoria to those in other states. Thus, for example, a political debate over the issue of 'truth in sentencing' contributed to a substantial review of the Victorian sentencing system (Victorian Sentencing Committee, 1989) and the Sentencing Act 1991 which abolished remission, albeit simultaneously instructing sentencers to reduce the lengths of the sentences they passed to compensate (Freiberg, 1995; Randla, 1995). Although this change did not initially appear to increase the Victorian prison population, increases were seen from 1994 onwards (Freiberg, 1997b: 161–2), doubtless because the instruction to reduce the lengths of sentences announced in court had little effect, but also because of a growing general punitiveness encouraging longer sentences for offenders convicted of serious crimes (Ministry of Justice, 1998: Appendix 2). The 1991 Act had been passed under a Labor administration which was replaced in 1992 by a radical conservative government elected on a platform of tough law and order policies. Legislation passed in 1993 introduced disproportionately long and indefinite sentences for serious violent and sexual offenders. Yet the *differential* in imprisonment rate between Victoria and its neighbours has remained; all have gone in similar directions but this has not resulted in homogenization of punishment levels.

New Zealand

Perhaps the most salient difference between New Zealand and Australia is that New Zealand has no federal structure and hence no separate jurisdictions which might exhibit the kinds of disparity we have noted in Australia. New Zealand is also, of course, much smaller than Australia; indeed its population of 4 million is less than that of either New South Wales or Victoria. It has, for example, only one maximum security prison.

Culturally and historically the two countries have much in common as well as being next-door neighbours. New Zealand's culture is an attenuated version of the Australian tradition described earlier (for example, a similar liking for sport, with a particular penchant for Rugby Union and strong national pride in the world-beating All Blacks). However, New Zealanders are often understandably annoyed at being mistaken for Australians or lumped together with them (as we are doing here) and keen to differentiate themselves from their neighbours. They have been known to take pride in being a small nation that at times leads the world, for example (paradoxically) both in creating one of the most highly regulated social-democratic welfare states prior to the arrival of David Lange in 1984, and in having taken particularly giant strides towards neo-liberalism thereafter.[15]

Another element of New Zealand's cultural and historical traditions, identified by our contributor John Pratt (1992) as being of particularly significance in its penal history, is the vision of New Zealand as the 'perfect society'. When New Zealand was colonized in the nineteenth century 'the settlers wanted to build a perfect society: a Britain of the South Pacific, but without any of the social problems of the home country' (Pratt, 1992: cover blurb) – and, unlike Australia, without the new country's population being largely based on Britain's rejected deviants (transported convicts and their descendants) messing up their perfection. And yet – if, indeed, 'yet' is the appropriate word – New Zealand has consistently had a high rate of imprisonment compared with Australia and most of Western Europe, including England (save for a brief period in the mid-1980s). Certainly imprisonment rates were higher than one would expect from a predominantly social-democratic country in the 1970s and early 1980s, and today they are high even for a nation which has turned so strongly towards neo-liberalism. Pratt's thesis is that the 'perfect society' syndrome on the one hand led New Zealand to be particularly intolerant towards its deviants, creating high levels of both social exclusion and punishment.[16] But at the same time, it also caused a degree of denial about the country's social problems and need for social control, so that New Zealand preferred punishment to take place invisibly behind the prison walls. Non-custodial alternatives such as probation, which retain deviants more visibly in the community, were introduced but for the most part never greatly developed or used as they were elsewhere (although the semi-custodial disposal of 'periodic detention', introduced in 1962, was a notable feature of the New Zealand penal system until its abolition by the Sentencing Act 2002).

Imprisonment was used for Maori offenders as well as for those of European descent, despite the prior existence of Maori penal practices which did not include imprisonment. The perfect society was to be British in its culture, without any room for the quaint customs of the natives, and this attitude persisted to create continuing resistance to the reinstatement of Maori modes of punishment – although the new system of youth justice which was introduced by the Children, Young Persons and their Families Act 1989 (see Chapter 13) was designed to be more sensitive to Maori values. We shall discuss the racial dimension of New Zealand's penality further shortly.

Official rhetoric and ideology – especially that emanating from official bodies such as Commissions of Inquiry, which have been numerous – was for a long time anti-custodial. By the early 1980s, although rehabilitative optimism had collapsed in New Zealand as elsewhere, its place had been partially taken by a humane version of 'just deserts' philosophy, while even the prison abolition movement was exerting a noticeable influence (Pratt, 1987). This anti-custodial ideology was reflected in legislation. New Zealand's Criminal Justice Act of 1985 – which followed a Penal Policy Review by an official commission which reported in 1981 (Department of Justice, 1981) – laid down the familiar principle that imprisonment should be used as a last resort, and even went so far as to provide that those who committed property offences punishable by seven years' imprisonment or less should not be imprisoned except in special circumstances. In terms of enacted statute law, this represents a far greater intrusion upon sentencers' discretion to imprison than is found even in countries with low levels of imprisonment. It did not, however, prevent the prison population from rising sharply after 1986 (following only a gradual increase over the previous quarter century). The prison population increased by 58 per cent between 1986 and 1996. (Interestingly, in view of our general thesis, this sharp increase in the rate of imprisonment coincided with New Zealand's switch to neo-liberal social and economic policies.) One might suspect that there was a serious gap between the anti-custodial 'law in the books' represented by the 1985 Act and the 'law in action' when courts passed actual sentences. Yet official research suggests that in fact the law has been applied by the courts in line with the legislative intent. The proportion of the prison population who are property offenders declined from 29 to 20 per cent between 1987 and 1995, and the average property offender in prison had 40 previous convictions. The increase in the prison population has been mainly in people convicted of *more serious violent offences*, who have increased in number, and have also been receiving harsher sentences from the courts and serving a higher proportion of these longer sentences in prison before being released (Ministry of Justice, 1998: Chapter 3). Thus the picture is very much one of *bifurcation*, with increasing penal harshness being directed towards those at the more serious end of the offending scale.

This bifurcatory policy found expression in the 1985 Act itself, which introduced a presumption in favour of imprisonment for seriously violent offenders, a tendency which was to be strengthened in subsequent years (Thorp, 1997). But parole was also liberalized at this time, leading to a (temporary) reduction of the prison population by several hundred in 1985–6. By the late 1980s the political climate had changed. A further Commission of Inquiry into the Prison System (1989; the 'Roper Report') expressed liberal scepticism about the desirability of imprisonment except where there was a significant risk of further violent offending and made a number of liberalizing recommendations. But this time the liberal line met a less welcoming response from the political realm, and only minor recommendations of Roper were effectively implemented, while new legislation in 1993 specifically increased sentences and post-release controls on sex offenders (Thorp, 1997), although it also increased parole eligibility for those who were not serious violent offenders. This followed a particularly notorious child rape/murder which – like the murder of James Bulger in England in 1993 – may have played a significant part in accelerating New Zealand's move towards a harsher penal climate. A further increase in 'populist punitiveness' in the late 1990s and early 2000s has been well charted by Pratt and Clark (2004).

On the political front, the 1984-1990 Labor government's introduction of economic neo-liberalism left the National Party (conservative) opposition to try to make capital on the law and order question in imitation of conservative parties elsewhere. Their call for tougher policing and punishments was met by a similar shift on Labor's part. The National Party government of 1990–9 toned down its penal stridency on coming to power, preferring to stress managerialism and limited privatization rather than ever-increasing harshness. There were no moves, for example, to introduce either 'three strikes and you're out' sentences, or to reduce early release by means of 'truth in sentencing' legislation. However, a citizen-initiated referendum on criminal justice was held in conjunction with the 1999 General Election, in which 92 per cent of those participating voted for minimum sentences and 'hard labour' for all serious violent offenders (although also for more restitution and compensation for victims).[17] The new Labor-led coalition under Helen Clark subsequently undertook a review of the legislative framework contained in the 1985 Criminal Justice Act and passed a Sentencing Act, a Parole Act and a Victims' Rights Act in 2002, replacing the 1985 Act. The 2002 legislation was a (one might say 'Blairite') mixed package which on the one hand abolished the mandatory life imprisonment sentence for murder while on the other increasing the terms that most murderers will serve, and sought to encourage the use of fines and restorative justice processes, but also, again, contained various measures designed to imprison serious and 'high risk' offenders for longer. (As the legislation was being passed, the Justice Minister encouraged judges to make more use of maximum penalties.) The Victims' Rights Act extended the rights of victims to be notified of decisions relating to 'their' offenders.

The campaign for the 2002 General Election (won by Labor) was notable in that all main parties other than the Greens competed on the basis of being 'tough on crime' (Pratt and Clark, 2004). There have since been signs of a further upsurge of populist punitiveness. In 2004 the opposition National Party leader Don Brash promised to abolish parole, a measure he himself estimated would increase prison numbers by 50 per cent; for its part the Labour-led government is now building four more prisons and planning to restrict the rights of prisoners.

Despite high levels of imprisonment and a heightened atmosphere of punitiveness, New Zealand does not as yet appear to be in any generalized state of 'penal crisis'. Prison conditions are generally relatively good – compared, for example, with England, if not (say) Sweden. Overcrowding is not a major problem, with most prisoners spending most of their sentences in a single cell with internal sanitation, although the current growth in prison numbers is certain to lead to an increase in 'double bunking'. Resource problems for the system are limited by the fact that around two-thirds of prison places are minimum security. Escapes from prison have not been a significant difficulty to date. There was some industrial unrest in the 1990s, with two major strikes by prison staff ending in comprehensive defeat for the unions, who have since been enfeebled.

One might expect punishment in New Zealand – as in Australia and the USA – to have a major problem of legitimacy surrounding the issue of race. New Zealanders in recent decades[18] have prided themselves on the steps that have been taken to meet the valid claims of the Maori people, backed by a strong political consensus.[19] However, grievances remain, in the sphere of criminal justice and elsewhere. Maoris make up around 15 per cent of New Zealand's population (whereas only 2 per cent of Australians are Aborigines) – but account for 45 per cent of New Zealand's male sentenced prisoners (Lash, 1996: 36). Maori prisoners (like Maoris generally) are significantly younger than their non-Maori counterparts, and the rates for young Maori men aged 18–30 has been estimated (perhaps conservatively) at around 650 per 100,000. Some commentators regard these statistics – along with others demonstrating the increasing decline of Maoris' economic position – as indicative of an institutionalized racism which perpetuates and magnifies the social and economic exclusion of the Maori people. In the past there have been claims that the (Western-style) New Zealand criminal justice system – and especially imprisonment – is inherently inappropriate, oppressive and illegitimate, with demands for an entirely separate system of justice to be set up. The greatest concession to such demands was the system of youth justice introduced in 1989; but successive Justice Ministers have refused to allow or recognize 'Maori justice' for adults,[20] and the 'Maori justice movement' has waned in recent years.

So far, despite the discontents engendered by law and order ideology, there does not seem to be any general crisis of legitimacy among the public at large in New Zealand. Periodically there have been problems leading to a feeling that punishment, and especially prisons, needed to be relegitimated by new initiatives, in a mood of crisis avoidance rather than crisis management. (A perfect society is one with the wisdom to see crises coming and take evasive action.) Hence the numerous official Commissions of Inquiry, such as the Roper Report of 1989, which had been preceded by comparatively minor disturbances in some prisons and Maori complaints that imprisonment was inappropriate to their culture. It is perhaps remarkable that there is no generalized crisis as yet, given New Zealand's high and increasing prison population, and given the scope for legitimate grievance on the part of the Maori people. If there is a continuance of the current increases in both prison numbers and in penal populism, the perfect society could be heading for trouble.

Notes

1 Australia's fast-rising population is thought to have reached 20 million in December 2003, up from 13.5 million in 1976.

2 However, this is mainly so in respect of their *adult* criminal justice systems. The picture is significantly and interestingly different in respect of youth justice in these two countries (see Chapter 13).

3 Representing 7,327 prisoners in August 2004 (John Pratt, personal communication).

4 And indeed that outstanding example of this phenomenon of the political 'Third Way', the American Democratic Party under Bill Clinton (President from 1993–2001), although of course the Democratic Party – while left of centre in the American political spectrum – could never fairly be called 'social democratic' in any but the most attenuated sense.

5 Western Australia introduced a minimum 12 months' custodial sentence for three-time domestic burglars in 1996. The Northern Territory introduced mandatory sentences for a wide range of property offences in 1997, but repealed them in 2001 in the face of criticisms (from, among others, the UN's Human Rights Committee in 2000) that they discriminated severely against young Aboriginal offenders and could be open to challenge on constitutional and human rights grounds.

6 There have, however, been some moves to extend restorative justice to adult offenders in New Zealand, and three recent Acts – the Sentencing Act 2002, the Parole Act 2002 and the Victims' Rights Act 2002 – all contain restorative principles and provide for restorative processes in respect of adults as well as juveniles.

7 Although not strictly speaking part of the penal system, there have also been numerous riots in immigrant detention centres in the last few years.

8 Strictly speaking this is probably untrue, although they may well be the race which is most *over-represented* in its country's prisons. About 1 per cent of persons of Aboriginal and Torre Strait Islander descent are in prison, compared with around 2.5 per cent of African-Americans, who achieve this higher score because of the phenomenally greater *overall* imprisonment rate in the USA.

9 See above, Note 5.

10 See above, Note 5.

11 One factor in recent Australian politics has been the rise (since the late 1990s) of Pauline Hanson's One Nation party, a right-wing party which calls for the end of Asian immigration and state aid to Aborigines, and also espouses particularly harsh policies on criminal justice. One Nation never made significant breakthroughs at either state or federal levels, peaking at 8 per cent of the vote in the 1998 federal election before declining amid in-fighting and other travails. However, it is thought to have played a part in encouraging 'bidding wars' between the larger parties on law and order issues.

12 Imprisonment rates for 1996 were as follows: ACT 35, Tasmania 80, Victoria 70, SA 85, NSW 133, Queensland 133, WA 171, NT 388; overall rate 119 (Brown, 1998: 372). Note that these are rates per 100,000 general population *aged 10 or over*, not the measure more commonly used in this book of rates per 100,000 total population of all ages. On the latter measure, the overall Australian rate at this time was around 95.

13 Brown (1998: 372–3). For example, the Northern Territory has by far the highest proportion of persons of Aboriginal or Torres Strait Island descent in its population of any jurisdiction (20 per cent) and also far and away the highest imprisonment rate (388 per 100,000 population aged 10 or over in 1996).

14 0.3 per cent compared with 2.4 per cent in Queensland and around 1 per cent in New South Wales.

15 The successful 'export' of restorative justice approaches in recent years which we mentioned earlier has generated a similar sense of pride, and has even stimulated a niche market in 'restorative justice tourism' involving visits by growing numbers of academics and practitioners from other Western countries to study the various approaches. Such tendencies afford an all-too-rare example of a non-USA-led convergence in penal policies.

16 This could be seen as in line with Durkheim's speculation (1964: 68–9) that 'a society of saints' would criminalize faults which appear trivial to us. (John Pratt, personal communication.)

17 Pratt (2000b: 433); Pratt and Clark (2004). The referendum was triggered by the collection of 380,000 signatures on a petition by Norm Withers, the son of a robbery victim. The full referendum question was 'Should there be a reform of our justice system placing greater emphasis on the needs of victims, providing restitution and compensation for them and imposing minimum sentences and hard labour for all serious and violent offences?'

18 And in particular since 1985, when a Labour government agreed to hear claims under the 1840 Treaty of Waitangi, whereby Maori leaders gave up their right of governance in return for guarantees of certain rights to land and resources.

19 Recently, however, concerns have arisen that this consensus may be being threatened, following a speech by National Party opposition leader Don Brash in early 2004 in which he denounced reparations to the Maori as a 'grievance industry' (*The Guardian*, 16 April 2004).

20 But see Note 6 above for recent moves to extend restorative justice to adult offenders.

6

South Africa: The Transition from Apartheid

As we noted in Chapter 1, South Africa does not fit neatly into our typology of political economies. Indeed, South Africa offers an interesting amalgam of neo-liberal and social democratic elements. Above all it is a transitional society, and in seeking to evolve from an authoritarian to a more democratic order it operates in a very different social, political and economic context from any of the others we have described. But what has so far seemed to be emerging is a predominantly neo-liberal polity, with the punitiveness that goes along with it.

It could be said that apartheid South Africa constituted two separate polities, one parasitic on the labour and poverty of the other. White society was almost social democratic[1] in its level of public services (although not in the nature of its tax base), with correspondingly low levels of punishment for white transgressors. The story was, however, very different for the black majority (who make up over three quarters of the South African population) whose cheap labour made this possible; for them welfare provision was minimal and punishment severe. At one stage in the 1980s, South Africa had the highest proportionate prison population in the world according to official figures, amounting to an estimated 423 per 100,000 general population in 1979/1980 and 373 in 1989.[2] Contributing to these figures were prisoners whose incarceration could be directly attributed to the apartheid system, including political prisoners and black people who were imprisoned for being in areas reserved for whites and other breaches of 'petty apartheid' laws.

The ruling African National Congress (ANC) party – which took power in the first democratic elections in 1994 following its 'unbanning' and the freeing from prison of Nelson Mandela in 1990 – could be described in terms of its general ideology as a social democratic party which aspires to a social welfare approach to governing South Africa. However, it faces a formidable challenge in putting such an approach into practice – and in meeting the expectations raised among the newly enfranchised black electorate – in a country where the apartheid system entrenched massive disparities in wealth and income between the white minority and the black majority and provided only the most basic of welfare provision. South Africa remains in most respects a *de facto* neo-liberal state. Moreover, there are severe economic constraints on the present government's ability to significantly alter the direction of its social welfare policies. Some critics of the ANC government (for example Pilger, 1998) berate it for not having introduced more radical measures to redistribute power and wealth in the new South Africa. Other commentators (such as Younge, 1998) feel that to date the ANC has moved as far and fast as it realistically could while maintaining both a peaceful transition and a functioning economy in a world increasingly dominated by free-market economics. It is common ground, however, that the gap between rich and poor remains vast – indeed, material inequality remains as great as it was under apartheid[3] – and that the government of Thabo Mbeki (who replaced Nelson Mandela as President in 1999) is more unambiguously wedded to the free market than ever.

Even though some progressive legislation has been enacted, for example in the field of labour relations, and despite the existence of various mechanisms to co-ordinate the labour market strategies of government, employers and trade unions in the national interest, these do not go far enough to justify South Africa's inclusion in the 'corporatist' category. The same can also be said about black empowerment strategies, which seem to be creating an elite of black entrepreneurs and civil servants rather than significantly narrowing the gap between rich and poor. There has been some success in starting to dismantle the artificial barriers which prevented any black people joining the top economic echelons of society, but little if any progress for those at the bottom, who are at the mercy of rampant unemployment (by some estimates in excess of 40 per cent)[4]. The problem of 'social exclusion' is even more acute in South Africa than in any of the other countries in our sample. And the South African welfare state remains minimalist. Despite democratization and the accession to power of politicians whose ideological aspirations were to transform society, South Africa's structure remains predominantly neo-liberal. It is perhaps no surprise, therefore, that its punishment levels in 2003 – nine years after the first democratic elections – were second only to the USA in our sample of countries. Nevertheless, South Africa is affected by the legacy not only of the apartheid system, but also of the struggle against it and of the progressive ideology developed by the ANC and others in the course of that struggle. This included a critique of South African penality under apartheid and its role in repressing the majority population, and a countervailing liberal/radical penal ideology.[5] Strands of this progressive penology live on in the ANC government, and accounts for some more humanitarian developments in areas such as prisoners' rights, police reform (Shearing, 1994; van Zyl Smit, 1999: 206; van Zyl Smit and van der Spuy, 2004) and non-custodial punishments. But it has to compete with the ideology of 'law and order', and the competition between the two has yielded some uneven results.

Penality has certainly altered significantly in South Africa since the transition, but it remains a country with high levels of punishment and a punitive public mentality which has intensified in recent years. Around 1,500 ANC prisoners were released by amnesties between 1990 and 1992, while petty apartheid laws were gradually dismantled prior to the transition to democracy. In 1990 and 1991 large general amnesties secured the release of many thousands of prisoners (van Zyl Smit, 1998: 408).[6] But prison numbers soon began to rise again. On 31 December 1995, the imprisonment rate based on official figures was 273 per 100,000 general population, very high by almost any standard. Since then it has increased to levels rarely seen even under apartheid, standing at 402 in 1999, a figure repeated in 2003 (Walmsley, 2000, 2003b). This represents a total in absolute numbers of 180,952 prisoners in South Africa in 2003, compared with 110,481 in 1989. (See Tables 2.1 and 2.2 in Chapter 2.)

The rise in the imprisonment rate between 1991 and the end of the 1990s can be attributed to two factors. The first was *an increase in the number of unsentenced prisoners*. Such prisoners had accounted for only 16 per cent of the South African prison population in 1976, but – despite the abolition of most provisions for detention without trial – for 24 per cent by 1996[7] and 36 per cent by 1999. This reflected both a decline in the efficiency of the court system leading to longer remand periods, and a tightening of the bail laws. A moral panic in 1994 and 1995 resulted in legislation designed to make bail more difficult to obtain,[8] which seems to have had an immediate effect: the number of prisoners awaiting trial rose from 23,908 on 31 January 1995 to 28,948 on 31 May 1996.[9] In 1997 laws were passed to restrict the right to bail even further.[10] However, from 2000 there was a modest decline in the number of unsentenced prisoners, largely thanks to 'a concerted campaign led by the Inspecting Judge, who has made the combating of overcrowding the primary objective of his work (van Zyl Smit, 2004: 233). The number of *sentenced* prisoners rose from 78,838 in 1976 to 88,838 in 1996, but this actually represented a *decline* in relation to the population as a whole during this period (van Zyl Smit, 1998: 417).[11] What had been and still is happening, in South Africa as in so many other countries, is *bifurcation*, the process whereby minor offenders are dealt with outside prison but more serious offenders are dealt with more harshly than ever. A decline in the number of offenders sentenced to prison between 1976 and 1996 was offset by an *increase in the length of sentences* (van Zyl Smit, 1998: 418–9), a bifurcatory trend that continued in subsequent years.[12]

It is a truism that crime is an appallingly serious problem in South Africa, with a high murder rate and the highest level of recorded rape in the world.[13] Few deny that the crime problem has worsened in recent years.[14] But some commentators feel that white South Africans have been exceptionally fortunate to have experienced such a peaceful transition to majority rule and such a limited diminution in their economic privileges, and find it galling that the whites who still wield disproportionate political and economic influence place so much emphasis on complaining about crime rather than the material and racial inequality which fuels it

[handwritten margin note: Whites complain about crime. However they don't think it could be due to lack of money & materials]

> To many white South Africans, 'crime' is the euphemism for the migration of impoverished, workless blacks across the old racial dividing lines. In one sense, the issue is quite useful to the corporate elite that controlled the economy under apartheid and controls it now, for it reminds the ANC government that it must discipline those frustrated with the lack of change. (Pilger, 1998)

This 'white whine' (Steele, 1997) disguises the fact that, as is always the case, the main victims of crime are poor and black, whereas the portrayal of crime in the media tends to concentrate on crimes against whites.[15] But it helps to fuel a law and order ideology which concentrates on trying to be tough on the criminal rather than on the causes of crime, and which has found strong echoes in sections of the black population. Following the transition to democracy, a wide range of the government's political opponents united to demand more punitive policies, including calls for the reintroduction of the death penalty and for minimum sentences (van Zyl Smit, 2000).

The government stood firm on the death penalty, which had been abolished by backdoor means. Capital punishment had been used by the apartheid regime and opposed by the ANC. When President de Klerk announced the unbanning of the liberation movements in February 1990, his speech also contained an undertaking to reconsider the death penalty (already the subject of a moratorium since 1989), perhaps in part motivated by a fear that capital punishment might in future be used against those guilty of political crimes in defence of the apartheid state. The Interim Constitution adopted in 1993 was ambiguous over the constitutionality of capital punishment, but in two of its earliest cases the new Constitutional Court held that both capital and corporal punishment were unlawful,[16] and the 'final' Constitution which subsequently came into force in 1996 contained substantially the same provisions. The ANC government of Nelson Mandela, a long-time personal opponent of the death penalty, argued before the court that capital punishment was unconstitutional. But the death penalty retains strong public support among all racial groups,[17] and there are vociferous calls for its return from widely varying parts of the political spectrum.[18]

[handwritten margin note: death penalty]

The government's stance on the death penalty increased the pressure on it to introduce punitive measures of other kinds. The first of these was the 1995 tightening of the bail laws mentioned previously, followed by a further tightening in 1997. Also in 1997 minimum sentences were introduced for certain serious offences.[19] Much of this had the effect of continuing and intensifying the bifurcatory tendencies we noted earlier, increasing the harshness of punishment especially for more serious offenders. Government rhetoric also assumed a tougher tone. Perhaps the most remarkable statement from a government source was the announcement in 1997 by the Commissioner of Correctional Services (backed by the then Minister) that prisoners could be kept in underground prisons converted from disused mineshafts (van Zyl Smit 2004: 232–3). This statement was perhaps something of a high water mark, and both the Commissioner and Minister had been replaced by the end of 1999.[20] More concretely, however, increased resources have been poured into the penal system. The March 1997 budget promised a 14 per cent rise in spending on the police and 23 per cent on prisons (Steele, 1997), and some new prisons (including a 'super maximum' security prison) were subsequently built. This, however, seems unlikely to solve the severe overcrowding problems of South Africa's prisons. In 1995 the prison system had been overcrowded by 19 per cent,[21] with some regions and individual prisons being even more overcrowded. Subsequently the position became bleaker still, with the system as a whole being overcrowded by no less than 63 per cent on 31 March 2004 (Department of Correctional Services, 2004). Many prisons have more than double the number of prisoners for which they officially have room, and prison conditions in general remain appalling, no better than they were prior to the transition to democracy (van Zyl Smit, 2004: 230).)

Although succumbing in some respects to the demands of law and order ideology, the ANC government has also attempted to humanize the penal system in certain other respects. A degree of official welfarism and rehabilitationist ideology survives – even if often at the level of lip service and belied by the brutal everyday realities of the penal system – encouraged by a recognition that offenders have been victims of a highly discriminatory social system. The collisions between the benevolent urge to reform and the countervailing forces of law and order ideology are well exemplified in the story we will be telling in Chapter 13 concerning the custodial remand of juveniles. To anticipate briefly, legislation was introduced in 1994 to make it more difficult to remand juveniles in prison, but the new law was ineffective and the government's attempt to enforce it led to a backlash and further legislation in 1996 which in effect restored the previous position (van Zyl Smit, 1998: 412). A further initiative by the government in 1997 aimed at keeping children out of prisons also seems to have proven ineffective.

The legal rights of prisoners had belatedly received some recognition from the South African courts in the 1980s and 1990s. The fact that one of the most important cases concerned a political prisoner by the name of Nelson Mandela[22] dramatizes what may be a significant factor, that many of those in government in the new South Africa have spent time in prisons themselves. The 1993 and 1996 Constitutions contained certain general and specific rights for all detained persons, including the right to be detained under conditions consonant with human dignity and rights to legal advice. The Correctional Services Act 111 of 1998 (brought into force in 2004) seeks to incorporate these constitutional rights (van Zyl Smit, 2001a; van Zyl Smit and van der Spuy, 2004). But in practice human dignity is often in short supply in overcrowded prisons, many of which are dominated by the violent inmate gangs which have long existed in South African prisons. In 1998 several prisoners were reported to have died following assaults by prison staff; in the same year the Department of Correctional Services launched a pilot project to train prisoners and staff in 'human rights norms' (Human Rights Watch, 1999).

Both inmate disturbances and staff unrest are new features of prison life which did not exist under apartheid. Riots were largely prevented by general repression and the promise of brutal retribution should disturbances occur. But, as can often happen, political change and the advent of an expected more liberal age encouraged greater boldness. As had happened in East Germany, there were prison disturbances during the period of political transition, as prisoners sought to gain concessions. The months from March to June 1994 saw probably the worst prison riots in South African history. The first issue on which prisoners protested was the right to vote. Initially the legislation for the first democratic election (which took place on 27 April 1994) excluded many sentenced prisoners. Demonstrations and hunger strikes took place in protest, orchestrated by SAPHOR (the South African Prisoners Human Rights Organisation), a prisoners' organisation which emerged in the early 1990s. The protests led to violence, riots and the deaths of a number of prisoners, but also concessions on voting rights (van Zyl Smit, 1998: 410). Following the election protests continued, with the main grievance now being release dates. The pre-transition amnesties had favoured political prisoners over so-called 'common law' or non-political prisoners. SAPHOR's charismatic leader Golden Miles Bhudu, himself a former common law prisoner, argued that they too were victims of apartheid and should also benefit from amnesties and improved conditions, and riots continued until June 1994 when the government set up a judicial inquiry into prison unrest, the Kriegler Commission (1995). Like the Woolf Inquiry in England in 1991 (Woolf and Tumim, 1991), Kriegler found that the main reason for the unrest had been the sense of injustice felt by prison inmates, and that many of their grievances were well founded.

Both unionization of prison staff and industrial action are also recent developments. In 1989 POPCRU (the Police and Prison Officers Civil Rights Union) was founded, and quickly became the focus for both police and prison officers who supported the liberation movements. Prison trade union activity was swiftly banned by legislation in 1990, but POPCRU survived. It has since been joined by COUSA (Correctional Officers Union of South Africa) which caters mainly for black prison officers, and by the PSA (Public Servants Association), a general civil servants' union which represents mostly white prison staff. Industrial relations are now highly unstable, and staff go-slows and outright strikes have become a feature of South African prison life.

Criminal justice in South Africa suffers from a widespread crisis of legitimacy. Of course, under apartheid the criminal justice system never held any legitimacy for the great majority of the population, and in the transition to democracy it has failed to acquire the legitimacy it needs. Although the gap between imprisonment rates for white and black South Africans has narrowed to some extent, it is clearly still dramatic.[23] Not only is the penal system saddled with the legacy of apartheid, but it also has to operate with a crisis of resources and the general perception that criminal justice is failing to stem a rapidly rising tide of serious crime.

In just about every respect, then, South Africa suffers from an acute penal crisis. In so far as a tendency to penal crisis seems to be associated with a neo-liberal polity – and given the degree of pre-existing economic and racial inequality and the continued reliance on neo-liberal economic governance – it seems all too likely that this crisis will continue and deepen. One response to this has been moves to introduce privatized prisons, which we discuss in more detail in Chapter 16. Another, discussed by van Zyl Smit (1996), is *managerialism*, which has become a significant influence on the correctional system here as elsewhere. This is true both within the Department of Correctional Services (as the Department of Prisons was renamed in 1991), and outside, with deliberate attempts being made at the highest levels of central government to coordinate the various departments and agencies involved in criminal justice. But no managerial techniques have managed to make any serious impact on the multiple massive problems of penality in South Africa.

If there is a potential ray of light in the gloom, it concerns the development of restorative justice, which has deep roots in traditional African society. Even under apartheid, urban black communities developed and practised their own communal mechanisms of social ordering alongside (and frequently in opposition to) the official structures (van Zyl Smit, 1999: 203). These alternative forms of communitarian justice were based on the application of African customary law in rural areas and 'makgotla' courts in the urban townships which had co-existed with state forms of justice from colonial times onwards. Some of these were further developed during and following the transition to democracy. Restorative justice also received the highest level of official backing in the unique form of the Truth and Reconciliation Commission (South African Truth and Reconciliation Commission, 1998), which from 1996 to 1998 inquired into the political crimes committed by all sides during the apartheid era. But although the TRC has been seen and presented as a massive symbol of restorative justice in the new South Africa, its development has been slow compared with the onward march of law and order ideology and its effects. The reality of South African penality remains overwhelmingly punitive. It remains to be seen, not only whether the nation's penal crisis can be contained (let alone solved), but also whether the new nation can emerge from its brutal past and attain a penal system in keeping with a modern constitutional democracy.

Notes

1 This had its roots at the very beginning of apartheid. The early Afrikaner nationalists were very concerned about the exploitation of white workers by English-speaking

capitalists and dedicated to uplifting the 'poor whites'. After 1948 – when the predominantly Afrikaner National Party came to power and enshrined apartheid into South Africa's laws and constitution – this became a primary function of the state welfare apparatus, and (it could even be said) of the penal system. (Particular thanks to Dirk van Zyl Smit for this note.)

2 1979/80 figure from Terblanche (1998: 176); 1989 figure calculated by Dirk van Zyl Smit from official sources for 30 June 1989. Calculating South Africa's imprisonment rate from official information over the years is complicated by a number of factors, including systematic underestimation of the numbers of black people in the general population in official statistics under apartheid and the exclusion of the supposedly independent black 'homeland' states of Transkei, Bophutatswana, Venda and Ciskei. This means that the 1989 imprisonment rate of 373 per 100,000 general population actually represents a smaller absolute number of prisoners (110,481 in a 'South Africa', population officially estimated at 29,617,000) than the 1995 rate of 273 (112,572 prisoners in a general population of 41,244,430) – van Zyl Smit, questionnaire response) and much smaller than the 2003 figure (180,952 prisoners; imprisonment rate 402).

3 In the mid-1990s the lowest 10 per cent of the population accounted for just 1.1 per cent of total national consumption while the highest 10 per cent accounted for 45.9 per cent, which is the biggest disparity by far of any of the countries featured in this book. In 2000 it was estimated that 50 per cent of the population was below the poverty line (*CIA – The World Factbook*).

4 In 2000 the *CIA World Factbook* estimated the South African unemployment rate at 30 per cent.

5 For a discussion of the role of different schools of criminological thought in the old and new South Africas, see van Zyl Smit (1999).

6 There was also an amnesty to mark Nelson Mandela's eightieth birthday in 1998.

7 Calculated from van Zyl Smit (1998: 416–7). 'Absolute' figures were 15,139 out of a total prison population of 93,977 in 1976 and 28,047 out of 116,885 in 1996.

8 Criminal Procedure Amendment Act 75 of 1995; see van Zyl Smit (1998: 413).

9 Calculated from van Zyl Smit (1996: 9).

10 Criminal Procedure Second Amendment Act 85 of 1997 (see van Zyl Smit, 2001b: 5–6).

11 This decline in the number of sentenced prisoners is not due to any decrease in crime or in the length of sentences (both of which appear to have increased). It could be due to any permutation of the following factors: fewer petty and first offenders receiving prison sentences rather than one of an increasing number of non-custodial alternatives; shorter terms being served as the result of amnesties and other early release policies; and (perhaps most of all) 'a dramatic overall decline in the rates of detection and successful prosecution of crime' (van Zyl Smit, 2001a: 590).

12 See for example Table 14 in Department of Correctional Services (2003), showing a significant increase in the proportion of prisoners sentenced to 10 years or more between 2002 and 2004, an increase the report ascribes to new mandatory minimum sentences.

13 Around 21,000 South Africans are murdered each year, with a similar number of attempted murders. Statistically, South Africans are more likely to be shot dead than die in a car accident. About 50,000 rapes are reported in South Africa each year (*Guardian*, 6 December 2001). In 1997, South Africa had the highest per capita rates of murder and rape, the second highest rate of robbery and violent theft and the fourth highest rates of serious assault and sexual offences, of the 110 countries with crime levels listed by Interpol (Schönteich, 2000).

14 Serious crime seems to have risen dramatically in the 1980s, with reported murders having increased by 135 per cent between 1983 and 1992 and large increases in other offences (Terblanche, 1998: 175). It is thought that 'organised crime mushroomed in the 1980s as a direct result of state-sanctioned alliances with the security services' (Pilger, 1998). In the 1990s, 'there was probably some overall increase in crime rates in South Africa, and certainly a dramatic increase in perceptions that crime was a major national problem' (van Zyl Smit, 2000: 200).

15 For example, a national survey in 2003 (Burton et al., 2004) found that black people accounted for 79 per cent of the population but 92 per cent of victims of armed robbery. Stock theft, one of the commonest crimes, had been experienced by 8 per cent of black and 5 per cent of white respondents in the previous year.

16 *S v Makwanyane and another* (1995) 3 SA 391 (CC); *S v Williams* (1995) 3 SA 632 (CC). The Constitution's provisions include the rights to life, to equality before the law to human dignity, and not to be subjected to cruel, inhuman or degrading treatment or punishment.

17 According to a 1990 public opinion poll, 74 per cent of black South Africans, 70 per cent of whites and 63 per cent of 'coloureds' and Asians believed that abolition would lead to an increase in crime (cited in Hood, 1996: 29n).

18 Those who have campaigned for the return of the death penalty include a radical Muslim-led group PAGAD (People Against Gangsterism and Drugs: see van Zyl Smit, 1999: 209).

19 Criminal Law Amendment Act 104 of 1997 (see van Zyl Smit, 2001a: 591).

20 The Minister (Sipho Mzimele) belonged to the ANC's conservative coalition partners the Inkatha Freedom Party. He was replaced by a more moderate successor in 1998. The Commissioner (Khulekani Sithole) was forced to resign in 1999 following widespread media allegations of corruption and mismanagement and scrutiny of the Department by the parliamentary Public Accounts Committee (van Zyl Smit and van der Spuy, 2004: 196–7).

21 The prison system officially contained cell accommodation for 94,381 prisoners but in fact housed 112,572 inmates (Dirk van Zyl Smit, questionnaire response).

22 *Mandela v Minister of Prisons* (1983) 1 SA 938 (A).

23 The statistics on this point are unsatisfactory and not up to date. Van Zyl Smit (1998: 417) calculated that between 1976 and 1996 the white imprisonment rate dropped from 79 to 57 per 100,000 population while the equivalent figure for blacks dropped more sharply from 350 to 198; since when the overall prison population has increased greatly. The imprisonment rate for 'coloureds' (people of mixed race) has historically been even higher than for blacks, but had also declined slightly from 776 in 1976 to 714 in 1996.

7

Germany: Archetypal Corporatism

The Federal Republic of Germany is made up of sixteen *Länder* (or states) which have a high degree of autonomy. Following World War Two, five of these Länder made up the communist state of East Germany (the German Democratic Republic), while the Federal Republic (or 'West Germany') comprised the remaining eleven. The fall of the Berlin Wall in 1989 led rapidly to the reunification of Germany in 1990, with the East joining the Federal Republic. The former East Germany contributes about 16 million to the total German population of 83 million. It is the Bundestag (the Federal Parliament) which makes Germany's criminal law (both substantive and procedural), and laws such as the Penal Code, Code of Criminal Procedure and the Prison Act 1977 which are binding on all states. Nevertheless, as we shall see later, and as is the case in other federal countries such as the USA and Australia (see Chapters 3 and 5), significant differences can be found between the different Länder (which each have their own ministries of justice) in terms of their penal practices.

Historically, Germany has been the archetype and model for conservative corporatism in Europe since the foundations of the German welfare state were laid by 'Iron Chancellor' Otto von Bismarck in the 1880s. (Bismarck, an ultra-conservative, was concerned to bind all classes in German society together with ties of mutual and communal interest to stave off the threat and appeal of socialism.) At the end of the twentieth century, Germany's welfare state was one of the most comprehensive and generous in the world, accounting for about one third of the national budget, and providing an average pension of 70 per cent of an individual's last income before retirement. The welfare state is largely run by 'tripartite' corporate arrangements; for example, the rates of insurance programmes are set by Parliament and administered by boards containing representatives of trade unions and employers. Benefits are not 'universal', however (in the sense of equal for all), but linked to the incomes of individuals during their working lifetimes. East Germany had a very different – more modest, but much more egalitarian – system during its time as a separate communist country from 1945 to 1990, when the West German system was extended to the East.

In general, German society is highly communitarian. The political culture prizes consensus and stability, with a 'social market' or 'stakeholder economy' based on consensus between workers, unions, employers, shareholders and politicians. The freedom of the free market is in practice significantly abridged by the duties of firms to act as good corporate citizens and take into account the interests and views of all sections of the community. Germany is also – in the terms employed by Savelsberg (1999) which we discussed in Chapter 1 and will revisit later in this chapter – a highly *bureaucratized* but in many respects *decentralized* polity.

For most of the late twentieth century, under coalition governments led either by the Christian Democratic Union (from 1949 to 1969 and 1982 to 1998) or by the Social Democratic Party (1969 to 1982), the corporatist welfare state remained intact, enjoying popular support. Serious cutbacks did occur under Christian Democrat Chancellor Helmut Kohl following the 1990 reunification and Germany's signing of the Maastricht Treaty in 1993;[1] the economic difficulties caused by these two developments in combination also led to record post-war unemployment in Germany (11 per cent in 2003). Kohl was replaced as Chancellor by the Social Democratic Party's Gerhard Schröder in 1998 (heading a Social Democrat–Green coalition), but the erosion of the German corporate welfare state is set to continue. Schröder – whose politics of *Die Neue Mitte* largely resemble those of Tony Blair in Britain, including presenting a 'tough on crime' image and rhetoric – is currently pushing through an unpopular programme of cuts to the welfare state entitled 'Agenda 2010'. The changes are dramatic by German standards, but would still leave the German welfare state as one significantly more generous than those found in neo-liberal countries such as the UK.

Since the late 1980s, Germany (and before 1990 West Germany) has borne out our general thesis about the relationship between political economies and cultures and punishment levels well enough: along with France, Italy and the Netherlands it is a conservative corporatist (and highly communitarian) country, which has lower imprisonment rates than neo-liberal economies such as England, Australia, New Zealand and the USA, but higher rates than the Scandinavian social democracies, a relationship displayed in Tables 1.2 in Chapter 1 and 2.2 in Chapter 2. Yet this was not always so. Despite its high level of corporatism and communitarian generosity, for a long time after World War Two West Germany had one of the highest imprisonment rates in Western Europe, exceeding 100 prisoners per 100,000 population for most of the 1960s. The rate then dropped quite suddenly, from 102 in 1968 to 75 in 1971, before increasing again to a peak of 105.5 in 1983 (Dünkel, 1996: 146). For much of the 1970s and 1980s, West Germany was the country with the very highest imprisonment rate in Western Europe, only being overtaken by the UK in 1986. But by 1987 the West German rate had declined to 88 (when the rate for England and Wales was 92 and for the UK 94).[2] It continued to decrease until 1991

(when the rate for the 'old West Germany' was 81); since then the imprisonment rate in both West and Eastern parts of Germany has risen and stood at 98
overall in 2003.[3]

To some extent the *relative* changes between (West) Germany and other countries may be explicable by developments in those other countries; for example the
rapid neo-liberalization of the UK in the 1980s under Margaret Thatcher and the
simultaneous rise in the prison population. By contrast, although West Germany
was under the relatively conservative rule of Helmut Kohl's Christian Democrats
from 1982 to 1998, nevertheless the corporatist welfare state remained largely
unscathed at least until the 1990s. But neither this nor any developments in West
Germany's own political economy serve to explain either the initially high rate of
imprisonment or its significant reductions from 1969 to 1971 and from 1983 to
1991. These must be explained by factors which are at least relatively autonomous
from the general nature of modern Germany's corporatist culture. First we must
examine the penal philosophies which have predominated in German penality.

The German Penal Code of 1871 (which predated the creation of the corporatist state) laid down the retributivist principle that sentences should be commensurate with the 'guilt' (culpability) of the offender. However, this notion that
the sentence should fit the crime was subsequently heavily modified, as rehabilitation established a significant place in German penal thinking in the 1960s.
A 'great reform' of West German criminal law in 1969 and further amendments
to the Penal Code (*Strafgesetzbuch*) in 1975 attempted to bring more forward-
looking considerations into judicial sentencing. Section 46 of the Penal Code (as
amended in 1975) now states that the guilt of the offender is the basis for fixing
the sentence, but that the effects of the punishment on the offender's future life
is also to be taken into account; hence rehabilitation and incapacitation are also
legitimate considerations. Moving in a similar direction, section 2 of the Prison
Act 1976 declared that the sole purpose of the *execution* of a prison sentence (as
opposed to its *imposition* by the sentencing court) is the reintegration of the
offender into society (Dünkel and Rössner, 2001: 288; Feest and Weber, 1998:
234–9). The influence of the rehabilitative notion is not surprising, since as we
noted in Chapter 1, rehabilitation (in particular in the form of 'resocialization')
is a philosophy which seems particularly well suited to a corporatist and communitarian mentality. Indeed, the 1976 Prison Act was passed just when international penological fashion was moving towards 'just deserts' thinking and
jettisoning the idea that rehabilitation could work. In West Germany, however,
such thinking was largely rejected across the political spectrum. Retributivism
has also had its adherents, however, and enjoyed something of a revival in the
1980s, being favoured by some prison administrations and encouraged by a decision of the Constitutional Court in 1983.[4] This revival stuttered in 1987, when
the efforts of some conservative Länder to amend the Prison Act failed.

We have not yet explained the variations in German punitiveness: the high
imprisonment rates in the 1960s, the sudden drop from 1969 to 1971, the rise

from 1971 to 1983, decline until 1991 and increase thereafter. We are least confident that we can account for the first of these, the punitiveness that held sway until the late 1960s. This punitiveness forms at least a partial exception to our general thesis, according to which a nation with a highly developed welfare system should have a relatively low prison population. It could be said – tentatively – that a punitive tendency in German culture predated the creation of the corporate state and persisted into the modern era, embodied in the retributivism of the 1871 Penal Code. In this respect it is tempting to contrast the relatively conservative and authoritarian ethos of German communitarianism with the more liberal tradition of the Netherlands, which as we shall see in Chapter 8, consistently had lower imprisonment rates until very recently. We must enter the caveat that it is at best simplistic and often misleading to equate retributivism with a harshly punitive approach (Cavadino and Dignan, 2002: 41; and see our concluding chapter). Nevertheless, it may be that in the German context the move from retributivism towards resocialization represented and facilitated a shift in attitudes and practices from relative punitiveness to relative leniency.

Certainly the 'great reform' of 1969 was intended, not only to embody forward-looking purposes of punishment as opposed to retribution, but also (and the two things were seen as intimately linked) to reduce the significance of imprisonment in penal practice. And the sharp decline in the imprisonment rate between 1969 and 1971 was brought about by these 1969 legislative reforms, which both fettered the discretion of judges to impose imprisonment and provided them with non-custodial alternative sentences. The legislation abolished sentences of one month or less and discouraged prison sentences of less than six months,[5] on the basis that such penalties were of no use for rehabilitative treatment, which required more time. At the same time, powers to impose suspended prison sentences – the equivalent of probation in other countries – were extended and particularly strongly encouraged for sentences of up to one year. The means related 'day fine' system was introduced as from 1975. The number of short prison sentences (which in 1968 had accounted for 83 per cent of all sentences of imprisonment [Weigend, 1997: 177] decreased, bringing about an immediate drop in the numbers in prison (from 102 per 100,000 population in 1968 to 75 in 1971).

However, from 1971 onwards the imprisonment rate began to climb again, reaching 105.5 in 1983 (Dünkel, 1996: 146). This appears to have been largely due, not to any great revival in short sentences, but to an increase in the lengths of longer ones, especially (from the end of the 1970s) for drug offences and for serious violent and sexual crimes (Albrecht, 1997: 186; Feest and Weber, 1998: 244; Weigend, 1997: 180). As in other countries (notably the USA), the 'war against drugs' has been significant. Drug offenders comprise between 10 and 20 per cent of the prison population, and legislation has repeatedly increased penalties for drug and drug-related offences (see Feest and Weber, 1998: 244–5). Penalties for violent and sexual offenders, which had already been lengthening without legislation, were also considerably strengthened by two law reforms in 1998 (Dünkel and Rössner, 2001: 292).

Some commentators have suggested that this lengthening of sentences was a perverse result of the philosophy of rehabilitation, because of the notion that more serious offenders were 'in need of more – and time-consuming! – rehabilitation' (Feest and Weber, 1998: 241). This is questionable, however. The severer sentences for more serious offenders were driven more by the 'guilt' of the offender (in the sense of s. 46 of the Penal Code) and by the felt need to protect the public by means of incapacitation; it was not that sentencers had rediscovered a belief in imprisonment as a means to reform offenders. What was definitely being witnessed, however, was a classic example of a steadily growing *bifurcation* of punishment (such as we have already noticed in other countries), whereby we see relatively lenient penalties, often decreasing in severity, for less serious offenders, but increasingly harsh punishments for those offenders deemed to be more serious or dangerous. In West Germany this took the form of fewer short prison sentences for lesser offenders but longer imprisonment for certain types of more serious case.[6]

The second reduction in the West German prison population took place in the years 1983 to 1991. Unlike the first reduction, this owed little to legislative change: the conservative Kohl government had come to power in 1982 and its inclinations were for tougher rather than more lenient criminal justice policies. Nor could demographic changes or variations in crime rates explain the decline in imprisonment. Rather, it was due to a change in attitudes and behaviours on the part of judges and prosecutors, many of whom became convinced that imprisonment was an ineffective method of responding to crime. (German prosecutors have wide powers to divert cases from court[7] and can impose fines or community service or accept a promise to perform reparation as an alternative to prosecution.) Also influential were forceful, high-profile movements by lawyers and other criminal justice practitioners who campaigned to oppose excessive use of custodial remands, which underwent a particularly dramatic reduction as a result, decreasing by nearly 30 per cent between 1982 and 1987 (Graham, 1990: 156). Practitioners also led 'the alternatives movement', working to provide non-custodial alternatives for juvenile offenders; while the emerging Green Party adopted semi-abolitionist policies and contributed to a strong movement resisting the construction of new prisons (Feest, 1988). Interestingly, the decrease in the prison population was again not brought about by any reduction in *lengths of sentences* (in fact, the lengths of prison sentences increased during this period), but was entirely due to a smaller number of offenders (and defendants pre-trial) being sent to custody at all (Graham, 1990).

Perhaps the most obvious explanation for the subsequent *increase* in the imprisonment rate since 1991 is that 'again the prosecutors and judges changed their behaviour', reflecting and expressing a harsher political climate, and in particular 'moral panics on the rise in crime in the course of the unification'

(Feest and Weber, 1998: 247). These moral panics were but one effect of the reunification of Germany in 1990 and the broader historical phenomenon of the fall of the Iron Curtain in the late 1980s and early 1990s. The effects of the collapse of the old West–East boundary – in Europe as a whole as well as in Germany in particular – have been unsettling in both material and mass-psychological terms.

In material terms, of course, acute economic dislocation in Eastern Europe and civil wars in the Balkans and elsewhere have caused mass movements of refugees and would-be economic migrants. The unification of Germany had a seriously deleterious effect on the economy of the West of the country, shortly to be exacerbated by the deflationary effects of budget cuts following the Maastricht Treaty and resulting record unemployment. Things were even worse in the East, as unification caused an immediate, dramatic and largely unforeseen collapse in the economy of the old East Germany and some influx of Easterners (*Ossis*) into the West. Perhaps a more significant migration for our purposes, however, have been *Aussiedler* – descendants of Germans from the former Soviet Union who were granted the automatic right to a German passport. The mass-psychological effects have been that Germans, no less than the people of other Western nations, have been feeling increasingly under siege from a tidal wave of impoverished foreigners who are seen as a threat to well-being and way of life. At the same time, budget cuts following the Maastricht Treaty contributed to record levels of unemployment in Germany. All of these dislocations can be seen as products of 'globalization' (see Chapter 1), and the insecurities they engender can lead to demonization and harsh treatment for the newcomer.

And so it has been in Germany. The demonization, as elsewhere, involved a moral panic about supposedly rising crime due to reunification and incoming foreigners. It is not clear how much basis this panic had in reality. There was little hard evidence of an alarming increase in crime in the Western Länder in the immediate aftermath of reunification, let alone one driven by newcomers (Feest and Weber, 1998: 247; Flynn, 1995; Messner and Ruggiero, 1995: 142–5), although there was a very significant increase in the Eastern states around this time. Thereafter there was a rise in recorded violent crime by young (German) offenders, notably in the West; but crime rates in the East have been relatively stable since 1995. What there has undoubtedly been, however, is a rise in *fear* of crime, and in xenophobia (the latter perhaps most dramatically manifested in violent attacks on foreigners and asylum seekers by neo-Nazi gangs). And in the famous words of American sociologist W.I. Thomas, 'if men define situations as real, they are real in their consequences'.

In Germany, around a quarter of the prison population is made up of foreign nationals and members of ethnic minorities.[8] Significantly, the recent rise in imprisonment levels is very largely attributable to a rise in the *remand* population (counteracting the reduction achieved in the 1980s) rather than in those *sentenced* to prison custodial *sentences*, and remands in custody appear to have been used particularly freely for non-German defendants and especially asylum seekers (Dünkel and Rössner, 2001: 298).[9] Thus much of the higher imprisonment rate may be due to increased *fear* of the crimes that outsiders *might* commit – rather than of any real increase in crime – leading prosecutors and judges to be more cautious about allowing non-German defendants to have their liberty pending their trials.[10]

At this point we should step back and insert an element of broader perspective. Although as we have seen there have been some significant shifts in the imprisonment rate of the Federal Republic both before and since reunification, it should be borne in mind that such shifts are relatively minor compared with those experienced by some other countries. Indeed, Savelsberg (1999: 63) describes West Germany's punishment as 'remarkably stable over a long time period'. West Germany's imprisonment rate at its lowest (75 per 100,000 in 1971) was 71 per cent of its peak value (105.5 in 1983). By contrast, the imprisonment rate of the USA at its lowest (162 in 1972) was 23 per cent of the figure in 2002 (701). The swings in penality in East Germany were even more dramatic. The highest imprisonment rate was 284 per 100,000 in 1974, but in 1991, the year following reunification, it was a mere 19, just 7 per cent of the former figure. In general, prison populations in East Germany fell during periods of political liberalization and rose at times of increasing repression. The falls can be largely accounted for by amnesties granted by governments – which typically, however, only reduced imprisonment rates in the short term – including a very wide-ranging amnesty just prior to reunification. The rises may not have been quite so directly the result of government and Communist Party policy, but in a political system where power was highly centralized in Communist hands, where judges were in effect subordinate to the wishes of the Party, the effect of central policy on penal decisions was just as real if not so direct and overt (Savelsberg, 1999: 58–61).

We noted in Chapter 1 that authoritarian societies such as the old East Germany do not fit our 'radical pluralist' frame of analysis, since the political power in such countries is not pluralized but monopolized. In the old communist nations of Eastern Europe, power was monopolized by the Communist Party both formally (through its grip on the official political institutions) and also informally, through the *Nomenklatura* network of Party members which permeated social institutions generally. Savelsberg (1999) has theorized that countries which, like East Germany, are highly bureaucratized and subject to highly centralized power structures can be subject to hectic swings in levels of penality as policy changes issue from the powerful political centre. Such swings will, however, presumably depend on there being dramatic policy changes at the centre – in East Germany's case at least, associated with recurring crises in the state socialist system, interspersed with more liberal periods where the political powers sought to gain public legitimacy by means of a gentler, less repressive approach. Whereas one can imagine that if there were to be policy stability at the political centre, a highly centralized and bureaucratic state could conceivably have very stable levels of punishment and imprisonment.

West Germany on the other hand, although also highly bureaucratized (as is inevitable in a corporatist system) was to a great extent decentralized politically, both in its regional structure and in the existence of political checks and balances in the organization of the state. (Both bureaucratization and some degree of decentralization in the latter sense can be seen as more or less inevitable components of a corporatized society.) Savelsberg sees this combination of bureaucracy and decentralization as being most conducive to relatively stable levels of punishment – as in West Germany. As we noted in Chapter 1, there are various features of the Federal Republic – relative lack of populist media, strong political parties, judges and prosecutors who are relatively insulated from the political process – which will tend to mitigate the effects of any tendencies towards 'populist punitiveness'. Less stable than the Federal Republic – though more stable than somewhere like East Germany – is a country such as the USA, which combines decentralization with 'personalism', a less bureaucratic structure of power. Such countries are, Savelsberg says, relatively stable in the short term (because decentralized power does not allow rapid short-term shifts) but highly dynamic in the long term (because the lack of rigidifying bureaucracy allows for a more populist politics and consequent changes in penality as a response to shifting public moods).

It could be said, though, that in all countries, however bureaucratized, there has been a tendency in recent decades towards 'personalism'. This does not mean that the amount of bureaucracy necessarily diminishes (in fact it is likely to increase), but politicians increasingly seek to gain popularity with the public 'over the heads' of institutional bureaucracies and state personnel such as civil servants and criminal justice practitioners (and indeed political parties). They are influenced relatively less by enduring bureaucratic institutions and more by what Savelsberg (1999: 63, using a Foucauldian[11] term) calls 'new types of knowledge' produced by 'opinion polls, new interest groups, and mass media', not to mention focus groups. This may have happened less in corporatist countries such as Germany than in nations such as the USA, but the trend has been in the same direction. It can be at least partly ascribed to the decline in the authority of traditional institutions, and in deference to them by public and politicians alike, leading to the greater 'popularization of crime politics' (Simon and Feeley, 1995: 168) we discussed in general terms in Chapter 1. We can see the recent increases in the German imprisonment rate, in the xenophobic and Other-phobic atmosphere of recent years, in this way. Certainly the impact of populist punitiveness has been more in evidence from the 1990s onwards, exhibited for example in 1998's tougher legislation on violent and sex offenders (Dünkel and Rössner, 2001: 292) and in Chancellor Schröder's 'tough on crime' rhetoric.

We must now say a little more about the general nature of the German Democratic Republic's penality and its legacy in the reunified Federal Republic.

As we have seen – and as is common under repressive regimes of all kinds – levels of imprisonment in the GDR were usually very high by West European standards, but fluctuated greatly as governments alternated between more repressive and relatively liberalized policies. There was a paradoxical contrast generated by the combination of what have been called a 'police state' and a 'welfare state' approach to prisons (Arnold, 1995). On the one hand, prisoners had few rights against the state, and prison conditions and regimes were in general very poor by Western standards. On the other hand, one right that did exist and was effective in practice was the right of every prisoner to work.[12] This was a manifestation of the state's Marxist ideology, leading to a penal philosophy– albeit in many ways neglected in practice – of resocialization through labour. Between the fall of the Berlin Wall in late 1989 and the reunification of October 1990, East German prisoners successfully demanded changes in prison conditions, reviews of sentences and wide-ranging amnesties (Arnold, 1995: 88–90), which brought down Eastern imprisonment rates to levels well below those in the West. Following reunification, it was seen as necessary to bring East German prisons up to Western standards – but the main priority was given to upgrading security rather than ensuring that conditions for prisoners reached even the minimum requirements laid down by the Federal Republic's Prison Act (Dünkel, 1995: 95). Other changes have included replacing the communal cells which were used in East Germany, but which contravene rules in the Federal Prison Act that prohibit housing more than eight prisoners in a cell; the introduction of open prisons and more generous granting of home leave (Dünkel, 1995).

Following reunification we have seen a gradual convergence between East and West German penality. In 1991 the Eastern imprisonment rate (immediately following an extensive amnesty) was 19 per 100,000 population compared to the West's 81, and for some years every single Eastern Land had a rate lower than that of every Western state. By 2000, however, the difference (92 in the East, 98 in the West) had narrowed and almost closed (Dünkel and Morgenstern, 2001: 166).

This is not to say that all Länder have identical, or even similar, imprisonment rates. In 2000 these ranged from 170 per 100,000 general population in Hamburg to 57 in Schleswig-Holstein (Dünkel and Morgenstern, 2001: 166). There is no strong correlation between the political ideology of a state's government and its imprisonment rate, certainly between CDU- and SPD-controlled Länder; for example, in 2000 the rate of conservative Baden-Württemburg was 79 compared with the 103 of social democratic North Rhine-Westphalia. In general, more urbanized states (with higher crime rates, especially for serious offences) have higher imprisonment rates than more rural states. But ideology and political initiatives can make a difference: Bremen has followed a policy of 'decarceration' over the past two decades, resulting in a relatively low rate of 85; while the lowest rate is to be found in Schleswig-Holstein, where since the mid-1980s an SPD–Green administration has pursued a policy of diverting offenders to community sanctions. The opposite picture can be seen in highly conservative

Bavaria, which combines a very low crime rate with a rather high imprisonment rate of 101.5. Another pattern – noticeable, but far from unbroken – is that imprisonment rates tend to increase as one travels down the map from Schleswig-Holstein in the North to Bavaria in the South.[13] The North–South penal divide is emerging more prominently than that between West and East.

Germany does not have a penal crisis – at least, not yet. Prison numbers are rising, and seem likely to continue to rise in the current climate. The Schröder government came to power promising (following the lead of Tony Blair in the UK) to be tough on crime and on the causes of crime, but – due in part to the restraining influence of the SPD's Green coalition partners – has to date done little of significance to encourage toughening of punishments generally.[14] The imprisonment rate of 98 per 100,000 in 2003 is relatively high historically for West Germany, but still below the 1983 peak of 105.5. Historically, both East and West Germany have suffered from severe prison overcrowding, and over-crowding in closed prisons has re-emerged as an issue in recent years, especially since the end of the 1990s, but not to the extent that prevailed previously, in the early 1980s.[15]

There have been some problems with prison security in the Eastern Länder since reunification, partly caused by the unification of the two penal systems. Security features such as electric fences and guard dogs were removed from Eastern prisons, leaving them relatively easy to escape from, and as mentioned previously large sums have been spent in improving security in Eastern prisons since reunification (Dünkel, 1995). But security has not been a serious problem in the West. Similarly, there was some inmate disorder in Eastern prisons in the run-up to reunification in 1990 by prisoners calling for better conditions and demanding to be included in amnesties – but nothing comparable in the West. The problem in the East seems to have been solved by application of a measure, which worked well in West Germany in the mid-1970s – reforms including the introduction of day leave and home furloughs for prisoners (which are of course not likely to be granted to prisoners who misbehave).

In general, conditions and regimes in German prisons are relatively good by international standards. Conditions in the East are still less good, but were greatly improved in the period prior to reunification (Arnold, 1995; see also Dünkel, 1995). As for prisoners' rights and justice within prisons, the Prison Act 1976 in theory guarantees the rights of prisoners, including the right to exten-sive judicial review of their complaints. It has been claimed that this law greatly improved the atmosphere within German prisons, leading to fewer disturbances.[16] Others doubt this, however, given the very low likelihood in practice of such procedures producing a satisfactory result from the prisoners' point of view (Feest, 1993), and there have even been claims that disillusionment with the reality of the new 'rights' led to *increased* disturbances following their imple-mentation (Messner and Ruggiero, 1995: 134). Maybe excessive claims have been made for the effectiveness and effects of these legal entitlements, and certainly it seems likely that the extension of home leave and work release programmes had more effect. Nevertheless, in the 1990s the Constitutional Court made some significant decisions about, for example, remuneration for prison labour and other aspects of prison regimes which had a significant positive impact on the daily living conditions of many inmates.

Overall, there is as yet no generalized crisis of either resources or of legitimacy in the German penal system. The legacy of the past reductions in imprisonment, together with the persistence of a relatively benign ideology of resocialization, leaves Germany with a certain amount of slack which would have to be used up before crisis point is likely to be reached. Yet there are danger signs, as imprisonment rates and a general climate of intolerance are both still on the rise. Trouble is simmering, and it remains to be seen whether it will cool down or come to the boil.

Notes

1 The Maastricht Treaty, agreed in 1991, transformed the European Community into the European Union and prepared for the adoption of a single currency (the euro) by those EU countries who wished to join it. Twelve countries (including, in our sample of nations, Germany, France, Italy and the Netherlands but not the UK or Sweden) adopted the euro from 1999. The Maastricht Treaty created economic 'convergence criteria' for countries adopting the euro, including the criterion that budget deficits be no more than 3 per cent of GDP. As a result, several nations cut their spending budgets, especially on welfare benefits.

2 Dünkel (1996: 146); HC Deb 29 April 1988. At this time, imprisonment rates in Scotland (109 in 1987) and Northern Ireland (121) were significantly higher than in England and Wales.

3 Sources: Dünkel (1996: 146); Walmsley (2003b). In 1991 (the year following reunification), the West German imprisonment rate was 82 and the East German rate a mere 19 per 100,000 (Feest and Weber, 1998: 242, 246–7). This followed a far-reaching amnesty for former East German prisoners at the time of reunification. Previously East Germany had had very high imprisonment rates of about 200 per 100,000 general population.

4 This was a ruling – no longer of importance – that prison administrations were entitled to take into account the particular gravity of guilt of two Nazi criminals serving life imprisonment for multiple murder in deciding whether they should ever be released (see Feest and Weber, 1998: 238).

5 Section 47, sub. 1 of the Penal Code allows imprisonment for less than six months 'only if special circumstances concerning the offence or the offender's personality make the imposition of a prison sentence indispensable for reforming the offender or for defending the legal order.' At the same time, section 56 requires courts to suspend prison sentences of up to one year whenever the offender can be expected to refrain from further offences without going to prison (Weigend, 1997: 178). Sentences of less than one month were abolished in 1969.

6 We should perhaps briefly mention the legacy of the terrorist threat (in particular from the Red Army Faction, or 'Baader-Meinhof Gang') in the 1970s, and the German

state's repressive response to that threat. This included special legislation to allow for longer remand periods and solitary confinement for defendants charged with terrorist offences, legislation which has not been repealed. However, there is little statistical sign that the terrorist threat resulted in any general intensification of punishment. More recently, terrorists have been replaced by newer folk devils of deviance – organized crime, hooligans, non-political violent offenders and foreigners.

7 In theory, German police and prosecutors are bound by the 'principle of legality' or *Rechtsprinzip* which lays down that a charge should always be brought when there is sufficient evidence that a person has committed a crime. In practice, and in the detail of the law – especially in less serious cases – this principle is cancelled out by the countervailing 'principle of opportunity', which allows non-prosecution for reasons of public expediency. Almost 50 per cent of prosecutable cases are in fact dismissed or discontinued (Dünkel and Rössner, 2001: 289).

8 In 1996, 23 per cent of all sentenced prisoners were foreigners (Dünkel and Rössner, 2001: 340).

9 The rise in the remand prison population, extremely noticeable following the opening of the Eastern European borders, peaked in 1993 – a year in which laws restricting the influx of refugees and other foreigners were introduced – and declined to some extent thereafter (Dünkel and Rössner, 2001: 298).

10 This may be partly explained by the fact that newly arrived foreigners with no fixed home address other than an asylum hostel would not normally be allowed bail for fear of absconding.

11 Derived from the theories of Michel Foucault: see Cavadino and Dignan (2002: Chapter 3).

12 Not for full pay – East German prisoners received 18 per cent of the wages of free labourers; but this was proportionately three times what a West German prisoner received. Prisoners were also integrated into the national pension scheme (Dünkel, 1995: 96).

13 It may or may not be relevant in terms of penal cultures that the Northern Länder are geographically (and historically and culturally) closer to Scandinavia, and that the South is more Catholic.

14 The SPD Minister of Justice has adopted a more moderate approach than Herr Schröder's rhetoric would suggest. However, the Schröder government has taken steps to extend the application of preventive measures for sex offenders, and Schröder himself has been reported as querying whether sex offenders ought to be released at all, on the grounds that they are 'untreatable'.

15 Section 18 of the Prison Act sets as a goal that every prisoner should be in single accommodation during rest periods, but this goal is still routinely not met. On 31 March 1993, 42 per cent of prisoners in Western Länder and 71 per cent of those in the East were sharing cells with another prisoner. For overcrowding rates in the different Länder, see Dünkel and Morgenstern (2001: 169–70).

16 Christian Pfeiffer, speaking on the BBC's *Panorama* programme, 4 June 1990.

8

The Netherlands: A Beacon
of Tolerance Dimmed

For several decades following World War Two, the Netherlands held a symbolic position as an example of penal enlightenment in the eyes of many liberal commentators. Speaking for ourselves as English criminologists, we were accustomed to pointing to the Netherlands as a prime symbol of a nation similar and close to England, yet whose penal policies were significantly less harsh. David Downes' 1988 book *Contrasts in Tolerance* embodied this admiring attitude to Dutch penality. Nor was the attitude – at the time – misplaced. On the (admittedly rough) standard measure of imprisonment rate, the Dutch figure prior to the 1990s was consistently the lowest of any medium- or large-sized country in Western Europe. From a relatively high figure following World War Two,[1] the Dutch imprisonment rate had declined to around 20 per 100,000 general population in the early 1970s, and in 1975 was only 17 (Rutherford, 1986: 136). Although it began to increase after 1975, by 1983 it was still only 28 per 100,000, at a time when the figures for West Germany, England and Wales, France, Italy and Sweden were 103, 87, 68, 65 and 65, respectively.[2] (Interestingly, these Dutch rates were considerably lower than Japan's current imprisonment rate – 53 in 2002 – and even lower than Japan's 1992 rate of 36. And yet Japan's rate of imprisonment has sometimes – although evidently wrongly – been seen as the kind of rate not easily imaginable in a modern, developed Western country.)

More recently, however, times have changed in the Netherlands. Actual numbers of prisoners rose from a low of 2,526 in 1975 to 10,200 in 1995, 13,618 in 1997 and 16,239 in 2002 – more than a 500 per cent increase from the 1975 figure. The Dutch imprisonment *rate* rose steadily from the 1975 low of 17 per 100,000, reaching 67 in 1995, 87 in 1997 and 100 by 2002. This current rate exceeds those of Sweden, Finland, Germany, France and Japan in our sample of countries, and indeed the majority of countries in Western Europe (equalling the rate of Italy, although still below those of England, Australia, New Zealand, South Africa and the USA). Since 1985, the Dutch imprisonment rate has actually increased at a faster rate even than that of the USA (Tak and van Kalmthout,

1998). A steadily increasing emphasis on tougher punishments and a decline in traditionally tolerant and lenient Dutch attitudes has led to severer sentencing and a deterioration in the quality of prison conditions and regimes (Kelk, 1993). We shall first examine how to explain the relative penal leniency of the Netherlands; then discuss the developments which have brought about the recent increasing harshness; and finally assess the current state of the Dutch penal system and its immediate prospects.

We take as our starting point *Contrasts in Tolerance*, David Downes's 1988 study of Dutch penality, which we find broadly convincing (Downes, 1988; see also Downes, 1982). Downes's account has a somewhat open-textured and speculative nature, which we consider to be something of a virtue at this present juncture in the history of comparative penology. We see Downes's approach as very much in line with our own 'radical pluralist' *modus operandi*: like us, Downes is prepared to allow a wide range of social factors into his explanatory framework without unconvincingly reducing any of them to mere epiphenomena of some putatively 'basic' factor. Downes says that in writing *Contrasts in Tolerance* he was 'striving to be a good Weberian' (Downes, 1990: 96), and Weberian sociology shares with radical pluralism both this non-reductive quality and an insistence on the importance of human agency. Consequently we feel no compunction in broadly purloining his account.

Downes dismisses resource factors as influential in the Netherlands' postwar 'decarceration', noting that neither national economic stringency nor lack of prison capacity have much plausibility as causes.[3] He (1988: 101) places most weight upon 'variables closely connected with the actual accomplishment of sentencing by the prosecutors and judges themselves'. Crucial to the Dutch record on punishment was leniency in sentencing and prosecutorial practice; but this in turn was conditioned by the cultures and belief-systems of these practitioners – what could be termed ideological rather than material factors. Both judges and prosecutors were imbued with a cultural belief in the wrongfulness and disutility of harsh (and especially custodial) punishments.

That this belief existed and was a potent cause of Dutch penal leniency is beyond doubt, although *why* exactly it existed to such an extent in the Netherlands is perhaps still a little mysterious. Constantijn Kelk (1993: 325) is one of those who ascribes it not only to the longstanding Dutch tradition of 'tolerance' but to 'a reaction to the extreme violence of which humanity had shown itself capable during the second world war' – and in particular the fact that 'many well-known and respectable Dutch citizens' – including many future judges – 'who would probably otherwise never have seen a prison from the inside, ended up there during the war as victims of the Nazis, and what they saw in the prisons shocked them so much that by 1947 a committee [the Fick Commission] ... had proposed drastic reforms'. (Downes [1998: 78] points out however that wartime internment was also experienced by Belgium and France, whose penal policies were less lenient until recently.)

One factor was the influence of the 'Utrecht school' of criminology, who promulgated strongly rehabilitationist and strongly anti-punitive and anti-custodial views between the late 1940s and mid-1960s.[4] Although there is some debate over exactly how strong their influence was it clearly had some important effect, not only in shaping the beliefs of practitioners but also in developing practical alternatives to custodial punishments. Their underlying message that offenders' welfare is the responsibility of the general community and that the aim should be to reintegrate and resocialize offenders rather than subject them to retributive punishment and social exclusion was one which harmonized with the general political culture of the Netherlands. And at this point Downes's analysis interfaces with the dimension we identified in Chapter 1 as a particular theme of this book – the relationship between penality and political economy.

As we noted in Chapter 1, the Netherlands can be seen as a nation basically corporatist and Christian Democratic in nature, while also having much in common with the Nordic social democracies. The modern Dutch state was largely founded upon the 'pillars' of the Catholic and Protestant churches whose combined membership encompassed the majority of the citizenry. But the Netherlands – with its generous welfare state provisions, traditional tolerance and social liberalism – saw the communitarianism of Christian Democracy combined (in a complex manner) with a libertarianism and egalitarianism more characteristic of a Nordic nation. This sprang from a culture of a relatively tolerant Christianity (and indeed of mutually tolerant Christian churches, including a famously liberal national Catholic church). Up to the 1990s, the result of this classically Dutch mixture of humane paternalism with libertarian social democracy was a penality that was even more lenient than that of most Nordic nations, despite the general rule we noted in Chapter 1 that social democratic nations tend to have lesser rates of punishment than corporatist ones. Perhaps the difference is that a secular and liberal social democracy is happy for every citizen to (as it were) go to hell in their own way, while a tolerant and liberal Christian Democracy with religious pluralism likes to think of everyone going to heaven by their own routes, and can be even kinder to sinners as a result. In this respect, however – as we shall see – the Netherlands has changed significantly in recent years.

Leniency, and an ideology of leniency, ran through the Dutch criminal justice system. Prosecutors were particularly likely to drop cases; judges were loath to impose custodial sentences, and especially long sentences of imprisonment; and prison regimes themselves were relatively liberal and humane. The ideology of 'law and order' was generally kept at bay; penal ideologies were a hybrid of Strategy C ideas of humaneness and human rights. Dutch penal law is still founded upon the Criminal Code of 1886, which in turn was originally based upon the ideas of Cesare Beccaria and the eighteenth-century 'Classical School' of criminal law which derived from general Enlightenment thinking (Beccaria, 1963; Cavadino and Dignan, 2002: 46–8). The Classical School, whose ideas are in many ways similar to those of the 'justice model' of the late twentieth century, stressed that penal sanctions should be no harsher than necessary and that the severity of punishments should be proportionate to the seriousness of offences. As Kelk (1993: 326) puts it, twentieth-century Dutch penal law was based both on this classicism and on later penal philosophies: 'It refutes retribution as an absolute goal in itself, but maintains it as the basis of all punishment and as a determinant of proportionality in relation to the offence. Within the limits of proportional retribution, actual retribution must be determined by specific aims (such as special deterrence, resocialization, general deterrence etc).'

In other words, the Netherlands' penal culture was one which traditionally (and very much in the tradition of Beccaria) saw punishment as justified only if it was *both* 'deserved' in the sense of being proportionate to the offence *and* useful in bringing about beneficial consequences. (This is, by the way, a philosophy very much in line with the one we ourselves espouse: see Cavadino and Dignan [2002: 54–8].) In general, this tends to be a recipe for penal leniency – provided, at any rate, that one is not too easily satisfied about what is deserved and what is useful. For most of the second half of the twentieth century the Dutch were not easily satisfied on either score. As to desert, Dutch tolerance and compassion for fellow humans has fostered a relatively sympathetic approach as to what just deserts require by way of punishment. And on the second point, Dutch criminal justice practitioners in particular have been highly sceptical of the notion that 'punishment works' in the sense of harshness effectively reducing crime. The occupational beliefs of judges and prosecutors were that harsh penalties were ineffective as deterrents to crime, but that humane treatment could effectively reduce crime by resocializing and reforming offenders.

Crucial in this mixture was the idea of *resocialization*, which underlay many of the reforms proposed by the Fick Commission in 1947 (whose membership included Gerrit Theodoor Kempe, a criminologist of the Utrecht School) and which was also embodied in the Prison Act of 1953. Kelk (1993: 325) aptly comments that 'the very idea of resocialisation suited a society in the process of being rebuilt'; it also suited a liberal Christian society concerned to bring as many lost sheep as possible back into the fold, being *inclusionary* rather than exclusionary (see Preface). Belief in resocialization of course both entails and necessitates that people retained a *rehabilitative optimism* – faith that reformative measures could actually be effective in turning offenders away from crime – and although (as in other countries) this rehabilitative optimism suffered in the 1970s and 1980s, it survived better and longer in the Netherlands than in many other countries. For example, a new law (the Penitentiary Principles Act) governing penal institutions which came into force in 1999 has been seen as toning down the importance of rehabilitation as opposed to security and control (von Hofer, 2002), but also continues to stress the principle of resocialization (Kelk, 2001: 479).

Although resocialization entails the reform of the offender, the Dutch philosophy never espoused full-blown *criminological positivism*, the deterministic school of thought, which is founded upon scepticism about human free will and which consequently denies any responsibility of offenders for their criminal actions. Rather the Dutch attitude contained 'an emphasis on offenders' own responsibility and on punishment as a means of making good the offence to society, after which rehabilitation could take place' (Kelk, 1993: 325). (Even the Utrecht School, who particularly favoured the use of psychiatric treatments for offenders,[5] mostly operated with an existentialist psychotherapeutic approach which was relatively voluntaristic rather than one which sees psychological troubles as illnesses over which the patient has no control and for which the patient has no responsibility.) This is a version of reformism which retains concern for the human dignity, freedom and civil rights of the offender, insisting for example that the severity of punishment is not disproportionate to the seriousness of the offender's transgression. In contrast, positivism has a tendency to justify grossly excessive punishment in the form of 'treatment' (Cavadino, 1997a: 17–18); this is not seen as a violation of the offender's rights to freedom since human freedom itself is regarded as a worthless illusion by those who really believe in positivism.

We have identified prosecutors and judges as particularly key figures in channelling this benevolent ideology into a practice of leniency. A word needs to be said in particular about the (in international terms) unusually vital role of the public prosecution service, which has been described as 'the spider in the web' of the Dutch criminal justice system (Downes, 1988: 13). It is the prosecutors who alone decide which cases should come to court, and their discretion is very wide. Dutch law holds to an 'opportunity principle' or 'principle of expediency' (*opportuniteitsbesingel*) whereby prosecution can be waived on (widely defined) policy grounds.[6] This power was increasingly used as part of a deliberate policy of 'diversion', and by 1983 only 39 per cent of criminal cases registered with the prosecutor's office resulted in formal prosecution, compared with around 60 per cent in 1960 (Bottomley, 1986: 203). Prosecutors can also in effect impose a fine without resorting to a court hearing by means of the 'transaction' (*transactie*), with the offender's consent (see Tak and van Kalmthout, 1998). (The power to agree a transaction was greatly increased by legislation in 1983; by 1996 35 per cent of cases were settled in this way, compared to 11 per cent discontinued for evidential or technical reasons and 4 per cent dropped on policy grounds.) When cases do proceed to court, the prosecution can also make (non-binding) recommendations as to the sentence the judge should impose. Since the early 1970s, the Ministry of Justice has sought to harmonize practice by the drafting of guidelines (in collaboration with senior prosecutors) regarding the waiving of prosecution and recommendations as to sentence for particular crimes (Downes, 1988: 14).

Crucial also, of course, are the judges who actually pass sentence on offenders – although it is said that Dutch judges generally feel bound to follow prosecution recommendations on sentence when they comply with the guidelines (Kelk, 1993: 331). The difference between sentencing in the Netherlands and comparable countries has primarily been, not that Dutch judges passed a great many *fewer* custodial sentences than other countries, but that prison sentences when passed tended to be much *shorter* (Bottomley, 1986: 202; Downes, 1988: 30). In the Netherlands, the judges who try criminal cases are a relatively small and wholly professional body (Downes, 1988: 18), and a group of people who, for a time at least, had a very definite collective prejudice against the use of severe custodial punishments, and even when feeling impelled to pass a sentence of imprisonment would seek to keep its length as short as possible.

Dutch prosecutors and judges form part of a relatively small 'joint moral community' (Christie, 1994: 41) – or 'penal elite' – who have shaped the country's criminal justice policy. Nils Christie (1994: 45) writes perceptively of

> a peculiar Dutch mechanism for coping with conflicts. The history of that country is filled with external as well as internal conflicts. The people have learned to live with their internal differences. They have learned the art of compromise. One mechanism to escape conflict has been to delegate decision-making up to the top of the system. Here representatives of opposing forces in Dutch society are given the mandate to sort out their differences and come up with solutions that can be lived with by all the various parties. It is an undemocratic solution, but preferable to civil war at the local level.

We might take issue with Christie's (characteristic) attractively flamboyant mode of expression. It is contentious to speak of such arrangements as 'undemocratic', although terms like 'bureaucratic' and 'archetypally corporatist' are surely apt. The set-up is certainly undemocratic if one adopts the American cynic H.L. Mencken's definition of democracy as the theory that 'the people' know what they want and deserve to get it good and hard. It goes against the kind of populist politics in which law and order ideology tends to thrive – as it has most notably in the USA in recent times. (Populist politics is also assisted by the existence of downmarket 'tabloid' media which tend to reinforce and amplify knee-jerk punitive responses among the public. The Netherlands has been relatively free of such print-based media, although the recent development of 'reality TV' [Downes, 1998: 153]) – which graphically depicts scenes of violent crime and police responses to it – represents a move in the direction of 'tabloid television'.) It is a more indirect, representative form of democracy than one in which politicians seek to translate populist common sense swiftly into policy, sometimes contrary to the better judgement of the elite of experts and practitioners.[7] 'Bureaucratization' of political and legal institutions of the kind found in the Netherlands has been identified by Savelsberg (1999) as a factor which tends to bring about stability in a country's penality – as long, that is, as the country is a decentralized, pluralist democracy. If, however, bureaucratization is combined with a highly centralized state or party monopolization of power, as it was in former Communist countries, then the mixture can lead to wild, centrally-dictated swings in the penal pendulum in response to political events.

And yet, as we noted at the beginning of this section, both the stability and the lenient nature of Dutch penality have suffered significantly in recent years. We now discuss some of the factors behind this shift towards harsher punishment.

In the Netherlands as elsewhere, the trend of late modernity has been towards a more individualized, less communitarian society. Allegiance to the Christian churches has declined both numerically[8] and in terms of the strength of the ties between individuals and church (and between churches and state), leading to what has been called the *depillarization* of the corporate state; workplace and local communities have declined and become more fragmented and less stable; lifestyles and personal concerns have become more privatized. Kelk (1993: 328) speaks of 'a depersonalised style of life and alienation between individuals. A lack of social attachments between people, and between people and social systems ... In general, people seem to have become more egocentric.' This late-modern trend towards individualized 'anomie' is hardly unique to the Netherlands, but may have progressed there faster, and from a lower base, than in many other countries.

In this respect, the Netherlands can be seen (by those who, such as Nils Christie and ourselves, liked the Netherlands the way it was) as a victim of globalization. American-style consumerist culture has had a much swifter impact on the Netherlands than on many other West European countries. Language doubtless plays a part: compared to France and Germany, for example, Dutch people are far more likely to enjoy media and entertainment in the English language, mostly of American origin. This has made them more open than more culturally sheltered nations to import American ideologies along with other American products. They – and their politicians – have also followed the lead of the neoliberal UK. One consequence has been a shift away from the Netherlands' mix of Christian and social democracy to incorporate an increasing degree of neoliberalism in economic and social policy. Importantly, however, the Dutch welfare state system remains to date fairly unscathed, despite a significant restructuring in the early 1990s (van der Veen and Trommel, 1998). And unlike several other European countries, the Netherlands did not find itself having to plan cuts in welfare state provision in order to achieve the 'Maastricht criteria' of economic convergence in order to join the single European currency in 1999.

One might have expected that a shift towards neo-liberalism would have concomitantly changed Dutch ideas about how to deal with crime. In a more Americanized, individualized, secularized and marketized world, one would expect to find less tolerance of criminals, who are no longer seen as troubled and troublesome members of our own society but as outsiders with whom we have no interests in common. The solution to crime would be seen as being the repression and exclusion of offenders – keeping the lawless minority either in fear or else well away from the law-abiding majority – not their resocialization and reintegration into the mainstreams of the community. We are no longer our brother's keeper, but his jailer – not that we recognize him as a brother any more. The trend would therefore be away from a humane and inclusionary

Strategy C mindset towards harsh and exclusionary Strategy A attitudes. It is not exactly this that has happened in the Netherlands, however. What has happened has been more like *a redrawing of the boundaries of the community* – to exclude those offenders who are seen as incorrigible lost souls, but still to include less serious and less persistent offenders. This is, of course, a policy of *bifurcation* – dividing offenders into two categories of less serious and more serious criminals, towards whom radically different approaches may be taken. The official aim is to seek to reduce the use of short-term imprisonment and expand the use of alternatives to imprisonment for lesser offenders at the same time as increasing punishments for more serious offenders. And this has indeed been happening: the average time served by a prisoner doubled between 1980 and 1999, as the number of short prison sentences declined and the length of longer ones increased (von Hofer, 2002).

Although there is an increasing tendency to write off the more serious offenders as irretrievably lost souls who cannot be resocialized and who may be excluded and incarcerated for long periods, this is far from the case for the less serious offenders. For these, the communitarian goal of resocialization is still alive. Indeed, it could be said to have taken on a new lease of life with the introduction and promulgation of new forms of community sentence, mostly aimed at the resocialization of the offender.[9] Prosecutors who recommend prison sentences of less than six months are required by guidelines to provide reasons explaining why a community sentence is not appropriate instead. However, community sentences are intended not only for some offenders who would previously have been sentenced to relatively short periods of imprisonment, but also some who might have been subjected to a fine or not faced prosecution at all – disposals which might be cheap, convenient and lenient, but which can hardly be said to represent strenuous efforts to rehabilitate offenders.

In all of this – and despite the increasing Americanization of the general Dutch culture – English developments in punishment have exerted a greater influence on Dutch penal thinking than has the USA. The *bifurcatory* tendency noticeable in the Netherlands is reminiscent of that seen in England, before and during the 'Hurd era' of 1987–92 (see Chapter 4). The same could be said of the 'strategy of encouragement' being pursued in the Netherlands, whereby an expanded range of community sentences are provided and their use is encouraged – by guidelines, rhetoric and attempts to make them attractive alternatives to custody – but not mandated by government or legislation. More recent themes in English policy and rhetoric have also been reflected in the Netherlands. The statements of ministers that punishments should be 'swift and sure' (Kelk, 1993: 328) echoed British New Labour's adoption, in milder form, of the American concept of 'zero tolerance'.

It is relevant here that, although Dutch social democrats and liberals have traditionally been more in favour of penal leniency than the Christian Democrats, the Dutch Labour Party (which led coalition governments from 1994 to 2002) is one of the many social democratic parties which have consciously imitated Tony Blair's New Labour in Britain (which in turn imitated American New Democrats such as Bill Clinton), including its quest for a 'tougher' image in the area of law and order. Consequently, there was no major change in the direction of policy when Labour-led coalitions took over from Christian Democrat-dominated administrations in 1994. In general, traditional party politics has played little part in the shift in Dutch penal attitudes. Unlike in some other countries (such as the UK and Australia) there has been no great 'bidding war' between different parties for which can pose as 'toughest on crime'; but there has been a cultural change across the entire political spectrum.

The pace of this cultural change has accelerated dramatically in the last few years, as the relatively pacific politics of the Netherlands have been thrown into turmoil. Two major causes have been the immigration issue and a more general collapse of confidence in government – both of these being factors which can be seen as implicated in the growing 'culture of control' (Garland, 2001: see Chapter 2) in late modern societies. The year 2002 saw a (Labour-led) Dutch government resign ignominiously, accepting that it had been at fault in failing to do more to prevent a massacre of thousands of Bosnian Muslims by Serb forces at Srebenica in 1995. The following elections of May 2002 were largely dominated by the anti-immigration campaign of the charismatic Pim Fortuyn. This movement had an intriguingly Dutch character untypical of other contemporary far-right developments in Europe in that it represented itself as not only non-racist but even as essentially liberal. Fortuyn, himself a flamboyant homosexual, argued that the Netherlands' liberal culture was at risk from immigrants who did not share it. Again, Fortuyn's pitch was a bifurcatory re-drawing of the boundaries of the Dutch community: those who were to be included were those who (whatever their race, he claimed) accepted the nature of that liberal community, while others were to be excluded. More typically for such right-wing parties, the *Lijst Pim Fortuyn* advocated hard-line policies on law and order as well as immigration, and sought to link the two issues. Shockingly, Fortuyn was assassinated during the election campaign, in which his party came second and entered a short-lived coalition led by the Christian Democrats. In-fighting in Fortuyn's party contributed to the collapse of this government, and the election of 2003 saw its electoral support slashed and the party removed from the coalition government. However, the Pim Fortuyn phenomenon has had a noticeable effect on hardening the policies of the mainstream parties on immigration issues. Most recently, the Netherlands has been experiencing its most serious intercommunal unrest of modern times following another murder, of anti-Muslim film director Theo van Gogh in November 2004. It may be to early to judge the long-term effects of such developments on Dutch penality, but they seem likely to contribute to its growing harshness. In October 2002 the government promised to reduce crime by 20 to 25 per cent by 2006 by measures including an extra 5,000 prison places and increased penalties for certain offenders (Ministerie van Justitie van Nederlands, 2002; Pakes, 2004; von Hofer, 2003b).

As well as this general trend in the direction of Strategy A harshness, the Netherlands has also seen a very notable rise in Strategy B managerialism. Its roots can be detected at least as far back as the early 1970s when the Ministry of Justice instigated the drawing up of guidelines for prosecution decisions and sentencing recommendations. Since then, managerialism has come on apace, with increasing bureaucratization and regulation of the criminal justice system and emphasis on standardized procedures, throughput, value for money and efficiency generally. As ever, the danger here is that compassion and concern for human beings and their rights and interests get lost in the wheels of the impersonal bureaucratic machine – as both Antonie Peters (1988) and Constantijn Kelk (1993) of Utrecht University have complained has happened. We ourselves favour the employment of managerialist techniques in combination with and furtherance of a humane Strategy C set of values (Cavadino et al., 1999, especially Chapter 2). But without such a moral basis, managerialism runs the risk of lapsing into an amoral instrumentalism or forging an anti-humanitarian alloy with Strategy A harshness, leading to what we have called 'punitive managerialism', or what Kelk (1993: 338) terms in the Dutch context 'efficient repression'.

Always bearing in mind the contextual point that the Netherlands today is still less punitive than some of its West European neighbours – not to mention such countries as the USA and New Zealand – a trend in the direction of such punitive managerialism has been very evident. An individual who played an important specific role in this development was Dato Steenhuis, who 'throughout the 1980s moved between senior posts within the prosecution service and the Ministry of Justice. Although a large number of academics and practitioners were influential during this period, it was Steenhuis who first articulated and actively promoted the new and distinctively managerial perspective within the Dutch criminal justice context' (Rutherford, 1996: 61). A watershed moment was reached in 1985 with the publication of the Ministry of Justice's policy document *Society and Crime (Samenleving en Criminaliteit)*, which represented both a step towards managerialism and a significant official break with the Dutch tradition of leniency. The document, produced in response to public and political concern about rising crime and the perceived ineffectiveness of the Dutch criminal justice system to control crime, promised swifter, surer and more effective sanctions against wrongdoers. The administration of the criminal justice system was to be more tightly and efficiently regulated, and a significant increase in both prosecution and imprisonment was envisaged: unconditional discontinuances of prosecution were to be reduced by 50 per cent,[10] and the number of prison cells was to be increased.

Subsequent government policy documents confirmed and reinforced this dual trend towards both harsher punishment for offenders and a more regulated managerial regimen for the criminal justice system – that is, in the general direction of a punitive managerialism *hollandaise*. The results included a prison building programme which commenced in the early 1990s (following on from a previous, less ambitious expansion programme in the early 1980s) leading to an increase in the Netherlands' prison capacity from 3,127 in 1975 to 12,030 cells by the end of 2002 with further expansion of around 5,000 places planned; and the extremely rapid rises in actual imprisonment rates which we have already noted. The latter were pre-eminently brought about by harsher sentencing, with significant increases in both the proportion of convicted offenders sentenced to non-suspended custody and in the lengths of custodial sentences passed. For example, 34 per cent of convicted drugs offenders were imprisoned in 1995 compared with 22 per cent in 1985, while the number of sentences of over four years' imprisonment passed in the Netherlands increased from 692 to 1,796 over the same period. Dutch courts imposed 10,900 years of detention in 1995 compared with 5,900 in 1985 (Tak and van Kalmthout, 1998: 13).[11]

All this has been despite the policy, mentioned earlier, of attempting to encourage the use of community penalties, including new ones, as alternatives to custody. Although community sentences have been increasingly used by the courts, this development has happened at the same time as an expansion in the use of imprisonment. It may well be, then, that these community penalties have tended to be used, not so much as an alternative to custody as to substitute for other non-custodial disposals such as fines and waivers of prosecution – an outcome not dissimilar to that found in other countries (such as England) which have adopted this 'strategy of encouragement' (see for example Cavadino and Dignan, 2002: 122, 153.)

These developments in the Netherlands suggest a need to clarify Savelsberg's (1999) thesis (mentioned earlier): that a 'bureaucratized' polity in a pluralist democracy tends to stabilize penal practices. Perhaps this is so where the bureaucratic elite are themselves stable in their penal philosophies; if so, their privileged positions of power will tend to act as a buffer insulating criminal justice from swings of public and political opinion. But in a country where a relatively small elite dictates penal policies, it may be that relatively rapid change is possible and even facilitated when that elite changes its mind and/or its personnel. In Savelsberg's terms, we could characterize the Netherlands as being quite 'centralized' for a pluralist democracy, although of course in power terms it is much less centralized than a Communist state. The Netherlands is a relatively small country without the degree of regional autonomy to be found in (say) Germany, Australia or the USA and power to determine the operation of criminal justice in particular is as we have seen concentrated in the hands of a comparatively small national 'penal elite'.[12] In the Netherlands during this period, the mindset of this penal elite altered significantly over a relatively short time. One possible factor mentioned by Kelk (1993: 331) is that 'the average age of judges has gone down enormously in a very short time, not only in the sense that more young judges have joined the judiciary, but also in the sense that one can now become a judge at a much earlier age'; there has been a generational change in personnel contributing to a sea change in penal attitudes in the 'joint moral community'.

So was there, and is there, a 'penal crisis' in the Netherlands?

In the 1980s there was certainly no *crisis of resources*. A system that uses both prosecution and imprisonment so sparingly without substituting expensive alternatives is almost bound to operate relatively cheaply. There would, however, have been a severe crisis had it not been for one characteristic Dutch policy which contributed to the low imprisonment rate: the practice of putting lesser offenders sentenced to custody on a waiting list and not actually detaining them until a prison place became vacant. This policy did, however, eventually create a kind of perceived – one might almost say imaginary – crisis of prison resources in the governmental mind following criticisms by a series of official agencies and reports. The backlog of sentenced offenders waiting to enter prison rose from the 1970s onwards to an extent which caused the Ministry of Justice increasingly serious concern (Tak, 1998: 2) and was one factor leading to the adoption of the prison building programmes of the early 1980s and 1990s. One aim of this was to eliminate the waiting list, which was achieved in 1999.

But the waiting list system had assisted a situation whereby conditions within Dutch prisons were relatively tolerable. Prisons were not overcrowded, and one prisoner per cell was the almost unbreakable rule (Downes, 1988: 23), until – after a long struggle between the Ministry of Justice and prison governors and staff – the policy was abrogated by Royal Decree in 1994 (van Swaaningen and de Jonge, 1995: 28). Nor were there crises of control or security, despite the odd moral panic caused by occasional high-profile escapes (van Swaaningen and de Jonge, 1995: 32). Industrial relations problems with prison staff were likewise generally absent.

The problem that the Dutch penal system had in the 1980s was essentially a *crisis of legitimacy*. This was not the sort of crisis of legitimacy wherein the system is perceived as being unacceptably inhumane to its subjects (cf. Fitzgerald and Sim, 1982: Chapter 1). The Dutch system was increasingly perceived as being excessively *lenient*, and consequently ineffective at controlling crime because it provided insufficient deterrents against offending. It was also seen as in some respects offending against liberal 'rule of law' principles, especially in respect of prosecutors' wide discretion to enforce or not to enforce the law and the delay in implementing prison sentences (Tak, 1998: 3). (Reforms to tackle these perceived flaws can be seen as 'modernizing' in a wide, Weberian sense: see Chapter 1.) The most popularly perceived remedies – whether rightly or wrongly[13] – were harsher and more consistent sanctions against wrongdoers, and an injection of more rigorous management into the criminal justice system.

Crime was indeed rising in the Netherlands, as it was elsewhere. Although there was little objective reason to believe that lenient Dutch penal policies were behind these rises, this belief nevertheless took hold within the Dutch penal elite. In particular, 'victimization surveys which purported to show that the Netherlands was becoming one of the most criminal countries in Europe were important in facilitating a more punitive mentality' (van Swaaningen and de

Jonge, 1995: 41). Another factor was the Netherlands' increasing drugs problem, complicated by the pressures placed upon the Netherlands by other countries – including the USA, but also Germany and Sweden – to introduce tougher measures against drug offenders, as lenient and liberal Dutch policies were perceived as exacerbating not only its own but international drug problems due to the Netherlands' strategic position in international narcotic trade routes (Christie, 1994: 46; Downes, 1988: Chapter 5). Here again, the Netherlands can be seen as a victim of globalization, in both the drugs trade itself and in strategies to combat it.

Globalization in penal ideologies also played its part. The notion that the antidote to crime is to be tough on offenders is one that has largely infected the Netherlands from the outside, being foreign to the previous Dutch tradition. As a result, resocialization and other humane impulses have been downgraded in favour of deterrence and managerialism: the Netherlands' traditional Strategy C approach has been eroded by a mixture of Strategies A and B. Prosecution serves as an example: the impersonal managerialist urge to exert control over the prosecution decision has undermined the more compassionate practices of diversion and discontinuance which prevailed previously.

There is a further factor with an international dimension which has also played its part in hardening penal attitudes in the Netherlands. This is the increasing phenomenon of transnational migration, now from the formerly Communist East as well as from the South, and especially from former Dutch colonies in the East Indies. Traditional Dutch tolerance towards the foreign migrant and hospitality towards the refugee has also been weakening, a development particularly dramatized by the brief meteoric political career of Pim Fortuyn, mentioned previously. As elsewhere in Western Europe, the Netherlands has seen a rising level of concern and debate about how to deal with migrants and refugees and an increasing willingness to detain them. As elsewhere, too, the image of immigrants and ethnic minorities has become conflated with images of criminality, and harsher policies towards both the migrant and the criminal have advanced in symbiosis (see Chapter 2). Quite apart from detention of alleged illegal immigrants and those claiming refugee status, an increasing number of non-Dutch people have found their way into penal institutions proper. The proportion of prisoners without Dutch nationality rose from 12 per cent in 1981 to 26 per cent in 1992 (Downes, 1998: 164). Overall, only 52 per cent are both Dutch and white (van Swaaningen and de Jonge, 1995: 29), making the Netherlands a prime example of the process Sim et al. (1995: 9) refer to as the casting of the migrant as an international scapegoat or 'folk devil' against whom harsh treatment is legitimated.

We do not mean to give the impression that Dutch governments have been deliberately attempting to stoke up punishment to the maximum possible level. On the contrary, they have attempted to keep punishment and the prison population under control. A Minister of Justice appointed for a four-year term in 1994 promised to reduce the imprisonment rate; although the promise was not kept, it was an indication that Dutch attitudes to punishment remain far distant from those in, say, the USA. The general policy is still one of *bifurcation*: seeking to reduce the use of short-term imprisonment and expand the use of alternatives to imprisonment for lesser offenders at the same time as increasing punishments for more serious offenders. But it remains to be seen how successful such official policies can prove in practice in the long run. At present the rapidly rising imprisonment rate suggests that, as has happened elsewhere (notably England and Wales since the 1980s: see Cavadino and Dignan, 2002, especially 333–42) the result is likely to be a toughening of punishments across the board as penal attitudes – and sentencing levels – harden generally.

At the moment there is not a crisis – yet – although the current Dutch penal situation is not a comfortable one. The expansion in prison capacity has not been keeping pace with the rise in the actual prisoner population. Although the prison system as a whole for a long time remained free from overcrowding, in 2001 mounting pressure on the capacity of the prison system led to cell occupancy exceeding 100 per cent. This led the government to introduce various emergency measures including the use of police cells to hold hundreds of prisoners and the accelerated and temporary release of thousands more. In 2003 the government agreed to further amend the law to allow greater routine use of cell sharing. Meanwhile, prison regimes have declined in quality, with less freedom of movement and fewer communal activities for inmates. The prison building programme has also meant that Dutch prisoners are now much less likely to be held in small prisons than previously, which is also likely to contribute to a poorer quality of life (Kelk, 1993: 332). Nevertheless, it could not be said that Dutch prisons as yet suffer from a severe general crisis of conditions. Nor is there any sign of an industrial relations crisis.

There has, however, been growing concern over prison security, which was heightened by a number of prison escapes and hostage-taking incidents during the early 1990s. There is also serious concern over the 'control' problems that are believed to be posed by the still relatively small number of exceptionally 'dangerous' inmates serving very long (in Dutch terms) prison sentences. The response to these anxieties has been predictable and consists of a 'closed door' approach to any act of hostage-taking and the designation of a temporary maximum security unit at Vught (Downes, 1998: 166). As has happened elsewhere (for example in England and Wales; see Cavadino and Dignan, 2002: 183–6), the growing preoccupation with prison security resulted in an oppressive regime at Vught that was not only unprecedentedly severe by Dutch standards but which has been compared with some of the worst conditions encountered in the UK.[14] The treatment of 'dangerous' inmates in a number of Special Detention Units has also drawn adverse comment from the European Committee for the Prevention of Torture (Council of Europe CPT, 1993: 33f.), following an inspection visit to the Netherlands in 1993. So far, with the exception of the 'closed door' policy which requires all exits to be sealed the moment there is a hostage-taking incident, the detrimental impact of security concerns on prison regimes and relations between prison officers and inmates appears to be largely confined to the small number of maximum security units. However, experience elsewhere (again particularly in the UK) serves as a warning sign that security concerns can all too readily generate a 'moral panic' that may have an adverse impact on prison conditions and regimes right across the prison system

Despite some scope for moral concern in other areas also – for example about needlessly rising levels of punishment, or about the wildly disproportionate numbers of foreigners and members of ethnic minorities in Dutch prisons – there is as yet still no generalized crisis of legitimacy. Only time will tell whether this will remain the case. Meanwhile a crisis of numbers and resources looms. The present upward trajectory of punishment trends in the Netherlands is so steep that the situation could easily spiral out of control. The harsher sentences being passed now are likely to fuel an accelerating numbers crisis within the prison system, and even the most vigorous and expensive prison building pro-gramme is likely to find it difficult to keep up, or could even itself encourage a greater use of custody by sentencers. Unless – which from experience elsewhere we doubt – the policy of encouraging greater use of non-custodial penalties proves more of a success than it has so far, the Netherlands could soon pay the price for jettisoning its old penal habits by facing a penal crisis of a kind it has never previously known.

Notes

1 In 1950 the rate per 100,000 total population was 66 (Rutherford, 1986: 136). This *followed* a dramatic reduction of the prison population from 8,577 in 1947 to 5,858 in 1950 (excluding political prisoners such as wartime collaborators).

2 Source: Council of Europe, *Prison Information Bulletin* (numbers 1–9); cited in *Hansard*, 29 April 1988.

3 More precisely, Downes says that constraints on the capacity of the criminal justice system have played a part in shaping Dutch penal policies, particularly from the mid-1960s to mid-70s, but rightly notes that the interesting question is why for so long the Dutch *treated* limited penal capacity as a constraint on penal practices, rather than sim-ply expanding that capacity by building more prisons (Downes, 1982: 337–9). Indeed, in 1972 prison capacity was knowingly *reduced* when the system was restructured (von Hofer, 2003: 24).

4 This was the 'old' Utrecht School (based at the Institute of Criminology within the Law Faculty at Utrecht University), whose members included Willem Petrus Joseph Pompe, Pieter Aart Hendrik Baan, Gerrit Theodoor Kempe and Rijk Rijksen. A later gen-eration at Utrecht (the 'new' Utrecht School), including Antonie Peters and Constantijn Kelk, place greater stress on the legal rights of offenders.

5 This is an oversimplification, which skates over some significant differences between individuals within the 'Utrecht School' (see Downes, 1988: 93–5).

6 In legal theory, the classic contrast to this is Germany, where the 'legality principle' theoretically requires all known offenders to be prosecuted. In practice, however, the working of prosecutorial discretion in Germany is not that different from in the Netherlands. A better contrast in practice is Finland, where there has traditionally been a more legalistic approach to mandatory prosecution.

7 This has been aptly satirized by the American folk singer Tom Paxton: 'We'll fearlessly take our positions when we know how you feel/We've taken the polls and we know it's the safe thing to do ... We'll be out there leading, about two or three steps behind you' ('We All Sound The Same', from *The Paxton Report*, Evolution Records, 1980). Note, however, the evidence that in the politics of law and order, politicians (and the media) have often recently seemed to *lead* public opinion in the direction of punitive polices (Beckett, 1997).

8 Church membership in the Netherlands was 99 per cent in 1900, 76 per cent in 1958 and 61 per cent in 1970 but only 42 per cent in 1991. According to official estimates, only a quarter of Dutch people were members of a Christian church by the year 2000 (J. Kerkhofs, in *The Tablet*, 24 July 1999).

9 The community service order has been in use since 1981; more recent innovations include training orders, combination orders and electronic monitoring; and, for younger offenders, measures such as the HALT programme (see Chapter 14), which combines elements of reparation and education as an alternative to prosecution.

10 Only 4 per cent of prosecution cases received an unconditional waiver for policy reasons by 1996 (plus another 11 per cent unconditionally dropped on technical and evidential grounds) – down from an estimated 28 per cent in the early 1980s (Tak, 1998: 7). The decrease in unconditional policy waivers did not lead to a similarly large increase in court cases, however, because an increasing number were waived under condition or settled by means of a 'transaction' (see above).

11 There was a 22 per cent increase in the number of cases tried by the criminal courts over this period (from 83,800 on 1985 to 102,300 in 1995), but this by no means accounts for these increases.

Downes (1998: 157) puts forward the view that, broadly speaking, it is 'the rise in the volume of the more serious offences, rather than any marked increase in punitiveness, which accounts for the continuing rise in prison numbers since the late 1980s' although 'some trends do not fit that pattern consistently'. It is doubtful whether Downes' own figures justify this conclusion. It seems to us more accurate to say that although some of the rise in prison numbers can be attributed to an increase in offenders processed for certain serious offences (notably involving hard drugs), rather more is attributable to harsher punishments.

12 One example of this centralization is the arrangement whereby the national Ministry of Justice issues guidelines which govern prosecution and sentencing decisions.

13 We would say wrongly: crime rates are mostly determined by social and economic factors rather than the operations of the criminal justice system, and the deterrent and other crime-reducing effects of the criminal justice system, while not non-existent, are all too easy to overestimate. See generally Cavadino et al. (1999: Chapter 2).

14 Downes (1998: 166) likened conditions in Vught to the notorious 'cages' that were once operated at Peterhead Prison in Scotland.

9

France and Italy: Corporatism and Catholicism

Two neighbouring countries on the main continent of Europe, with much in common but some striking differences. Their languages are Romance, their religion is overwhelmingly Roman Catholic, and their urbanites pride themselves on their style, sophistication, cuisine, fashion and general sexiness. They have similar size populations (an estimated 59 and 56 million in France and Italy, respectively in 2002) and GDPs ($1.45 and $1.27 trillions respectively in 2000). (In each of these latter respects, both countries are similar to the UK – 59 million and $1.36 trillion.) Their prison populations are also similar – 64,813 in France in July 2004 and 56,574 in Italy in September 2002, representing 109 and 100 inmates per 100,000 general population respectively. This makes them both mid-ranking countries in Western European penality and in our sample of countries, with similar rates to the Netherlands and Germany. As one might expect of mid-ranking countries in an age of general penal inflation, both countries have seen a rise in their prison populations since the mid-1980s. The two countries' rates were also similar in 1985, but since then both rates have fluctuated, unevenly and out of synch with each other, as shown in Table 9.1.

The general levels of imprisonment in these two countries are more or less what we would expect, given that both countries can be given the general description of 'conservative corporatist' or 'Christian Democratic', with the kind of communitarian ethos typical of such countries. They occupy the middle reaches of penality between neo-liberal nations on the one hand and social democracies on the other, along with the other conservative corporatist countries. Yet things are not quite so simple, for neither country is corporatist in quite the same sense as Germany, the Netherlands or the Nordic social democracies. Importantly, the trade unions are not incorporated into the state and its provision of welfare benefits and services, as is the case in these other

Table 9.1 *French and Italian prison populations and imprisonment rates per 100,000 general population*

Year	France: prison population	France: imprisonment rate	Italy: prison population	Italy: imprisonment rate
1985	40,354	72	43,585	76.5
1986	47,628	84	43,685	76
1987	50,639	89	34,838	61
1988	52,494	92	34,675	60
1989	45,102	78.5	30,594	54
1990	46,798	81	31,234	55
1991	48,675	84	32,368	56
1992	49,323	84	46,152	80
1993	51,100	87	50,800	88
1995	53,178	91	49,102	86
1997	54,442	90	49,477	85
1998	53,259	91	49,864	87
1999	53,948	92	51,427	89
2000	48,835	80	53,481	93
2001	46,376	78	55,136	95
2002	50,714	85	56,574	100
2003	55,382	93	*	*
2004	64,813	109	*	*

Sources: Council of Europe; Walmsley (1999, 2000, 2002, 2003b); Home Office (2001a: Table 1.21); Ministère de la Justice (2004); Robert Cario (personal communications). Figures are for 1 September wherever possible.

* – Figures not available.

countries.[1] Their trade unions are strong and influential in other ways, however. Agreements with Italy's trade unions (representing around 40 per cent of the labour force in the early 1990s) set wages and salaries in every major field. France has a much lower rate of union membership (10 per cent in the early 1990s), but they combine a tradition of militancy with a habit of being listened to by governments. Thus in 1995–6 significant cuts in the French welfare state, proposed by the conservative Prime Minister Alain Juppé in the context of France's preparations to meet the Maastricht criteria for entry into the European single currency, met resistance in the form of large-scale strikes which had the effect of delaying and mitigating the planned cuts. In 2003 similar scenes recurred as a one-day strike paralysed the nation in protest against proposed cuts in pension benefits.

Until relatively recently, France and Italy differed sharply on their levels of welfare state provision, a difference that can be traced back to the immediate aftermath of World War Two. In France, a highly statist approach to industry, the economy and welfare were adopted at this time, laying the foundations of the modern French state. Key industries were nationalized as the government assumed direction of the economy. In 1946 a comprehensive system of health and social insurance was established in France, as it was in her neighbours in Western and Northern Europe. The French welfare system remains much more comprehensive and well-funded than those of most countries, although not at the same level as those of Germany, the Netherlands or the Nordic social democracies. Italy on the other hand – in common with other states in Southern Europe such as Greece, Spain and Portugal – has only had a relatively rudimentary welfare state. For example, she only established a national health service in 1980, and it is still poorly resourced by EU standards. However, Italy's public social spending has been increasing in recent years, to the point where it now (as a proportion of GDP) exceeds that found in the UK and is not too far behind that found in France.[2] One might as a result (or perhaps more precisely, as a correlative) expect Italy to have had much higher punishment levels than France for many years, but as we have seen this was not so.

This may indicate that what is of significance in influencing imprisonment rates is not the cost or level of welfare provision so much as the degree and nature of communitarianism, egalitarianism and tolerance or authoritarianism in a country's *culture*, which because of local political and historical differences will not always translate evenly into the formal political economy. In Italy the Christian Democratic Party – which dominated politics from World War Two until it finally imploded under the weight of monumental corruption scandals in 1994 – did not try to introduce a Western Europe-style welfare state. This may have had much to do with the influence of a conservative Catholic church whose own style of communitarianism contained an ideological element which feared that too much state welfare might undermine the alternative social support structures of the church and the family. By contrast, the French republican tradition has an enduring anti-clerical streak suspicious of church interference in politics and favouring a strong state as the focus of the national community, clearly an attitude far more favourable to the creation of a welfare state. Such pro-welfare anti-clericalism was of course also characteristic of the Italian Communist Party. But although second in popular support only to the Christian Democrats, the PCI was rigorously excluded from power until 1996, by which time it had metamorphosed into a 'Third Way' social democratic party, the Left Democrats (PDS).

France

France has since World War Two been ruled mostly by Christian Democrats of a Gallic stamp and most notably by Charles de Gaulle and his 'Gaullist' successors. From 1981 to 2002 governments led by the Socialist Party predominated: the Socialists governed from 1981–6, 1988–93 and 1997–2002, the 1997–2002 government being one in which a parliamentary majority led by Socialist Prime Minister Lionel Jospin 'cohabited' with the Gaullist President Jacques Chirac. The dramatic elections of 2002 eventually saw President Chirac re-elected with a large right-wing parliamentary majority. In the early 1980s, the Socialist government attempted to move the country in the direction of social democracy but encountered severe difficulties, and thereafter they made little serious attempt to alter the nature of the French political economy. Nevertheless, French socialism has resisted adopting the 'Third Way' ideology to a greater extent than elsewhere in the West – in a league table of the Third Way, the French Socialist Party would rank well below the leading left-of-centre parties in the USA, the UK, Australia, New Zealand, Germany and the Netherlands, although above the Nordic social democratic parties.

The political economy of France contains some social democratic elements, particularly in the areas of industrial relations and a health service which provides an enviable level of care but is currently experiencing serious budgetary difficulties. It is also unusually statist and 'dirigiste' for Western Europe, with more nationalized industries and services even than in the Nordic countries, although there have been some privatizations and welfare cuts from the 1980s onwards (including the cuts initiated by Alain Juppé in the mid-1990s, mentioned previously, with further cuts being proposed by the current government under President Chirac). These were first pursued by conservative governments influenced by neo-liberal ideology. (The Right in France today is essentially a *mélange* of free-market conservatism and a traditional Gaullism which still favours a strong, corporatist national state.) Privatizations continued under the Chirac-Jospin 'cohabitation' of 1997–2002. The general French public ethos, however, remains corporatist: it is usually assumed, for example, that large private firms should and will take account of the interests of the nation and their workforce, and that the national government is entitled to have an influential say on such matters. The national state is strong, and French bureaucracy is notoriously formidable.

Until the 1970s, punishment in France was not a matter of great public controversy. The officially dominant penal ideology – as elsewhere in the West at the time – was a humane positivism: 'rehabilitation, individualization of the penalty and the dual approach of probation and imprisonment, to avoid sending petty offenders and first offenders to prison' (Faugeron, 1991: 249).[3] And indeed, humanity and the reintegration of the prisoner remain the official aims of punishment in France. But the consensual nature of French penality was to change. Prison riots in the years 1971 to 1974 were followed by major reforms with a liberal intent in 1975. These reclassified prisons, attempted to improve prison conditions and regimes introduced some reforms to detention on remand and created new community penalties intended as alternatives to custody. (These alternatives to custody were little used by sentencers, however, accounting for less than 2 per cent of sentences: Faugeron, 1991: 250.) A right-wing backlash

against these reforms was supported by sections of the media and the conservative government at the time. From this time onwards, punishment has been a
party political issue in France. In general, right-wing governments have tended
to toughen penal legislation and practice while Socialist governments have tried
to reduce the prison population.

At least until recently the penal ideology of French socialism, like its more
general ideology, retained a more traditional flavour than did parties elsewhere
which adopted the 'Third Way' approach with its 'tough on crime' orientation.
Until the beginning of the twenty-first century the gap on law and order issues
between the main parties of the left and right was significantly wider in France
than in most Western European countries. Even so, the differences should not
be exaggerated. Conservative governments have combined law and order
rhetoric and some repressive measures with other pragmatic moves to try to
keep the prison population under some control. One such pragmatic measure,
employed by both left and right, is the collective amnesty, traditional on the
election of Presidents and Bastille Day. For example, there was a notable drop
in the number of prisoners following the re-election of the Socialist President
Mitterand in 1988. As a result 'periodically, prisons are emptied a little, before
the number of prisoners increases again' (Combessie, 2001: 253), leading to an
'upwards zig-zag' just as marked as the one described in England in Chapter 4,
and clearly visible in Table 9.1.

In the late 1970s and early 1980s, the conservative government of President
Giscard d'Estaing espoused law and order ideology and castigated their Socialist
opponents as being soft on crime, much as Margaret Thatcher's Conservatives
were doing in the UK (in opposition and subsequently in government) at the same
time. An Act of 1978 restricted the early release of prisoners by introducing
'security periods' during which release was forbidden. The *Sécurité et Liberté* Act
of 2 February 1981 attained a certain mythic status as the symbol and apogee of
conservative penal repression. It increased scales of punishments for certain
offences, restricted the use of alternatives to custody, reduced prisoners' rights
and the ability of magistrates to supervise the treatment of prisoners. (However,
it also included one of many attempts to tackle France's chronic problem of
imprisonment on remand.) The recurrence of the word *'sécurité'* to legitimize
penal repressiveness is symptomatic: it is commonly said that law and order ideology in France is fuelled by a feeling of *insecurity* in the modern French psyche,
an insecurity which owes something to fear of crime but rather less to real
increases in real crime (see, for example, Gallo, 1995: 75) – all of which fits in well
with the analysis presented in Chapter 2.

Following the electoral victory of the Socialist President François Mitterand in
the summer of 1981, the death penalty was abolished, the *Sécurité et Liberté* Act
was partially repealed and an Act of 1983 introduced more alternatives to custody. The prison population was reduced by a quarter within three months
(Gallo, 1995: 76). A potentially important managerialist initiative (resembling in

some respects the 'systems management' approach applied in youth justice in England from the 1980s onwards: see Cavadino and Dignan, 2002: Chapter 9) was the establishment of a National Commission for the Prevention of Delinquency (CNPD) in 1983, a body with national and local arms which sought to use multi-agency cooperation at local level to prevent crime and promote rehabilitation in the community. But this, along with the generally reductionist approach of the Socialist government, was scrapped when the pendulum swung back with the election of a right-wing parliamentary majority in 1986 (led by Jacques Chirac) to 'cohabit' with Mitterand. The new government further restricted early release, ceased to question the continued growth of the prison population, sought to build new prisons to provide 15,000 places (with the aim of expanding total capacity to 70,000 places), and pursued a policy of prison privatization (see Chapter 16). 1988 saw Mitterand's re-election as President, a new Socialist parliamentary majority, and a scaling down of the prison building programme from 15,000 to 13,000 places. (This programme, which commenced in 1986, became known as the 'Programme 13,000'.) The prison population had in the meantime risen from 40,354 in 1985 to 52,494 in 1988 (see Table 9.1).

The efforts of Socialist governments after 1981 to control the prison population were largely ineffective, apart from Mitterand's two major amnesties in 1981 and 1988. Although France has not seen penal inflation of the kind experienced by the USA, England or the Netherlands in recent years, nevertheless the general picture has been of a 'constant and unchecked rise in the prison population' (Faugeron, 1991: 252), except for the temporary dips engineered by presidential amnesties. The introduction of community penalties as supposed alternatives to custody failed to have its intended effect because sentencing judges by and large did not use them as alternatives to custody. Nor were they required to do so by binding legislation. This was what we term a 'strategy of encouragement' (Cavadino and Dignan, 2002: Chapters 4 and 5), whereby government provides alternatives to custody and encourages sentencers to use them, but sentencing discretion remains with the judges. As in England, the strategy failed.

The policy of French Socialist governments has essentially been one of bifurcation,[4] with harsher sentences being reserved for more serious offenders and a policy of diverting lesser offenders from custody. In practice, and especially in an atmosphere thick with law and order rhetoric from politicians and media, judges failed to discern an appropriate distinction between the serious offenders who should get more severe sentences and the middling offenders for whom alternatives to custody were intended. There was a reduction in shorter sentences, but along with some diversion of lesser offenders from custody went a significant increase in the imposition of longer sentences (Gallo, 1995: 80–1). The result was that sentences in general – and the prison population – were dragged upwards (Alderson, 1989). The performance of the French judges in the 1980s contrasts with that of German judges at the same time (see Chapter 7).

The German judicial culture was much more anti-custodial, and it was essentially the practice of judges and prosecutors that significantly reduced the German prison population from 1983 to 1991 despite the lack of any major legislation to encourage this trend. In France, by contrast, the legislation was put in place but judicial practice kept the prison population rising.

More recently the Socialist party began responding to conservative criticisms with assertions that it too was and would be tough on crime. One practical manifestation of this was the announcement in 2000 that another half a dozen large prisons would be built. Then came the national elections of 2002, which threatened to prove a watershed in French penal politics. In the presidential elections, Jacques Chirac adopted the American slogan of 'zero tolerance' of crime, while Socialist candidate Lionel Jospin put forward very similar policies under the Blairite slogan 'tough on crime, tough on the causes of crime'. With all the major parties putting their faith in tough law and order rhetoric, (and with many voters and commentators professing that it was difficult to discern any difference between Chirac and Jospin on any major issue) the first round in April 2002 resulted in a stunning defeat for Jospin, who came third behind both Chirac and the far-right National Front candidate Jean-Marie Le Pen. (Le Pen is a more typical far-right European than the Netherlands' Pim Fortuyn, who rose to prominence and was murdered in this same year of 2002 – see Chapter 8.) Le Pen's first round success was largely attributable to his populist appeal to voters on law and order, on which he promised to be even tougher than his mainstream opponents, also deploying the slogan la tolérance zéro and advocating a referendum to restore the death penalty and an extra 200,000 prison places. One poll found that 74 per cent of Le Pen voters put crime at the top of their list of concerns (at least when talking to pollsters), above immigration at 60 per cent (Le Figaro, 23 April 2002). A frequent comment was (again) that French people felt 'insecure', a term used to conflate concerns about both crime and immigration.

Chirac's response was to appoint a new right-wing Prime Minister, Jean-Pierre Raffarin, together with a hardline and highly popular minister for the interior (Nicolas Sarkozy[5]) with a brief to lead a 'law and order drive'. Chirac and his supporters subsequently won both the second round of the presidential election and the ensuing parliamentary elections by massive majorities. Initially this 'law and order drive' concentrated on policing rather than punishment, with promises of increased pay and rubber bullets for the police and new rapid reaction squads to tackle organized crime. Clampdowns were also promised on truancy, prostitution, begging and loitering. In 2003 a programme to create an extra 13,200 prison places was announced. Since the natural effect of such a heightened 'law and order' atmosphere and rhetoric is always to make sentencing harsher, it is not surprising that the prison population is now reaching record levels: by 1 July 2004 there was a total of 64,813 inmates in French prisons.

As with our other mid-range corporatist countries, France does not suffer from a generalized penal crisis, but shows some definite signs of incipient crisis.

On the positive side, prison regimes have been ameliorated in various respects in recent decades, and specifically since the liberal reforms of 1975. Prisoners' access to news and entertainment media has increased greatly, and the prisons have been opened up to the outside world in a variety of ways. However, prisoners' rights in respect of complaints and disciplinary procedures are relatively undeveloped (Combessie, 2001: 262–8). Prison security is not a major problem, however, although since the early 1980s there has been a number of spectacular escapes involving the use of helicopters to lift prisoners out of high-security prisons. Nor have prison riots featured strongly since major upheavals in the 1970s and especially in 1974 – what has been called the 'May '68' of French prisons, which precipitated the liberal reforms of 1975. There has been the occasional localized upheaval, however, such as at the *maison d'arrêt* in Dijon in 1996.

Understaffing is not generally severe in French prisons by international standards, with a ratio of one staff member to three prisoners. Moreover, new prison officers are younger and better educated than in the past, with longer periods of training required (Combessie, 2001: 262–8). This does not, however, seem to have improved staff morale or industrial relations in prisons. Prison officers complain that they are (despite what we just said) understaffed, starved of resources and threatened by a growing number of psychologically disturbed inmates. The number of resignations of staff members has increased, and 1998 saw a nationwide week of protests by the prison workers' union, who were calling on the government to allocate funds to employ more prison officers.

A particularly notorious and chronic feature of the French penal system is its high numbers of remand prisoners. On 1 January 1999, remand prisoners constituted 39 per cent of the total prison population, whereas in Western Europe generally proportions of 20 to 30 per cent are more common. Faugeron (1991: 252) points out that defendants jumping bail is a significant problem in France, with a large number of verdicts and prison sentences being passed on defendants who cannot be found because they are no longer at the same address, or gave a false address in the first place which was never checked. It seems likely that this problem exists because of inefficient French bureaucracy, and in particular the length of time it takes cases to come to trial in France's inquisitorial criminal justice system. These chronic delays mean that defendants can stay on remand for long periods of time, reducing the throughput of the remand population and in consequence inflating its size at any one time. A salient characteristic of French criminal procedure is the *juge d'instruction* (or 'examining magistrate'), who only actually figures in around 10 per cent of criminal investigations but is prominent in the most serious cases. The *juge d'instruction* combines the roles of investigator, prosecutor and judge, supervising the police investigation of a crime. Until 2001, the *juge d'instruction* could also authorize the pre-trial detention (*détention provisoire*) of a suspect for long periods. The criteria for detention were both wide and vague, including 'to preserve public order from the disturbance caused by the offence'.[6]

There has been no shortage of legislative initiatives which have repeatedly tinkered with the law and procedure of remand detention – in fact *'il pleut des lois'* on the topic (Robert, 1992: 287). But none have so far succeeded in bringing about a sustained and significant reduction in the remand population. Even conservative governments have endeavoured to address the remand problem; for example, the *Sécurité et Liberté* Act of 1981 contained provisions which it was (vainly) hoped would reduce the reliance on remand detention. Short-lived laws passed by Socialist governments in the 1980s envisaged the creation of a three-judge court to authorize pre-trial detention instead of the *juge d'instruction*, but these were abandoned in the face of strong resistance from magistrates (Combessie, 2001: 279). Further reforms were introduced in 1984 and 1989 by Socialist governments, limiting the remand period for lesser periods and requiring the *juge d'instruction* to hold an adversarial hearing before authorizing *détention provisoire*. The remand population did decline slightly in the late 1990s, down to 19,212 on 1 January 1999 from a peak figure of 22,159 in January 1995[7] (Combessie, 2001: 281), but this was still high in relative terms.

The most radical package of legislative reform was passed in 2000 and implemented in 2001. Perhaps the most significant change was the one which arguably attacked the root of the problem, to wit the entire system of long-term detention at the behest of the officials in charge of investigation, who could thereby legitimize their own dilatoriness at the expense of suspects' liberty. This reform finally removed the power of the *juge d'instruction* to order pre-trial detention, transferring it to a new judge called *le juge des libertés et de la détention*. The new laws also stated that pre-trial detention should be regarded as the exception, and placed time limits on remands in custody, with an absolute maximum of four years in the most serious cases. These reforms were expected to reduce the remand population further: doubtless time will tell, but in July 2004 the number of remand prisoners was 22,110 – 34 per cent of the total prison population.

Another important factor in France's imprisonment rate is the large number of foreign nationals in prison. This is against a general background of racial disharmony (belied by the much-celebrated multi-racial character of the French football team which won the World Cup in 1998 and the European Championship in 2000). Stricter immigration laws were introduced in 1993, and – like many Western countries – France has been singularly unwelcoming to the waves of refugees and would-be migrants who have tried to move westwards and northwards in recent years. The National Front party was already one of the strongest ultra-right parties in Western Europe when immigration and race became salient issues in the 1990s, and in 2002 the party's leader Jean-Marie Le Pen achieved second place in the first round of the presidential elections, with opinion polls showing strong public support for Le Pen's hardline policies on both immigration and law and order. It is in this context that we must see the fact that on 1 July 2004, 21 per cent of prisoners in Metropolitan France were foreign nationals

(Ministère de la Justice, 2004: 28). (The figure had been 14 per cent in 1969, but was as high as 31 per cent in 1993–4 – Combessie, 2001: 277.) This compares with around 6 per cent of foreign nationals in the general population resident in France. A significant minority of these foreign prisoners are *sans-papiers* – in prison because of violations of regulations relating to work permits and permission to stay in France (Gallo, 1995: 82). Due to a general French policy forbidding the keeping of ethnic data, there are no statistics about the *racial* make-up of the prison population, but it is inevitably a safe guess that non-whites are also substantially over-represented.

Above and beyond anything else, the French prison population is on a long-term upward trend, likely to be exacerbated by the current political mood for tough law and order policies and rhetoric. On 1 July 2003 French prisons held a then-record 60,963 inmates in a prison system with an official capacity of 48,600 – overcrowding by a factor of 25 per cent (1.25 prisoners per place), since when the prison population has increased still further. Overcrowding is particularly concentrated in the *maisons d'arrêt*, which house remand and short-term sentenced prisoners and have been known to be overcrowded by 50 per cent, as opposed to the *maisons centrales* and *centres de détention* which cater for longer-term prisoners and may have unfilled spaces. Government plans in 2002 projected the construction of thirty new prisons with 13,200 more places by 2007.

Such overcrowding inevitably affects conditions and regimes adversely, which in turn has generated a growing crisis of general legitimacy. In recent years there have been some particularly outspoken criticisms of the prison system. In 2000, Véronique Vasseur, the chief doctor at La Santé prison in Paris, published a best-selling book condemning conditions at La Santé (Vasseur, 2000), and two parliamentary reports in July 2000 condemned what one called 'the humiliation of the Republic'. Much publicity has also been given to suicides by prisoners (of which there were 124 in total in 1999), and opinion polls have found nearly half of the French population believing that the country's prison system is rotten (*The Guardian*, 21 January and 26 August 2000). One factor in the legitimation crisis of French penality is the damage that has been caused to the general legitimacy of French political and legal institutions by a variety of scandals in recent years, including the involvement of high-ranking politicians in policies concerning the contamination of donor blood with HIV and a number of corruption scandals which have increased public cynicism about the likelihood of well-connected miscreants facing justice.

But perhaps also relevant to this burgeoning crisis of legitimacy is the fact that – despite their feelings of 'insecurity' and willingness to voice support for tough law and order policies in general terms – ordinary French people do not seem to have a particularly punitive mindset. There is an interesting anomaly apparent in France's showing in international league tables concerning public attitudes to punishment and imprisonment in particular, as measured by opinion surveys. As we saw in Chapter 1 (see especially Table 1.3), it is sometimes possible to detect a rough correspondence between the extent to which a country's public favours the use of imprisonment and its actual imprisonment rate, although this association is by no means as strong as one might expect. France is one country that does not fit. As Table 1.3 shows, the 'punitiveness score' of the French public is lower than that of any other country in our sample except Finland.[8] On this basis, France should be almost at the very bottom of our imprisonment league table instead of midway. Even at the height of National Front popularity in mid-2002, a poll found that only 36 per cent of French people wanted the death penalty reintroduced (*The Guardian*, 29 May 2002), whereas similar polls in Britain usually find strong majorities in favour. It may be that French politicians, in following the international bandwagon of populist punitiveness, have misjudged their own people.

Italy

Italy is one of a 'southern cluster' of European Union nations identified by Hanns von Hofer (2001), along with Greece, Spain and Portugal.[9] These have all had much lower levels of state welfare provision than the European countries to their north, whether conservative corporatist, social democratic, or (in the case of Britain) neo-liberal but with some social democratic trace elements. Southern Europe is generally poorer than are the countries further north; but Italy has become more prosperous since World War Two and as we saw previously she has recently been spending a higher proportion of her increased GDP on welfare.

The Christian Democratic rule of Italy from World War Two until the demise of the Christian Democratic Party in 1994 can be contrasted with the Netherlands. Dutch society was said to rest on the 'pillars' of the different (but all relatively liberal) Christian churches, whereas Italy had the single and more authoritarian pillar of the Catholic Church and its Christian Democratic political arm, opposed by its weaker rival in the shape of the Communist Party which had its own ethos of communitarian loyalty. The Communists never achieved the share in government which they had long coveted, despite coming agonizingly close in the 1970s and evolving more and more into a social democratic party. Reformed and renamed as the Left Democrats (PDS) the ex-Communist Party became the largest party in Romano Prodi's 'Olive Tree' coalition government in 1996 (led from 1998 to 2000 by the PDS's Massimo D'Alema and from 2000 to 2001 by the Socialist Giuliano Amato), only to lose power in 2001 to a right-wing coalition under Silvio Berlusconi. Berlusconi (who had previously been Prime Minister for seven months in 1994 before his coalition fell as a result of corruption charges against Berlusconi personally) represents a new, much less corporatist and more neo-liberal ideology than the Christian Democracy that

Italy is used to, fittingly for someone in the 'capitalist robber baron' mould. The Berlusconi government plans to reduce pensions spending and reduce the legal rights of trade unionists, proposals which have sparked off strikes and demonstrations similar to those seen in France.

In Italy as in other conservative corporatist countries, the notion of reform of the offender has endured as the officially dominant penal philosophy despite its rejection and downgrading in both neo-liberal and social democratic countries, and despite losing popularity among Italian criminologists from the mid-1970s onwards (Pavarini, 1994: 56). (Indeed, as we shall see, at this very time reforms were being introduced based on the notion of rehabilitation.) Retributivism plays little part in the official penal ideology and was not revived from the 1970s onwards in the way that it was in many other countries, including the USA, England and the Nordic countries. Indeed, under Article 27(3) of the Italian Constitution adopted in 1948, 'Punishments may not consist of measures contrary to a sense of humanity and shall aim at re-educating the convicted'. (Article 27(4) outlaws the death penalty in peacetime, and indeed Italy as a nation is one of the world's staunchest opponents of capital punishment, a stance strongly encouraged by the Catholic Church and endorsed by Italian public opinion.) The emphasis on reform is understandable, since this is a philosophy congruent with both Christian Democratic and Communist communitarianism. Nevertheless, although reform is enshrined as something which all punishments must aim at, is also permitted the pursuit of other aims, and the Constitutional Court has repeatedly stated that punishment can be polyfunctional, with retributivism and individual and general deterrence recognized as legitimate purposes as well as reform. Indeed, it could be said that in general Italian penality does not in practice differ greatly from other countries, insofar as punishments are generally distributed on a proportionate 'just deserts' basis, despite the official ideology stressing rehabilitation.

This mixture of penal ideologies, not untypical of many countries, can be traced back through a history of successive influences. Italy prides herself on her long-standing humanitarian tradition in criminology, from the classical penal reformer Cesare Beccaria in the eighteenth century and the later 'Italian school' of pioneering positivist criminologists including Lombroso, Ferri and Garofalo. Although all could be seen as humanitarian reformers in their own times (and all rejected retribution as a penal aim), their penal philosophies were sharply divergent. Beccaria proclaimed that the criminal law should be clear and definite, with fixed penalties proportionate to the seriousness of the offence and deterrence as the only permissible aim of punishment. His ideas – a development of the philosophies current in the eighteenth-century European Enlightenment – were to a great extent enshrined in the French Revolutionary and Napoleonic Penal Codes of 1791, 1795 and 1810 which strongly influenced subsequent Italian penal codes. The positivist school, on the other hand, rejected deterrence and proportionality as penal aims and favoured measures to reform and incapacitate offenders by way of indeterminate sentences. A penal code drafted by the positivist Enrico Ferri in 1921 was rejected as too radical, and a rather different code – the 'Rocco Code' – was introduced in 1930. This was again modified in 1948 but remained essentially intact.

The Beccarian (or 'just deserts') approach is embodied in section 71 onward of the penal code, which state the principle that the punishment should fit the crime. However, this is largely negated by other legal provisions. The reformative approach – and in particular the legacy of criminological positivism – can be seen in the existence of provisions for indeterminate sentences and flexible release. For example, 'safety measures' (*misure di sicurezza*), including custody, may be imposed on offenders who are deemed to be 'socially dangerous'; these 'safety measures' have no maximum length and cannot be revoked unless a judge decides that the individual is no longer dangerous. There are also 'double-track' provisions which allow indeterminate measures to be imposed on both adult and juvenile offenders *in addition to* determinate sanctions if they are deemed to be dangerous to society. The Rocco Code was adopted in 1930 under Mussolini's Fascist dictatorship, and the maximum penalties laid down were, as one would expect under such an authoritarian regime, very severe. In addition, almost every offence carries a statutory minimum sentence. Prison was the primary method of punishment under the code, which only envisaged two alternative penalties for felonies and misdemeanours (*delitti* and *contravenzioni*): conditional suspension and judicial pardon for offenders under the age of 18; while conditional release for prisoners who were deemed to be successfully resocialized was also possible (Giunta, 1991: 359). But actual sentencing practice has always been much more lenient than the code would suggest: 'To some extent, the very existence of a severe legislation lacking political legitimacy (since it was the offspring of fascism) has fostered the process of leniency in sentencing' (Pavarini, 1994: 50). This combination – of judicial 'softening' of legislation intended as harsh, along with elements of positivism in the law – meant that 'the model of penality that slowly established itself in Italy is one of flexibility' (Ruggiero, 1995: 56). This should not be exaggerated, for other countries such as England and the Netherlands have also been characterized by wide scope for judicial discretion in sentencing, together with flexibility for the executive and administration to determine actual release dates for many prisoners. Nevertheless, the gap between an apparently harsh 'law in the books' and the 'law in action' on sentencing was wide, with judges regularly applying 'only the minimum sentences provided by law ... coupled with the virtually automatic application of both suspended sentences and release on licence or remission', together with a generous use of general amnesties and pardons on the part of the national legislature (Pavarini, 2001: 414).

Commentators have suggested that in implementing this 'softening' of punishment in practice, the Italian judges (many of whom were politically progressive) and other authorities were embodying the sentiments of the public (one might say, in Durkheimian vein, expressing the Italian *'conscience collective'*) (Ruggiero, 1995: 51). According to Pavarini, in Italy 'the actual demand for punishment has long been weak at the social level ... The "law and order" campaigns repeatedly launched by conservative political forces and often feared by many, have always yielded meagre results'.[10] Pavarini attributes this to the fact that 'legitimization of the penal system has always been weak', with criminal justice being perceived by many as inherently political, and even 'as a violent means of preserving social inequality' (Pavarini, 2001: 414–15). At any rate, Italy had 'one of the lowest rates of incarceration in the western world in the mid-1970s' (Pavarini, 2001: 413).

Thereafter, however, the rate fluctuated, rising in the 1970s, dipping in the early 1980s, rising again to a level of 76.5 per 100,000 in 1985, dropping sharply to 54 in 1989, rising dramatically between 1991 and 1993 and then continuing to climb steeply to the level of 100 in 2002. (See Pavarini, 2001: 407, 411; and Table 9.1 above.) Ruggiero (1995, 1998) attributes these fluctuations to a succession of 'emergencies' (or 'moral panics') which demonized particular categories of criminals and gave rise to specific new legislative provisions aimed at these specific categories, but also had the effect of increasing punishment levels for offenders in general.[11]

As has happened elsewhere, moral panics and concern about crime has led to an injection of 'law and order ideology' into penality – when crime is perceived as a problem which is becoming dangerously out of hand, the response is to adopt 'tough' measures to combat it, with the popular emphasis shifting towards deterrence and retribution and away from rehabilitation.[12] This process has been increasingly assisted, as elsewhere, by tabloid journalism deploring the crime problem and promoting law and order ideology as its solution. The successive 'emergencies' concerned: armed robbers in the 1960s; political terrorists and terrorist suspects in the mid-1970s (who accounted for 4,000 of Italy's prisoners at the start of the 1980s); drug crime and the Mafia[13] in the 1980s and 1990s; and corrupt politicians – the massive *Tangentopoli* ('Bribesville') scandal – in the early 1990s. The latter three emergencies were linked, with drug trafficking and some prominent politicians being associated with the Mafia. The effects of the 'war' on organized crime have been especially felt following the murders in 1992 of Giovanni Falcone and Paolo Borsellino, two prosecutors who had led investigations into the Mafia. The 'war on drugs' has also had enduring effects, with around 30 per cent of Italian prisoners being drug addicts (Pavarini, 2001: 401).[14] In some cases, remarkably given the generally prevailing Italian penal ideology, emergency legislation specified certain types of offender (drug traffickers, recidivist drug users and extortionists) as not capable of rehabilitation (Ruggiero, 1998: 219–20). Even more remarkably, rules introduced in 1991 lay down that alleged members of criminal organizations cannot be given non-custodial alternatives to prison unless the *police* report that they are not dangerous and have severed their links with their organizations (Ruggiero, 1998: 219).

Ruggiero (1995: 67) goes so far as to suggest that these intermittent emergencies are 'vital for the very existence of prisons in Italy', because the legitimacy of the prison comes under severe question except when the demonization of these categories of offender serve to legitimize prison as a response to their crimes. We suspect that the prison – in Italy and elsewhere – is a rather more robust institution than this, but what is true is that the surges in punishment kicked off by these 'emergencies' have repeatedly led to government concern about soaring prison populations and attempts to reduce them.

However, like other countries (including France and England at different times), Italy has found that it is one thing to introduce legislation intended to foster a reduction in the prison population and quite another thing for such a reduction to occur. The first legislative attempt was the Prison Act (Act 354 of 1975), introduced in response to overcrowding and unrest in the prisons. The law contained liberal measures to recognize the rights of prisoners, and also introduced three provisions aimed at reducing the time prisoners spent in prison: release on parole, semi-liberty (day release from prison) and early release as a positive sanction for participation in resocialization programmes. Subsequently, Act 689 of 1981 introduced three new penalties aimed at reducing short-term prison sentences: monetary fines, 'controlled liberty' (freedom with a variety of restrictions and conditions), and semi-liberty (imprisonment for at least ten hours per day). All of these could be imposed as substitutes for prison sentences not exceeding, respectively, thirty days, three months and six months (Giunta, 1991: 360). Further legislation in 1986 and 1988 introduced special leave for prisoners and significantly increased the scope for allowing semi-liberty and parole.[15] One overall effect of these changes was very largely to shift the power to determine how long a prisoner spent in incarceration from the sentencing judge to the prison administration, who made the decisions about early release (Ruggiero, 1998: 213–15). This is just as the positivistic 'treatment model' prescribes. For although positivism and the associated ideal of rehabilitation had in many other countries lost ground to the ideologies of 'just deserts' and 'law and order', it gained ground in Italy at this time, and with a wide measure of political support: Pavarini (2001: 418) notes the 'singular political consensus that prison reform has encountered' in Italy since 1975, based on a general acceptance of 'the idea of punishment as medicine'.

As for the intended effects on the prison population, the results were disappointing. The 1975 reforms had no noticeable impact on imprisonment rates, although there was subsequently a drop in the prison population (possibly due to a waning of the anti-terrorist 'emergency'). From 1986 until 1991 there was a significant drop in imprisonment rates, but one which only stored up trouble for the future. After 1985 the number of *short* prison sentences dropped sharply, but at the same time there was a significant increase in *longer* prison sentences. Some of the decline in short sentences was presumably due to judges using the new provisions to pass non-custodial sentences instead, but in other cases they will have passed *longer* sentences. It is possible that this shift to longer sentences represented a reaction by sentencers to the new measures which allowed greater scope for early release at the discretion of others, leading the judges to increase sentences to compensate (Pavarini, 2001: 406–9). Such a shift would have the natural tendency of reducing the prison population in the short run, as fewer short-term inmates enter the prison system, but increasing it in the longer run because of the greater number of prisoners who remain incarcerated for longer. At any rate, imprisonment rates did indeed leap significantly in the early 1990s, and (following a slight dip between 1993 and 1997) have continued to increase thereafter (see Table 9.1).

Italy thus provides yet another example of penal *bifurcation*, with penalties for some offenders getting harsher (with the increase in longer sentences) but those for others becoming more lenient (with non-custodial measures replacing prison in some cases). Bifurcation has also occurred within the prison. There has been a general trend, exemplified by the 1975 Prison Act, to give greater recognition to the rights of prisoners, and a general 'opening' of the prison in terms of prisoners' opportunities for contact with the outside world (Giunta, 1991). But at the same time, certain prisoners who are regarded as being particularly dangerous have been subject to specially restrictive measures. Thus, Act 663 of 1986 introduced special leave for prisoners and extended judicial responsibility for overseeing measures relating to the personal liberty of prisoners while simultaneously instituting 'special surveillance' for prisoners deemed to be dangerous. It should be noted, however, that the latter was intended as a liberalizing measure. Previously, section 90 of the 1975 Prison Act had authorized the Minister of Defence to suspend the normal rules about the treatment and resocialization of prisoners in specified prisons where necessary for purposes of order and security. Although intended only to allow such suspension for limited periods where absolutely necessary, its implementation in practice led to the creation of permanent maximum security prisons despite the fact that only a small number of prisoners in these institutions were actually thought to be dangerous.

The 1986 legislation provided instead for individualized security whereby only the prisoners defined as dangerous lost normal privileges, leading to the creation of high-security *sections* within prisons in which a smaller number of inmates are kept out of contact with the rest of the prison population (Giunta 1991: 370–1). Legislation in 1992, following the murders of the prosecutors Falcone and Borsellino, further restricted the rights of Mafia prisoners to contact with other prisoners and the outside world. Proposals to extend the laws until 2006 led to prisoners refusing prison food and other protests in 2002 (*The Guardian*, 11 July 2002).

Two further factors should be mentioned as contributing to the problems of Italian penality. One is the 'principle of legality', or of mandatory penal action. As in Germany – but to a greater degree in theory, and perhaps also with a greater impact in practice – this precept requires, at least in principle, that wherever there is evidence of an alleged offence, the criminal justice agencies must respond, and there is no legal provision for either the police or prosecution to divert detected offenders from prosecution by administering a caution or the equivalent. Although, as elsewhere, there are ways around this in practice (thus creating another gap between the 'law in the books' and the 'law in action'), it is believed to have real effects in Italy.[16] It leads to an overloading of the criminal justice system, and possibly to a ratcheting up of sanctions generally so that imprisonment levels are higher than they would otherwise be.

Another, chronic problem is that of pre-trial detention. Although perhaps less notorious than the similar problem in France, it is actually worse in Italy, with around half the prison population consisting of remand prisoners. Again, the institutions and practices of a Latinate inquisitorial tradition of criminal justice are implicated. Like France, Italy had an examining magistrate (*giudice istruttore*) who was responsible for the investigation of serious crimes and also had the power to authorize pre-trial detention. As in France, this system led to many defendants being imprisoned for long periods awaiting trial; recognition in practice of the right to a speedy trial not being one of the most distinctive features of criminal justice in either country. A new Code of Criminal Procedure adopted in 1988 represented a significant notional shift towards a more adversarial system, abolishing the *giudice istruttore*. Now investigation and the charging of offenders are the responsibility of the public prosecutor, who has to apply to a judge to authorize detention on remand (a system not dissimilar to that adopted in France from 2001). Nevertheless, numbers held on remand remain high.

The law lays down the maximum length for remand (varying according to the severity of the offence), but under 'emergency' legislation these can be extended for defendants accused of involvement in organized crime. Ruggiero (1998: 212, 223) suggests that remand imprisonment in Italy is in effect a system for 'punishing defendants in advance', thereby bypassing both the rule of law and the official ideology of reform as the aim of imprisonment. Various legislative attempts have been made to ameliorate the situation. One such was a law passed in 1995 allowing remand prisoners charged with offences carrying sentences of less than four years to be released after one month in custody – which led to the release of all the politicians currently charged with corruption offences, provoking spectacular protests (Ruggiero, 1998: 223).

Like France, and like the other conservative corporatist countries in our sample, Italy shows definite signs of incipient penal crisis at present. Certainly the prison population is climbing steeply, prompting the government in 2003 to announce plans to build twenty-two new prisons. International experience suggests that by the time such places are provided in such an expansionist climate there will be plenty more prisoners to fill them; in any event in the meantime there are inevitable consequences for overcrowding and prison conditions. In 2003 prisons were operating at 36 per cent over capacity. Conditions are particularly bad in southern Italy: for example, in Catania prison in Sicily in 1998 each cell was holding four to eight prisoners, despite the official rule that inmates should be accommodated in single cells. Nevertheless, riots and escapes are not particularly salient problems at present. Disturbances were rife in the 1970s, and exacerbated by arrival of politicized prisoners in the mid-1970s (Ruggiero, 1995: 64). Since then, disturbances have not been a particular feature of Italian prisons, although protests about deteriorating conditions and alleged ill-treatment have recently been becoming more frequent. Escapes happen now and again, as for example when a Mafioso murderer managed to saw through the bars of his high-security prison using dental floss (*The Guardian*, 10 April 2000). But one of the most serious problems, linked to the main issue of the numbers of inmates, is said to be the understaffing of prisons.

The racial dimension to penality which is to be found in many countries – certainly in the USA, England, South Africa, Australia, New Zealand and France in our sample – is also present in Italy, despite the fact that Italy's population is almost all white and home-born. More than 25 per cent of prisoners are foreigners, although immigrants account for only around 2 per cent of the general population (Pavarini, 2001: 401; see also Ruggiero, 1998: 221–2). The context is one Italy shares with many other Western countries: issues of immigration and the treatment of asylum-seekers have come to the fore in recent years, with the south of Italy being an important entry point for would-be migrants and the Berlusconi government in particular assuming hardline policies against them.

The Italian version of the crisis of legitimacy is probably exacerbated by the penal system's traditional lack of legitimacy, discussed earlier. Nor is this helped by the peculiar intertwining of crime, corruption, politics and the Mafia in Italy in recent years: cynicism about criminal justice is fuelled by the feeling that the system – with its agonising slowness, inefficiencies, bias and indeed corruption – will always ensure that the most serious criminals (and in particular senior Mafiosi and politicians) will never receive justice. In this connection, the position of Prime Minister Silvio Berlusconi himself is remarkable. Accused of bribing a judge during a corporate takeover battle in the 1980s, he was put on trial in 2003, but the trial was halted by legislation hastily passed by his own parliamentary majority granting high-ranking officials immunity from prosecution while in office. Berlusconi has been fighting a long-running battle against the Italian judiciary (which includes prosecutors), accusing them of persecuting him out of political motives. In December 2004 he was dramatically acquitted (on technical grounds) of the bribery charge. Meanwhile, a Mafia informer has alleged that Berlusconi's *Forza Italia* party agreed in the early 1990s to alleviate the position of Mafia defendants and prisoners in return for support.

Public cynicism is perhaps understandable in such circumstances. Italian people are exceptionally aware of the likelihood of inequities in criminal justice, but also feel frustrated and helpless that many criminals are not being punished. This could be fertile ground for law and order ideology and for further upward spirals in punishment. But whether politicians like Silvio Berlusconi could successfully exploit such a mood without being perceived as even more hypocritical than they presently are, remains to be seen. Italian cynicism and general lack of belief in the system could, paradoxically, prove to be something of a restraining factor in the headlong rush to law and order.

Notes

1 As a result, Pampel et al. (1990: 541) give both France and Italy low scores (below Australia and New Zealand but above the UK and USA) on the dimension of 'corporatism' on their definition.

2 Italy's public social expenditure was 26.9 per cent of GDP in 1997, compared with 33.3 per cent in Sweden, 29.6 per cent in France, 29.3 per cent in Finland, 26.6 per cent in Germany, 22.9 per cent in New Zealand (1992 figure), 21.6 per cent in the UK, 18.1 per cent in Australia, 16 per cent in the USA and 14.4 per cent in Japan. By contrast, the figures for Greece, Spain and Portugal in 1993 were 16.8 per cent, 22.4 per cent and 17.5 per cent, when Italy's was 25.0 per cent (source: OECD Social Expenditure Database.) Italy now has very high expenditure on pensions compared with other countries, but still ranks low on some other social services such as health and family services.

3 This is despite the survival until the early 1990s of the Napoleonic Penal Code of 1810, largely based on the approach of Cesare Beccaria (discussed in the ensuing section on Italy), which was to prescribe punishment in proportion to the seriousness of the offence. There had been many subsequent legal reforms aimed at individualizing punishments and suiting them to individual offenders. A new Penal Code was presented in 1992, coming into force in 1994.

4 This bifurcatory theme is strongly present in the new Penal Code adopted under a Socialist government in 1992 (coming into force in 1994), which made provision both for non-custodial penalties and for reinforced severity of punishment for those who commit more serious crimes.

5 M. Sarkozy, seen as a potent rival to President Chirac, was moved to the post of finance minister in 2004, but back to the interior ministry in 2005.

6 *Code de Procédure Pénale*, Art. 144.

7 Proportionately this represents a drop from 43 per cent of the total prison population in 1995 to 39 per cent in 1999. The highest ever proportion of remand prisoners in French prisons (52 per cent) occurred in 1984. (These figures relate to 1 January in each year, and include only Metropolitan France, i.e. excluding the overseas departments.)

8 The 'punitiveness score' is explained in Chapter 1. The French anomaly is even more dramatic when a slightly different measure of punitiveness is used (see Chapter 1, Note 33). In 2000, only 12 per cent of French respondents thought that imprisonment was the most appropriate sentence for a recidivist burglar aged 21 – a lower figure than in Finland and Italy, much lower than in Sweden, the Netherlands and England and higher only than those found in Austria and Catalonia in a survey of fifty-eight countries (Mayhew and van Kesteren, 2002).

9 For reasons we do not pretend to fully understand, this 'southern cluster' of European nations exhibits wide differences in punishment levels. Greece has an imprisonment rate

below the European norm, although higher than that found in the Nordic countries (80 in 2003), while Spain and Portugal have relatively high prison populations, not far behind England (138 and 137 in 2003). Italy's rate of 100 in 2003 is intermediate between these other countries.

10 It may be relevant here that the International Crime Victimization Survey (see Chapter 1, especially Table 1.3) shows an average level of punitiveness among the Italian public for the countries in our sample.

11 Such an effect is far from unknown in other countries. In England, for example, a moral panic about young offenders exacerbated by the murder of 2-year-old James Bulger by two 10-year-old boys in 1993 (mentioned in Chapters 4 and 12) seems to have contributed to an increase in sentencing levels across the board, including the sentences for adult and petty property offenders (see Home Office, 2000: 151, Figure 7.4.)

12 Historical comparisons show that this punitive reaction to perceived increases in crime is not always inevitable. In the late nineteenth century in England and in the 1960s in many countries the response was often to seek better ways of reforming offenders. But these were times when public policy-making was dominated by a middle class elite which had a strong faith in science as likely to provide solutions to society's problems. More recently a more populistic politics has coincided with a decline in faith in science and in deference to experts, and a powerful reversion to the 'common sense' view that harsh punishment is likely to be the most effective method of reducing crime.

13 Simply being involved in a 'Mafia-type' organization (*associazione per delinquere di tipo mafioso*) makes the offender liable to imprisonment for up to fifteen years.

14 Pavarini (1994: 57) notes that in the two-year period 1991–2, which saw a massive increase in the Italian prison population, the proportion of drug abusers within that population rose from under 20 to over 60 per cent.

15 Other non-custodial and semi-custodial measures can also be substituted for imprisonment by the Tribunal of Surveillance, made up of two judges and two experts, after conviction. The tribunal can impose probation, house arrest or semi-liberty as alternatives to imprisonment.

16 Nelken (2002) argues that it has provided 'a marvellous shield' for prosecutors bringing charges against powerful politicians and business defendants in corruption cases, notably during the 'clean hands' prosecutions of 1992 which destroyed the Christian Democratic Party.

10

Sweden and Finland: Nordic Social Democracy[1]

Sweden and Finland are two of the 'Nordic countries'[2] (along with Norway, Denmark and Iceland). These countries – all advanced, prosperous, industrialized welfare states – have much in common with each other. Not only are they close to each other geographically, historically, ethnically and culturally,[3] they also cooperate in legal and non-legal fields in many ways and via a variety of bodies (including governments, parliaments and non-governmental organizations). For example, in 1996 the Nordic countries combined to produce a joint strategy on warring motorcycle gangs. Quite apart from such formal efforts at cooperation and harmonization, the Nordic countries are often more influenced by each other than by other countries when they frame their policies and laws.

The Nordic countries in general, and Sweden in particular, constitute the archetypal example of social democratic corporatism. Their welfare states are comprehensive and egalitarian, with generous universal benefits (lower on average in Finland). Although they have all had periods of government by 'centre-right' coalitions, these countries have retained social democratic welfare states despite (for example) cuts in welfare provision such as those implemented in Sweden in the 1990s. There has been some degree of movement in a 'neo-liberal' direction in recent years, but it has been small compared with many other countries, and of course the starting-point was much more social democratic than in other countries. Such things are hard to measure, but it could be that, if anything, the gap in this respect between the Nordic countries and others has widened over the last two decades rather than narrowed. The cultures of these (historically Protestant) nations are secular, classless, egalitarian and liberal. In penal terms they are all – comfortably in line with our general thesis about the relationship between political economy and punitiveness – comparatively lenient, with relatively low levels of imprisonment per head of population.[4] Indeed, at times in recent decades both Sweden and Finland have bucked the international trend and reduced their prison populations. In Sweden there was a reduction (which, however, appears to have been only temporary) between

Table 10.1 *Swedish and Finnish prison populations and imprisonment rates per 100,000 general population*

Year	Sweden: prison population	Sweden: imprisonment rate	Finland: prison population	Finland: imprisonment rate
1988	4,716	56	3,598	73
1989	4,796	57	3,103	62
1990	5,046	60	3,537	71
1991	4,731	55	3,130	63
1995	5,767	65	3,018	60
1997	5,221	59	2,798	55
1998	5,290	60	2,585	51
1999	5,484	62	2,389	46
2000	5,678	64	2,703	52
2001	6,089	68	3,040	59
2002	6,506	73	3,617	70

Sources: Council of Europe; Walmsley (1999, 2000, 2002, 2003a, 2003b); Home Office (2001: Table 1.21). Figures are for 1 September wherever possible.

1995 and 1998. Finland saw a dramatic and sustained reduction in imprisonment commencing in 1976 and continuing until 1999, although it commenced at a time when (anomalously) Finnish prison numbers were high by contemporary European standards. (Table 10.1 tells part of the story from 1987 onwards.)

The communitarianism of these social democratic societies is rather different from that of 'conservative corporatist', Christian Democratic countries such as Germany. In the latter, the rights and responsibilities of citizens and the state have a more traditionalistic and collectivist basis. Citizens of different social rank have their own (unequal) allocated places and are looked after (unequally but conscientiously) by the community and its institutions. In a not entirely metaphorical sense, one's place in society is 'God given'. The society comes first, but it cares for all its members. They, conversely, must behave according to the traditional morality of the society. Social democracy, being secular and egalitarian, has a different ethos. It is (although this may sound strange to some ears) more *individualistic* – society is extremely important, but at the end of the day it is there to serve the needs of all its individual members, not the other way round. The spirit is that of a (particularly egalitarian) version of John Rawls's (1972) social contract theory, whereby the social contract is reached by the imagined consensus of rationally self-interested individuals negotiating behind a 'veil of ignorance', not knowing what their individual characteristics or place in society will be. Such a procedure is not likely to produce a state with a religious tinge or one where individual freedom is infringed for reasons of cultural tradition, but will produce a high level of material security for all.[5] All citizens will have important responsibilities to support the just state, which in turn supports all its citizens on an equal basis. Within that framework of social support and social responsibility, the individual is then free to pursue his or her own individual goals and own conception of the good life, which is not prescribed by society, religion or traditional culture.[6]

One possible effect of this has been that the Nordic countries have been more open than the conservative corporatist ones to the ideas represented by the 'justice model of corrections', which seeks to ensure that offenders are punished in proportion to the 'just deserts' they are due from having committed the offence (see Cavadino and Dignan, 2002: Chapter 2). Justice model theory owed much to the philosophy of the 'social contract': it bore a strong resemblance to the eighteenth century 'Classical School' of Cesare Beccaria (1963), whose theories were based on Enlightenment social contract theory, and some of its most prominent proponents (von Hirsch, 1976) appealed to the contractarian retributivist theory of the American writer Jeffrie Murphy (1979). In its original and more liberal versions (which emanated from leftish American criminologists in the late 1960s and 1970s) this was in no way an attempt to make punishments harsher; quite the reverse. The previously prevailing 'treatment model', with its indeterminate sentences and the wide discretionary power over offenders, which it handed to officials, was seen as oppressive and as potentially leading to grossly excessive punishment. The principle of proportionality was seen as a necessary safeguard for the individual offender against disproportionately severe sanctions. The individualism of this critique meant that it made relatively little headway in conservative corporatist polities, who tended to retain a strong belief in the more collectivistic notion of the 'resocialization'[7] of offenders. The more liberal social democracies were more likely to accept that individual offenders had a right not to be incarcerated indefinitely until society deemed them to have reached an acceptable level of socialization.[8]

Another feature of these countries has been the nature of their power structures, as explained by Finnish criminologist Patrik Törnudd (1993: 4–5): 'In some countries the direction of reforms is largely dominated by the public debate, by the relative strength of the different political parties and their reform agendas and also by the personal convictions and preferences of the Minister in charge of crime control issues. Other countries have a more bureaucratic power structure, where the convictions of the senior civil servants and the experts consulted by these civil servants decide the shape and direction of the reforms. If countries are ranked according to this dimension – which depending on your point of view may be called the dimension of eliticism or the dimension of populism – the Nordic countries can generally be characterized as fairly expert-orientated and Finland has been said to be the most expert-orientated among the Scandinavian countries.' Although, as we shall see, this picture is not static and both Sweden and Finland have seen a move towards populism in recent years, this general ranking remains in force.

Thus, in terms of the concepts expounded by Joachim Savelsberg (1999), the Nordic countries have a *bureaucratic* political structure, as opposed to a 'personalized' one with a higher reliance on individual political and legal decision-makers. (Although certain public servants and experts can make an important personal difference, as we shall see shortly.) They are also, in terms of Savelsberg's other dimension, relatively *centralized* in their power structures – not unlike the Netherlands (see Chapter 8), and perhaps more so – although this may be mitigated to some extent by the fact that they are invariably governed by multi-party coalitions. This centralization is abetted by the fact that all the Nordic countries have small populations – 8.9 million in Sweden, 5.4 million in Denmark, 5.2 million in Finland and 4.5 million in Norway (and 290,000 in Iceland). All of this contributes to maximizing the influence in these countries of a relatively small group of criminal justice experts who are a significant part of the 'penal elite' of these countries – what Nils Christie calls the 'joint moral community' of people who are responsible for shaping a society's criminal policy (Christie 1993, discussed by Rutherford, 1996: 129f.).[9] Indeed, identifiable individuals have played major roles in both Sweden and Finland. Nils Jareborg (a close associate of the American 'justice model' theorist Andrew von Hirsch) played an important part in Sweden's adoption of the 'just deserts' principle; in Finland Inkeri Anttila (a lawyer and criminologist who was Minister of Justice in 1975 and was also prominent in the reform of Finland's criminal law and crime control system) and Patrik Törnudd are among those who deserve special mention.

Savelsberg (1999) says that a country whose political structures are highly centralized and highly bureaucratic can exhibit great instability in their penalities. His examples are the 'state socialist' regimes of Poland and East Germany prior to the fall of communism, where punishment levels saw dramatic fluctuations in levels of punishment over both short and long terms in response to central party *diktats*. But his thesis (as Savelsberg recognizes, and as we also investigate in Chapters 8 and 11) needs some development and qualification. It is likely that such tendencies to penal instability are mitigated in a bureaucratized and centralized *democracy*, for power is never quite as centralized in a democracy as it can be in a country where all power flows (in effect) from the Central Committee of the Communist Party. An independent judiciary doubtless makes a big difference, especially one whose judges exercise a great deal of discretionary power over the choice and length of penal sentences. Moreover, such dramatic changes are only likely if the penal elite of the country keeps changing its mind about punishment. If the penal elite – as for so long in Sweden – retains its faith in a lenient mode of punishment, we are likely to see stable and low levels of punishment. As indeed has been the case in Sweden, although as we shall see there have been some changes in methods of punishment and in determining the amount of punishment an individual should receive, and recent sharp increases in levels of punishment. (We shall also see a similar stability in punishment levels when we come to consider the case of Japan in Chapter 11, where political power is monopolized by a small elite.) In contrast, if the penal elite becomes convinced that it has been punishing too much up until now, a fairly rapid fall in levels of punishment is possible (although not of the magnitude of change seen in some communist countries at times). And this happened in Finland in the years following 1976, whereas something like the reverse has occurred in recent years in the Netherlands (see Chapter 8), and seems now to be occurring in Sweden.

Sweden: the archetypal social democracy[10]

Sweden is a peaceful place. Not only was she proudly neutral throughout the twentieth century, she has not been involved in any war since 1814. This has helped the Swedes to create the archetypal social democratic welfare state. Extremely generous, egalitarian and expensive (and financed by high taxation levels), it is also highly bureaucratic and marked by strong incorporation of trade unions into its structure. For example, unemployment insurance is funded by the government but administered by the trade unions. The Social Democratic Party, the architect of Sweden's welfare state, has been the dominant force in Swedish politics since 1932. It has been in power as the leader of coalition governments since that date, with the exception of periods of (relatively) right-wing rule by the so-called 'Bourgeois' parties from 1976 to 1982 and (more significantly for our purposes) from 1991 to 1994. It was during the latter period of Bourgeois rule that there was serious questioning of the nature of the Swedish welfare state, at a time when economic recession and record unemployment constituted the most daunting challenge to date to the 'Swedish model' of political economy. The Swedish model (which has relatively little provision for those outside the labour market and is funded by contributions from those within it) is very dependent on full employment, including high levels of female participation in employed work. For a long time unemployment in Sweden was kept low by European standards by proactive government employment policies.[11] But in the 1990s the jobless rate rose to 8 per cent, raising questions about the general viability of the Swedish model. The Bourgeois government engineered some serious cutbacks in welfare provision (and presided over a severe economic recession) but did not funda-mentally alter the nature of the welfare state. In 1994 the Social Democrats returned to power and have remained there ever since.

As one would expect if our general thesis is correct, this social democratic welfarism has been associated with low levels of punishment, although Sweden has never had the very lowest imprisonment rates in Europe. In the 1980s the Netherlands had a much lower rate (34 per 100,000 general population in 1986 compared with Sweden's 56), and as the Netherlands' rate increased and over-took Sweden's in the 1990s, Finland's rate reduced to below the Swedish level.

But just as Sweden was consistently a prime example of a social democratic state, so was she a consistently lenient one up to the end of the twentieth century. Finland and the Netherlands have oscillated in their punitiveness over the years; Sweden's leniency remained relatively stable until very recently. As Table 10.1 shows, imprisonment rates did briefly rise to some extent in the early 1990s (when the 'Bourgeois' government was introducing cutbacks in the welfare state) but then declined again to a low of 59 per 100,000 population in 1997. Since 1998, however, there has been a very sharp and accelerating rise: indeed, by the second quarter of 2004 the imprisonment rate had reached a record level of 80 per 100,000.[12] Sweden nevertheless remains well within the 'relatively lenient' zone by international standards, ranking below all the countries in our sample bar Japan and Finland for rates of imprisonment.

It is not so much that Sweden is particularly sparing in its use of custodial sentences, but more importantly that Swedish prison sentences tend to be short. In 1997, the number of people sentenced to immediate imprisonment in Sweden amounted to 161 per 100,000 of the population, whereas the equivalent rate in England and Wales was 178.[13] But a third of all sentences are of three months or less, and only a tenth exceed one year (von Hofer et al., 1997: 65). The short average sentence is, paradoxically, partly due to a particularly punitive attitude to one particular crime. Drinking and driving often attracts a sentence of imprisonment – although less often than it used to[14] – but sentences are usually very short (between one and two months [Leander, 1995: 175]). But prison sentences for most other offences are also short when measured against those prevalent in other European countries.[15] Moreover, conditions for those within prison are relatively far from harsh, with 22 per cent of prison places for sentenced inmates being within open prisons (von Hofer and Marvin, 2001). The Swedish prison system has a long-standing reputation for being open and liberal, with generous provision for visits and home leave. The Prison Treatment Act of 1974 requires imprisonment regimes to promote resocialization and counteract the deleterious effects of confinement. Prisoners' rights are also formally recognized by the Prison Treatment Act, although many of these rights can be restricted on the grounds of considerations such as security. Notably, prisoners have rights to organize themselves (including electing inmates' councils) and to be consulted by the prisons directorate on issues of policy and administration.[16]

The dominant philosophy of punishment in Sweden until the 1980s was rehabilitation. In the Nordic countries generally (although, as we shall see, to a lesser extent in Finland), 'a general attempt was made in criminal justice to adopt a medical and therapeutic model ... most evident in Scandinavia in the adoption of special sanctions for young offenders, mentally abnormal offenders, recidivists (chronic offenders), vagrants and misusers of alcohol. It was typical of these new forms of sanctions that they were imposed for an indeterminate period and were to achieve one of two goals – either the treatment or the incapacitation of the offender' (Lahti, 1985: 61). In 1965, during the period of international 'rehabilitative optimism', Sweden adopted a new Penal Code (or 'Criminal Code', *Brottsbalken* in Swedish) which instructed sentencing courts to 'foster the sentenced offender's rehabilitation in society' (see Jareborg, 1995: 95-6). It should not be thought, however, that this positivistic approach had an all-pervading hegemony. Along with the other Nordic countries, Sweden's tradition of penal philosophy also justified punishment on the grounds of *general prevention* – not only general deterrence, but also the prevention of crime by denouncing the criminal's actions in order to influence the public's sense of morality (Lahti, 1985: 67).[17] Again, special preventive sentences were reserved for particular categories of offenders such as young or allegedly dangerous offenders, and common sentences such as imprisonment and fines were generally imposed in proportion to the seriousness of the offence (Jareborg, 1995: 97). But rehabilitation (and the associated notion of 'incapacitation' of serious offenders by incarceration pending their rehabilitation) could be said to have dominated in penal discourse and abstract ideology.

Rehabilitation is a philosophy that one might expect to appeal to a social democracy at least as much as to a conservative corporatist country (Tham, 1995). Social democratic ideology, with its emphasis on equality and social solidarity and caring for those at the bottom of society, is likely to see the criminal as a victim of adverse social conditions – the social 'causes of crime'. There but for fortune go any of us. Such an approach tends to deny the individual responsibility of individual offenders for their wrongdoing, along the lines spelt out by the 'positivist' school in criminology. The offender should not so much be blamed as treated and helped to reform. Moreover, the social democratic left has normally seen itself as generally 'progressive' and in favour of modern scientific solutions to social problems, and thus is likely to be attracted to ideas in any field which portray themselves in this way. Thus was criminological positivism imported to Sweden from elsewhere in Europe and from the USA and arguably accepted and applied more consistently than anywhere else. It is noteworthy, for example, that in the 1960s the rehabilitationist Penal Code was initially attacked by KRUM, the forceful and left-wing national prisoners' movement, essentially for not being rehabilitative enough – initially because insufficient treatment was provided within prison, and later on the grounds that rehabilitation could not be effectively pursued within prison at all (Tham, 1995: 105).

From the late 1960s onwards, however, the tide turned against positivism and the rehabilitative approach both internationally and within Sweden. The KRUM critique moved on to criticizing the notion of treatment itself, on the grounds of justice and due process (essentially the 'justice model' critique of the treatment model). As a result, a working group was set up by the National Swedish Council for Crime Prevention, which in 1977 produced a report entitled *A New Penal System: Ideas and Proposals (Nytt Straffsystem: Idéer och Förslag)*. This report adopted a 'justice model' approach, recommending that sanctions should be determined not by treatment possibilities but by the 'penal value' – the blameworthiness – of the offence. (A proposal which had been anticipated by legislation in neighbouring Finland in 1976, as we shall see shortly. The Finnish reform was an important influence on the authors of *A New Penal System*.) The report also, albeit in minor vein, suggested that more emphasis be placed on general deterrence. General deterrence theory was growing in popularity as the treatment model waned, promoted by economistic criminologists and the 'rational actor' analysis of crime, eminently represented in Sweden by the Nobel Prize-winner Gary Becker (1968; see Tham, 1995: 106). Following a long bureaucratic parliamentary process (which is the Swedish way of legislating) the 'just deserts' principle made its way into a central position in the Penal Code by way of a Sentencing Reform Act which was passed in 1988 and came into force in 1989. Chapter 29 of the Penal Code now states that punishment shall be imposed 'according to the penal value of the crime', the penal value to be determined 'with special regard to the harm, offence or risk which the conduct involved'.[18]

This shift from treatment to just deserts was not a matter of great party political controversy. The 1977 report *A New Penal System* had been published under a centre-right coalition, while the legislation was passed under the Social Democrats, following a long pre-legislative process of a kind designed to produce inter-party consensus (Jareborg, 1995: 99). Some Social Democrats resisted the change from the traditional treatment philosophy, and it was more popular with right-wing newspapers than with the Social Democratic press (Tham, 1995: 110). To some extent the new Penal Code may have been the result of some Social Democrats lacking the courage of their convictions and fearful of giving their (increasingly confident) political opponents greater opportunities to attack them on the subject of law and order and paint them as being 'soft on crime'. (In Sweden, as often elsewhere, the political left has often tried to take a low profile on crime, not taking a 'law and order' approach but at the same time believing that a 'softer' approach is electorally disadvantageous [Tham, 1995: 101].) But there were also aspects of Social Democratic ideology and tradition which on the one hand were not averse to taking a tougher line on crime, and on the other hand may have found a different kind of attraction in a 'just deserts' approach.

Henrik Tham (1995: 101–3) points to certain tendencies in Swedish social democracy which are less opposed to a 'law and order' approach to crime. One is the attitude, backed by traditional Marxist theory and the 'workerist' outlook, that criminals are actually class enemies of the respectable working population, forming a 'lumpenproletariat' likely to betray the workers to the bourgeoisie, and predominantly preying on decent proletarians in committing their crimes. Again, the Swedish social democratic tradition is associated with a strong state, seen as necessary to redistribute resources and protect trade union power. Combined with the relative historical absence of an urban liberal community and culture[19] and the fact that Sweden has not been occupied by a foreign power for several centuries,[20] this contributes to a weak civil liberties tradition. But it may also be that, as mooted earlier, the secular and humanistic basis of Nordic social democracy also facilitated the acceptance of the 'justice' philosophy among many Social Democrats of a more liberal point of view, who saw just deserts (as indeed did its original American proponents) as a more humane mode of punishment with greater protection for the individual from disproportionate punishment. Paradoxically (and this has wider application than just to Sweden) the justice model may have appealed to some because it seemed to them less liberal, and to others because it seemed more liberal. It may also have been attractive to 'progressives' as the latest notion in international leftist criminology, and for some leftists KRUM's radical critique of the treatment ideology and its effects may have inclined them in favour of the justice model as an alternative and potentially less repressive philosophy of punishment.

The authors of *A New Penal System* hoped that the adoption of the just deserts principle would limit punishment.[21] However, the Bourgeois parties saw it as an opportunity to demand harsher sanctions. Following the lead of conservative parties elsewhere – notably the British Conservatives in the 'law and order' General Election of 1979 – they attacked the Social Democrats for being 'soft on crime', berating the Swedish welfare state and its associated treatment philosophy as being criminogenic.[22] This attack was particularly fierce prior to and during the second Bourgeois government of 1991-4, but it is true to say that from the early 1980s onwards there has been a clear change of the crime policy climate in Sweden towards 'law and order', albeit mild by the standards of many other countries. The dominating influence of liberal experts has decreased; 'law and order' has become a part of party politics, the role of popular movements has decreased while that of populist thinking has increased,[23] and most parts of the mass media have adopted an illiberal stance with regard to crime policy matters. But none of this was a serious threat to the 'just deserts' framework. The desert principle was perfectly palatable to the Bourgeois parties, as its emphasis on individual responsibility and punishment rather than treatment fitted 'market state values' more obviously than it did the social democratic tradition; indeed, its rise in Sweden has been linked to a loss of confidence in the Swedish model welfare state (Tham, 1995).

Even so, it should not be thought that the philosophy of rehabilitation has entirely died – far from it. Although it is no longer so influential in determining the lengths of prison terms, the Swedish penal system is still characterized by serious ambitions to reform and rehabilitate its subjects within a sanctions framework defined by just deserts. By law (the Prison Treatment Act 1974), the official primary goals of the execution of the prison sentence remain promoting the inmate's adjustment to the community and counteracting the detrimental effects of incarceration, although since the late 1980s there has also been an increased emphasis on 'security' (von Hofer and Marvin, 2001: 638, 642–3). Elements of a rehabilitationist approach are also evident in measures such as the laws which provide that drug users may be subjected to compulsory treatment.

The overall pattern of criminal justice policy over the decades has been as follows. In the early 1970s, the Social Democratic government passed a number of laws of a decriminalizing and depenalizing nature along with legislation to restrict the use of imprisonment and make imprisonment less severe. The prison population was reduced, and the Prison Treatment Act 1974 was passed, which stressed humanitarian values and prisoners' rights (Tham, 1995). Following the first Bourgeois government (1976–82), the Social Democratic record in the harsher climate of the 1980s was more mixed. Parole eligibility was increased, with release at the halfway point in the sentence being introduced for medium length prison terms, but prison regimes became harsher for those serving longer sentences, with greater stress on security and less eligibility for home leave (Tham, 1995: 97). New, stricter laws were passed concerning white-collar crime and violence against women, while the already strict anti-drugs laws were made harsher (under pressure from opposition parties) and the number of prison sentences increased. Under the Bourgeois government of 1991–4 the (relative) harshness increased further, with yet tougher drugs legislation, eligibility for release on parole being moved back from halfway through the sentence to the two-thirds point in 1993, and legislation to increase the permitted punishments for some twenty categories of crime (Jareborg, 1995: 119–20; Leander, 1995: 186–7; Tham, 1995: 110–11). Probably as important as anything else, the conservative Minister of Justice (from the Moderate Party) engaged in a campaign of law and order rhetoric, publishing a policy document announcing her intention *To Restore a Degenerated Criminal Policy* (Justitiedepartementet, 1993). As we have seen, the prison population rose significantly during this period of law and order, peaking in 1994.

1995 was the first full year of a new Social Democrat-led government. The Social Democrats had continued to adopt a low profile on law and order, while adopting the British Labour Party's popular if enigmatic slogan 'tough on crime and tough on the causes of crime'. Their 1994 election campaign stressed crime prevention and alternatives to imprisonment, and argued that the conservative cutbacks to the welfare state were a cause of crime; but they committed themselves to continuing conservative policies such as parole at the two-thirds point (Leander, 1995: 189–91). In the next few years the Swedish prison population declined to levels just above those of the mid-1980s. This is thought to be attributable to two main factors. One was the introduction and nationwide deployment of electronic monitoring of offenders (von Hofer, 2000) as an alternative to short prison sentences of up to three months. This innovation was favoured by all main political parties, introduced on a trial basis under a Bourgeois government in 1993, and extended nationwide under the Social Democrat-led government in 1997. Unlike in some other countries (for example England), the Swedish version of tagging is not a separate sentence of the court but is a way of serving a short prison sentence which has already been passed by the court. It is generally believed – and the decline in the prison population suggests that this belief may be well founded – that this legislative arrangement has meant that tagging in Sweden genuinely functions as an alternative to prison rather than largely as an alternative to other non-custodial penalties. A second possible factor in the decline was that internal reorganizations within the police and prosecutorial services led temporarily to fewer offenders being processed.

This relative stability in the Swedish prison population at this time (along with the Finnish experience, to be discussed shortly) suggests at least two points of more general interest. One is that it may be by no means inevitable in the modern Western world for punishment levels to continue to rise inexorably. Another is that the adoption of a 'just deserts' sentencing framework does not have to be associated with increased levels of punishment:[24] in the right social and political context, punishment levels can be as or more lenient with just deserts as with a more positivistic sentencing system.

Until very recently it could be said with confidence that Sweden does not suffer from a penal crisis (von Hofer and Marvin, 2001: 648). In the late 1990s the imprisonment rate was around 60 per 100,000 of the general population. Prison conditions were very good by international standards, with modern buildings and single cells as the norm. Staff–inmate ratios were favourable (1.1 or 1.2: 1). Riots and disorder were rare events, with only one major riot (at the Tillberga maximum security prison in July 1994; see Leander, 1995: 169–70) in the last twenty years. Escapes from prisons had declined (from 647 in 1988/9 to 409 in 1994/5).[25] There were no industrial relations problems (in line with the Swedish industrial scene generally). There was no general crisis of resources, and the main legitimacy problem of the Swedish penal system was a relatively mild popular feeling that it was not tough enough. Those of us who live in countries with more troubled penal systems could be excused a wistful sigh as we gazed towards Sweden.

Much of this remains true. Prison conditions are still relatively very good in Sweden, and prison numbers are still relatively low in international terms. However, in the last few years it has been increasing sharply and indeed has reached levels never seen in the twentieth century. The 'penal Zeitgeist'[26] in Sweden is moving in the same direction as in most of the West. As, indeed, is the general Zeitgeist: as Sweden's social democratic ethos and political economy continue to erode (albeit under a Social Democrat-led government at present), so her penality is becoming harsher and more crisis-prone. The public debate on crime and punishment has become marked by calls for greater use of imprisonment, and sentencing scales have been tightened for many offences (von Hofer, 2003b: 30). Sentences for crimes of violence have become increasingly harsh, as have those for drug offences. (Official Swedish policies on drugs had become significantly harsher in the 1980s, and the last few years have seen a further punitive twist manifested in more and longer prison sentences.) Restrictions on the conditional release of longer-term prisoners (effective from January 1999) have also made a significant contribution to the rising prison population.[27] Whereas in 1996 the occupancy rate in prisons was 82 per cent, in 2000 it was 101 per cent and in 2002 95 per cent, compared with an official target maximum of 90 per cent. Some prisons are now overcrowded, an almost unheard-of situation in Sweden. In previous times the governmental response to such a situation might have been to introduce measures to reduce the prison population and ensure that the customary Swedish normality of a prison population between 4,000 and 6,000 was retained. Instead, there seemed to be a wide political consensus that prison numbers should be allowed to exceed 6,000 on a continuing basis, and the Social Democratic government decided to create an extra 1,400 extra prison places by 2008.

Our Swedish colleague Hanns von Hofer describes the Swedish prison system as currently in a deep crisis marked by rising prisoner numbers, overcrowding, unrest and spectacular escapes, leading to the resignation of the Director General of the Prison and Probation Service in September 2004 (von Hofer, 2004, and personal communications). Official rhetoric from the government and the new Director General (a former senior police officer) has concentrated on security and increasing prison capacity: the penal elite was changing its tune. Thus, several classic signs of penal crisis have made quite a sudden appearance. It is unusual to see such signs in a country with a relatively low rate of imprisonment; their appearance in Sweden can be attributed to the severe strains, particularly in terms of penal resources, brought about by a swift upward shift in punishment levels in a nation that has for a long time needed a relatively small prison capacity. It is too soon to know whether the crisis will pass, perhaps with Sweden's penality settling down to a less lenient but still fairly stable state, or whether the future holds a further spiralling of penal severity and recurrent crisis. But current events in Sweden are an uncomfortable warning that even a country long renowned as a haven of peaceful social democracy and penal leniency is not immune to the forces of punitiveness and the penal crises they create.

Finland: the new beacon of enlightenment? (Now dimming slightly)

Much of what we have said about Sweden applies also to Finland, but there are some interesting differences. Not least is the fact that, despite its social democratic nature, Finland in the 1970s had a surprisingly high prison population by contemporary European standards. But thereafter, at least until the turn of the century – and as a result of a quite deliberate reorientation in official policy – Finland reduced its imprisonment levels to such an extent that it could be regarded as having taken over the Netherlands' traditional role as the beacon of penal enlightenment in Western Europe. As in Sweden, however, imprisonment rates have been rising again in the last few years.

The year 1976 was important for Finnish penality. That was the year when – anticipating the Swedish reform of 1989 – the Finnish Penal Code of 1889 was amended by the addition of a chapter which enshrined 'just deserts' as the main principle of sentencing.[28] It also marked the beginning of a long and steep decline in the use of imprisonment in Finland, from a peak of 118 per 100,000 population in 1976 (high by Western European standards even today). By 1989 the rate was 68, and in 1999 it stood at 46 – the lowest rate in Europe for any country with a population of over a million except for the Bosnian Federation (Walmsley, 2000). The title of a well-known article by Patrik Törnudd (1993), 'Fifteen Years of Decreasing Prisoner Rates in Finland' (referring to the years 1976 to 1991), proved to be over-modest, for apart from a slight upturn in 1992,[29] Finland's prison population declined for no less than twenty-three years. As Table 10.1 demonstrates, only in 2000 did it start to rise. The rise over the next few years was very steep, however, with a rate of 46 inmates per 100,000 general population in 1999 becoming one of 70 in 2002: more than a 50 per cent increase in the prison population in the space of three years. The Finnish imprisonment rate is currently higher than that of Nordic neighbours Norway (59 in 2002) and Denmark (64), although still below that of Sweden (73 in 2002), and indeed the vast majority of European countries. We shall first consider the 1976 revision of the Penal Code and its context.

Finland's legal and penal culture differs from that of Sweden in a manner that can perhaps be explained historically. Whereas Sweden has been intact, unoccupied and almost unthreatened since 1658,[30] Finland only achieved independence in 1917. Ruled by Sweden until 1809, Finland was thereafter a Grand Duchy in the Russian Empire, supposedly autonomous but fighting a long battle against 'Russification'. In 1917 Finland took advantage of the turmoil of the Russian Revolution to declare independence, undergoing a bloody civil war between left and right before peace and a new republican constitution were achieved in 1919. Finland twice found herself at war with the USSR during World War Two, but the two countries signed a peace treaty in 1947. Thereafter Finland's policy was neutrality and a generally Scandinavian orientation, but also importantly a prudent friendship with the Soviet Union, seen by some Western observers as subservience. The effects of these turbulent events included a strong attachment to the safeguards afforded by legalism and the rule of law in Finland; although 'relatively strict legalism is typical of all the Scandinavian criminal justice systems ... Finns have been *particularly* inhibited in extending the discretionary powers of criminal justice agencies – especially those of the police and prosecutors' (Lahti, 1989: 64). This is despite the Finns having not only a typically Nordic attachment to the welfare state but also a particularly strong belief and trust in the Finnish state and its agents (and therefore not suffering from the collapse of trust in the state identified in Chapter 2 as one possible factor contributing to a harsh penality). Yet such trust is perhaps conditional upon the strict regulation of the state by the rule of law and the state's continued good behaviour in abiding by the rules.

Perhaps partly for similar reasons, Finland never accepted the positivist treatment ideology of punishment – with the high degree of discretion it places in the hands of state-employed treatment experts – as fully as Sweden did. (Another reason could be that opportunities to introduce positivistic treatment methods were limited by the dire economic circumstances consequent on Finland's harsh history [Lappi-Seppälä, 2001: 92].) The 1889 Penal Code is usually described as being classical in orientation, with reform and incapacitation being subordinated to the principles of desert and general prevention. The 'general prevention' of crime by punishment was traditionally seen as operating largely by the denunciation of the crime represented by the penalty rather than by way of deterrence. In the ensuing decades Finnish criminology and criminal law did become influenced by criminological positivism (and especially by the German-based International Union of Criminologists). Among the measures introduced in the first half of the twentieth century were legislation permitting lengthy semi-indeterminate sentences for 'dangerous recidivists', special educative sanctions for young offenders, a greatly expanded parole system, and compulsory castration for sex offenders (Lahti, 1977). But as Törnudd (1993: 3) says,

> the war years and the opposition by influential old-school experts slowed down the process. While neighbouring Sweden wholeheartedly accepted the rehabilitation ideology in the 1940s and 1950s, the Finns did not seriously begin to reform the criminal justice system before the 1960s. But it was too late for the rehabilitation ideology to become dominant. The wave of criticism against the ideology of coercive treatment had at that time already reached Finland.

From the 1960s on, the individual treatment ideology was subjected to severe critical scrutiny throughout the Nordic countries, as indeed it also was in much of the English-speaking West (if less so in Christian Democratic Europe). The 'just deserts' approach was in the ascendancy. In Finland, castration of offenders fell into disuse in the 1960s and was abolished in 1970, while the criteria for indefinite incarceration of recidivists were considerably tightened in 1971, reducing the numbers so detained to single figures (Lahti, 1989: 67). The new chapter added to the Penal Code in 1976[31] stated that 'punishment shall be measured so that it is in just proportion to the damage and danger caused by the offence and to the guilt of the offender manifested in the offence.' But there was an 'asymmetry' to this proportionality principle: the Code allowed courts to impose sentences which were more lenient than proportionality would indicate, but – so as to guarantee citizens against the excessive use of state force – not generally to pass disproportionately harsh penalties (Lappi-Seppälä, 2001: 124). The overall result is similar to the principle of 'limiting retributivism' favoured by Norval Morris (1974: 75) and ourselves (Cavadino and Dignan, 2002: 56) among others.

Our Finnish colleague Raimo Lahti (1989: 69) expresses the opinion that it is misleading to call these developments neo-classical. Certainly there was more to it than just just deserts, and even the phrase 'humane neo-classicism' (Lappi-Seppälä, 2001: 115) may be inadequate. An influential figure in reforming Finnish penality was the criminologist Patrik Törnudd, who advocated a rational cost-benefit approach to the social costs of crime and crime control policies (a pragmatic, managerialist strategy). (Törnudd (1993) modestly plays down his own starring role in Finnish developments.) This approach was applied in the context of Finland's traditional attachment to the notion of general prevention as the rationale of punishment. 'The aim of punishment is to demonstrate society's disapproval of the act and to teach the public the limits of acceptable behaviour. As the new generation of criminologists were sociologists, this thesis is usually supplemented with the observation that while every society needs a criminal justice system, the immediate impact of penalties is very small, as the general preventive effect mainly operates through indirect mechanisms ... A prison sentence of a few weeks may be almost as effective in demonstrating society's condemnation as a prison sentence of a few months' (Törnudd, 1993: 3). The implementation of this approach led to reforms in the penal law which had not only the intention but also the practical effect of reducing the prison population (Lahti, 1989: 67). Lahti, himself an influential member of the Finnish penal elite, describes Finnish penal thinking as a largely *pragmatic* search for an efficient criminal justice system, but within the boundaries set by principles of justice and humanity.[32]

Questionable in terms of all three of these values – efficiency, justice and humanity – was Finland's use of imprisonment, which was very high by contemporary Western European standards and much higher than those of neighbouring countries. The few Finns who were aware of this fact tended to assume that it must be due to a high rate of violence in Finland. Statistical analysis disproved this assumption (Törnudd, 1993: 1), but there is no single clear explanation for the high imprisonment rate of Finland at the time. Nils Christie's (1968: 181) suggestion is that Finland's troubled history led to a cultural climate whereby severity was measured on a different scale than those used by her neighbours – when the populace has suffered so much, judicial punishments are likely to seem trivial by comparison. Another possible explanation concerns the Finnish combination of strict legalism with some particularly rigid and ageing legislation which, for example, prescribed a high minimum sentence for aggravated theft (Törnudd, 1993: 2) and discouraged prosecutors from dropping charges. It may even have been that Finland's less welfare-oriented penal tradition made punishment harsher than in neighbouring countries, for a rehabilitative ideology often (though not necessarily always) has the general effect of making punishment more lenient.[33] Or maybe it was just an irreducible piece of Finnish idiosyncrasy of the time. If so, the ensuing reduction in punishment was also idiosyncratic, for Finland did not merely regress to the Nordic mean but for a while became the least punitive Nordic country (if we exclude Iceland).

The debates and developments in Finland were led by professional criminologists, who wield much more influence in Finland's especially 'expert-orientated' society than in more populistic polities. This was doubtless assisted by the fact that 'crime control has never been a central political issue in election campaigns in Finland, nor have Ministers of Justice ever seen crime control as a primary area of interest' – except occasionally and briefly when a Minister of Justice (one of them a criminologist herself)[34] has been strongly committed to liberalizing punishment (Törnudd, 1993: 5). Even today, 'none of the "heavyweight" politicians has called for populist policies, such as three-strikes laws or "truth in sentencing"' (Lappi-Seppälä, 2001: 140).

Criminologists were the first to define Finland's relatively high prison population (by contemporary European standards, and certainly compared with the other Nordic countries) as a problem. The Norwegian criminologist Nils Christie

> recalls speaking to Finnish judges and criminologists in Helsinki in 1968. At the time, Mr Christie and others were developing the first international comparisons of prison populations, so he was the first to tell the Finns that their incarceration rate was totally unlike that of their Scandinavian neighbours and was 'really in the Russian tradition'. The audience was shocked, Mr Christie recalls ...'and some of them then decided that this was not a very good policy.' (Gardner, 2002)

Criminologists also demonstrated that the high imprisonment rate was not due to high crime rates in Finland but to more offenders being sent to prison for longer periods. They 'shared an almost unanimous conviction that Finland's [then] internationally high prisoner rate was a disgrace and that it would be possible to significantly reduce the amount and length of prison sentences without serious repercussions on the crime situation' (Törnudd, 1993: 5). And it was experts such as these who were in charge of planning reforms in Finland's criminal law, which they set to amending with the express intention of reducing the prison population. It again may say something about Finland's legal culture that when the amendments were made, they were not resisted or subverted by practitioners such as sentencing judges but were applied in accordance with their letter and spirit, with the result that they had the consequences intended. Perhaps a vital factor was that the judiciary generally strongly supported the legislative changes, and even anticipated the legislature in reducing sentencing levels (Lappi-Seppälä, 2001: 114, 122) as well as taking advantage of the new laws to continue the process.

A wide variety of mechanisms were utilized in pursuit of the reductionist end: decriminalization, diversion from prosecution, the encouragement for courts to pass not only fewer but also shorter prison sentences, amnesty[35] and extension of early release. Legislative reforms (see Törnudd, 1993) included decriminalization of public drunkenness and conscientious objection by Jehovah's Witnesses, new laws allowing greater use of 'conditional imprisonment' (suspended sentences), criminal law reforms allowing lesser sentences for theft and drunken driving, and liberalization of parole rules. Perhaps of particular interest – although doubtless not making the largest contribution to reducing imprisonment rates – was a change in the law, effective in 1991, regarding the dropping of prosecutions. This had previously hardly occurred at all in Finland, which had stuck rigidly to the so-called 'principle of legality' prescribing prosecutions whenever evidence existed against a suspect. (This principle also exists in Italy, and – in less rigid form, with wide exceptions – in Germany and Sweden, whereas the more discretionary 'opportunity principle' has held sway in the Netherlands, Denmark and Norway.)

Another particularly Finnish aspect to the story is the way in which Finland has reduced her dependence on imprisonment without introducing an array of community penalties based on ideas of rehabilitation and individual prevention. We have mentioned conditional imprisonment; in addition, community service was introduced on a trial basis in 1991 and nationally in 1994, and seems to have been generally used by sentencers as a genuine alternative to custody, as intended, especially for drink-driving offences (Lappi-Seppälä, 2001: 116). But otherwise what has happened is that imprisonment sentences have either been shorter than previously, or been replaced with the classicistic community penalties of conditional sentences and fines. Both the *number* of prison sentences and their average *lengths* were reduced significantly between 1976 and 1991. These changes have, however, been limited to non-violent offences, most notably theft and drunken driving. Conversely, sentences for violent crimes have become longer (Aho, 1997: 270), so Finland has clearly participated in the international trend towards *bifurcation* of punishment. Indeed, this is bifurcation in its truest sense, with sentences for violent offences becoming harsher while those for other crimes have become more lenient (as opposed to all punishments becoming harsher but some more dramatically than others). Finally, thanks at least in part to administrative measures to speed up proceedings, the number and proportion of remand prisoners has been reduced. It now stands at around 10 per cent of the prison population, whereas elsewhere in Europe it tends to be 20 to 30 per cent (Aho, 1997: 273).

Finland did not suffer either a real or perceived crime wave in the wake of these changes. Indeed, the decline in the prison population had no measurable effect on crime rates or trends (Lappi-Seppälä, 2001: 119–22), and Finland's crime rate is still relatively low. Nor was there a notable backlash[36] against the softening of punishment levels. This is not to say that Finland has been immune from the general international trend towards law and order ideology. In the last few years there have been more demands, especially in the media, for tougher crime policies (see Lappi-Seppälä, 2001: 141; 2002: 425). This must be seen in perspective: 'the Finnish debate on crime policy issues would appear fairly peaceful and idyllic to someone used to the controversies raging around law-and-order issues in, e.g., the USA or England – or even in neighbouring Sweden' (Törnudd, 1993: 29). Nevertheless, as we have seen, punishment levels are currently rising steeply in Finland, and if she is Europe's new beacon of penal enlightenment then it is dimming slightly at present.

Conditions and regimes in Finnish prisons are not overall as favourable as in Sweden. Overcrowding is no longer a problem, and the situation of prisoners in the newer prisons is good by international standards. Around a quarter of prison places are in open conditions (Lappi-Seppälä, 2001: 100). However, there remain a number of older prisons with poor conditions (including a lack of access to toilet facilities at night) and problematic regimes. One of these (Turku Central Prison) experienced several inmate strikes in 1998 in protest against the way prisoners were being treated in this particular institution. These disorders, the inmates' sense of injustice which provoked them, and the actual conditions and regime at Turku, do not seem to be typical of Finnish prisons generally. Security and control are not perceived to be major or generalized problems, nor are there major difficulties with prison staff (who, like agents of the Finnish state generally, are seen as trustworthy). Nor is there a general 'crisis of resources'. However, the recognition of prisoners' formal rights is not far advanced – perhaps partly as a result of the fact that Finland did not join the Council of Europe until 1989 and thus was not previously a signatory to the European Convention on Human Rights. Prisoners still largely lack an opportunity to appeal against decisions taken by the prison authorities.

There is no major problem of racial legitimacy in the Finnish penal system. Like the other Nordic countries – but even more so – Finland is ethnically quite homogeneous, with only very small indigenous – Romany and Sami (Lapp) – minority populations,[37] and hardly any foreign residents until very recently. The opening of the borders to former communist countries has not so far caused either a noticeable increase in crime or the kind of fear of crime by foreigners seen in Germany (Aho, 1997: 275–6). Foreigners are over-represented by a factor of three in the prison population, but absolute numbers are very small (103 in 1996).

So Finland is a country whose penal elite perceived it as having, if not a crisis, at least a problem of legitimacy (in international terms) as a result of its high prison population in the 1970s, and which responded to the crisis by determined and successful efforts to reduce its prison numbers. This reduction has contributed to a situation which is about as far from penal crisis as can readily be imagined in present-day Europe, on almost all counts. Some elements of the Finnish experience may not be generalizable to other countries, including the nation's idiosyncratic strong belief and pride in the rectitude of its own state. Yet some aspects surely have a wider relevance, such as the association between penal leniency and social democracy. Also of interest is the wide variety of measures which have been utilized in Finland in the cause of leniency, which do not however include a vast array of new non-custodial penalties. Törnudd (1993: 13) is surely right to stress that 'attitudinal and ideological readiness to bring down the number of prisoners is more important than the choice of technique to achieve this end'. (The same is surely true, for example, of the Netherlands.) A lenient ideology with roots in the culture – and, we would venture, political economy – of a nation, is what has been of the greatest significance. Even more so than in Sweden, Finland also shows that such an ideology need not place any strong emphasis on reform and rehabilitation. Elsewhere – such as the Netherlands between World War Two and the 1980s, and in Ontario in the 1960s and early 1970s (McMahon, 1992) – there has been such an association between rehabilitative ideology and reduction in punishment levels, but not in Finland.

We do not know whether either Sweden or Finland can maintain their current relative leniency into the twenty-first century; let alone increase it. Certainly the latest trends in both countries are in the direction of increasing harshness. There is a danger that global trends towards the politicization of penal policy and international harmonization of criminal justice will lead to a greater harshness (Lappi-Seppälä, 2001: 142-3; 2002: 425). In Finland's case this would be ironic, since it was the earlier internationalization (or at least 'Nordicization') of her penality which helped move punishment in a more lenient direction. But at least it can be said that the recent pasts of both of these countries can still be seen as providing encouraging object lessons which may – hopefully – suggest that the spiralling rises in imprisonment which so many countries have witnessed in recent years need not be accepted as inevitable.

Notes

1 We should confess that our Finnish associate Raimo Lahti dislikes our use of the term 'social democracy', which can of course connote particular political parties. In our usage – common among non-Nordic analysts – we mean to characterize these countries broadly, as explained in Chapter 1, with no implication that they cease to be generally 'social democratic' in their political economy when non-Social Democrats are in power (although they do tend to move away from the social-democratic archetype at such times).

2 Often (less accurately) called the 'Scandinavian' countries. Strictly speaking, Scandinavia is the peninsula shared by Sweden and Norway.

3 All but Finland are also close linguistically. They have their own languages, but they are so closely related that speakers of different 'Scandinavian' languages can usually understand each other.

4 Norway and Denmark have imprisonment rates (59 and 64 respectively in 2002) which are fairly stable (having risen slightly since the 1980s) and currently a little lower than that of Sweden. Iceland, with a population of only 289,000, has one of the very lowest imprisonment rates in Europe (37 in 2002) (Walmsley, 2003b).

5 In Rawls's opinion, at least. There is of course a voluminous literature on Rawls's theory of justice: see e.g. Barry (1973).

6 This illustrates the somewhat abstract but important point that a liberal or socialist communitarianism can be fundamentally individualistic in that it is based on the interests of human individuals. Communitarianism need not be collectivistic (giving primacy to the collective entity which is 'society' or 'the community'); nor is there any necessary connection between individualism of this ilk and the atomistic philosophy that 'there is no such thing as society'. See further Cavadino (1997b: 236–7), Lukes (1973).

7 It may be significant that the word 'resocialization' tends to be used in conservative corporatist countries, whereas in the individualistic US terms such as 'reform', 'rehabilitation' and 'treatment' are used instead. Individual offenders 'reform' or are reformed by individualized treatment. Similarly, 'rehabilitation' and 'treatment' are things done to individual offenders, in all probability by individual treatment experts, but 'resocialization' is by definition something achieved by society as a whole.

8 This corresponds to a distinction drawn by Gallo (1995: 71) in the context of French penality, between 'a secular, "neutral" model born with the Enlightenment, and a religious, confessional model aimed at the redemption of the offender.' (For Protestant countries, the term 'penitential' should perhaps replace 'confessional'.)

9 John Pratt has pointed out that New Zealand is also a small country – indeed, smaller than any of the Nordic countries apart from Iceland – but it lacks such an influential small group. This is presumably because New Zealand today (having moved from a non-corporatist social democracy to neo-liberalism) is less centralized and less bureaucratic in its power structure, having a more personalized politics.

10 We have to record a note of dissent on behalf of our Swedish associate Hanns von Hofer. He disagrees with the general 'look and feel' of the section on Sweden, taking the view that we should place less emphasis on Sweden's past reputation for leniency and more stress on the harsh penal climate that has developed more recently. We share his disquiet at recent developments and would doubtless express ourselves rather differently if we were writing within a Swedish rather than a comparative context.

11 'During the 1980s, when unemployment figures for the EU rose to between six and ten per cent, Swedish figures remained at between two and three per cent' (Tham, 1996: 3).

12 Hanns von Hofer, personal communication.

13 This seems to represent a significant change (for both countries) from the late 1970s. Pease (1982) found adult prison admission rates of 69 per 100,000 for England and Wales and 121 for Sweden, based on figures between 1978 and 1980. Pease noted at the time that this seemed to represent a substantial change in Swedish penal practice between 1974 and 1978. It may have been due to an increase in short prison sentences for drunken driving in the late 1970s.

14 In 1992 around 50 per cent of those found guilty of 'aggravated drunken driving (driving with 1.5 mg alcohol per millilitre of blood) received custodial sentences (Jareborg, 1995: 120n). This reflects Sweden's traditionally puritanical attitude towards substance abuse (as opposed to other aspects of personal life). Drugs laws are also severe in Sweden. However, following a change in the law in 1990, and the introduction of electronic tagging nationwide in 1997 (von Hofer, 2000) admissions to prison for drink-driving plummeted from 4,425 in 1990 to 1,005 in 2000.

15 However, the international trend towards 'bifurcation' of punishment, with increasing sentences for offenders deemed to be particularly serious or dangerous, is very visible in Sweden as well. For example, the number of prisoners serving life sentences at one time increased from 15 in 1983 to 101 in 2000.

16 In the 1970s the prisoners' movement KRUM succeeded in making its voice forcefully heard in debates about penal policy, although it ceased to exist in the 1980s.

17 See Cavadino and Dignan (2002: 43–4) for an explanation and discussion of the denunciatory theory of punishment, and Chapter 2 therein for a general introduction to the philosophy of punishment.

18 As translated by Jareborg (1995: 101).

19 As Tham (1996: 2) says, 'being a predominantly rural society with few towns of substantial size, Sweden did not develop a strong tradition of liberalism in the late nineteenth century'.

20 Sweden threw off Danish rule in 1521, regained the last occupied provinces from Denmark in 1658, and last fought in a war (in an alliance against Napoleon) in 1814.

21 A leading architect of the 'just deserts' reform in Sweden was Nils Jareborg – although not an author of the 1977 report, he has been called its 'spiritual father'. He was also a member of the working group that proposed the draft sentencing bill which became law in 1989 (Jareborg, 1995: 101). Jareborg is a close associate of the leading liberal American 'justice model' theorist Andrew von Hirsch.

22 One element of the Bourgeois critique of the Swedish welfare state was that it encouraged crime by undermining individual responsibilities and important non-state institutions such as the family (Tham, 1995). Tham's (1998) comparison of crime trends in England and Sweden in the 1980s suggests the opposite conclusion, however. During this period the egalitarian Swedish welfare state remained intact while that of Britain was cut back under Margaret Thatcher's Conservative government; at the same time crime increased much more sharply in England and Wales. This supports the traditional left/ liberal thesis that material inequality, unemployment, poverty and the lack of social solidarity engendered by a neo-liberal economy are criminogenic and that a generous welfare state *reduces* crime.

23 A populist party entered the Swedish Parliament for a few years around 1990.

24 Barbara Hudson (1987: 93) claimed, largely on the basis of American experience in the1970s and 1980s, that

> far from bringing about a new regard for defendants' rights, restricting the powers of correctional personnel over offenders' lives, and returning to a more modest, minimalist role for the state's coercive apparatus, the justice model has provided ideological legitimation for the new right's policy of incarcerating more people, for longer periods, in the name of public protection.

Andrew von Hirsch (1993: Chapter 10) argues to the contrary that increased levels of punishment are far from being an inevitable consequence of the adoption of a just deserts framework, and cites Finland and Sweden as examples.

25 Increased emphasis was however placed on security in the late 1980s and 1990s. Following the escape of a spy, provisions were introduced (effective in 1988, but relaxed in 1999) that prisoners in certain categories had to be kept in maximum security prisons if there was reason to believe they were likely to try to escape (von Hofer and Marvin, 2001: 642–3).

26 A phrase provided by our Swedish colleague Hanns von Hofer. Von Hofer (2003b: 32) identifies the issues of drugs and immigration as potent factors in making punishment harsher in Sweden, and as relatively absent in Finland. Around 7 per cent of the Swedish population is made up of migrants from outside the EU, yet foreigners comprise 25 per cent of the Swedish prison population (1,258 persons on 1 March 1996).

27 Prior to 1999 prisoners sentenced to more than two years could be conditionally released after half of their sentences had elapsed; this has been changed to two-thirds. Another possible factor in the rise in imprisonment is an increase in the number of offenders reaching the courts following the previous decline caused by reorganization of the police and prosecutorial services.

28 Further important revisions of the Penal Code came into effect on 1 January 2004. However, as regards punishments the revised version largely reproduces and codifies previous provisions.

29 Törnudd (1993: 24) gives figures which clearly must have been compiled and/or calculated on a basis different from that employed to produce the numbers in Table 10.1, and for this reason have not been included in that table. His figures indicate that the Finnish imprisonment rate rose slightly from 69 per 100,000 in 1991 to 70 in 1992.

30 See above, Note 20.

31 The revised version of the Code effective from 2004 (see above, Note 28) reads similarly.

32 Finland may differ from Sweden in this respect, for Törnudd's (pragmatic and managerialist) cost-benefit analysis has had little influence in the formation of penal policy in Sweden.

33 See for example McMahon (1992), who found that a reduction in imprisonment rates in Ontario occurred in the 1960s and early 1970s at a time of rehabilitative optimism. On the other hand, Finland herself has recently demonstrated that it is perfectly possible to be lenient without much in the way of rehabilitative ideology. See also above, Note 24.

34 The reference is to Inkeri Anttila, who became Minister of Justice in 1975.

35 Sentences were reduced by one-sixth in 1977 to celebrate the sixtieth anniversary of Finland's independence.

36 There was a slight backlash against the lesser punishments for drink-driving in the sense that the lower blood alcohol limit for aggravated drink-driving was lowered in 1994, with 'vigorous support from a group of law and order orientated members of parliament' (Törnudd, 1997: 264–5).

37 Finns account for 93 per cent of the population, Swedes for 6 per cent and the remaining indigenous Roma, Sami (Lapps) and Tatar peoples between them comprise less than 1 per cent of the population.

11

Japan: Iron Fist in a Velvet Penal Glove

Japan is the sole exemplar in this study, and perhaps anywhere in the world, of a distinctive type of late capitalist state to which we have given the name 'oriental liberal corporatism'. Penologically speaking also it is highly distinctive. Indeed, in many respects it is easily the most paradoxical of all the countries we have been examining. Firstly, for many years it has succeeded, uniquely, in maintaining a comparatively low and stable crime rate[1] in spite of the pace and scale of its urbanization and industrial growth,[2] and despite the severe economic and social dislocation it also experienced during the course of the twentieth century. Secondly, although in many ways its criminal justice and penal institutions and processes look extremely familiar to Western eyes, the way they operate can often seem surprising since they are still strongly imbued by traditional Japanese attitudes and values. Thirdly, the Japanese criminal justice system has a reputation in many quarters for the remarkably lenient way in which many offenders appear to be dealt with, which (combined with the low crime rate) ensures that Japan's proportionate rate of imprisonment is the lowest of any of the countries covered in this book (53 per 100,000 in 2002).[3] Yet at the same time aspects of the Japanese penal system have been likened by international human rights organizations and some domestic critics to those more normally associated with repressive totalitarian regimes. Fourthly, and finally, although the Japanese appear to rely heavily on informal methods of social control that promote the ideal of social *inclusion*, yet Japan retains and continues to use the death penalty and other *exclusionary* forms of punishment when dealing with certain types of offenders. Japan hence employs a mode of penal *bifurcation* which is of an intriguingly different character from those of other countries. Perplexing as these paradoxes may seem at first glance, Japan's penal practices are nevertheless still entirely congruent with our overall thesis about the relationship between political economy (taking particular account of the social context in which it operates) and punitiveness; as we shall see in the course of this section.

Japan is an island society and until the mid-nineteenth century had experienced two-and-a half centuries of relative isolation from outside influences under a quasi-feudal system of warlords known as *shoguns*.[4] Indeed, even after this period of isolation came to an end, Japan has remained an unusually homogeneous society ethnically to this day – even in comparison with the Nordic social democracies that are also thought of as extremely homogeneous.[5] The combination of one race, a single language, relative absence of entrenched class divisions and a long history of shared customs has contributed to a strongly developed and resilient sense of national identity.[6] Perhaps this long-standing geographical and cultural isolation helps in part to explain Japan's continuing penological insularity despite its more recent participation in such international penal organisations as the United Nations Asia and Far Eastern Institute for the Prevention of Crime and Treatment of Offenders (UNAFEI),[7] and the Asian and Pacific Conference of Correctional Administrators (APPCA).

Japan's distinctive legal and penal culture is a product of both the historical developments that have helped to shape its institutional and procedural forms, and also the indigenous value system, social attitudes and cultural practices that continue to influence the way the Japanese criminal justice and penal systems operate in reality.[8] As its long period of isolationism was drawing to a close in the second half of the nineteenth century, Japan embarked on a rapid process of modernization which, in the case of its legal system, involved the conscious but selective adoption and adaptation of various Western models. Initially Japan looked to France when drafting its Criminal Law and the Law of Criminal Procedure in 1880, but thereafter the main source of influence was Germanic. A new Code of Criminal Procedure introduced in 1890 borrowed more heavily from Prussia, and a replacement Criminal Code introduced in 1907 was likewise inspired by a more authoritarian German model. Japan's first written Constitution, in 1889, also drew heavily on the Prussian Constitution of 1850, which vested strong power and authority over Parliament in the hands of the Kaiser. This was felt by the imperial political elite of the time to be more in keeping with the desire to retain the central power and focus of the Japanese emperor than the more liberal, democratic and egalitarian constitutional models that had been adopted in Western countries.

After World War Two, a new, more democratic, American-inspired Constitution – sometimes referred to as 'the Peaceful Constitution' because it enshrined the principles of pacifism and peaceful cooperation with other countries – was introduced in 1947. The Constitution also incorporated a provision requiring due process of law and guaranteed the right to a legal defence for those accused of committing a crime. The adoption of this new Constitution heralded a significant change in the sources shaping the Japanese polity, with American influence dominating in the major political, economic and social reforms that were introduced during the postwar period. Within the criminal justice sphere, the most important changes consisted of a new Code of Criminal Procedure, introduced in 1948, and its accompanying Rules of Criminal Procedure that were brought into force in 1949. (Another important change involved the introduction of a new system of youth justice, which we discuss more fully in Chapter 12.) The effect of these changes was to introduce a number of Anglo-American rights-based precepts into the Japanese criminal process, though the Criminal Code itself was not significantly altered, and in many respects the implementation of the revised procedural rules continued to be influenced by Germanic law.

The outcome of these successive waves of influence is a criminal justice system whose outward form still owes much to its civil law origins, despite the more recent accretion of Anglo-American rights-based principles. In terms of its content, as we shall see, Japanese penal law can often appear authoritarian, even draconian; yet in terms of its application the wide-ranging discretion that is often vested in Japanese criminal justice officials is frequently, albeit selectively, exercised in a manner that can appear remarkably lenient to Western observers. In other words, the gap that exists in all countries between 'the law in the books' and 'the law in action' is more of a yawning chasm in Japan. The reason for this is that the day-to-day functioning of the Japanese criminal justice system is far less influenced by the ostensibly Western-style legal, institutional and procedural *forms* we have been considering, and much more by the persistence of quintessentially Japanese-style values, concepts and their associated social *norms*. It is also shaped by the very different social context in which it operates. Or, as Komiya (1999: 372) has pithily put it, the Japanese legal system is 'Western in guise but Japanese in spirit'. In order to understand the prevailing legal and penal culture in Japan, therefore, it is even more important than usual to probe behind the formal legal structure and investigate the underlying social configurations and the informal norms with which they are associated. It is these to which we must now turn.

Japan is without doubt the most strongly and comprehensively communitarian and least individualistic of all the societies we have been examining. Indeed it could be said to epitomize the more collectivist and authoritarian end of the communitarian spectrum, in the sense that the interests of the group or community to which an individual belongs are widely believed to override the latter's individual rights and entitlements. In this respect the Japanese form of communitarianism offers an interesting contrast to the much more egalitarian and individualistic version to be found in the Nordic social democracies. Japan is also a highly 'relational' society in the sense that the Japanese concept of 'self-identity' is inextricably linked to the expectations of other members of the various social groupings to which an individual belongs, and at the same time is moulded by the reciprocal social obligations that accompany those expectations.

The most important of these Japanese social groupings are also the main agencies of primary socialization to which individuals might expect to belong during different phases of their lives: families, schools, workplace and local communities (see also Moriyama, 1989, 1995). Japanese family relationships are characterized by the unusually high degree of dependency (both physical and emotional) by children on their parents,[9] in return for which children are expected to accept parental authority and conform unquestioningly to their often exacting expectations in matters of home discipline.[10] Japanese schoolchildren are socialized by the 'hidden curriculum' that not only demands respect for school authority and strict conformity with meticulously detailed school regulations, but also fosters a shared responsibility for the poor academic performance and unacceptable social behaviour of other members of their group (see also Masters, 1997: esp. Chapters 7 and 8). Likewise, Japanese companies have also traditionally exerted a strong socializing influence over their employees. In return for providing a range of security benefits that are more usually thought of as being (or even exceeding) the responsibility of the welfare state[11] – such as a job for life, medical assistance, company housing, recreational facilities, retirement benefits and 'a sense of belonging' to a corporate family – Japanese workers are expected to show unstinting loyalty and commitment to the firm, and to abide by the company's many informal social norms. Finally, in the past, local communities also exerted powerful informal social control functions, based on the provision of mutual assistance, the exercise of mutual oversight and the threat of social ostracism ('murahachibu') for non-conformists. Even today, groups of 15–20 households or residential blocks are organized in community associations known as 'chonaikai', which discharge a variety of functions including the dissemination of information from the local council, co-ordinating crime or fire prevention activities and organizing festivals. They also organize sporting and other activities for children and, in this way, continue to exert a strong socializing influence over children within a particular locality.

The exercise of informal social control within each of these social groupings, and others like them, tends to conform to a similar pattern and revolves around the concept (and power) of interdependent relationships. An important aspect of these relationships is the principle of showing respect for one's elders and social superiors. Such relationships are also fostered and maintained through the performance of reciprocal obligations and the granting of rewards to those who comply with their social obligations. Behaviour is regulated in part by a plethora of highly detailed rules and regulations,[12] but also by a more nebulous type of informal conduct norm or social expectation, the Japanese term for which is 'giri'. Komiya (1999: 372) has described this as a Japanese traditional duty or psychological burden that is owed to another individual to whom one might be indebted. The precise content and scale of this duty is highly personal and subjective, since it depends in part on the nature and intensity of the relationship as well as the degree of 'indebtedness'. Nevertheless, the (informal) pressure to comply with the duty is remarkably strong because it helps to reinforce one's membership of the group or relationships to which one belongs, and with it the sense of security that such relationships impart. Conversely, a failure to act in accordance with the appropriate norms and social expectations is likely to induce a sense of shame, and demands an apology in order to reaffirm one's commitment to the group or relationship and ensure one's reintegration within it.

This distinctive form of informal social control is for the most part highly effective (if somewhat oppressive-sounding to most Western ears). It thus helps to explain Japan's remarkably low crime rate since the Japanese are, constantly and from a very early age, socialized to exercise self-control, which makes it much more likely that most will tend unthinkingly to comply with the law. But, as we will now try to demonstrate, the existence of such an effective form of social control also helps to explain much more besides, including Japanese attitudes towards the law and the formal legal system; their attitudes towards other norma-tive concepts such as 'right', 'wrong' and 'justice'; their philosophy of punishment; and also the reasons why the formal criminal justice system operates in the way that it does.

At least within the sphere of the kind of close-knit personal relationships we have been considering, one Japanese commentator has pointed out that 'there is a strong expectation that a dispute should not and will not arise; even when one does occur, it is to be solved by mutual understanding' (Kawashima, 1963: 44). Within this context, dispute resolution is much more likely to come from within the group and is far less likely to involve an appeal to judicial intervention based on the application of universal external norms. Moreover, the inclination to avoid confrontation and to eschew external intervention when it does occur extends not only to hierarchical relationships, but also to those involving mem-bers who are equal in social status. In cases such as these, disputes are usually resolved once again by the informal intervention of a third party go-between who is also a member of the same social group rather than an outsider. Kawashima (1963: 51) points out that, in discharging this role, 'the go-between should not make any clear-cut decision on who is right or wrong or inquire into the existence and scope of the rights of the parties'. Perhaps this preference for informal consensual modes of dispute-settlement, at least within the sphere of close reciprocal relationships, helps in part to explain the relatively small number of practising lawyers in relation to the size of the Japanese population as a whole, compared with other countries.[13]

Not all relationships are of this close and reciprocal kind, however, and in their dealings with strangers or other non-members of the groups to which they belong, Japanese people may feel less inhibited about defending their interests and assert-ing their entitlements (Komiya, 1999: 374). Indeed, they may even resort to litiga-tion in defence of their rights and interests,[14] since the same informal rules of conduct no longer apply in such settings. It is in this sense that the Japanese could be said to have a 'dual' legal culture, with two very different types of norms. One, based on the Japanese notion of *giri*, or traditional duty, helps to regulate rela-tionships *within* the social groupings to which an individual belongs. The other, which approximates more closely to the Western concept of legal rights and responsibilities, may more readily be invoked when dealing with strangers.

This same dualism also extends to other normative concepts. The Japanese attitude towards rules, for example, contrasts sharply with prevailing Western attitudes. In the West, rules are universalistic in application, relatively few in number and are frequently permissive in the sense that they enable independent individuals to determine the basis on which they mutually agree to interact with one another. In Japan, however, although there are some universalistic rules, for example those laid down in the criminal codes, there is a far greater number of highly detailed context-specific norms and expectations that are particularistic or personalistic in content. They are also repressive in their effects both because they are highly prescriptive and also because meticulous compliance is expected on the part of those subject to them. Consequently, Japanese people are inclined to worry constantly that they may not be observing the rules, and will thereby expose themselves to shame-inducing criticism or disdain by others.

Likewise, Japanese notions of 'right' and 'wrong', and even the concept of justice itself, are much more context-specific and far less universalistic than in the West, since the important thing is to do what is right *in the circumstances relating to this particular actor* rather than according to some absolute standard. This may help to explain the very high levels of discretion conferred on Japanese criminal justice officials and also the apparent leniency to which this gives rise, both of which, as we shall see, are among the most characteristic features of the Japanese criminal justice system. It may also help to explain why universalistic penological precepts such as those associated with the concept of 'just deserts' and the justice model of corrections have had very little impact on Japanese attitudes towards the philosophy of punishment, to which we now turn.

As we have seen, Japan's low crime rate is mainly attributable to the preventive effects of its informal social control mechanisms whereby most are successfully socialized into complying with the law without having to resort to punitive sanctions on anything like the scale that is required in most other industrialized countries. Not surprisingly, therefore, the philosophy of punishment in Japan has been strongly characterized by a pronounced emphasis on the resocialization of offenders, as in other states with a strong corporatist and communitarian mentality, such as Germany. In keeping with the idea that the most effective socialization agents are the social groupings to which most individuals belong, moreover, Japanese criminal justice agencies are prepared to show remarkable leniency[15] towards those who behave in a socially approved manner following their offence. Provided offenders admit their wrong-doing, apologize for it and show willingness to make amends for what they have done, the formal response on the part of almost all criminal justice agencies can appear very lenient to Western observers.

This seemingly very lenient approach is consistent with a Japanese saying 'We hate crime but not criminals' which, as Johnson (1996: 21) points out, has a double meaning. First, offenders are liable to be judged and dealt with according to their *moral* as well as their legal responsibility, in marked contrast with the Western tendency to concentrate almost exclusively on the latter element. Second, the Japanese tend to view offenders[16] as fellow countrymen who therefore share an innate capacity for self-correction and the future resumption of harmonious relationships with others. Accordingly, they are deemed to deserve to be read-mitted into society once they have demonstrated this capacity by apologizing and making restitution for what they have done. In reality, however, the Japan-ese approach is not as uniformly benevolent as it is sometimes made out to be. For, as we shall see, both the law and also the everyday practice of Japanese criminal justice agencies are strongly geared towards ensuring that suspected offenders do indeed comply with these expectations, with scant regard for some of the due process safeguards that are taken for granted in the West.

Those who do not respond in a socially approved manner, or who repeatedly offend without showing any remorse, present much more of a problem for the authorities. This is particularly true in cases where (as is likely) persistent behav-iour of this kind results in their exclusion from the small-scale social groupings to which they may previously have belonged.[17] Thus, although the Japanese penal system remains formally committed to the principle of resocialization, with the aim of correcting the offender's criminal tendencies and securing their readmission into the community, in reality the reintegrative capacity of Japanese society is severely limited in such cases. Consequently, offenders who deliber-ately and persistently flout the expected norms and standards of the community are apt to be dealt with by means of overtly repressive measures and exclusion-ary punishments, the principal aim of which appears to be to bludgeon them into conformity or punish them for their continued intransigence.

Turning now to the operation of the Japanese criminal justice system, this is also strongly influenced by the distinctive social context in which it operates, despite its superficial resemblance to Western systems. For example, the police in Japan – uniquely in the industrialized world – maintain a community-based system of policing that is centred upon local mini-police stations known as 'Koban'[18]. Police officers also tend to patrol on foot, and are required to visit all local residents in their area once or twice each year, dispensing information and advice,[19] and, of course, obtaining information. This relatively 'intimate' style of policing, with its comparatively close police–community relations, constant per-sonal surveillance and detailed local knowledge has been credited in the past with clear-up rates that were far higher than those achieved in the West. Thus, as recently as 1985, the clear-up rate for penal code offences excluding those involving traffic accidents was as high as 64 per cent. Since then it has declined rapidly, however, reaching a record low of 19.8 per cent in 2001 (Japanese Ministry of Justice, 2003: Appendix 1–3).[20]

A second important feature is that the police in Japan operate within the con-text of an uncompromisingly 'enabling' legal framework that is strongly geared to 'crime control' values – particularly aimed at the inducement of confessions – at the expense of 'due process' safeguards (Miyazawa, 1992). 'Crime control' values favour the repression of crime by giving the police and other state authorities wide discretionary powers aimed at maximizing the prospects of detection; whereas 'due process' prioritizes the protection of innocent suspects and defendants from being wrongly convicted or otherwise unjustly treated.[21] Miyazawa's ethnographic study (see also Terrill, 1999: 370) of a Japanese police station disclosed that the standard method of investigating an offence was to question a suspect until a confession was received, and only then to seek corroborating evidence if necessary. This approach may not sound all that different from police investigation methods in other countries, but in Japan it is greatly facilitated by the generally very relaxed rules relating to detention for questioning. Thus, although the police are obliged in most cases to refer a case to the public prosecutor within forty-eight hours of a detained suspect's arrest, the prosecutor may authorize detention for a further twenty-four hours. Moreover, if additional time is thought to be required, this may be granted by a court for a further ten days, which can be further extended on application by the prosecutor, making it possible to detain a suspect for a total of twenty-three days before a decision on prosecution has to be made.[22] In 1996, the detention period of almost half (46 per cent) of all pre-trial detainees was extended in this way (National Police Agency, n.d.). Moreover, pre-trial detention is the norm rather than the exception.[23] Suspects who are detained before trial may be held either in prison or in a police jail, which is known as 'Daiyo-Kangoku' or 'substitute prison'. The latter are far more numerous, and are preferred by the police (on grounds of convenience), but have provoked complaints by the Japanese Federation of Bar Associations (1990) that the denial of access to a lawyer[24] and conditions in which they are interrogated violate the human rights of detainees and may often result in forced confessions.[25] Perhaps not surprisingly, the majority of Japanese defendants plead guilty (approximately 90 per cent of those tried in the district courts), and the acquittal rate following a trial is truly minuscule.[26]

Only a minority of cases get to court, however, as we shall see. In the case of certain minor offences (including theft, fraud and handling of stolen property), the police have discretion to terminate the case without referring it to the prosecution provided the damage is settled and the victim does not insist on punishment. Moreover, this discretionary power to divert offences that have been informally resolved away from the criminal justice system is even more powerfully entrenched within the Japanese prosecution service and is one of the principal factors that has contributed to the sparing use of imprisonment in Japan during the postwar years.

Article 248 of the 1948 Code of Criminal Procedure authorizes public prosecutors to grant a 'suspension of prosecution' in any case in which prosecution is deemed to be unnecessary even though there is enough evidence to prove the suspect's guilt. The factors that have to be taken into account in reaching this decision include the character and circumstances of the offender, the gravity of the offence,[27] the circumstances under which the offence was committed and the conditions subsequent to the offence. Clifford (1976: 69) has suggested that one consequence of this broad discretion has been to turn public prosecutors in effect into 'interpreter(s) of public morality', since it is they who decide who should be made an example of, and who shall be given another chance. In practice this has been one of the principal legal mechanisms enabling the formal legal rules to be 'reconciled' with the informal social control context in which they operate in Japan. It thus enables the public prosecutor to have regard to events that may have happened following the offence, including the extent to which the offender shows regret for the offence, the making of restitution to the victim or other amends, and any action to prevent future offences that may have been taken by the offender's family. In 2001, 36.4 per cent of all cases processed by public prosecutors' offices were dealt with by means of suspension of prosecution, and the prosecution rate for adult Penal Code Offenders (excluding traffic cases) was 37.5 per cent (Japanese Ministry of Justice, 2003: App. 2–3).

When prosecution does take place, the same discretion to exercise leniency in deciding how an offender should be dealt with extends also to Japanese judges. This in itself is not surprising from a Western viewpoint, as wide judicial discretion in sentencing is common in Western countries also. However, what is perhaps most notable is that Japanese judges appear just as willing as public prosecutors to avail themselves vigorously of this power – even where the police and prosecutors have not – at least in the case of offenders for whom they deem formal punishment to be unnecessary. Article 25 of the Penal Code authorizes judges to suspend a prison sentence[28] under 'extenuating circumstances'. Over the years the proportion of offenders[29] who are dealt with by means of a suspended sentence has grown from 45.9 per cent of all sentenced offenders in 1951 (Shikita and Tsuchiya, 1992: 165)[30] to 61.2 per cent in 2001 (Japanese Ministry of Justice, 2003: Table 2-3-2-2). If those who are placed under probationary supervision are added to this total[31] the proportion is 66.4 per cent. Nor is it simply minor offenders who qualify for suspended execution of sentences. The discretion to suspend a sentence is not available for offenders where a prison term in excess of three years is imposed, or for certain categories of recidivist offenders.[32] However, this does not prevent the imposition of suspended sentences on many who are guilty of serious offences but who lack such a sentencing record. In recent years suspended sentences have been imposed on 18 per cent of those convicted of murder,[33] 53 per cent of those committed of rape and other sexual offences and 58 per cent of those convicted of causing non-negligent bodily injury.[34] Another important factor that has contributed to the low rate of imprisonment relates to the *length of prison sentences* that are imposed on offenders who do not qualify for suspension of execution. In 2001, the great majority of those imprisoned (80 per cent) received sentences (including suspended sentences) of three years or less, compared with 2.4 per cent of sentences of five years or more.[35]

Thus, Japan's remarkably low rate of imprisonment clearly owes much to the continuing willingness on the part of prosecutors and judges (and to a lesser extent the police also)[36] to withhold the full force of the penal law from those whose behaviour and circumstances indicate that they remain committed to the values of the community. Provided they show a willingness to conform to society's expectations as to the way they should behave in future there is a good chance that they will escape the imposition of exclusionary (and potentially counter-productive) sanctions such as imprisonment. By incorporating extensive discretionary powers for public prosecutors and judges in particular, the Japanese have been able to adapt the Western-style legal framework they adopted to their own particularistic sense of justice. In stark contrast with Western universalistic principles of abstract justice, the Japanese approach, as we have seen, insists on taking into account the particular personal circumstances and moral attributes of each offender, and only applying the formal sanctions that are authorized by the law when this is seen as unavoidable. Usually this is because the offender is felt to be beyond the reach of the informal social control mechanisms that continue to regulate the lives of most Japanese so effectively.

So far we have concentrated mainly on the *cultural* factors that help to promote such ostensible leniency on the part of Japanese prosecutors and judges, but it would be a mistake to overlook or belittle the *structural* factors that help to powerfully reinforce this approach. It is particularly important to have regard for such factors in the context of an authoritarian communitarian polity such as Japan. For, as Peters (1992: 284) has rightly pointed out, to *over*-emphasize the cultural aspects runs the risk of neglecting the important dimension of power, and its very uneven distribution within the Japanese state.

Japanese prosecutors and Japanese judges are members of a relatively small, highly centralized, intensely bureaucratized and immensely powerful penal elite. Partly because Japan has continued to rely on private sector employers to discharge many of the functions (notably those relating to social welfare and health care[37]) that in the West were considered the responsibility of central governments, Japan's national bureaucracy has remained relatively small in comparison with other industrial nations. Unlike the USA (but in common with most European countries), Japanese public prosecutors and judges are neither elected nor politically appointed, but are careerists who have to undergo a series of highly competitive national examinations combined with rigorous training. It would be difficult to exaggerate the power and influence of Japanese public prosecutors in particular. They not only dominate the pre-trial criminal process in Japan, as we have seen, by virtue of their *de facto* power to determine whether a defendant should face formal criminal proceedings. But – in the case of defendants who are brought to trial – the sentence (if any) that they receive is also likely to be directly influenced by recommendations made by the prosecution.[38] Moreover, public prosecutors have also been described (Clifford, 1976: 72) as forming a powerful elite within the Japanese Ministry of Justice ('*Homu-sho*') from which is drawn the permanent civil service head of the ministry, the director of the corrections bureau (responsible for prison administration), and also the director of the rehabilitation bureau (responsible, *inter alia* for probation and parole).[39]

As well as being highly bureaucratic, Japan's criminal justice and correctional apparatus is also strongly centralized. For example, all Japan's probation and parole activities are handled on a nationwide basis within a single Rehabilitation Bureau; prison administration is handled by the Corrections Bureau; and both come under the jurisdiction of the Ministry of Justice. For well over a hundred years the trend within the correctional sphere has been towards the unification and centralization of administrative responsibility. Even though there is a degree of devolution at regional and local levels, Japanese criminal justice and penal administration nevertheless remains highly centralized in another, even more important, sense: namely the virtual absence of a system of institutional or procedural checks and balances. Moreover, this state of affairs is also replicated in the organization and distribution of political power within the state itself.

Not only are Japan's criminal justice and correctional agencies organized along highly bureaucratic lines, the same could also be said of the entire pre-trial investigation and decision-making process (Peters, 1992: 270). What is striking about the Japanese criminal process is the absence of what Peters refers to as a 'juridical balance of powers' between different officials including police, prosecution authorities, judicial officials and defence counsel, which in most other countries together constitute a system of procedural checks and balances. Instead, the Japanese criminal process is characterized by a bureaucratic division of labour in which the investigating prosecutor is the official who is exclusively in charge of the pre-trial process, working, in secret, to determine whether there is evidence of the accused's guilt.

Peters has suggested (1992: 287) that one reason for the Japanese preference for a bureaucratic rather than a juridical division of labour among the different criminal justice agencies may be because the modern administration of justice in Japan has remained an exclusive, centralized state function, responsibility for which is discharged by a ruling elite that is made up of state bureaucrats, and from which private lawyers are systematically excluded. To some extent this may reflect the concentration of political power in the hands of Japanese state bureaucrats whereas in other countries, for example the Netherlands, political power (including the administration of justice) was often wielded by independent local magistrates and professional lawyers. Against this background, Peters suggests, the extent to which state bureaucrats exert supreme dominance over the criminal process in Japan may be more readily understood, and this may also help to explain the relative impotence of Japanese defence lawyers and, consequently, their apparent inability to influence the proceedings by upholding due process safeguards.

Indeed, the authoritarian communitarianism of Japan can be seen as at least a partial exception to our 'radical pluralist' frame of analysis since political power in Japan is largely monopolized instead of being pluralized as in most of the other countries we have been examining. In Japan, political power is vested largely in the hands of a relatively small, centralized, state elite, comprising members of the ruling Liberal Democratic Party (which has been in government continuously, save for one year, since World War Two)[40] and unelected officials such as public prosecutors and judges. Indeed, until recently, both the policy-making process and the responsibility for the day-to-day running of government departments was in practice vested in a small cadre of powerful bureaucrats as opposed to elected politicians.[41] This monopolization of power may be less extreme than it formerly was in Communist bloc countries such as East Germany (which we discussed in the section on Germany). In the 'command economies' of Communist countries there was little or no privately-owned industry and the whole economy was under the formal or informal control of the state and the Communist Party *Nomenklatura*. In Japan economic power is divided between different (but often large and formidable) blocs of privately-owned industry with important links to political factions, including competing factions within the ruling party. The fact that the LDP's rule is subject to the constraints of democratic election may also attenuate its monopoly of power to some degree. Nevertheless, power relations in Japan are far from the 'pluralism' which characterizes Western democracies.

We have already mentioned (in Chapters 1, 7, 8 and 10) Savelsberg's (1999) hypothesis that countries which are highly bureaucratized and subject to centralized power structures may be subject to hectic shifts in penality. Although this was certainly the case with East Germany (see Chapter 7), it is equally certainly not true of Japan. Indeed, the Japanese example supports the suggestion we made in Chapter 8 that where there is a stable penal policy at the political centre, a highly centralized and bureaucratic state is likely to experience very stable levels of punishment and imprisonment, possibly over a prolonged period of time.

One explanation for this sharp contrast in the degree of dynamism that is exhibited by the evolution of penality in Japan and East Germany may be that the political elite in East Germany was seeking to impose its will on a reluctant and, at times, defiant populace, and consequently found it extremely difficult to secure lasting public legitimacy. In sharp contrast, the relative homogeneity of Japanese society – culturally, ethnically and also socially – may have made it easier for certain elements of the Japanese state bureaucracy[42] to project themselves as the embodiment of the 'moral community'. In which case, it is perhaps not so surprising that it appears acceptable for its criminal justice officials – police, prosecutors and judges – to concern themselves with the moral attitudes and attributes, as well as the legal responsibilities, of private individuals. In general, the Japanese populace appears to have retained a higher level of deference towards traditional institutions (including the police, public prosecutors and courts) and values than in most other countries, even when the comparison is restricted to those within the 'corporatist' sphere. Consequently, it is perhaps not surprising that Japan has so far shown correspondingly greater level of resistance towards the 'politics of personalism' in which politicians elsewhere have sought to appeal 'over the heads' of institutional bureaucracies and the state personnel – civil servants and criminal justice practitioners – who work within them.

Having reflected on the general nature of Japan's highly distinctive penality, we are able to turn now to the question whether Japan is presently experiencing, or may possibly be about to experience, a penal crisis. At first glance Japan does not appear to have a penal crisis – at any rate not in the conventional sense – since, at least in recent years it appears to have avoided many of the classic 'symptoms' in the form of excessively high prison population, overcrowding, prison riots, assault rates, and prison escapes. However, there are signs that Japan's long period of relative immunity from such crisis-related symptoms may be drawing to a close. Moreover, as we shall see, Japan's prison system has long suffered from other serious problems, which show no signs of abating, and which, collectively, could be considered symptomatic of an incipient penal crisis, albeit one that is rather different in kind from that experienced by most of the other countries we have been considering.

For many years, the rate of imprisonment in Japan has been far lower than that associated with most other industrialized nations, and has indeed declined steadily during much of the postwar period. It declined from 198.3 per 100,000 in 1950 to 63.7 in 1970,[43] and reached a low of 36.1 per 100,000 in 1992. In terms of absolute numbers also, the Japanese prison population trend has also been consistently downwards for most of the postwar period, falling from 103,170 in 1950 to 44,876 in 1992. Since then, however, the Japanese prison population has been increasing steadily, rising by 29 per cent between 1995 and 2000 (Barclay and Tavares, 2002: Table 3) and reached a total of 67,255 by mid-2002 (Walmsley, 2003b). The recent increase in the size of the prison population has, not surprisingly, also had an impact on Japan's rate of imprisonment, which rose particularly steeply to 53 per 100,000 in 2002 (from 42 in 1999 [Walmsley, 2000, 2003b]). The growth in the prison population is also beginning to have an impact on the rate of occupancy, since the overall capacity of Japan's prison system[44] has remained relatively stable in recent years, and was 65,264 at the end of 2002 (International Centre for Prison Studies, 2004). In December 1998 the total occupancy rate was reported as 82.9 per cent, but because there is less capacity for convicted prisoners than for unconvicted inmates, the occupancy rate for the former was 89.1 per cent. Recent newspaper reports record that, following the steady increase in prison numbers, the capacity for convicted inmates was exceeded by 3.6 per cent in the year 2000, the first overflow of prisoners since 1972 (*Mainichi Shimbun,* 16 November 2001).[45] The problem of overcrowding is particularly acute in respect of Japan's women's prisons, where the recorded occupancy rate was 119 per cent in 2000 (APCCA 2001).

Prison conditions in Japan are poor by international standards – many prisons are old and in need of reconstruction and refurbishment – and prison life for inmates is harsh and often inhumane.[46] Indeed, many aspects of the prison regime in particular have been castigated by both domestic critics (Japan Federation of Bar Associations, 1992; Kaido, 2001) and international observers (e.g. Human Rights Watch, 1995; Stern, 1998: 95ff.) alike as an affront to human rights and human decency. One of the most striking aspects of Japanese prison life, at least in the eyes of Western observers, is the extent to which it appears to be repressively regimented by a highly detailed and restrictive set of prison rules, covering virtually every aspect of a prisoner's daily life. They include severe restrictions[47] on permitted movement within cells – effectively confining prisoners to a prescribed seating position at all times with the exception of bedtime and one fifty minute period after lunch – and a version of the 'silent system' that prohibits conversation during work time, inspection time and bedtime and also in prohibited areas such as dressing rooms, bathrooms and offices. When viewed in a Japanese context, however, this may simply represent an even more extreme manifestation of Japan's support for an authoritarian form of communitarianism that, as we have seen, is by no means confined to the prison population. Certainly among the Japanese public at large, there appears to be strong support for the application of exclusionary forms of punishment including harsh prison regimes and even, in extreme cases, the death penalty,[48] at least in respect of persistent and unrepentant law-breakers. Having rejected the constraints imposed by an informal, inclusionary, 'familialist'[49] framework of social control, such offenders are effectively 'disowned' by their own social groupings and criminal justice agencies alike. Consequently, little compunction is felt when they are exposed to harsh exclusionary social control measures. This is another manifestation of the rather extreme Japanese form of bifurcation to which we referred earlier.

One aspect of the Japanese prison system that frequently attracts incredulous comment from outsiders – as well as being a source of evident pride to Japanese prison authorities – is its apparent orderliness, which is reflected in the extraordinarily low recorded incidence of disruptive incidents. Thus, prison riots, which are relatively commonplace in many Western prison systems, are virtually unheard of in Japan. The level of other security-related incidents also appears to be remarkably low.[50] There are very few recorded escapes from Japanese prisons,[51] in comparison with other countries. And yet Japan's prison population contains a relatively high proportion of recidivists, as many as one-fifth of whom have previously been admitted to prison on at least four previous occasions (Ministry of Justice, 2003: 134),[52] and many of whom are members of the 'yakuza'[53] or Japanese Mafia.[54] Inmates such as these might be thought to pose particularly acute control problems for the prison authorities on the grounds that they are likely to be among the most resistant to the social values and informal norms that inhibit most Japanese from engaging in criminal conduct. The obvious question to which such reflections give rise is how such a high level of orderliness is maintained within the Japanese prison system. Part of the explanation, as we will now explain, lies in the application of a range of social control techniques that mirror – albeit in an even more intensive and often oppressive form – those operating *outside* the prison walls.

Among the many factors that contribute to the maintenance of control by the Japanese prison authorities some commentators (e.g. Clifford, 1976: 93; Johnson, 1996: 136, 1998: 359; see also Shikita, 1972: 19) have drawn attention to the interpersonal relationships between inmates and prison staff, which are portrayed as being largely deferential and submissive on the part of the former[55] and paternalistic or even benevolent on the part of the latter. Such accounts are apt to stress factors encouraging prison staff to feel concerned about inmates' interests and long-term welfare, and to assist inmates in obtaining future employment while not betraying their prison experience.

Those who adopt a more critical standpoint (e.g. Human Rights Watch, 1995; Japan Federation of Bar Associations 1992; Stern, 1998) have tended to place greater emphasis on the normative and structural contexts in which these relationships are conducted. They include an insistence by the authorities on the strict observance by inmates of the rigid and incredibly detailed prison rules to which we have already referred, which is reinforced by the imposition of a quasi-militaristic form of discipline that extends even to control over inmates' bodily movements.[56] The scope for associating with (and, in the case of recalcitrant inmates, even the scope for communicating with) other inmates is also strictly controlled by the authorities. Virtually all inmates (including those given life terms) are sentenced to imprisonment with forced labour,[57] and most of these are required to undertake intensive industrial work for a standard forty-hour week within workshops that are attached to each prison. As for the *yakuza*, it is organized along similar lines to the rest of Japanese society and its members are expected to abide by strict codes of conduct. Indeed, the parallel even extends to the kinds of reciprocal obligations that regulate relationships between *yakuza* bosses and their subordinates. Somewhat ironically, therefore, it may also be capable of discharging an informal social control function over its members even though most of them may have been 'disowned' by more mainstream informal social control agencies. Perhaps it is not surprising that, within the Japanese prison system, senior members of the *yakuza* who are prepared to be compliant – as most are, in order to expedite their release date – are dispersed among the workshops and cell-units and are even relied upon to exert control over other inmates.[58]

Japanese prisons also operate a rigid four-category grade system of incentives that rewards compliance with the rules, but only after a set period of time has been served on each stage. Contact with the outside world is severely restricted, particularly for those on grade 4, which is the lowest grade, and both incoming and outgoing mail is routinely censored. Parole is also used as an incentive for good behaviour on the part of inmates,[59] particularly since the application to the parole board for parole has to be initiated by prison wardens rather than the inmates themselves.

The greatest cause for concern in the eyes of its critics relates to the punitive treatment that is meted out by Japan's prison authorities to those who offend against the prison rules, since this is felt to be arbitrary, frequently abusive and, on occasion, to constitute inhumane treatment of inmates (Amnesty International, 1998; Japan Federation of Bar Associations, 1998). The number of inmates who are punished each year is said to be high (Stern, 1998: 99), and in 2001 penalties for rule violations were imposed on inmates in 34,565 cases.[60] Domestic critics (for example, Kaido, 2001: 434) have complained that the catalogue of disciplinary offences and their punishments is not set out in law or official regulations, and that, although they are outlined instead in the *Handbook of Life in Prison*, the latter is not published.[61] Other critics, such as the Japanese Federation of Bar Associations, have also complained that making a protest to a prison officer may be taken as a punishable offence *per se*, regardless of reason, and that even asking guards the reason for instructions or orders may be taken as a protest.

The most commonly administered penalty for disciplinary infractions is 'minor solitary confinement' ('*keiheikin*'), which may last for a period of up to two months (Amnesty International, 1998). During this period all contact and communication is severed – except between prisoner and guards, and only then when the latter deem it essential – and inmates are not permitted to take exercise or bathe. Inmates who are confined in this way are required to remain motionless in a kneeling or cross-legged position in the middle of a single cell (instead of the communal cell holding 6–8 prisoners, in which most inmates are kept) for hours on end (reportedly between 7.00 a.m. and 5.00 p.m.). They may sometimes be required to stare continuously at a single place on the cell wall, where a poster exhorting the inmate to reflect may have been hung.

Each prison also contains blocks of single cells for 'strict solitary confinement' or solitary confinement as treatment ('*gensei dokkyo*'), where certain categories of prisoners – including those held on death row, those who are considered to be unsuited to living and working with others and those who are felt to be disruptive – are detained for twenty-four hours a day, sometimes for very prolonged periods of time.[62] Critics complain that decisions as to who is subjected to this treatment, and for how long, are left entirely to the discretion of the prison warden (Japan Federation of Bar Associations, 1998). When detained in this way inmates are forced to maintain a particular sitting posture on pain of punishment. Although the exact number of inmates who are subject to strict solitary confinement is not made public, Kaido (2001: 436) suggests that about 10 per cent of all convicted prisoners may be detained in this way.

An even more severe form of treatment that is possibly open to still greater abuse takes the form of confinement in a special 'protection cell' ('*hogobo*'), which is intended for those who are deemed to show aggravated signs of instability or vulnerability. Such cells are said to be a common feature of all centres of detention in Japan (Amnesty International, 1998), and are subject to twenty-four hour video monitoring. Prisoners who are held in protection cells are strip-searched on entry, and are often bound with leather or metal restraints that immobilize the hands at all times, even when eating and carrying out other bodily functions.[63] According to the Japanese Ministry of Justice, protection cells are intended for the following categories of prisoners only: those who are suspected of trying to escape, acting violently, or who threaten harm to themselves or others; those who repeatedly exhibit abnormal behaviour, for example resulting in the dirtying of their cells or damage to property; those who persist in making a noise and who refuse to obey orders to stop; and those whom it is deemed inappropriate to hold in a normal cell.

Critics, such as Amnesty International, are concerned about the vagueness of such criteria, which appear to allow considerable scope for abuse. They also suspect that 'protection cells' are used – unlawfully – as a form of punishment, but this is impossible to verify since, together with other human rights organizations, Amnesty International has always been denied access to prisoners, and has even been unable to inspect the protection cells themselves. This refusal to grant access is symptomatic of the curtain of secrecy that cloaks every aspect of Japanese prison administration, fuelling suspicions that it provides a convenient screen for further human rights violations.

The treatment that is meted out to particular categories of prisoners – notably those on death row, women prisoners and foreign inmates – has also given rise to acute concern on the part of both domestic and international critics alike. Japan's retention of the death penalty (although not mandatory for any offence) is highly controversial *per se*, and seems to be at odds with its overall support for inclusionary social control measures. However, this and other exclusionary forms of punishment are, as we have suggested, not reserved solely for those who have committed particularly heinous offences, but are also applied to those deemed to be beyond the influence of such inclusionary mechanisms. Three people were executed and fifteen sentences of death were imposed (including five on members of the religious cult formerly known as '*Aum Shinriyko*') in 2000 (Amnesty International, 2001),[64] just over half of whom had had their sentences confirmed by the Supreme Court. The conditions in which death row prisoners are held are particularly restrictive since they are all subject to solitary confinement, thereby depriving them of human contact with inmates, and are entitled to visits and correspondence only from members of their immediate family and, in the case of those who are petitioning for retrials, their attorney. Such prisoners are generally notified of their impending execution only one hour before it takes place, and even their families may not be informed until after the execution has taken place (Kaido, 2001: 437).

There were 3,325 female prisoners in Japan in mid-2002 (APCCA 2002: Table 1) – a similar proportion (5 per cent) to that found in most countries – but the 44 per cent increase in the number of women prisoners over the past six years far outstrips that of men. Almost half of all Japanese female prisoners are admitted for offences relating to the use of stimulant drugs. Although there are six prisons that are specially designated for female prisoners, many are held in special units within the large detention centres, in police jails ('*daiyo-kangoku*') or smaller detention centres. Many allegations of sexual violence are reported, particularly in these latter institutions, where the guards are male. Another complaint relates to the aim of treatment for female prisoners, which has been characterized as one of 'genderization'[65] since the role of women's prisons is to enable women to 'acquire stability of emotion, to learn the skills and manners of housekeeping, to become cultured, to acquire a hobby, to pay attention to health care and to maintain the relationship with her guarantor' (Standing Order of the Director of Corrections Bureau, 1996, cited by Kaido, 2001: 440).[66]

The treatment of foreign inmates is also highly problematic since many of these, unsurprisingly, find it extremely difficult to adapt to 'Japanese-style treatment', quite apart from the language problems they may experience. The number of foreign inmates has also increased rapidly in recent years. Thus, there were approximately 3,980 such inmates at the end of 2000,[67] compared with 1,909 at the end of 1989 (Judicial System and Research Department, 1998, cited in Kaido, 2001: 441). Although some foreign inmates (those who have arrived in Japan recently and who do not speak the language) are assigned to a special category and receive different treatment from Japanese prisoners, they still suffer acute restrictions with regard to visits and communications with the outside world. Perhaps it is no coincidence that many of the complaints received by international non-governmental organizations such as Amnesty International and Human Rights Watch relate to such inmates.

The absence of adequate and effective grievance procedures has also fuelled criticism of Japan's prison system which, unlike most of those studied in this book, lacks any external monitoring system – such as a prison inspectorate, review boards, ombudsman or visitation committees – that is independent of the prison administration authorities. There are administrative and judicial complaints procedures that are nominally available to Japanese prison inmates, but most of the former are open to abuse or manipulation by the prison authorities, while the latter are largely ineffective. Among the administrative complaint mechanisms, aggrieved inmates are supposed to be entitled to an interview with a prison warden, though in practice the interview is likely to be conducted by a guard who is responsible for the day-to-day treatment of inmates (and who may even be the object of the complaint). A second possibility is to petition the prison inspector who visits each prison once every two years. Alternatively, an inmate may petition the Minister of Justice. However, both these mechanisms are in practice routinely subject to censorship, and success rates are extremely low. Moreover, as we have seen, there is a high probability that the making of a complaint may be seen as an act of insubordination that is apt to be met with retaliatory action on the part of the prison authorities.

Judicial grievance procedures include administrative lawsuits and also civil lawsuits brought against the state seeking damages in respect of allegations of unlawful treatment, but these are not free from problems either (Kaido, 2001: 430). One of the biggest difficulties is the absence of a state-funded legal aid scheme, which severely restricts the availability of judicial remedies. Even if a lawyer is available, however, correspondence is liable to be censored, and prison guards may be present even during meetings between a prisoner and his or her attorney. Moreover, the grounds for succeeding with an administrative lawsuit are extremely difficult to establish. The number of civil actions against the authorities has been increasing in recent years, however, as has the proportion of cases in which the complainant is successful, though the courts continue broadly to recognize the very wide discretionary powers that are exercised by prison staff in their treatment of inmates, so success is by no means assured.

Even after due allowance is made for the highly distinctive social context in which it operates, Japan's prison system epitomizes a particularly extreme variant of Goffman's (1961) concept of the 'total institution' since virtually all aspects of an inmate's life are regulated in minute detail. But perhaps this is a predictable response on the part of an authoritarian communitarian polity for those who refuse to abide by its prescribed ethos and social *mores*. In most other types of societies, a penal system of the kind we have been describing would almost certainly be subject to a massive and destabilizing crisis of legitimacy. However, this is clearly not the case in Japan. There are legitimation problems in Japan also; but for the most part they are restricted to particular constituencies and do not appear to resonate widely with the Japanese populace as a whole. Some prison inmates, as we have seen, clearly do not accept the legitimacy of the current prison regime, and do their best to challenge it, mostly by exploiting the few legitimate channels that are available. However, the combination of a highly repressive system for maintaining control, a virtually impenetrable cloak of secrecy surrounding the prison system, and the virtual absence of a culture of protest on the part of prison inmates all serve to minimize the scope for unorthodox expressions of dissent.

The Japanese prison system also engenders legitimation problems on the part of prison staff, for whom the practical conditions of employment are said to be appalling (Kaido, 2001: 429). In addition, all staff are required to be interviewed twice a year to ensure their continued suitability for the various responsibilities they have to discharge. Moreover, staff are also held responsible in the event of prisoner escapes or other scandals,[68] which may result in staff relocations, often at very short notice. Consequently, staff morale is reported to be low, and Kaido has suggested that the rate of suicides among prison staff may be even higher than that of inmates.[69] However, prison staff[70] are not allowed to belong to trade unions, and it may be this fact, rather than an absence of staff grievances, that explains the relative absence of the kind of industrial relations problems that are experienced in other penal jurisdictions with comparable prison staff legitimation problems.

Finally, as we have seen, the Japanese penal system is widely perceived by international human rights organizations to lack legitimacy and, indeed, has been frequently condemned for systematically violating the human rights of Japanese prison inmates in particular. With the exception of a few domestic critics – notably the Japan Federation of Bar Associations – who have campaigned tirelessly over such issues, however, these concerns are not shared by the bulk of the Japanese populace, politicians[71] or (with few exceptions) the media.

Within the Japanese context, such compliant attitudes towards the penal system are perhaps not surprising. And no radical change seems likely, at least for as long as the relatively limited use that is made of the Japanese penal system continues to be perceived as contributing to Japan's remarkably low crime rate in recent years. Yet there are clear danger signs, as both the crime rate[72] and also the prison population now appear to be rising sharply, and doubts are increasingly being expressed in the media[73] about the effectiveness of Japan's crime control agencies. There are also signs of a quickening of interest on the part of opposition politicians in the problems faced by the prison system, which were recently debated in the Standing Committee for Judicial Affairs. Moreover, there are even signs that the Japanese people may be becoming less tolerant of, and more punitive towards, offenders, than they were in the past. In part this may be because of moral panics induced by particularly notorious offences such as the Sarin gas attack at a Tokyo subway station in March 1995, in which twelve people died.[74] But in part it may also reflect a growing sensitization towards the needs and views of victims of crime in general, which could conceivably result in greater pressure on prosecuting authorities and sentencers alike in the future to take such views into account[75] when dealing with offenders. Thus, although it would be premature to speak of a generalized crisis of legitimacy for the Japanese penal system at the present time, many of the ingredients for such a crisis are already in place. And it remains to be seen whether Japan can continue to maintain its apparent immunity from the symptoms of penal unrest that have afflicted other jurisdictions, particularly if greater demands are placed on the penal system in the future.

Notes

1 Japan's low crime rate in recent decades is well-documented. (See, e.g. Clifford, 1976; Haley, 1991; Johnson, 1996, 1998). The recorded crime rate for Penal Code offences (which includes all the main offence categories but excludes 'special law offences' such as traffic law offences) during the postwar period declined from a rate of 2,000 per 100,000 population in 1948 to below 1,500 per 100,000 in 1957, reaching an all-time low of 1,091 in 1973. Since then, the crime rate has climbed steadily, however, and reached

2,149 in 2001, suggesting that the era of 'low and stable crime rates' may now have ended (Japanese Ministry of Justice, 2003: Appendix 1-1). However, Japanese crime rates remain low in comparison with other major industrialized countries in the west. The comparable crime rates for some other industrialized countries (relating to 2000) are as follows: US 4,125; France 6,421; Federal Republic of Germany 7,625; UK 9,961 (Japanese Ministry of Justice, 2003: Table 1-4-1-1).

2 Western commentators have often lauded this achievement as Japan's social 'miracle', and some have likened it to the 'economic miracle' for which Japan was also once known, during the 1970s and 1980s (Clifford, 1976; see also Komiya, 1999: 369).

3 A year earlier it was 48 per 100,000 (Walmsley, 2003a).

4 Shoguns were military overlords who presided over a feudal hierarchy comprising 'daimyos' who were local feudal overlords, 'samurai' and their followers. Feudalism was not formally abrogated until 1869.

5 Non-Japanese ethnic groups (mostly Korean) account for only 0.6 per cent of the population. By way of comparison, in Finland, Finns account for 93 per cent of the population, Swedes for 6 per cent and the remaining indigenous Roma, Sami (Lapps) and Tatar peoples between them comprise less than 1 per cent of the population.

6 Notwithstanding Japan's relative homogeneity in comparison with most other countries, it would be misleading to imply that there are no social divisions. One sector of Japanese society that has consistently been marginalized and excluded comprises 'the Burakumin', who are descendants of the outcasts of feudal days. Some 3 million Burakumins live in 6,000 ghettos throughout Japan, where they are widely regarded as the social equivalents of India's 'untouchables' (Moriyama, 1995: 54). Other minority groupings, including Korean and Chinese residents, have also been marginalized and excluded by mainstream Japanese society.

7 UNAFEI is a United Nations regional institute that was established in 1962 by an agreement between the United Nations and the Japanese government with the aims of promoting the sound development of criminal justice systems and mutual co-operation in Asia and the Pacific region.

8 For a general overview of the Japanese criminal justice system, see Moriyama (1992); Terrill (1999: 355–412).

9 Conversely, in later life parents tend to become highly dependent on their children who, in the absence of a state-organized system of care for the elderly, are expected to assume responsibility for their elderly relatives.

10 See Komiya (1999: 382). We have drawn heavily on his very helpful account in this next section.

11 Mawby (1990: 118) refers to this as 'Gemeinschaft capitalism'.

12 Komiya (1999: 379) explains that the main reason for having so many rules and regulations is that many groupings to which a person may belong are not based on personal affiliations such as friendships or shared interests, but consist of large-scale social entities comprising people with heterogeneous attributes and interests. The function of the rules is to regulate the behaviour of all members of the group in order to strengthen the links between them.

13 In Japan there is approximately one practising lawyer for every 7,000 people whereas in the UK the figure is one lawyer for every 700 people (Dean, 2002: 5). The ratio of lawyers to inhabitants in the United States is one per 450 (Moriyama, 1992).

14 However, Moriyama (personal communication) has suggested that even when faced with a dispute involving a stranger, decisions about whether to resort to legal action are likely to be influenced by moral judgements as to whether or not the disputant is

thought to be a 'good person'. Conversely, legal action may sometimes be contemplated against non-strangers, for example in the case of a dispute involving a neighbour who is felt to be a 'bad person'.

15 At least with regard to 'ultimate outcomes' and, in particular, the severity of any formal sanction that may be imposed. With regard to the *criminal process*, however, the treatment that is accorded to suspects prior to any 'dispositional' decision is frequently far from lenient, as we shall see.

16 Similar feelings of empathy extend also to criminal justice officials including policemen, prosecutors, judges, prison guards and probation officers, all of whom are likewise viewed as fellow countrymen and, because they are all descended from the same ancestors, as members of the same Japanese 'family'. This sense of 'familialism' is considered by some to be an important component in Japan's overall informal social control mechanism (see for example, Moriyama, 1995: 55ff.).

17 Families in particular are expected to offer assistance to any members who may be in trouble with the law, but they, in turn, expect wrongdoers to make efforts to reform and, unless they do so, will ultimately forsake them. Likewise, criminal justice agencies may be prepared to favour lenient outcomes for first, second or, at best, third time offenders but, beyond that, are far more likely to resort to harsh, exclusionary 'non-familial' forms of punishment.

18 And '*chuzaisho*', their counterparts in rural areas.

19 On matters relating to crime prevention for example, though they also offer advice and assistance on a wide range of other non-criminal matters, including the giving of directions, advice on dealing with disputes and providing more generalized services for the community and its residents.

20 The comparable clear-up rate in England and Wales was 23.5 per cent in 2002–3 (Home Office, 2003: 13). Moriyama (personal communication) has suggested that one reason for the decline in the Japanese clear-up rate is an increase in the number of emergency 110 calls to the police, resulting in part from the nationwide diffusion of mobile phones.

21 The terms 'crime control' and 'due process' were coined by the American writer Herbert Packer (1969). Note, however, that Packer envisaged 'crime control' operating via a high rate of *convictions* contributing to effective *deterrence* of crime; in the Japanese context it seems rather to operate via a high rate of *confessions*, which do not usually lead to prosecution and conviction but to *resocialization* of the offender by informal methods.

22 By contrast, in England a suspect may only be held for an absolute maximum of four days without being charged with an offence, and detention beyond thirty-six hours requires an order issued by a magistrates' court (Police and Criminal Evidence Act 1984). In practice, 99 per cent of suspects are released or charged within twenty-four hours.

23 In 2001, the proportion of arrests in respect of which the public prosecutor made a request for detention was 93.4 per cent, and the rate at which such requests were granted by the judge was 99.8 per cent (Ministry of Justice, 2003: Table 2-2-3-1). Bail is seldom granted to suspects awaiting trial and, in any event, is only available once a suspect has been indicted. In 2001, the bail rate in district courts was only 13.6 per cent, and 27 per cent of defendants were detained for longer than three months; in summary courts the bail rate was 5.7 per cent, and 9.6 per cent were detained in excess of three months (Japanese Ministry of Justice, 2003: Table 2-3-4-1). There is no limit to the length of detention once a suspect has been indicted.

24 State-funded legal advice is only available to suspects after they have been indicted. Moreover, the Code of Criminal Procedure sanctions restrictions on access to counsel 'when it is necessary for the investigation' (Yoshida, 2000: 4).

25 The Human Rights Committee was asked to consider the issue at a meeting in Geneva on 27 and 28 October 1993, but decided that the system did not constitute a violation of the International Covenant on Civil and Political Rights, though the way it is administered was felt to require due care (Kurata and Hamai, 1998: 3).

26 In 2001, only forty-four defendants were acquitted, yielding an acquittal rate of just 0.005 per cent of the total (Japanese Ministry of Justice, 2003: 118). Since conviction rates are high in most countries that allow defendants to plead guilty, however, a more meaningful measure for comparative purposes is the 'residual conviction rate' that relates only to those cases that are contested. In one of the few comparative studies of conviction rates, Ramseyer and Rasmusen (1999: 5) calculated that the residual conviction rate in Japan was 98.8 per cent in 1994, compared with 30.9 per cent for defendants in federal courts in the USA.

27 Prior to 1948, the discretionary power of the prosecutor was even wider since no reference was made to the gravity of the offence. This factor was inserted in the 1948 code, presumably at the insistence of the American occupation authorities who may have found such a broad discretionary power unpalatable.

28 The Japanese power to suspend the execution of a prison sentence was originally influenced by nineteenth-century Franco-Belgian systems. There the power was intended to serve as an intimidatory warning to deter the offender, though in a Japanese context it enables the court to withhold the imposition of an exclusionary punishment that might sever the offender's ties with the potentially far more powerful informal social control mechanisms to which s/he may still be subject.

29 Those who are dealt with in district or family courts as opposed to those processed by summary courts, which are responsible for processing the vast majority of (relatively minor) offenders. In 2001, 93.3 per cent of defendants were dealt with by way of summary proceedings (calculated from Japanese Ministry of Justice [2003: 118–120] statistics.

30 In 1931 it was only 13.7 per cent.

31 In Japan those put under probationary supervision (which is obligatory for those given repeat suspended sentences) are included among those dealt with by means of suspension of execution of sentence. In contrast to most other countries in this study, there are no 'community sentences' apart from probation. The commonest sanction is the fine (which was imposed on 95 per cent of all offenders (including summary offences) in 2001 (calculated from Japanese Ministry of Justice [2003: Table 2-3-2-1] statistics. In district or family courts, however, the fine only accounts for less than one per cent of all disposals.

32 Those who have previously been sentenced to a term of imprisonment in excess of three years or to a lesser prison sentence which ended less than five years previously.

33 In many such cases it is likely that the murder involves members of the same family. 'Inter-generational' murders are relatively common in Japan, which may reflect the pressures that can arise when members of the same extended family live in close proximity within the same household.

34 Figures calculated from Japanese Ministry of Justice (2003: App. 2-4) statistics.

35 Figures calculated from Japanese Ministry of Justice (2003: App. 2-4) statistics. By way of comparison, approximately 11.5 per cent of the Dutch prisoners were serving sentences of four years or more on 30 September 2003 (Statistics Nederlands), while the corresponding figure in England and Wales (excluding lifers) was 42 per cent in October 2004 (UK Prison Statistics).

36 The police are obliged to refer cases to the public prosecutor, who alone is authorized to determine whether a defendant is prosecuted or not, with the exception of 'trivial

cases' that may be disposed of by the police according to criteria designated by the public prosecutor.

37 But not exclusively, since the private sector is also actively involved in the criminal justice and correctional spheres. Japan's probation service, for example, is heavily dependant on unsalaried voluntary probation officers, who not only greatly outnumber their professional colleagues but are also responsible for almost all supervision of probation clients and parolees. In 2001 there were just 880 professional probation officers, compared with 48,760 volunteer probation officers (Moriyama, personal communication). As we shall see, Japanese prisons are run on industrial lines and, as such, are also heavily dependent on private companies. Finally, the operation of half-way houses catering mainly for discharged prisoners is also undertaken by private organizations.

38 Murayama (1992: 237, n.42) suggests that the proportion of cases in which the judge follows the prosecution's recommendation may be as high as 80 per cent.

39 According to Clifford, prosecutors are also frequently used to draft laws and, even after retirement, act as advisors to government in various capacities.

40 During the period 1955–93, the LDP was the only ruling party. After a short period out of office the LDP regained power at the head of a coalition, a position that it has retained since 1994.

41 Electoral reforms introduced in January 2001 were intended to strengthen the power of elected Ministers, thereby curbing the influence of non-accountable bureaucrats (Gilhooly, 2004: 145–6).

42 As opposed to the Japanese *political establishment* which, notoriously, has been periodically rocked by political/industrial corruption scandals such as the Lockheed affair of 1976, and the Recruit-Cosmos bribery scandal of 1989, which resulted in the resignation of the then Prime Minister (whose successor was also forced to resign over a sexual scandal).

43 Source: Annual Reports of Japanese Corrections Bureau, cited by Johnson (1998: 351).

44 On 1 April 2002, there were fifty-nine prisons, five branch prisons, seven detention houses, 110 branch detention houses and eight juvenile prisons (Japanese Ministry of Justice, 2003: 129).

45 In 2001 the total prison population was reported to be 9.7 per cent above the capacity figure, and 80 per cent of prisons were said to be overcrowded (*Mainichi Daily News*, 20 November 2002).

46 Critics have complained *inter alia* about the inadequate provision of outdoor exercise (amounting to approximately ninety minutes per week), inadequate standards of lighting, heating and ventilation and the requirement for male prisoners to have shaven heads (Human Rights Watch, 1995: 6ff.).

47 The official explanation for such restrictions is 'to make it easy for officers to quickly and accurately discover persons who are ailing, who have committed suicide or inflicted self-injury, when they make their inspection rounds' cited by Japan Federation of Bar Associations (1998).

48 An opinion poll survey in 1994 indicated that only 13.6 per cent of respondents supported total abolition of the death penalty. The poll was conducted by the Information Centre of the Cabinet Secretary, and was published in the Yearbook for Public Opinion Polls, 1995 (Yoshida, 2001).

49 A term coined by Moriyama, 1995.

50 The number of recorded cases involving homicides or bodily injury against other inmates was in single figures for each of the four years 1997–2000, and no such incidents were reported among staff (Japanese Ministry of Justice, 2000: Table II-21). These were

'official figures', however and, as in other countries, may be liable to under-reporting. See Note 60, below, for the number of inmates who were penalized for assaults, fighting, etc.

51 In 2001, two such escapes were recorded, but this is exceptional, as no such incidents were reported during the preceding four year period (Japanese Ministry of Justice, 2000: Table II-21, 2003: Tables 2-4-3-4. Levels of security appear to be high throughout the Japanese prison system. This is particularly true of prisons housing long-term recidivists, which have been likened to 'supermax' prisons (Kaido, 2001: 436). But even detention centres, which house all unconvicted detainees – in addition to death-row prisoners – are maximum security institutions.

52 Assuming that such prisoners are likely to receive somewhat longer sentences, it is not surprising that they constitute such a sizeable proportion of the overall prison population.

53 The term 'yakuza' technically refers to the members of organized Mafia-style syndicates that are known as 'kumi'. There are estimated to be about 3,300 gangs, which have a total membership of around 90,000 (Gilhooly, 2004: 211).

54 A total of 3,376 new inmates in 1999 were said to be members of organized crime groups, accounting for 13.8 per cent of the 24,496 inmates who were newly admitted that year (Japanese Ministry of Justice, 2000).

55 Japanese inmates are obliged to call prison guards 'sensei', which is a general term of respect meaning 'teacher' or 'master', that is normally reserved for persons with superior knowledge.

56 Instruction in military drill, including marching, forms part of the orientation training for new recruits and, like other aspects of Japanese prison life, is designed to induce habitual conformity on the part of inmates.

57 In 2001, 28,420 persons were given determinate prison sentences, only 194 (0.7 per cent) of whom were sentenced to imprisonment *without* forced labour (figures calculated from Japanese Ministry of Justice (2003: 132) statistics).

58 A small but significant minority of multiply recidivist offenders are relatively old and therefore are unlikely to pose serious control problems for the authorities. In 2001, 8 per cent of newly admitted prisoners were aged 60 or over (Japanese Ministry of Justice, 2003: 132).

59 Though the parole rate is very low. According to statistics published by APCCA, (2002: Table 4), the parole rate in Japan was only 5.6 per 100.000 population in mid-2000, compared with 45.9 per 100,000 in New Zealand and 44.7 per 100,000 in Australia.

60 The highest proportion of rule violations related to assaults on other inmates (15.3 per cent of the total), neglect of work duty (13.9 per cent) and fighting (8.4 per cent) (Japanese Ministry of Justice, 2003: 140).

61 This is contrary to the United Nations Standard Minimum Rules for the Treatment of Prisoners, Rule 29, which stipulates that any conduct that is capable of constituting a disciplinary offence together with the type and duration of any punishment that may be inflicted should always be provided by law or regulation. Moreover, Principle 30(1) of the United Nations Body of Principles for the Protection of All Persons under any form of Detention or Imprisonment stipulates that such laws or regulations must be duly published.

62 Kaido reports (2001: 437) that according to a government response to an official question from a member of the House of Councillors, in 1999 twenty-three life sentenced prisoners were held in solitary confinement, six of whom had been detained in this way for more than twenty-five years.

63 They may be forced to wear specially designed trousers with a slit in the seat ('metaware pants') that enable them to go to the toilet, though not to maintain adequate personal hygiene.

64 Since then, nine death sentences were imposed in 2001, fifteen in 2002 and twelve as of September 2003 (Masanori, 2003).

65 Such complaints are by no means confined to the Japanese prison system.

66 Though training in fork lift truck driving and boiler operation is also said, to be on offer, somewhat incongruously, in addition to training in care service for the elderly (APCCA, 2001).

67 Figures calculated from statistics provided by the International Centre for Prison Studies 2004 (Prison Brief for Japan) and Walmsley (2003a). This is equivalent to 6.5 per cent of the 2001 prison population, which is very much higher than the proportion of foreigners in the general population at the time; see Note 5, above.

68 For example, the smuggling out of a list of inmates by a former prisoner of Japan's third largest prison, Nagoya (*Mainichi Shimbun*, 4 August, 2000).

69 It is difficult to confirm this since, although inmate suicides are recorded in the official statistics compiled by the Ministry of Justice, prison staff suicides are not officially reported. The number of *inmate* suicides (10 in 1999 and 2000) is equivalent to a suicide rate of 40.8 per 100,000 receptions, compared with 67 per 100,000 receptions in England and Wales in 1999 (Cavadino and Dignan, 2002: 189).

70 In common with other emergency staff such as police officers and fire fighters. There is a National Personnel Authority for government employees in general, which deals with matters such as working conditions, though this is criticized as ineffective (Kaido, 2001: 428).

71 The Japanese Minister of Justice has been described (Kaido, 2001: 431) as 'a mere puppet of the bureaucrats of the Ministry of Justice'. Moreover, most of the executive officials within the ministry, as we have seen, are former prosecutors, and hence are likely to be more interested in maintaining the efficiency of the prison system as an instrument of social control than in upholding the human rights of prison inmates.

72 The lowest recorded crime rate in recent times was 1,091 per 100,000 in 1973. Since then there has been a gradual increase in the crime rate, which reached 1,506 by 1997, the highest since 1956 (Kurata and Hamai, 1998). Since then the rate of increase has quickened markedly and by 2000 had reached 1,925 per 100,000, which is the highest since 1949. (Latest figures are calculated from statistics obtained from the National Police Agency [http://jin.jcic.pr.jp/stat/stats/14CRM21.html] and those obtained from the Census of Japan [http://www.jinjapan.org/stat/stats/01CEN21.html].)

73 Reflected in the newspaper headline: 'Government report: crimes peaking and prisons overflowing' (*Mainichi Shimbun*, 16 November 2001).

74 There have also been severe moral panics relating to young offenders in particular (see Chapter 14).

75 In the first Japanese victimization study, conducted by the Ministry of Justice, 54 per cent of all victims whose views were canvassed indicated that they thought the sentence was 'too lenient', and this proportion rose to 66 per cent in the case of victims whose offender had been sentenced to a long sentence of imprisonment in respect of a serious violent offence (Hamai et al., 2000).

Part 3

PATTERNS OF
PENALITY?

In Part 1 we saw that our selected countries may be differentiated according to their political, social and economic arrangements, their material circumstances and also their ideological predilections. We argued that, at least in general terms, it is possible to relate the different types of political, economic and-social cultures to which each country belongs to significant *penological* differences between them. Thus, the countries we have been examining offer striking contrasts with regard to their penal ideologies and the schools of penal thought to which they subscribe, the nature of their penality and also their specific forms of penal practice, including the degrees of punitiveness with which they are each associated. In this part of the book we extend this analysis *thematically* by selecting two more specific sets of penological issues – youth justice and prison privatization – and considering the extent to which they may display similar 'patterns of penality'.

12

Comparative Youth Justice

The very emergence of a separate 'youth justice system' that is distinct from the adult criminal justice system is perhaps one of the earliest examples of a globalizing tendency at work within the penological realm. Indeed, it seems highly probable that the adoption of specific social control measures from the nineteenth century onwards for dealing with problematic groups of young people may be associated with much broader processes of industrialization, urbanization and contemporary developments in the social sciences that fostered new ideas about childhood. More recently there have been a number of international texts calling for the adoption of common strategies for dealing with juvenile delinquency.[1] Not surprisingly, perhaps, some (e.g. Dünkel, 1998; Dünkel et al., 1997) have sought to identify major recent trends in the development of youth justice systems that apply 'across the board'. However, our analysis suggests that the youth justice systems that have emerged in the countries covered by this study not only adopted different initial responses to 'the youth justice' problem but continue to follow distinctively different developmental trajectories.

The question that we will now begin to address is whether these differences can be satisfactorily explained in terms of the radical pluralist framework we set out in the introduction, and which is depicted in slightly adapted form in Figure 12.1. This suggests, firstly, that any attempt to compare youth justice systems will need to take account of their philosophical underpinnings (including the philosophy that each society holds in regard of adult criminality and penality), their institutional arrangements and the processes whereby young offenders are dealt with. And secondly, that the most satisfactory explanation for any differences that emerge is one that focuses on the interplay between ideological and material factors and which takes into account the social and cultural context within which these relationships are played out.

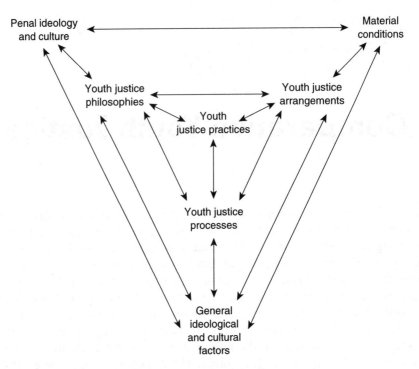

Figure 12.1   *A radical pluralist analysis of youth justice systems*

Approaches to youth justice

The origins, history and continuing development of 'youth justice' (or 'juvenile justice')[2] systems have been particularly complex and often paradoxical with regard to each of the countries featured in this book, and this presents a major challenge when seeking to compare them. One analytical aid that we propose to use seeks to differentiate between a number of distinct approaches that (in keeping with our radical pluralist framework) encapsulate different philosophical assumptions, institutional arrangements and operational policies and processes. These five youth justice 'models' are presented in diagrammatic form in Table 12.1[3] and will be discussed more fully below. One very important preliminary observation, however, is that these models are intended to serve solely as 'conceptual tools' with a view to capturing some important distinctions between the different approaches to the treatment and processing of particular categories of young people. It should not be assumed that any of the youth justice systems we will be examining have ever corresponded exclusively and unequivocally to any of the models presented here, since most have been, and continue to be, influenced by a variety of approaches, and virtually all have changed, to a greater or lesser

Models	Philosophical assumptions	Institutional arrangements	Policies and processes
Welfare model	Determinist: crime is 'caused' Paternalistic and protectionist Focus on 'needs' not 'deeds' Child as dependent Help/treatment or education, not punishment	'Socialized welfare tribunal' based on parens patriae Unified care/criminal jurisdiction	Pre-delinquent interventions Informal procedures 'One-track adjudication' Unfettered discretion Social science expertise Use of diagnostic custody Indeterminate, flexible orders
Justice model	'Free will' and 'accountability' Child as responsible agent Focus on 'deeds' not 'needs' Young offender as 'bearer of rights' Focus on 'just deserts'	'Modified criminal court' Distinct care/criminal jurisdiction	'Two-track adjudication' Procedural safeguards in court Procedural formality Determinate sentencing Proportionality in punishment Treat like cases alike
Minimum intervention model	'Labelling perspective' Dangers of secondary deviance Avoidance of 'net-widening'	'Gate-keeping mechanisms' Alternatives to custody	Decriminalization Diversion from prosecution Decarceration Systems management approach Targeting, monitoring
Restorative justice model	Focus on restoration for victims Focus on reintegration (and accountability) of offenders Empowerment of parties New role for state: 'subsidiarity'	'Family group conference' Victim-offender mediation Changes in role of youth court Unified care/criminal jurisdiction	Diversion from courts combined with reparation Decarceration Flexible/innovative outcomes Need for cultural sensitivity
Neo-correctionalist model	Primacy of offending prevention 'Law and order' ideology 'Responsibilization' of offenders and their parents Young offender as bearer of responsibilities and obligations Offender accountability towards victims and community Efficiency and effectiveness Focus on community safety	Reform of court process Closer links with adult courts New 'civil' forms of punishment	Early interventionism Pre-delinquent interventions Relaxation of age limits 'Zero tolerance' Reparation by offenders Focus on persistence 'Progressive' sentencing Quasi-mandatory sentences 'Fast-tracking' Systems management approach

extent, over time. Nevertheless the typology may be helpful in analysing the balance of influence between various different youth justice approaches in each of the countries covered by the study.

The 'welfare model'

The 'welfare model' encapsulates a positivistic approach that is based on the assumption that juvenile wrongdoing is the product of social or environmental factors for which the young person cannot be held individually responsible. Accordingly, the primary goal of the youth justice system is to provide appropriate help or treatment[4] for offenders; rather than punishment. Indeed, young people who are vulnerable or in trouble are considered to be in need of protection from the potentially harmful and corruptive influences of the adult world, including the adult criminal justice system. Consequently, the primary emphasis is on the 'needs' and 'best interests' of the child rather than the 'deeds' they may have committed.

These paternalistic assumptions are also reflected in the institutional arrangements that – in some jurisdictions at least[5] – have come to be associated with the welfare model. The most distinctive of these arrangements has been the creation of a separate set of 'socialized welfare tribunals'[6] as alternatives to the regular criminal courts, in which the state invokes the principle of *parens patriae* to assume the role and responsibilities of a surrogate parent in respect of troublesome and vulnerable children. Two aspects of the socialized welfare tribunal are particularly noteworthy. First, it combines two conceptually distinct jurisdictional strands: one relating to young offenders and the other to children in need of care and protection. And second, consistent with the fact that its proceedings are characterized as civil or welfare in nature, rather than criminal, the tribunal's jurisdiction encompasses not only conventional criminal offences but also so-called 'status offences'. The latter include 'dissolute' or 'wayward' behaviour on the part of young people, such as truancy, illicit sexual activity, and other forms of non-criminal 'delinquency'.

Consequently, one of the policies and processes that is associated with the welfare model involves the authorization of 'pre-delinquent interventions' in respect of a wide range of 'inappropriate' behaviour by young people. A second relates to the use of informal procedures that are designed to elicit the 'whole truth' about the child, unfettered by restrictive constructs such as the concept of legal relevance and the need to prove the commission of an offence. Indeed, there is a tendency to downplay the significance of the offence itself, and concentrate instead on the social facts and circumstances that have precipitated the child's appearance in court. This aspect is linked to a third characteristic which relates to the use of social scientific 'experts' (social workers, psychologists, psychiatrists, those trained in pedagogy), either as decision-makers in their own right or, more commonly, as advisers and report-writers to assist judges. Another closely related feature involves the conferral of wide-ranging discretion on the part of decision-makers who are responsible for determining and providing for the 'best interests' of the child. This is reflected in the use of a 'one-track' adjudication procedure for all 'troubled' children, whether they are offenders, non-criminal delinquents, or victims of abuse or neglect, since all are liable to be dealt with by means of 'ward of court proceedings'. It frequently involves a willingness to use custody (or at least compulsory removal from home) both for diagnostic purposes and also to remove the child from its harmful environment. There is also a marked preference for court orders and disposals that are flexible, individualized, and open-ended or indeterminate in duration. Such disposals have the effect of investing a high degree of discretionary power over the young person's life in the practitioners who are charged with implementing them.

Turning now to the impact of the welfare model: aspects of the welfare approach have at various times influenced the youth justice systems in all of the countries in our study, though both the extent and duration of its influence have been highly variable. Generalizing very broadly, we will see that the welfare approach was adopted in its 'purest' form during the early part of the twentieth century in much of the USA and, somewhat later, in the Scandinavian countries (especially Sweden) and also Japan. Key elements of the welfare approach have also influenced the development of youth justice systems in most of the conservative corporatist countries, particularly Germany, but also Italy, France and (at least until recently) the Netherlands. The remaining common law countries have not been totally immune from its influence although in most of them, as we shall see, its impact has been far less pervasive, particularly with regard to the development of youth justice institutions and their associated jurisdictional arrangements.

However, it is also true to say that the impact of the welfare approach has considerably diminished since its heyday during the first two-thirds of the twentieth century. Nowhere is this more apparent than in the USA, which has since the 1960s comprehensively abandoned many aspects of its erstwhile welfare-oriented youth justice system. Elsewhere, the welfare approach has also come under pressure, but while the influence of other approaches has become more apparent, it shows no signs in these countries of being abandoned altogether. This is particularly true of Sweden, and it also applies to a lesser extent to several of the conservative corporatist countries (notably Germany and France) and to Japan, where the welfare approach still retains much of its former pre-eminence.

The 'justice model'

In contrast to the positivism of the welfare model, the 'justice model' espouses a 'classicist' approach that is based on the assumption that even young people are – with certain limited exceptions – reasoning agents who are endowed with free will. Because they are considered to be responsible for their actions, it is felt acceptable for them to be held accountable in law for what they have done, which means that the primary focus is on the 'deeds' of the child rather than their welfare 'needs'. Accordingly, the principal goal of the youth justice system – as of the adult criminal justice system – is initially to determine the suspect's legal guilt or innocence and next, if convicted, to assess the degree of culpability that they bear. Punishment should then be apportioned in accordance with the seriousness of the offence and the offender's corresponding 'just deserts'. Because the system is acknowledged to be unequivocally engaged in the administration of punishment that often entails a loss of liberty, and that cannot be assumed to be benign 'treatment' that is in the interests of the offender, there is a greater emphasis – formally at least – on the need for procedural rights of 'due process' and for appropriate constraints to be placed on the punitive power of the state.

Not surprisingly, perhaps, the institutional arrangements that are most closely associated with the justice model consist of modified 'junior criminal courts' rather than the socialized welfare tribunals that help to characterize 'pure' versions of the welfare approach. The notion that young people need to be protected from 'contamination' by mixing with older offenders is still present – albeit in highly attenuated form – but is addressed by introducing relatively minor modifications to the standard lower-tier criminal courts that deal with adult offenders. The most common modifications relate to the provision of separate juvenile court proceedings that are held either in a different building or at least at a different time from adult court proceedings; the restriction of access to the public; and the imposition of constraints on the freedom of the media to identify the young people who appear before the court. A second tendency is to introduce a much clearer differentiation between the two jurisdictional strands relating on the one hand to young offenders and on the other to those in need of care and protection. When taken to its logical conclusion, this might entail a complete separation between the two strands, and an institutional separation between children who are 'in trouble' for what they have done, and those who are vulnerable to abuse or neglect, with completely separate courts and procedures for each category.[7] But even where the two strands are united, there is a tendency to adopt a 'two track' adjudication model, with different procedures for dealing with each group of children. In some jurisdictions (as we shall see) there has also been a tendency in practice for the 'criminal' strand to be prioritized (ideologically and, frequently also, numerically) in comparison with the 'care' jurisdiction of the juvenile court.

The procedural safeguards that are associated with the justice model include the following rights: to be notified in advance of the specific charges a young person is facing; to legal representation (paid for out of public funds if necessary); to a fair and impartial hearing; to confront and cross-examine witnesses and to be presumed innocent until proven guilty, which includes a privilege against self-incrimination). The range of sentencing 'outcomes' that are associated with the justice model more closely resemble those available in adult criminal courts, with a strong emphasis on the need for proportionate, finite and consistent penalties rather than the open-ended, indeterminate and highly individualized orders that are characteristic of the welfare model.

As for the impact of the justice model, its influence – particularly with regard to the adoption of 'modified criminal courts' as opposed to socialized welfare tribunals – may be seen in the early development of juvenile justice systems in many of the common law jurisdictions, with the notable exception, initially, of the USA. However, its most dramatic impact was subsequently to be felt in the USA itself, as we shall see, following a series of landmark decisions by the Supreme Court during the 1960s. The ultimate effect of these rulings was to transform the juvenile court 'from a nominally rehabilitative welfare agency into a scaled-down second-class criminal court for young offenders' (Feld, 1999), thereby paving the way for further, even more radical, changes to come. The influence of the justice approach on youth justice systems has also been felt in many other jurisdictions, including conservative corporatist states and Nordic social democracies. But although it has moderated certain aspects of their predominantly 'welfare-based' systems – notably with regard to the elimination of 'indeterminate' sentencing practices – it has failed to bring about a wholesale transformation of the systems themselves on anything like the scale experienced in the USA.

The 'minimum intervention model'

The philosophy that underpins the 'minimum intervention model' is derived in part from criminological 'labelling theory', which suggests that all official forms of processing young offenders are potentially harmful to them since they 'label' and stigmatize them as criminals. This makes it more, rather than less, difficult for them to desist from crime in future since it may make it harder for them to engage in lawful activities, for example by rendering them unemployable. Indeed, it may also increase the risk of them participating in illicit activities, for example by confining them in custodial institutions where they can meet other offenders, learn from them and be drawn into criminal subcultures. Placement in custodial institutions could for this reason constitute the most harmful and counter-productive of all official interventions. There is indeed criminological evidence[8] that lends support to the idea that official responses to crime may frequently promote 'secondary deviance' on the part of young offenders, thereby fuelling the 'deviancy amplification spiral' that they are ostensibly designed to prevent! Such considerations have given rise to a 'minimum intervention' strategy – particularly popular with certain youth justice practitioners – incorporating some or all of the following elements:

1 avoiding the use of custodial or residential institutions wherever possible because of the adverse effects they can have on the social development and criminal propensities of young people (linked with a policy of decarceration and deinstitutionalization);[9]

2 using community-based alternatives to custody wherever possible in cases that do call for a punitive intervention (linked with a policy of diverting young offenders from custody);

3 avoiding prosecution altogether where possible, by encouraging prosecutors to discontinue proceedings and encouraging the police to 'caution' or warn young offenders instead (linked with a policy of diversion from prosecution);

4 taking care to avoid 'net-widening' by ensuring that the above interventions are never used for young people who would otherwise have been dealt with informally (linked with a policy of targeting and monitoring);

5 advocating a policy of 'decriminalization', certainly with regard to 'status' offences where they exist, but also at the very least in respect of minor criminal offences which, when committed by young people, would no longer carry even the threat of criminal sanctions; and

6 advocating a policy of 'depenalization' whereby even young offenders who commit more serious offences would no longer come within the jurisdiction of the criminal courts, but would be dealt with instead by means of civil proceedings administered by an appropriate 'child-sensitive' institution or tribunal.

Another important feature of the minimum intervention philosophy is that it applies as much to interventions that are ostensibly 'welfare-based' as it does to those that are imposed with criminal justice objectives in mind. The 'helping' professions are seen as potentially just as harmful to young people as their more openly coercive criminal justice counterparts, since they are apt to pathologize young people and consequently they too are likely to intervene in their lives far too readily and too intensively, with damaging consequences. For this reason, the minimum intervention approach opposes the indiscriminate use of 'welfare' considerations, whether in respect of sentencing (or remand) decisions, or in deciding whether to prosecute or caution young people.

As for the institutional arrangements that might be expected to feature within a minimum intervention model, a distinction perhaps needs to be drawn between a 'pure' version of the model, which would incorporate the full range of policies itemized above, and the more limited version that is more likely to be encountered in practice. Different institutional methods have been adopted in order to instantiate the minimum intervention principle. In Canada, for example, a largely welfare-based system for dealing with young offenders was modified in 1984 by the introduction of criminal law based proportionality principles in order to reduce the intrusion of the justice system into the lives of young people in pursuit of welfare goals (Doob and Sprott, 2004: 190-8; Doob and Tonry, 2004: 14). Scotland, on the other hand, has until now retained a relatively 'pure' welfare approach that is strongly committed to the principles of diversion and minimum intervention (Bottoms and Dignan, 2004). Indeed, perhaps one of the reasons for the continuing international interest that has been shown in the Scottish Children's Hearings system (which we describe below) since its inception in 1971 relates to the 'unique nature' of the Scottish youth justice system, one important feature of which is its commitment to implementing such a radical minimum intervention model in practice (Bottoms, 2002: 455).[10] In reality, however, most other youth justice systems continue to rely on either a modified criminal court or a more traditional form of socialized welfare tribunal, neither of which is fully committed to the principle of minimum intervention. In circumstances such as these the use of diverse 'gatekeeping' mechanisms is especially important, in order to secure the diversion of offenders from prosecution or custody, though the precise form they take varies widely within different jurisdictions, as we shall see. Another institutional feature that may often (though not invariably) be associated with a diversionary approach involves the adoption of various 'alternatives to custody'.

Apart from the various diversionary processes themselves, another policy that has often been associated with the minimum intervention model involves the use of a distinctive implementational strategy that is known in England as 'systems management'. This involves a number of managerialist techniques. They include the use of research and analysis in order to ascertain how the youth justice system is operating in a particular local area, the setting of targets and the adoption of appropriate procedures (for example 'gatekeeping' mechanisms) by criminal justice agencies. The latter work in collaboration with one another in pursuit of shared diversionary objectives, and monitor the outcomes of their interventions to ensure that these objectives are achieved.

In terms of its impact, the minimum intervention model came to prominence much more recently than either of the other two models we have looked at so far and was particularly influential during the 1970s and 1980s in a wide variety of penal jurisdictions. One of the key tenets of the minimum intervention model – that custody should by imposed on those under the age of eighteen only as a last resort and for the shortest possible period – was incorporated in Article 37 of the UN Convention on the Rights of the Child. The Convention was established in 1989 and has been ratified by 191 of the 193 members of the United Nations, the two exceptions being the USA and Somalia.

So potent was the model for a time that it almost assumed the status of 'the new orthodoxy',[11] particularly when the practitioners who were often instrumental in promoting the 'minimum intervention' agenda succeeded for a time in gaining the interest and active support of governments. Despite these short-term successes, however, the influence of the model has waned more recently, especially in some of the neo-liberal countries, where it has lost ground to two even more recent models. Ironically, however, one specific feature of the minimum intervention model that seems destined to continue to shape the youth justice agenda in these countries – even after the eclipse of the 'new orthodoxy' itself – relates to its use of managerialist techniques, most notably in the sphere of inter-agency cooperation. The difference is that these techniques are increasingly being pressed into service in pursuit of other, sharply contrasting, youth justice objectives, as we shall see.

The 'restorative justice model'

The 'restorative justice model' is based on a radically different set of assumptions about the concept of crime itself, the relationship between offenders, victims, citizens and the state, and also about the most appropriate ways of responding to crime. Whereas traditional criminal justice theorists have portrayed crime first and foremost as an offence against the state, the restorative justice model places particular emphasis on the harm that is done to the victim, whose interests were for many years neglected by mainstream criminal justice agencies and policy-makers alike. Traditional approaches have tended to place the responsibility for dealing with crime firmly in the hands of state-appointed agencies, who are expected to deal with offenders (and almost exclusively with offenders) in accordance with 'the public interest'. In marked contrast, the restorative justice model advocates a policy based on involving those who are most directly affected by a particular offence – victims, offenders and their 'communities of care'[12] – in decisions about how it should be resolved. Moreover, such a policy gives primacy to those interests as opposed to the more general and abstract 'public interest'.

The restorative justice model also advocates a very different set of goals for the criminal justice system instead of the predominantly offender-focused goals – retribution, deterrence, rehabilitation, and incapacitation – that are associated with traditional approaches. With regard to victims, the aim is *restoration*, which encompasses the repairing of the physical, emotional and psychological harm that may have been experienced. With regard to offenders, the primary aims include the promotion of accountability towards those who have been harmed by an offence, and the active reintegration of offenders themselves back into the community. With regard to communities the goal is one of empowerment and a reinvigoration of civil society founded on a network of constructive and largely self-repairing social relationships. Many of those who favour the restorative justice model advocate a radical reformulation of the state's role and responsibilities with regard to crime, which can be expressed in terms of the 'principle of subsidiarity'.[13] Instead of the state – or its representatives within the criminal justice agencies – assuming direct and primary responsibility for 'dealing with' crime and its aftermath, its chief function should be to act as facilitator, information giver, provider of resources and deliverer of services. Only in cases that cannot be satisfactorily resolved by the relevant communities of care should the state serve as the ultimate arbiter of fairness, and provide a court-based forum for delivering restorative outcomes.

In terms of criminal justice policies and processes, the restorative justice model – like the minimum intervention model – favours the diversion of (many if not most) offenders from prosecution, and also strategies aimed at decarceration (since custodial interventions often make it very difficult to secure restorative outcomes). Moreover, in some jurisdictions, as we shall see, the approach has accorded a high priority to the need to develop culturally sensitive and appropriate procedures for dealing with particular categories of young offenders (notably those belonging to indigenous racial or ethnic minorities) and their victims. Not surprisingly, the emphasis on meeting the needs of victims while promoting the accountability and well-being of offenders – and at the same time securing the empowerment of victims, offenders and communities – has resulted in a quest for new and more suitable institutional arrangements and procedures. The best known of these procedural innovations include the use of 'family group conferencing', 'community conferencing' and other variants on the conferencing theme, which enable offenders, victims and their respective families to informally resolve matters by reaching an agreement as to how the offence should be dealt with. Another, very closely related, innovation involves the use of 'victim–offender mediation', which differs from conferencing mainly with regard to its more restricted focus on the principal 'stakeholders' themselves (victims and offenders) rather than their respective communities of care. The adoption of a 'full-blown' restorative justice model would clearly entail major changes in the role (and prominence) of the juvenile court, which would largely be confined to determining issues of guilt or innocence in contested cases, and providing a back-up in cases that could not be satisfactorily resolved by the standard restorative justice procedures. It might also be noted in passing that a conferencing approach need not be confined to young people who are in trouble with the law, but would in principle be equally appropriate for those in need of care and attention[14] and, in this sense, the adoption of a restorative justice approach is compatible with a 'unified' jurisdiction dealing with both criminal and care matters.

The effects of the restorative justice model have so far been highly variable. Although the term 'restorative justice' itself did not come into widespread use until much later, victim–offender mediation schemes originated in North America (where they were initially known as 'Victim–Offender Reconciliation Projects', or 'VORPs') during the 1970s and 1980s. However, these are not in any sense integrated into the criminal justice system since they are not legislatively mandated and where they do operate it is solely on a 'stand-alone' basis. Elsewhere, as we shall see, notably in France and Germany, the use of victim–offender mediation forms an integrated part of the regular criminal justice system, since it is now authorized by law, though the extent to which it is used in practice in these countries remains patchy. The family group conferencing approach was initially introduced and pioneered in New Zealand which, as we shall see, remains unique in the extent to which it has adopted a reasonably 'pure' version of the restorative justice model as the basis of its youth justice system.[15] Other forms of conferencing programmes have been developed elsewhere which differ from the New Zealand approach in a number of important respects, most notably insofar as they mainly involve the police rather than social workers as facilitators. This variant on the conferencing approach was originally pioneered in a number of Australian states, though most have now adopted the New Zealand model. However, police-led conferencing has also been introduced on a stand-alone, trial, basis in a number of other jurisdictions including the USA, England and Wales and also South Africa. In many of the countries in which restorative justice initiatives have been introduced, however, their restorative potential has been somewhat blunted by the emergence and growing predominance of a very different youth justice model, to which we now turn.

The 'neo-correctionalist model'[16]

The 'neo-correctionalist model' resembles the justice model inasmuch as both adopt an uncompromisingly punishment-oriented approach, but in other respects they are very different. Whereas the justice approach views the offender as a bearer of rights – and therefore entitled to protection against excessive punitive interventions on the part of the state – the neo-correctionalist approach is more likely to emphasize the responsibilities that young offenders, and even their parents,[17] owe towards others, including the victim, the community and the state. And whereas the justice model makes at best modest claims as regards its ability to achieve any reduction in the incidence of crime – preferring to ensure that offenders receive the punishment which is most just rather than the most effective in terms of crime reduction – the neo-correctionalist approach espouses a much more ambitious crime control goal for the youth justice system. The prevention of offending by young people is accorded primacy, and all other aims are subordinated to it. Thus, reparation – for victims and also the wider community[18] – is favoured chiefly insofar as it may contribute to a reduction in reoffending rates rather than something to which recipients should be entitled as of right, as restorative justice proponents would advocate.

Another aim of the neo-correctionalist model is to improve the efficiency of the youth justice system, for example by co-ordinating the activities of the various criminal justice agencies, speeding up the criminal justice process and increasing the effectiveness of the various interventions that are directed at young offenders. In addition to these purely pragmatic considerations, however, the principal philosophical foundation for the neo-correctionalist approach derives from an unashamedly populist 'law and order' ideology that equates effectiveness with the imposition of tough, intensive and unashamedly punitive interventions. In certain other respects, the neo-correctionalist model more closely resembles the welfare model than the justice model with which it is more commonly compared. This is particularly true with respect to the type of behaviour it seeks to prevent, which is not confined to purely criminal behaviour but often extends also to acts of 'pre-delinquency', including truancy and other non-criminal forms of rowdy or anti-social behaviour.[19] To some extent this change of focus reflects the adoption of a much broader agenda for the criminal justice system as a whole, which is no longer restricted to responding to crime *per se*, but has to do with the preservation of 'community safety' and public order in general.

These broad assumptions are reflected in a number of more specific policies and processes that help to characterize the neo-correctionalist model. They include a marked preference for strategies based on the principle of 'early intervention', which in this context can take a number of different forms. Firstly, there is a tendency to adopt various preventive measures for dealing with acts of pre-delinquency, including the creation of new quasi-criminal forms of 'civil' penalties[20] to combat anti-social and related forms of behaviour. Secondly, there is a tendency to extend the principle of criminal responsibility to younger age groups. One way of doing this involves the abolition of the protective legal doctrine of *doli incapax* whereby children of a certain age are presumed to be incapable of committing a crime unless they can be shown to appreciate the difference between right and wrong. Another such strategy involves the use of 'transfer procedures', whereby young offenders may be subjected to the jurisdiction of adult criminal courts instead of dealing with them in juvenile courts, where the type and severity of any punishment to which they may be liable is likely to be limited. Thirdly, there is a tendency to adopt more intensive and punitive interventions even in respect of petty and first-time offending, in order to 'nip it in the bud': the policy of 'zero tolerance'. Other measures that are associated with the neo-correctionalist approach include the use of mandatory or semi-mandatory penalties for certain categories of offenders, and the adoption of so-called 'progressive' sentencing strategies whereby persistent offending is met by increasingly punitive responses regardless of the seriousness of the offences themselves. Finally, the emphasis on efficiency is reflected in the adoption of two related sets of measures. One involves the introduction of 'fast-tracking' procedures that are designed to reduce the time taken to deal with young offenders. The other involves the extension of 'systems management' techniques – such as inter-agency collaboration – that are intended to unite all criminal justice agencies in pursuit of a common set of preventive goals.

The institutional arrangements that are associated with the neo-correctionalist model include the adoption of the 'transfer' procedures mentioned above which enable certain young offenders to be dealt with in adult criminal courts, and also modifications of juvenile court proceedings in order to make them more meaningful to young people, thereby supposedly enhancing their preventive potential.

In terms of its effect, the first signs of an emergent neo-correctionalist model could be detected in the USA during the late 1970s, and during the next two decades the transformation of American juvenile courts from a nominally rehabilitative welfare agency into a modified criminal court for young offenders was increasingly influenced by an overtly neo-correctionalist agenda. Similar tendencies can also be discerned in most other neo-liberal countries during this period, with the notable and interesting exception of New Zealand. Beyond the neo-liberal sphere of influence however, as we shall see, the impact of the neo-correctionalist model has so far been much less pervasive.

One possible general explanation for this fairly pronounced 'pattern of penality' in the youth justice realm is that the emergence of the justice model in many neo-liberal societies coincided with a severe and widespread economic downturn. This resulted in high levels of unemployment in which the young, the poor and the disadvantaged were particularly badly affected by the disruption of one of the main socialization processes during the transitional period from childhood to adulthood. Perhaps not surprisingly, the same period also coincided with growing moral panics – by no means confined to neo-liberal countries – over various youth crime issues. In several neo-liberal countries, however, this disruption was compounded by attempts on the part of mainly right-wing governments to restructure the welfare state, notably by restricting young people's access to unemployment benefits and other forms of welfare support. Within this context, the prior (or in some instances contemporary) adoption of a justice model that was based on an explicitly punitive orientation – even though nominally tempered by just deserts principles – provided a fertile medium for the emergence of a still more punitive approach in pursuit of an openly neo-correctionalist agenda.

The fact that most conservative corporatist societies and social democracies appear not to have succumbed to the same tendencies despite their exposure to the same economic downturn, and in spite of their willingness to embrace at least some aspects of the justice model, may be attributable to two important sets of differences, operating respectively at the material and ideological levels. Firstly, such countries did not set about the systematic dismantling of their welfare state provisions on anything like the scale experienced within the neo-liberal camp. And secondly, they did not entirely reject the philosophy underlying the welfare model, which continued to provide an alternative and still vibrant mode of discourse to the harsher punitive rhetoric that underlies both the justice and, in particular, the neo-correctionalist models.

Now that we have identified the principal influences that have helped to shape youth justice systems in most of the developed world over the last century or so, in the next two chapters we will examine the differential impact that they have had on each of the countries in our sample. Since our main purpose is to ascertain the presence or absence of 'patterns of penality' that might be related to the political, social and economic circumstances affecting each country we will group them according to the four types of political economy that we set out in Chapter 1.

Notes

1 The most important of these are the United Nations Convention on the Rights of the Child (1989), that has been ratified by almost every country in the world with the exception of the USA and Somalia, the Beijing Rules (United Nations, 1985) and two sets of recommendations published by the Council of Europe (1987, 2003).

2 The terminological shift that took place in the latter part of the twentieth century would make an interesting etymological study in its own right. But for present purposes it is sufficient to note that these two terms are broadly interchangeable and that the phrase 'youth justice' has largely come to supersede the older usage 'juvenile justice' in most of the jurisdictions that are included in this study. However, the older term continues to be more commonly used in some jurisdictions, notably Japan. Likewise many countries continue to employ the term 'juvenile court' even though some (e.g. England and Wales) have renamed them as 'youth courts'.

3 In compiling this typology we have inevitably drawn on a number of sources, though we have freely adapted all of them. The most important sources (and the models to which they relate) are as follows: 'welfare' and 'justice' models: Faust and Brantingham (1979), Alder and Wundersitz (1994), Cavadino and Dignan (2002); 'minimum intervention' Model: Bottoms et al., (1990), Cavadino and Dignan, (2002); 'correctionalist' model: Bottoms and Dignan (2004); and 'restorative justice' model: O'Connor (1998) and Morris (2004). See also Morris et al. (1980); Thorpe et al. (1980).

4 The 'welfare' approach encompasses at least two distinct positivistic tendencies. The first is a pseudo-medical 'treatment model' that can also be applied to adult offenders, and the second is a 'social welfare' model that is based on the provision of social work intervention. The latter approach is more likely to be directed at 'problem' or dependent children and their families (Rutherford, 1992: Chapter 2). A third (less overtly positivistic) variant that has gained a firm hold in several conservative corporatist countries, as we shall see, consists of a 'resocialization' model, which adopts a pedagogical approach that is aimed at offenders who are immature or inadequately socialized.

5 Notably Norway (see Stang Dahl, 1985) and, as we shall see, other Scandinavian jurisdictions; and also certain states in the USA (Fagan and Feld, 2001).

6 The term is derived from the very helpful distinction drawn by Faust and Brantingham (1979) between countries that deal with juvenile offending by means of modified criminal courts and those that establish separate juvenile tribunals for this purpose. The primary focus in the latter is not on the criminal act that may have been committed by the child, but the social facts and circumstances that have resulted in proceedings being instigated with regard to the child.

7 As advocated, for example, by Morris et al. (1980); and as more or less instituted in England since the Children Act 1989.

8 See, for example, in a British context West (1982: 104–11); Brody (1976: 14–16).

9 The terms 'decarceration' and 'deinstitutionalization' are used to refer respectively to the general movement to reduce or abolish custodial and other institutional methods (for example residential children's homes) of dealing with offenders and other deviants.

10 For details, see Bottoms and Dignan (2004). The Scottish system's commitment to a thoroughgoing diversionary approach is epitomized by the legal principle that no requirement or order shall be made with respect to a child unless 'it would be better for the child that the requirement or order be made than that none should be made at all' (s. 16(3) of the Children (Scotland) Act, 1995).

11 Which was indeed the term by which it became known in England and Wales (see for example, Jones, 1984). However, as Dünkel (1996a) has pointed out, diversionary measures and alternatives for dealing with minor crimes and status offences have also been introduced in many other European countries.

12 Within the restorative justice movement (as opposed to this ideal-typical model) there are a number of important differences of emphasis, notably with regard to the issue of 'community involvement' and what this entails. The term 'community of care' refers principally to those who are concerned for the well-being of either the victim or the offender. A somewhat broader term that is sometimes used is the 'community of interest', which also encompasses others who have concerns about the offence and its consequences, and those who may be able to contribute towards a solution to the problem presented by the offence. Conversely, other restorative justice advocates prioritize the involvement of victims and offenders themselves, and place far less emphasis on the involvement of others. See Dignan (2002; 2005) for these and other tensions within the restorative justice movement itself.

13 The principle of subsidiarity refers to the decentralizing doctrine that nothing should be done by larger, more complex organizations that cannot be done as well by smaller and simpler organizations. It originated as a key precept in Catholic social thought in opposition to the assumption by the state (as opposed to the church and families, etc.) of responsibility for promoting social welfare, but has subsequently been applied to the allocation of decision-making responsibility within the European Union.

14 In some jurisdictions, including England and Wales, conferences have established a more secure footing in the child welfare field than in the criminal justice sphere (Dignan and Marsh, 2001: 89).

15 There are plans to extend the use of diversionary conferencing initiatives for certain categories of adult offenders also, but these have so far not come to fruition.

16 In terms of the strategies to which we refer in the introduction, this model can perhaps best be thought of as representing an amalgam of Strategies A and B, an approach that we have also referred to elsewhere as 'punitive managerialism' (Cavadino et al., 1999: 54). See also Muncie and Hughes (2002).

17 We shall later refer to this as 'responsibilization' (Muncie, 1999: 169). It is true that the concept of 'responsibility' also features in both the justice and restorative justice models. However, the neo-correctionalist variant differs in compromising the procedural safeguards that are associated with the justice model while rejecting the participatory and inclusive elements associated with a restorative justice approach.

18 The tension between restorative justice and neo-correctionalist values is also illustrated in the strong government support that is currently given in England to the idea of 'community payback', which may include physical work, such as clearing up litter, graffiti or vandalism and other forms of conservation work, in addition to the provision of social support to vulnerable groups (Home Office et al., 2002). In marked contrast with this, the degree of support for direct victim reparation or victim participation in restorative justice processes since 1997 has been far more restrained.

19 Whereas the welfare model favours (ostensibly at least) early intervention as a means of protecting the child, the neo-correctionalist approach is more interested in its moralizing and controlling potential with a view to protecting adults and an adult-oriented social order against disruption and disorder on the part of children and young people (Qvortrup, 1997: 80).

20 See, for example, the introduction of anti-social behaviour orders in England and Wales, which we refer to below.

13

Neo-Liberal Youth Justice Systems

Generalizing broadly, we will see that neo-liberal youth justice systems are the most divergent and also, in many ways, the most volatile of all. Nevertheless, a number of broad tendencies can be discerned. Firstly, the effect of the welfare approach has been far more uneven within this group of countries than in most other types of penal polity. Secondly, irrespective of its original impact, the welfare approach has shown far less endurance in neo-liberal than in most other types of youth justice systems. Thirdly, neo-liberal youth justice systems have been particularly receptive to the justice model.[1] And finally, with the singular and fascinating exception of New Zealand, neo-liberal youth justice systems have in recent years shown a far greater affinity towards an uncompromisingly *neo-correctionalist* approach than any other type of penal polity.

Youth justice in the USA[2]

In 1899, the state of Illinois created the first juvenile court in the USA.[3] This took the form of a socialized welfare tribunal that was presided over by special judges who were not necessarily legally trained. It also incorporated a new procedure – the delinquency petition – the intended effect of which was to put in issue the characteristics of the individual children and the circumstances of their backgrounds rather than the specific offences they may have committed. This approach reflected the *parens patriae* principle that delinquent children and those in need should be protected by the benevolent authority of the state, which would help them overcome their delinquency or misfortune. As such, it was intended to provide a welfare-based alternative to the adult criminal courts and, despite the many subsequent changes, the American youth justice system formally still remains largely separate from the adult criminal justice system.[4] However, the boundaries between the two systems are now more porous for children charged with criminal offences[5] than at any time since 1899.

The first change in the ostensibly welfare-based philosophy that underpinned the juvenile court was prompted by a series of Supreme Court decisions, beginning with the landmark cases of *Kent* v. *the United States* and *In re Gault*, decided in 1966 and 1967 respectively.[6] The combined effect of these legal challenges was to 'legalize' the procedure of the juvenile court, which had hitherto relied upon informal processes, confidential hearings and an absence of procedural rights. Notwithstanding its benevolent-sounding 'child-saving' rhetoric and the humanitarian concerns that may have inspired its early development, critics of the welfare approach[7] viewed the early juvenile court system as an essentially coercive and discriminatory system of social control. In their view, one of its most important functions in reality was to control, assimilate and 'Americanize' the children of recently arrived immigrants and those from racial and ethnic minorities (Platt, 1977; Sutton, 1980). The 'due process' revolution that was unleashed by the Supreme Court was part of a broader contemporary liberal commitment to the protection of human rights in general and the civil rights of racial minorities in particular.[8] Although from a strict legal point of view, the Warren Court's 'due process' rulings were confined to the extension of juveniles' procedural rights, they ultimately transformed the substance of the youth justice system as well. Thus, the effect of the Supreme Court's interventions was not only to substitute an adversarial trial process for the welfare-based paternalistic model, but also to undermine the welfare model in respect of many of the process's substantive outcomes. The characteristics of the welfare model included an emphasis on 'treatment' rather than 'punishment' as the basis for coercive interventions, an ostensible focus on the young person's future welfare rather than any offence they may have committed, and a marked preference for indeterminate, non-proportional sentences. All these were threatened by the procedural revolution that was underpinned by a radically different set of philosophical foundations, based on the 'justice model'.

However, the new youth justice edifice that was ultimately to emerge from the ruins of the welfare model did not in the end reflect the penologically restrained styling of the classicist justice model so much as the far more brutalist architectural style that we have come to associate with the neo-correctionalist model. Several factors contributed to this unanticipated turn of events. One was the escalating crime wave that coincided with the due process revolution as the demographic bulge created by the postwar baby boom began to make an impact on juvenile delinquency rates during the 1960s. This provoked a succession of moral panics which came to a head during the 1980s over issues such as the 'epidemic' of crack cocaine and the proliferation of guns among young black males, resulting in a steep escalation in the homicide rates among this sector of the population. A second factor was the urban racial disorders of the 1960s, during which American cities were rocked by violent black protests fuelled by decades of discrimination, deprivation and segregation. Moreover, structural and economic changes during the 1970s and 1980s exacerbated both sets of problems by contributing to the deindustrialization of many inner-city areas. This has resulted in the emergence of an increasingly isolated largely black urban 'underclass' living in acute poverty which is hardly alleviated by the extremely limited welfare provision that is available.

This confluence of structural, economic, and demographic changes was increasingly exploited by conservative politicians for their own electoral advantage from the late 1960s onwards, by fanning public concerns over youth crime, violence, and racial disorder to whip up support for their own much more punitive law and order policies. By successfully attributing the rise in crime to fecklessness on the part of individual offenders rather than social structural forces, and by pinning the blame for failing to halt the rise in crime on 'excessively lenient' criminal justice agencies they have been able to garner electoral support for their own hardline law and order policies.

The overwhelming predominance of the current neo-correctionalist approach in the American youth justice sphere is reflected in two complementary sets of trends. The first relates to a continuing tendency to blur the formerly distinct boundaries between the juvenile court and adult criminal courts, thereby exposing increasing numbers of juvenile offenders to the more punitive disposals that are available in the latter. And the second relates to the increasingly punitive strategies that are likewise being adopted for those who remain subject to the jurisdiction of the juvenile court.

The boundaries between the juvenile and criminal courts have never been completely watertight since juvenile court judges have always had the power to waive the jurisdiction of the juvenile court, though traditionally this was only exercised in respect of a small number of 'chronic' or 'heinous' offenders (Tanenhaus, 2004). During the 1980s and 1990s, however, a majority of states and also the federal jurisdiction adopted statutory mechanisms that facilitate the transfer of juvenile offenders to criminal courts. One such device is the 'legislative exclusion' clause, the effect of which is to automatically exclude the jurisdiction of the juvenile court, either for certain categories of offence (for example violence) or for specific types of offenders.[9] Another device is the 'prosecutorial waiver' clause that enables a prosecutor to select the forum in which a juvenile offender will be tried. Although the prosecutor's discretion is subject to statutory guidelines (for example relating to age, offence or previous convictions) these are frequently very broad and, in some cases, permit the transfer of young people charged with property offences or even merely misdemeanours. Between 1992 and 1997, no fewer than forty-four states and the District of Columbia passed laws making it easier for juveniles to be tried as adults. Once transferred in this way, juvenile offenders are liable upon conviction to be sentenced in the same way as if they were adults, sent to the same prisons, and until a Supreme Court decision in March 2005, could even be sentenced to capital punishment for crimes they committed as children.[10]

Between 1988 and 1994, the number of delinquency cases transferred to adult courts as a result of judicial waivers grew by 73 per cent and, although the numbers have declined somewhat since then, this is partly a result of an increase in the number of serious cases involving juvenile offenders that bypass the juvenile court altogether as a result of statutory exclusion or prosecutorial waiver provisions. Although the number of cases transferred to adult courts constitutes a small proportion of the total caseload that is formally processed by the juvenile court,[11] the upward trend in recent years reflects a fundamental legal, political and cultural shift in the way juvenile offenders are conceptualized. From being seen as innocent, dependent and often vulnerable children they are increasingly viewed as responsible, autonomous and often predatory 'quasi-adults'. Moreover, this reconceptualization of the juvenile offender is also discernible in the way young people who remain within the jurisdiction of the juvenile court are dealt with.

In the past, the welfare-oriented *parens patriae* philosophy of the juvenile court placed greater emphasis on the social circumstances of the young people appearing before them – with a view to determining the kind of treatment that would promote their 'best interests' – than the need for judicial safeguards or even proof of legal guilt. Now, however, juvenile sentencing laws increasingly adopt offence-related principles either based on 'just deserts' notions of proportionality and determinacy or 'get tough' mandatory minimum sentence criteria[12] in order to 'guide' sentencing discretion and thereby restrict the scope for judicial leniency. According to Fagan and Feld, (2001), just under half (twenty-two) the states had adopted such criteria by the mid-1990s. Moreover, by the end of 1995, seventeen states had adopted 'blended sentencing' provisions that authorize courts to impose juvenile and/or adult correctional (custodial) sanctions on serious and violent juvenile offenders whether they have been dealt with in a juvenile or adult criminal court. The growth in popularity of boot camps for juveniles as a form of 'shock incarceration' during the 1980s and 1990s[13] is another example of the tendency to treat delinquent youth as if they were adult criminals. Another illustration of the way in which the boundaries have been blurred between juvenile and adult courts relates to the growing tendency to 'open up' the former, at least in respect of serious offences, by admitting the public and allowing offenders to be identified (Torbet and Szymanski, 1998). This has the effect of removing the protective screen of confidentiality that previously may have helped to reduce – for juveniles at any rate – some of the adverse consequences associated with 'labelling'.

Perhaps not surprisingly, one obvious effect of this increasingly punitive orientation has been a dramatic increase in the incarceration rate for juvenile offenders. By 1999,[14] 371 juveniles were in custody for every 100,000 in the population[15] (compared with 245 in 1995), though this masks a huge variation in the custody rate for individual states, which ranged from ninety in Vermont[16] to 704 in the District of Columbia (Sickmund, 2004). It also conceals an enormous – and widening – disparity in the incarceration rates for offenders of different ethnic origins. Thus, national custody rates for black juveniles were substantially higher than for other groups. For every 100,000 non-Hispanic black juveniles in the population, no fewer than 1,004 were in a residential placement facility on census day in 1999, which compares with a rate of 485 for Hispanics and 212 for non-Hispanic whites.[17] Moreover, a study examining proportional changes in the racial composition of institutional populations for the period 1985–95, which corresponds with the era of 'get tough' legislative sentencing initiatives, revealed that while the percentage of black juveniles who were confined in public facilities *increased* by almost 63 per cent, the corresponding figure for white juveniles actually *declined* by 7 per cent (Feld, 1999), thereby increasing the differential still further.[18]

So far, the trends we have been examining suggest that, at least in the case of more serious and persistent juvenile offenders, there has been a sustained and dramatic shift in the orientation of the American youth justice system away from the welfare approach which characterized it until the 1970s. However, the current orientation is most appropriately characterized not in terms of the justice model – with its emphasis on consistency and restraint in the administration of punishment – but rather in terms of the much more punitive and regressive variant that we have called the neo-correctional model. But this is only part of the picture, since we have not yet said anything about the way the US youth justice system deals with less serious non-persistent offenders. Here the pattern becomes rather more complex.

Firstly, it is important to note that the retreat from the welfare approach since the mid-1970s has also been accompanied by a steep reduction in the use of detention for 'status offence' cases (those that would not constitute an offence if committed by an adult). In 1975 an estimated 143,000 status offence cases involved detention, whereas by 1996 the figure was down to just over 39,000 (Snyder and Sickmund, 1999). And whereas status offence cases were twice as likely as delinquency cases to involve secure detention prior to disposition in 1975, by 1992 the likelihood of detention was only half that for delinquency cases.[19] Secondly, it should also be noted that very many non-status offence cases that are referred to the juvenile court are dealt with informally following a decision by the prosecutor or court intake officer that a satisfactory resolution is possible without any formal intervention on the part of the court. This is in addition to the informal diversion (which is unrecorded and therefore unquantifiable) that occurs as a result of the police deciding to lecture or warn a juvenile wrongdoer prior to release. In 1999, 42 per cent of all juvenile delinquency cases were handled informally by the juvenile courts (Puzzanchera et al., 2003). Both these tendencies might be thought to indicate at least a residual commitment to the minimum intervention approach in the case of less serious offenders.[20] It could also be argued that they are consistent with a 'bifurcatory' approach that adopts a tough approach when dealing with really serious offenders while exercising leniency towards minor transgressors. However, the position is not quite that straightforward.

Firstly, although it is true that significant numbers of cases are dealt with informally, the proportion of cases that are handled in this way has declined substantially in recent years. In 1988, for example, over half of all cases were resolved informally, compared with 42 per cent just over a decade later. Secondly, most of the cases that are informally resolved (just over 60 per cent in 1999) still entail some form of intervention service and/or sanction to which the young person agrees in return for the charges being dropped. These might include a term of voluntary probation supervision, voluntary restitution, community service, or referral to another agency such as a specialized drug or alcohol rehabilitation centre or mental health treatment centre.[21] This tendency reflects a growing dissatisfaction with diversion for its own sake in recent years, and a preference for 'conditional' diversion, frequently linked to the making of reparation. To this limited extent there is some slight support for at least a rudimentary restorative justice approach, but little in the way of official commitment.[22] Thirdly, there is a growing tendency to adopt 'pre-emptive' interventions even in respect of juveniles who have not offended. Thus, since 1990, over 1,000 localities have introduced curfew provisions to keep young people off the streets during the late evening and early morning periods. And fourthly, there is also a growing tendency to hold parents responsible for the consequences of their children's offending, either by making them attend parenting classes or by requiring them to pay restitution or reimburse the state for the costs associated with the care, support, detention of treatment of their children. Both the latter tendencies are more consistent with a neo-correctionalist than a minimum intervention approach.

Perhaps we can summarize recent trends in the US juvenile system by saying that they combine a strategy of harshly punitive correctionalism for serious and persistent offenders with a tendency towards a somewhat milder but still punitive form of correctionalism (sometimes incorporating an element of reparation) in respect of less serious offenders. Moreover, these tendencies are supplemented by the development of new forms of preventive correctionalism that are increasingly being directed at non-offenders. The overall effect has been to substantially increase the degree formal social control that is exerted over young offenders compared with the position even as recently as two decades ago. Contemporaneously, many of the special protective measures that young offenders have traditionally benefited from have been curtailed, for example by 'opening up' juvenile court proceedings and official records to the public and the media.[23]

Youth justice in Great Britain[24]

The English and Scottish youth justice systems share a common early history that differs in several important respects from the US model. During the nineteenth century children in both jurisdictions were treated as adults in the eyes of the law, and were liable to adult penalties, including imprisonment, transportation or the death penalty, if convicted of a criminal offence. In the Children Act of 1908, however, courts catering specifically for juveniles were introduced in both England and Scotland. Unlike the US-style socialized welfare tribunals, these were intended from the outset to operate as conventional criminal courts, subject to relatively minor modifications. One distinctive feature was that hearings were either held in a separate court building or at a different time from adult proceedings, and the other was that public access was restricted. In most other respects, however, they continued to resemble adult criminal courts both with regard to their largely due process based procedures and also in terms of their personnel, though subsequently separate specialist panels of magistrates were appointed to preside over hearings involving young offenders.[25] These early juvenile courts also retained a punitive ethos, the main differences from the adult system being that restrictions were placed on the use of imprisonment, which was abolished altogether for children under the age of 14; alternative disposals including probation supervision were introduced; and new, separate, custodial institutions were developed for young people.

One respect in which these juvenile courts did resemble their US counterparts was that they too combined the two distinct jurisdictional strands relating on the one hand to young offenders and on the other hand to children in need of care and protection. However, in contrast to many other countries that adopted the socialized welfare tribunal model, the juvenile court's 'care jurisdiction' was always subordinate, both ideologically and numerically, to its criminal jurisdiction (Bottoms and Dignan, 2004).

In terms of the youth justice models we referred to above, the early history of the juvenile justice system in England and Scotland owed more to the justice than the welfare model and, generalizing somewhat, this state of affairs persisted until the late 1960s. During that decade however, the juvenile justice systems in both England and Scotland underwent a radical reappraisal, resulting in both cases in significant (but rather different) legislative reforms that were intended to totally transform each system. In each case the dominant ideology underlying the reform programme was an explicitly welfare approach in which much greater precedence was to be accorded to the welfare of the child, even when dealing with criminal allegations. As such, the apparent ascendancy of the welfare approach in England and Scotland during this period provides an interesting counter-example to the globalizing tendencies that are more normally remarked upon in a youth justice context, since it coincided with the first wave of legal challenges that were ultimately to undermine and subvert the welfare-based approach to youth justice in the USA. At this point, however, the hitherto common trajectory of the English and Scottish juvenile justice systems began to diverge, giving to rise to two sharply contrasting sets of arrangements on either side of the border.[26]

In Scotland, the former juvenile court structure was completely dismantled and replaced by a new system of children's hearings, operating entirely within the civil jurisdiction, which deals both with suspected child offenders and those in need of care and protection. With regard to the former category, the hearings system deals with young persons aged 8–15 who are alleged to have committed a criminal offence. With regard to the latter category, it has jurisdiction over children under 16 who are thought to be in need of care and protection.

One of the most distinctive features of the Scottish system is the priority that is ostensibly accorded to the 'welfare of the child' as the paramount consideration whether dealing with offence or care and protection cases. But whereas in other jurisdictions that have adopted a welfare-based approach (including the USA, as we have seen) this has often resulted in an excessively coercive interventionist approach, this has not been the case in Scotland. There, the system has been strongly influenced from the outset by a version of the 'minimum interventionist' ethos. This is reflected in two key aspects of the Scottish system. The first distinctive feature is that most child offence cases that are not dealt with informally by the police[27] are referred to an official called the 'Reporter to the Children's Hearing', who exercises a pivotal 'gatekeeping' role within the process. For the reporter has to be satisfied both that there is evidence to support the ground on which the case has been referred – i.e. that the child has committed the offence, if it is a criminal case[28] – and that the child is potentially in need of compulsory measures of care. And second, the minimum intervention ethos is now encapsulated in Scottish law (Children [Scotland] Act 1995, s. 16(3)), which states that the court should not make any order or requirement of any kind unless it would be better for the child than not to do so. (The 'no beneficial order' principle, see Kearney [2000: 25] and Bottoms and Dignan [2004].)

A second distinctive feature of the Scottish system is that the hearings themselves are conducted by lay panels, each comprising three members of the public, who differ from English lay magistrates in two important respects. First, in terms of their responsibilities, they are specifically recruited, trained and required to deal with children according to their needs within an explicitly welfare-based system. And second, in terms of their occupational background, they are much more likely than their counterparts in the English lay magistracy to be drawn from the spheres of health, education and welfare (Asquith, 1983: 134; see also Bottoms and Dignan, 2004).

A third feature of the Scottish system is that the range of disposals available to panel members is remarkably limited, particularly since they apply to both offence-based and care-based cases. The first option is for the Hearing panel to discharge the case, taking no action; a second option is to make a non-residential supervision requirement, which allows the child to remain at home under the supervision of a social worker; and the third possibility involves placing the child in a specified kind of residential establishment, such as a hostel, local authority home or residential school.

In practice, the commission of a criminal offence simply constitutes one of a number of possible grounds that, if proved or accepted, might result in a child being brought before a hearing. Moreover, even in such cases, the paramount consideration for panel members is the child's welfare needs rather than his or her criminal deeds. In terms of practical outcomes, three trends are particularly noteworthy in the present context.

Firstly, there has been a strong and, indeed, continuing diversionary ethos ever since the inception of the Children's Hearing system (for details see Bottoms and Dignan, 2004: Table 3). This is reflected in a steady increase in the proportion of potentially eligible offence-based cases that are diverted away from the Hearings, and in which no action is taken (rising from 39 per cent in 1980 to 71 per cent in 1999). This trend is matched by a corresponding decline in the proportion of cases that are referred to a Hearing (from 48 per cent in 1980 to 20 per cent in 1999).

Secondly, a closely related trend consists of a marked change in the proportion of offence-based as opposed to care and protection cases coming before the Hearings. In 1975, the great majority of all referrals (88 per cent) involved alleged offences, and only 4 per cent related to care and protection issues, which is consistent with the historical tendency we remarked upon earlier for the care jurisdiction to be ideologically and numerically subordinate to the offence jurisdiction within both England and Scotland. By 1999, however, the proportion of referrals involving alleged offence grounds had declined to 45 per cent, whereas the proportion of cases involving care and protection issues had increased to 41 per cent (see for details Bottoms and Dignan, 2004: Table 7).

Thirdly, there has been a steady decline in both the number and proportion of cases dealt with by means of residential placements of whatever kind. Thus, in 1980 there were 4,634 placements in total, 33 per cent of which involved a residential placement of some kind; but by 1999 there were just 1,204 placements in total, of which only 22 per cent involved any kind of residential placement Bottoms and Dignan, 2004: Table 6).[29] This trend is also consistent with a strong commitment to the minimum intervention model, which places an emphatic emphasis on the use of custody only as a last resort. Despite this emphasis, Scotland nevertheless shares with England and Wales the dubious status of being among the countries with the highest proportion of prison inmates under the age of 21. An explanation for this apparent paradox lies in the fact that the relatively lenient and non-interventionist Scottish youth justice system only has jurisdiction over young people who are below the age of 16 (whereas the English youth justice system deals with 16 and 17 year olds). Scottish offenders who are over the age of 16[30] come under the jurisdiction of the adult criminal justice system which, in comparison, is far more punitive and much less influenced by either welfare or minimum interventionist principles. Nevertheless, it is worth noting at this point that the average daily prisoner population of young offenders (under the age of 21) under sentence has declined somewhat in recent years from 798 (comprising 16 per cent of the total prison population) in 1996–7 to 602 (comprising 11.5 per cent of the prison population) in 2002–3 (Scottish Prison Service, 2003: Appendix 3; see also Bottoms and Dignan, 2004: 145).

One final noteworthy feature of the reformed Scottish youth justice system – at least during the period prior to the creation of a devolved Scottish Parliament in 1999 – is that it had persisted for thirty years in largely unchanged form, during which period it continued to enjoy widespread backing among the Scottish political, legal and policy-making establishment. These features – its hitherto long-term stability, distinctiveness and consensuality – stand in sharp contrast with most of the other neo-liberal polities dealt with in this section, and in particular with the far more turbulent and contentious English experience during the same period.

At one stage in the late 1960s it appeared as if the English youth justice system was embarking on a very similar welfare-inspired programme of reform to the one that was adopted north of the border. One of the original aims of the Children and Young Persons Act 1969 was to provide an alternative to prosecution for the majority of young offenders by prescribing pre-trial consultation between police and social work agencies. They were intended to act as gatekeepers, and also to direct young people who required them to appropriate forms of treatment and assistance. A second aim was to replace the system of criminal prosecutions with civil care proceedings for those under the age of 14, and for all but the most serious juvenile offenders above this age. A third aim was to substitute non-punitive and semi-indeterminate residential care placements of the kind currently available in Scotland for punitive custody. Unlike Scotland, however, the outward form (and also the personnel) of the existing English juvenile courts was to be retained, including its adversarial style of proceedings.

For various complex domestic political reasons, however, the English legislation was only ever partially implemented. Indeed, the existing custodial powers of the magistrates were not only retained but, in certain respects, were subsequently reinforced. Moreover, those provisions that did take effect proved highly controversial, and the resulting changes in the youth justice system were diametrically opposed to the original intentions (for details see Cavadino and Dignan, 2002: 289–90).

Thus, there was a dramatic decline in the use of community-based disposals for young offenders, a massive rise in the use of custody (from 3,000 in 1970 to nearly 8000 by 1982) and a doubling in the proportion of 14–16-year-olds who were given custodial sentences (from 6 to 12 per cent between 1970 and 1978). Shortly after the incomplete reform of the English youth justice system, support for the welfare principle in England (as in many places elsewhere) was undermined by the collapse of confidence in the 'rehabilitative ideal'. However, the influences that began to shape the English youth justice system during the final quarter of the twentieth century were derived from a variety of often conflicting ideological approaches, none of which have achieved total supremacy.

The growth in the use of custody during the 1970s and early 1980s was indicative of an early switch towards a more correctionalist approach, and coincided with a rightward shift in the political spectrum. However, the increasingly strident law and order rhetoric of the early 1980s belied a more complex picture at the level of penal reform and particularly with regard to penal practice. A second, very powerful influence on the development of juvenile justice during the 1980s was the minimum intervention philosophy, which was actively embraced by a 'juvenile justice movement' of juvenile justice practitioners and supporting academics. They pioneered the development of a 'systems management' approach, based on the principles of decarceration, diversion from court and from custody, gatekeeping, inter-agency cooperation, targeting and monitoring that we described earlier. Moreover, they also elicited the active support of the government of the day, which (largely for pragmatic managerial reasons rather than the humane concerns of the 'juvenile' justice movement) officially supported and promoted the use of formal police cautioning as an alternative to prosecution. The practical impact of this accommodation between the ideologically committed practitioners associated with the youth justice movement and the pragmatic support of the government was enormous. Cautioning rates increased dramatically during the 1980s: for example 82 per cent of known indictable offenders under the age of 17 were cautioned in 1992, compared with 49 per cent in 1980.[31] And the use of gatekeeping tactics to reduce the levels of custody and residential care were so successful that some parts of the country prided themselves on achieving the status of 'custody-free zones' for juveniles under the age of 17.

A third source of influence on the development of the youth justice system during this period took the form of 'justice model' thinking, which was reflected in a number of developments. The first of these involved the replacement in 1982 of a semi-indeterminate treatment-oriented form of custody known as 'borstal training' with a determinate, more explicitly punitive custodial sentence, known as 'youth custody'. The introduction (also in 1982) of 'gatekeeping' criteria which needed to be met before a custodial sentence could be passed on young offenders was also consistent with 'justice model' thinking insofar as it was intended to promote greater consistency and parsimony in the application of punishment. And third, the introduction of a variety of procedural reforms during the final quarter of the twentieth century – including the growth of state-aided legal representation for defendants, and advance disclosure of the prosecution case – was likewise consistent with a 'justice model' approach. However, these reforms also resulted in increased delay and expenditure, and thereby helped to fuel concerns about the efficiency and effectiveness of the youth justice system that were to come to a head during the 1990s. Another significant, though often overlooked, change that took place during this period involved a disaggregation of the previously combined care/offence jurisdictions of the English juvenile courts, which took effect in 1989. Thereafter, a separate care jurisdiction was established with its own family proceedings court, leaving the juvenile court, which was soon to be renamed the youth court, to deal exclusively with criminal matters.

One of the most characteristic features of the English youth justice system in recent years has been its instability and turbulence. A second is the extent to which significant shifts in youth justice policy have been prompted by external events, and the (perceived) public response they elicit. During the early 1990s a succession of 'moral panics' about various youth crime issues contributed to a 'demonization of young offenders' (Graef, 1995). These prompted a succession of policy changes that have culminated in an attempt to fundamentally reform the entire youth justice system, which is still ongoing, and to which we now turn.

A 'New Labour' government came to power in 1997 after a period of eighteen years in opposition. Reform of the English youth justice system was one of its principal policy priorities, and a flurry of legislative changes was introduced during its first two years of office. Although these built to some extent upon changes that had already been adopted by the outgoing Conservative administration[32] much was new. Indeed, the system as a whole has been so significantly altered since 1998 that it has been referred to as the 'New Youth Justice' (for example, Goldson, 2000). At a philosophical level the 'new youth justice' system is based on a repudiation of many aspects of the youth justice orthodoxy that had prevailed until the mid-1990s. One was the principle of minimum intervention. A second was the alleged preoccupation with 'processing' young offenders through the system (or out of it), often without any effective remedial action being taken. And the third involved an alleged 'culture of excuses' whereby, according to Labour Home Secretary Jack Straw (1997–2001), the youth justice system 'excuses itself for its inefficiency, and too often excuses the young offenders before it, implying that they cannot help their behaviour because of their social circumstances' (Home Office, 1997: 1).

In place of this 'old orthodoxy', the government's youth justice reform policy was chiefly influenced by 'neo-correctionalist' thinking, partially attenuated by – or at any rate incorporating – certain elements of a restorative justice approach. These philosophical underpinnings are reflected in five key principles that have informed its strategy.[33]

(i) **The primacy of preventing offending** The prevention of offending by children and young people has been adopted as the principal aim of the entire post-1998 youth justice system. This represents a symbolic shift of focus that further undermines the hitherto influential principles of minimum interventionism and justice model thinking. The principle is reflected in the introduction of two new non-criminal measures for dealing with pre-delinquents. The first authorizes the imposition of local *child curfews* on children under the age of ten, thereby widening the criminal justice net. A second measure – the *child safety order* – enables courts to place under supervision children under the age of ten who have committed (or are thought to be at risk of committing) acts for which they might have been prosecuted if older. Although little used in practice as yet, measure has been criticized for effectively abandoning the minimum age of responsibility[34] (Fionda, 1999: 45), and also for its potentially drastic ning effect. Both measures are somewhat redolent of the nineteenth- welfare approach which also sought to control analogous non-criminal forms of behaviour. This combination of a punitive neo-correctionalist approach with a quasi-welfarist agenda is symptomatic of a tension that lies at the heart of the current youth justice reform programme.[35]

(ii) Effective interventionism Two key features of the new preventive approach are early intervention and intensive community supervision. Early intervention is intended to be effective in 'nipping offending in the bud', and is reflected in the introduction of a new statutory pre-trial diversion process to replace the old system of cautioning. This is based on a graduated response in which young offenders now normally at best receive a single reprimand, followed by a more serious 'final warning' that can (and usually does) entail some additional action or intervention apart from the warning itself, before being prosecuted if they reoffend. Another example of 'early intervention' involves the use of 'Anti-Social Behaviour Orders' (ASBOs) that were introduced in 1998 to cover forms of behaviour (including persistent nuisance, harassment, verbal abuse, intimidation and minor damage) that were felt not to be adequately regulated by the criminal law. The measure, which applies to anyone over the age of ten, is controversial since it is a civil measure, which means that the standard of proof is lower than that required for a criminal conviction. Yet it can result in the imposition of long-lasting (for a minimum of two years) restrictions including bans on entering certain areas and curfews. Moreover, a breach of an order constitutes a criminal offence that is punishable by up to five years in prison. Finally, a new system of intensive supervision in the community known as 'Intensive Supervision and Surveillance Programmes' has been introduced as an additional sentencing option when dealing with persistent offenders. Such programmes may run alongside certain other pre-existing community penalties.[36]

The notion of effective interventionism itself is predicated on a new form of correctionalism that differs from the old-style treatment model with its emphasis on the personal rehabilitation of convicted offenders. Instead, the new approach sets out to address a relatively limited range of 'risk factors' – for example truancy, poor parenting and dysfunctional peer relationships – that are taken to be predictive of future offending behaviour. As we have seen, it frequently involves pre-emptive action taken against those who have not yet been convicted of a criminal offence. And although ostensibly based on an 'evidence-led approach', the strategy has been criticized for neglecting empirical findings that call into question the causative status of the selected range of aetiological factors (Pitts, 2001: 9).

(iii) Responsibilization Muncie (1999: 169) adopted this somewhat inelegant term in order to elucidate an important feature of the new youth justice system. Its most obvious connotation relates to the increased expectation that young offenders themselves should take responsibility for their own actions. The recent abolition of the former doctrine of *doli incapax*[37] (see above) is one obvious manifestation of this principle. But a secondary connotation draws attention to the fact that parents are also expected to face up to their responsibilities for their offspring's offending behaviour. Thus, parents of children who have offended or acted anti-socially may find themselves subject to a parenting order, requiring them to attend compulsory counselling and guidance sessions or face a substantial fine. Once again the combination of welfare aspirations with overtly punitive enforcement sanctions arguably betrays a degree of tension within the reform strategy itself.

(iv) Reparation   In addition to – but also explicitly subordinate to – the primary aim of prevention, the new youth justice system also seeks to ensure that young people are helped to understand the harm that is done to victims and communities, for example by making appropriate reparation. Reparation can be made to serve a double purpose: firstly, by providing a tangible manifestation of an offender's willingness to take responsibility for their actions; and secondly, by demonstrating a greater commitment (not least on the part of the government itself) to meeting the needs of victims.

Accordingly, measures have been introduced to promote the use of reparation and, to a lesser extent, mediation as part of the sentencing process.[38] One of the most obvious of these measures is the so-called 'reparation order', which requires young offenders to make reparation to their victims (provided they are willing to receive it) or the local community. This incorporation of a relatively modest element of restorative justice was potentially boosted by the introduction in April 2002 of a new procedure for dealing with young offenders who are being prosecuted for the first time, provided they are willing to plead guilty and provided the offence in question is not serious enough to merit a custodial sentence. In almost all such cases the court now makes a 'referral order' referring the young person to a youth offender panel, thus providing a significant new avenue for diverting offenders from court. The panels are a non-judicial forum within which the panel members, together with the young offender and possibly others – including the offender's parents and the victim – are able to agree on a 'youth offender contract'. Such contracts may embody a wide range of possible activities and requirements, including (but not restricted to) reparation to the victim or the community, or programmes designed to address the young person's offending behaviour. Despite their undeniable restorative justice potential, however, early empirical findings have shown a disappointingly low level of victim participation and input (Newburn et al., 2002).

(v) Efficiency   A perception that the old youth justice system was excessively preoccupied with procedures at the expense of delivering effective interventions to prevent offending has contributed to an emphasis on the need for greater efficiency and value for money. One of the most obvious manifestations of this principle has been the drive to speed up procedures, by a series of 'fast-tracking' initiatives focused in particular on persistent young offenders, though it is also associated with a number of institutional changes that have been introduced since 1997, and to which we now turn.

The first and most significant of these changes involves the creation of new localized multi-agency *youth offending teams* which are responsible for providing a comprehensive range of youth justice services within each local authority area. A national Youth Justice Board has also been established with wide-ranging powers including the promotion of good practice, funding of new initiatives, setting of national standards, monitoring of the youth justice system and advising the Home Secretary on the operation of the system. Finally, the reform programme also entails an attempt to bring about a radical *change of culture* on the part of youth justice agencies and practitioners.

One obvious target group comprises the practitioners who are now employed within the youth offending teams, many of whom may well have sympathized with the minimum intervention philosophy as espoused by the 1980s juvenile justice movement, but who are now being cajoled into supporting the new correctionalist strategy. Attempts to change the culture of youth justice also extend to the youth court itself. One set of initiatives involves changes to the layout of the court that are aimed at producing a less intimidating setting within which everyone present might be encouraged to talk more directly about the reasons for a young person's offending behaviour and what needs to be done about it (Allen et al., 2000). The government has also complained about the 'culture of secrecy' surrounding the youth court, which has been pejoratively described as a 'secret garden'. This has prompted a range of initiatives designed to make the court more open to the victim and the general public and also, in certain cases,[39] to facilitate greater access to the media, though this process has not gone as far in the direction of 'naming and shaming' young offenders as in some US states (see above).

As for their impact on youth justice practice, the above reforms have contributed to a significant reduction in the proportion of young offenders who are cautioned as opposed to being prosecuted and, conversely, a marked increase in the proportionate use of custody. Both trends are in marked contrast to recent developments in Scotland, which we remarked upon earlier. The caution rate for juveniles was already in steep decline during the period leading up to the implementation of the new English system, but in the year that it took effect nation-wide (in June 2000), the number of juveniles who were dealt with by means of cautions, reprimands and final warnings declined by 8 per cent. According to the latest criminal statistics (for 2003), the downward trend in the juvenile caution rate continued across all the juvenile age ranges and in respect of both males and females until 2002[40] though in 2003 it appears to have stabilized or even been reversed in the case of male offenders and also in respect of female offenders aged 15–20 (Home Office, 2003: Table 2.3).

With regard to the use of custody the picture is a little more complicated. In the year 2000, a new custodial sentence for young people – the detention and training order – was introduced, half of which was to be served in custody, and half under supervision in community. During its first year of operation, the number of custodial sentences imposed increased by 10 per cent, despite a 12 per cent reduction in the number of recorded offences in the eight categories of offences most likely to attract a custodial sentence (Youth Justice Board, 2001). In the following year, 2001, a new intensive community-based 'Intensive Supervision and Surveillance Programme' was introduced, which appears to have contributed to a slight short-term decrease in the proportion of young offenders given custodial sentences,[41] though this was offset in part by a slight increase in the proportion of young offenders given a secure remand during the same period[42] (Audit Commission, 2004: Appendix 5). Nevertheless, by 2002, the number of 15–17-year-old boys who were sentenced to some form of custodial disposal was 70 per cent higher than it had been a decade earlier, while the number of girls had increased by a factor of five (Home Office, 2003; Table 4.9). Of the 6,944 young people who were given custodial disposals in 2003–4, a total of 794 (11.4 per cent) were under the age of 15. Moreover, in the first few months of 2004, the number of young people who make up the 'secure estate' population[43] had begun to rise again, after a short period of stability, and in March 2004 it was 10.5 per cent higher than it had been at the end of 2003 (Youth Justice Board, 2004: 76).

As we have seen, the UK has not one, but two remarkably different youth justice systems. The Scottish system until recently seemed to be relatively stable and apparently securely established on the basis of a welfare-oriented but strongly diversionary approach that caters for both offence and care cases. The English system is highly volatile and constantly contested, incorporating as it does an eclectic mix of approaches; but it is increasingly influenced by neo-correctionalist principles, at least with regard to offence-based cases. However, these have been deliberately segregated in the main from those raising care and protection issues.

Is it possible to account for the coexistence of two such very different systems operating side-by-side, as they do, within the confines of a single non-federal nation state? We believe that a tentative explanation can be provided that is broadly compatible with the radical pluralist account.

Very briefly, penal policy-making in England and Wales (as in many other European countries) during the early postwar period, was largely the prerogative of a small, 'penal elite', comprising a restricted group of senior civil servants, influenced and supported by academic 'experts' and leading criminal justice professionals. They pursued a relatively liberal penal agenda epitomized by the abolition of the death penalty in 1965, the introduction of parole in 1967 and, in the context of juvenile justice, the welfare-based 1969 Children and Young Persons Act. After the 1960s, however, this elitist policy-making model was gradually supplanted by a harsher, more populist approach. This coincided with a major political realignment in which the Conservative Party set out to appeal to disaffected 'blue-collar' workers, and also with an era of radical changes in the ownership, management and editorial leanings of many national newspapers. The first decisive intimations of such a shift were evident in the campaign rhetoric that accompanied the 1979 General Election, but it was not until the early 1990s that politicians began to pursue an unequivocally populist penal agenda, unencumbered by the more pragmatic concerns of previous decades. The election of a Labour government in 1997 served only to confirm the ascendancy of this more populist penal policy-making model as it set out to honour its pre-election pledge to be 'tough on crime' as well as being 'tough on the causes of crime'.

This dramatic shift in the penal policy-making process did not extend north of the border, however, since – at least in the era prior to devolution[44] – Scotland remained relatively immune from the populist tendencies that were rapidly infecting its southern neighbour. Indeed, the successful introduction and subsequent entrenchment of the unique Children's Hearings system in Scotland during the last thirty years represents a remarkable triumph for an older, more elitist penal policy-making model.[45] Its resilience may be due in part to the very different political and ideological climate in Scotland during the latter part of the twentieth century. This was reflected in the gradual elimination of all Scottish Conservative Members of Parliament despite the Conservatives' preponderance south of the border. An equally important factor, however is that, prior to devolution, the responsibility for much domestic policy-making lay in the hands of senior civil servants within the UK Scottish Office. Compared with their English counterparts they were far less susceptible to populist pressures, whether from Scottish MPs (since these overwhelmingly belonged to 'opposition' parties), the Scottish press (which had to take account of the domestic political climate'[46] or even Conservative politicians in Westminster who were, in any event, already deeply unpopular in Scotland. In this respect, the penal policy-making process in Scotland much more closely resembled that to be found in other European countries than in the neo-liberal camp to which its English neighbour so clearly belongs.

Whether this state of affairs continues to prevail in a post-devolution era, however, is open to serious doubt. Indeed there are already signs of significant changes in the Scottish youth justice policy agenda linked with a discernible politicization of debates on youth justice issues following the establishment of a separate Scottish Parliament in 1999, and the election of a Scottish Executive comprising a coalition of Labour and the Liberal Democrat Party. Thus, the subject of youth crime formed part of the Scottish Cabinet's first strategy meeting in 1999 (see Bottoms and Dignan, 2004). A newly created Advisory Group on Youth Crime highlighted the problem of 'persistent young offenders', and advocated the development of a national strategic framework, backed by local 'multidisciplinary teams' to address the problem of youth crime. Not only were these recommendations accepted, in June 2000, but the Scottish Executive (2002) subsequently announced a further package of measures[47] including the launch of a pilot scheme involving 'Specialist Children's Hearings', whose task would be to 'fast-track persistent offenders under the age of 16'. It also announced a 'youth court feasibility project' to assess the feasibility of special Youth Courts for

16- and 17-year-olds, 'with some flexibility to include 15 year olds'. All these measures are redolent of policy developments south of the border. It thus appears distinctly possible that one effect of devolution has been to establish a national assembly whose elected members are more responsive to public and media concerns over youth justice issues,[48] and that this could ultimately change the conceptual framework underpinning the juvenile policy-making process, shifting it from a holistic welfare based approach towards a more neo-correctionalist 'youth crime' agenda. If so, one paradoxical long-term effect of devolution may ultimately be to undermine the distinctiveness of the Scottish system and to push it closer in some respects towards a more populist English model.

Youth justice in New Zealand[49]

New Zealand differs from the other neo-liberal polities we have examined so far inasmuch as it not only underwent a process of colonization by European (chiefly British) settlers, but has retained a sizeable indigenous population, currently around 15 per cent.[50] Prior to colonization, the indigenous Maori population had its own justice system that differed fundamentally from the English system of law and jurisprudence brought in by early colonists.[51] From the 1890s, however, it was the latter that prevailed, and for much of the next century youth justice developments in New Zealand were chiefly influenced by those taking place elsewhere: notably (but by no means exclusively) in England. Accordingly, young offenders were likewise treated initially as adults and, when separate procedures were introduced (as in the Juvenile Offenders Act of 1906), these conformed to the English-style 'modified criminal court' model rather than the socialized welfare tribunals that were adopted elsewhere.

More overtly welfare-oriented reforms were also introduced early on in New Zealand. They included the Child Welfare Act of 1925, which set up a Child Welfare Branch that became responsible for the care and supervision of both neglected children and also child offenders (thereby eradicating the distinction between these two categories). Although the primary focus was ostensibly on the 'needs' and 'best interests' of the child, it resulted in large numbers of young people – many of them Maori – being processed through the courts (whose powers and practices were largely unaffected by the changes) often for minor offences. Moreover, many of these young people were placed in institutions 'for their own good' for indeterminate periods that might last for any length, until they reached the age of 20. New custodial powers were also introduced in the early postwar period, including English-style borstal training and also periodic detention for boys and girls aged 15 and 16, and detention centres for boys aged 16.

New Zealand juvenile justice reforms continued to reflect mainly external influences until as recently as the 1970s, as for example in the Children and

Young Persons Act, passed in 1974, which was influenced by both minimum interventionist and justice model thinking. Thus, the Act sought to prevent children under the age of 14 from being prosecuted altogether, and to encourage the pre-existing practice of diversion from prosecution for older children (aged 14–16), whereby police and social workers acted in effect as gatekeepers. The Act also increased the procedural rights of young people by providing them with legal representation and giving them access to social work reports. And it introduced separate procedures for dealing with neglected children and those who had offended (but only in the case of those over the age of 14).

In one important respect, however, the reforms introduced during this period were innovative rather then derivative. For the 1974 Act also sought to encourage greater involvement on the part of families and local communities rather than the courts in decisions about young offenders. Although heavily criticized, and largely ineffectual in practice, this development can nevertheless be seen as a very early step in a communitarian direction, and a precursor of far more radical changes to come. These later changes were prompted a variety of concerns, including complaints that the 'imported' youth justice system was not only culturally inappropriate but also institutionally racist in the way it dealt with young indigenous offenders.[52] Moreover, the Labour government had undertaken in 1984 to honour the 1850 Treaty of Waitangi, which set out relationships between Maori and the Crown, adding further leverage to these complaints.

A second influence on subsequent youth justice developments was New Zealand's role as co-sponsor of the United Nations Convention on the Rights of the Child. Among its more influential principles are the following: that children's views should be taken into account in any judicial or administrative hearing affecting them (Article 12); that children's cultural roots should be maintained (Article 30); and that children should be treated with dignity, should be reintegrated into society and should be dealt with as far as possible without resorting to judicial proceedings provided their rights are safeguarded (Article 40). Finally, a third important source of influence on New Zealand's present youth justice system was the United Nations Declarations of Basic Principles for Victims of Crime, which helped to shape the Victims of Offences Act 1987. Although the latter stopped short of giving victims a role in decisions about how offenders should be dealt with, it did reflect a much greater awareness on the part of the New Zealand criminal justice system of the needs and entitlements of victims.

Morris (2004) suggests that these three sets of sensitivities – directed towards the need to protect children's rights, to acknowledge the interests of victims and, above all, to reflect the cultural diversity of New Zealand's population – have chiefly contributed to the emergence of a distinctive and increasingly influential youth justice system: one that is now widely hailed as the principal exemplar of a fully fledged restorative justice model. The present system was brought into being by the Children, Young Persons and their Families Act 1989. One of its most innovative and distinctive features involved the introduction of a novel decision-making procedure known as the 'family group conference', which can be used for dealing with both offenders and young people in need of care and protection. It aims to encourage young offenders and their families together with victims and their supporters, to reach an agreement about how offences should be dealt with, taking into account both the interests of the victim(s) and also the accountability and well-being of offenders.

The way the system operates in practice is that children between the ages of 10 and 13 cannot be prosecuted even though they are over the age of criminal responsibility. They are dealt with in the same way as those in need of care and protection, and the focus of any intervention (such as a police warning, 'diversion' or family group conference) is on the child's welfare as opposed to its responsibility. Only as a final resort can an application be made to the Family Court that the child is in need of care and protection, as a result of which the child may be placed in care.

With regard to young offenders between the ages of 14 and 16, many are simply warned by the police, or else 'diverted', which usually involves some action in addition to a warning. This often takes the form of an apology, but may also include an agreement to undertake community work or to make reparation to the victim. Thus, in New Zealand, even straightforward 'diversion' is consistent with restorative justice values by attempting to make amends to victims wherever possible.

Family group conferences operate at two distinct stages in the criminal justice process: as a semi-mandatory alternative to court for young people in respect of whom the police propose to lay charges in the youth court;[53] and, for most of those who are prosecuted, as a pre-sentence mechanism for making recommendations to the judge.[54] In most cases the judge is likely to follow its recommendations, which is in line with the principle of empowering the parties, though it represents a marked departure from the role that is conventionally ascribed to judges in neo-liberal youth justice systems. Another distinctive feature of the conferencing process relates to the very important part that is played by the co-ordinator, most of whom are social workers employed by the Child, Youth and Family Service (which is also responsible for care and protection matters). They are responsible not only for convening and facilitating the conference, but also for notifying appropriate people of its outcome and generally upholding the objectives and principles of the legislation. Occasionally they may also be involved in monitoring compliance with the outcome of the conference.

Restorative justice values are commonly reflected in the agreed outcomes that result not only from family group conferences themselves, but also from many of the cases dealt with by police diversionary measures. Thus, with regard to the latter, a study conducted by Maxwell et al. (2002) found that two-thirds of young offenders apologized to their victims, one-third agreed to do community work, and just over one-fifth undertook some kind of reparative activity. In respect of family group conferences themselves, a separate study found that apologies were again the most frequent recommendation (in over three-quarters of all cases), followed by some kind of community work (in around two-thirds of cases) and reparative activities (in approximately half of all cases) (Maxwell et al., 2003).[55] In the absence of effective monitoring procedures, however, the extent to which offenders comply with agreements reached at conferences remains largely a matter of conjecture.[56]

Quite apart from its restorative ethos, the present New Zealand youth justice system has also had a pronounced diversionary effect, since it resulted in an immediate (and largely sustained) steep drop in the rate of prosecutions involving young people, from 630 per 10,000 young people prior to the introduction of the 1989 reforms to 240 per 10,000 in 2000/1 (Morris, 2004: 269). According to Maxwell et al. (2002), 43 per cent of young offenders under the age of 17 coming to the attention of the police in 2000/1 were warned, and 32 per cent were diverted. Just 8 per cent were referred directly by the police to a family group conference, and a further 17 per cent were prosecuted, most of whom would be referred to a family group conference by a youth court judge prior to sentence (see also Morris, 2004: Table 1).

The reforms also resulted in a substantial fall in the number of young offenders who were given custodial sentences (including corrective training and imprisonment), from 295 in 1987 to 104 in 1990, and, after some fluctuations, down to 73 by 2001. Reductions on this scale are likely to have resulted in significant financial savings, though these are more difficult to quantify. Indeed, some have suggested that it may not be entirely coincidental that the era in which the reform package was introduced was also characterized by severe economic recession and a huge national debt. Duncan and Worrall (2000) and Watt (2003), for example, are among those who see a possible link between these economic factors and the political pressures to which they give rise, and an increased willingness to bring about a partial shift in responsibility from the state to families and local communities.[57] And one of the main criticisms that has been directed at the reform programme is that any financial savings that might have been generated have not been passed on to the conferencing system, which according to Maxwell and Morris (1996: 102–3) has been starved of resources. More recently, concerns have been expressed at the building of four new specialist youth custody units (with plans for a further three), which will ultimately provide 220 places. Even though the units are intended to cater for offenders up to the age of 19, this substantial increase in the amount of accommodation that is available has raised fears that it will encourage a greater use of custody for boys under the age of 17 (Morris, 2004: 271). Despite these and other criticisms, however, the scale of the 'restorative justice revolution' that has transformed the New Zealand youth justice system in recent years remains unique, both within the neo-liberal camp and also beyond it.

Youth justice in Australia

Like New Zealand, Australia also experienced a process of colonization by European (chiefly British) settlers but, unlike New Zealand, the indigenous aboriginal population today makes up only a very small proportion (less than 2 per cent) of the total population.[58] Another important contrast between the two countries is that Australia's federal structure encompasses eight separate youth justice systems which manifest significant variations in youth justice legislation and procedures for dealing with young offenders and delinquents.[59] Nevertheless some general trends are discernible.

Thus, by the early twentieth century most states had established a separate system of 'modified criminal courts'[60] for children, following South Australia's very early lead that many believe dates back to 1895.[61] Subsequently, many states moved towards a hybrid model by adopting a variety of welfare-oriented measures including a more prominent court-room role for social workers, departures from a tariff-based approach to sentencing and a move towards indeterminate sentencing aimed at the rehabilitation of young offenders. Moreover, the jurisdiction of the juvenile court was in many cases extended to encompass 'status' offences (i.e. acts by young people whose behaviour was judged to be inappropriate or immoral rather than criminal), and children who were felt to be in need of care and protection. In Western Australia responsibility for the entire juvenile justice system including the Children's Court was, for a time (1947–88), entrusted to the Department for Community Services. Then in 1971, South Australia enacted a highly welfare-oriented measure, the Juvenile Courts Act which, in many respects, closely resembled its English precursor, the ill-fated Children and Young Persons Act 1969 (see above). Thus, it became the first Australian state to introduce 'children's aid panels', comprising social workers and senior police officers to provide warnings and counselling for minor offenders under the age of 16 (Daly, 2001: 69). And it required that more serious offenders of this age should be dealt with by means of care proceedings identical to those used for children in need of care and protection, instead of being prosecuted.

This proved to be the zenith of the welfare model's influence in Australia, however, and from the mid-1970s to the late 1980s, it was increasingly eclipsed by the growing ascendancy of the US version of the justice model. Ironically, South Australia was also the first state to experience the gravitational pull of the 'back to justice' movement, the influence of which can clearly be seen in a further reform of its youth justice system introduced in 1979. This resulted in a clear separation of the state's civil and criminal jurisdictions, the introduction of determinate sentencing policies and the abolition of the 'offence' of uncontrollability, together with the introduction of various justice-inspired procedural entitlements, though certain welfare-inspired measures were retained, including the juvenile aid panels. By the early 1990s, every state with the exception of Tasmania had modified its youth justice system in accordance with justice model principles and, although they all retained some welfare-based elements, the influence of the former appeared to be strengthening over time. The most obvious manifestation of this tendency was the adoption of constraints on the sentencing powers of the courts, which featured in juvenile justice reforms in New South Wales, Victoria and Queensland. These generally take the form of a scale of penalties, and a requirement for the court to consider whether a less serious penalty than the one proposed might be more appropriate.

Interestingly, the adoption of such constraints coincided with a halving in the overall incarceration rate for juvenile offenders, which declined from 65 per 100,000 in 1981 to 32 per 100,000 in 2000 (Australian Institute of Criminology, 2002).[62] This reflects an annual rate of decline in the number of male and female juveniles detained in corrective institutions of 3 per cent and 6 per cent respectively during this period. This marked decline in the juvenile incarceration rate is in stark contrast to the experience in other neo-liberal countries such as the USA during the same period, though the youth custody rate in England also declined during the 1980s. As we saw in the USA, however, the overall figures for Australia likewise mask a marked disparity in the incarceration rates for offenders of different ethnic origins. Thus, the incarceration rate for indigenous offenders in December 2000 was 16 times higher than that for non-indigenous juveniles, and indeed the rate of indigenous incarceration actually increased between 1993–7, at a time when the rate for non-indigenous juveniles was stable. Since 1998, however, the rate of indigenous detention has declined faster than that for non-indigenous juveniles (Australian Institute of Criminology, 2002).

As we have already noted with regard to other neo-liberal polities, however, the waxing influence of the justice model coincided with a severe economic downturn. This resulted in a serious deterioration in the state of the youth employment market, which was compounded by a reduction in welfare benefits including income support for young people who were out of work. Perhaps it is no coincidence that this period also witnessed an upsurge in moral panics focusing on juvenile crime and the rise in some states of a 'neo-correctionalist' approach with regard to youth justice policy-making.

In Western Australia, for example, public outrage over a perceived escalation of violent youth crime and an increased threat to public safety resulting from high speed car chases involving the police and juvenile car thieves or 'joy riders' prompted the adoption of increasingly draconian legislative measures during the early 1990s.[63] They included increases in maximum penalties for offences committed while driving a stolen vehicle and the introduction of mandatory minimum sentences of eighteen months' detention for repeat violent offenders.[64] Moreover, there is also provision for such offenders to be imprisoned in adult jails, which overrides a ban on the use of adult imprisonment for youths under the age of 16. The switch in Western Australia from a 'welfare-based approach' to one inspired by the justice model in 1988 had previously resulted in a sharp, albeit short-term, increase in the incarceration rate (by more than 50 per cent) the following year, following a period of decline. Moreover, the adoption of tougher measures in 1992 also resulted in an increase in the rate of juvenile imprisonment, and even though it has fluctuated somewhat thereafter, it remains one of the highest in Australia.[65] Western Australia was also the first Australian state to introduce, in 1995, an American style boot camp for non-violent young offenders, though it ultimately shied away from the strict military model under-pinning many of the US programmes, as was also the case in England and Wales (Atkinson, 1995). Western Australia is also one of four states to have introduced curfew provisions for young offenders (Mukherjee et al., 1997: 3).

As in other neo-liberal polities, the philosophy of minimum intervention has also influenced the way juvenile offenders are dealt with in Australia. Queensland was the first Australian police jurisdiction to establish a Juvenile Aid Bureau, in 1963, which pioneered the use of police cautions. Although the practice had no statutory basis initially, it proved popular with the police (since they control it and can determine the outcomes), and was given statutory support and encour-agement in 1992. By the mid-1990s over half (55 per cent) of all juvenile offend-ers in Queensland were cautioned. Cautioning is now authorized in every other Australian jurisdiction, either on a statutory basis (in the case of five jurisdic-tions) or on the basis of police instructions (in the case of three), though in Tasmania it has only been authorized since the Youth Justice Act 1997.

Since the early caution-based minimum intervention initiatives of the 1970s and 1980s, however, the Australian quest for diversionary measures and also for more constructive ways of responding to crime has, as elsewhere, increasingly revolved around developments in the field of restorative justice. Shortly after the pioneering introduction of family group conferences in New Zealand, a modified version of the conferencing model was adopted in New South Wales. This was based on the concept of 'reintegrative shaming' that had recently been formulated by Australian criminologist John Braithwaite (1989), and in 1991 was piloted by the police in Wagga Wagga as a new-style 'effective cautioning scheme' for juve-nile offenders. Although this police-led 'scripted conferencing' model was sub-sequently also piloted in a number of other Australian jurisdictions (including the Northern Territory, Queensland and Tasmania), it has since fallen from favour in almost all of them.[66] The only surviving scheme operates in the Australian Capital Territory, which is also the location of the internationally renowned Canberra Reintegrative Shaming Experiment (or RISE) (Sherman et al., 2000; Strang et al., 1999).

More recently, there has been a marked preference for non-police run confer-encing schemes, which in many respects more closely resemble the New Zealand model. The first state to introduce restorative conferencing on a statutory basis as an integrated component within its juvenile justice system was once again

South Australia, in 1993 (Wundersitz, 1994). The system that was introduced involved a two-tier diversion process, the first of which involves police cautioning (both formal and informal) and, as in New Zealand, may also entail 'reparative outcomes'. Conferences are reserved for more serious cases, and thus constitute a second tier of diversion though, unlike New Zealand, the police retain discretion to direct the most serious cases to the Youth Court instead of referring them to a conference.

Since then, all other jurisdictions with the exception of the Australian Capital Territory and Victoria have introduced statutory schemes, though there are considerable jurisdictional variations between them (see Daly and Hayes (2001) for details). For example, Western Australia differs from South Australia in conferencing a high proportion of less serious cases (including traffic offences), while prohibiting its use for more serious cases. In several states (including New South Wales, Northern Territory, Queensland, Tasmania and Victoria) conferencing may be used by the court as a sentencing option. It would be misleading to depict conferencing as a purely diversionary process, whatever form it takes, since it will often entail the offender undertaking some form of reparative activity, either for the victim or for the community. Indeed, in a number of states (for example South Australia) it has been introduced as part of a package of youth justice measures with a variety of aims including holding young offenders accountable for their actions, and increasing the range and severity of sanctions at all levels of the system 'to provide an appropriate level of deterrence', as well as protecting the rights of victims. In this respect most of the recent Australian restorative justice developments exhibit the English tendency to *supplement* the existing youth justice system and be subordinated to its traditional aims. This contrasts sharply with the New Zealand tendency to more or less *supplant* the traditional aims with (or largely subordinate them to) an alternative set of aims derived from a radically different philosophical approach.[67]

Youth justice in South Africa

South Africa is not the only country within our neo-liberal sample to have been colonized by European settlers, but it is unique in having been ruled for a considerable period of its history by a white political elite that comprised only a small minority of the total population.[68] The ultra-conservative apartheid system that resulted from this state of affairs had a profound impact on every aspect of penality in South Africa including its youth justice system. Until the late 1980s the dominant approach could broadly be characterized as 'justice'-oriented, though it was a far more punitive and repressive variant than that associated with any of the other neo-liberal polities including, in many respects, even the USA. Attempts to reform the youth justice system since the transition have proved immensely challenging, particularly in the context of a notoriously high crime rate and the increasingly punitive attitudes of the public at large, and progress has often been faltering. Nevertheless, a blueprint for reform has been taking shape in recent years that attempts to incorporate a mixture of welfare-oriented, diversionary and restorative justice aims as part of a comprehensive package of measures. The reform package had not yet, at the time of writing, been adopted. But if it were to be successfully implemented, it would at least remove some of the most glaring anomalies and injustices that are associated with the present system.

Of the countries we have examined so far, South Africa is unique in that it does not at present have a comprehensive youth justice system that differentiates clearly and consistently between the way juvenile and adult offenders are dealt with. This state of affairs is compounded by the retention, until now, of the old common law rules relating to age and criminal capacity. Thus, the minimum age of criminal responsibility is currently 7, which is the lowest in our sample, although children between the ages of 7 and 14 years are presumed to lack criminal capacity unless there is evidence to the contrary (the principle of *doli incapax*). But because such evidence is readily accepted by the courts, young children are regularly held responsible for their criminal conduct and can, in law, even be sentenced to imprisonment.[69]

There is no separate juvenile court as such in South Africa – not even a modified criminal court – and young offenders may be tried in any of the ordinary criminal courts[70] (District, Regional or High court) according to the normal rules of criminal procedure, except that the hearings are held *in camera* and parents or guardians may legally be compelled to attend. There is a separate children's court, which exercises jurisdiction over children in need of care and protection, and it is possible for children who are charged with criminal offences to be diverted to this court either by the prosecutor or by a magistrate if this is felt to be appropriate. Such cases are dealt with by means of an inquiry rather than a criminal trial, and may result in a child being placed under supervision (with parents or foster parents), or in a children's home, a reform school or an industrial school. However, this option is rarely utilized, and it is estimated that only 5 per cent of cases are dealt with in this way (Zaal and Matthias, 1996). Moreover, reform schools are widely regarded as 'universities of crime' (Sloth-Nielsen and Muntingh, 2001: 8), and children who are placed there are known to be at risk of serious human rights abuses (Robinson, 1997: 175).

Compared with other neo-liberal countries, the scope for diversion in the case of young offenders who are not in need of care and protections is also highly restricted. Since there is no legislative authorization for diversion, the chief mechanism has involved a voluntary withdrawal of charges by the prosecution and a referral to one of a number of diversion programmes, for example those run by the National Institute for Crime Prevention and the Resettlement of Offenders (NICRO).[71] However, NICRO diversion services were only introduced in 1992, are still not available in all parts of the country and, even where they do exist, are only able to handle a small proportion of cases that would be suitable for diversion (estimated at 5 per cent). Moreover, much depends on the knowledge of individual prosecutors of the programmes that are available, and their willingness to make use of them. Until recently, South African courts have been reluctant to interfere with prosecutorial discretion, though there are signs of an increased willingness on the part of the High Court to review such administrative decisions, either on the grounds of bad faith, or a failure by the prosecutor even to consider the issue of diversion (Sloth-Nielsen and Muntingh, 2001).

The relatively undeveloped scope for diversion from prosecution has also exacerbated the problem of pre-trial detention, which is further compounded by the fact that juveniles are routinely remanded into custody to await trial, even for minor offences, when no guardian can be found into whose custody they may be released. The number of children who were detained in this way was a cause for concern for the post-transitional government which tried, unsuccessfully, to tackle the problem (van Zyl Smit, 1999). The existing law was amended in 1994 to prevent altogether the detention in prison of children under the age of 14 and to restrict their detention in police cells to twenty-four hours; and, in the case of older juveniles, to limit (to forty-eight hours in most cases) the period in which they could be detained in either prison or police cells. Although the intention was to implement these amendments gradually, and only after alternative places of detention were made available for more serious juvenile offenders, this did not happen. Instead, the amendments were made applicable nationwide in May 1995, whether or not alternative secure 'places of safety' were available. This resulted in the wholesale release of many juveniles regarded as highly dangerous, and an outcry in the media, which linked the strategy with rapidly rising crime rates. In the wake of the ensuing 'moral panic', a private member's bill was adopted in 1996 that effectively restored the *status quo*, with the result that children continue to be detained before trial even for relatively trivial offences (including shop-lifting and minor theft). In 1997 the government again launched a national programme aimed at keeping children out of prisons, but by the end of October 1998 there were 1,440 children awaiting trial in prison (van Zyl Smit, 2001a: 604). At the time of writing the latest official statistics showed that 2,232 children under the age of 18 who were awaiting trial were detained in correctional centres (Department of Correctional Services, 2004: Table 13).

For those juveniles who are convicted, the most prevalent sentence under apartheid was corporal punishment, in the form of whipping, which was imposed on approximately 35,000 child offenders annually prior to its abolition in 1995 (South African Law Commission, 1997: para. 9.3). This practice was ruled to be unconstitutional by the Constitutional Court in the landmark case of *S. v. Williams.*[72] Since then, however, there appears to have been a significant increase in the number of juveniles who are sentenced to imprisonment, despite a long-term decline in the number of children who are convicted each year.[73] Although reliable contemporary statistics on sentencing trends are difficult to obtain, figures supplied by the Department of Correctional Services (2000; cited by Sloth-Nielsen and Muntingh, 2001) indicate that from January 1995 to July 2000, the overall number of children under the age of 18 serving prison sentences increased by over 150 per cent. This is the highest increase in any age category, even though the total comprises less than 2 per cent of the global sentenced prison population. Almost exactly half of those serving custodial sentences had been convicted of property crimes, while approximately one-third had committed offences of violence.[74]

The total number of juveniles[75] who are deprived of their liberty has also increased dramatically in recent years after a long period of stability. Thus, on 30 June 1988, there were 14,571 juveniles in South African prisons (Arndt et al., 1989: 23), a figure that was almost unchanged by the end of 1997 (Community Law Centre 1997: 4). By 31 March 2004, however, a total of 28,827 were detained in custody, just under half of whom were unsentenced (Department of Correctional Services, 2004: Table 13).[76] This figure includes 1,926 children under the age of 18[77] who are serving sentences of imprisonment, and a further 2,232 who are unsentenced, making a total of 4,158.[78] Moreover, during the period 1998–2003 a total of 74 children between the ages of 7 and 13 (inclusive) were sentenced to prison, 16 of whom were between the ages of 7 and 11 (Sloth-Nielsen, 2003: 5). A further 125 children aged 12 or less were detained in prison awaiting trial despite the fact that Section 29 of the Correctional Services Act proscribes such treatment for children under the age of 14. As for their ethnic composition, a recent survey of juvenile prison inmates has shown that 'coloured' inmates are over-represented by 8.5 per cent compared with the general population, while white inmates are under-represented by 12.7 per cent, but unfortunately corresponding figures are not cited for black inmates (Luyt, 2001).

However, it is the conditions faced by young offenders and the way they are treated while they are in detention that has aroused the greatest concern on the part of penal reformers. The physical conditions are almost certainly worse than in any other country in our sample, with an average of 23.3 persons (and a maximum of 60 persons), housed in each prison cell, which only contains a single toilet (Luyt, 2001). A recent survey (Luyt, 2001) indicated that a significant minority of juveniles in detention had experienced the use of either whipping (19 per cent) or smacking (26 per cent in prisons and 33.8 per cent in places of safety), even though both forms of chastisement are now illegal. Moreover, nearly 30 per cent of respondents reported experiences of fear and victimization (involving assaults or sexual assaults) by other inmates during detention. In 1992, a 13-year-old child was brutally murdered by his cell mates while being held in custody in a police cell[79] on a charge of shoplifting. And nearly five years later another child of similar age was also murdered by his 21-year-old cell mate while being detained in a holding cell on a shoplifting charge (Shapiro, 1997).

The first of these incidents sparked a campaign Justice for the Children: No Child Should be Caged, led by human rights lawyers. In 1995 an inter-ministerial committee was set up to examine ways of transforming the child and youth care system in South Africa, and in 1997 the South African Law Commission (2000) established a Juvenile Justice Committee to develop a coherent and comprehensive system for dealing with juvenile offenders. This eventually resulted in the drafting of a Child Justice Bill but, although it was introduced to Parliament in August 2002, it still had not been approved at the time of writing (December 2004). The Bill contains a number of key changes, the most important of which are summarized below (see also Sloth-Nielsen and Muntingh, 2001).

Firstly, the minimum age of criminal responsibility is to be raised from 7 to 10, though the principle of *doli incapax* will continue to apply to children between the ages of 10 and 14.[80] Secondly, two new statutory procedures – assessment and diversion – will form central components of the reformed system (Chapters 4 and 5 of the Bill). The aim is for all children to be assessed by a probation officer as soon as practical after arrest, and for an informal 'conference-style' preliminary inquiry (involving the child suspect, his or her family and prosecution, chaired by a magistrate) to be conducted within forty-eight hours of arrest. The aim of the inquiry will be to ensure that the child is dealt with in an appropriate manner by establishing whether (and on what basis) the child can be diverted, whether there are grounds for proceeding to trial and, if so, to determine the release or suitable placement of the child while awaiting trial. The Law Commission (2000: para. 8.23) anticipates, on the basis of a predictive impact assessment, that as many as 60 per cent of cases brought before the inquiry will be diverted, converted to a children's court inquiry (see above) or dropped due to lack of evidence.

The Bill sets out three levels of diversion – incorporating varying degrees of onerousness – the aims of which are to channel young offenders away from courts and prison wherever possible, while still holding them accountable. The least onerous diversionary options available at level one include an oral or written apology, a formal caution, symbolic restitution to a specified person, group or institution or restitution to the victim(s) of a specified object.[81] Level two diversionary options include those available at level one but the maximum duration (where applicable) is six months rather than three. However, various additional diversionary measures are available at this level, including the possibility of community service or the performance of some service or benefit for the victim(s) of an offence, or payment of compensation (up to a maximum of R500). Other restorative justice options including the use of victim offender mediation and referrals to family group conferences also feature among the diversionary measures that are available at this level.[82] Level three diversionary options are restricted to children over the age of 14, who would be liable upon conviction to a custodial sentence not exceeding six months. Measures that are available at this level include the possibility of longer periods of community service, compulsory attendance at a specified centre for vocational or educational training for thirty-five hours per week for a period not exceeding six months, or compulsory attendance for up to six months at a programme that contains a residential element comprising up to thirty-five days in total and not more than twenty-one consecutive days (s. 47(5)).

Thirdly, the Bill provides for the designation of 'child justice courts', which will be presided over by designated 'child justice magistrates' at district court level, though it allows for children to continue to be tried at either regional or high court level where the seriousness of the offence warrants a more severe sentence. Fourthly, with regard to sentencing, the Bill sets out the purposes of sentencing, which include the following three key principles: encouraging the child to understand the implications of, and be accountable for, the harm caused by an offence; promoting an individualized response that is appropriate to the child's circumstances and proportionate to the circumstances surrounding an offence; and promoting the reintegration of the child into the family and community (s. 63). The Bill also differentiates between and authorizes the imposition of community-based sentences,[83] restorative justice sentences,[84] correctional supervision[85] and sentences with a residential requirement (which involve a deprivation of liberty for periods of up to twenty-one consecutive nights with an overall maximum of sixty nights during the course of a programme). With regard to the use of custody, the Bill proposes the abolition of imprisonment for children under the age of 14 (s. 69), and would require there to be substantial and compelling reasons for the imposition of such a sentence on children above that age: normally the conviction must be for a serious or violent offence, although imprisonment is also authorized for children who have failed in the past to respond to alternative sentences.

If these measures are enacted and implemented (a major proviso in the light of previous experience), the youth justice system in South Africa would much more closely resemble that found in several other neo-liberal countries. This is particularly so with regard to the adoption of a modified system of criminal courts dispensing a wide range of straightforwardly punitive measures; encouragement of diversion from prosecution and custody in less serious cases; and a growing support for restorative justice interventions at various stages in the process. Indeed, additional support for a restorative justice approach is also to be found in the objects of the Act, which include promoting the principle of ubuntu[86] in the child justice system, one aspect of which 'supporting reconciliation by means of a restorative justice approach' (s. 2(b) of the Bill).

In the next chapter we will contrast the highly variable pattern of development that characterizes neo-liberal youth justice systems with the rather different sets of influences that have helped to shape the youth justice systems in corporatist countries.

Notes

1 To some extent this is unsurprising. The neo-liberal states in our sample, which are predominantly English-speaking and with legal systems based on the English common law, have traditionally favoured 'adversarial' legal processes rather than the 'inquisitorial' procedures traditional in many other countries (including continental Europe and Japan). Adversarial systems tend to emphasize – at least formally – the need for procedural safeguards for those charged with criminal offences, which is in line with the 'due process' aspect of the justice model.

2 In outlining the trends and developments that are briefly summarized in this section we have drawn on an unpublished paper by Fagan and Feld (2001).

3 Credit for establishing the world's first separate court for juveniles is contested. Although this honour is often accorded to Cook County Juvenile Court, Chicago Illinois in 1899 (e.g. Tanenhaus, 2002: 42), others have pointed out that this was preceded by South Australia's State Children's Act enacted in 1895 (Freiberg et al., 1988). See also Watt (2003).

4 We have drawn attention elsewhere (Cavadino and Dignan, 2002: 7) to the *unsystematic* nature of the *English* penal and criminal justice systems, which also encompass the youth justice system. In the USA it is even more misleading to think of there being a single youth justice system, and the multiplicity of separate systems in each of the states is consequently exceedingly complex.

5 The juvenile court was originally set up to handle cases involving the care of neglected and dependent children, status offenders and incorrigible juveniles as well as those children alleged to have committed an act that would constitute a criminal offence if committed by an adult.

6 *Kent v. the United States* (1966) 386 US 541 conferred due process safeguards on juveniles whose cases were to be transferred to the adult system. *In re Gault* (1967) 387 US 1, 87 S.Ct. 1428, 18 L.Ed.2d 527 extended the constitutional right to a hearing to juveniles facing commitment to an institution.

7 See, for example, Grubb and Lazerson (1982); Feld (1999). But see Grossberg (2002) for a more balanced account.

8 One of their most important consequences was to divert and/or 'deinstutionalize' status offenders and juveniles deemed to be 'incorrigible'.

9 At present twenty-three states plus the District of Columbia have at least one provision enabling the transfer to the criminal court of juveniles even as young as 10 years old. Most of the remaining states (eighteen) permit this to happen in respect of children aged 14 or above (Allen et al., 2004: 344–5).

10 On 1 March 2005, just as this book was going to press, the United States Supreme Court voted 5–4 to outlaw the death penalty for juveniles under the age of 18 at the time of the offence. Until then, the USA was one of only a handful of countries still to allow offenders who committed their crimes as juveniles to be executed (the others being Iran, Nigeria, Saudi Arabia, and Pakistan). Two other countries which formerly allowed the execution of juvenile offenders – China and Yemen – have also recently abolished the practice (*Guardian*, 12 January 2000). Of the forty states, plus the federal jurisdiction, that authorize the death penalty, nineteen permitted the execution of offenders for crimes committed when they were not yet 18 years of age. Between 1973 and 31 December 2000, death penalties were imposed on 200 offenders who were younger than 18 at the time of

their offence (representing approximately 3 per cent of all individuals sentenced to death since 1973) (Sickmund, 2004). Since 1973, just over half (51 per cent) of those under sentence of death for crimes committed when they were under 18 had their death sentences reversed, 9 per cent have been executed, and 39 per cent remain under sentence of death (Sickmund, 2004: 22).

11 For every 1,000 juvenile delinquency cases that are formally processed, only 8 – less than 1 per cent – were waived to adult criminal courts (Puzzanchera, 2003). In part this is because prosecutors appear to exercise their discretion sparingly, and in one recent study fewer than one in four potentially eligible offenders were in fact transferred to the criminal court (Sridharan et al., 2004).

12 These include mandatory minimum sentences based on age, and stipulations that certain offences are punishable by minimum terms of confinement or minimum levels of security placement. (Sheffer, 1995; Torbet et al., 1996)

13 Boot camps subject young people to short periods (90–120 days) of residential military-style training that frequently includes hard physical labour and demeaning verbal degradation. By 1994 there were over forty-seven boot camps across the United States, six of which were for juveniles (MacKenzie, 1994).

14 Which, at the time of writing, was still the most recent date for which statistics were available. The Office of Juvenile Justice and Delinquency Prevention (OJJDP) was planning to publish an updated version of its national report on offenders and victims early in 2005.

15 At that time, just over 134,000 young people were under some form of custodial supervision in detention, correctional or sheltered facilities (Sickmund, 2004: 3). On 30 June 2000, 7,600 young offenders under the age of 18 were held in local adult jails, which is close to the level recorded in 1995 (Source: Bureau of Justice Statistics Correctional Surveys in Correctional Populations in the United States, 1997 and Prison and Jail Inmates at midyear 1998, 1999 and 2000).

16 Though this was almost double the rate of 49 in 1997.

17 The latest census of juveniles in residential placements relates to 2001, and shows an overall incarceration rate of 336 per 100,000 juveniles. The racial breakdown shows a rate of 863 for black offenders, 366 for Hispanics and 209 for white offenders (Sickmund et al., 2004).

18 However, a more recent analysis shows that between 1990 and 1999, the number of cases involving detention increased at a faster rate for white juveniles (17 per cent) than for black juveniles (3 per cent) (Harms, 2003).

19 Consequently, 'status' offenders account for only a small proportion of all juveniles detained in custodial facilities (4 per cent in 1999) (Sickmund, 2004: 3).

20 Meanwhile, however, the US government has consistently refused to commit itself, even notionally, to the principle of minimum interventionism that – as we have seen – is enshrined in the United Nations Convention on the Rights of the Child. For it is one of only two United Nations members (the other being Somalia) not to have ratified the Convention.

21 A growing tendency towards the medicalization of treatment for deviance appears to be another distinctive feature of the correctionalist approach, at least in the USA, where young people in public detention facilities are routinely sedated, and public school teachers insist that disruptive children are given ritalin and other behaviour modifying drugs (Don Anspach, response to questionnaire).

22 In the USA it is estimated that in the year 2000 there were around 773 restorative justice programmes aimed at young offenders (Schiff and Bazemore, 2002: 180) Over half

of these (393) were victim offender mediation programmes. However, these were not in any sense integrated into the criminal justice system since they were not legislatively mandated and the great majority are operated by non-public agencies, mostly private community-based or church-based initiatives, though some are linked with particular probation departments, prosecuting attorney's offices, correctional facilities or victim service agencies.

23 Snyder and Sickmund (1999: 89) report that during the 1990s, no fewer than forty-seven states increased public access to juvenile records and proceedings, forty-six allowed young offenders to be photographed and fingerprinted, and forty-two allowed the names of young offenders (and in some cases photographic or other official records) to be released to the media (Snyder and Sickmund, (1999: 101).

24 Although the British sections of this book are principally concerned with the penal system in England and Wales, it would be difficult and possibly misleading – for reasons that will become apparent – to ignore Scotland altogether in any comparative analysis of contemporary youth justice developments. We will, therefore make very brief reference to the sharply contrasting Scottish youth justice system, but see Bottoms and Dignan (2004) for a more detailed account. See also Cavadino and Dignan (2002: Chapter 9) for a more detailed commentary on the English youth justice system.

25 The fact that English magistrates are currently not permitted to sit in the youth court for more than seven days a year places obvious limits on the degree of specialization, though the Audit Commission (2004) has criticized the lack of continuity to which this restriction in part gives rise.

26 Though, as we shall see, the degree of divergence has begun to diminish in recent years, somewhat ironically, following the establishment of a devolved Scottish Parliament, in 1999.

27 In a restricted range of (more serious) offences, the police may refer the case to the procurator fiscal (public prosecutor), who has the discretion to prosecute the case in the sheriff court. In 1989, which is the most recent year for which full figures are available, of the cases in which the police initiated formal steps with regard to an alleged offence by children under 16, 13 per cent were reported to the procurator fiscal, compared with 76 per cent who were referred to the reporter and 11 per cent who were issued with a police warning. See Bottoms (2002: 490, n.17).

28 If the charge is denied, the case is referred the sheriff court for the facts to be established; and assuming that they are, the case is then referred back to the Children's Hearing.

29 The figures for 2000, however, show a slight increase in the proportion of residential placements, to 24 per cent.

30 Together with the small proportion of under 16 year olds who are referred by the police to the procurator fiscal and who are then prosecuted in the sheriff court (see note 27, above).

31 Calculated from official Home Office statistics; see also Cavadino and Dignan (2002: 296–7).

32 A number of more punitive responses had been introduced during the mid-1990s though these were short-lived. They included the introduction of a new detention measure – the Secure Training Order – for persistent offenders aged 12–14, and an experiment with US-style boot camps (see above).

33 This analysis is slightly adapted from Bottoms and Dignan (2004).

34 Though purists might object since such cases are dealt with in the civil Family Proceedings Court rather than the criminal Youth Court.

35 And also the 'Tough on crime, tough on the causes of crime' soundbite (see Chapter 4) with which it has long been associated.

36 See Cavadino and Dignan (2002) for additional information about the wide range of sentencing powers that are currently available to the courts. However the government has recently announced plans to replace the present range of eight discrete community sentencing options with a single new generic juvenile community sentence to be known as the 'Juvenile Rehabilitation Order' (Home Office, 2004). This will enable sentencers to select from a wide range of interventions including supervision, curfews, electronic monitoring, unpaid work in the community and treatment programmes aimed at drug, alcohol or mental health problems.

37 By the Crime And Disorder Act 1998. At the other end of the age scale, the law has been amended so that offenders between the ages of 18 and 20 who are given custodial sentences will no longer be detained in separate institutions for young adult offenders, as in the past, but in adult prisons. However, the relevant provision (s. 61 Criminal Justice and Court Services Act 2000) is not yet in force.

38 Note that restorative justice interventions are also available for young offenders at the pre-trial stage as part of the diversionary system of reprimands and final warnings that replaced the old system of cautioning in 1998.

39 For example, in cases where the nature of the offending is serious or persistent, or has affected a number of people living in the local community, or where it is felt that alerting others to the young person's behaviour could reduce the likelihood of further offending by an offender. Such provisions are controversial, however, since they appear to contravene Article 40(2b) of the UN Convention on the Rights of the Child, which proclaims a right to privacy throughout criminal proceedings in respect of offenders under the age of 18.

40 The decline in the caution rate for the different age groups between 1992 and 2002 is as follows (the rate for females is shown in brackets): age 10–11 down from 96 (99) to 83 (94); age 12–14 down from 86 (96) to 63 (84); age 15–17 down from 59 (81) to 41 (62).

41 From 8.6 per cent of offenders prior to the introduction of the new order to 7.8 per cent in the period after its implementation.

42 From 5.1 per cent to 5.9 per cent.

43 The secure estate comprises a number of young offender institutions managed by the Prison Service that house the bulk of the 2,869 young offender population (83 per cent of the 10–17-year olds detained therein); local authority-run secure children's homes (10.1 per cent); and a small number of secure training centres run by the private sector (6.6 per cent). See Youth Justice Board (2004: 78).

44 In 1999 a devolved Scottish Parliament was established, the first national assembly for Scotland since the 1707 Acts of Union.

45 Although the Scottish Children's Hearing system was undoubtedly the subject of considerable interest among those with a professional interest, civil servants and some social elites in Scottish society (Lockyer and Stone, 1998), for whom it was also a source of national pride (Bottoms, 2002: 455), knowledge of the system outside these circles was much more limited (Hallett and Murray, 1998).

46 The main 'opposition' party during this period not only boasted a considerable majority of Scottish Members of Parliament, but was in many respects decidedly more 'Old Labour' in its political orientation than its counterpart south of the border.

47 The package also included a proposal to consider the introduction of a national system of police warnings which would include the possibility of introducing restorative cautions similar to those developed in Australia and elsewhere, including the Thames Valley in England.

48 And also to political pressures emanating from the predominantly English 'New Labour' Party.

49 See Morris (2004) for a much more detailed account of the trends and developments that are briefly summarized below.

50 Moreover, of the million or so children under the age of 18, approximately one quarter are from the indigenous Maori population, and a further ten per cent are of Pacific Island descent (Morris, 2004).

51 See Pratt (1992: Chapter 2) for details. It was only after the Magistrates Court Act of 1893 that a single English-based justice system was prescribed by law.

52 A Department of Social Welfare report called *Puao-Te-Atu-Tu* (Daybreak), published in 1986, proved highly influential in sensitizing policy-makers to the discriminatory nature of much social welfare policy and practice, particularly in the much more receptive climate brought about by the election of the Lange government in 1984 after years of rigid state regulation.

53 Morris (2004: 264) points out that the police in New Zealand have three main options:

1 to deal with the young person informally;
2 to refer the case to a specialist branch of the police named 'youth aid', which can issue a warning, divert the young person (which may also entail some additional reparative element) or refer to a family group conference; and
3 to arrest the young person and lay charges in the youth court.

The third of these options is only available in certain statutorily defined circumstances, and where the offence is 'purely indictable'.

54 Judges in the youth court cannot sentence a young person without first referring them to a family group conference, though cases can be transferred to the district court for trial where the offence is purely indictable, the young offender is at least 15 years of age and elects to be tried by judge and jury. Alternatively, cases may be transferred for sentence when the court is satisfied that the nature and circumstances of the offence are such that, if the offender were an adult, only a custodial sentence would be appropriate. Such 'transfer' cases are exceedingly rare and, according to a retrospective sample investigated by Maxwell et al. (2003) comprised only 7 per cent of the total in 2001.

55 Other frequently agreed recommendations were restrictions on an offender's movements or participation in some kind of programme.

56 See Morris (2004: 280) for a more detailed discussion of the available evidence.

57 Not all are convinced by such arguments, however. John Pratt, for example, in commenting on an earlier draft, points out that it would have been cheaper still to have adopted a policy of straightforward diversion without needing to incur the expense required to set up the family group conferencing infrastructure.

58 The only exception being the sparsely populated Northern Territory, where the indigenous population comprises 27 per cent of the total population (Australian Bureau of Statistics, 1997).

59 See Mukherjee et al., (1997), for an overview of these differences.

60 Although most of these are closed to the public, in keeping with most other specialized juvenile courts, juvenile proceedings are open to the public in Victoria and in the Northern Territory.

61 Which would make it, and not Chicago Illinois, the first such court in the world. As we have seen (Note 23), credit for establishing the world's first juvenile court is a matter of controversy. However, Daly (2001: 69) is among those who refer to South

Australia's State Children's Act of 1895, which she refers to as the first in a century-long tradition of pioneering juvenile justice developments, making it 'arguably the first' jurisdiction in the world to establish a separate court for juveniles.

62 The decline was particularly marked in New South Wales (down from 88 per 100,000 in 1981 to 39 per 100,000 in 2000) and Victoria (down from 60 per 100,000 in 1981 to just 10 per 100,000 in 2000), both of which had adopted similar constraints.

63 The Crime (Serious and Repeat Offenders) Sentencing Act of 1992 had initially been aimed exclusively at juvenile offenders, but was amended to include adults in some of its provisions immediately prior to its enactment (Naffine and Wundersitz, 1994: 214).

64 The introduction of mandatory minimum sentences for convicted juveniles by Western Australia and the Northern Territory attracted forthright criticism from the United Nations Committee on the Rights of the Child: Government of Australia *Joint Senate Committee on Treaties Report on the Convention on the Rights of the Child* (1998), 346. This led to the repeal of this legislation in the Northern Territory in 2001.

65 In 2000, Western Australia's juvenile incarceration rate of 51.9 per 100,000 was exceeded only by Tasmania (66.46) and Northern Territories (60.7). Tasmania's high rate of juvenile incarceration is relatively recent, and follows the enactment of a new Youth Justice Act in 1997, which was based on a mixture of neo-correctionalist, justice model and restorative justice principles. Three years later its rate of juvenile incarceration had almost doubled.

66 Despite its widespread adoption in numerous other countries, including the Thames Valley police force in England (see Hoyle et al., 2002), the USA (see McGold and Wachtel, 1998) and Canada.

67 The most likely explanation for this difference in approach relates to a gradual acknowledgement in New Zealand that its cultural insensitivity towards such a substantial segment of New Zealand society and its resulting lack of legitimacy rendered the entire youth justice system in need of radical reform. Conversely, in Australia, where the indigenous population represents a much smaller proportion of the population as a whole, the legitimacy of the youth justice system is less vulnerable to such 'systemic' challenges and, consequently perhaps, the perceived scale of any reforms that might be needed have been correspondingly more modest.

68 In 1996, the ethnic composition of the population was as follows: black 79 per cent, white 9.5 per cent, 'coloured' 9 per cent, Indian 5 per cent.

69 Alternatively, however, children (who are defined as persons under the age of 18) may be placed under the supervision of a probation officer or sent to a reform school, 'in lieu of punishment' (s. 290, Criminal Procedure Act 1977).

70 In some urban areas where there are sufficient numbers of defendants under the age of 18, courts may be assigned to deal exclusively with such cases, but this is an administrative designation only, and does not constitute a separate system of juvenile courts (South African Law Commission, 1997).

71 NICRO is a non-governmental organisation similar to those found in other countries, such as Nacro (the National Association for the Care and Resettlement of Offenders) which operates in England and Wales. The diversion options that are available are described in Muntingh and Shapiro (1997).

72 1995 (3) SA 632 (CC).

73 The total number of children under the age of 18 who are convicted each year decreased from a high of more than 50,000 in 1980/1 to 17,526 in 1995/6, a decline of 66 per cent (Sloth-Nielsen and Muntingh, 2001: 9). Moreover, as a proportion of the total

number of convictions, children comprised only 7.8 per cent in 1995/6 compared with 13.9 per cent in 1980/1.

74 In 1997, the concept of minimum sentences for certain categories of juvenile offenders was introduced, but those under the age of 16 are excluded and, even for older offenders, the onus is on the state to show that there are serious and compelling reasons for imposing such a sentence. Subsequent case law has effectively restricted the scope of the legislation still further (Sloth-Nielsen, 2001).

75 Although the terms are not always used consistently, references to 'children' in South Africa normally apply to those under the age of 18; the term 'juveniles' strictly applies (as here) to those under the age of 21. In addition, the Department of Correctional Services (2001) also uses the term 'youth' to encompass those aged between 4 and 25 years.

76 Although statistics are incomplete, it is estimated that in 2001 those children awaiting trial who were detained in prison accounted for just half of the total, the rest being detained in other facilities, including those operated by the police and the Department of Social Development (Muntingh, 2003: 105, Table 74).

77 The comparable figure for 1994 is approximately 600 (South African Law Commission, 1997: para. 9.19).

78 The proportion of imprisoned children who are awaiting trial has increased from 33 per cent of the child prison population in 1996 to over 54 per cent in 2001 (Muntingh, 2003: 101, Table 69). During the same period child prison inmates increased as a proportion of the total prison population from just under 1 per cent in 1995 to 2.37 per cent in 2000, before declining slightly to 2.19 per cent in 2001 (Muntingh, 2003: 102, Table 70).

79 At the end of 2000, 18 per cent of juveniles awaiting trial were detained in police cells, compared with 45 per cent who were detained in prisons and 37 per cent in other facilities such as places of safety (Sloth-Nielsen and Muntingh, 2001: 16).

80 Section 5 of the Bill: As we have seen, this was also the position in England and Wales prior to the 'new youth justice' reforms introduced in 1998.

81 Section 47(3) of the Bill. These by no means exhaust the range of level one diversionary options, which also include inter alia the possibility of compulsory school attendance orders, family time orders, positive peer association orders, and good behaviour orders, the maximum duration of which in each case is three months.

82 Section 47(4) of the Bill. Hitherto, in the absence of any statutory recognition, these practices have only been available on an ad hoc basis, and consequently, recourse to them has been sporadic and inconsistent.

83 Which include some of the more onerous diversionary measures available at levels two or three, with a maximum duration (where applicable) of twelve months (s. 64).

84 These involve a referral to either a family group conference or victim offender mediation though the child justice court has the power to either approve the ensuing recommendations or substitute (giving reasons for doing so) its own order (s. 65).

85 Which can last for up to three years, but which may only be imposed on child offenders who are over the age of 14 (s. 66).

86 Ubuntu is a term derived from the Zulu and Xhosa languages, the closest equivalent for which in English is probably 'humane compassion towards others', which encompasses caring, sharing and being in harmony with all of creation. It has been adopted as one of the founding principles of the post-Apartheid Republic of South Africa.

14

Youth Justice Systems: Corporatist Variants

Conservative corporatist youth justice systems

The youth justice systems that are found in conservative corporatist countries mostly include the existence of specialized criminal courts for juveniles. And all have been shaped, to a greater or lesser degree, by a version of the 'welfare model', in which the primary justification for judicial intervention (or non-intervention) has been the 'best interests of the child', while the principal goal of the entire youth justice system could be defined as 'resocialization through education'. Indeed, this pedagogical purpose is likely to be reflected in several key aspects of the court process itself including, for example, a much more active role for the judge than is associated with most neo-liberal youth justice systems. Moreover, the trial procedure is also designed to encourage a higher level of participation on the part of the juvenile accused and any accompanying family members. In part, these 'orientational' differences between the two types of juvenile justice systems may be attributed to deeper structural differences in the legal systems themselves (Weijers, 2002). Thus, it is probably no coincidence that the more pedagogically oriented youth justice systems are to be found in conservative corporatist states that have traditionally favoured a civil law based inquisitorial approach. Conversely, the adversarial system that is associated with the common law tradition favoured by neo-liberal states tends to minimize the scope for interaction or dialogue between judge and accused during the trial process itself, and thereby inhibits the development of an explicitly pedagogical approach. Within common law-based youth justice systems, the scope for pedagogical dialogue is at best confined to the period after conviction and may often depend on the type of sentence that is imposed instead of being a central and routine part of the trial process itself.[1]

Another interesting feature of the welfare model that has been adopted by most of the conservative corporatist juvenile justice systems is that it has become imbued with a strong 'minimum interventionist' ethos. This also stands in marked contrast to the more coercive and interventionist approach that is associated, for example, with the ostensibly welfare-oriented US youth justice system. The minimum intervention approach may also be consistent with a belief in, and a commitment to enhancing, the pedagogical role of the trial process itself, which, if successfully accomplished, may be thought to preclude the need for further intervention. In common law-based adversarial systems, however, the trial process is much more narrowly focused on the establishment of the guilt or innocence of the defendant, as an abstract legal subject rather than as a whole human being. Sentencing is often seen as something of a hurried afterthought, and is certainly largely divorced from the guilt-finding process. In the inquisitorial tradition, by contrast, the court is seen as actively engaging with the defendant as a whole person throughout a relatively seamless process. So it is perhaps no coincidence that in neo-liberal states minimum interventionist developments tend to be chiefly associated with pre-trial diversionary processes whereas in conservative corporatist states they are equally likely to be associated with court-based processes.

The welfare approach was much slower to take hold in many conservative corporatist countries than it was in the USA but, once established, it has tended to show a greater degree of resilience in the face of challenges posed by the justice model and neo-correctionalist approach. Consequently, the youth justice systems that are found in most conservative corporatist countries – with the possible exception of the Netherlands – tend to show a much greater degree of stability than those associated with neo-liberal polities. In the main, the degree of homogeneity they exhibit is also greater compared with their neo-liberal counterparts. One of the most significant internal differences among this group of countries is that Germany has retained separate jurisdictional strands for dealing, respectively, with juvenile offenders and those in need of care and protection, while in several other conservative corporatist countries these jurisdictional strands have been united.

Youth justice in Germany[2]

As might be anticipated in the light of our foregoing analysis, the German youth justice system is distinctly different in several important respects from its counterparts in both neo-liberal and social democratic polities, but bears a distinct 'family resemblance' to those in other conservative corporatist states. As we shall see, German youth justice was never completely dominated by a Scandinavian-style social welfare model since it has always maintained a clear distinction between children in need of care and protection and those who have offended against the law. And even though its approach towards juvenile offenders has been strongly influenced by welfare-based principles of education and resocialization, these have mainly had the effect of modifying the kind (and intensity) of punishments that are meted out, rather than displacing the idea of punishment altogether. But while the German youth justice system has always remained a 'sub-system' within the general criminal justice system (Albrecht, 2004), the extent to which juvenile offenders are dealt with differently from their adult counterparts is far greater in Germany than in many neo-liberal states. And, far from emulating the neo-liberal tendency to erode those differences that do exist by exposing increasing numbers of young offenders to adult forms of trial and punishment, the trend in Germany has been to try and sentence an ever-increasing proportion of young adult offenders (aged 18–20) on the same basis as juveniles. Moreover, in marked contrast to the volatility that has characterized most neo-liberal juvenile justice systems, the German approach towards young offenders has shown a remarkable degree of stability apart from one brief aberration under the influence of Nazism during World War Two.

The emergence of a separate legal framework for dealing with juvenile offenders (between the ages of 14 and 17 inclusive)[3] did not occur in Germany until 1923, when the Youth Court Law (*Jugendgerichtsgesetz*) entered into force. Prior to that, juvenile offenders[4] came under the same jurisdiction as adults, albeit that the penalties to which they were exposed were mitigated on account of their age. Although juvenile offenders remain subject to the same substantive criminal laws as adults,[5] many of the procedural rules are different, notably those relating to the organization of the prosecution system, the juvenile criminal courts and also the conduct of juvenile criminal trials. According to the Youth Court Law this process of specialization also extends to youth court judges themselves, who are required to have special (psychological and sociological) knowledge of young people, though research has shown that despite these requirements most youth court judges are newcomers to youth justice (Adam et al., 1986). In the year preceding the enactment of the Youth Court Law another important reform was introduced – the Youth Welfare Law (*Jugendwohlfahrtsgesetz*, 1922) – which laid the foundations for a separate jurisdiction for those[6] in need of care and protection. This is administered by the family courts, though the same set of judges are entitled to sit in both courts. Those who are deemed to be in need of care and education are dealt with by youth welfare departments, though – as might be expected of a conservative corporatist polity – there is a preference for private[7] rather than public youth welfare provision, except as a last resort.

The Youth Court Law established a number of important general principles that have continued to characterize the orientation of the German juvenile justice system ever since its introduction. The first of these involved a curtailment of the traditional 'principle of legality' – which states that known offenders must be prosecuted – authorizing public prosecutors[8] to dismiss proceedings not just in the case of petty offences (as for adults); but also if an adequate 'educational measure' has been undertaken, either by an institution or by individuals including teachers, parents or other relatives. Various forms of diversion are thus possible.

They include diversion without any sanction; diversion in combination with measures undertaken by other agencies (such as parents or school) or linked with mediation; and diversion that is combined with a more formal intervention such as a warning, a fine, community service, an apology to the victim, reparation or mediation.[9] The latter are imposed by the juvenile court judge acting on a recommendation by the prosecutor. Between them diversionary measures were imposed in respect of 69 per cent of all juvenile offenders in 2001, leaving just 31 per cent to be dealt with by means of formal court sanctions.

The second and even more fundamental principle relates to the primary purpose of the juvenile criminal justice system, which is aimed at the education and resocialization of the young offender, and is thus focused mainly on the latter's personal circumstances and rehabilitative needs. Consequently, both prosecutors and judges are obliged to consider factors such as the offender's family background and school achievements when deciding how a young person should be dealt with,[10] in contrast to the purely offence-related factors that have to be taken into consideration when dealing with adult offenders.

This difference in the overall orientation of the German youth justice system is also reflected in the type of penalties that are available when dealing with young offenders. In place of the normal offence-specific penalties (each with its own maximum and minimum range) that are prescribed by the German penal code, the Youth Court Law contains a specific system of measures that are divided into three categories: educational measures, disciplinary measures and youth imprisonment. Educational measures are intended to have a positive effect on the behavioural patterns of young offenders by securing and enhancing the conditions of socialization. They include community service, participation in social training courses or traffic education, attendance at vocational training, participation in victim offender mediation or supervision by a social worker.

The second category of juvenile sanctions comprises disciplinary measures[11] and includes three sub-categories: cautioning by the juvenile judge; fulfilling certain obligations (for example paying a fine, performing community service, compensating a victim or formally apologizing to the victim); or short-term detention (*Jugendarrest*). The latter is the most severe disciplinary measure and involves intermittent detention (imposed during weekends or spare time) in a special unit (separate from youth prison) that may last for up to four weeks. One important distinction between these disciplinary measures and youth imprisonment itself is that they are not entered onto a juvenile's criminal record and therefore, in theory at least, entail fewer adverse consequences for the juveniles concerned.

The final category comprises youth imprisonment, the minimum sentence for which is six months. The maximum is generally five years, but in the case of exceptionally serious offences it may be ten years. The reason for the six months' minimum sentence (compared with one month in the case of adult offenders) stems from a belief that the treatment and education of a young offender cannot be accomplished within a shorter time-span. Sentences of youth imprisonment are served in separate juvenile prisons and are only supposed to be imposed when educational or disciplinary measures are not sufficient, either because of the juvenile offender's 'criminal tendencies'[12] or because of the gravity of the offender's guilt, taking into account the seriousness of the offence that has been committed. Youth imprisonment sentences of up to two years can be suspended,[13] though the offender is then subject to a period of probation (between two to three years) part of which (one to two years) will be subject to probationary supervision.

With regard to the choice between these different types of measures, the governing principle is again based on educational need, though this is tempered by the requirement of proportionality that is derived from the German constitution (Albrecht, 2004: 453). In practice this entails a hierarchy of responses whereby disciplinary measures may only be applied if educational measures alone are not sufficient in meeting the educational needs of the offender, and juvenile imprisonment may only be resorted to if the offender's educational needs are unlikely to be met by educational or disciplinary measures alone.[14] In determining the kind of educational measure that is appropriate, however, a judge has to ensure not just that it is sufficient to meet the offender's educational needs, but also that it is the least severe measure that is required to effect this aim and that – taking into account the seriousness of the offence – it is proportional to the goal to be achieved.

It is sometimes suggested (see, for example, Albrecht, 2004: 483–4) that this welfare-based sentencing orientation for juvenile offenders can paradoxically render them liable in practice to be dealt with *more severely* than an adult offender would be for an offence of comparable seriousness despite the formal requirements of minimum intervention and proportionality. This argument is backed by figures suggesting that juvenile judges make considerably more use of sanctions involving deprivation of liberty than those who are responsible for sentencing adult offenders. Thus, Heinz (1990), for example, has suggested that 25 per cent of juvenile offenders are sentenced to unconditional terms of youth imprisonment or short-term detention compared with a detention rate of approximately 5 per cent in the case of adult offenders even though juvenile crimes tend to be much less serious, on average, than those committed by adult offenders. However, the figures cited by Heinz exclude the use of informal sanctions and, when these are included, the rate of unconditional youth imprisonment is a mere 2 per cent; suspended youth prison sentences account for another 4 per cent, and the sanction of youth detention (which is milder than adult imprisonment) accounts for a further 5 per cent.[15] Moreover, the proportionate use of custodial measures for juvenile offenders has declined significantly in Germany during the 1980s and 1990s: by 55 per cent in respect of short-term detention and by 25 per cent in the case of youth imprisonment (Dünkel, 2003: 116–17).

In terms of youth justice policy development, the general trend over the years has been to confirm and consolidate the principle of education on the one hand, and to reduce the punitive impact of juvenile criminal justice on the other hand (Albrecht, 2004). The biggest aberration occurred in 1943 under the influence of Nazi ideology (Kerner and Weitekamp, 1984) and took the form of a special amendment, the aim of which was to replace rehabilitation with retribution as the primary goal of the youth justice system. The age of criminal responsibility was lowered to 12 years for juveniles who had committed serious offences. Suspended sentences of imprisonment and short-term imprisonment were abolished,[16] and new forms of youth imprisonment were introduced instead. Finally, the amendment also made it possible to transfer serious juvenile offenders aged 16 upwards to adult criminal courts where they could be dealt with by adult criminal sentences, including the death penalty. The law was in force for three years but was abolished immediately after the war as part of a concerted attempt to cleanse the German legal system of Nazi ideology. (Ironically, such measures are now more likely to be associated with the ultra neo-liberal orientation of contemporary youth justice policies in the USA).

Under the Youth Court Law Amendment of 1953, young adults aged 18–20 were also brought within the scope of the Youth Court Law, making it possible for them to be dealt with as juveniles, which may be thought of as a 'reverse transfer' strategy. In recent decades a growing proportion of young adult offenders (now amounting to slightly more than 60 per cent on average) are dealt with as juveniles.[17] This is in marked contrast to developments in many neo-liberal jurisdictions, though the policy has been coming under pressure in recent years as a result of growing concern over the incidence of 'hate crimes', many of which are committed by right-wing extremist offenders within this age range, particularly within the East German Länder.

During the 1960s and 1970s Germany experienced a vigorous debate over the merits of assimilating the juvenile crime and care jurisdictions, and proposals were tabled which would have abolished juvenile criminal law measures altogether, requiring juvenile offenders to be dealt with instead under the juvenile welfare law regime. As we have seen, similar debates were also taking place at the same time in a number of neo-liberal countries including England. In Germany, however, this more radical version of the welfare approach towards juvenile offenders foundered in the face of strong opposition from criminal justice professionals, despite strong backing from the student and trade union movement, and also the Social Democratic-Liberal government (in office from 1969 to 1982).

The only other significant development in German juvenile justice policy was the Youth Court Law Amendment of 1990, which reflected a number of wider influences including those associated with the justice model, the minimum intervention approach and also the restorative justice movement. The influence of the justice model can be seen most clearly in the adoption of restrictions on the pre-trial detention of juveniles[18] and the abolition of the indeterminate youth prison sentence, though the overall educational orientation of the juvenile justice system was left unscathed. The influence of justice model thinking can also be discerned in the growth in official support for policies promoting 'equal opportunities', particularly on the part of deprived young people.[19] This resulted in the eventual closure of a system of prison-like closed foster homes (known as 'Fürsorgeerziehungsheime') which were seen by many critics as a symbol of purely repressive policies towards working-class youth. After a long campaign a new child welfare law in 1990 emphasized the voluntary nature of all welfare services for children, and restricted foster care to open homes.[20]

The influence of the minimum intervention approach has been even more pervasive and has contributed to a growth in official support for policies aimed at diversion and decarceration. At first, however, developments in this direction were largely practitioner-led, as was also the case in a number of neo-liberal juvenile justice systems. Since the 1970s, for example, public prosecutors have shown an ever greater willingness to dismiss juvenile criminal cases rather than prosecuting them, and by 1990 diversion by the public prosecutor accounted for every second case involving a juvenile offender (Heinz, 1989, 1990). A growth in the number of victim-offender schemes in recent decades may also have contributed to this tendency. As a result, the rates of adjudication and sentencing of juvenile and young adults have remained stable in spite of a pronounced increase in the number of suspects in these age groups.

A similar tendency is also apparent with regard to imprisonment rates, which decreased during the 1980s and 1990s to 6 per cent of all youth court dispositions (compared with 8 per cent during the 1970s) despite a steady increase in the number of juvenile suspects. The proportionate use of short-term detention has also declined (from 24 per cent in 1976 to 18 per cent in 1998), while the number of measures requiring community service and social training by the offender has increased markedly during the same period. Following these developments, the Youth Court Amendment of 1990 explicitly adopted the principle that adjudication and formal sentencing should be a 'last resort'. The Amendment also extended the range of alternatives to imprisonment by encouraging the use of suspended sentences for terms of imprisonment between one and two years and by 1995 59 per cent of such sentences were suspended (Dünkel, 1998: 287). Albrecht (2004) has suggested that the reason for the pronounced and continuing influence of the minimum intervention approach is that it fits well with the general welfare approach (Sozialstaat) which emerged during the second half of the nineteenth century, and that the labelling theory on which it is founded appealed to youth justice practitioners.

As for the restorative justice approach, this is represented in Germany almost exclusively by various victim offender mediation and reparation initiatives as opposed to 'conferencing' procedures. The latter model is much less well developed in most conservative corporatist countries than in many neo-liberal ones.[21] At first these initiatives were largely practitioner-led, but the 1990 Youth Court

Law Amendment also authorized the practice. Thus, under current juvenile criminal law, public prosecutors may refrain from prosecution if, after the conclusion of victim offender mediation, it appears that no further educational measures are required. Similarly, if the young person is convicted an offender may be instructed – by means of an educational order – to try to reach a settlement with a victim. Alternatively, reparation or a personal apology may be ordered as conditions to be fulfilled in complying with a disciplinary measure. Despite this statutory backing, however, the impact has been relatively modest. On the one hand there has been a substantial (60 per cent) increase in the number of mediation projects established since the legislative amendment of 1990 (Dünkel, 2003: 129). On the other hand, however, a national poll conducted in 1995 showed that while 74 per cent of all local authorities provided mediation schemes, most of them resorted to mediation only infrequently and mostly on an *ad hoc* basis (Dünkel, 2003: 127).

It would be wrong to suppose that the German juvenile justice system has remained completely unscathed by the 'law and order' tendencies that have influenced the direction of juvenile justice policies in many neo-liberal systems, however. Ever since World War Two there has been a succession of moral panics over youth crime issues, culminating during the 1990s in concerns relating to violent and persistent juvenile offenders, young immigrant offenders, and chronic child offenders who appear to be beyond the control of conventional juvenile justice and juvenile welfare measures. Albrecht (2004) highlights the case of a young boy called 'Mehmet', born in Germany but of Turkish descent, who managed to combine all these concerns. Having committed sixty offences before the age of 14, he was given a sentence of youth imprisonment and a deportation order (which was enforced immediately) when he continued offending beyond his fourteenth birthday. Not surprisingly, perhaps, cases like Mehmet's have fuelled calls by conservative political parties and mainstream public opinion for a more repressive approach to be adopted towards juvenile offenders.

In April 2000, the opposition Christian Democratic Party/Christian Social Union proposed a reform package,[22] supported by a number of Länder containing (*inter alia*) the following measures:

- requiring young adults normally to be tried and sentenced as adults rather than juveniles;
- increasing the maximum sentence of imprisonment for young adults from ten to fifteen years;
- introducing a new supervision order that would impose tight controls on the movement of juveniles;
- extending to the family court powers to impose a similar range of restrictive and punitive orders to those currently available in the youth court (including participation in social training courses and community service but also victim offender mediation); and
- strengthening the powers of family courts to deal with parents who have allegedly failed to supervise and control their delinquent or criminal offspring.

The overall tenor of these proposals is more redolent of the neo-correctionalist approach that has come to characterize the youth justice systems in many neo-liberal countries. This is particularly true of the proposal to hold parents responsible for their errant offspring. If adopted, such a programme, would represent a major departure for the German youth justice system which has until now been chiefly characterized by its remarkably firm and stable attachment to a mildly welfarist approach. Even if it were to be adopted, however, its main thrust appears to be directed at the treatment of young adult offenders and at extending the punitive powers of the more welfare-oriented family courts, leaving the overall orientation of the German youth justice system itself largely intact. Thus, although a shift towards a more correctionalist approach cannot be entirely ruled out, the German youth justice system appears set for the foreseeable future to retain a far higher degree of resilience in the face of 'law and order' forces than most of the neo-liberal systems we examined in the previous section.[23]

Youth justice in Italy

Italy is unusual inasmuch as the welfare approach for juvenile offenders took hold there somewhat later than in many other countries and has in certain respects strengthened its grip in recent years. The Italian youth justice system has also been influenced by both diversionary and (to a lesser extent) restorative justice tendencies, though the justice model has had rather less impact than in most other countries. There have been relatively few signs to date of a pronounced 'neo-correctionalist' backlash, though the influence of the youth justice system has to some extent been strengthened since 1988, at the expense of the social welfare authorities.

A separate system of juvenile courts was not established in Italy until 1934; moreover, for the next two decades it continued to apply mainly penal measures that were only to a limited extent tempered by rehabilitative elements (Gatto and Verde, 1998: 357). It was not until 1956 that a series of welfare-based reforms was introduced, which were further strengthened in 1962 by the establishment of social service agencies with wide ranging powers and responsibilities. The still relatively undeveloped social welfare system was radically overhauled in 1977, which resulted in a transfer of responsibility for administering social services from the social services department of the Justice Ministry to the various local authorities. Although the juvenile courts retained their powers to make court orders in respect of young offenders, any rehabilitative measures that they imposed were actually administered by these much more autonomous local authorities. In many districts, especially in the north of Italy, social service departments increasingly assimilated the treatment of young offenders into the general social welfare system catering for children in need of care and protection.

The overall effect was to strengthen the influence of a welfare-based approach that aimed at the avoidance of stigmatization and embodied a preference for community intervention rather than detention in closed institutions.

In 1988, however, Italy introduced a new Code of Criminal Procedure which replaced the former inquisitorial system with an adversarial model. At the same time a separate code of criminal procedure for juveniles was introduced. The reform package incorporated a number of competing ideological perspectives that have to some extent moderated the influence of the welfare approach. The rehabilitation of young offenders by means of personalized social programmes remains an important aim of the system, but the power of the Justice Ministry and the juvenile courts has been reasserted by once again subordinating local authority social services departments to their control. Another aim of the reforms was to strengthen the accountability of young offenders while safeguarding their rights[24] during the course of legal proceedings. The reform package also promoted the use of diversionary measures, but at the same time (as we shall see below) authorized the use of a wide range of 'preventive' measures at the pre-trial stage.

One unusual feature of the current Italian youth justice system is the very high degree of specialization on the part of all the agencies concerned, including a specialist body of police officers, specialist prosecutor and the very highly specialized juvenile court ('*Tribunale per i minorenni*') itself. Another distinctive feature is the lack of any autonomous pre-trial diversionary mechanisms, whether on the part of the police or prosecution, which results from an unusually strict application of the 'legality principle'. Diversion is still possible,[25] but formally this is only possible under the auspices of the court, which exercises jurisdiction over offenders between the ages of 14–17 inclusive. Below the age of 14, juveniles are presumed to be '*doli incapax*' and cannot be prosecuted, but even above that age the court is obliged to assess whether the suspect has the full 'capacity to understand and consciously act' ('*capace di intendere e di volere*') and is responsible, before any charges may be laid.[26]

Thereafter, judicial proceedings may pass through three distinct phases. The first phase consists of a preliminary investigation. This is conducted by the public prosecutor under the supervision of the 'magistrate for preliminary investigations', who is a single professional judge. The latter has the power to dismiss the case, order the defendant to face questioning or confirm the arrest and/or preliminary detention. Although this is not strictly a judicial phase, the magistrate may also decide to impose preventive measures ('*misure cautelari*') in advance of any hearing. Such measures include the possibility of educationally useful activities, home curfew, placement in a group home or 'preventive detention' in either a 'reception centre' or a juvenile prison. The second phase consists of a preliminary hearing, and is conducted by a panel of three judges (one professional magistrate and two honorary 'lay' magistrates). And the third phase involves a trial before the juvenile criminal court itself, which involves a panel of four judges (two professional magistrates and two lay magistrates).

The predominant influence of the welfare model manifests itself in a variety of ways. Firstly, all those working in the field of juvenile justice (including police, prosecutors, defence lawyers and judges) are not only specialists, as we have seen, but are required to undertake specialist training programmes arranged by their respective professional bodies (Corghi, 2000). Secondly, the judges themselves comprise both legal experts and those who are expert in the field of psychology, psychiatry, pedagogy, criminal anthropology or biology. Thirdly, the juvenile court has competence over both criminal and civil proceedings (the latter involving care and protection matters and also the delinquent acts of those under the age of 14 if they are regarded as being dangerous to society).[27] Fourthly, the court is assisted by social workers – often located in the courts – whose task it is to identify the socialization problems that may account for the young person's behaviour. Fifthly, the court proceedings themselves are intended to serve an explicitly pedagogical function by actively involving the young person and his or her parents in a process that is aimed at rehabilitation. And finally, the influence of the welfare model is also apparent in certain of the disposals that are available to the court, though in many respects the minimum intervention model appears to have exerted a far more powerful influence on both the range of disposals and also the use that is made of them.

Many of the disposals are available not only after trial, but also following the preliminary hearing, providing the offender's responsibility has been established by that stage. One of the most important disposals, numerically, takes the form of a judicial pardon ('*perdono giudiziale*'), which is issued in cases when it is thought more advisable in order to aid the maturation process not to inflict a criminal sanction. In the first few years following its introduction, this power was being used in as many as 80 per cent of all cases involving 14–17-year olds (Picotti and Strobel, 1996). Alternatively, cases that are thought to be trivial ('*irrilavanza del fatto*') may also be dismissed by the judge. Another possibility is to suspend the proceedings (for a maximum period of one year, or three years in the case of serious offences) by placing the young person on probation ('*suspensione del processo con acasa alla prova*') under the supervision of a social worker. If there is a positive report at the end of the period the charges will be dropped. Measures such as these may be thought of as functionally equivalent to the pre-trial diversion processes that are available in other countries such as the Netherlands and Sweden.

Other disposals including fines and custody are also available, the latter being served in special custodial institutions ('*Istituti Penali Minorili*') for young people, though the length of sentence that may be imposed is reduced[28] on account of the offender's age (as in France). Moreover, two alternative measures were introduced in 1981 as substitutes for short terms of imprisonment of up to three and six months respectively. The first – '*libertà controllata*' – is a form of police supervision requiring an offender to report regularly to them. The second – '*semidetenzione*' – takes the form of an intermittent custodial sentence, enabling the offender to be free for part of the day to take part in employment or educational activities while spending ten hours a day in prison, usually at night. These 'substitutive' sanctions are now available for juveniles sentenced to terms of custody of up to two years (Dünkel, 1998: 292). As a result of these various mitigatory alternatives, Italian juveniles tend in the main to be incarcerated only for very serious violent offences, and the numbers involved are very small. However, detention is used more extensively as a preventive measure, particularly with regard to foreign juveniles, who are not eligible for local authority social assistance and other welfare-based measures, since these are conditional on having a fixed address and a residence permit.[29]

Finally, the second half of the 1990s witnessed a surge of interest in restorative justice, which was reflected in the opening of a number of victim offender mediation services within the juvenile justice system. Although not specifically authorized by law[30] at that time, some judges began to refer cases to these services, frequently at the preliminary hearing stage, and often in conjunction with probation. If the outcome is positive, the judge may then dismiss the case or give a judicial pardon. Eight such services were operative at the time of writing. Since 2002, when a new law was introduced relating to minor offences, mediation has been available either 'officially', within the context of a probation order ('*messa alla prova*'), or unofficially at the pre-trial stage if the juvenile court is willing to adjourn a hearing. If an attempt at mediation is successful during this period (which may be for up to two months), the final outcome is likely to take the form of a dismissal of the case.[31] If unsuccessful, the case proceeds in the normal way.

Despite these tentative recent moves towards a restorative justice approach, however, and the conflicting ideological approaches that were embodied in the 1988 juvenile criminal procedure, the principal influences on the Italian juvenile justice continue to be those associated with the welfare approach and minimum intervention philosophy. Compared with these, the impact of both the justice model and neo-correctionalist tendencies have been relatively muted and there are few indications that this state of affairs is likely to change, at least in the immediate future.

Youth justice in France[32]

The French youth justice system resembles the Italian system in being a relatively late convert to an ostensibly welfare-oriented approach, which – in theory at least – has largely maintained its pre-eminence despite increasing competition from rival influences. Although a separate youth justice system was first introduced as long ago as 1912, comprising a children's court, reformatories and probation system ('*liberté surveillée*') that were inspired by US influences, the new measures were unpopular with judges and the reformatories in particular were dogged by scandal (Gazeau and Peyre, 1998: 221). Consequently, juvenile offenders continued to be liable to much the same kinds of penalties as adults, even though their severity was mitigated on the grounds of youthfulness ('l'excuse de minorité'). In 1945, however, responsibility for administering youth justice was transferred from the Ministry of the Interior to the Ministry of Justice, and a new rehabilitative and paternalistic model – based on the education and (re)socialization of juvenile offenders – was adopted. This welfare orientation is ostensibly reflected in four key principles: specialization, continuity of treatment, flexibility of treatment and a preference (again in theory at least) for treatment to be administered in an open environment.

The degree of specialization in the French juvenile justice system is less pronounced than in Italy, and is largely confined to particular institutional structures rather than the functions they perform. Unlike Italy, the principle of specialization is chiefly restricted to the juvenile court, and does not fully extend either to the police[33] or public prosecutors. The role of the public prosecutor[34] is, however, very important and incorporates a gatekeeping function since cases can be dismissed if prosecution is felt not to be in the pubic interest, or on grounds of insufficient evidence. In principle, the police are obliged to refer all cases to the prosecutor, though in practice minor offences, particularly if committed by a first time offender, are liable to be simply registered and dismissed, sometimes accompanied by an unofficial caution (Gazeau and Peyre, 1998: 227).

Minor criminal cases are heard by a single full-time professional youth court magistrate ('juge des enfants'), who does receive specialist training. As in Italy, the juvenile court combines criminal and civil care-and-protection jurisdictions, and most dispositions at this level involve educational rehabilitation measures or those intended to protect the juvenile from neglect or abuse.[35] Children under the age of 13 cannot be prosecuted, and may only be dealt with by educational measures though exceptionally these could involve an institutional placement. More serious cases are dealt with by a juvenile court ('tribunal pour enfants') comprising a professional juvenile court magistrate, who presides, and two lay 'assesseurs' who are selected from specialist panels. Older juveniles (those aged 16 and 17) who are charged with very serious crimes are liable to be dealt with by a juvenile assize court ('cour d'assises des mineurs'),[36] comprising a judge from the district court of appeals, two juvenile court magistrates and nine jurors. In accordance with its welfare orientation, the law recommends the use of educational or 'care' measures for juvenile offenders,[37] though if the circumstances of the offence or personality of the offender are deemed to require it, 'penal measures' may also be applied[38] on a case by case basis to those aged 13 and above.

The principle of continuity is chiefly reflected in the belief that the same judge[39] should be engaged (actively) throughout the proceedings, both in questioning the young person and also in negotiating the outcome that is most likely to promote their best interests. By restricting participation to a single judge it is assumed that the decision will be taken by the person who best knows the offender's personality, and by encouraging active participation on the part of the offender it is believed that the prospects for a successful resolution, including compliance, will be improved. However, the judge's responsibility also continues after the sentence has been pronounced since he or she is authorized to revise, revoke, supplement or terminate the sanction in the light of the offender's progress. This continuing responsibility on the part of the judge is also consistent with the preference for flexible, individualized, treatment measures, which reflects a belief that they must be capable of responding to the unstable personalities of many young offenders.

The preference for treating juvenile offenders in an open environment is reflected in the priority that is supposed to be accorded to 'educational measures', though the sentencing practice of the courts suggests that this privileged status has gradually eroded over time. Thus, in 2002 'educational measures' accounted for less than half (41.7 per cent) of all sanctions pronounced in that year while 'penal measures' accounted for 48.4 per cent[40] (Ministère de la Justice, 2003: 22). This represents a sizeable increase in the proportionate use of penal measures, which only accounted for one-third of all sanctions in the early 1980s, and for just over one-quarter at the start of the 1960s.

In terms of their content, two-thirds of the 'educational measures' that were imposed in 2002 consisted of a simple warning ('admonestation'), and all but a tiny fraction of the remainder resulted in the child simply being handed over to its parents or other responsible person to be dealt with. The number who were assigned to protective or 'secure' placements of any kind amounted to just over 1 per cent, and a fractionally higher proportion were assigned to some form of supervised educational activity without removing them from their normal surroundings. At the level of penal practice, therefore, there is little evidence of any serious commitment to a 'treatment-oriented' (as opposed to a more straightforward 'diversionary') approach. As for the penal measures, just over half (57 per cent,) were 'custodial', though just under half of these (43 per cent) were 'fully suspended', while just over one-third (36 per cent) were completely unsuspended. Fines accounted for 16 per cent of the penal sanction imposed, and alternatives to custody ('peines de substitution'), for example community service ('travail d'intérêt general' or TIG) accounted for the remainder (26 per cent).

Those juveniles who are sentenced to immediate custody[41] are supposed to be sent to special penitentiary centres, where the emphasis is on social rehabilitation programmes, but not all are fully equipped for this purpose. The centres are supposed to be entirely separate from adult prisons, but in practice usually take the form of a juvenile wing that is attached to an adult prison.[42] The number of juveniles who were detained in this way fell during the 1980s, reaching a record low in 1991 (when they accounted for just 0.8 per cent of the total prison population, compared with 2.1 per cent in 1980). However, it began to rise again during the 1990s, and by 1999 juveniles accounted for 1.3 per cent of the total prison population (Combessie, 2001: 272),[43] though most of them (more than two-thirds) were serving sentences of less than two months, which is difficult to reconcile with the official 'treatment' orientation of the youth justice system as a whole.

Until recently, there were no closed facilities for the treatment of juvenile offenders apart from these juvenile prison wings. The only other facilities took the form of community-based juvenile treatment centres (providing either long-term or temporary care facilities), known as *'foyers'*, or group homes. These are run by public agencies, private organizations or religious orders, and are used to house both delinquent and non-delinquent youths (those in need of care and protection). A distinctive feature of the foyer system is the continuing involvement of the judge, who not only decides whether a child should be sent there for long-term or temporary care, but also remains responsible for monitoring the young person's progress with the probation officer or social worker who has been assigned to the case. More recently, however, the foyer system has been augmented by the opening of several additional hostel and care centres, and the creation of a variety of stricter reformatory youth centres. Thus, in 1999 two new types of educational institutions were established. *'Centres de Placement Immédiat'* (or 'emergency placement centres'), of which there were forty-six in 2004, are designed for young offenders who are in urgent need of removal from their family and social environment in order to deal with temporary crises. *'Centres Éducatifs Renforcés'* (or 'secure educational centres'), of which there were seventy-two in 2004, are designed for serious young delinquents who are at risk of reoffending and incarceration. They provide intensive educational activity programmes lasting for between three and six months.

These developments have taken place amid growing public concern over the extent of youth crime, and may presage a shift towards a more neo-correctionalist approach, as may the recent introduction of electronic monitoring for young offenders. The clearest indication to date of a move in this direction can be seen in the law of 9 September 2002,[44] whose principal aim was to reinforce the responsibility of young offenders. Under this law, young people who commit more serious offences can be brought more swiftly before a *juge des enfants*. It also introduces a new type of penalty, known as *'sanctions educatives'* ('educational sanctions'), that are interposed between the two more traditional sets of sanctions: educational measures and penal measures. Controversially, *sanctions educatives* can be imposed on children between the ages of 10 and 18, provoking concerns over a lowering of the age of criminal responsibility (normally 13) (Castaignède, 2003: 782).[45] Various measures can be imposed under this new ordinance: the confiscation of property that has been used to commit an offence, as well as the proceeds of an offence; prohibitions on returning to the scene of the crime, mixing with accomplices or meeting the victim; attending a course in 'civic training'; and undertaking some form of reparation. With the exception of the latter two measures, the 'educational' value of such sanctions is somewhat obscure. Indeed, they are somewhat more redolent of the 'early intervention' strategies associated with some of the recent English youth justice reforms, as is also the case of the 'fast-tracking' procedures.

Another innovation that is associated with the 2002 ordinance is the creation of a new set of closed educational centres (*'centres éducatifs fermés'*) combining educational provision within a closely monitored and controlling environment.[46] Such centres are intended for young people aged 13–18 who are subject to a supervision order or conditional detention sentence after other educative measures have failed. They are designed to operate as a 'last chance saloon' since offenders who breach the rules or escape are explicitly threatened with imprisonment.[47] In September 2004 there were ten such centres, and a further fifteen are expected to open during 2005 (Ministry of Justice press release dated 15 September 2004). Finally, seven new penal establishments specifically for young offenders are due to be opened by 2006, each with a capacity of 60 places.[48]

As a result of these recent developments, it appears that the French youth justice system has in many respects become harsher and more repressive than it used to be. Indeed, many of these developments are much more redolent of recent changes in the English youth justice system than the more welfare-oriented approach of the postwar French system. In spite of these tendencies, however, up to now, the overall welfare orientation in France, as in most other conservative corporatist countries we have examined, has not completely succumbed to the even more repressive tendencies that are associated with the neo-correctionalist approach. Indeed, lip service continues to be paid to the founding welfare-based principles governing the postwar French juvenile justice system, as in the 2002 ordinance, which expressly reaffirmed them.

With regard to other influences on the French juvenile justice system, the impact of the justice model has been less pronounced until recently than in many other countries, though juveniles are entitled to legal advice from the beginning of police detention. Moreover, since 2000, they have been granted the right of silence, and any police interviews must be videotaped. As we have seen already, in many respects the operation of the youth justice system in practice appears to reflect a 'minimum intervention' philosophy rather than the treatment-oriented 'welfare-based' approach to which it is officially committed. Diversion is also carried out by both prosecution and, to a lesser extent, by the police. Furthermore, since 1993, French prosecutors have also had the power to refer young offenders to 'penal mediation' as an alternative to prosecution. This results in the prosecution being dropped, provided the attempt at mediation is successful. The introduction of penal mediation is the most conspicuous example to date of the influence that the restorative justice approach has had on the French juvenile justice system, though in practice, as in many other conservative corporatist countries, the measure has been relatively seldom used.[49]

Youth justice in the Netherlands[50]

The development of a separate system of youth justice has had a longer history in the Netherlands than in most other countries, though the foundations of the modern system were laid in the early part of the twentieth century. For almost a century thereafter, the prevailing influence on the system was essentially welfarist in orientation (Junger-Tas, 1982), but since 1995 this has been supplanted, initially by justice model tendencies, and more recently by increasingly neo-correctionalist impulses. These have resulted in a far more radical change in direction, and a much greater degree of volatility than that experienced in most other conservative corporatist polities, though the underlying welfare orientation has not been entirely effaced by any means.

Another general feature of the Dutch youth justice system is that it retains a formal distinction between the care and protection system and the juvenile criminal law even though in practice the two are intertwined to a considerable extent. In 1901 the Dutch parliament adopted a child care law, dealing with care and protection issues, and a child penal law which established a specific system of proceedings and sanctions for dealing with juvenile delinquents.

On the civil law side, guardianship orders were introduced whereby parental rights could be abrogated, either temporarily (*'ontheffing'*) in respect of those incapable of bringing up their children adequately, or permanently (*'ontzetting'*) in cases of serious neglect or ill-treatment. Private, mostly church-affiliated organizations (corresponding to the three main confessional 'pillars': orthodox Calvinism; Reformed Protestantism; and Catholicism) were subsidized by the state to provide child care places. In 1922, the supervision order was introduced;[51] this involves the appointment of a family guardian for periods of one year at a time, either in respect of children living at home or those living in institutions or with foster families.

On the criminal law side, the 1901 Act clearly stated that children who offended were wherever possible to be re-educated and not punished but, if punishment was felt to be required, that it should also be educative in character. The Act introduced three main sanctions – the reprimand, fine and reform school – and conferred wide discretionary power on the judge to determine whether a child[52] should be (re)-educated or punished, and for how long. In reaching this decision, a judge was obliged to take account of a preliminary inquiry, the aim of which was to determine the family's socialization capacity, and also the child's state of development, character and behaviour. Unusually for a welfare-oriented system children were afforded the same procedural rights as adults, including access to a lawyer.[53] A system of specialized, professional juvenile judges with competence in both civil and penal matters was introduced in 1921, and their powers were further extended in 1961, when they were authorized to intervene in the execution of sanctions.

During this 'welfare era' all criminal justice agencies – police, public prosecutor and juvenile judge – were supposed to act 'in the best interests of the child', though the interpretation given to this principle has evolved over the years. By the 1980s most youth justice agencies and many practitioners subscribed to a version of the 'minimum interventionist' philosophy, and this resulted in a dramatic reduction in the number of juveniles who were subjected to formal interventions of any kind. For example, the discretionary power of the police to divert juveniles from court by taking 'no further action' or dismissing the case with an informal caution or warning gradually became institutionalized and studies revealed a diversion rate ranging between 54 and 80 per cent (Junger-Tas, 1983; Van der Hoeven, 1985). Moreover, public prosecutors also exercised a diversionary role, relying in part on their inherent discretion (deriving from the expediency principle) to dismiss less serious cases. They also routinely engaged with juvenile judges and social workers employed by the council for child protection in tripartite consultations to determine which cases should be prosecuted and which could be dismissed with an official reprimand.[54]

As a result of these various diversionary mechanisms, it was estimated that in the early 1980s, only about 15 per cent of all children coming into contact with the police eventually appeared before the juvenile judge (Junger-Tas, 2004). Moreover, social workers began placing greater emphasis on voluntary supervision and guidance of young people in need of care and protection, resulting in sizeable reductions in the number of child care placements during the 1970s.

However, the 1980s represented the high-water mark of the minimum interventionist approach in the Netherlands, as in many other countries, and developments since then (whether in the sphere of youth justice practice or the legislative framework within which they operate) have been increasingly influenced by 'justice model', reparative and 'neo-correctionalist' tendencies. One of the first indications of a significant change of direction involved the growing preference for 'conditional diversion', which has largely replaced the erstwhile policy of unconditional dismissals. Instead, juvenile offenders may be required either to pay compensation to their victims, or to attend a diversion programme known as HALT (*'Het ALTternatief'*). The latter may involve apologizing to victims, reparative work (up to a maximum of twenty hours) carried out on a free Saturday, or the payment of damages to victims, and is used mainly for petty offences, particularly minor property crimes and criminal damage. Since its introduction in Rotterdam in 1982, it has spread all over the country, and there are now some sixty-five schemes, jointly financed by the Ministry of Justice and local municipalities. By 1999, nearly 23,000 juveniles were being diverted on this basis, mostly for property crimes (40 per cent), criminal damage (20 per cent) or offences involving fireworks (20 per cent) (Netherlands Ministry of Justice, 2001a).[55]

A similar change was adopted by prosecutors, who came under growing pressures from government and the general public during the 1980s to relinquish their former practice of dismissing the majority of juvenile offenders unconditionally in favour of conditional dismissals involving an apology, the performance of community service, or payment of compensation to victims.[56] Both sets of developments are consistent with a switch from diversion for its own sake to a philosophy of 'early interventionism' with the aim of holding offenders accountable, promoting restorative outcomes for victims and, thereby, reducing the likelihood of reoffending. The number of young people appearing in court has also increased in recent years, from around 6,000 young people who were prosecuted in the 1980s and early 1990s to 9,200 cases in 2000 (van der Laan, 2003: 82).

A third, broadly contemporaneous, development involved an extension to the range of sanctions available to the court by 'importing' from England and adapting two non-custodial penalties: the community service order (or work projects) and intermediate treatment programmes (or training projects). The former involves practical tasks that are intended to benefit the community, while the latter aim to improve an offender's social and/or practical skills. They were first introduced on an experimental basis in 1983 (van der Laan, 1988), but received legislative endorsement in 1995, and in the year 2000 almost 12,000 juvenile offenders were required to undertake alternative sanctions,[57] just over half of which (6,500) were imposed by the courts (van der Laan, 2003: 83). This expansion in the use of alternative sanctions appears largely to have been at the expense of the fine, the use of which has dwindled substantially since the early 1980s. Other measures available to the court include juvenile probation (imposed in 6,000 cases in 2000), detention[58] and compensation orders (imposed in 1,000 cases in 2000).

These changes at the level of juvenile justice practice were echoed and reinforced in 1995 by an important legislative change (the Juvenile Criminal Law, 1995), which placed both the HALT scheme and the prosecutor's power to impose a conditional diversion on a statutory footing. This effectively converted them into de facto penal sanctions (Junger-Tas, 2004) rather than straightforward diversions from prosecution and punishment. The Act also increased the maximum terms for those sentenced to detention, doubling (from six to twelve months) the length that may be imposed on juveniles aged between 12 and 16, and quadrupling (from six to twenty-four months) the length that may be imposed on those aged 16–18, though even these new maxima are considerably shorter than those available in many other European countries.[59] The legislation also made it possible to detain serious violent and sexual offenders in special treatment-oriented custodial institutions for up to six years in order to administer appropriate forms of remedial treatment. One of the biggest departures was to facilitate the transfer of juvenile offenders to adult criminal courts, by relaxing the criteria that need to be satisfied for this to happen.[60] However, this power has not so far resulted in a significant long-term increase in the number of juveniles being tried in adult courts; indeed, quite the reverse. For whereas in 1995, when the new legislation was introduced, 16 per cent of cases that were submitted to juvenile judges were transferred to the adult criminal court, by 1999, this had fallen to 2.5 per cent (Junger-Tas, 2004: 333, Table 7).[61] As for the other measures, an evaluation of practitioners' views and statistical sources covering the first five years after the reforms suggested that the changes – in particular the increase in the length of confinement that may be imposed – did not appear to have resulted in sentencing practice becoming more repressive (Kruissink and Verwers, 2001). Indeed, Junger-Tas, (2004: 328) noted that the three years following the 1995 reform package witnessed substantial reductions in the number of juvenile court detention sentences imposed, regardless of length, despite a slight increase in 1999. These optimistic assessments may turn out to be premature, however, for – as we shall see in Chapter 15 – the most recently available statistics show a dramatic increase in both the number of young offenders in detention and also in the rate of juvenile detention relative to other countries in the study.

At the other end of the spectrum, a special pilot project known as STOP was introduced in 1999, which allows police officers to arrest children under the age of criminal responsibility and propose some form of educative social work intervention, provided their parents agree.[62] This initiative (which is now available on a national basis) echoes the introduction of child safety orders in England and Wales (see above), and has similar implications regarding the minimum age of criminal responsibility. Each year between 1,000 and 1,400 young children (mostly aged 10 and 11) are referred to STOP, which falls under the jurisdiction of the public prosecutor (Klooster et al., 2003).

Thus, in marked contrast to the position in Germany, the Dutch youth justice system has adopted a number of 'neo-correctionalist' measures that more closely resemble recent initiatives in some of the neo-liberal polities than those associated with conservative corporatist states.[63] As a result, some of the former differences between the youth justice system and the adult system have now been eroded. Juvenile offenders are much more likely to be held accountable for their criminal actions and many of the interventions to which they are increasingly exposed seem intended to serve explicitly repressive as opposed to welfare or treatment aims. Nevertheless, it would be wrong to infer from these developments that the Netherlands has abandoned its welfare-oriented heritage altogether.

Among the countervailing tendencies, the following developments affirm the resilience of at least some welfare-based impulses (see also Junger-Tas, 2004). Firstly, the Dutch police have recently reintroduced a special 'youth police' section, and some forces have appointed specialist educators or social workers to assist them in youth cases. Secondly, judges continue to take account of the personal circumstances and personalities of the young people who appear before them when deciding what criminal or care and protection measures to impose, and appear not to have lost total confidence in treatment-based or educational interventions. And thirdly, for those young offenders who are detained, there is now a possibility for them to be released early (after serving at least half the term) in order to take part in a vocational training course or equivalent treatment programme (along the lines of the detention and training order that has recently been introduced in England and Wales; see above). Moreover, there is continuing interest in the Netherlands, as elsewhere, in the development of different forms of sanctioning based on the principles of restorative justice, including a variety of mediation-based and conferencing projects. Consequently, it is perhaps too soon to predict the imminent demise of the Netherlands' traditional attachment to the welfare model. Not only does the Dutch juvenile justice system as a whole remain formally committed to promoting the welfare of young offenders but, as we have seen, it also continues to retain at least a residual attachment to this approach in practice.

Social democratic youth justice systems

The most obvious and distinctive feature of social democratic youth justice systems is the complete absence of a separate set of criminal courts for dealing with juvenile offenders, most of whom are dealt with instead by a specialist institution known as the child welfare board. The board is also responsible for dealing with young people in need of care and protection, and has traditionally placed a strong emphasis on the welfare of the child, paying particular regard to the latter's needs and social circumstances rather than the deeds they may have committed. In Nordic countries, therefore, the child welfare system rather than the court system is for the most part seen as the most appropriate way of dealing with the problematic behaviour of, and exercising social control over, young people. One of the most interesting internal differences *within* the small social democratic group of countries relates to the influence of the restorative justice model, which has had a relatively significant impact on the juvenile justice system in Finland (and also Norway), but has been very slow to take hold in Sweden (and also in Denmark).

Youth justice in Sweden[64]

The Swedish youth justice system is conceptually very different from most of the others we have been examining, since it has retained a reasonably pure version of the 'socialized welfare tribunal' model rather than the 'modified criminal court' model that has come to be favoured more prevalently elsewhere. This model is characterized by the adoption of a separate set of tribunals for dealing with both delinquent and non-delinquent children who are in need of specialized care. All agencies responsible for dealing with young offenders – public prosecutor, court and social welfare agencies – retain considerable discretion, and priority is given to the application of sanctions outside the court, leaving the traditional criminal justice agencies with a largely residual role in such cases. Consequently, there is no separate juvenile court system as such, and those who do come before the courts are for the most part subject to the same procedural and substantive rules as adults, though the sanctions to which they may be liable are in some respects more lenient in the case of younger offenders.[65] But although the system remains committed to a version of the welfare model, it has also been heavily influenced during the last twenty-five years by the justice model and, to a much lesser extent more recently, by restorative justice thinking.

During the 1970s and 1980s (as we saw in Chapter 10), the hitherto prevailing treatment philosophy in Sweden increasingly gave way to a just deserts approach, at least with regard to adult offenders, epitomized by the Sentencing Reform Act, which came into force in 1989. The effect of this change on the youth justice system has to some extent been more muted, but a number of changes are nevertheless discernible, with regard to both policy and practice. Thus, in 1990 a parliamentary committee was established to examine the role and responsibilities of, and also relations between, the social welfare system and criminal justice system with regard to juvenile offenders. The Committee focused specifically on the methods of intervention adopted for juveniles and the sanctions imposed on them, which it felt should be guided by four key desert-based principles (Swedish Committee on Juvenile Delinquency, 1993). Firstly, the system should be based on a commitment to humanitarian principles, which should regulate the use of coercive sanctions and also the time that elapses between the commission of a crime and the imposition of a sanction.[66] Secondly, sanctions should be predictable in the sense that the penalty should be fixed, and the consequences of committing a criminal act should be known in advance. Thirdly, the severity of the sanction should be proportional to the seriousness of the offence. And finally, sanctions should be perceived as fair, which entails equality before the law and consistency, as well as proportionality.

The age of criminal responsibility in Sweden is 15, which is one of the highest among the countries in this study. Children below that age who commit a crime cannot be prosecuted or subjected to a penal sanction, but may be dealt with instead by the social welfare authorities that are appointed by each municipal council.[67] In the past the police only became involved when offences were committed by juveniles over the age of 15, but since 1982 they have been authorized to investigate offences committed by those aged twelve or more. However, if any compulsory intervention is deemed necessary, the case will then be referred to the social welfare committee for the area in which the young person resides.[68] According to Doek (2002: 507), social welfare authorities are entitled to request the suspension of an investigation involving a person below the age of 15. Young offenders who are dealt with by the social welfare authorities may be admonished, warned, supervised, referred for out-patient treatment or placed in an institution for treatment.[69] Those not placed in an institution may receive various forms of intermediate care, comprising a wide range of structured activities during the day while continuing to live at home. With offenders of this age, the guiding principle remains that any intervention should be determined by the needs of the child rather than the deed(s) they may have committed, which shows a continuing commitment to the traditional welfare approach. However, the strength of this commitment is becoming more tenuous in respect of older offenders, as we shall see.

Juvenile offenders who are aged between 15 and 20 are liable to be prosecuted and sentenced in the normal way, though this is relatively unusual, especially for suspects under the age of 18. Indeed, over the last 25 years the prosecution rate[70] for young people aged 15–20 has almost halved from 6,050 per 100,000 in 1975 to 3.728 per 100,000 in 2002 (official Swedish criminal statistics, cited by von Hofer, 2003a). Moreover in 2002, the three principal disposals in the case of young offenders aged between 15 and 17 were prosecutorial fines (56 per cent), waivers of prosecution[71] (21 per cent), or transfers by the court to the social welfare agency (16 per cent).[72] Even in the case of young adult offenders aged between 18 and 20 fines remain the commonest disposal (56 per cent) followed by prosecution waiver (10 per cent), though the proportion of cases transferred to social welfare agencies was under 2 per cent for this age group.

The influence of 'just deserts' thinking on the deliberations of the Juvenile Delinquency Committee was so pervasive that its final report of 1993 advocated the complete cessation of court referrals to social welfare agencies[73] on the grounds that the sanction bore no relation to the seriousness of the offence. This proposal was not adopted by the incoming Social Democratic government, however, which retained the practice, and the number of judicially arranged transfers has continued to rise since then (from 601 in 1975 to 2,428 in 2002: a four-fold increase; Swedish official criminal statistics, cited by von Hofer, 2003a). Even so, there has been a substantial decline in the *proportionate* use of the measure since no less than 44 per cent of 15 to 17 year olds were dealt with in this way in 1998 (National Council for Crime Prevention, 2000) but just 16 per cent in the year 2002 (Swedish official crime statistics).[74]

Changes have also been made to the way the transfer procedure itself operates. Prior to 1999, the court had no say over the outcome of cases that were transferred, which were dealt with either in accordance with an agreement negotiated between the social welfare committee and the young offender or in one of the ways outlined above in respect of young offenders under the age of 15. Since 1999, however, the social welfare committee is obliged to submit a concrete treatment plan to the court, which has to satisfy itself that the proposed measures are commensurate with the seriousness of the offence and the previous convictions of the young offender before ratifying it. In addition, the court now has the power to combine the transfer with one of the following penalties: day fine; reparation; or unpaid work (a form of community service) of between 20 and 100 hours. Moreover, the transfer can be rescinded at the request of the public prosecutor, and another sanction imposed, in the event of continuing non-compliance following a warning (von Hofer, 2003a). These changes provide further confirmation of the extent to which the traditional welfare approach has been supplemented and partially supplanted by a combination of just deserts and reparative impulses.

As for the remaining judicial sanctions, they include an obligation to undertake unpaid work in conjunction with the youth service, probation and a form of judicial caution, but the use of such sanctions is rare for the youngest age group and collectively they accounted for just under 6 per cent of all disposals in 2002.[75] Although imprisonment is a legally valid sanction for offenders over the age of 15, it is very rarely imposed on those under the age of 18, for whom it is restricted to 'exceptional cases' only and, according to the official sentencing statistics, only 7 young offenders received such a sanction in 2002. Youth prisons were abolished in 1980,[76] and the few who are sentenced to custody are held in special youth wings that are attached to, but separate from, normal prison establishments. Imprisonment can only be imposed on those aged 18–20 in special circumstances, and life imprisonment can never be imposed on those under the age of 21.

As part of the youth justice reforms of 1999, however, a new penalty of youth detention was introduced, the duration of which may be as short as fourteen days or as long as four years, without the possibility of release on parole that is available for adult offenders. Such sentences are served in special closed wings of reformatories or youth centres[77] (not in the separate youth wings of the regular prisons), which also house other young people whose behaviour is considered to require special supervision. The commonest reasons for placing a young person in such centres other than on offence grounds are for substance abuse or absconding from another placement. Although the length of sentence is determined by the nature (and seriousness) of the offence, the primary purpose of the measure is still the care and treatment of the young person. The imposition of youth detention is in principle subject to the same 'exceptional circumstances' proviso that applies to the use of imprisonment for young offenders. In practice, however, the take-up of the two measures has been very different. For whereas the number of young offenders aged 15–17 who are sentenced to imprisonment has remained low and fairly static in recent years (between 4 and 11 each year), the number of young people sentenced to youth detention has been far higher. In 2002 no fewer than 122 offenders under the age of 20 were given youth detention, ninety-nine of whom were under the age of 18.[78] In reality, therefore, the new measure has been associated with a dramatic escalation in the use of the most severe sanction that is available for dealing with young offenders.[79]

More generally, the influence of 'just deserts' thinking is also evident in other recent reforms to the Swedish social welfare system for dealing with young people, including offenders, one effect of which has been to reinforce their rights. Thus, the Social Services Act 1998. Section 1 stipulates that in imposing measures that affect children, the best interests of the child are to be specially observed;[80] the child's right to be heard has also been strengthened; and social welfare committees are required to take into account the wishes of the child where this is possible, depending on the child's age and level of maturity.

Apart from the justice model, other approaches have had little significant impact on the still predominantly welfare-based Swedish juvenile justice system. Some interest has been shown in victim offender mediation, and in 1998 the Swedish government commissioned the National Council for Crime Prevention to introduce, support and evaluate a trial of mediation projects for young offenders (Nehlin, 2000). In the year 2000 there were reported to be approximately 50 active projects, mostly organized by municipal social welfare authorities, operating in close conjunction with the police.[81] During the late 1990s, the Swedish welfare authorities began piloting New Zealand-style family group conferencing, initially in the context of decisions about children and young people thought to be in need of care and protection, though in 1998 a new project was initiated involving young offenders. Compared with other Scandinavian countries such as Norway and Finland, however, the restorative justice approach has had only a very minor effect to date on the operation of the Swedish youth justice system.

Youth justice in Finland[82]

Finland's youth justice system resembles Sweden's in the following main respects, which we simply note here without elaborating in detail. It has the same age of criminal responsibility (15); there is no separate juvenile court;[83] offenders between the ages of 15 and 17 may be dealt with either by the child welfare system or the regular adult criminal justice system, but if by the latter then they are likely to be dealt with more leniently;[84] and the way juvenile offenders are dealt with continues to be strongly influenced by 'welfare model' thinking, even though the rest of the criminal justice system has been reformed in accordance with 'justice model' precepts. In a number of other important respects, however, the Finnish system differs significantly from the Swedish system, and it is these differences that we will concentrate on in this section.

One of the biggest differences relates to the much more prominent role that victim offender mediation now performs in Finland (as indeed it also does in Norway) as a way of responding to offences committed by offenders of all ages, but particularly those committed by juveniles.[85] The first mediation project was launched in the city of Vantaa, in the Helsinki metropolitan area, in 1983. Just over a decade later the practice had steadily expanded over much of the country, being offered by over 175 municipalities (serving approximately three quarters of the population of Finland) by 1996.[86] In 1997, over 3,600 criminal cases involving 4,800 suspects were referred to mediation, just under two-thirds of which (64 per cent) involved suspects under the age of 21 (Iivari, 2000: 13).

Mediation in Finland is not prescribed by law – unlike in Norway – though it has achieved at least a measure of legal recognition[87] since a successful outcome may influence the decision of the prosecutor[88] to waive further measures, or that of the court to waive punishment. Also in contrast to Norway, Finland has not adopted a community mediation approach in which responsibility for organizing the practice is conferred on local communities themselves, with only a minimal role for the authorities. Instead, mediation has been based on the Anglo-American victim–offender model, which requires good cooperation with justice and social welfare authorities. Thus, in many areas, mediation offices are located in municipal social welfare departments, and work in close collaboration with both the police and child welfare authorities (Iivari, 2000: 13).

The appeal of victim offender mediation in a Finnish context has been attributed (Iivari, 1986, 2000) in part to a reaction against the neo-classical reforms that were introduced in Finland during the 1970s and 1980s under the influence of the justice model (see Chapter 10).[89] Critics felt that this approach placed a disproportionate emphasis on the appropriate punishment for an offence without regard to the needs of either victim or offender. And mediation was welcomed by many of those responsible for dealing with young offenders and child welfare cases who felt frustrated at the lack of feasible options when dealing with such cases.

A second important difference between Finland and Sweden relates to the special provisions that have been adopted in Finland with regard to juvenile offenders who are prosecuted and sentenced by the courts. In 1989 the law was amended to prevent the use of immediate imprisonment for offenders who are under the age of 18 in the absence of 'weighty' reasons for imposing such a sentence. And shortly after this, the Supreme Court overturned a sentence of two years' imprisonment that had been imposed on a juvenile for attempted manslaughter since the court took the view that there were no weighty reasons to justify such a sentence notwithstanding the seriousness of the offence itself. On 1 May 1999 the daily prison population included just three 15–17-year-old prisoners compared with some twenty or so before the reform was enacted (Joutsen et al., 2001: 33). Moreover, the number of prisoners aged between 18 and 20 also declined substantially from over 200 before the reform was introduced to 61 in 1999. On 1 May 2003 there were three inmates aged between 15–17 and 93 aged between 18–20.[90]

Until recently, Finland – unlike Sweden – did have one separate juvenile prison (Kerava Prison) for offenders under the age of 21 who were sentenced to immediate custody. The juvenile prison differed from its adult counterparts in a number of respects including the kind of training courses and educational provision that were available and also with regard to the more generous arrangements for early release. For example, those in juvenile prison were eligible for release on parole after just one-third of the sentence had been served instead of half as in the case of adult prisoners. In addition, a special administrative body known as the Prison Board determined whether an offender who might be eligible should be sent to juvenile prison or an ordinary prison.

Following a major administrative reorganization of the Finnish prison service in 2001, however, the separate categorization of Finland's prisons by function has been dropped. One beneficial consequence of the change is that it enables juvenile prison inmates in principle to be sent to a prison closer to their place of residence.[91] Other consequences have been less beneficial including the abolition of the special status that was previously accorded to juvenile inmates and with it the more generous rules covering parole eligibility. So while the number of juvenile prison inmates may have declined substantially in recent years, those who are sentenced to imprisonment are undoubtedly dealt with more harshly now than they were in the past.

An alternative to unconditional imprisonment that has for many years helped to reduce its use is conditional imprisonment, whereby an offender is placed on probation for between one and three years. In 1997, another non-custodial sanction known as 'juvenile punishment' was introduced in seven district courts for an experimental period that has subsequently been extended to the end of 2004. The penalty consists of a modified form of community service involving between ten and sixty hours' regular unpaid work that is carried out under supervision and is intended to provide an intermediate sanction for juvenile offenders for whom a fine is deemed insufficient but custody is unnecessary (Aalto, 2002). The measure has been described as a hybrid, as it incorporates elements of a neo-classicist approach, since it entails a degree of censure for an offence, combined with a rehabilitative orientation, since it also aims to reintegrate offenders with their immediate community (Marttunen, 2003: 180). One of the purposes of the new penalty was to insert an additional rung in the system of sanctions in the hope of deferring or avoiding altogether the imposition of unconditional imprisonment. The measure has been somewhat slow to take off, however, and by the end of 2001, its rate of usage in those districts in which it was available was roughly equivalent to one-fifth of the number of conditional sentences of imprisonment imposed on juvenile offenders (Marttunen and Takala, 2002). Following a recent report on the reform of the Finnish youth justice system[92] the government appears poised to extend the availability of juvenile punishment as a permanent sanction from 2005. At the same time, it seems probable that its content will be modified by strengthening its educational/rehabilitative features at the expense of the more punitive aspects including both the emphasis on unpaid work and the length of the supervisory period.[93]

Apart from these few relatively minor exceptions, however, in most other respects the Finnish and Swedish juvenile justice systems have much more in common with each other (and with those of other Nordic countries) than with any of the others we have examined so far in this study.

Oriental liberal corporatist youth justice

As we saw in Chapter 11, Japan's unique status within this study – as the sole exemplar of an oriental liberal corporatist welfare model – is a product of the distinctive fusion that has taken place between selective overseas influences and Japan's own indigenous cultural traditions and values. Nowhere is this more vividly illustrated than in the field of youth justice. For more than a century, the Japanese youth justice system has been profoundly influenced by US youth justice principles and precepts while still retaining a distinctively Japanese orientation at the level of practice. For most of the lost fifty years the system displayed a remarkable stability, and during most of this period appeared largely immune to the reformist tendencies that have dramatically reshaped many other juvenile justice systems around the world, including its own US *alma mater*. In recent years, however, the Japanese youth justice system has itself come under enormous strain, resulting in unprecedented and inexorable demands for fundamental reform that ultimately proved impossible to withstand.

Youth justice in Japan

The history of the modern Japanese youth justice system can be divided into two main phases, corresponding roughly to the first and second halves of the twentieth century. Morita (2002: 363) has pointed out that US 'child-saving' philosophy helped to shape Japan's Reformatory Act in 1900, which was the first national law providing for the compulsory housing and correction of children prone to committing misdemeanours. Moreover, the Juvenile Law of 1922 (also known as the Taisho Juvenile Law) was likewise influenced by the Anglo-American doctrine of *parens patriae* which, as we saw earlier, favoured the use of 'protective measures' that were intended to be guided by parental compassion to rehabilitate rather than punish young delinquents. ('Protectivism' is a term often used to describe the Japanese version of the welfare model.) The doctrine appealed to Japanese youth justice reformers in part because it resonated with the Japanese concept of *'amae'*, which encompasses the notions of 'dependence' and also 'attachment' and is valued as a source of morality in its own right (Morita, 2002). However, instead of being incorporated wholesale into Japanese youth justice law, the *parens patriae* principle was adapted in the light of Japanese cultural values and selectively applied. Thus, although rehabilitation was adopted as the juvenile law's primary objective, the principle of criminal accountability was also retained, together with the possibility of punishment for offenders who were beyond hope of rehabilitation. This 'bifocal model' contrasted with the 'unifocal' orientation of the US juvenile justice system of the early to mid-twentieth century with its exclusive attachment to the goal of rehabilitation.

A second departure from the US juvenile court model was to confine the scope of Japanese juvenile law to juvenile offenders and delinquents (including those guilty of 'status offences'). But it excluded neglected and dependent children in need of care and protection rather than combining these two jurisdictional strands as in the USA. A third departure involved an active screening role for the prosecutor, who was called upon to divert juvenile offenders to be dealt with by means of protective measures wherever possible, while reserving prosecution and punishment for those who were otherwise unlikely to repent, or in respect of whom deterrent measures were deemed to be called for. Juveniles who were deemed to be eligible for protective measures were referred, by either the police or prosecutor, to a semi-judicial body known as the Juvenile Inquiry and Determination Office ('shonen shimpano'), which had complete jurisdiction over the investigation, disposition and subsequent treatment of juveniles. The minority of juvenile offenders for whom protective measures were deemed inappropriate[94] were tried in special criminal proceedings for juveniles. This distinctive reworking of the US doctrine of *parens patriae* was characterized by contemporary Japanese practitioners as combining a 'strict-father, tender-mother approach' (Morita, 2002: 367) in contrast with what they perceived to be the 'maternal protectivism' of the US juvenile justice system.

Following its defeat in World War Two, Japan was obliged to undertake a wholesale revision of its juvenile law based on a much more purist adoption of the US doctrine of *parens patriae,* whose ideological supremacy at home was as yet unchallenged. The new juvenile law was enacted in July 1948 and entailed a number of major reforms. The first of these involved the creation of a new non-criminal 'Family Court', with primary jurisdiction over all juvenile criminal offenders below the age of 20. Secondly, and in keeping with the imposition of a 'socialized welfare tribunal' model, the sole objective of the new system was geared to the application of 'protective' measures. Thirdly, the erstwhile involvement of the prosecutor in 'screening' cases for diversion or prosecution and punishment was terminated. And fourthly, an US-style waiver system was introduced whereby, in exceptional cases only, juveniles aged 16 and older might be prosecuted in the regular criminal courts.

In spite of this radical overhaul, however, the revised Japanese youth justice system still did not fully integrate the treatment of neglected and dependent children with those who offend against the law as in the American juvenile justice system. Instead, the jurisdiction of the family courts extended only to juvenile offenders and delinquents who are over the age of 14 and under 20 years of age. Those who are deemed to be in need of care and protection (together with those under the age of 14 who perform an act that would constitute a crime if committed by an older person) are dealt with by a separate system of child guidance centres which provide temporary shelter, foster care or other appropriate measures for children under the age of 18. Such centres are set up by local authorities and administered under a different jurisdictional strand by the child welfare law as opposed to the juvenile law. Moreover, children cannot normally be compulsorily placed in a child guidance centre without parental consent. Child guidance centres only refer juveniles to family courts when they are thought to need the protective measures available in the latter, but this happens very rarely.[95]

Less than two decades after the revision of Japan's juvenile law, the doctrine of *parens patriae* that had underpinned the US juvenile justice system was fatally undermined, as we have seen, by the so-called 'due process revolution' that was instigated by the United States Supreme Court. But although the *Gault* decision reignited a vigorous debate over the need for further reform of the Japanese youth justice system,[96] the principle of *parens patriae* remained entrenched in Japan, and the Juvenile Law of 1948 remained substantially intact for the remainder of the century. We will now briefly describe the key features of this system and its operation before turning to the factors that ultimately precipitated a further series of reforms in 2001.

Under the 1948 Juvenile Law the Family Court was given primary jurisdiction firstly with regard to all juveniles (over the age of 14 and under 20 years of age) who are suspected of committing *any* offence regardless of seriousness; and secondly over those who are deemed – by virtue of their behaviour or circumstances[97] – to be likely to commit an offence (referred to as 'pre-delinquent juveniles'). In respect of minor offences (punishable by means of a fine or lesser penalty), the police are required to refer a suspected juvenile directly to the Family Court. Where the offence is more serious (punishable by imprisonment or worse), the suspect is referred to a public prosecutor for further investigation. Provided there is sufficient evidence, however, the prosecutor is then obliged to refer the case to the Family Court and has no discretionary power not to prosecute (in marked contrast with cases involving adult suspects).

Once a juvenile case is filed in the Family Court it is assigned to an official known as a *kateisaibansho chousakan*[98] who co-ordinates a thorough assessment of the juvenile (including mental, aptitude, personality and psychological tests) and his or her family background and surrounding environment. If the court considers it necessary for the child to be taken into 'protective custody' while these tests and observations are undertaken, it may order a period of detention in a Juvenile Detention and Classification Home for up to four weeks. After the investigation is concluded reports – including recommendations as to the most appropriate form of treatment – are submitted to the court prior to the hearing together with those from other agencies (such as the police, prosecution or welfare authorities).

Until very recently Family Court hearings were conducted by single professional judges on an informal and non-adversarial basis in accordance with the doctrine of *parens patriae*.[99] The hearings themselves are not open to the public, and the only people who are permitted to attend apart from the juvenile are the probation officer, court clerk, parent(s) or guardian(s) and, where appropriate, a court-approved lawyer. The juvenile law did not recognize the right to a defence lawyer in the conventional sense because the adoption of such adversarial features was considered to do more harm than good in fostering the sound development of juvenile offenders. Instead, the court allowed the juvenile or his guardian to appoint an 'attendant' from a list of approved persons, the attendant's role being to serve as 'defence counsel' and at the same time cooperate with the court in finding the most appropriate form of treatment for the juvenile. Indeed, everyone present is expected to assist the judge in discharging the protective role of the court. Although the court is required to establish findings of fact beyond reasonable doubt, it does not employ the rules of evidence that are stipulated in the adult Code of Criminal Procedure. However, in 1983 the Japanese Supreme Court upheld the due process right of a juvenile to receive legal representation in a case where the defendant wished to examine a witness in order to establish an alibi.[100] This limited due process concession initiated a modest but significant change in both the number of lawyers present in juvenile court hearings[101] and also their role with regard to the hearing, which we will return to later. One final characteristic feature of the Japanese Family Court hearing is that (as with adult cases) the processes of adjudication and disposition are combined rather than being differentiated as in many of the juvenile justice systems we have been examining.

As for the dispositional powers of the Family Courts, the five principal options that are available include the following: dismissal without a hearing, dismissal after a hearing, imposition of protective or educational measures, referral to the child welfare authorities after a hearing or referral to the public prosecutor. The commonest outcome by far involves a dismissal of the case without a hearing, which in 2001 accounted for almost 72 per cent of all cases dealt with by the Family Court (Japanese Ministry of Justice, 2003: Fig. 4-2-2-5).[102] This may sound like a straightforward diversionary process, but this is not necessarily the case since it comes at the end of an intensive investigation and assessment procedure (often including casework) that is conducted prior to any hearing. Before the case can be dismissed an offender must not only have confessed but must also have shown repentance and a commitment not to repeat the offence. Moreover, the juvenile's parent, guardian or supporter must also undertake to work for the offender's rehabilitation. And even where the case is dismissed the court may stipulate a variety of informal (legally non-binding) protective measures designed to reinforce these undertakings. Cases may also be dismissed following a hearing and, in 2001, this was the outcome in 10.6 per cent of all cases dealt with by the Family Courts. In approximately half of these cases the offender was already under the supervision of a probation officer during the investigation stage (a procedure known as 'tentative probation') and the judge ordered this to continue while reserving final determination of the case (effectively dismissing it).

Alternatively, the Family Court may impose a variety of so-called formal protective (or educative) measures, one of which involves probationary supervision by a court appointed probation officer who is assisted by volunteer probation officers recruited from members of the public. In 2001, just over 13 per cent of all cases handled by the Family Court were dealt with in this way, rising to 37 per cent of cases involving status offences and just over 43 per cent of cases involving robbery (Japanese Ministry of Justice 2003: 227-9). Another option involves compulsory commitment to a juvenile training school[103] that is run by the Corrections Bureau of the Ministry of Justice. Juvenile training schools are divided into four types which each deal with different categories of offenders: juveniles aged 14-15 who do not require medical care; juveniles over the age of 15 without aggravated criminal tendencies; juveniles aged 16-22 who have aggravated criminal tendencies; and, finally, any juveniles between the ages of 14 and 25 who need medical treatment. The correctional education that is provided at juvenile training schools is based on an individualized treatment programme that is designed to meet the inmate's rehabilitative needs. The programme includes vocational and living guidance, academic and physical education in addition to other activities. Even in cases where very serious acts have been committed, the period of custody (which is semi-indeterminate) is set at 'two years or less, with a maximum extension of one year'.[104] The average length of commitment to a training school is eleven months (Morita, 2000: 372). Despite the overall protective ethos of the Japanese juvenile justice system, only 3.8 per cent of all juvenile cases in 2001 involved commitment to a juvenile training school (Japanese Ministry of Justice, 2003: Fig. 4-2-2-5).[105] Another possibility is for the Family Court to refer a child after a hearing to the child welfare authorities, which could result in committal to a residential home (for example where the child is neglected, abused or dependent), but such cases are rare and in 2001 only 0.3 per cent of juvenile cases were dealt with in this way.

The remaining option that is available to the Family Court is to refer the case, after the investigation or hearing, to the public prosecutor for criminal trial with a view to the imposition of a punitive (as opposed to a 'protective') measure following a conviction. However, under the 1948 juvenile law this was only possible where the juvenile was over 16 years of age, had committed an offence that, if committed by an adult, was punishable with imprisonment or death, and where the Family Court considered it appropriate to do so, having regard to the nature and circumstances of the offence. In such cases the prosecutor is obliged to prosecute, and the juvenile defendant is normally treated in the same way as an adult.[106] Very few juvenile offenders are referred to the public prosecutor, however, and in 2001 this happened in only 0.4 per cent of cases. The number of juveniles under the age of 20 who were prosecuted, convicted and committed to a juvenile prison for an indeterminate sentence was only fifty-eight (including three given life sentences) in 2001 (Japanese Ministry of Justice, 2003:

Table 4-2-2-8), though this was the highest figure since 1994. A further 113 defendants were given determinate sentences, but almost all of these (109) were suspended (with or without probationary supervision). Such figures affirm the persistence of a radical non-punitive tendency on the part of Family Court judges, who are reluctant to commit juveniles to trial, and on the part of ordinary first instance court judges in dealing with those juveniles who do come before them.

For over fifty years since the adoption of the 1948 juvenile law, the Japanese youth justice system appeared relatively unscathed by the pressures that had precipitated radical reforms elsewhere and, in comparison with the USA, the doctrine of *parens patriae* remained far more securely entrenched in Japan. This apparent stability is somewhat deceptive, however, for – as we indicated earlier – the United States Supreme Court decision in *Gault* and in subsequent due process cases quickly unleashed a vigorous debate in Japan also about the appropriate balance between protectivist policies and due process safeguards. The absence of any substantive reforms to the juvenile law during this period has been attributed by one commentator (Morita, 2002: 368–9) to the existence of deep-seated ideological differences between two principal protagonists: the Ministry of Justice[107] which favoured radical reform and the Japanese Supreme Court which was opposed to any major attempts to dilute the protectivist ethos of the Family Court. Nevertheless, the Supreme Court did make limited concessions, as we have seen, and in subsequent years there has been a gradual increase in the number of lawyers participating in juvenile hearings and in the frequency with which juveniles contest some of the allegations made against them. Although the numbers involved were still relatively small, the move towards a more adversarial approach in such cases had a profound effect on the traditional informal, inquisitorial, consensual model, which was ill equipped to meet the challenge that it posed to the authority of the court.

The Supreme Court responded to the challenge in 1996 by tabling proposals to amend the juvenile hearing procedure and, having gained the support of the Ministry of Justice and Japanese Bar Association, a Bill was submitted to the legislature in 1999. The partial amendment of the juvenile law incorporating these proposals took effect in 2001. The due process amendments have resulted in a 'twin-track' approach enabling the existing informal non-adversarial format to be retained for the great majority of juvenile hearings while introducing a special modified procedure for certain exceptional cases. The new procedure will come into play where the judge considers it appropriate in cases involving serious crime where there is a need for fact-finding to be conducted on a contested basis. In cases such as these, the due process reform package incorporates five important modifications to the traditional juvenile hearing system.

Firstly, there is now provision for juvenile cases to be heard by a panel of three Family Court judges, instead of a single judge (many of whom were relatively young and inexperienced) as in the past. Secondly, Family Court judges now have discretion to admit prosecutors to the hearing, to assist the court in fact-finding, albeit still under the direction of the court. Thirdly, in cases such as these, the judge is also obliged to allow participation by a lawyer to represent the juvenile, thereby authorizing a more formal, adversarial approach. Fourthly, the maximum period during which a juvenile defendant may be detained in a Juvenile Detention and Classification Centre prior to trial has been doubled from four to eight weeks.[108] And finally, it is now possible for both prosecutor and defence to seek a retrial by reason of error in fact-finding in such cases. It is too soon to assess the impact of the reform package, but two cautionary notes have already been sounded (Morita, 2002: 377). Firstly, the Ministry of Justice has estimated that fewer than 200 juveniles per year will be tried under the new procedure. And secondly, the decision to invoke the new procedure lies within the sole discretion of the Family Court judge, leading Morita to suggest that the effect of the reform package may paradoxically be to tame the gradually strengthening assertion of juvenile rights over the last two decades.

Since the late 1990s, however, the debate over the reform of the juvenile justice system has been overtaken by three other related sets of developments. These in turn have precipitated a series of much more far-reaching reforms that may come to pose the biggest challenge to the protectivist ethos of the youth justice system since its inception. The first development took the form of a growing moral panic over the perceived scale and nature of the juvenile crime problem. One incident that especially inflamed public opinion in Japan,[109] and came to epitomize public concerns over the issue, involved the particularly gruesome murder of two elementary school children by a 14-year-old junior high school boy in Kobe in 1997.[110] Because of his age, the juvenile who was responsible for the murders was tried in the Family Court, which found him to be mentally unstable and sent him to a medical juvenile training institution in October 1997.[111]

Although this was by no means an isolated incident, the statistical trends show a far more mixed picture than that suggested by popular public perceptions. Thus, the juvenile homicide rate (0.74 per 100,000 juveniles in 2000[112]) was only half that recorded in 1969 and just under one third of the rate recorded in 1954 (Japanese Ministry of Justice, 2002: App. III-5). The juvenile robbery rate has increased substantially in recent years (the 2000 rate of 11.82 is more than double that of 1995) but is still below the rate recorded in 1961 and most years prior to that. The equivalent rate for rapes committed by juveniles at 2.2 per 100,000, is also higher than it was throughout the 1990s but is only a fraction of the rate recorded in 1958 (when it was 24.3 per 100,000) or even as recently as 1971 (when it was 12.3). Meanwhile, the rate of assaults committed by juveniles has fallen dramatically over a long period, and hit a postwar low of only 11.5 per 100,000 in 1999 compared with 53 per 100,000 in 1970 and 69.2 at its height in 1964. Nevertheless, the Japanese public has been assailed in recent years with media reports that highlight the incidence of violent crimes – some of which involve acts of seemingly gratuitous cruelty – that in many cases have been committed by young high school age offenders. One predictable consequence of this exposure has been to stimulate public debate about both the aims and content of the juvenile law, and this in turn has fuelled unprecedented demands for reform of the law.

A second important, and to some extent related, development has been the emergence of an embryonic but increasingly influential victims' movement in Japan. Victim consciousness was slower to develop in Japan than in many other countries; for example the Japanese Society of Victimology was only established in 1992. But the subsequent publication of academic research on victim perceptions has highlighted the high levels dissatisfaction felt by victims with the personal apology and material restitution that may have been offered by their offenders (Hosoi and Nishimura, 1999; Miyazawa et al., 1996; see also Hamai et al., 2000). Moreover, the growing public concern over high profile cases involving juvenile offenders such as the Kobe killing has also exposed a serious imbalance on the part of the 1948 juvenile law with regard to its treatment of juvenile offenders and their victims. Thus, whereas the identity of the Kobe juvenile murderer was protected from disclosure, in accordance with the 'protectivist' ethos of the juvenile law, the identity of one of his victims was repeatedly publicized by the media, together with personal information relating to his mental deficiency and family background. In the wake of a second murder, also committed at about the same time by a group of teenage boys, the victim's mother set up a group campaigning for the rights of crime victims after she was excluded from the investigation process and denied information about the Family Court's decision (Levinson, 2001). Concerns raised by and on behalf of victims in cases such as these have fuelled further public outrage at what was considered to be the excessively lenient treatment of the juvenile offenders who were responsible for the killings.

The third important development, which is again directly related to the first two, has involved an unprecedented mobilization of political support for radical reform of the juvenile law on the part of politicians from three of the main political parties. This represents a very significant departure from the traditional tendency to leave such matters in the hands of the elite policy-making establishment, as illustrated by the history of the 'due process' reform package that we examined earlier. An amendment to the juvenile law incorporating several radical reform proposals was passed by the Japanese Diet late in 2000 and took effect in April 2001. The main effects of the changes are as follows.

In response to the growing public concern over the juvenile crime issue, the revised legislation lowers the age at which juvenile offenders may be sent to the ordinary criminal courts for prosecution and punishment from 16 to 14.[113] Consequently, offenders as young as 14 could be given sentences of imprisonment for the first time, though the revised law allows them to be sent either to youth prison or a juvenile training institution. In addition, Family Courts are now advised that they should normally refer serious juvenile offenders who are over the age of 16 to prosecutors to stand trial as adults, instead of leaving this decision to their discretion as in the past, and reasons have to be given for not doing so. The revised law also lowers the age at which life sentences of imprisonment may be imposed. In the past, offenders below the age of 18 could only be given a limited term of between ten and fifteen years' imprisonment. Now, however, it is up to the court to decide whether to impose a life sentence or a limited term of imprisonment. And finally, victims will receive more information about what happens in Family Courts, and for the first time will also be allowed to make statements to the court.

Taken as a whole, the package of reforms represents a substantial dilution of the protectivist ethos that has underpinned Japan's juvenile justice system in the past, and introduces a number of neo-correctionalist tendencies, most notably by exposing greater numbers of juvenile offenders to the adult system of prosecution and sentencing. Radical though this recent shift in direction undoubtedly is in Japanese terms, however, it is important not to exaggerate its importance. Not only does the youth justice system retain its overall protectivist ethos for the great majority of younger and less serious juvenile offenders, in some respects this ethos has even been strengthened – in typical Japanese balancing fashion. Consistent with this approach, attempts are to be made to improve the educational facilities available in youth prisons, and young offenders are to be given guidance on atonement. They will also be expected to write letters of apology to the victims of their crimes or to family members. As the Ministry of Justice has said in a notification to juvenile prisons and reformatories, the aim of the revised law is still to rehabilitate young offenders, rather than punish them.

Notes

1 As we noted above, however, some recent reforms to the English youth justice system are intended to promote a greater degree of dialogue between young offenders and youth court magistrates (Allen et al., 2000).

2 See Albrecht (2004) and Dünkel (2003) for much more detailed accounts of the trends and developments that are briefly summarized below.

3 Offenders under the age of 14 may only be dealt with under the Youth Welfare Law (see below). Offenders between the ages of 14 and 17 inclusive are liable to be dealt with under the Youth Court Law provided they are capable of differentiating between the concepts of right and wrong and acting accordingly. Offenders between the ages 18 and 20 inclusive may also be dealt with under the Youth Court Law if this is felt to be appropriate (see below).

4 The minimum age of criminal responsibility had previously been 12.

5 Accordingly, there is no provision for 'status offences' within German youth justice laws.

6 The Youth Welfare Law applies to those below the age of majority (currently 18, but 21 at the time the law was enacted).

7 For example involving placement in foster family. Dünkel (2003: 126) sees the preference for privately-run projects as another practical illustration of the principle of 'subsidiarity' – see also Chapter 12 Note 13 – whereby the state cedes responsibility to 'civil society' organizations.

8 Unlike most neo-liberal countries, with the exception of South Africa, the police in Germany have lacked any general discretionary power to dismiss cases, though in some state jurisdictions they are now able initiate diversionary measures.

9 Dünkel (2003: 108) refers to these respectively as 'non-intervention', 'diversion with education' and 'diversion with intervention'.

10 Trained social workers belonging to municipal youth departments are responsible for evaluating juvenile defendants' social background, personality and the circumstances of the offence. They are also responsible for making recommendations to the court regarding the kind of action that should be taken and (in appropriate cases) whether the defendant should be dealt with according to juvenile or adult criminal law.

11 'Zuchtmittel', s. 13, Youth Court Law.

12 Controversially, this is taken by many courts to authorize the imposition of youth imprisonment on 'petty persistent' offenders, even though their offences are minor, as in the case of shoplifting, and despite the incompatibility between this approach and the underlying educational philosophy of the Youth Court Law (Weitekamp et al., 1998).

13 Around 70 per cent of all youth prison sentences are suspended in Germany, rising to 80 per cent in respect of sentences of up to one year.

14 Dünkel (2003: 107) refers to this as the 'principle of subsidiarity' or 'minimum intervention'.

15 We are grateful to Frieder Dünkel for pointing this out; see also Dünkel (2003: 116, Figure 11) for details.

16 The 1943 amendment also introduced the third category of juvenile sanctions known as 'disciplinary measures', referred to above. These changes were retained even though the amendment itself was repealed.

17 Albrecht (2004), citing Statistisches Bundesamt (1982–2000); see also Dünkel (2003: 121). The tendency is particularly pronounced for more serious offences, including murder, robbery and serious sexual offences. Albrecht attributes this phenomenon to a judicial reluctance to impose the high minimum penalties that are prescribed for adult offenders in such cases.

18 Pre-trial detention is only authorized in the case of juvenile offenders who are under the age of 16 where the alternative of placement in foster care is not a suitable option. Moreover, Youth Court aid workers have a duty to provide information to the court relating to the need for detention and absence or unavailability of suitable alternatives to it.

19 In addition, Dünkel (2003: 111) points out that young offenders are also protected by much the same rights-based procedural rules as apply in the case of adult offenders, deviations from which are only authorized when warranted on educational grounds.

20 Subsequently, however, a few closed residential institutions were re-opened, though the number of available places is very small, and accounts for only around 0.2 per cent of all placement measures within the welfare system (Dünkel, 2003: 107; Sonnen, 2002: 330).

21 Walgrave (2004: 566) has suggested that the different developmental trajectories of restorative justice in the two groups of countries can be explained by differences in their respective legal systems. Anglo-Saxon nations, which are more likely to fall into the neo-liberal camp, share a common law heritage that is less prescriptive in terms of its legal procedures and sentencing disposals, affords more discretion to criminal justice officials, and hence allows more scope for experimentation including the possibility of greater input by victims or other members of the community. Most other continental European countries, on the other hand, share a civil law heritage that incorporates the legality principle, prescribes strict legal procedural rules and affords little scope for discretionary decision-making on the part of criminal justice officials. Consequently, the range of

possible disposals in any given case is more circumscribed, and the scope for involvement by non-professional lay people is correspondingly restricted.

22 For many years conservative parties in Germany have also advocated a reduction in the age of criminal responsibility, from 14 to 12, and have opposed the application of the Youth Court Law to young adult offenders (Dünkel, 2003: 133).

23 Dünkel (2003: 135) attributes this resilience in part to the fact that most youth justice practitioners remain deeply committed to the 'culture of education', which is continually reinforced through their participation in further educational programmes that are organized by various professional bodies.

24 These include the presumption of innocence, right to state-funded legal assistance and entitlement to secrecy.

25 One such diversionary mechanism – 'irrilivanza del fatto' – authorizes the dismissal of a case 'for irrelevance of the fact' by either a single judge at the preliminary investigation or under the auspices of a court following a preliminary hearing (see below).

26 Juveniles below the age of 14 and those who are considered to be incapable of understanding and acting with criminal intent are normally transferred to the general welfare system that is administered by local authorities. Exceptionally, juveniles in either of these categories who are considered to be 'socially dangerous' may be retained within the penal system and dealt with by means of 'security measures' ('misure di siccurezza'), which may include detention in a reformatory or control in the community.

27 Formerly, the jurisdiction of the juvenile court also extended to juveniles who were deemed to be 'wayward in behaviour or character' ('irregolarità della condotta o del carattere'), a category which is broadly comparable to 'status' offenders within Anglo-American countries. However, the measures that were available in such cases have now largely fallen into disuse following the introduction of the 1988 Code of Criminal Procedure (Gatti and Verde, 1998: 364).

28 By one-third compared with the adult sentence. Juveniles cannot be sentenced to life imprisonment.

29 On 1 September 2001, a total of 477 juveniles were detained in juvenile detention centres (IPM), 38 per cent of whom were awaiting a court decision and 33 per cent of whom were under sentence (the remainder either awaiting sentence or under appeal). On 30 April 2004, a total of 519 juveniles were detained in IPMs, over half (54 per cent) of whom were foreigners. However, the juvenile court also has the power to apply alternative measures such as house detention or committal to social services. Maurizio (2003) has suggested that because prison staff are inadequately trained in the treatment and detention of juveniles the power to detain is infrequently exercised.

30 Magistrates have a general power to impose 'prescriptions' ('prescrizioni') when placing a juvenile offender on probation, either at the preliminary hearing stage or during the course of a trial. Some magistrates use this power in order to encourage offenders to make amends for their offence or to seek a reconciliation with the victim.

31 On the grounds of 'irrilevanza del fatto' (see above, Note 25).

32 See Cario (2000) for a much more detailed account of the French youth justice system.

33 Although, as in Italy, there were once specialist 'brigades des mineurs' (or 'juvenile brigades') these have now disappeared in many districts and, even where they do still exist, they often concentrate on young persons who are victims. However, the issue of police specialization with regard to juvenile offenders is currently under review following a partial revival of the practice in a number of districts (see Commission d'Enquête sur la Délinquance des Mineurs, 2002; Lazerges and Balduyck, 1998). Even so, the gendarmerie has no specialist units dealing with minors.

34 As with the police, some courts have a specialist prosecutor dealing with young offenders ('*parquet des mineurs*'), but others do not.

35 When adjudicating on a case in chambers the juvenile court magistrate is only empowered to impose educational measures. If some other disposition is felt to be appropriate, or if the offence would incur a sentence of seven years' imprisonment or more, the case has to be sent to the juvenile court, which has the power to impose either educational or penal measures.

36 During the mid-1990s, only around 100 cases per year out of a total of 70,000 judgments (0.14 per cent) were tried in this way (Gazeau and Peyre, 1998: 223). However, by 2003, the latest year for which figures are available, the number had risen to 443, accounting for 0.7 per cent of the 63,950 young offenders who were tried by the criminal courts (Ministère de la Justice, 2003: 22).

37 Moreover, before any charges are brought against a young person, a social report focusing on the juvenile offender's domestic and social circumstances is prepared by a social worker and passed on to the public prosecutor together with the police report.

38 Either by themselves or, as in Italy, in combination with protective 'care' measures (a technique known as the '*double dossier*').

39 With the assistance of social service agencies, including the Department for the Judicial Protection of Minors at the Ministry of Justice, which offers courts a range of services including the conduct of social and psychological investigations, advising the judiciary on educational matters, proposing solutions, finding a home in an emergency and operating short or long-term residential units. In 1999, the Department employed 6,400 officers, half of whom were youth workers, and dealt with 146,000 young people including both young offenders and children in need of care and protection (Ministry of Justice website).

40 The remainder, accounting for just under 10 per cent, were dismissed ('*Mesures rejetant la poursuite*').

41 Custodial sentences are only supposed to be imposed in 'exceptional circumstances', and even then cannot be longer than half the length that would be imposed on an adult offender.

42 A decade ago, only 4 of the 51 institutions that had been formally designated for this purpose were equipped with separate facilities for juvenile inmates. By September 2004, 58 of the 64 establishments designated to take juvenile offenders had separate wings; but not until 2007 will all establishments have separate provision (Ministry of Justice press release dated 15 September 2004).

43 On 1 April 2004, juveniles accounted for 1.2 per cent of the total prison population of 62,569 (Ministère de la Justice, 2004: 6).

44 La loi n° 2002–1138 du 9 September 2002.

45 However, only 331 sanctions éducatives were imposed in 2003, which represents less than 0.5 per cent of the 88,488 measures and sanctions imposed in 2003 (Ministère de la Justice, 2004: 22).

46 Unlike other educational centres they have strengthened security measures including a perimeter fence, and young residents are not allowed to leave the centre without an escort.

47 Prior to 2002, young offenders under the age of 16 could only be imprisoned if convicted of a serious offence.

48 The new institutions are intended to provide basic educational training (twenty hours per week) and also sporting opportunities, while seeking to maintain contact with families and after-care professionals (Ministry of Justice press release dated 15 September 2004).

49 The number of penal mediations involving juvenile offenders almost doubled during the first three years after its introduction, but in the year 2000 (the most recent year for which statistics are available), only 5,110 cases were dealt with in this way, of which 90 per cent were ordered by the juvenile prosecutor ('*parquet des mineurs*', and just 10 per cent by the '*juge des enfants*' (figures supplied by Robert Cario). See also Cario (1997).

50 See Junger-Tas (2004) for a much more detailed account of the trends and developments that are briefly summarized below. See also van der Laan (2003).

51 This is also available as a criminal sanction for young offenders, though it is far less frequently used for this purpose.

52 The principle of *doli incapax* was abolished, as was the minimum age of criminal responsibility, though in 1961 the age of 12 was (re-)established as the minimum age, as it had been under the first Dutch Criminal Code, adopted in 1809.

53 De Rooy (1982) suggested that during this period the Netherlands had one of the most progressive systems of children's legislation in the whole of Europe.

54 Until this 'gatekeeping function' was discontinued in 1995, following criticism from the European Court of Human Rights that the tripartite consultations blurred the separate judicial and prosecutorial competencies (Dünkel, 1998: 305).

55 The number of juveniles referred to HALT bureaux represents approximately half the total number of cases that are investigated by the police each year.

56 In 2000, 4,600 cases were dismissed, and a further 5,500 task sanctions or alternative sanctions were imposed by the prosecutor, either as a condition of dismissal or as a condition imposed as part of a 'transaction' (van der Laan, 2003: 82).

57 Around 70 per cent of the alternative task-based sanctions involved work projects or community service orders, 21 per cent involved training orders and 9 per cent a combination of both work and training projects (van der Laan, 2003: 83).

58 Sentences of detention may either be unsuspended (imposed in approximately 1,050 cases in 2,000 or suspended (imposed in a further 3,000 or so cases). In addition, a further 3,000 young people were taken into pre-trial detention in the same year (van der Laan: 2003: 83).

59 The increase in the length of confinement that may be imposed did not at first appear to have resulted in sentencing practice becoming more repressive. Indeed, the three years following the 1995 reform package witnessed substantial reductions in the number of juvenile court detention sentences imposed, regardless of length. However, they appear to have increased slightly in 1999 (Junger-Tas, 2004: 328) and, as we shall see in the final section, the latest figures show a dramatic increase in the juvenile detention rate, suggesting that over the longer term sentencing practice may well have become significantly more repressive than before.

60 It also remains possible, as in Germany, for 18–20-year-old offenders to be tried in juvenile courts, though it is unusual for educational measures to be imposed on them.

61 Junger-Tas (2004: 333) suggests that the decline is largely attributable to the increase in sentencing powers available to juvenile court judges and an expansion in the number of places available in youth detention institutions. Capacity in juvenile offender institutions increased from 1,045 places in 1995 to 2,477 places in 2004 (Dutch Ministry of Justice Press Release, 24 September 2004).

62 In cases where more intractable problems are suspected, as in cases involving the commission of a serious offence by a child under the age of criminal responsibility, the young person may be referred to the Council of Child Care and Protection ('*Raad voor de kinderbescherming*'), and may result in a civil protection order being imposed.

63 On 24 September 2004, the Dutch Ministry of Justice reported that the Cabinet had accepted proposals including the possibility of confiscating possessions from juvenile offenders, increasing the number of hours of community service that can be imposed by the prosecutor and introducing new behavioural measures.

64 The following section draws on Janson (2004) and van Hofer (2003).

65 The penal code states (Chapter 29, s. 7) that offenders under the age of 21 may be given a milder sanction than the one prescribed for adults in respect of a similar offence.

66 'Fast-tracking' provisions now apply to offenders under the age of 18, whereby those charged with offences punishable with more than six months in prison have to be tried within six weeks of being charged. A survey of crime investigation reports from four prosecution districts undertaken by the Swedish National Council for Crime Prevention (2000) showed that the time taken to process cases involving young offenders fell from an average of forty days in 1993 to twenty-five days in 1998.

67 Each local authority appoints members to serve on a small social welfare committee that is supported by a staff of professional social workers, day-care attendants, preschool teachers, etc. The social welfare boards are responsible for local social community planning; the provision of generalist social services to specific categories who need them, such as children, the elderly and the disabled; and the provision of care and social assistance for specific individuals and families in need, including those responsible for children and young persons with problems (see Janson, 2004).

68 Sweden also has a special police unit known as the social police, whose responsibilities include liaison with schools, plainclothes street patrolling and the diversion of youths, where appropriate, from the criminal justice system.

69 In the year 2000, 226 young persons aged 10–14 were placed in an institution for treatment, 105 of whom were placed in so-called 'special homes' (see below) (Janson, 2004: 415).

70 The 'prosecution rate' in this context refers to all forms of prosecution measures including waivers and prosecutorial day fines in addition to those committed to the court for trial and sentence.

71 The use of prosecution waivers for this age group fell from 9,164 in 1975 to 2,621 in 2002, a decline of more than two-thirds (Official Swedish criminal statistics, cited by van Hofer, 2003).

72 While the fine is a classically deserts-based measure, the substantial decline in the prosecution rate and the residual use of prosecution waivers are more redolent of a 'minimum intervention' approach, while the 'transfer procedure' reflects a more traditional 'welfare' approach.

73 A similar policy stance has also been adopted by Sweden's Moderate (conservative) party (van Hofer, 2003).

74 The latest figure is lower even than in 1985, when approximately one quarter of young offenders were transferred to social welfare authorities (Swedish National Council for Crime Prevention, 2000).

75 They are somewhat more prevalent for 18–20 year-olds, in respect of whom they account for just under one in four disposals (Swedish official statistics, cited by van Hofer, 2003).

76 In order to comply with Art. 37 of the Convention on the Rights of the Child.

77 They are formally designated as 'paragraph 12 homes', which refers to the provision of the Care of Young Persons (Special Provisions) Act 1990 (*LVU, Lagen om vård av*

unga). Note that since 1993, all institutions within the social welfare sector have been administered by a new national board, the National Board of Institutional Care (SiS).

78 The average length of stay in a closed youth centre is 9.7 months, compared with an average stay of just 5.6 months for those young offenders serving 'regular' sentences of imprisonment (van Hofer, 2003, personal communication).

79 In 2002 a committee on juvenile sanctions was appointed to review the penalty system for 15–21 year olds in the light of the 1999 reforms. The committee, which is due to report in December 2004, was asked *inter alia* to examine the impact of youth detention and to consider the case for the introduction of additional alternative sanctions including the greater use of mediation.

80 This was partly to ensure compliance with the UN Convention on the Rights of the Child.

81 Moreover, since 1988 the police have been authorized to instruct offenders to repair the damage of any offence if permission has been given by the injured party, and prosecutors may consider an offender's willingness to do so when deciding how to proceed.

82 A very useful account of the Finnish juvenile justice system has been written by Marttunen (2003).

83 Unlike Sweden there is no separate 'youth police' section either.

84 With regard to offenders aged between 15 and 17, a reduction rule applies to the sentence, which cannot exceed three quarters of the amount that would be imposed on an adult offender.

85 Finland also differs from Sweden by rendering all offenders, even those under the age of 15, liable to provide compensation for any damage caused by an offence, irrespective of any criminal prosecution or conviction.

86 Although Finland has 450 municipalities, those offering mediation included many of the most populous parts of the country. By 2002 80 per cent of the population had access to a mediation agency and some 5,000 cases were referred to mediation each year (Finnish Ministry of Justice, 2003a).

87 By means of an amendment to the law in 1996 (Joutsen et al., 2001).

88 In 1997, prosecutors were responsible for 45 per cent of referrals to mediation, compared with 39 per cent from the police, 8 per cent from the parties themselves and the rest from social welfare and other authorities (Iivari, 2000: 11, Table 1).

89 Iivari (2000: 2) also cites the influence of Nils Christie (1977) who not only criticized the formal criminal justice system for 'stealing conflicts' – including those involving allegations of criminal behaviour – from the parties involved, but also helped to popularize North American models of mediation within Norway and more broadly in other Scandinavian countries including Finland.

90 According to statistics obtained from the Finnish prison service website at: http://www.rikosseuraamus.fi/11143.htm

91 Once the inmate has completed a risk and need assessment and provided the prison in question has been certified as being appropriate by the administrative Prison Board referred to above.

92 The 'Juvenile Commission' was set up in 2001 to reassess the entire Finnish juvenile justice system and give consideration to strengthening its rehabilitative aspects (Marttunen, 2003: 170). The Commission report was published in 2003 (Finnish Ministry of Justice, 2003b).

93 Based on information provided by Raimo Lahti.

94 In 1942 only 2.8 per cent of cases were prosecuted, 26.5 per cent were dismissed after some kind of informal protective treatment had been ordered, and 70.7 per cent were referred to the Juvenile Inquiry and Determination Office (Morita, 2002: 366).

95 Morita (2002: 370) reports that only 222 juveniles were referred to the family court by child guidance centres in 1997, which is 0.13 per cent of the total number of juveniles (164,327) who were dealt with by the family court in that year.

96 See Morita (2002: 368–70) for details.

97 For example those who are prone to habitual disobedience, who repeatedly abscond from home, who associate with disreputable persons or who undertake activities that are harmful to the morals of themselves or others. This category of 'pre-offence juveniles' is broadly equivalent to the concept of 'status offenders' in the United States.

98 The role of the *kateisaibansho chousakan* has been likened by one commentator to a cross between a probation officer and a mentor (Nagel, 1999).

99 Article 22 of the Juvenile Law stipulates that 'hearings shall be conducted softly and mildly with warm consideration'.

100 Supreme Court decision of 26 October 1983, *Keishu* 37, no. 8 (1983): 1260, as cited by Morita (2000: 380).

101 In 1977, lawyers appeared in fewer than 700 cases, but twenty years later this figure had quadrupled (Morita, 2002: 373), though this was still only equivalent to 1 per cent of all juvenile cases dealt with by the Family Court. One reason for this very low participation rate presumably has to do with the equally low incidence of contested allegations that we mentioned in connection with adult offenders in Chapter 11.

102 Dismissal without a hearing is much less common (accounting for just 3.7 per cent of final disposals) in respect of more serious offences such as robbery, and even in respect of status offences (it accounts for just over 10 per cent of disposals (Japanese Ministry of Justice 2003: 228–9).

103 In 2002, fifty juvenile training schools accommodated approximately 4,800 juveniles (Japanese Ministry of Justice 2003: 239, Appendix 4–11).

104 According to a 1977 notice issued by the Director-General of the Justice Ministry's Corrections Bureau, as cited by Seto (n.d.).

105 However, the proportion of juveniles who are committed to a juvenile training school following conviction of a serious offence is much higher (61.3 per cent in the case of murder and 42.3 per cent in the case of robbery). Likewise in the case of 'status offences', some 18 per cent of family court disposals result in a commitment to juvenile training school (Japanese Ministry of Justice 2003: 228–9).

106 Except that the death penalty is not available for juvenile offenders who are under the age of 18 at the time of committing a capital crime. Moreover, until recently juveniles under the age of 18 whose offences would otherwise merit life sentences of imprisonment were dealt with instead by fixed terms of ten and fifteen years.

107 In 1970 the Ministry of Justice drafted an *Outline for the Amendment of the Juvenile Law* in response to the *Gault* judgment that included a package of due process rights for defendants including (*inter alia*) a right to remain silent, to appoint a lawyer and to examine the evidence. The proposals were referred to at the time as 'Gaulting the system' (Morita, 2002: 369).

108 Unlike the other amendments, this particular modification is seriously at odds with the underlying due process ethos, and perhaps reflects a Japanese tendency to seek where possible to 'balance' opposing forces. However it cannot be denied that the effect of such a lengthy process of pre-trial investigation and assessment is likely to massively

offset the advantage that might be gained by strengthening the defendant's due process entitlements at the subsequent trial hearing.

109 In England, an incident involving the killing of 2-year-old James Bulger by two 10-year-old boys in February 1993 had a similar impact on public opinion and likewise hardened attitudes towards juvenile offenders in that country.

110 The severed head of one of the victims was placed on the gates of his school with a note in its mouth in which the killer taunted the police and threatened to strike again.

111 In July 2002 the offender became eligible for release after turning 20, but the Family Court ordered his continued detention until 31 December 2004 (as authorized by the juvenile law), by which time he would be 23 years of age (*Mainichi Interactive News Archives*, 22 May 2002, 12 July 2002).

112 The latest year for which figures are available.

113 The Japanese Criminal Code also stipulates 14 as the minimum age for criminal responsibility, but the higher age limit laid down in the juvenile law took precedence over this prior to the recent amendment.

15

General Patterns
in Youth Justice?

We will conclude our account of youth justice approaches by drawing attention to two very striking 'patterns of penality' that are also very much in line with the radical pluralist thesis. The first of these patterns relates to the various age thresholds that determine the extent to which young offenders may be exposed to the imposition of formal social control measures based on the application of criminal sanctions. Two age thresholds are of particular interest. The first relates to the 'age of criminal responsibility', which normally refers to the age at which young people first become liable to be prosecuted for criminal offences,[1] while the second relates to the minimum age at which young offenders become liable for penal detention. Two other age thresholds are also worth noting, one of which relates to the minimum age at which it is normally possible for a young offender to be tried according to the adult criminal law. The other – which is normally referred to as 'the age of criminal majority' – marks the upper age at which any special measures designed to protect the welfare of young offenders cease to apply. Offenders who have reached that age can normally expect to be dealt with by the normal provisions that operate in the case of adult offenders.

The relationship between these age thresholds and the four main groups of penal jurisdictions is depicted in Table 15.1. When the four different groups of countries we have been considering are compared, there does appear to be a fairly consistent pattern in the degree of protection that is afforded to young offenders against the risk of prosecution and the imposition of formal sanctions including the use of imprisonment.

Thus, the group of states which operate with the highest overall minimum age of criminal responsibility comprises the Scandinavian social democracies. In Sweden and Finland (and also in Norway and Denmark) the minimum age of criminal responsibility is 15, and offenders who are below that age cannot normally be prosecuted at all, whether in adult courts or even in specialized juvenile criminal courts. In both Sweden and Finland, as we have seen, even though young offenders who are between the ages of 15–18 may be prosecuted in the

Table 15.1 Age thresholds relating to juvenile criminal responsibility by penal jurisdictions

Penal jurisdiction	Age of criminal responsibility	Minimum age for penal detention	Minimum age at which adult criminal law may normally be applied	Adult criminal law must be applied ('Age of criminal majority')
South Africa	7	7	18	18
USA	Generally 10 (but can be as young as 6)	7*	16/17/18	Generally 18 but can be 20 or even 25
England and Wales	10	12/15	18	18
Australia	10/14	10	17/18**	17/18
New Zealand	10/14***	15	17	17
The Netherlands	12	12	18	18
France	13	13	18	18
Germany	14	14	18	21
Italy	14	15	18	18
Japan	14/16	14/16	14/16	20
Finland	15	15	15	20
Sweden	15	15/18	15	18/21

*Age determined by state, but many states have retained the common law minimum age of 7.
**Generally 18, but 17 in Queensland and Victoria. However, these states have been asked to review their youth justice laws.
***The age of criminal responsibility in New Zealand is 10, but the minimum age at which children can be prosecuted is 14.

ordinary courts, this is relatively unusual, and offenders of this age are more likely to be dealt with instead by the social welfare authorities. Indeed, in Sweden, offenders even up to the age of 20 may be dealt with in this way, though this only applies to a minority of such offenders.

In Japan, the age of criminal responsibility is also fairly high, at 14, and young offenders between the ages of 14 and 20 are normally dealt with by welfare-oriented family courts although recently, as we have seen, the minimum age at which juveniles may be prosecuted in the ordinary criminal courts has been lowered from 16 to 14 years of age.

The minimum threshold age for criminal responsibility in most of the conservative corporatist states[2] is somewhat lower than that found in the Nordic social democracies. In Germany and Italy, for example, the corresponding age is 14, which in turn is slightly higher than that in France,[3] where it is 13, and the Netherlands, where it is 12.

Within the majority of social democratic states and corporatist states, therefore, there is a tendency to systematically divert most young people from the criminal justice system altogether. This is achieved by adopting a relatively high age of criminal responsibility, which thus operates as a fairly rigid bar on prosecution, and protects young offenders from exposure to the exclusionary effects of conviction and formal punishment. In sharp contrast, most non-corporatist states, and especially those that have pronounced neo-liberal tendencies, appear much less reluctant to expose young offenders to the exclusionary risks of prosecution, conviction and the imposition of a variety of formal punishments. Moreover, even this limited degree of protection has been further eroded in several neo-liberal states recently.

In England and Wales, for example, the position until recently was that only children below the age of 10 were completely immune from prosecution. Children between the ages of 10 and 14 were presumed to be incapable of knowing that what they were doing was wrong, unless the prosecution were able to prove otherwise. The operation of this doctrine attracted considerable publicity in 1993 following the killing in Liverpool of a 2-year-old toddler, James Bulger, by two 10-year-old boys. They were not only tried (unusually in an adult court) but, after being pronounced capable of knowing that what they were doing was wrong, were convicted and sentenced to detention for life. However, the doctrine of *doli incapax* on which this 'individual capacity' approach was based was abolished by Section 34 of the Crime and Disorder Act 1998. England and Wales already had one of the lowest ages of criminal responsibility, 10, in the whole of Europe, and the latest change reinforced its reputation for being one of the countries affording young offenders the least protection against the risk of criminal prosecution.[4]

The position is broadly similar in many American states (though some retain the common law minimum age of 7,[5] while others have a minimum age of 11 or 12). In South Africa also, the minimum age of criminal responsibility is currently 7 although, as we saw earlier, there have been recent moves to raise this to 10. The doctrine of *doli incapax* continues to apply in South Africa, and also – in respect of offenders between the ages of 10 and 14 – in several Australian states. Prior to 1997, the state of Queensland was an exception by applying the presumption to children up to their fifteenth birthdays. However, the Criminal Law Amendment Act of 1997[6] brought the state into line with the majority of other states in Australia, where 14 remains the general age of criminal responsibility, subject to the rebuttable presumption of incapacity in the case of children as young as 10-years-old.

In addition to the 'entry avoidance' measures we have just been considering, most countries, as we have seen, also apply special measures that are designed to protect young offenders from being exposed to the full rigours of the adult criminal law even after they have reached the minimum age of criminal responsibility. These often include the provision of specialized courts or tribunals (usually sitting in private) and also restrictions on the range of sentences that may be imposed. As with the age of criminal responsibility, there is also some variation in the upper age threshold (the age of criminal majority) at which special provisions that are applied in the case of juvenile offenders give way to those applicable to adults.

Once again there is a tendency for countries that have a higher minimum age of criminal responsibility threshold to also adopt a more pronounced welfare approach even in respect of offenders above that age, who find themselves caught up in the criminal justice system (Johnson, 1995: 14). And again the greatest degree of protection is to be found in some of the Scandinavian states such as Sweden, where special welfare measures may be applied to young offenders up to the age of 20;[7] and in Finland where juvenile courts are competent to try offenders up the ages of 18 or 19. In Japan also, the majority of offenders below the age of 20 are kept out of the regular criminal courts and dealt with instead by welfare-oriented family courts. In most other European countries, including England and Wales,[8] the normal age of criminal majority is 18. In other neo-liberal countries, including New Zealand and two Australian states, the age of criminal majority is just 17. Germany is somewhat unusual, as we saw above, inasmuch as it has adopted a 'reverse transfer' strategy whereby a significant proportion of 'young adult offenders' between the ages of 18 and 20 are dealt with under the auspices of the Youth Court Law rather than the adult criminal law.

The position in the USA is complicated by the variation in the ages of criminal majority within the different states, ranging from a low of 16 in Connecticut, New York and North Carolina to 24 years in California, Montana, Oregon and Wisconsin (Hallett and Hazel, 1998: 24). However, there has been a growing tendency in the USA recently, as we saw earlier, for the jurisdiction of the juvenile courts to be waived, which then exposes the juvenile offender to the full rigours of the adult criminal justice system.[9] Pressure to restrict the ambit of special protective measures for juveniles has come about largely as a result of neo-correctionalist demands, which appear to be much less prevalent and influential in corporatist states than in neo-liberal and non-corporatist ones. The major aberration within the neo-correctionalist camp is New Zealand, whose distinctive restorative justice inspired approach we examined earlier.

Generally speaking, therefore, it can be seen that the countries which afford young offenders the greatest degree of protection against the risks of prosecution and, consequently, the imposition of formal sanctions are the Nordic social democracies together with the rather special case of Japan. The conservative corporatist states form an intermediate group in which young offenders are offered a moderate degree of protection against the risks of prosecution and the imposition of formal sanctions, while the states affording the most minimal levels of protection are the neo-liberal states.

A second, equally striking, pattern of penality relates to the proportionate use of imprisonment for young people within each of the four main groups of penal jurisdictions, as depicted in Table 15.2.[10] Once again, when the four different groups of countries are compared, there appears to be a fairly consistent pattern in the extent to which imprisonment is resorted to, whether this is measured in terms of the proportionate size of the juvenile prison population in relation to the overall prison population or the imprisonment rate for young people per 100,000 of the relevant age sector of the population in each jurisdiction. Thus, with only one exception, the jurisdictions fall into four distinct bands according to their propensity to imprison juvenile offenders, with neo-liberal states at the most punitive end of the spectrum, and the Scandinavian social democracies and Japan at the most lenient end,[11] while the conservative corporatist states tend to occupy the middle ranking.

The one exception is the Netherlands, whose juvenile detention rate far exceeds that of all other conservative corporatist states, and indeed outstrips several neo-liberal countries also. Moreover, the column showing juvenile inmates as a proportion of the total prison population tells a similar story. Figures published by the United Nations Survey of Crime Trends (2004) suggest that the Netherlands has been becoming steadily more punitive with regard to juveniles in recent years, as the number of juveniles imprisoned for criminal offences was as low as 209 in 1995 and was still below 400 in 1997. If calculated on the same basis as the current figure, the detention rate in 1995 would have been around 18.7, which is much closer to the conservative corporatist 'norm'. But although the current detention rate seems to be moving increasingly 'out of line', this aberration is nevertheless consistent with other findings in this study. It is also consistent with our radical pluralist thesis since, as we saw in Chapter 8, of all the conservative corporatist states the Netherlands has been most heavily influenced in recent years by neo-liberal tendencies with regard to penal policies and practices.

In conclusion, it can be seen that these two related patterns of penality – which are closely in line with similar trends relating to the imprisonment rate for adult offenders – are broadly consistent with our radical pluralist hypothesis, and provide further support, should any be needed, for the contention that penal practices in different jurisdictions are crucially influenced by the social, economic and political context in which they operate.

Table 15.2 *Proportion of the prison population comprising juveniles under the age of 18*

Penal Jurisdiction	Prisoners under 18 years of age (unless otherwise stated)		YP per 100k relevant pop	Remarks
	Number	Per cent of prison population		
USA	135,107	6.5		Of those in state and federal prisons at 30.6.2003; source: Int. Centre for Prison Studies.
	104,413		336.0	Based on juvenile offenders in public and private residential facilities on 24.10.01; source Sickmund et al. 2004.
New Zealand	369 (130)	6.4 (2.25)	68.0 (30.5)	At 15 November 2001. New Zealand Department of Corrections (2003).
England and Wales	2,869	3.8	46.8	At March 2004. Source: Youth Justice Board annual statistics 2003/4 and HO Quarterly prison statistics for 2004.
Scotland	170	2.6	33.0	At 30.6.03. Source: Scottish Executive (2004).
Australia	545	2.4	24.9	At 30 June 2002. Source: Bareja and Charlton (2003); and AusStats, Australia Yearbook.
South Africa	4,158	2.2	69.0	At 31.3.04. Source: Departments of Correctional Services.
The Netherlands	574	3.1	51.3	At 1.9.2003. Source: Council of Europe Annual Penal Statistics, 2002 and WODC personal communication.
France	751	1.2	18.6	At 1.7.2004. Source: Ministère de la Justice (2004).
Germany	841	1.38	23.1	As of 31.3.2001. Source: Statistisches Bundesamt
Italy	(267)*	0.5	(11.3)	In 2003. Source: Ministero di Giustizia (2003).
Finland	7	0.2	3.6	At 15.4.04. Source: International Centre for Prison Studies prison brief for Finland www.prisonstudies.org.
Sweden	14	0.2	4.1	At 1.10.03. Source: official statistics of Swedish Prison Administration (KVS) Stockholm 4.5, 5.5.
Japan	7**	0.01	0.12	Japanese White Paper statistics for 2002.

Table 15.2 (Continued)

Comment on methodology

The above table has been compiled specifically for this book since comparable statistics are not routinely compiled for juvenile offenders, though some comparable statistics for adult offenders are now published on a regular basis (see Walmsley, 2003b). The International Centre for Prison Studies also publishes some statistical information relating to juvenile prison inmates in respect of a wide variety of jurisdictions.

The table has been compiled on the basis of data obtained from a variety of sources but wherever possible using figures published by the national prison administration or its equivalent. In each case the most recently available figures relating to the number of young people under the age of 18 who are held in penal detention has been used, since it would have been impossible to obtain comparable information relating to all the countries in the study for any given year. In compiling the table, information was sought relating to all young prisoners under the age of 18, whether detained in adult prisons, juvenile prisons or equivalent detention centres, including both sentenced inmates and those who are awaiting trial or sentence, but excluding civil prisoners or those awaiting deportation. In most cases it is possible to state the number of offenders under the age of 18 with some precision, but not always. In the case of New Zealand, for example, the only available information is derived from a census of prison inmates, and this only differentiates between those under 17 and those aged between 17 and 19. Two sets of figures are therefore shown for New Zealand, the first of which includes those aged 18 and 19 and the second (in parentheses) is based on an estimate of the number of offenders under the age of 18. Likewise with regard to the United States, the census data of those detained in juvenile institutions (which is used as the basis for calculating the juvenile detention rate) contains a small number of offenders who have reached the age of 18, though it has not been possible to adjust for this in making the calculations.

Juvenile detention rates have been calculated on the basis of *relevant* national population rates as opposed to the total national population as in some published studies. In the case of neo-liberal jurisdictions the relevant age range is assumed to be 10 to 17. For all other countries the relevant age range has been adjusted according to the age of criminal responsibility. Because relatively few very young offenders are imprisoned even in neo-liberal countries, it should be noted that the adoption of a broader age sector of the population has the effect of *lowering* the detention rate somewhat, so the differences between neo-liberal and other jurisdictions are, if anything *under*-stated. It should also be noted that the inclusion of females as well as males has the effect of lowering the overall detention rate, which would undoubtedly be much higher in each case if only males had been included in the analysis.

Wherever possible national population figures are derived from the most recent official census data for the precise age ranges in each country where these are available. In some cases, however, census data is not published in this form since age bands are grouped together. In such cases calculations are based on the *estimated* proportion of the population and so should not be regarded as absolutely precise. Where official census data was not available the US Bureau of the Census International database has been used instead (e.g. in the case of Italy and Japan).

*Italian juvenile detention centres (of which there are 21, for juveniles convicted of very serious crimes) held on average 475 juveniles each day in 2003, of whom 62 were aged 14–15, 205 were aged 16–17 and 208 were young adults aged between 18 and 21. In terms of nationality, 241 were Italian and 234 were foreigners.

**In addition to the relatively small number of juveniles who are imprisoned, there are also approximately 4,800 who are detained in juvenile training schools, unfortunately no statistical breakdown according to age is available.

Notes

1 The law regulating entry into the youth justice system is typically complex, and conceptually encompasses two distinct sets of issues even though this distinction is not always consistently observed in practice. The first relates to the age at which children are deemed to have the mental capacity to commit a crime. The second relates to the age at which they may be liable to prosecution and formal sanctions provided they are deemed capable of committing an offence. The same term – 'age of criminal responsibility' – is often used to cover both sets of issues, though this can cause confusion since in some countries (e.g. New Zealand) different age limits may apply in respect of each set of issues.

2 Though a notable exception is Belgium, where the age at which criminal responsibility begins is 18, as is also the case in Luxembourg.

3 France is one of a number of countries that applies an individual capacity test in respect of children between the ages of 13–17, in order to determine whether a particular child knew that what they were doing was wrong, or were capable of forming the requisite criminal intent. Germany and Italy also operate an individual capacity test, as do Norway and the Republic of Ireland.

4 The age of criminal responsibility in Scotland is even lower at 8. Moreover, young offenders in Scotland are dealt with in the adult courts from their sixteenth birthday onwards.

5 In North Carolina children as young as 6 years of age may be liable to be referred to a delinquency hearing. In three states the minimum age is 7, in one it is 8 and in eleven states the age is 10.

6 S. 29 of the Queensland Criminal Code as amended.

7 In effect, the public prosecutor is empowered to waive prosecution in such cases, but is normally required to notify the social welfare authorities, to ensure that appropriate action will be taken.

8 Offenders in England and Wales who are between the ages of 18 and 20 inclusive are liable to be tried in adult courts; although they are not liable to the full range of sentences that may be imposed on adult offenders, those over the age of 15 (or 12 if they are categorized as 'persistent young offenders') may nevertheless be detained in special institutions for young offenders.

9 Including the imposition of the death penalty: see Chapter 13 above, note 10.

10 Readers are advised to read the notes that accompany the table for information relating to the methodology that has been used in order to construct it.

11 Although Japan imprisons very few young people indeed, under the age of 18 as we saw earlier it does maintain a network of 52 juvenile training schools of various kinds, to which juvenile offenders may be committed by the courts. The latest figures show that in 2002, some 4800 'juveniles' were accommodated in such institutions. However, the term 'juvenile' normally encompasses those under the age of 20 and, for some purposes may extend to those under the age of 26 (for example in the case of those with a serious physical or medical disorder). Unfortunately, no breakdown by age is available for those detained in juvenile training schools. The only information that is available relates to age on admission, which indicates that 42.2 per cent of males are aged 18 or 19 at the time of admission, most of the remainder being younger than this.

16

Prison Privatization

Our analysis so far suggests not only that there is a coherent 'pattern of penality' – in respect of both its nature and also its relative severity – across the main types of late capitalist societies we are comparing; but also that it is possible to account for this, broadly, within the context of a radical pluralist framework of analysis. In this section we turn to the changing balance between public and private sector involvement in the operation of prison services and facilities: a process that is commonly referred to as 'prison privatization'. Although the term conjures up an image of a shift in the ownership and control of the entire prison system from the public to the private sector, which is what has happened in recent years in other sectors of the economy, the reality with regard to prison privatization is somewhat different. Nowhere in the world as yet has an entire prison system been privatized in this way,[1] and the term is best understood as a contractual process that 'shifts public functions, responsibilities and capital assets, in whole or in part, from the public to the private sector' (Austin and Coventry, 2001: 2).

Privatization within a penal context can assume a number of different forms. The first entails a 'contracting out' (or outsourcing) of ancillary services such as catering, education, health or the escort of prison inmates to and from the courts. A second entails the use of private contractors to design and build prison facilities for the public sector, which continues to manage them. A third possibility entails the contracting out of management responsibilities – including security and control over inmates – to private sector companies while ownership of the prison buildings remains within the public sector. A fourth, and even more radical option, is for the private sector to be given responsibility for the design, construction, management and finance of individual prisons (known as 'DCMF' prisons), which are then leased to the state on a per capita basis for a predetermined period (usually 25 years). Finally, there is also, at least in theory, a fifth possibility, which would entail contracting out not only the *delivery of penal services* but also some or all of the strategic functions relating to the commissioning, monitoring and enforcement of prison service contracts.

One of the most striking 'patterns of penality' relates to the extent and also the nature of private sector involvement in the provision of penal services and facilities within the different countries we have been examining. Once again, four distinct groups of countries can be identified which, broadly speaking, correspond to our four-fold categorization. In the first group, comprising countries which exhibit pronounced neo-liberal tendencies, there has been a sudden and rapid shift towards a policy of privatizing a wide range of prison and other penal services – including the construction and management of entire prisons – that shows few signs of abating. In the second group of conservative corporatist countries, private sector involvement in the provision of penal facilities and services has been much slower to develop, and has not so far extended to the contracting out of prison management to profit-making private enterprises. In the third group, comprising the Scandinavian social democracies, there has so far been little or no interest in the issue of penal privatization. Finally, in a category of its own, is the special case of Japan, which until recently seemed strangely resistant to the lure of privatization despite its highly developed market economy, but which now seems poised to take its first tentative steps down the prison privatization pathway. We will briefly examine the nature and extent of private sector involvement in the provision of penal facilities and services within each of these four groups of countries before seeking to account for these differences in terms of a radical pluralist framework of analysis.

Neo-liberal countries: origins and recent revival of prison privatization

Private sector involvement in prison administration is not exclusively a recent phenomenon by any means. In the USA, for example, it has been linked to the system of prison labour leasing, which was especially common in southern states from the end of the Civil War (Austin and Coventry, 2001: 9–13; James et al., 1997: 1–4; Ryan and Ward, 1989: 18; and Shichor, 1995: 34–43).[2] Under this arrangement, prisoners (who were predominantly black) were expected to work for private contractors, who were paid by the state to feed, house and clothe them for the duration of the 'contract', which corresponded to their prison sentence. Northern and eastern states operated a variation on the prison leasing theme whereby the state, rather than the private contractor, was responsible for operating and managing the prison, but outside contractors operated the prison workshops (or factories) for a profit. Gradually, this 'contract' system came to replace the system of leased prisons that had prevailed in southern states, as the states' correctional authorities began to assume control over the management of the prisons themselves, and confined the 'leasing' arrangement solely to the labour element. However, private sector involvement in the exploitation of prison labour continued until the early part of the twentieth century, when it was finally phased out in the wake of humanitarian concerns, economic changes (including the effects of the depression) and growing labour opposition (Austin and Coventry, 2001; DiIulio, 1990; Shichor, 1995).

In England and Wales also, private jail keepers were often responsible for the running of prisons from the Middle Ages to the nineteenth century (Cavadino and Dignan, 2002: 229; McConville, 1981: 9; Porter, 1990: 67; and Pugh, 1968). Although they received no official payment for doing so, they were entitled to charge their captive 'customers' for the services they provided[3] until the fee system was abolished in 1815 (McConville, 1981: 247–8). By this stage, private sector involvement in the penal system was beginning to assume a rather different form as a result of the rapid growth of penal transportation after 1788 (Ammon et al., 1992; Feeley, 2002; Hughes, 1987; James et al., 1997: 10–11; and Shaw, 1966). This involved the use of convict ships that were operated by private contractors who were regulated by highly detailed specifications set out in contracts drawn up by the British government. Responsibility for monitoring performance and enforcing the terms of the contract was entrusted to government-employed 'surgeon-superintendents' and naval agents who accompanied each consignment of convicts.

This early experience with 'contracting-out' was a precursor for the privatization of 'prison escort' duties in the UK and elsewhere during the latter part of the twentieth century. But it also foreshadowed other forms of joint ventures between government and private enterprise in the operation of the penal system. For once the convicts arrived at the penal settlements (those who survived the voyage), a practice developed of 'assigning' them to work for free settlers. Since these settlers became responsible for feeding, clothing and housing the convicts, the cost to the government was far less than the expense it would otherwise incur in keeping them captive. Although the practice of penal assignment was abolished in 1849,[4] it foreshadowed a very dramatic revival of interest in private sector involvement in prison administration in Australia about a century and a half later.

The contemporary renaissance of prison privatization began in the USA and can be traced back to the contracting-out of non-secure correctional facilities such as community treatment centres and half-way houses during the late 1960s (James et al., 1997: 5–6; Krisberg et al. 1986: 28). However, responsibility for operating these facilities was entrusted in the main to philanthropic not-for-profit private sector organizations, a move that was largely supported by juvenile justice reformers. The first *secure* facility to be contracted-out, in 1975, was the small scale Weaversville Intensive Treatment Unit housing just 20 juvenile offenders, in Pennsylvania (Logan and Rausch, 1985: 307). This was followed by the somewhat larger Okeechobee School for Boys, in Florida, which was opened in 1982 and catered for 400 juveniles.

Private sector involvement in the operation of the prison system in America took a qualitatively different turn, however, once commercial enterprises sought to become actively involved during the early 1980s. The birth of a private prisons industry in the USA was marked by the formation of the Corrections Corporation of America in 1983 (Thomas and Logan, 1993). In that same year CCA was awarded its first contract – with the United States Immigration and Naturalization Service – to design, build and manage a 350-bed minimum security detention facility in Houston, Texas (McDonald, 1994). Since then, this nascent private prisons industry has experienced a steady, albeit relatively modest, period of growth. It has now established a significant foothold in the rapidly burgeoning market for correctional services, whether this is measured in terms of the number of corporations involved, the size of the private prisons sector, its market share, the depth of market penetration or the scale of its international presence.

By the end of 1998, fourteen private security corporations based in the USA were responsible for operating 158 privatized prison facilities[5] with an estimated bed capacity of 116,626,[6] mainly in the southern and western USA (Austin and Coventry, 2001: 4). The total number of inmates detained in privatized facilities in June 2003 was 94,361 according to the US Bureau of Justice (2004), which represents about 6.5 per cent of all state and federal adult prisoners.[7] (However, this proportion is lower than the 91,953 recorded in June 2001, when the private prison population accounted for 6.8 per cent of the total.) At first these facilities were exclusively confined to 'shallow-end' institutions catering for relatively low-risk inmates such as juveniles, prisoners awaiting trial and those with a low security categorization, but they now include several maximum security facilities catering for high security risk adult offenders.[8] In 2002, privatized prison facilities were located in thirty-one state jurisdictions,[9] and in 2003 four of these – New Mexico (44 per cent), Alaska (29 per cent), Montana (26 per cent) and Wyoming (26 per cent) – had at least a quarter of their prisoners in private facilities (US Bureau of Justice, 2004). Moreover, an additional six states at the time had contracted to house prisoners in private facilities located beyond their geographical boundaries.[10] However, there is considerable variation in the degree of support for prison privatization since thirteen states (mainly in the northeast and midwest) currently have no privately held prisoners.

Moreover, the expansion of private correctional services in the USA has not gone unopposed, and resistance has been fuelled by widely publicized failings in a number of privately operated facilities.[11] Even in states where there is legal authority to proceed, proposals to establish new privatized facilities have met with stiff local opposition from residents in many areas. There are also signs of increasingly vocal professional opposition, and a national protest by correctional officers was mounted in October 1998.[12] Partly as a result of this resistance, a majority of prison authorities at state and local level had still not awarded any contracts to the private sector well over a decade after the first contract had been placed with CCA. Moreover, the state of North Carolina passed legislation in 2000 preventing any future 'speculative' prison building by the private sector and forbidding corporations from importing 'out of state' prisoners.[13] However, the federal prison authorities' policy of commissioning the private sector to detain thousands of low security 'criminal aliens' appears to have provided a lifeline for the ailing private prisons industry, at least in the short term.[14]

The private for-profit sector has responded to the relatively sluggish growth in domestic demand for its services by means of a three-fold strategy. First, within the domestic arena, private sector security firms have aggressively marketed specialized ancillary services (such as design, catering, medical and regime programmes) within publicly managed prison facilities. A second, simultaneous response has been to diversify the services they provide beyond what they see as their core areas of expertise. Many have branched out into the delivery of intermediate sanctions such as treatment facilities and supervised release programmes, for example, or are developing new technologies of surveillance and control (Thomas et al., 1997: viii). From the beginning, however, entrepreneurial private security corporations in North America also appear to have been aware of the lucrative opportunities that might be presented by expanding their activities overseas, which constitutes their third response. Moreover, they have achieved considerable success by virtue of a combination of active political[15] and financial lobbying,[16] in order to create a market for their services, combined with more conventional business expansion and marketing tactics.[17]

Attempts to exploit overseas opportunities for expanding the market for US-owned or part-owned private correctional services tend to conform to a fairly well-established pattern. In the first instance, invitations are sent out by private security corporations in the USA to carefully selected policy-makers, legislators and potential domestic lobbyists in specific target jurisdictions to view one of the growing number of 'show-case' private prison facilities. This serves as an important prelude to the political lobbying that will generally be required in order to promote the necessary legislative changes to create a market for private prison services within that particular jurisdiction. Only after this has been successfully accomplished is the climate right for the massive investment that will be required for the establishment of a sufficiently developed and experienced commercial infrastructure that is capable of responding to government invitations to develop prison or correctional facilities.

This provides the entrée for well-resourced and well-informed commercially-minded representatives from both the local jurisdiction and also from US parent corporations to establish locally-based (but usually internationally-financed-and-led) consortia to take advantage of the newly established marketing opportunities. An additional refinement that frequently occurs involves the recruitment of key personnel from both the penal policy-making sector and also the publicly managed prison sector. The aim is partly to cultivate the necessary expertise within the organization to lend credibility to the tendering process. However, it probably has not gone unnoticed in corporate planning departments that a carefully crafted combination of helpful contacts and 'inside information' might be expected to provide a more successful formula for winning the growing number of highly lucrative prison privatization contracts than relying on mere serendipity (or even conventional competitive acumen) alone.

The process that we have outlined is both politically sophisticated and commercially astute. It has been repeated with considerable success in a number of different penal jurisdictions.[18] Most of these involve other English-speaking common law countries (for reasons we will consider below): notably Australia, England and Wales, and New Zealand, though there have also been some significant recent developments in South Africa, as we shall see. We turn next to Australia, however. This was not only the second country, chronologically, to resuscitate the hitherto dormant 'mixed economy' regime of public and private sector involvement in the operation of the prison system; but, by the close of the twentieth century, it was easily the most significant in terms of the 'market share' that had been contracted out to the private sector.[19]

As in the USA, the recent renaissance of prison privatization in Australia has been far from even across its eight penal jurisdictions: the states of New South Wales, Queensland, South Australia, Tasmania, Victoria and Western Australia, together with the Northern Territory, and the Australian Capital Territory. Apart from the ACT, each of these has its own separate criminal justice system and correctional services. So far, four jurisdictions – Queensland, Victoria New South Wales and South Australia – have already introduced privately managed prisons and another – Australian Capital Territory – is planning to do so. Only Tasmania and Northern Territory so far seem immune from the trend, despite the latter's phenomenally high rate of imprisonment.[20]

Queensland is the state with the longest experience of privatization to date. There, the roller-coaster process began after a review of corrections policy in 1988 which was conducted by J. Kennedy, who was a businessman. The 'Kennedy Review' (1988), which was implemented in full, recommended a restructuring of the old prisons department. This was renamed the Queensland Corrective Services Commission, and the ensuing process of 'corporatization' set a precedent which has subsequently been copied in other state territories. Also in line with Kennedy's recommendation to create a market for penal services and engender competition,[21] the Correctional Centre at Borallon became Australia's first privately managed (but still state-owned) prison when it opened in January 1990. The contract for this medium security prison was awarded to Correctional Corporation of Australia which, as the name implies, is a subsidiary of Corrections Corporation of America operating as part of a consortium.[22]

A second privately-managed prison – the Arthur Gorrie 'campus-style' reception and remand centre – opened in 1991. Although it had originally been commissioned as a public sector prison, the then Labor government put its management out to tender after negotiations with the prison officers unions broke down. The contract was eventually awarded to Australasian Correctional Management, which is a subsidiary consortium of the American corrections giant formerly known as Wackenhut[23] and a local Australian private security company (providing armed guards and security technology services) known as ADT. (Although private commercial corporations are exclusively involved in the privatization of custodial institutions in Queensland, a number of not-for-profit community organizations have additionally been contracted to provide non-custodial programmes, particularly for juvenile and Aboriginal offenders).

Subsequently, the process of prison privatization was taken a stage further in Queensland when the already 'corporatized' Queensland Correctional Services Commission (QCSC) was further restructured in April 1997. This took the form of an administrative division into separate purchaser and provider organizations.[24] The name 'Queensland Correctional Services Commission' was retained by the 'purchasing' or commissioning body, while the original service delivery or provider 'arm' was established as an independent government corporation in its own right, known as Queensland Corrections or (QCORR). The 'privatization plot' thickened still further in 1996 when QCORR successfully 'tendered' against both the main private sector competitors, ACM and CCA, and other contenders, to secure the contract for the new maximum security Woodford Prison. The tendering process was surrounded in controversy after allegations about the use of inside information called its probity into question. Further controversy was caused in 1997 when it was announced that QCORR was to become the first public corrections authority in the world to compete for prison contracts abroad, including not only other Australian states but also other countries in South East Asia and the South Pacific.[25]

Next it was announced that virtually all the remaining publicly managed correctional services in Queensland were to be 'market tested', presumably with a view to further privatization.[26] And in 1998, following an approach from the companies concerned, it was announced that the two privately-run prisons were to be sold to their operators, releasing funds which would be used to build new prison accommodation in response to the rapid increase in the number of prison inmates.[27]

Since then, however, there have been signs of a dramatic rethink, suggesting that a halt may have been called to the hitherto seemingly inexorable shift towards wholesale privatization of the state's entire prison estate. The change of heart appears to have been prompted by a highly critical review of the state's corrections system, conducted by a senior civil servant. The Peach Report (1999), which was published in January 1999, concluded, *inter alia*, that the purchaser/provider concept had created inefficiencies, and that any cost efficiencies had resulted not from corporatization, but from more intensive use of prison facilities (i.e. from overcrowding, involving the doubling-up of prisoners, in both public and private facilities).[28] The Government of Queensland responded by adopting the review's call for an abolition of corporatization, and announced legislation that would bring corrections back under direct ministerial control, under a new Department of Correctional Services. Indeed, the future expansion of prison privatization in Queensland was itself called into question by an announcement by the Minister of Corrective Services in 2001 that 'The Labor government's policy is to ensure that prisons remain publicly owned with a limited number of privately operated prisons'.[29] Whether this really does herald a lasting policy reversal in Queensland, however, remains to be seen.

Elsewhere in Australia, the development of prison privatization has also been uneven. In the state of Victoria, for example, the experience has if anything been even more dramatic and erratic. Until 1992, the state of Victoria was controlled by a Labor government that was opposed to prison privatization. The election of a strongly pro-privatization conservative Liberal government in the same year resulted in a change in the law, and the adoption of a vigorous privatization programme that was to catapult Victoria into pole position in the world prison privatization stakes. By November 1999, Victoria had more than 45 per cent of its prison population held in three privately run prisons that were owned and managed by Corrections Corporation of Australia, Australasian Correctional Management and Group 4.[30] The same administration also proposed in 1998 to 'corporatize' the Public Correctional Enterprise (known as CORE), by converting it from a service agency within the Department of Justice into a public authority.[31] The change was intended to bring about a Queensland-style separation between service purchaser and policy-maker (the Department of Justice), and service provider and regulator (Correctional Services Commissioner). Moreover, further privatization was promised if an evaluation set up by the government found that the private sector was more cost efficient and also more effective in rehabilitating prisoners.

In a sign that the politicians' enthusiasm for prison privatization had possibly outstripped that of the electorate, however, the state general election in autumn 1999 resulted in the election of a minority Labor government, and electoral defeat for three erstwhile ministers who had been responsible for developing a privatized youth detention facility.[32] Moreover, the incoming government was much less ideologically committed towards prison privatization, while accepting the need to respect the contractual obligations imposed by their predecessors. On 3 October 2000, however, the state of Victoria invoked emergency powers to resume control over the privatized Metropolitan Women's Correctional Centre, which was subsequently bought back from the private sector in the wake of a series of default notices issued against the company operating the prison.[33] When the government thereafter decided to commission three new prisons, it announced that two of these were to be privately financed, designed, built and maintained but publicly operated and managed,[34] while the third was to be publicly built and operated.[35] Finally, the government of Victoria decided to (re-)integrate the Office of the Correctional Services Commissioner with the Public Correctional Enterprise (CORE), to reconstitute a single business unit with effect from July 2003. The decision to follow Queensland in reversing the 'corporatization' strategy was taken in the wake of a critical report on the operation and management of Victoria's private prisons. The Kirby inquiry (2000) concluded that the strategy of encouraging competition between service providers had resulted in fragmentary service delivery and was no longer appropriate. Once again, it is too soon to say whether this represents a permanent reversal of fortunes for the policy of prison privatization in Victoria, as some would claim,[36] or simply a temporary check in its erstwhile seemingly unstoppable momentum.

New South Wales, which has the largest prison system in Australia, has also embarked on a policy of prison privatization. Indeed, it was the second state in Australia to do so, though the pace of development was soon eclipsed, as we have seen, by the state of Victoria. Although New South Wales had experienced a dramatic increase in its prison population during the late 1980s,[37] the initial impetus in support of privatization has been attributed (Baldry, 1994) to the promotional activities of Corrections Corporation of America (CCA), which was then making a loss in the United States. Successful lobbying by CCA of New South Wales' then Minister of Corrections, Michael Yabsley, resulted in the commissioning of a private consultant's report (Kleinwort Benson Australia Ltd, 1989), which recommended privatization on the basis of overseas experience. Paving legislation was adopted in 1990,[38] and in 1993 the contract for the operation of Junee Correctional Centre, a prison for medium and maximum security inmates, was awarded to Australian Correctional Services Pty (ACS). This was a consortium of Thiess Contractors, ADT Security and American private prisons operator Wackenhut Corrections Corporation.

Since then, the policy of prison privatization has failed to take off in the way that it has done in Queensland and Victoria, in spite of unsuccessful attempts to promote a 'zero crime' policy linked to a prison privatization strategy during the state election in 1999. But although the incoming Labor government had been opposed to the private management of Junee Correctional Centre while in opposition, it decided not to allow an in-house bid when the tender for Junee came up for renewal in 2001. Subsequently the government announced the adoption of a private finance initiative modelled on the one developed in the UK (see below), but three new prisons are to are to be run by the public sector in return for an agreement by the Public Services Association to accept flat rate overtime payments (*Prison Privatisation Report International* 2004, 61: 2; see also Roth, 2004).

Two of the remaining four jurisdictions have also proceeded, albeit more tentatively and cautiously, down the same prisons privatization pathway. For a time it seemed as if Western Australia might pioneer a somewhat different approach, which appeared to owe more to Western European style corporatism than the more brutal 'corporatization' approach that was adopted by Queensland. Instead of using prison privatization as a blunt instrument with which to bludgeon 'recalcitrant' labour unions into submission, the government in Western Australia appeared content to rely on the unspoken threat posed by privatization to inject greater 'realism' on the part of the Australian Prison Officers Association (POAA) in discussions over working practices and the need for restructuring. For its part, the POAA appeared to view the prospect of 'genuine consultative labour relations' as preferable to wholesale privatization. The outcome was a package of measures, somewhat reminiscent of the 'Fresh Start' package which the government in England and Wales imposed on prison officers in 1987 (see Cavadino and Dignan, 2002: 16). In return for improvements in basic pay, prison officers in Western Australia agreed to the removal of overtime payments and other entitlements. The 'hidden benefit' that the deal secured for the workforce was a three-year moratorium on market testing, while the government conceded greater consultation and a devolution of some power and responsibility to staff in return for more efficient working practices and a voluntary commitment to restructuring.

However, the respite which the deal seemed to offer to both sides proved to be relatively short lived, since the more consensual and consultative approach appeared to be giving way towards the end of the 1990s to the 'free collective combat' approach that is more usually associated with neo-liberal style industrial relations strategies. One symptom of this gradual 'reversion to type' was the announcement by the Western Australian Government in 1998 of plans to put out to tender ancillary services relating to the management of court and police custody, prisoner transportation and court security.[39] This was followed by a call for expressions of interest from private consortia that might wish to build and run a new 750-bed medium-security prison near Perth.[40] The Upper House of Western Australia's Parliament tabled legislation paving the way for prison privatization in August 1999. Although the Democratic Party, who held the balance of power in the Upper House, was previously opposed to the idea, they withdrew their opposition in return for a commitment to introduce an independent prisons inspectorate.[41] The contract to build and operate Acacia prison, near Perth, was subsequently awarded to Corrections Corporation of Australia.[42] The prison opened in May 2001, was fined A US$1.05 million in its first year of operation, and was reported to be on Western Australia's alert list of prisons 'at real risk of significant failure' following its first review by the inspector general of custodial services (*Prison Privatisation Report International*, 2003, 55: 5).

In South Australia, the management of Mt Gambier prison for women was awarded to Group 4 Securitas, and the facility opened in 1996. The state has subsequently announced plans for a new privately financed women's prison, and a juvenile detention centre, both of which were provisionally due to be operated by public sector staff, plus a new privately designed and operated prison for men.[43] The latter proposal had previously been shelved by the former Liberal government following a decrease in the state's prison population. The decision to revive the plan was prompted by an anticipated increase in inmate numbers as a result of recently introduced law and order measures.[44] The quickening pace of prison privatization initiatives in South Australia is associated with the provision of UK assistance in the use of private finance in the provision of public infrastructure (see below).[45]

The ACT, which hitherto has sent its prisoners to serve their sentences in New South Wales prisons, also decided in 2001 to commission a privately built and operated prison (though opting for public finance and ownership). However, these plans were put on hold as a result of economic problems caused by disastrous bush fires in January 2003.[46] Australia's immigration detention centres, which are run by the federal government, are also operated by private contractors. The only two jurisdictions to have resisted the trend towards prison privatization to date are Tasmania, which has enjoyed one of the lowest rates of imprisonment in Australia in recent years (see Chapter 5 Note 12), and the Northern Territory. The Tasmanian government considered the possibility of private sector involvement in a new prison to be built in the south of the island, but decided in 2001 that the new facility would, after all, be publicly owned and operated. Meanwhile, the Northern Territory government likewise rejected prison privatization and enacted legislation in 2001 that retained the status of prison officers as public servants.[47]

In spite of its uneven pattern of development, the speed and scale of support for the policy has ensured that Australia can claim by far the highest proportion of prisoners accommodated in privately managed facilities, though estimates vary as to the precise figure, which has almost certainly peaked in the light of recent reverses.[48] The only other countries that can claim to have overtaken the USA, relatively modest proportion of approximately 6 per cent of inmates who are detained in private facilities are England and Wales and Scotland. By the end of 2001, over 6,000 adults and young offenders were held in English private pri ons, which represents around 8 per cent of the overall prison population.[49] Scotland, with its separate prison service, had just one private prison (Kilmarnock), though its 600 inmates represent approximately 10 per cent of Scotland's total prison population (Nathan, 2003a: 165).

We have described the early moves towards prison privatization in England and Wales in some detail elsewhere, and will not repeat this account here (Cavadino and Dignan, 2002: 229–34; see also Nathan, 2003a). Suffice it to say that the early history and subsequent implementation of the policy prior to the General Election of 1997 conforms very closely to the general pattern we have already outlined in several Australian states. Two early developments are worthy of note, however, because of their influence on privatization initiatives elsewhere (including, most notably, Australia and South Africa).

The first of these entailed an important shift in the mode of privatization, since the first three prisons involved 'management-only' contracts, whereby the Prison Service retained ownership of the buildings and merely contracted out the operational responsibility (including custodial and managerial functions) to the private sector. Since 1996, however, private contractors have been responsible for financing, designing, constructing and managing all the more recent private prison ventures (the so-called 'DCMF model', referred to above). In October 2003 there were nine privately managed prisons in England and Wales, of which two involved 'management-only' contracts while seven (with a further two in the pipeline) conformed to the 'DCMF model'. Private sector involvement in the criminal justice system has not been restricted to prisons, however, but also extends to immigration detention centres and secure training centres for the detention of young offenders. Prison–court escort services have also been privatized, as has the provision of other ancillary services (for example, education and health) within prisons and the provision of electronic monitoring programmes. Moreover, a 'DCMF' model has also been adopted for the development and maintenance of new police stations, court complexes and probation hostels, making the English criminal justice system the most heavily privatized in Europe (Nathan, 2003a: 165).

The second development, which is even more significant since it paved the way for the DCMF model, involved the adoption, in 1992, of the highly controversial 'Private Finance Initiative' (PFI) as the standard method of procurement for all public sector infrastructure. The initiative consists of a self-imposed doctrine whereby the Treasury refuses to sanction any new public expenditure unless the use of private finance has first been considered. The chief attraction for the government is that the involvement of private finance avoids the need for public sector borrowing,[50] which successive governments have sought to reduce, in pursuit of a tight fiscal policy. However, critics[51] point out that this apparent fiscal benefit is illusory since the public purse will ultimately pay considerably more for assets and services that are provided by the private sector. This is partly because private sector borrowing costs are considerably higher than those of the state (which, unlike private contractors is unlikely to go bankrupt or renege on its debts) but also because of the need to ensure sufficiently attractive profit margins in order to tempt potential investors. In the case of prison facilities these inflated costs are recouped by means of *per capita* payments from the Treasury to the private contractors over the duration of the twenty-five-year private prison contracts in a public-sector equivalent to paying for goods and services by means of hire purchase.

For a short time after the General Election of 1997 the future of prison privatization in England and Wales appeared to be in some doubt since the victorious Labour Party had unequivocally pledged to take private prisons back into public ownership.[52] However, this 'principled opposition' began to melt away within days of the election victory. One week later the new Labour Home Secretary announced that he would be prepared to sign contracts that were already in the pipeline if this proved to be the only way of providing new accommodation quickly. Just over ten days later the Home Secretary confirmed[53] that a complete *volte face* had taken place when he announced that, in the wake of two secret Prison Service reviews, all new prisons in England and Wales would be privately built and run. The reviews were said to have concluded, first, that the option of using private finance to build new prisons while retaining the management function within the public sector was not affordable and did not offer value for money; and second that the immediate transfer of private prisons to the public sector could not be justified, citing the same grounds. As for the private finance initiative, it has been embraced by the New Labour government with even more enthusiasm that that shown by their Conservative predecessors.

In spite of the incoming Labour government's 'U-turn' on the issue of prison privatization, the private sector has experienced mixed fortunes since then, including a number of significant reverses. Thus, two former privately managed prisons (Buckley Hall and Blakenhurst) reverted to public sector management when their contracts came up for renewal (in 1999 and 2000 respectively) after Prison Service bids were judged to be of higher quality and lower cost than their private sector counterparts. The first public-sector prison to be 'market tested', Manchester,[54] also remained in public sector control after the in-house bid was preferred to those of private sector rivals. And when Brixton prison was threatened with privatization in 2001 after being publicly lambasted by the then prisons minister Paul Boateng as a 'failing' institution, not a single bid was received from a private sector company.[55]

Another set-back followed in the wake of a disturbance, at a detention centre for illegal immigrants (Yarl's Wood) in 2002 (Molenaar and Neufeld, 2003). This resulted in a destructive fire and the (temporary) closure of the facility but, more importantly, contributed to a growing reluctance on the part of the insurance industry to provide cover for private prisons, thereby delaying the signing of the contracts to build two new ones (*Prison Privatisation Report International*, 2002, 47: 6).

Like their counterparts elsewhere, private prisons in England have experienced a number of significant failings (see Cavadino and Dignan, 2002: 234–55 for details) but even these were eclipsed by the spectacular shortcomings of Ashfield young offender institution, which opened in 1999. In May 2002, the Prison Service took the unprecedented step of removing the director from his post and imposing public-sector management amid fears for the safety of both inmates and staff, prompted by concern that the private operators might lose control of the prison. The outgoing Director General of the Prison Service, Martin Narey, described it as the worst prison in England and Wales 'by some measure', and threatened to take it back into public ownership if performance did not improve.[56] Another measure of the depth of concerns over the safety of the prison was the decision by the Youth Justice Board to withdraw hundreds of sentenced young offenders from the institution (though somewhat bizarrely this did not affect those on remand).

Not surprisingly, perhaps, there have also been some tentative (and short-lived) signs of second thoughts about the direction of the prison privatization strategy both within government and the Prison Service itself. Thus, both the former Director General of the Prison Service and the prisons minister have floated the idea of adopting an alternative approach, in which prisons would continue to be designed, financed and built by the private sector, but operated by the public sector. This approach has more in common with the French concept of 'semi-private' prisons based on a mixed management model (see below) and was inspired by an internal report commissioned in 2001 by the prison service (Carter, 2002). This report did not appear to herald an imminent volte-face, however, for it also extolled what it claimed to be the virtues of the existing fully privatized model and the PFI scheme in general and called for an ambitious renewal programme designed to replace many of the existing prisons. This would involve the sale of up to thirty prisons, many in prime urban locations, and their replacement with eight much larger regional or 'super jails' holding up to 1,500 inmates instead of the normal complement of around 500 (*The Guardian*, 27 February 2002). If adopted, such a strategy would provide a way of circumventing continuing private sector reluctance to take on existing 'failing institutions' and could herald a further significant expansion in private sector involvement in the English prison system.

In December 2003, the government published a second Carter report, which proposed a radical restructuring of the prison and probation services intended to integrate the operation of both services under the auspices of a single organization, the National Offender Management Service (or NOMS) (Carter, 2003). Although this restructuring was motivated partly by a desire to achieve a more 'seamless' partnership between the two services, it was also clearly intended that both should be more routinely and systematically exposed to the disciplines of the market place.[57] Thus, with regard to prisons the report recommends the introduction of 'fixed term management contracts for all prisons, which would be open to competition at the end of the contract' (Carter, 2003: 37). And while the report envisages that the majority of offender managers who would be responsible for supervising offenders in the community would initially be drawn from the public sector, it anticipates that new providers will emerge over time, which could be drawn from public, private or voluntary sectors. The government's response to the Carter proposals was broadly positive (Blunkett, 2004). Even if they are not fully adopted, the future of the private prison industry seems assured for the foreseeable future at least while the PFI doctrine holds sway with the government, which continues to be the case despite growing doubts elsewhere about the wisdom of such a strategy (Centre for Public Services, 2002; Kochan, 2003). But if they were to be fully and vigorously implemented, the Carter strategy would herald a further significant expansion in private sector involvement in the penal system, this time extending beyond the prison system itself.

New Zealand is another English-speaking common law jurisdiction that has also shown pronounced neo-liberal tendencies in recent years. Prison privatization has made some limited headway here also, but progress has been much more hesitant and faltering than in any of the other countries we have been examining so far. As in England and Wales and several of the Australian states, limited forms of private sector involvement – including court escort and ancillary services such as catering, plus the operation of remand centres – were advocated by two official policy reports towards the end of the 1980s (Roper, 1989; Strategos Consulting Limited, 1989). The initial response was lukewarm, however. Not only was the notion of 'full-blown' privatization rejected, but even more limited forms of private sector involvement were put on hold until the US and Australian experience became clearer.

However, the 1990s coincided with a period of conservative rule, which not only boosted the promotion of free-market economics that had begun under a Labour administration in the mid-1980s, but also extended the concept to the operation of the prison service. The service itself was 'corporatized' as in Queensland (see above). Plans for two private prisons in Auckland – a remand prison and a medium secure facility – were introduced in 1991, and in 1994 the Penal Institutions Amendment Bill (No. 3) provided the enabling legislation that was required to authorize the private operation of these privately designed and constructed institutions. Progress was still faltering, however, and the original tenders – comprising an integrated package of design, construction, finance and management – were rejected as unsatisfactory. New tenders were called for, which disaggregated the 'design and build' element from the management and operational element.[58]

By the time of the 1999 General Election, contracts for prisoner escort and court security services in the Auckland and Northland regions had been allocated to the private sector, and the first privately managed prison (Auckland Central Remand Prison) was commissioned, becoming operational in mid-2000. The outgoing conservative National Party government, which had held power since 1990, had by that stage committed itself to five new privately managed prisons plus seven specialist youth facilities.[59] However, the government's enthusiasm for privatization in other sectors of the economy had proved electorally unpopular, and the November 1999 General Election returned a coalition led by a Labour Party that was pledged to halt the prison privatization programme. In 2000, the then minister for corrections stated that 'there has been an experiment overseas – driven by ideology – to introduce private prisons and it hasn't worked ... this government won't let New Zealanders become guinea pigs for an experiment here'.[60] Following a lengthy gestation period a new Corrections Bill,[61] which stipulates that no new prison management contracts may be entered into, received its third reading on 3 June 2004, prompting claims that New Zealand was the first national government in the world to legislate against private prisons.[62] Somewhat ironically, given its principled objection to the use of coercive powers by bodies other than the government itself, the government of New Zealand has been taken to task by the United Nations Human Rights Committee, which has voiced concerns about the operation and monitoring of the privately managed remand prison at Auckland and the contracted-out prison escort service. The Committee is concerned that the practice of privatization and lack of effective monitoring may be incompatible with the obligations of contracting states under the International Covenant on Civil and Political Rights, and their accountability for any violations of those rights.[63]

The only other country in which prison privatization has progressed as far as it has in the above group of English speaking common law countries is South Africa which, like them, has also experienced pronounced neo-liberal tendencies over the years. Moreover, South Africa, too, has a long history of private sector involvement in the prison system. Indeed, the first private prisons were built and operated by the De Beers Mining Company which, by the end of the nineteenth century, was using 10,000 prison labourers daily, for whom it met the incarceration expenses and also made a payment to the state (Goyer, 2001, Chapter 2; van Heerden, 1996: 4–6). Convict labour continued to be used by South Africa's mining industry until 1952, and thereafter by the agriculture sector until the practice was abolished by Act of Parliament in 1959.

The contemporary prison system in South Africa suffers from many of the same problems experienced in other countries, though rarely on such a scale, as we saw in Chapter 6. They include chronic overcrowding,[64] which is particularly acute in the remand sector, an institutionalized gang culture (Haysom, 1981), dilapidated and squalid prison estate, poor security and major public health concerns.[65] Moreover, the prison system still suffers from the legacy of the apartheid system, with its militarized system of prison management and accompanying ethos of deplorable staff-inmate relations in which human rights abuses occurred without effective monitoring or redress (Berg, 2003: 180). In some respects, the transition to democracy has increased the scale of the challenge still further, since the adoption of a new constitution in 1996, with its associated Bill of Rights, conferred new rights on prison inmates and heightened expectations of reform. At the same time, the government adopted an economic strategy that aimed to reduce public expenditure, while facing competing pressures from other public services such as health and education. And although some foreign aid and assistance was provided, this was frequently tied to deficit reduction strategies or heavily promoted the adoption of private finance initiatives, particularly in the sphere of correctional services.

Perhaps unsurprisingly, therefore, the option of prison privatization was considered as a significant element in South Africa's prison reform programme as early as 1994 (Goyer, 2001: Chapters 5). However, it was not until 1997 that the decision was taken in principle to embark on a programme of prison privatization, following a fact-finding visit by members of the Department of Public Works and the Department of Correctional Services to the USA and the UK.[66] This was seen in part as a means of providing new facilities to mitigate the serious overcrowding without having to raise the capital in advance of construction, and in part as an attempt to improve staff-inmate relations and also to reform prison management practices. What is more surprising is the decision to introduce the relatively untried 'full-blown' DCMF model, the speed with which it was adopted, and the fact that, unlike most other countries which have begun by privatizing 'shallow end' facilities, the first two private prisons in South Africa are both maximum security institutions. In this respect at least (and also the fact that it is the first developing country to embrace such a strategy), the South African pattern of prison privatization is unique.

The Correctional Services Act of 1998, which provides statutory authorization for contracted-out prisons was supported by the South African cabinet, in which both the largely social democratic ANC and the more conservative Inkatha Freedom Party were represented. There appears to have been very little debate over the issues of principle raised by the policy of prison privatization, and the main sources of controversy at the time were confined to the revelation that the Youth League of the ANC was involved in one of the local consortia bidding for the construction and operation of two prisons.[67]

In the initial flush of enthusiasm for the project, the South African government was originally reported to be planning to privatize no fewer than seven new prisons including pre-trial, super-maximum security and maximum security prisons and at least one youth development centre, between them holding a total of 10,000 inmates.[68] The proposed contracts were valued at more than R10.5bn (£208m) and were expected to cover the finance, design, construction, maintenance and operation of the new facilities, with financial returns being guaranteed by the government. In the event, however, these ambitious plans were drastically scaled down in the light of the country's impoverished financial situation.[69]

The revised programme involved two separate extremely large maximum security prisons[70] that were financed, designed, built and managed by the private sector. South Africa's first private prison, at Bloemfontein, opened in 2001 and is operated by a consortium led by Copenhagen-based Group 4 Falck, acting in conjunction with a number of South African construction and investment firms. The second prison is situated in Louis Trichardt, in Northern Province, and is operated by a consortium led by South African Custodial Services (SACS), which is the South African subsidiary of US private prisons corporation Wackenhut.[71] Both prisons were commissioned by the South African government's Asset Procurement and Operating Partnership System (APOPS), a government agency which was set up in 1996, though it was closely modelled on the United Kingdom's private finance initiative.

Although the initial decision to embark on a prison privatization strategy in South Africa was relatively uncontroversial, concerns have subsequently been raised regarding the proportion of the prison service budget that is consumed by the costs of the two private prisons.[72] This has precipitated a financial crisis for the department of corrections and, in particular, for South Africa's other 236 prisons, which have been faced with a freeze on posts and other cutbacks. Moreover, while the private prisons are protected from overcrowding, the public sector suffers from 68 per cent overcrowding (*Prison Privatisation Report International* 2003, 58: 1). Allegations of corruption have also been levelled against a former commissioner of prisons relating to the allocation of private prison contracts, and a commission of inquiry has been appointed to investigate the charges.[73] The experience of prison privatization in South Africa (mirroring that in other countries), seems to confirm that, while it may be possible to provide superior standards of care and facilities in a limited number of 'showcase' institutions, this is frequently at the expense of the rest of the system, which may even be worse off than before. As for the future of the prison privatization strategy, it is too soon to say how this might be affected by the recent controversy. The immediate response involves an attempt to renegotiate the terms of the contract taking account of the Department of Correctional Service's 'affordability constraints',[74] and there have been reports that the department may be considering a French-style 'semi-privatization' model in any future prison commissions.[75] In the meantime, the extent of any private sector involvement in the proposed four new prisons remains undecided.

Although unique in some respects, South Africa's embrace of prison privatization is nevertheless consistent with the fact that significant private sector involvement in the operation of prison systems has so far been confined, for the most part, to a relatively small group of countries that are united above all by their neo-liberal tendencies.

Conservative corporatist countries and the limited impact of prison privatization

In marked contrast with the above group of neo-liberal countries, the impact of prison privatization to date has been much more limited within the group of conservative corporatist countries that is included in this study. This is despite the fact that some of these countries (for example, France) have also been faced with the problem of chronic overcrowding, while others (for example, the Netherlands and also Italy to a lesser extent; see Chapters 8 and 9) have experienced an extremely rapid increase in the size of their prison population in recent years. As we shall see, the concept of prison privatization is not unknown, even within this second group of countries, but so far there have been significant differences, both quantitative and qualitative, in the nature and scale of its development compared with the current state of prison privatization in neo-liberal countries.

Within the group of conservative corporatist countries, France has by far the greatest experience of private sector involvement in corrections policy generally, though much of this involves the voluntary not-for-profit sector (Vagg, 1994: 305). Since the middle of the last century, for example, the main responsibility for juveniles held in custody has been assumed by private voluntary associations, though the commercial sector has also been involved for many years in the provision of ancillary services such as prison industries and workshops.

More recently, France has also experienced the same kinds of problems affecting the prison system in the UK and elsewhere, of excessive prison numbers resulting in the chronic overcrowding of prisoners, many of whom were held in antiquated prison facilities. Moreover, French penal policy-makers have been exposed to the same classic 'hard sell' marketing ploys by US private prisons corporations that have also been directed at their English, Australasian and South African counterparts. Indeed, the French Minister of Justice also visited selected private prison establishments in the USA in 1987, at around the same time as a visit paid by the British Parliamentary Home Affairs Committee. However, attempts by American corporations to export their expertise, technology and private prison services as a ready-made solution to the penal requirements of governments seeking to expand their penal estate without, at the same time, expanding their public sector borrowing requirements, have so far met with a distinctly different response in France.

Instead of opting for the kind of 'full-scale' prison privatization programme that has been adopted elsewhere, France has embarked on a qualitatively different 'semi-privatization' strategy. Here, the role of the private for-profit sector has been restricted to the design and construction of new prisons, and the provision of various ancillary services,[76] but has so far stopped short of private sector ownership and management of those facilities.

In 1986, a right-wing French government responded to the rapid increase in the prison population by launching 'Programme 13,000', which was intended to provide 13,000 additional places for prisoners in twenty-five new penal establishments between 1987 and 1992. The original proposal envisaged full-scale privatization, but this was opposed by prison administrators and by members of the French Parliament, and a compromise resulted in the adoption of a watered-down form of semi-privatization. Thus, a law of 22 June 1987 authorized public or private sector involvement in the construction and fitting out of prisons or the provision of functions *other than that of prison management, security and control* (emphasis added). By 1997 there were twenty-one such 'semi-private' prisons accommodating over 10,000 additional inmates, and the construction of another six such prisons was announced in October 2001, prior to the presidential and parliamentary elections of May 2002.[77] Ownership of the new facilities (which were financed by public money) remains with the French government, however, as does responsibility for management, security and control. The only functions that have been privatized to date apart from construction include catering, plant maintenance, transport for inmates, drug rehabilitation and other medical services.

'Full-scale' privatization of French prisons cannot be ruled out in the future, particularly since there is not felt to be any constitutional bar on private sector involvement in the administration of the prison system. Moreover, French corporations such as SIGES (which is a subsidiary of Sodexho SA) are not only actively involved in the provision of a range of ancillary services in French prisons; they are also linked with other transnational corporations with interests in prison privatization. In 2003 another right-wing French government announced another massive construction programme involving twenty-eight new prisons creating a further 13,200 beds. This time the proposal extends to private finance with lease-back arrangements (to avoid an increase in the budget deficit), and the possibility of 'full-scale' privatization involving the contracting out of custodial services is also under consideration once more. Invitations to tender were expected to be issued at the end of 2003,[78] but still on the basis of the state retaining responsibility for custodial services.

Until now, therefore, the French attitude towards the concept of prison privatization[79] appears to be qualitatively different from the Anglo-American variant that prevails within the neo-liberal sector. So far, it has stopped well short of the fundamental challenge that Anglo-American style prison privatization has posed to hitherto unquestioned assumptions concerning the responsibility of the state for administering penal policy. Nor has it resulted in the frontal assault on the working practices of private sector prison officer unions that has accompanied the development of prison privatization within the neo-liberal countries we have examined.

Elsewhere in Europe, there has so far been equally little enthusiasm for Anglo-American style full-scale prison privatization. In Germany, only the state governments of Hesse and Saxony-Anhalt, have shown any interest in the issue; but even here progress to date has been limited to the proposal to build a single semi-private prison at Hunfeld, 130 km north east of Frankfurt and another in the village of Warmsdorf, 150 km south west of Berlin.[80] Another state government, that of North-Rhine-Westphalia, decided against the adoption of private prisons in 1998.[81] The use of private custody staff in state prisons would in any event be unconstitutional in Germany, so for the moment it seems unlikely that full-scale privatization will be adopted in the foreseeable future.[82]

In the Netherlands also, prison privatization has, so far, been seen as a 'non-issue', in spite of the massive four-fold increase in the prison population in less than twenty years, and the huge prison building programme to which this has given rise. Until now – apart from one experiment involving the private financing of a publicly operated facility – the necessary infrastructure has been financed, constructed and operated by the public sector, and a proposal to engage private companies to build prisons and then lease them back to the state was rejected by the government.[83] A range of ancillary services (including catering, education and laundry plus prison escort services) has been privatized, however (Beyens and Snacken, 1996: 247).

The Dutch government has also conferred executive agency status on the prison service,[84] allowing budgetary devolution and a substantial decentralization of authority to the individual prison governors. This has been described as a form of 'backdoor privatization' by two Dutch commentators (van Swaaningen and de Jonge, 1995: 25ff.) since in principle it is said to make it possible for 'every service except the actual control functions' to be carried out by private enterprise (van Swaaningen and de Jonge, 1995: 26). This may be so in theory, but in reality the only functions that even fully independent prison governors would be authorized to privatize are those relating to ancillary services. So while it is true that the administrative restructuring to which van Swaaningen and de Jonge refer bears some similarities to the adoption of 'executive agency status' for prison departments that has taken place elsewhere,[85] it seems unlikely that this move will of itself result in a significant prison privatization programme in the Netherlands.

However, in a penal climate that is becoming increasingly influenced by law and order concerns, the Dutch subsidiary of the British private security firm Securicor has been awarded a contract to run detention facilities for offenders imprisoned for offences relating to drug-trafficking.[86] And in 2001, the Dutch Ministry of Justice commissioned a report on public–private partnerships which called for further investigation into the potential for increased collaboration in relation to the prison system. The Minister of Justice was reported to have stated that he did not intend to reduce state control in this area, but nor did he reject outright the idea of such partnerships.[87]

In other conservative corporatist states, such as Italy, prison privatization has so far made even less headway, in spite of the steady increase in the size of the prison population in recent years, as a result of which they were operating at 36 per cent over capacity by 2003. However, the Italian government announced a prison building programme in 2003 comprising twenty-two new prisons, half of which are to be financed, procured and operated in the conventional manner (*Prison Privatisation Report International*, 2003, 57: 2). As for the other half, the government has commissioned a feasibility study to consider the use of a semi-private model, using private finance and construction and the private operation of ancillary services.

However, even in those European countries that have not adopted full-scale prison privatization as part of their official penal policy (such as France, Germany and the Netherlands) banks and other commercial and financial institutions have shown some interest in the UK's 'Private Finance Initiative',[88] which, as we have seen, has underpinned the development of prison privatization in England and Wales since its launch in 1992. It is conceivable that pressure from European financial institutions could help to promote the spread of prison privatization in other European countries in the future.

Oriental liberal corporatist Japan: first tentative moves towards privatization

In Japan, all prisons are at present run by the state and, according to the Prisons Department, the authorities have a reputation for effective and efficient administration.[89] Japan's penal code requires convicted prisoners to work, and there is some private sector involvement in the provision of prison industries and related work-based facilities.[90] Likewise, some ancillary services have also been contracted out (APCCA, 2002). Beyond that, there did not appear to be much public support for any greater private sector involvement in the running of Japanese prisons. In response to growing pressures from an expanding prison population,[91] however, the Ministry of Justice[92] has in recent years been gathering information about the operation of private prisons in countries such as the USA, UK and Australia, and is thought to be particularly interested in the 'agency' status of the Prison Service in England and Wales.[93] In 2003, the government announced that it was planning to use private finance in order to procure a new 1,000 cell prison for both male and female inmates. Although it was initially reported that custodial services were to be retained by the public sector (*Prison Privatisation Report International*, 2003 57: 2), it now appears that the 'MIYA Rehabilitation Promotion Centre' is to be administered by a private contractor under a 20-year PFI-style contract.[94] And there are unconfirmed reports that the government may be contemplating a second public./private partnership prison (*Prison Privatisation Report International*, 2004. 61: 2).

Nordic social democracies: absence of prison privatization

In sharp contrast to the enthusiastic promotion of prison privatization in neo-liberal countries, and the more tentative interest that has been shown in conservative corporatist states and also Japan, prison privatization has failed to make any real headway to date in the group of 'low imprisonment' countries comprising the Nordic social democracies. In both Finland and Sweden there has been no large-scale commercial private-sector involvement in the penal system so far.[95] The entire penal system, and particularly the state administration and operation of the prison system, is state-organized, and there appears to be a strong political and public consensus in support of the state's continuing role in this field. The state's role is seen as essential for the continued legitimacy of the penal system and the protection of individual prisoners' rights, while the state itself and its civil servants enjoy a high level of trust and public support. So far there has been no support for prison privatization at the level of penal policy.[96] Although the cost effectiveness of public administration is contrasted unfavourably in some quarters with the private sector, it seems unlikely that prison privatization will take hold in the Nordic social democracies, at least while the prison population there remains stable and the rate of imprisonment continues to be comparatively low.

Conclusion: accounting for the revival and uneven pattern of prison privatization to date

It is almost certainly not coincidental that the recent revival of private sector involvement in the provision of prison facilities and services should have origi- nated in, and made most progress to date within, the neo-liberal group of coun- tries. For these are the ones in which the material and ideological contexts appear to be most conducive to the resurgence of prison privatization. Among the material factors that have helped to transform official attitudes in favour of encouraging private sector involvement in the provision of prison-based facili- ties and services, the most significant has undoubtedly been the recent rapid increase in the size of the prison population – particularly (but not exclusively) in the USA.

However, the rightwards shift in political attitudes that took place during the 1980s in both the USA and the UK, was equally instrumental in establishing an ideological climate that favoured a strategy based on prison privatization. For the rapid increase in the size of the prison population in many neo-liberal juris- dictions during the 1980s and 1990s was itself largely stimulated by the increas- ingly strident and punitive 'law and order' rhetoric that shattered the more liberal consensus that had prevailed during the earlier period of rehabilitative optimism. However, this pronounced ideological shift also threatened to unleash a massive demand for increased expenditure in order to drastically increase the amount of prison accommodation that would be required in a more punitive sentencing climate.[97]

Meeting this demand in the conventional way – by increased public borrowing or imposing additional taxes – would not only have been electorally unpopular. It would also have undermined another key right-wing ideological commitment, which was to 'roll back' those commitments and financial responsibilities of the state that were felt to be provided more efficiently by the private sector. Only by inviting private contractors to make the initial substantial investments that were required in return for guaranteed payments at a sufficiently attractive rate was it possible for 'neo-liberal' governments to indulge their punitive predilec- tions without at the same time sustaining and expanding the politically reviled public sector. Hence, the ideological preferences of neo-liberal governments in the USA and the UK during the 1980s and early 1990s created a potentially lucrative marketing opportunity to meet the increased demand for additional prison capacity which the private sector was quick to exploit.

As for the subsequent, rather uneven, spread of prison privatization, our account provides telling additional evidence of the existence and activities of a powerful international 'corrections-commercial complex' (Lilly and Knepper, 1992), (or 'penal-industrial complex')[98] and also its influence on domestic penal policy-making in a variety of countries. The countries in which prison privatization has made most headway to date are not only characterized by their neo-liberal tendencies. Most of them[99] also share a common language, culture and legal traditions, and have long-standing financial, investment and trade links. It might be thought that these factors could help to explain both the apparent sphere of influence that is wielded by the international penal-industrial complex and hence, also, why prison privatization has made more headway in these countries than it has elsewhere to date.

However, this does not in our view provide a complete explanation for its uneven pattern of development. Nor does it adequately explain the much greater resistance that is shown in other countries, such as the Netherlands, or the rather different nature of prison privatization that has been adopted in countries such as France. Both of these are countries that appear to share at least some of the material and ideological conditions that have been conducive in promoting full-scale prison privatization elsewhere. We would suggest that one reason why prison privatization has failed to make greater headway in France and the Netherlands has to do with more deep-seated ideological assumptions that are prevalent in these and also in many other countries about the relationship between individual citizens (including prisoners), the state and the market place.

Again it is no coincidence, in our view, that the countries in which prison privatization has so far made greatest headway are also those in which, historically, the survival and well-being of individual citizens has been most dependent on the relatively unfettered operation of 'market forces'. The term 'commodification' has been coined (Esping-Andersen, 1990) to refer to the tendency for a person's status and well-being to be treated as a commodity, and the societies that have shown the greatest degree of commodification, historically, have themselves been neo-liberal in orientation. Indeed, the most extreme example was the systematic practice of slavery in the southern states of the USA in the period prior to the Civil War in which people themselves were, quite literally, traded as 'commodities' on the market-place. It seems highly probable that in societies that still exhibit a relatively high degree of commodification the ideological resistance towards the concept and practice of prison privatization will be much less intense than elsewhere.

Conversely, it might be expected that in societies that have pursued more active policies of 'decommodification' – by according individual citizens social rights that are designed to insulate their status and economic well-being from the vagaries of market forces – the degree of resistance towards prison privatization will be much more intense. This could help to explain why there appears to be such strong public and official resistance towards the policy of prison privatization in the Nordic social democracies, where the degree of 'decommodification' has been greatest. It could also help to explain why there is much less support for the policy in the Netherlands, in spite of the very dramatic increase in the rate of imprisonment in recent years. And it could help to explain why, in countries such as France, private sector involvement has been limited to the design and construction of new prison facilities and the provision of ancillary services, but has stopped short of private ownership and operation of those facilities. Perhaps it could also help to explain the apparent ambivalence towards the policy of prison privatization on the part of the public in New Zealand, where the recent adoption of neo-liberal social and economic policies appears to be at risk of foundering on the older bedrock of social democratic political sentiment that had prevailed there until relatively recently.

In this part of the book we have attempted to undertake a thematic comparison of the main penal jurisdictions we are investigating, in terms of two distinct dimensions of penality. Based on this analysis, we have suggested that there is evidence of a fairly consistent 'pattern of penality' that appears to apply across a wide range of penal practices. This provides us with additional evidence that countries with similar social and economic characteristics are indeed also likely to share at least some common characteristics with respect to their penal practices.

Notes

1 This is not to say that it won't happen. In 2003 a Bill was introduced in Texas that would have allowed the entire state jail division to be privatized (*Prison Privatisation Report International*, 2003, 55: 2). Although this particular proposal was thwarted by intense opposition and a lack of legislative time (*Prison Privatisation Report International*, 2003, Vol. 56: 8), a somewhat similar proposal that would allow private companies to run all state prisons except maximum security and juvenile facilities in Arizona is expected to become law in 2004.

2 Indeed, Feeley (1991) has traced the practice back to the arrival of early English colonists in Virginia in 1607. They were followed by a handful of convicted felons who were granted a conditional pardon that involved them being transported to America by private entrepreneurs and sold into slavery.

3 Like the practice of prison privatization itself, the imposition of charges for inmates has also been revived in some jurisdictions, notably at Ocean County, New Jersey where prisoners are charged $200 for the first ten days of detention and $10 a day thereafter; though this is in fact, a public sector jail (*Prison Privatisation Report International*, 1997, 8: 3).

4 Over a decade after the publication of a highly critical official report by the Molesworth Committee on Transportation in 1838.

5 However, just two corporations – Corrections Corporation of America and Wackenhut Corrections Corporation – accounted for almost three quarters of the US market at 50.1 per cent and 20.4 per cent respectively (*Prison Privatisation Report International*, 2003, 55: 3).

6 This accounts for less than 7 per cent of the total bed capacity for the USA (Austin and Coventry, 2001: 6).

7 The federal system held 12.6 per cent of its inmates in private facilities on 30 June 2002 whereas the average across all the states was 5.2 per cent (US Bureau of Justice, 2003).

8 However, the federal bureau of prisons has expressed concerns about the ability of the private sector to manage high security prisoners for long-term confinement, and has

drawn attention to comparative cost findings suggesting that publicly operated prisons were somewhat cheaper to operate than their private sector counterparts (*Prison Privatisation Report International*, 2002, 49: 11).

9 Including the District of Columbia. Prisoners are also detained in private prison facilities in Puerto Rico and three federal jurisdictions with prisoner custody responsibilities: the Federal Bureau of Prisons, the US Immigration and Naturalization Service and the US Marshall's Service.

10 In 1997 the state of Arizona proposed that a private prison should be built and operated in Mexico to enable the state to reduce its construction and operational costs. The proposal was not adopted because of legal and constitutional concerns, but has since been revived (*Prison Privatisation Report International*, 2002/2003, 52: 9).

11 They include management failings, structural problems, staffing deficiencies and inadequate security systems (Greene, 2000: 6). Not surprisingly, perhaps, stock market valuations for private sector security firms have also dropped substantially in recent years (Austin and Coventry, 2001: 6). This has prompted calls for the Justice Department to develop contingency plans to deal with possible disruption of services resulting from bankruptcy or other financial problems (*Prison Privatisation Report International*, 2002, 46: 9–10).

12 See *Prison Privatisation Report International* (1997, 8: 2–3; 11:3); and (1998 23: 4).

13 Other states have also legislated to prohibit private sector involvement in the prison system; for example Pennsylvania, which enacted the Private Prison Moratorium and Study Act in 1986 (Beyens and Snacken, 2000: 253; Sellers, 1993).

14 *Prison Privatisation Report International*, 2001, 38: 6-7 Moreover, the Department of Homeland Security's goal of increasing the number of 'illegal immigrants who are apprehended and detained is likely to strengthen the lifeline still further (see *Prison Privatisation Report International*, 2003 59: 6).

15 One of the most prominent and influential lobbying organizations is the American Legislative Exchange Council (ALEC), which has provided model legislation for state politicians with a view to promoting a range of right-wing policies including prison privatization, harsher sentencing measures and tax cuts (*Prison Privatisation Report International*, 2003, 54: 8, 55: 2).

16 Private prison companies contributed more than $1.1m in campaign contributions to state level candidates in fourteen southern states during the 2000 elections, most of which was targeted on candidates they particularly wished to influence, such as those serving on key committees responsible for considering prison related legislation (Institute on Money in State Politics, 2001).

17 There may be parallels here with other industrial sectors, such as the nuclear industry, in which an inability to make significant inroads in the domestic market following the Three Mile Island disaster in 1979 was offset to some extent by the 'export' of American expertise and investment in overseas nuclear programmes.

18 See, for example, our own more detailed account of the history of prison privatization in England and Wales (Cavadino and Dignan, 2002: 229–35). This is closely corroborated by Andrew McLean Williams' account of recent prison privatization experience in Queensland, which he provided us with in response to our questionnaire. We have drawn on Andrew's account, both in our analysis of the process of international expansionism, and also in describing the current state of prison privatization in Australia, below.

19 As at 30 June 2003, the overall proportion of Australian inmates held in private prisons across all state jurisdictions was 17.8 per cent (Nathan, 2004: 7). This compares with around 9 per cent at the same time in England and Wales, and only around 6.5 per cent (federal and state prisoners) in the USA.

20 See Chapter 5, Note 12.

21 An additional motive for promoting greater competition was to challenge the power and influence of the Prison Officers' Union in Queensland, which had been resisting the introduction of new working practices (Steering Committee for the Review of Commonwealth State Services, 1997: 133).

22 The other partners being Wormald Security and John Holland Constructions. All are large multinational corporations.

23 In November 2003, it changed its name to the Geo Group Inc.

24 There are echoes here of a similar restructuring of the British National Health Service, which was reorganized on a similar purchaser and provider model as part of the then Conservative government's quasi privatization reform programme during the late 1980s.

25 See *Prison Privatisation Report International* (1997, 9: 1). Ironically, the private sector CCA had previously announced that it regarded SE Asia as a no-go area, at least until United Nations minimum standards applied there.

26 The announcement, in the 1996/7 Annual Report of QCSC, covered ten remaining correctional centres, two community corrections centres, the South Queensland Transport and Escort Service and four community corrections regions, sparing only three juvenile detention centres (*Prison Privatisation Report International*, 1997, 9: 1).

27 See *Prison Privatisation Report International* (1998, 21: 7).

28 See also *Prison Privatisation Report International* (1999, 28: 1).

29 Press statement issued on 11 December 2001 and reported in *Prison Privatisation Report International* (2002, 45: 8).

30 Some reports suggest that the proportion is even higher, and could exceed 50 per cent. See, for example, *Prison Privatisation Report International* (1999, 26: 5, 32: 1). Also Harding (1998). Roth (2004: 6), however, cites a figure of 35 per cent in 2004.

31 See *Prison Privatisation Report International* (1998, 20: 7).

32 See *Prison Privatisation Report International* (1999, 32: 1).

33 See *Prison Privatisation Report International* (2001, 38: 4). This is by no means the only serious failing associated with Victoria's privately operated prisons, however. Port Phillip prison, operated by Group 4, has also been heavily criticized for its high rate of inmate deaths and attempted suicides during the first three years of operation since its opening in August 1997 (see Hayward and Aspin, 2001:4 and also *Prison Privatisation Report International* (2000, 35: 2–4, for details)).

34 As we shall see, this 'semi-privatization' model was first adopted by France, but has subsequently found favour in a number of other jurisdictions including some which, like Victoria, had initially opted for a 'total privatization' approach.

35 See *Prison Privatisation Report International* (2001, 43: 7); (2002, 46: 6); and (2004, 61: 5).

36 It was roundly denounced as a 'failed social experiment' by one critic, Fr.Peter Nordern, who is director of Victoria's Jesuit Social Services, as reported in *Prison Privatisation Report International* (1999), 32: 1.

37 The rate increased from 101 per 100,000 in 1988 to 129 per 100,000, the second highest in Australia, in 1991 (Baldry, 1994: 129).

38 The Prisons (Contract Management) Act 1990.

39 *Prison Privatisation Report International* (1998, 16: 2).

40 *Prison Privatisation Report International* (1998, 19: 2).

41 *Prison Privatisation Report International* (1999, 30: 7).

42 Now owned by Sodexho SA of France, and known as Australian Integration Management Services (AIMS); see *Prison Privatisation Report International* (2002, 46: 6). In June 2004, the same company was fined A$300,000 dollars and lost the contract to provide security at the Supreme Court in Perth following a security lapse that enabled nine prisoners to escape; *Prison Privatisation Report International* (2004, 64: 10).

43 See *Prison Privatisation Report International* (2002, 48: 3, 50: 9).

44 See *Prison Privatisation Report International* (2003, 55: 6).

45 See *Prison Privatisation Report International* (2002, 50: 9).

46 See *Prison Privatisation Report International* (2003, 55: 7). In 2004 it was reported that the ACT was planning to build a new publicly owned and operated prison for both male and female prisoners in Canberra, though private contractors would be involved in its design and construction. *Prison Privatisation Report International* (2004, 64: 12).

47 See *Prison Privatisation Report International* (2002, 48: 2).

48 James et al. (1997: 11), citing Harding (1994), state that 28 per cent of Australian prison inmates were accommodated in privately managed prisons, whereas Coyle et al. (2003: 214), citing Biles and Dalton (1999: 1–3) suggest that the proportion peaked at 15 per cent in 1999. The most reliable recent estimate is probably the Australian Bureau of Statistics' estimate of 17.8 per cent on 30 June 2003 (cited earlier; see Note 19).

49 Beverley Hughes, who was Minister for Prisons, in response to a Parliamentary question, Hansard, 6 December 2001, cited by Nathan (2003a). In 2004, 9 privately run prisons held approximately 5,000 inmates, representing around 7 per cent of the total prison population (Prison Reform Trust, 2004: 25). A tenth private prison opened its gates in June 2004.

50 In jargon parlance, it has the effect of appearing to move capital expenditure – which would otherwise appear as a deficit – 'off balance sheet'.

51 Who include the *Economist* (28 January 1995), which described the PFI as a 'sham', and 'a boon only for politicians and those businessmen keen to profit from the public purse'. See also Cavadino and Dignan (2002: 239ff.).

52 Both John Prescott (who was to become the Deputy Prime Minister) and Jack Straw (who was to become the Home Secretary) reiterated the party's clearly stated opposition to the policy and practice of prison privatization in speeches to the annual conference of the Prison Officers' Association (in 1994 and 1996 respectively). See *Prison Privatisation Report International* (1998, 21: 1).

53 In a speech made, ironically, at another annual conference of the Prison Officers' Association, on 18 May 1998.

54 Formerly known as Strangeways, and the scene of the worst riot in British prison history in 1990 (see Cavadino and Dignan, 2002).

55 Other public sector prisons have since been 'performance tested', which carries the implicit threat of privatization if they fail to improve their level of performance, despite the evident lack of enthusiasm on the part of private sector companies to take on some of the more difficult prisons. Indeed, all public sector prisons are due to be performance tested over the next seven years starting in June 2003.

56 BBC, 5 February 2003 (< www.news.bbc.co.uk/1/hi/england/27726981.stm >). See also *Prison Privatisation Report International* (2003, 53: 2).

57 Although the report mainly refers to the euphemistic term 'contestability', its implications are spelt out clearly enough in the introductory summary, which asserts that 'The benefits of competition – from the private and the voluntary sector – could be extended further, across both prison and probation (Carter, 2003: 4).

58 See *Prison Privatisation Report International* (1997, 11: 2).

59 See *Prison Privatisation Report International* (2000, 34: 1).

60 Cited in *Prison Privatisation Report International* (2003, 54: 1).

61 Initially introduced in September 2001.

62 However, the Bill only prevents private sector involvement in the correctional system where this involves the use of coercive powers, thus enabling private sector involvement in prison escort work and the construction of prisons to continue. Moreover, it authorizes the existing private management contract to continue until its expiry date in mid-2005.

63 United Nations Human Rights Committee (2002: para. 13). See also *Prison Privatisation Report International* (2002, 51: 6).

64 On 31 March 2004, the prison population totalled 187,640 while the prison estate was designed to accommodate 114,787, making for an 'official overcrowding rate' of 63.5 per cent (Department of Correctional Services, 2004: 45). However, this understates the true extent of the overcrowding problem, since much of the accommodation consists of dormitories that are intended to house between nine and eighteen prisoners, but which in practice sometimes contain as many as sixty inmates (Goyer, 2001: Chapter 2).

65 It has been estimated that as many as one-third to one half of all inmates returning to the community after serving their sentence will suffer from tuberculosis, syphilis or HIV/Aids (Goyer, 2001: Chapter 5).

66 The then Minister of Corrections, Dr Sipo Mzimela, had apparently been a prison chaplain in the United States for a time, where he became an enthusiastic advocate of the practice (Berg, 2003: 182).

67 *Prison Privatisation Report International* (1998, 16: 6); see also Berg (2003: 184); and Sloth-Nielsen (2003: 23).

68 *Prison Privatisation Report International* (1997, 10: 1).

69 An additional factor may have been unconfirmed reports suggesting that the lowest contract bids for the operation of South Africa's proposed privately run prisons compared very unfavourably at R200 per day with the then current cost to the state of R71 per day (*Prison Privatisation Report International* 1998, 20: 8, 1999, 30: 1). However, an increase in costs is not that surprising since the standard and quality care specified in the private contracts was also intended to be very much higher than in public sector prisons.

70 With around 3,000 beds each, South Africa's two private prisons are currently the largest in the world (Nathan, 2003b).

71 Or Geo Group Inc, as it is now known; see Note 23 above.

72 Estimates range from 50 per cent (*Prison Privatisation Report International* 2002, 51: 2) to 75 per cent (*Prison Privatisation Report International* 2002, 50: 10) of the entire prison budget.

73 *Prison Privatisation Report International* (2000, 34: 2, 2002, 51: 2).

74 *Prison Privatisation Report International* (2002/2003, 52: 2).

75 *Prison Privatisation Report International* (2003, 54: 3).

76 They include accommodation, catering, healthcare, buildings maintenance, transportation, work or vocational training. Functions such as reception, supervision, rehabilitation and management are discharged by the public sector, however.

77 *Prison Privatisation Report International* (2001, 44: 1).

78 *Prison Privatisation Report International* (2002/2003, 52: 2).

79 This more restricted variant is not confined to France. The Belgian government, which also faces problems of prison overcrowding and the need to expand as well as

refurbish elderly and substandard prison accommodation at a time of financial stringency, has followed the French example by involving the private sector in the construction of two prisons. So far, however, the Belgian government has likewise ruled out the possibility of privatized prison management since it is not convinced that this would be cheaper, despite the marketing efforts of Sodexho/CCA; *Prison Privatisation Report International* (1997, 8: 4). See also Beyens and Snacken (2000: 247).

80 A previous proposal to locate the semi-private prison at Schluechtern was abandoned after an adverse ruling from the Hesse Administrative Law Court which came in the wake of an opposition campaign fought by local residents (*Prison Privatisation Report International* (2003, 55: 7).

81 *Prison Privatisation Report International* (1999, 30: 2).

82 On 12 November 2004, the Serco Group announced that it had been awarded a five year contract to provide ancillary services by the Ministry of Justice for Hesse.

83 Ministerie van Justitie (1988); Haan (1990).

84 So called '*interne beheersverzelfstandiging*'; see Beyens et al. (1992) for details.

85 Notably in England and Wales (see Cavadino and Dignan, 1997: 136) and several of the Australian states,

86 *Prison Privatisation Report International* (2002, 46: 4).

87 *Prison Privatisation Report International* (2001, 44: 2).

88 *Prison Privatisation Report International* (1997, 7: 3). See also Cavadino and Dignan (1997: 158-9).

89 *Prison Privatisation Report International* (1997, 15: 2).

90 A new agency, the Correctional Association Prison Industry Cooperation (CAPIC) has been established in collaboration with the Japanese Correctional Association, with a view to achieving efficiency savings by adopting private company management style (APCCA, 2002).

91 Prisons across Japan have become increasingly overcrowded in recent years, and in 2001 the overall occupancy rate topped 100 per cent for the first time in 35 years. *Japan Today*, 3 September 2001. Accessed online at: www.japantoday.com/gidx/news163422.html (accessed on 9 October 2003).

92 Likewise, the Governor of Tokyo has asked the private sector to draw up plans to build and operate additional police cells in order to alleviate overcrowding in police detention facilities (*Prison Privatisation Report International*, 2001, 42: 2).

93 *Prison Privatisation Report International* (1997, 7: 3). See also Cavadino and Dignan (1997: 136-7) for more about the agency status of the Prison Service in England and Wales.

94 The tender is due to be allocated in April 2005, and the prison is expected to open in March 2007 (Moriyama, personal communication).

95 Note that not-for-profit organizations are involved in the provision of after-care services and in organizing the unpaid work undertaken by offenders on community service.

96 This is reflected in the decision taken by the recently elected right-wing government in Denmark, which is another Nordic social democracy, to opt for public finance and operation for a new prison it is about to commission (*Prison Privatisation Report International* (2002, 45: 2)).

97 The early prospects for prison privatization in the USA were also boosted, rather ironically, by rulings by the American courts first that states which housed prisoners in overcrowded conditions were in violation of the American Constitution's ban on the use of 'cruel and unusual punishment'; and second that individual inmates

could sue state governments if the conditions in which they were detained were unsatisfactory.

98 Wood (2003:16) points out that the related term 'prison industrial complex' refers to the corporate colonization of public policy decision making structures.

99 Including even South Africa which, despite some obvious differences, belongs in many respects – historically, legally and even linguistically (with regard to the language of government) – to the same socio-cultural as well as politico-economic bloc of states.

Part 4
IN CONCLUSION

17

'A Boot Stamping upon a Human Face Forever'?

'If you want a picture of the future, imagine a boot stamping on a human face – for ever. (Orwell, 1990)

Some patterns, some lessons, some puzzles

We never thought that this book would be the last word on comparative penology. We do hope, however, that it is a useful contribution to a subject which is only just starting to develop. At the risk of stating what may be fairly obvious by now, certain patterns emerge from the stories we have been telling about punishment in the countries we have studied; we hope there are some lessons to be learnt; but we are inevitably left with some puzzles about why punishment has taken the turns it has in these countries – and indeed more generally – and *how* such developments occur. And there are puzzling problems about the direction penality might take in the future, and how its direction might best be influenced.

First, some patterns.[1] one of these has dominated this book, namely the link between penality and different types of political economy – neo-liberal, conservative corporatist, social democratic corporatist and oriental corporatist – with declining levels of punishment as we progress through this list. Even this pattern is far from watertight when viewed in a historical context – it is not an iron law of penality – for as we have seen, Finland and the Netherlands used to be exceptions to the rule. We have also found intermittently useful Savelsberg's (1999) two-dimensional typology that focuses on whether a country's political system is centralized or decentralized, bureaucratized or 'personalized', although we have suggested a couple of refinements to his theory (see Chapters 7, 8, 10 and 11). More generally, we have found that our general 'radical pluralist approach' (a framework which can accommodate analyses such as Savelsberg's) seems to work well enough to encompass the phenomena we have studied.

A pattern which is also a lesson – if hardly a surprising one – is that penal crisis is associated with high levels of punishment, and in particular with a high imprisonment rate, which tends to bring with it a crisis of stretched penal resources and strains giving rise to prison overcrowding and problems of conditions, control and legitimacy. These problems are exacerbated by the prominence of the 'law and order ideology' which gives rise to such levels of punishment; this ideology is a ravenous beast which rarely seems satisfied however much punishment we feed it with. But even here, crisis and punishment levels are not invariably associated with perfect precision. It would seem that, as we write, New Zealand (imprisonment rate 179 per 100,000 population in 2004) is suffering fewer signs of crisis than Sweden (imprisonment rate 80), because of the strains brought on by a *sudden* upward rise in punishment in Sweden.

We have also seen, to our gratification, that as we have argued elsewhere *sentencing is the crux of penal crisis* (Cavadino and Dignan, 2002: Chapter 4). That is, we have invariably found that – while for example laws and policies regarding the remanding of suspects in custody can have an important effect – it is the sentences passed on offenders by courts which have the greatest impact on both prison numbers and on how near or far a country is to penal crisis.[2] But the lesson is not that crisis can be easily avoided by doing something simple about sentencing, such as passing new laws to encourage more lenient sentencing, or providing attractive new alternatives to imprisonment. These can have their place, but are likely to be insufficient on their own: sentencing seems to have a relative autonomy from both legislation and the provision of non-custodial alternatives. In Germany, for example, the legislative 'great reform' of 1969 was successful in bringing about a sharp immediate (but temporary) drop in prison numbers, but a later reduction in imprisonment between 1983 and 1991 owed little to legislation but much to a change in attitude on the part of judges and prosecutors (see Chapter 7). On the other hand, in France in the 1980s (see Chapter 9) Socialist legislation aimed at curbing imprisonment failed due to the way it was implemented by the judges. In Finland, a 'strategy of encouragement' to use alternatives to imprisonment was successful despite a relative paucity of non-custodial penalties; yet similar strategies in France and England have been failures despite much wider provision of alternatives (see Chapters 4, 9 and 10). More crucial than any such legislative and governmental measures appears to be *the penal culture among sentencers* – although this is of course by no means hermetically insulated from the more general mood and temper of the times. The challenge for would-be penal reformers is to find ways of successfully encouraging the desired shifts in sentencing culture.

Note, however, that when we refer to a penal or sentencing *culture*, we do not mean a penal *philosophy*. One might imagine that a nation's adherence to such differing abstract philosophies as retributivism or criminological positivism might make a consistent difference to its levels of punishment. One might further imagine that, given the traditionally harsh image of the retributive philosophy and the 'softness' of a positivistic welfare approach in the public mind, that the latter would necessarily lead to a more lenient penality. The reality seems not to be so simple (see also Cavadino and Dignan, 2002: 41). We have seen that imprisonment rates decreased in the USA in the 1960s when positivism was at its most popular and increased from the 1970s onwards when other approaches (mostly, however, not retributivist in nature) supplanted it (see Chapter 3).[3] And it seems likely that there is some association between the continuing belief in the notion of resocialization in conservative corporatist countries – and indeed in Japan – and their relative leniency compared to some nations with different ideas on the subject. We also suggested in Chapter 7 – though more tentatively – that the older retributive tradition in Germany may have contributed to a relatively harsh penality prior to the late 1960s. And yet the adoption of sentencing laws based on the retributive principle of 'just deserts' in Sweden and Finland in the 1970s and 1980s did not lead to greater harshness; indeed, in Finland the change was followed by a substantial decrease in the prison population. Retributivism in penal philosophy, it seems, can have harsh or lenient results. It is 'law and order ideology' – most often associated with an emphasis, not on desert, but on deterrence and incapacitation – which gives rise to the harshest results. At bottom, however, we would venture that the lesson to be learnt is this: it is not so much the abstract penal philosophy that counts so much as the prevailing *inclusionary or exclusionary* attitude towards offenders which counts for most.

Some patterns give rise to puzzles. One which continues to trouble us is this. We think we have demonstrated that the position of a country within our typology of political economies has an important effect on the punishment level of that country. But why, exactly? In Chapter 1 we talked, mostly in rather general terms, about the different 'cultures' associated with these political economies, and the 'attitudes' to offenders which tend to go along with them. A simple explanation for the penal pattern would be that in neo-liberal countries *people generally* have harsher attitudes towards offenders than people do in conservative corporatist countries, who in turn are less tolerant of the deviant than those in social democracies, and these attitudes feed through into the political realm, into legislation, and into the attitudes and sentencing practices of judges. So public sentiments form the link between political economy and penality. The problem is that, as we saw in Chapter 1 (see especially Table 1.3), the association between *public attitudes* and political economy seems to be much weaker than that between political economy and punishment levels, and so is the link between public sentiments and punishment. For example – assuming that the findings of the public attitude surveys can be trusted – going by public attitudes, conservative corporatist France should have a lower imprisonment rate than social democratic Sweden, but she doesn't. The intermediary variable of public attitudes does not appear to be doing its work properly.

One possible (but doubtless only partial) solution to this conundrum could be found in Marx's dictum that 'the ruling ideas of each age have ever been the ideas of its ruling class' (Marx, 1977: 236). A harsh neo-liberalism and a harsh penality, for example, tend to go together because those with power – the socio-political elite and the penal elite – have similar ideas and attitudes, and it is they who can do most to shape both the political economy itself and the nation's penality. They do not necessarily take the populace with them all the way on either score. It is notable that developments in the direction of neo-liberalism have met with strong popular resistance in many countries – in our sample, France, Germany, Italy and Sweden are clear examples of this – despite being represented by the political establishment as economic necessities in the modern globalized marketplace. Similarly, a country's imprisonment rate cannot be assumed to be some perfect Durkheimian reflection of the sentiments of 'the people'. But perhaps – as political systems currently work – both political economy and punishment are largely the result of the sentiments of those people whose wishes count for most.

'A boot stamping upon a human face forever?'

Perhaps the biggest issue, and the biggest puzzle, is whether penality is fated to become harsher and harsher – as it has been doing in most of the countries surveyed – or whether there are any lessons to be learnt from our studies which indicate how an ever more punitive future could be avoided, or might simply fail to come to pass.

We are not gifted penal futurologists – we know of few people who are – and in any event it may well be that the future is open, not only in the sense of being uncertain and unpredictable, but also in being not inevitable. There may be several possible penal futures, and it could be a combination of chance and human endeavour that determines which one comes to pass. Having said that, we can perceive two possible general directions for penality, one involving a continuing increase in harshness and another (which, it will surprise few, we would rather see) in which there is a turning away from an ever more punitive society.

The penal pessimist would argue for the first scenario in the following manner. We know the penal trends of the recent past and the present, and we have some idea what has caused them (see especially Chapter 2). There is no reason to believe that such trends will stop in the foreseeable future, let alone reverse themselves. For they are in turn brought about by other trends, including the onward march of neo-liberal globalization, increased 'personalism' and populism in politics and the media, collapse of trust in government and the state, and a runaway burgeoning of individualism which is spreading from neo-liberal countries into the more communitarian world of conservative corporatist and social democratic nations. And there is in turn no reason to predict the halting of these trends either. Admittedly several of our countries have seen occasional reductions in imprisonment rates over the last half-century, but these have almost always proved to be temporary in the long run. As we highlighted in Chapter 4 (in the context of England and Wales), the long-term trend is upwards, even if there are zig-zags. The Netherlands went from being a 'beacon of enlightenment' to a nation with a fast-escalating prison population (Chapter 8); and even Finland's remarkable slashing of her imprisonment rate from 118 per 100,000 population in 1976 to 46 in 1999 has been followed by a sharp bounce back (Chapter 10). The penal optimist, on the other hand, could argue that trends never last forever. We saw at the end of Chapter 3 that there have even been detectable signs of a slight weakening of the law and order tide in the USA recently, and noted Michael Tonry's (2004) theory that a 'cycle of intolerance' is coming to an end (see Cavadino, 2005). So far, however, the evidence for this looks slim to us.

But there is no need to accept that the pessimistic scenario is inevitable. The social developments which have contributed to greater punitiveness (see especially Chapter 2) may have made greater penal harshness explicable, even maybe predictable (though we cannot recall many criminologists who did predict it). And the increasing populism of politics doubtless makes it advantageous in electoral terms for politicians to deploy 'tough' rhetoric and policies. But none of this makes harsh punishment a *rational* response to crime. Excessive punishment remains not only inhumane but demonstrably inefficient and ineffective as a means of controlling crime in any kind of political economy (see, for example, Cavadino et al., 1999: 37–40). It is also, of course, extremely expensive. Indeed, one reason for relative optimism (or at least for less than total pessimism) is the consideration that continually increasing levels of punishment must surely eventually become too intolerably expensive for political economies to cope with (see Chapter 3). Such an economic crunch point could be a long way off, but in the meantime its prospect – and the growing strains of developing penal crisis – could lead the more far-sighted to seek ways of avoiding it. The unpleasant counter-thought is that it could take a severe penal crisis or even catastrophe before such solutions are seriously pursued.

The irrationality of penal harshness suggests that the way forward might lie in pursuing policy-making frameworks which have a chance of fostering rational discussion and deliberation about how to respond to crime. Thus, for example, Michael Tonry (2004) recommends that the USA should abolish the direct election of judges and prosecutors and moving towards a European model whereby these officials are more like career civil servants than politicians, along with delegation of the task of making penal policies and rules to administrative agencies such as sentencing commissions. In other words, punishment in the USA should be more insulated from the world of electoral politics and kept in a semi-autonomous realm in which rational and informed thought has a chance to predominate over the knee-jerk reactions which are the stuff of populist politics. This recipe is one which seeks to claw back penal policy-making from the realm of populism (and indeed from the people) by largely reserving it to members of a free-floating penal elite – as has typically been the case in Western countries in the past. The problems with this are that, first, this is a genie which is likely to strongly resist being put back in its bottle. And second, that even if this is achieved the genie may well burst out some time in the future with alarming results. One could say that the penal elitism strategy as pursued in the Netherlands has come horribly unstuck since the 1980s (see Chapter 8). Generational change in the penal elite combined with a growing susceptibility to populist pressures for harshness has led to a rapidly rising prison population. Something similar may be happening in Sweden, and could also happen in Finland and Japan.

Gerry Johnstone (2000) puts forward a strategy which is in some respects the opposite of the elitist one. He calls for 'a move towards much more regular and meaningful public participation in penal policy making' (p. 172). Some will doubtless find this an alarming recipe for populist punitiveness, but Johnstone's intention is to combat populism – where elite politicians exploit the unthought-out prejudices of uninvolved voters – by involving and informing citizens, and thereby generating *reasoned* responses to crime. Such reasoned responses are a goal which Johnstone shares with Tonry. Models for such meaningful citizen participation include certain crime prevention and public safety initiatives and certain community-oriented versions of restorative justice. While a strategy such as this may have its dangers and drawbacks, and require much laborious effort over a long time period, Johnstone is surely right that a purely elitist approach is no longer tenable. The public cannot be excluded from penal policy-making; if they are, their voice will make itself heard through the channels of populist politics. The challenge is to encourage rational and informed public debate about punishment. The era of globalized information poses obstacles to this, with the domination of tabloid media and the contemporary citizen's supposed three-minute attention span; but it must surely present some opportunities as well.

We can hardly be blindly optimistic about the prospects. But one final lesson that does seem clear to us from the patterns we have perceived is that the pursuit of a humane and rational penality is intimately bound up with the struggle for a humane society generally. As Downes and Hansen (forthcoming) say, 'a substantial Welfare State is increasingly a principal, if not the main protection against the resort to mass imprisonment'. If we can achieve a decent society, we will be able to punish with decency.

Notes

1 We are only picking out a few notable patterns here. Several other patterns – relating to, for example, the development of managerialism and bifurcation in most or all of

these countries, the effects of 'wars on drugs', racial injustice and panics surrounding immigration – are also apparent, but we will leave these for another time.

2 This is not to belittle the serious problems posed by the use of pre-trial detention in some of the countries we have been studying, notably France and Italy.

3 Similarly, McMahon (1992) found a decline in Ontario's imprisonment rate in the 1960s and early 1970s, which she attributes to a strong prevailing belief in the rehabilitative philosophy.

References

Aalto, M. (2002) 'The Finnish juvenile justice system'. Paper presented at the 2nd International Association of Prosecutors (IAP) European Regional Conference held at the Hague, 20–22 March 2002.

Adam, H., Albrecht, H.-J. and Pfeiffer, C. (1986) *Jugendrichter und Jugendstaatsanwälte in der Bundesrepublik Deutschland*. Freiburg: Max-Planck-Institut für Strafrecht.

Aho, T. (1997) 'Land of decreasing prison population', in HEUNI (1997) *Prison Population in Europe and in North America: Problems and Solutions*. Helsinki: Ministry of Justice, pp. 269–76

Albrecht, H.-J. (1997) 'Sentencing and punishment in Germany', in Tonry and Hatlestad (1997), pp. 181–7.

Albrecht, H-J. (2004) 'Youth justice in Germany', in M. Tonry and A.N. Doob (eds), *Crime and Justice: A Review of Research*, 31. Chicago: University of Chicago Press, pp. 443–93.

Alder, C. and Wundersitz, J. (eds) (1994) *Family Conferencing and Juvenile Justice: The Way Forward or Misplaced Confidence?* Canberra: Australian Institute of Criminology.

Alderson, J. (1989) *Off the Treadmill*, BBC Radio Four, 15 August 1989.

Allen, C., Crow, I. and Cavadino, M. (2000) 'Evaluation of the youth court demonstration project'. Home Office Research Study No. 214. London: Home Office.

Allen, H., Simonsen, C. and Latessa, E. (2004) *Corrections in America: An Introduction*. Upper Saddle River, NJ: Pearson Prentice Hall, 2004.

American Friends Service Committee (1971) *Struggle for Justice*. New York: Hill and Wang.

Ammon, D., Campbell, R. and Somoza, S. (1992) *The Option of Prison Privatization: A Guide for Community Deliberations*. Athens, GA: University of Georgia.

Amnesty International (1998) *Japan: Abusive Punishments in Japanese Prisons*. Amnesty International Report – ASA 22/004/1998. 1 June 1998. Also available online at: http://web.amnesty.org/ai.nsf/Index/ASA220041998?OpenDocument&of=COUNTRIES\JAPAN

Amnesty International (2001) *Japan: Annual Report Covering Events from January to December 2000*. Also available online at: http://www.web.amnesty.org/web/ar2001.nsf/webasacountries/JAPAN?OpenDocument

Arndt, H. et al. (1989) *Children and Juveniles in Prisons in South Africa: Report by an Interdisciplinary Group from Switzerland and Germany*. Heidelberg: Druckerei Gebard.

Arnold, J. (1995) 'Corrections in the German Democratic Republic: a field for research', *British Journal of Criminology*, 35: 81–94.

Asian and Pacific Conference of Correctional Administrators (APCCA) (2001) *Prison Statistics, Asia and the Pacific, 2000*. Record of the 20th APCCA conference. Available online at: http://www.apcca.org/pubs/20th/appendixG.html

Asian and Pacific Conference of Correctional Administrators (APCCA) (2002) *Prison Statistics, Asia and the Pacific, 2002*. Record of the 22nd APCCA conference. Available online at: http://www.apcca.org/main_statistics_22nd_APCCA.htm

Asquith, S. (1983) *Children and Justice: Decision-Making in Children's Hearings and Juvenile Courts.* Edinburgh: Edinburgh University Press.

Atkinson, L. (1995) 'Boot camps and justice: A contradiction in terms?', *Trends and Issues in Crime and Criminal Justice* No. 46, Canberra: Australian Institute of Criminology.

Audit Commission (1996) *Misspent Youth: Young People and Crime.* London: Audit Commission.

Audit Commission (2004) *Youth Justice 2004: A Review of the Reformed Youth Justice System.* London: Audit Commission.

Austin, J. and Coventry, G. (2001) *Emerging Issues on Privatized Prisons.* National Council on Crime and Delinquency Bureau of Justice Assistance Monograph. Available online at: http://www.ncjrs.org/pdffiles1/bja/181249.pdf or at: http://www.ncjrs.org/txtfiles1/bja/181249.txt

Australian Bureau of Statistics (1997) '705.0 Population, distribution, indigenous australians 1996'. Press Release.

Australian Bureau of Statistics (1999) 'Australia now – a statistical profile: crime and justice corrective services'. Available at: http://www.abs.gov.au/Ausstats/ABS@.nsf/

Australian Institute of Criminology (2002) *Australian Crime – Facts and Figures 2001.* Canberra: Australian Institute of Criminology.

Baldry, E. (1994) 'USA prison privateers: neo-colonists in a southern land', in P. Moyle (ed.), *Private Prisons and Police: Recent Australian Trends,* pp. 125–38. Leichhardt, NSW: Pluto Press Australia.

Baldus, D.C., Woodworth, G.W. and Pulaski, C.A., Jr (1989) *Equal Justice and the Death Penalty: A Legal and Empirical Analysis,* NorthEastern University Press.

Barclay, G. and Tavares, C. (2002) *International Comparisons of Criminal Justice Statistics 2000.* Home Office Statistical Bulletin 05/02. London: Home Office. Also available online at: http://www.homeoffice.gov.uk/rds/pdfs/hosb601.pdf

Barclay, G., Tavares, C. and Siddique, A. (2001) *International Comparisons of Criminal Justice Statistics.* Home Office Statistical Bulletin. 06/01. London: Home Office.

Bareja, M. and Charlton, K. (2003) *Statistics on Juvenile Detention in Australia, 1981–2002.* Australian Institute of Criminology Technical and Background paper series. No. 5. Canberra: AIC.

Barry, B. (1973) *The Liberal Theory of Justice.* Oxford: Oxford University Press.

Beccaria, C. (1963) *On Crimes and Punishments.* Indianapolis, IN: Bobbs-Merrill.

Beck, A.J. et al. (1997) 'Correctional populations in the United States, 1995', Washington DC: Bureau of Justice Statistics.

Becker, G. (1968) 'Crime and punishment: an economic approach', *Journal of Political Economy,* 76: 169–217.

Beckett, K. (1997) *Making Crime Pay: Law and Order in Contemporary American Politics.* Oxford: Oxford University Press.

Beckett, K. and Western, B. (2001) 'Governing social marginality: welfare, incarceration, and the transformation of state policy', *Punishment and Society,* 3: 43–59.

Berg, J. (2003) 'Prison privatization developments in South Africa', Chapter 15 in Coyle et al. (2003).

Beyens, K. and Snacken, S. (1996) 'Prison privatization: an international perspective' in R. Matthews and P. Francis (eds), *Prisons 2000: An International Perspective on the Current State and Future of Imprisonment.* Basingstoke: Macmillan Press Ltd.

Beyens, K., Snacken, S and Eliaerts, C. (1992) *Privatizing van Gavangenissen,* Brussels: VUB Press.

Biles, D. and Dalton, V. (1999) 'Deaths in private prisons, 1990–1999: a comparative study', *Australian Institute of Criminology, Trends and Issues in Crime and Justice*, June 1999.

Blunkett, D. (2004) *Reducing Crime, Changing Lives*. London: Home Office.

Bonczar, T.P. (1997) *Characteristics of Adults on Probation, 1995*. Washington DC: BJS.

Bonczar, T.P. and Beck, A.J. (1997) *Lifetime Likelihood of Going to State or Federal Prison*. Washington DC: Bureau of Justice Statistics, March.

Bottomley, A.K. (1980) 'The "justice model" in America and Britain: development and analysis', in A.E. Bottoms and R.H. Preston (eds), *The Coming Penal Crisis: A Criminological and Theological Exploration*. Edinburgh: Scottish Academic Press, pp. 25–52.

Bottomley, A.K. (1986) 'Blue-prints for criminal justice: reflections on a policy plan for the Netherlands', *Howard Journal of Criminal Justice*, 25: 199–215.

Bottoms, A.E. (1983) 'Neglected features of contemporary penal systems', in D. Garland and P. Young (eds), *The Power to Punish: Contemporary Penality and Social Analysis* London: Heinemann, pp. 166–202.

Bottoms, A.E. (1995) 'The philosophy and politics of punishment and sentencing', in Clarkson and Morgan (1995), pp. 17–49.

Bottoms, A.E. (1995) 'The philosophy and politics of punishment and sentencing', in C. Clarkson and R. Morgan (eds), *The Politics of Sentencing Reform*. Oxford: Clarendon Press, pp. 17–49.

Bottoms, A.E. (2002) 'Policy and practice in England and Scotland', in M.K. Rosenheim, F.E. Zimring, D.S. Tanenhaus and B. Dohrn (eds), *A Century of Juvenile Justice*. Chicago: University of Chicago Press, Chapter 8.

Bottoms, A.E. and Dignan, J. (2004) 'Youth justice in Great Britain', in M. Tonry and A.N. Doob (eds), *Crime and Justice: A Review of Research*, 31. Chicago: University of Chicago Press, pp. 21–183.

Bottoms, A.E., Brown, P., McWilliams, B., McWilliams, W. and Nellis, M. (1990) *Intermediate Treatment and Juvenile Justice*. London: HMSO.

Braithwaite, J. (1989) *Crime, Shame and Reintegration*, Cambridge: Cambridge University Press.

Brody, S.R. (1976) *The Effectiveness of Sentencing*. Home Office Research Study No. 35. London: HMSO.

Brown, D. (1991) 'The state of the prisons in NSW under the Greiner government: definitions of value', *Journal of Justice Studies*, 4: 27–60.

Brown, D. (1998) 'Penality and imprisonment in Australia', in Weiss and South (1998) pp. 367–400.

Brown, M.J.A. (2000) *Care and Protection Is About Adult Behaviour: The Ministerial Review of the Department of Child, Youth and Family Services*. Report to the New Zealand Minister of Social Services and Employment.

Burton, P., du Plessis, A., Leggett, T., Louw, A., Mistry, D. and van Vuuren, H. (2004) *National Victims of Crime Survey, South Africa 2003*. Monograph No. 101. Available online at: http://www.iss.co.za/pubs/Monographs/No101/Contents.html

Cahalan, M. (1979) 'Trends in incarceration in the US since 1880', *Crime and Delinquency*, 25: 9–41.

Cahill, L. and Marshall, P. (2002) *Statistics on Juvenile Detention in Australia: 1981–2001*. Australian Institute of Criminology Technical and Background Paper Series No. 1. Also available online at: http://www.aic.gov.au/publications/tbp/tbp001.pdf

Cario, R. (ed.) (1997) *La Médiation Pénale: Entre répression et réparation*. Paris: L'Harmattan.

Cario, R. (2000) *Jeunes Délinquants. A la Recherche de la Socialisation Perdue*. 2nd ed. Paris: L'Harmattan.

Carter, P. (2002) *Review of PFI and Market Testing in the Prison Service*. H.M. Prison Service. Extracts from the executive summary are available online at: http://www.hmprisonservice.gov.uk/library/dynpage.asp?Page=964 (accessed 25 September 2003).

Carter, P. (2003) *Managing Offenders, Reducing Crime*. London: Home Office.

Castaignède, J. (2003) 'La Loi No. 2002-1138 du 9 September 2002: Un nouveau regard porté sur le droit pénal des mineurs. *Le Dalloz*, no. 12, pp. 779-85.

Cavadino, M. (1997a) *The Law of Gravity: Offence Seriousness and Criminal Justice*. Sheffield: Joint Unit for Social Services Research.

Cavadino, M. (1997b) 'A vindication of the rights of psychiatric patients', *Journal of Law and Society*, 24: 235-51.

Cavadino, M. (2005) 'Review of M. Tonry, "*Thinking about crime: sense and sensibility in american penal culture*"', forthcoming in *Crime, Media, Culture*, 1: 124-7.

Cavadino, M. and Dignan, J. (1997) *The Penal System: An Introduction*. 2nd edn. London: Sage.

Cavadino, M. and Dignan, J. (2002) *The Penal System: An Introduction*. 3rd edn. London: Sage.

Cavadino, M., Crow, I. and Dignan, J. (1999) *Criminal Justice 2000: Strategies for a New Century*. Winchester: Waterside Press.

Centre for Public Services (2002) *Privatising Justice: The Impact of the Private Finance Initiative in the Criminal Justice System*. London: Justice Forum/Centre for Public Services. Also available online at: http://www.centre.public.org.uk/briefings/privatisingjustice.pdf (Accessed 2 October 2003).

Cesaroni, C. and Doob, A.N. (2003) 'The decline in support for penal welfarism: evidence of support among the elite for punitive segregation', *British Journal of Criminology* 43: 434-41.

Christie, N. (1968) 'Changes in penal values', in N. Christie et al. (eds), *Scandinavian Studies in Criminology*. Halden: Universiteitsforlaget, pp. 161-72.

Christie, N. (1977) 'Conflicts as property', *British Journal of Criminology*, 17: 1-15.

Christie, N. (1993) *Crime Control as Industry: Towards Gulags Western Style?* London: Routledge.

Christie, N. (1994) *Crime Control as Industry: Towards GULAGS, Western Style*, 2nd edn. London: Routledge.

CIA, *The World Factbook*. Available online at: http://www.odci.gov/cia/publications/factbook/index.html

Clarkson, C. and Morgan, R. (eds) (1995) *The Politics of Sentencing Reform*. Oxford: Clarendon Press.

Clifford, W. (1976) *Crime Control in Japan*. Lexington, MA: D.C. Heath and Co.

Collier, P. and Tarling, R. (1987) 'International comparison of prison populations', *Home Office Research Bulletin*, 23: 48-54.

Combessie, P. (2001) 'France', in van Zyl Smit and Dünkel (2001), pp. 253-87.

Commission d'Enquête sur la Délinquance des Mineurs (Commission of Inquiry into Juvenile Delinquency) (2002) *La République en quête de respect*. Les Rapports du Sénat, no. 340, 2001-2, pp. 163ff.

Commission of Inquiry into the Prison System (1989) *Report of the Commission of Inquiry into the Prison System (Roper Report)*. Wellington: Department of Justice.

Community Law Centre (South Africa) (1997) *Children in Prison in South Africa: A Situational Analysis*. Bellville: University of the Western Cape.

Corghi, C. (2000) 'Minors under the Italian juvenile justice system'. Paper delivered at the conference on Strengthening and Implementation of Effective Judicial Protection of Minors in the Russian Federation, St Petersburg, 20-1 April 2000.

Council of Europe (1987) *Recommendation No. R(87) 20 of the Committee of Ministers to Member States on Social Reactions to Juvenile Delinquency.* Adopted by the Committee of Ministers on 17 September 1987 at the 410th meeting of the Ministers' Deputies. Strasbourg: Council of Europe.

Council of Europe (1987 and 2003) *Recommendation Rec (2003) 20 of the Committee of Ministers to Member States Concerning New Ways of Dealing with Juvenile Delinquency and the Role of Juvenile Justice.* Adopted by the Committee of Ministers on 24 September 2003 at the 853rd meeting of the Ministers' Deputies. Strasbourg: Council of Europe.

Council of Europe (1993) *Report to the Dutch Government on the Visit to the Netherlands Carried out by the European Committee for the Prevention of Torture and Inhuman or Degrading Treatment or Punishment (CPT) from 30 August to 8 September 1992.* Strasbourg: Council of Europe.

Council of Europe (2000) *Penological Information Bulletin.* No. 22. Strasbourg: Council of Europe.

Coyle, A., Campbell, A. and Neufeld, R. (2003) *Capitalist Punishment: Prison Privatization and Human Rights.* London: Zed Books.

Criminal Justice Commission (2001) *Criminal Justice System Monitor Volume 5.* Brisbane: Criminal Justice Commission.

Cullen, F.T., Van Voorhuis, P. and Sundt, J.L. (1996) 'Prisons in crisis: the American experience', in R. Matthews and P. Francis (eds), *Prisons 2000: An International Perspective on the Current and Future of Imprisonment.* London: Macmillan, pp. 21–52.

Currie, E. (1985) *Confronting Crime.* New York: Pantheon.

Currie, E. (1996) *Is America Really Winning the War on Crime and Should Britain Follow its Example?* London: NACRO.

Currie, E. (1998) *Crime and Punishment in America.* New York: Henry Holt.

Daly, K. (2001) 'Conferencing in Australia and New Zealand: Variations, research findings and prospects', in A.M. Morris and G. Maxwell (eds), *Restorative Justice for Juveniles: Conferencing, Mediation and Circles.* Oxford: Hart Publishing, Chapter 4.

Daly, K. and Hayes, H. (2001) 'Restorative justice and conferencing in Australia', *Trends and Issues in Crime and Criminal Justice*, No. 186. Canberra: Australian Institute of Criminology.

Dean, M. (2002) 'Major reforms ahead for legal education in Japan', *Cavendish Publishing Academic Reporter* Issue 3, Summer 2002.

Department of Correctional Services (South Africa) (2000) *Trends in the Offender Population: January 1995 to July 2000.* Report prepared for the National Council on Correctional Services.

Department of Correctional Services (South Africa) (2001) *Annual Report 2000/2001.* Cape Town: Formeset Printers.

Department of Correctional Services (South Africa) (2003) *Annual Report 1 April 2002 to 31 March 2003.* Cape Town: Formeset Printers. Also available online at: http://www.dcs.gov.za/annual_report/Annual_Report2002/Content.htm

Department of Correctional Services (2004) *Annual Report 2003/04.* Available online at: http://www-dcs.pwv.gov.za/annual_report/Annual_Report2003.

Department of Justice (1981) *Report of the Penal Policy Review Committee.* Wellington: Department of Justice.

Department of Social Welfare (New Zealand) Ministerial Advisory Committee on a Maori Perspective (1986) *Puao-Te-Atu-Tu (Daybreak)*, Wellington: Department of Social Welfare.

de Rooy, P. (1982) 'Armenzorg in Nederland', in B. Kruithof, J. Noordman and P. de Rooyeds (eds), *Geschiedenis van Opvoeding en Onderwijs*, pp. 96–105. Nijmegen: SUN.

Dignan, J. (1999a) 'Restorative crime prevention in theory and practice', *Prison Service Journal*, 123: 2–5.

Dignan, J. (1999b) 'The Crime and Disorder Act and the prospects for restorative justice', [1990] *Criminal Law Review*, 48–60.

Dignan, J. (2002) 'Restorative justice and the law: the case for an integrated, systemic approach', in L. Walgrave (ed.), *Restorative Justice and the Law*. Leuven: Leuven University Press.

Dignan, J. (2005) *Understanding Victims and Restorative Justice*. Buckingham: Open University Press.

Dignan, J. and Cavadino, M. (2003) 'Globalisation and comparative penal policy'. Paper delivered at the Sheffield Globalisation Conference, University of Sheffield, April 2003.

Dignan, J. and Marsh, P. (2001) 'Restorative justice and family group conferences in England', in A. Morris and G. Maxwell (eds), *Restorative Justice for Juveniles: Conferencing, Mediation and Circles*. Oxford: Hart Publications, Chapter 5.

Dilulio, J. (1990) 'The duty to govern: a critical perspective on the private management of prisons and jails', in D. McDonald (ed.), *Private Prisons and the Public Interest*. New Brunswick: Rutgers University Press, pp. 155–78.

Doek, J.E. (2002) 'Modern juvenile justice in Europe', Chapter 16 in M.K. Rosenheim, F.E. Zimring, D.S. Tanenhaus and B. Dohrn (eds), *A Century of Juvenile Justice*. Chicago: University of Chicago Press.

Doob, A.N. and Sprott, J.B. (2004) 'Youth justice in Canada', in M. Tonry and A.N. Doob (eds), *Crime and Justice: A Review of Research*, 31. Chicago: University of Chicago Press, pp. 185–242.

Doob, A.N. and Tonry, M. (2004) 'Varieties of youth justice', in M. Tonry and A.N. Doob (eds), *Crime and Justice: A Review of Research*, 31. Chicago: University of Chicago Press, pp. 1–20.

Downes, D. (1982) 'The origins and consequences of Dutch penal policy since 1945', *British Journal of Criminology*, 22: 325–62.

Downes, D. (1988) *Contrasts in Tolerance: Post-War Penal Policy in The Netherlands and England and Wales*. Oxford: Oxford University Press.

Downes, D. (1990) 'Response to Harman Franke', *British Journal of Criminology*, 30: 94–6.

Downes, D. (1997) 'Prison does wonders for the jobless figures', *The Guardian*, 25 November 1997.

Downes, D. (1998) 'The buckling of the shields: Dutch penal policy 1985–1995', in Weiss and South (1998), pp. 143–74.

Downes, D. (2001) 'The *macho* penal economy: mass incarceration in the United States – a European perspective', *Punishment and Society*, 3: 61–80.

Downes, D. and Hansen, K. (forthcoming) 'Welfare and punishment in comparative context', in S. Armstrong and L. McAra (eds), *Perspectives on Punishment: The Contours of Control*. Oxford: Oxford University Press.

Duncan, G. and Worrall, J. (2000) *The Impact of Neo-liberal Policies on Social Work in New Zealand*. See Brown (2000).

Dünkel, F. (1994) 'Untersuchungshaft als Krisenmanagement? Daten und Fakten zur Praxis der Untersuchungshaft in den 90er Jahren', *Neue Kriminalpolitik*, 6: 20–9.

Dünkel, F. (1995) 'Imprisonment in transition: the situation in the new states of the Federal Republic of Germany', *British Journal of Criminology*, 35: 95–113.

Dünkel, F. (1996a) 'Current directions in criminal policy', in W. McCarney (ed.), *Juvenile Delinquents and Young People in Danger in an Open Environment*. Winchester 1996, S. 38–74, 214–222 (Erweiterte und überarbeitete Fassung von Nr. 163).

Dünkel, F. (1996b) *Empirische Forschung Im Strafvollzug*. Bonn: Forum Verlag Godesberg.

Dünkel, F. (1998) 'Juvenile justice systems in Europe – legal aspects and actual developments', in UNAFEI Resource Material Series No. 52. Fuchu, Tokyo 1998, S. 275–321.

Dünkel, F. (2003) 'Youth violence and juvenile justice in Germany', in F. Dünkel (ed.), *Youth Violence: New Patterns and Local Responses – Experiences in East and West*. Mönchengladbach: Forum Verlag Godesberg, pp. 96–141.

Dünkel, F. and Morgenstern, C. (2001) 'Überbelegung im Strafvollzug – Gefnangenraten im internationalen Vergleich', in G. Britz, H. Jung, H. Koriath and E. Müller (eds), *Grundfragen Staatlichen Strafens*. Munich: Verlag C.H. Beck, pp. 133–70.

Dünkel, F. and Rössner, D. (2001) 'Germany', in van Zyl Smit and Dünkel (2001), pp. 288–350.

Dünkel, F., van Kalmthout, A. and Schüler-Springorum, H. (eds) (1997) *Entwicklungstendenzen und Reformstrategien im Jugendstrafrecht im Europäischen Vergleich*. Mönchengladbach: Forum Verlag Godesberg.

Durkheim, É. (1964) *The Rules of Sociological Method*. New York: Free Press.

Elkins, M. and Olagundaye, J. (2001) *The Prison Population in 2000: A Statistical Review*, Home Office Research Findings No. 154. London: Home Office.

Esping-Andersen, G. (1990) *The Three Worlds of Welfare Capitalism*. Cambridge: Polity Press.

Eysenck, H.J. (1954) *The Psychology of Politics*. London: Routledge and Kegan Paul.

Eysenck, H.J. (1958) *Sense and Nonsense in Psychology*, revised edn. Harmondsworth: Penguin.

Fagan, J. and Feld, B.C. (2001) 'Juvenile justice in the United States'. Paper presented at a conference on 'Crime and justice' – a review of research on comparative juvenile justice, held at Cambridge, 18–20 October 2001.

Faugeron, C. (1991) 'Prisons in France: stalemate or evolution?' in van Zyl Smit and Dünkel (1991) pp. 249–78.

Faulkner, D. (1996) *Darkness and Light: Justice, Crime and Management for Today*. London: Howard League.

Faust, F.L. and Brantingham, P.J. (1979) *Juvenile Justice Philosophy: Readings, Cases and Comments*, 2nd edn. St Paul, MN: West Publishing Co.

Feeley, M. and Simon, J. (1992) 'The New Penology', *Criminology*, 39: 449–74.

Feeley, M.M. (1991) 'The privatization of prisons in historical perspective', *Criminal Justice Research Bulletin*, 6: 1–10.

Feeley, M.M. (2002) 'Entrepreneurs of punishment: the legacy of privatization', *Punishment and Society*, 4: 321–44.

Feest, J. (1982) *Imprisonment and the Criminal Justice System in the Federal Republic of Germany*. Bremen: Universität Bremen.

Feest, J. (1988) *Reducing the Prison Population: Lessons from the West German Experience?* London: NACRO.

Feest, J. (1990) *New Social Strategies and the Criminal Justice System*. Strasbourg: Council of Europe, PC-CRC(90)14.

Feest, J. (1993) 'Institutional resistance against prisoners' rights', *Howard Journal*, 32: 127–35.

Feest, J. and Weber, H.-M. (1998) 'Germany: ups and downs in the resort to imprisonment – strategic or unplanned outcomes?', in Weiss and South (1998) pp. 233–61.

Feld, B. (1999) *Bad Kids: Race and the Transformation of the Juvenile Court*. New York: Oxford University Press.

Fick Commission (1947) *Rapport van de Commissie voor de Verdere Uitbouw van het Gevangeniswezen*. The Hague: Staatsdrukkerij.

Finnish Ministry of Justice (2003a) *Summary: Crime Trends in Finland*. Helsinki: Ministry of Justice.

Finnish Ministry of Justice (2003b) *Nuorisorikostoimikunnan mietintö*, [English translation: Report of the Juvenile Justice Commission], Committee Report 2003:2, Ministry of Justice, Edita Publishing 2003.

Finnish Prison Service (2001) 'Principal offence of prisoners serving a sentence according to their age on 1 May 2001'. Vankeinhoito – Vankien päärikos. Available online at: http://www.vankeinhoito.fi/11143.htm

Fionda, J. (1999) 'New Labour, old hat: youth justice and the Crime and Disorder Act 1998', *Criminal Law Review*, pp. 36–47.

Fitzgerald, M. (1977) *Prisoners in Revolt*. Harmondsworth: Penguin.

Fitzgerald, M. and Sim, J. (1982) *British Prisons*, 2nd edn. Oxford: Basil Blackwell.

Fleisher, M. (2001) 'United States of America – the federal system', in van Zyl Smit and Dünkel (2001), pp. 676–94.

Flynn, N. (1995) 'Germany's crime backlash', *Prison Report*, no. 30, Spring 1995: 8–9.

Foote, D. (1992) 'The benevolent paternalism of Japanese criminal justice', *California Law Review*, 80: 317–90.

Freiberg, A. (1995) 'Sentencing reform in Victoria: a case study', in Clarkson and Morgan (1995), pp. 51–94.

Freiberg, A. (1997a) 'Sentencing reform in Victoria', in Tonry and Hatlestad (1997), pp. 148–52.

Freiberg, A. (1997b) 'Sentencing and punishment in Australia in the 1990s', in Tonry and Hatlestad (1997), pp. 156–63.

Freiberg, A. (2001) 'Three strikes and you're out – it's not cricket: colonization and resistance in Australian sentencing', in Tonry and Frase (2001), pp. 30–61.

Freiberg, A., Fox, R.G. and Hogan, M. (1988) *Sentencing Young Offenders*. Commonwealth Youth Bureau and Australian Law Reform Commission, Sydney, pp. 1–12, 56–9.

Furniss, J. (1996) 'The population boom', *Corrections Today*, 58: 38–434.

Galbraith, J.K. (1993) *The Culture of Contentment*. London: Penguin Books.

Gallo, E. (1995) 'The penal system in France: from correctionalism to managerialism', in Ruggiero et al. (1995) pp. 71–92.

Gardner, D. (2002) 'Why Finland is soft on crime', *Ottawa Citizen*, 18 March 2002.

Garland, D. (1985) *Punishment and Welfare: A History of Penal Strategies*. Aldershot: Gower.

Garland, D. (1995) 'Penal modernism and postmodernism', in T. Blomberg and S. Cohen (eds), *Punishment and Social Control: Essays in Honour of Sheldon Messinger*. New York: Aldine De Gruyter, pp. 181–209.

Garland, D. (2001) *The Culture of Control: Crime and Social Order in Contemporary Society*. Oxford: Oxford University Press.

Gatto, U. and Verde, A. (1998) 'Italy', in J. Mehlbye and L. Walgrave (eds), *Confronting Youth in Europe: Juvenile Crime and Juvenile Justice*. Copenhagen: AFK Forlaget, Chapter 9.

Gaucher, B. and Lowman, J. (1998) 'Canadian prisons', in Weiss and South (1998), pp. 61–98.

Gazeau, J.-F. and Peyre, V. (1998) 'France', in J. Mehlbye and L. Walgrave (eds), *Confronting Youth in Europe: Juvenile Crime and Juvenile Justice*. Copenhagen: AFK Forlaget, Chapter 6.

Giddens, A. (1990) *The Consequences of Modernity*. Cambridge: Polity.

Gilhooly, H. (2004) *World Cultures: Japan*. London: Hodder & Staughton Ltd.

Giunta, F. (1991) 'Italy – the right to communicate with the outside world: between the "opening" of prisons and the protection of society', in van Zyl Smit and Dünkel (1991), pp. 357–82.

Goffman, I. (1961) *Asylums*. Garden City, New York: Doubleday Anchor.

Goldson, B. (ed.) (2000) *The New Youth Justice*. Lyme Regis, Dorset: Russell House Publishing.

Gorta, A. (1997) 'Truth in sentencing in New South Wales', in Tonry and Hatlestad (1997), pp. 152–6.

Goyer, K.C. (2001) *Prison Privatization in South Africa: Issues, Challenges and Opportunities.* Monograph No. 64. Pretoria: Institute for Security Studies. Also available online at: www.iss.co.za/Pubs/Monographs/No64.html (accessed 18 September 2003).

Graef, R. (1995) 'The demonization of young offenders: the new enemy within'. Paper presented at the British Criminology Conference, University of Loughborough, 20 July 1995.

Graham, J. (1990) 'Decarceration in the Federal Republic of Germany: how practitioners are succeeding where policy-makers have failed', *British Journal of Criminology*, 30: 150–70.

Greenberg, D. (1999) 'Punishment, division of labor, and social solidarity', in W.S. Laufer and F. Adler (eds), *The Criminology of Criminal Law,* Advances in Criminological Theory Vol. 8. New Brunswick: Transaction Books, pp. 283–361.

Greenberg, D. (2001) 'Novus ordo saeclorum? A commentary on Downes, and on Beckett and Western', *Punishment and Society*, 3: 81–93.

Greene, J. (2000) 'Prison privatization: recent developments in the United States'. Paper presented at the ICOPA conference, Toronto, Canada on 12 May 2000.

Greenwood, P., Rydell, C.P., Abrahamse, A., Caulkins, J.P., Chiesa, J., Model, K.E. and Klein, S.P. (1995) *Three Strikes and You're Out: Estimated Benefits and Costs of California's New Mandatory Sentencing Law* (Report No. MR-509-RC). Santa Monica: Rand Corporation.

Grossberg, M. (2002) 'Changing conceptions of child welfare in the United States, 1820–1935', in M.K. Rosenheim, F.E. Zimring, D.S. Tanenhaus and B. Dohrn (eds), *A Century of Juvenile Justice.* Chicago: University of Chicago Press, Chapter 1.

Grubb, W.N. and Lazerson, M. (1982) *Broken Promises: How Americans Fail Their Children.* New York: Basic Books.

Haan, W. (1990) 'Profyt by Privatisering van Straf: een Besprekingsartikel', *Recht en Kritiek*, 16: 135.

Haley, J.O. (1991) *Authority without Power: Law and the Japanese Paradox.* Oxford and New York: Oxford University Press.

Haley, J.O. (1996) 'Crime prevention through restorative justice: lessons from Japan', in B. Galaway and J. Hudson (eds), *Restorative Justice: International Perspectives.* Amsterdam: Kugler.

Hall, S. (1979) 'The great moving right show', *Marxism Today*, 23: 14–20.

Hall, S. (1980) *Drifting into a Law and Order Society.* London: Cobden Trust.

Hall, S. (1988) *The Hard Road to Renewal.* London: Verso.

Hall, S., Clarke, J., Critcher, C., Jefferson, T. and Roberts, B. (1978) *Policing the Crisis.* London: Macmillan.

Hallett, C. and Hazel, N. (1998) *The Evaluation of Children's Hearings in Scotland, vol. 2. The International Context: Trends in Juvenile Justice and Child Welfare.* Edinburgh: Scottish Office Central Research Unit.

Hallett, C. and Murray, C. (1998) *The Evaluation of Children's Hearings in Scotland: vol. 1: Deciding in Children's Interests.* Edinburgh: Scottish Office Central Research Unit.

Halliday, J. (2001) *Making Punishments Work: Report of a Review of the Sentencing Framework for England and Wales.* London: Home Office Communication Directorate.

Hamai, K., Villé, R., Harris, R., Hough, M. and Zvekic, U. (1995) *Probation Round the World: A Comparative Study.* London and New York: Routledge.

Hamai, K., Yokochi, T. and Okada, K. (2000) 'Victims of crime in criminal justice in Japan: a comprehensive study of victims, views of offenders and criminal justice system and offenders' views of victims'. Paper presented at the 10th international symposium of Victimology in Montreal on 7 August 2000. Also available online at: http://www.jcps.ab.psiweb.com/survey.htm

Harding, R. (1994) 'Privatising prisons: principle and practice'. Unpublished paper.

Harding, R. (1998) 'Private prisons in Australia: the second phase'. *Trends and Issues in Crime and Justice*. Number 84. April 1998. Australian Institute of Criminology.

Harms, P. (2003) 'Detention in delinquency cases, 1990–1999'. Available online from the OJJDP website at www.ojp.usdoj.gov/ojjdp

Harrison, P.M. and Karberg, J.C. (2004) *Prison and Jail Inmates at Midyear 2003*. Bureau of Justice Statistics Bulletin. NCJ203947, May 2004.

Hart, H.L.A. (1961) *The Concept of Law*. Oxford: Clarendon Press.

Haysom, N. (1981) *Towards an Understanding of Prison Gangs*. Cape Town: Institute of Criminology, University of Cape Town.

Hayward, D. and Aspin, R. (2001) *Contracting Out: Time for a Policy Rethink?* Swinburne Institute for Social Research. Also available online at: http://www.sisr.net/program-csp/seminarpapers/contracting_asphayward.PDF (accessed 23 September 2003).

Heinz, W. (1989) 'Jugendstrafrechtsreform durch die Praxis – eine Bestandsoufnahme', in Bundesministerium der Justiz (ed.), *Jugendstrafrechtsreform durch die Praxis*, Bonn: Berg Verlag, pp. 13–44.

Heinz, W. (1990) 'Gleichheit vor dem Gesetz in der Sanktionspraxis? Empirische Befunde der Sanktionsforschung im Jugendstrafrecht in der Bundesrepublik Deutschland', in H. Göppinger (ed.), *Kriminologie und Strafrechtspraxis. Tagungsberichte des kriminologischen Arbitreises*. Vol. 7, pp. 171–209. Tübingen: Aktuelle Probleme der Kriminologie.

Heinz, W. (1992) 'Abschied von der "Erziehungsideologie im Jugendstrafrecht"? Zur Diskussion über Erziehung und Strafe'. *Recht der Jugend und des Bildungswesens*, 40: 123–43.

Hill, S. (1981) *Competition and Control at Work: the New Industrial Sociology*. London: Heinemann Educational.

Hoeven, E. van der (1986) *Allochtone Jongeren by de Jeugdpolitie* (Minority juveniles at the juvenile police). Den Haag: CWOK.

Home Office (1980) *Young Offenders*, Cmnd 8045. London: HMSO.

Home Office (1988) *Punishment, Custody and the Community*, Cm 424. London: HMSO.

Home Office (1990) *Crime, Justice and Protecting the Public: The Government's Proposals for Legislation*, Cm 965. London: HMSO.

Home Office (1996) *Prison Statistics, England and Wales 1995*, Cm 3355. London: HMSO.

Home Office (1997a) *No More Excuses: A New Approach to Tackling Youth Crime in England and Wales*, Cm 3809. London: Stationery Office.

Home Office (1997b) *Prison Statistics, England and Wales 1996*, Cm 3732. London: The Stationery Office.

Home Office (2000) *Criminal Statistics England and Wales 1999*, Cm 5001. London: The Stationery Office.

Home Office (2001) *Prison Statistics England and Wales 2000*, Cm 5250. London: The Stationery Office.

Home Office (2003) *Criminal Statistics, England and Wales 2002*, Cm 6054. London: The Stationery Office.

Home Office (2004a) *Statistics on Race and the Criminal Justice System 2003*. London: Home Office.

Home Office (2004b) *Youth Justice – The Next Steps: Summary of Responses and the Government's Proposals*. London: Home Office Juvenile Offenders' Unit. Published

4 March 2004. Also available online at: http://www.homeoffice.gov.uk/docs3/youth justiceresponse.html

Home Office (2004c) *Criminal Statistics, England and Wales 2003*, Cm 6341. London: The Stationary Office.

Home Office, Lord Chancellor's Department and Youth Justice Board (2002) *Referral Orders and Youth Offender Panels: Guidance for Courts, Youth Offending Teams and Youth Offender Panels*. London: Home Office/Lord Chancellor's Department/Youth Justice Board. Also available online at: http://www.homeoffice.gov.uk/docs/referral_orders_and_yop.pdf

Hood, R. (1962) *Sentencing in Magistrates' Courts*. London: Stevens.

Hood, R. (1972) *Sentencing the Motoring Offender*. London: Heinemann.

Hood, R. (1996) *The Death Penalty: A World-Wide Perspective*, 2nd edn. Oxford: Clarendon Press.

Hosoi, Y. and Nishimura, H. (1999) 'The role of apology in the Japanese criminal justice system'. Paper presented at the Restoration for Victims of Crime Conference convened by the Australian Institute of Criminology in conjunction with the Victims and Referral Service, Melbourne, September 1999.

Hough, M. and Roberts, J. (1998) *Attitudes to Punishment: Findings from the British Crime Survey*, Home Office Research Study No. 179. London: Home Office.

Hoyle, C., Young, R. and Hill, R. (2002) *Proceed with Caution: An Evaluation of the Thames Valley Police Initiative in Restorative Cautioning*. York: Joseph Rowntree Foundation.

Hudson, B. (1987) *Justice Through Punishment: A Critique of the 'Justice Model' of Corrections*. London: Macmillan Education.

Hughes, R. (1987) *The Fatal Shore: A History of Transportation of Convicts to Australia 1787-1868*. London: Collins Harvill.

Human Rights Watch (1995) *Prison Conditions in Japan*. New York: Human Rights Watch.

Human Rights Watch (1999) *World Report 1999: South Africa: Human Rights Developments*. Available online at: http://hrw.org/worldreport99/africa/southafrica.html

Iivari, J. (1986) 'Mediation in Finland', *The Newsletter of FIRM, the forum for initiatives in Reparation and Mediation*, Volume 2, no. 3, 1986.

Iivari, J. (2000) 'Mediation in Finland', in T. Peters (ed.), *Victim–Offender Mediation in Europe. Making Restorative Justice Work*. European Forum for Victim-Offender Mediation and Restorative Justice. Leuven: KU Leuven. Also available online at: http://www.restorativejustice.org/rj3/Feature/April02/Finland.htm

Institute on Money in State Politics (2001) 'A contributing influence: the private-prison industry and political giving in the south'. Available online at: http://www.follow themoney.org/press/prisons.phtml

International Centre for Prison Studies (2004) *Prison Brief for Japan*. Available online at: http://www.kcl.ac.uk/depsta/rel/icps/worldbrief/continental_asia_records.php?code=97 (Accessed 30 July 2004).

James, A.L., Bottomley, A.K., Liebling, A. and Clare, E. (1997) *Privatizing Prisons: Rhetoric and Reality*. London: Sage.

Janson, C.-G. (2004) 'Youth Justice in Sweden', in M. Tonry and A.N. Doob (eds), *Crime and Justice: A Review of Research*, 31. Chicago. University of Chicago Press, pp. 391–441.

Japan Federation of Bar Associations (1990) *What's Daiyo-Kangoku?* Tokyo: Japan Federation of Bar Associations.

Japan Federation of Bar Associations (1992) *Prisons in Japan*. Tokyo: Japan Federation of Bar Associations.

Japan Federation of Bar Associations (1998) *Alternative Report to the Fourth Periodic Report of Japan on the International Covenant on Civil and Political Rights.* Available online at: http://www.nichibenren.or.jp/hrsympo/jrt/hreng4.htm

Japan Federation of Bar Associations (1999) *Looking for Criminal Procedure for the New Century (Atarashi seiko no keiji tetsudduki wo motomete).* Tokyo: Japan Federation of Bar Associations.

Japanese Ministry of Justice (1999) 'Summary of the White Paper on crime, 1998'. Available online at: http://www.moj.go.jp/ENGLISH/RATI/1998/rati-01.html

Japanese Ministry of Justice (2000) 'Penal code crime cases known to the police, cases cleared up and arrestees by type of crime (1980-99)' National Police Agency Criminal Investigation Agency, Table 23-1. Available online at: http://www.stat.go.jp/english/data/nenkan/1431-23.htm

Japanese Ministry of Justice (2002) *White Paper on Crime 2001.* Tokyo: Research and Training Institute, Ministry of Justice.

Japanese Ministry of Justice (2003) *White Paper on Crime 2002.* Tokyo: Research and Training Institute, Ministry of Justice.

Japanese Ministry of Justice (n.d.) *Public Prosecutor's Office.* Available online at: http://www.moj.go.jp/ENGLISH/PPO/ppo-01.html

Jareborg, N. (1995) 'The Swedish sentencing reform', in Clarkson and Morgan (1995), pp. 95-123.

Johnson, E.H. (1996) *Japanese Corrections: Managing Convicted Offenders in an Orderly Society.* Carbondale and Edwardsville, IL: Southern Illinois University Press.

Johnson, E.H. (1998) 'The Japanese experience: effects of decreasing resort to imprisonment', in Weiss and South (1998), pp. 337-66.

Johnston, H. (1995) 'Age of criminal proceedings in Europe'. *Howard League Report,* 10-4.

Johnstone, G. (2000) 'Penal policy-making: elitist, populist or participatory?', *Punishment & Society,* 2: 161-80.

Jones, R. (1984) 'Questioning the new orthodoxy', *Community Care,* 11 October: 26-9.

Joutsen, M., Lahti, R. and Pölönen, P. (2001) *Criminal Justice Systems in Europe and North America: Finland.* Helsinki: HEUNI (European Institute for Crime Prevention and Control). Also available online at: http://www.heuni.fi/uploads/mw1ahyuvuylrx.pdf

Junger-Tas, J. (1982) 'Holland', in M.W. Klein (ed.), *Western Systems of Juvenile Justice,* Beverly Hills: Sage, pp. 121-47.

Junger-Tas, J. (1983) *Jeugddelinquentie – Achtergronden en Justitiële Reactie.* WODC. Den Haag: Staatsuitgeveij.

Junger-Tas, J. (2004) 'Social welfare and youth justice in the Netherlands', in M. Tonry and A.N. Doob (eds), *Crime and Justice: A Review of Research,* 31. Chicago: University of Chicago Press, pp. 293-347.

Justitiedepartementet (1993) *Att Renovera en Förfallen Kriminalpolitik.* Stockholm: Justitiedepartementet.

Kaido, Y. (2001) 'Japan', in van Zyl Smit and Dünkel (2001), pp. 425-47.

Kangaspunta, K., Jouttsen, M., Ollus, N. and Nevala, S. (eds) (1999) *Profiles of Criminal Justice Systems in Europe and North America, 1990-4.* Helsinki: European Institute for Crime Prevention and Control (HEUNI).

Kawashima, T. (1963) 'Dispute resolution in contemporary Japan', in A.T. von Mehren (ed.), *Law in Japan: The Legal Order in a Changing Society.* Cambridge, MA: Harvard University Press, pp. 44-72.

Kearney, B. (2000) *Children's Hearings and the Sheriff Court,* 2nd edn. Edinburgh: Butterworths.

Kelk, C. (1993) 'The penal climate of the Netherlands', in *Dutch and Japanese Laws Compared.* Tokyo: International Center for Comparative Law and Politics, pp. 325-39.

Kelk, C. (2001) 'The Netherlands', in van Zyl Smit and Dünkel (2001), pp. 478–507.

Kennedy, J. (1988) *Commission of Review into Corrective Services in Queensland, Final Report*. Brisbane: QGPS.

Kerner, H.-J. (2003) 'Prisoners in the Federal Republic of Germany' *Krim-Dok-Online*. http://www.ifk.jura.uni-tuebingen.de/krimdok

Kerner, H.J. and Weitekamp, E. (1984) 'The Federal Republic of Germany', in M.W. Klein (ed.), *Western Systems of Juvenile Justice*. Beverly Hills, CA: Sage, pp. 147–70.

Kinko, S. (1984) *Why is there Less Crime in Japan?* Orientation Seminars on Japan: No. 15, The Japan Foundation, Office for the Japanese Study Center. Tokyo: Japan.

Kirby, P. (2000) *Report of the Independent Investigation into the Management and Operation of Victoria's Private Prisons* (Chairman P. Kirby), 2 vols, Melbourne: State of Victoria.

Kleinwort Benson Australia Ltd (1989) 'Investigation into private sector involvement in the New South Wales corrective services system'. Unpublished Government Report, Sydney.

Klooster, E., Slump, G.J., Nauta, O. and Burman, A. (2003) *Stopreactie: Redenen van Niet Bereik*. Amsterdam: DSP-groep.

Kochan, N. (2003) 'Is the PFI about to hit the buffers?', *The Banker*. Available online at: http://www.thebanker.com/news/archivestory.php/aid/224/Is_the_PFI_about_to_hit_the_buffers_.html (Accessed on 8 October 2003).

Komiya, N. (1999) 'A cultural study of the low crime rate in Japan', *British Journal of Criminology*, 39(3): 369–90.

Kriegler Commission (1995) *Report of the Commission of Inquiry into Unrest in Prisons*. Pretoria: Government Printer.

Krisberg, B., Schwartz, I., Litsky, P. and Austin, J. (1986) 'The watershed of juvenile justice reform', *Crime and Delinquency*, 32: 5–38.

Kruissink, M. (1990) 'The HALT programme: diversion of juvenile vandals', *Dutch Penal Law and Policy: Notes on Criminological Research from the Research and Documentation Centre*. The Hague: Dutch Ministry of Justice.

Kruissink, M. and Verwers, C. (2001). *Het Nieuwe Jeugdstrafrecht: Vijf Jaar Ervaring in de Praktijk*. Den Haag: Ministry of Justice/WODC.

Kurata, S. and Hamai, K. (1998) *Criminal Justice System at Work 1998: Outline of Crime Trends, Criminal Procedure and Juvenile Justice System in Japan*. Available online at: http://www.jcps.ab.psiweb.com/con1.htm

Lahti, R. (1977) 'Criminal sanctions in Finland: a system in transition', in F. Schmidt, *Scandinavian Studies in Law 1977*, vol. 21, pp. 121–57.

Lahti, R. (1985) 'Current trends in criminal policy in the Scandinavian countries', in N. Bishop (ed.), *Scandinavian Criminal Policy and Criminology 1980–85*, Stockholm: Scandinavian Research Council for Criminology, pp. 59–72.

Lahti, R. (1989) 'On Finnish and Scandinavian criminal policy', *Cahiers de Défense Sociale*, 1989: 64–73.

Lambie, A. (2002) 'When colour is an issue', *Howard League Magazine*, vol. 20 no. 1, February 2002: 14.

Lappi-Seppälä, T. (1992) 'Penal policy and sentencing theory in Finland', in R. Lahti et al. (eds), *Criminal Policy and Sentencing in Transition: Finnish and Comparative Perspectives*. Helsinki: Department of Criminal Law and Judicial Procedure, pp. 3–47.

Lappi-Seppälä, T. (2001) 'Sentencing and punishment in Finland: the decline of the repressive ideal', in Tonry and Frase (2001) pp. 92–150.

Lappi-Seppälä, T. (2002) 'Proportionality and other values in the Finnish sentencing system', in P. Asp, C.E. Herlitz and L. Holmqvist (eds), *Flores Juris et Legum: Festskrift till Nils Jareborg*. Uppsala: Iustus Förlag, pp. 401–28.

Lash, B. (1996) *Census of Prison Inmates 1995*. Wellington: Ministry of Justice.

Lash, S. and Urry, J. (1987) *The End of Organised Capitalism*. Cambridge: Polity.

Lash, S. and Urry, J. (1994) *Economies of Signs and Space*. London: Sage.

Lazerges, C. and Balduyck, J.P. (1998) *Réponses a la délinquance de mineurs*, rapport au Premier Ministre, Paris: La documentation française.

Leander, K. (1995) 'The normalization of Swedish prisons', in Ruggiero et al. (1995), pp. 169–93.

Lenin, V.I. (1965) *The State and Revolution*, 2nd revised edn. Moscow: Progress.

Levinson, H. (2001) 'Japan cracks down on youth crime'. BBC News Asia internet archive service, 1 March 2001.

Lilly, J.R. and Knepper, P. (1992) 'An international perspective on the privatization of corrections', *Howard Journal of Criminal Justice*, 31: 174–91.

Llewellyn, K. (1940) 'The normative, the legal and the law-jobs: the problem of juristic method', 49 *Yale Law Journal*, 1355–1400.

Lockyer, A. and Stone, F.H. (eds) (1998) *Juvenile Justice in Scotland: Twenty-Five Years of the Welfare Approach*. Edinburgh: T&T Clark.

Logan, C.H. (2002) The prison privatization research site. Available online at: http://www.ucc.uconn.edu/~logan/

Logan, C. and Rausch, S. (1985) 'Punishment for profit: the emergence of private enterprise prisons', *Justice Quarterly*, 2: 303–18.

Lukes, S. (1973) *Individualism*. Oxford: Basil Blackwell.

Luyt, W.F.M. (2001) 'The deprivation of liberty of children in South Africa'. Conference paper presented at the second world conference on the Investigation of Crime at Durban, South Africa, on 2–7 December 2001. Also available online at: http://www.tsa.ac.za/conf/papers/luyt.pdf

McConville, S. (1981) *A History of English Prison Administration, Volume 1, 1760–1877*. London: Routledge and Kegan Paul.

McCurry, J. (2004) 'Capital questions', *The Guardian*, 12 October 2004.

McDonald, D.C. (1994) 'Public imprisonment by private means: the re-emergence of private prisons and jails in the United States, the United Kingdom, and Australia.' *British Journal of Criminology*, 34: 29–48.

McDonald, D.C., Fournier, E. and Russell-Einhorn (1998) *Private Prisons in the United States: An Assessment of Current Practice*. Cambridge, MA: Abt Associates Inc.

McGold, P. and Wachtel, B. (1998) *Restorative Policing Experiment: The Bethlehem Pennsylvania Police Family Group Conferencing Project*. Pipersville, PA: Community Service Foundation.

McKee, J.-Y. (2001) *Criminal Justice Systems in Europe and North America: France*. Helsinki: HEUNI. Also available online at: http://www.heuni.fi/uploads/fq98onbf0fojy.pdf

MacKenzie, D.J. (1994) 'Boot camps: a national assessment', *Overcrowded Times*, vol. 5, no. 4, Aug.

McMahon, M.W. (1992) *The Persistent Prison? Rethinking Decarceration and Penal Reform*. Toronto: University of Toronto Press.

Maguire, K. and Pastore, A.L. (1996) *Sourcebook of Criminal Justice Statistics, 1995*. Bureau of Judicial Statistics, US Department of Justice, Washington, DC: USGPO.

Maguire, M., Morgan, R. and Reiner, R. (eds) (2002) *Oxford Handbook of Criminology*, 3rd edn. Oxford: Oxford University Press.

Mainichi Shimbun. (2002) 'Government report: crimes peaking and prisons overflowing', Mainichi Interactive News, 26 November 2001. Available online at: http://mdn.mainichi.co.jp/news/ archive/200111/16/20011116p2a00m0dm00900c.html

Marttunnen, M. (2003) 'Finnish juvenile criminal justice', reproduced in J. Francis and B. Whyte (eds) *Collection of Symposia Papers on European Youth Involved in Public Care and Youth Justice Systems*, Annex 7, as part of the ENSA Youth Project. Available online at: http://www.ensayouth.cjsw.ac.uk

Marttunnen, M. and Takala, J.-P. (2002) *Juvenile Punishment 1997–2001: Evaluation of a New Punishment*. Helsinki: The National Research Institute of Legal Policy, Publication no. 192. A summary in English is also available online at: http://www.om.fi/optula/15811.htm

Marx, K. (1977) *Selected Writings*, ed. D. McLellan. Oxford: Oxford University Press.

Masanori, Y. (2004) 'Death penalty and the media', *Japan Focus*. Available online at: http://japanfocus.org/article.asp?id=161

Masters, G. (1998) 'Reintegrative shaming in theory and practice: thinking about feeling in criminology'. Unpublished Ph.D. thesis, Lancaster University, UK.

Maurizio, R. (2003) 'Juvenile justice and social policy in Italy', in J. Francis and B. Whyte (eds), *Collection of Symposia Papers on European Youth Involved in Public Care and Youth Justice Systems*, Annex 7, as part of the ENSA Youth Project. Available online at: http://www.ensayouth.cjsw.ac.uk

Mawby, R.I. (1990) *Comparative Policing Issues: The British and American Systems in International Perspective*. London: Unwin Hyman.

Maxwell, G. and Morris, A. (1996) 'Research on family group conferences with young offenders in New Zealand', in J. Hudson and G. Maxwell (eds), *Family Group Conferences: Perspectives on Policy and Practice*. Leichhardt: The Federation Press (Australasian Studies in Criminology), pp. 88–110.

Maxwell, G., Robertson, J. and Anderson, T. (2002) *Police Youth Diversion: Final Report*. Wellington: Crime and Justice Research Centre.

Maxwell, G., Robertson, J., Kingi, V., Morris, A. and Cunningham, C. (2003) *Achieving Effective Outcomes in Youth Justice Research Projects: Final Report*. Wellington: Ministry of Social Development.

Mayhew, P. (1994) *Findings from the International Crime Survey*. Home Office Research Findings No. 8. London: Home Office.

Mayhew, P. and van Dijk, J.J.M. (1997) *Criminal Victimisation in Eleven Industrialised Countries: Key Findings from the 1996 International Crime Victimisation Survey*. The Hague: Research and Documentation Centre, Ministry of Justice.

Mayhew, P. and van Kesteren, J. (2002) 'Cross-national attitudes to punishment', in Roberts and Hough (2002), pp. 63–92.

Mayhew, P. and White, P. (1997) *The 1996 International Crime Victimisation Survey*. Home Office Research Findings No. 57. London: Home Office.

Messner, C. and Ruggiero, V. (1995) 'Germany: the penal system between past and future', in Ruggiero et al. (1995), pp. 128–48.

Miers, D. (2001) *An International Review of Restorative Justice*. Crime Reduction Research Series, Paper 10. London: Home Office.

Ministère de la Justice (2003) *Les Chiffres-Clés de la Justice. Octobre 2003*. Paris: Ministère de la Justice. Also available online at: http://www.justice.gouv.fr/chiffres/chiffres.htm

Ministère de la Justice (2004) *Les Chiffres Clés de la Justice, Octobre 2004*. Paris: Ministère de la Justice. Also available online at: http://www.justice.gouv.fr/chiffres/chiffrescles 2004.pdf

Ministerie van Justitie van Nederlands (1988) *Van Gedeelde Naar Verdeelde Verantwoorde-lykheid: Rapportage Inzake de Mogelykheden van Deconcentratie en Privatisering by de Addeling Arbeid van de Directie Genvangeniswezen*. The Hague: Ministry of Justice.

Ministerie van Justitie van Nederlands (2002) *Naar een Veiliger Samenleving*. The Hague: Ministry of Justice/Ministry of Home Affairs.

Ministero di Giustizia (2003) *Flussi di Utenza dei Servizi della Giustizia Minorile – Anno 2003*. Also available online at: http://www.giustizia.it/statistiche/statistiche_dgm/analisi_statistiche/Flussi2003.htm

Ministry of Justice (1985) *Samenleving en Criminaliteit (Society and Crime)*. The Hague: Ministry of Justice.

Ministry of Justice, (1991) *Annual Report of Statistics on Corrections, Vol. 1*. Tokyo: Corrections Bureau.

Ministry of Justice (1998) *The Use of Imprisonment in New Zealand*. Wellington: Ministry of Justice.

Mishra, R. (1999) *Globalization and the Welfare State*. Cheltenham: Edward Elgar.

Miyazawa, S. (1992) *Policing in Japan: A Study on Making Crime*. Translated by F.G. Bennett, Jr and J.O. Haley. Albany, NY: State University of New York Press.

Miyazawa, K., Tomita, N. and Tatsuno, B. (1996) *A Study on Victims of Crime*. Tokyo: Seibundo.

Molenaar, B. and Neufeld, R. (2003) 'The use of privatized detention centres for asylum seekers in Australia and the UK'. Chapter 11 in Coyle et al. (2003).

Morita, A. (2002) 'Juvenile justice in Japan: a historical and cross-cultural perspective', in M.K. Rosenheim, F.E. Zimring, D.S. Tanenhaus and B. Dohrn (eds), *A Century of Juvenile Justice*. Chicago and London: University of Chicago Press, Chapter 13.

Moriyama, T. (1989) 'Informal mechanism of crime control in Japan', *Takushoku University Journal*, Vol. 178: 17–37.

Moriyama, T. (1992) 'Japan' in G.R. Newman, (ed.), *World Factbook of Criminal Justice Systems*. Available online at: http://www.ojp.usdoj.gov/bjs/pub/ascii/wfbcjjap.txt

Moriyama, T. (1995) 'The structure of social control in Japan: why do we enjoy a low crime rate?', in R. Jakob, M. Usteri and R. Weimar (eds), *Psyche, Recht, Gesellschaft: Widmungsschrift für Manfred Rehbinder*. Bern: Verlag Stämpfli + Cie, AG, pp. 47–66.

Morris, A. (2004) 'Youth justice in New Zealand', in M. Tonry and A.N. Doob (eds), *Crime and Justice: A Review of Research*, 31. Chicago: University of Chicago Press, pp. 243–92.

Morris, A., Giller, H., Swed, E. and Geach, H. (1980) *Justice for Children*. London: Macmillan.

Morris, N. (1974) *The Future of Imprisonment*. London: University of Chicago Press.

Mukherjee, S., Carcach, C. and Higgins, K. (1997) *Juvenile Crime and Justice*. Australian Institute of Criminology Research and Public Policy Series No. 11. Also available online at: http://www.aic.gov.au/publications/rpp/11/index.html

Muncie, J. (1999) 'Institutionalized intolerance: youth justice and the 1998 Crime and Disorder Act'. *Critical Social Policy*, 19: 147–75.

Muncie, J. and Hughes, G. (2002) 'Modes of youth governance: political rationalities, criminalization and resistance', in J. Muncie, G. Hughes and E. McLaughlin (eds), *Youth Justice: Critical Readings*. London: Sage, Chapter 1.

Muncie, J. and Sparks, R. (eds) (1991) *Imprisonment: European Perspectives*. London: Harvester Wheatsheaf.

Muntingh, L.M. (2003) *Children in Conflict with the Law: A Compendium of Child Justice Statistics 1995–2001*. Cape Town: NICRO. Also available online at: http://www.childjustice.org.za/research.htm

Muntingh, L.M. and Shapiro, R. (1997) *NICRO Diversion Options*. Cape Town: NICRO. Also available online at: http://www.nicro.org.za/articles-DiversionOptions.PDF

Murayama, M. (1992) 'Postwar trends in the administration of Japanese criminal justice: lenient but intolerant or something else?', *Journal of the Japan-Netherlands Institute*, 4: 221–56.

Murphy, J. (1979) *Retribution, Justice and Therapy: Essays in the Philosophy of Law.* London: D. Reidel Publishing.

Murray, C. (1997) 'The ruthless truth: prison works', *Sunday Times*, 12 January 1997.

NACRO, (1995) 'Life sentence prisoners', National Association for the Care and Resettlement of Offenders Briefing Papers.

NACRO (1999) *Contrasting Judgements: Report on Two International Sentencing Seminars.* London: NACRO.

Naffine, N. and Wundersitz, J. (1994) 'Trends in juvenile justice', in D. Chappell and P. Wilson (eds), *The Australian Criminal Justice System: The Mid-1990s.* Sydney: Butterworths, Chapter 11.

Nagel, P. (1999) 'A comparative overview of the Japanese and American juvenile justice systems'. Available online at: http://www.nichibei.org/je/nagel.html

Nagle, J.F. (1978) *Report of the Royal Commission into NSW Prisons.* Sydney: NSWGPS.

Nathan, S. (2003a) 'Prison privatization in the United Kingdom', in Coyle et al. (2003), Chapter14.

Nathan, S. (2003b) 'Prison privatisation'. Seminar held on 26 August 2003 at the Vineyard Hotel, Cape Town.

Nathan, S. (2004) 'Globalisation and private prisons', *Howard League Magazine*, 22: 7–8.

National Police Agency (n.d.) 'Overviews of the system of suspect detention'. Available on-line at: http://www.npa.go.jp/ryuchi/Eseido1.html

National Swedish Council for Crime Prevention (1977) *Nytt Straffsystem: Idéer och Förslag.* Rapport 1977: 7. Stockholm: Brottsförebyggande rådet.

Nehlin, C. (2000) 'VOM trial in Sweden provides opportunity for progam support and evaluation', *VOMA Newsletter* Volume 7, pp. 9–10. Also available online at: http://www.voma.org/docs/connect7.pdf

Nelken, D. (2002) 'Comparing criminal justice', in Maguire et al. (2002), pp. 175–202.

Netherlands Ministry of Justice (2000) *Inflow into Juvenile Judicial Institutions.* Available online at: http://www.minjust.nl:8080/a_beleid/thema/jeugd/jcp/stats/dji/table/tab_001.htm

Netherlands Ministry of Justice (2001a) *HALT-diversion Statistics.* Available online at: http://www.minjust.nl:8080/a_beleid/thema/jeugd/jcp/def_jcp.htm

Netherlands Ministry of Justice (2001b) *Alternative Sanctions for Juveniles.* Available online at: http://www.minjust.nl:8080/a_beleid/ thema/jeugd/jcp/stats/kinderbs/table/tab_001.htm

New Zealand Department of Corrections (1999) *Census of Prison Inmates, Time Series Data.* Also available online at: http://www.corrections.govt.nz/publications/index.asp?parent_id=574

New Zealand Department of Corrections (2003) *Census of Prison Inmates and Home Detainees 2001.* New Zealand Dept. of Corrections. Also available online at: http://www.corrections.govt.nz/public/pdf/research/census/census2001.pdf

Newburn, T., Crawford, A., Earle, R., Goldie, S., Hale, C., Hallam, A., Masters, G., Netton, A., Saunders, R., Sharpe, K. and Uglow, S. (2002) *The Introduction of Referral Orders into the Youth Justice System: Final Report.* Home Office Research Study no. 242. London: Home Office Research, Development and Statistics Directorate. Also available online at: http://www.homeoffice.gov.uk/rds/pdfs2/hors242.pdf

O'Connor, I. (1998) 'Models of juvenile justice' in C. Alder (ed.), *Juvenile Crime and Juvenile Justice.* Australian Institute of Criminology Research and Public Policy Series, No. 14.

Ormerod, P. (1997) 'Stopping crime spreading', *New Economy*, 4: 83–8.

Orwell, G. (1990) *Nineteen Eighty-Four.* London: Penguin Books.

Packer, H.L. (1969) *The Limits of the Criminal Sanction*. Stanford, California: Stanford University Press.

Pakes, F. (2004) 'The Politics of Discontent: The Emergence of a New Criminal Justice Discourse in the Netherlands', *Howard Journal of Criminal Justice*, 43: 284–98.

Pampel, F.C., Williamson, J.B. and Stryker, R. (1990) 'Class context and pension response to demographic structure in advanced industrial democracies', *Social Problems*, 37: 535–47.

Pavarini, M. (1994) 'The new penology and politics in crisis: the Italian case', *British Journal of Criminology*, 34, Special Issue: 49–61.

Pavarini, M. (2001) 'Italy – the politics of punishment: the death of prison reform in Italy', in van Zyl Smit and Dünkel (2001), pp. 400–24.

Peach, F. (1999) 'Corrections in the balance: a review of corrective services in Queensland, January 1999. Queensland Corrective Service Review, Level 15, 215 Adelaide Street, Brisbane, Queensland 4000, Australia. Also available online at: www.qcsc.qld.gov.au/globals/what's new/corrserv.pdf

Pease, K. (1982) ' Prison sentences and population: a comparison of some European countries', *Justice of the Peace*, 146: 575–9.

Pease, K. (1991) 'Talk at the Annual General Meeting of the British Society of Criminology'. Unpublished paper.

Pease, K. (1992) 'Punitiveness and prison populations: an international comparison', *Justice of the Peace*, 156: 405–8.

Pease, K. (1994) 'Cross-national imprisonment rates: limitations of method and possible conclusions', *British Journal of Criminology*, 34, Special Issue: 116–30.

Penal Affairs Consortium (1999) *The Prison System: Regime and Population Trends*. London: Penal Affairs Consortium.

Peng, I. (2000) 'A Fresh Look at The Japanese Welfare State', *Social Policy and Administration*, 34: 87–114.

Peters, A. (1988) 'Main currents in criminal law theory', in J. van Dijk, C. Haffmans, F. Rüter, J. Schutte and S. Stolwijk (eds), *Criminal Law in Action: An Overview of Current Issues in Western Societies*. Deventer: Kluwer Law and Taxation Publishers.

Peters, A. (1992) 'Some comparative observations on the criminal process in Holland and Japan', *Journal of the Japan-Netherlands Institute*, 4: 247–94.

Picotti, L. and de Strobel, G. (1996) 'Freiheitsentziehende Maßnahmen gegenüber Minderhährigen und Jugenstrafvollzug in Italien', in F. Dünkel and K. Meyer (eds), *Jugenstrafe und Jugendstrafvollzug* vol. 2. Freiburg: Eigenverlag des Max-Planck-Instituts Eür ausländisches und internationales Strafrecht, pp. 905–96.

Pilger, J. (1998) 'Freedom next time', *The Guardian Weekend*, 11 April 1998.

Pitts, J. (2001) 'Korrectional karaoke: New Labour and the zombification of youth justice'. *Youth Justice*, 1(2): 3–16.

Platt, A. (1977) *The Child Savers*, 2nd edn. Chicago: University of Chicago Press.

Porter, R.G. (1990) 'The privatization of prisons in the United States: a policy that Britain should not emulate', *Howard Journal of Criminal Justice*, 29: 65–81.

Pratt, J. (1987) 'Dilemmas of the alternative to custody concept: implications for New Zealand penal policy in the light of international evidence and experience', *Australian and New Zealand Journal of Criminology*, 20: 148–62.

Pratt, J. (1992) *Punishment in a Perfect Society: the New Zealand Penal System 1840–1939*. Wellington: Victoria University Press.

Pratt, J. (2000a) 'The return of the wheelbarrow men: or, the arrival of postmodern penality', *British Journal of Criminology*, 40: 127–45.

Pratt, J. (2000b) 'Emotive and ostentatious punishment: its decline and resurgence in modern society', *Punishment & Society*, 2: 417–39.

Pratt, J. and Clark, M. (2004) 'Penal populism in New Zealand'. Unpublished paper.

Prison Reform Trust (2004) *Prison Reform Trust Factfile*. July 2004. Available online at: http://www.prisonreformtrust.org.uk

Pugh, R.B. (1968) *Imprisonment in Medieval England*. Cambridge: Cambridge University Press.

Puzzanchera, C.M. (2003) 'Delinquency cases waived to Criminal Court, 1990–1999. Available online from the OJJDP web-site at www.ojp.usdoj.gov/ojjdp

Puzzanchera, C., Stahl, A., Finnegan, T.A., Tierney, N. and Snyder, H. (2003) *Juvenile Court Statistics 1999*. Office of Juvenile Justice and Delinquency Prevention. Washington: US Department of Justice, Office of Juvenile Justice and Delinquency Prevention.

Qvortrup, J. (1979) 'A voice for children in statistical and social accounting: a plea for children's rights to be heard', in A. James and A. Prout (eds), *Constructing and Reconstructing Childhood*. London: Falmer.

Ramseyer, J.M. and Rasmusen, E.B. (1999) 'Why is the Japanese conviction rate so high?' Available online at: http://econwpa.wustl.edu:8089/eps/le/papers/9907/9907001.pdf

Randla, R. (1995) 'Community based corrections: an integral part of the Victorian penal system (Australia)'. Paper presented to the Socio-Legal Studies Association, University of Leeds, 27–29 March 1995.

Rawls, J. (1972) *A Theory of Justice*. Oxford: Oxford University Press.

Research and Training Institute (1993) *Summary of the White Paper on Crime*: Tokyo: Ministry of Justice.

Robert, V.P. (1992) *Entre l'Ordre et la Liberté: La Détention Provisoire. Deux Siècles de Débats*. Paris: L'Harmattan.

Roberts, J.V. and Hough, M. (eds) (2002) *Changing Attitudes to Punishment: Public Opinion, Crime and Justice*. Cullompton: Willan.

Robinson, J.A. (1997) *The Law of Children and Young Persons in South Africa*. Durban: Butterworths.

Roper, C. (1989) *Prison Review: Te Ara Hou – The New Way*. Wellington, New Zealand: Ministerial Inquiry into the Prisons System.

Roth, L. (2004) 'Privatisation of prisons', Background Paper No. 3/04 produced for the New South Wales Parliament. Available online at: http://www.parliament.nsw.gov.au/prod/parlment/

Royal Commission into Aboriginal Deaths in Custody (1991) *National Report*. Canberra: AGPS.

Ruggiero, V. (1995) 'Flexibility and intermittent emergency in the Italian penal system', in Ruggiero et al. (1995), pp. 46–70.

Ruggiero, V. (1998) 'The country of Cesare Beccaria: the myth of rehabilitation in Italy', in Weiss and South (1998), pp. 207–32.

Ruggiero, V., Ryan, M. and Sim, J. (eds) (1995) *Western European Penal Systems: A Critical Anatomy*. London: Sage Publications.

Rusche, G. and Kirchheimer, O. (1939) *Punishment and Social Structure*. New York: Columbia University Press.

Rutherford, A. (1986) *Prisons and the Process of Justice*. Oxford: Oxford University Press.

Rutherford, A. (1992) *Growing Out of Crime: The New Era*. Winchester: Waterside Press.

Rutherford, A. (1996) *Transforming Criminal Policy: Spheres of Influence in the United States, The Netherlands and England and Wales during the 1980s*. Winchester: Waterside Press.

Ryan, M. and Ward, T. (1989) *Privatization and the Penal System: The American Experience and the Debate in Britain*. Milton Keynes: Open University Press.

Sanders, A. (2002) 'Victim participation in an exclusionary criminal justice system', in C. Hoyle and R. Young (eds), *New Visions of Crime Victims*. Oxford: Hart Publishing, Chapter 8.

Sato, N. (1996) 'Honouring the individual', in T. Rohlen and G. LeTendre (eds), *Teaching and Learning in Japan*. Cambridge: Cambridge University Press.

Savelsberg, J.J. (1994) 'Knowledge, domination and criminal punishment', *American Journal of Sociology*, 99: 911–43.

Savelsberg, J.J. (1999) 'Knowledge, domination and criminal punishment revisited: incorporating state socialism', *Punishment and Society*, 1: 45–70.

Schiff, M. and Bazemore, G. (2002) 'Restorative conferencing for juveniles in the United States: prevalence, process and practice', in E.G.M. Weitekamp and H.-J. Kerner, (eds), *Restorative Justice: Theoretical Foundations*. Cullompton: Willan Publishing, Chapter 9.

Schönteich, M. (2000) 'South Africa's position in Africa's crime rankings', *African Security Review*, Vol. 9 No 4. Available online at: http://www.iss.co.za/Pubs/ASR/9No4/Schonteich.html.

Scottish Executive (2002) *Executive's Youth Crime Review: Report and Statement on Recommendations*. Edinburgh: Scottish Executive.

Scottish Executive (2004) *Prison Statistics, Scotland 2003*. Statistical Bulletin. Criminal Justice Series CrJ/2004/6. August 2004. Also available online at: http://www.scotland.gov.uk/stats/bulletins/00356-00.asp

Scottish Prison Service (2001) *Annual Report and Accounts 2000–2001*, SE/2001/280. Available online at: http://www.sps.gov.uk/keydocs/2000–2001/default.asp

Scottish Prison Service (2003) *Annual Report and Accounts 2002–2003*, SE/2003/190. Edinburgh: The Stationery Office. Also available online at: http://www.sps.gov.uk/reports/2002–2003/default.asp

Sellers, M.P. (1993) *The History and Politics of Private Prisons. A Comparative Analysis*. Cranbury: Associated University Press.

Seto J. (n.d.) 'Juvenile crime'. Foreign Press Centre, Japan. Available online at: http://www.fpcj.jp/e/shiryo/jc/jc.html

Shapiro, R. (1997) 'The quest for juvenile justice' in L.M. Muntingh and Shapiro (eds) (1997) *NICRO Diversion Options*. Cape Town: NICRO.

Shaw, A. (1966) *Convicts and the Colonies*. London: Faber.

Shearing, C. (1994) 'Participatory policing: modalities for lay participation', *Imbizo*, 2: 5–10.

Sheffer, J.P. (1995) 'Serious and habitual juvenile offender statutes: reconciling punishment and rehabilitation within the juvenile justice system' *Vanderbilt Law Review*, 48: 479–506.

Sherman, L., Strang, H. and Woods, D.J. (2000) *Recidivism Patterns in the Canberra Reintegrative Shaming Experiments (RISE) (Final Report)*, Canberra: ANU. Also available online at: http://www.aic.gov.au/rjustice/rise/recidivism/index.html

Shichor, D. (1995) *Punishment for Profit: Private Prisons/Public Concerns*. London: Sage.

Shikita, M. (1972) 'The rehabilitative programmes in the adult prisons in Japan' *International Review of Criminal Policy* 30: 11–19.

Shikita, M. and Tsuchiya, S. (1992) *Crime and Criminal Policy in Japan: Analysis and Evaluation of the Showa Era, 1926–1988*. New York: Springer-Verlag.

Sickmund, M. (1999) 'States with statutory exclusion, 1997', adapted from Torbet, P. and Szymanski, L. *State Legislative Responses to Violent Juvenile Crime: 1996–7 Update*. Washington DC: Office of Juvenile Justice and Delinquency Prevention, 1998. *OJJDP Statistical Briefing Book*. Available online at: http://ojjdp.ncjrs.org/ojstatbb/html/qa087.html. 1 July 1999.

Sickmund, M. (2000) *Offenders in Juvenile Court, 1997*. Washington DC: Office of Juvenile Justice and Delinquency Prevention. Also available online at: http://ojjdp.ncjrs.org/pubs/court.html#OJC

Sickmund, M. (2004) *Juveniles in Corrections*. Washington: US Department of Justice. Also available from the OJJDP website at: www.ojp.usdoj.gov/ojjdp

Sickmund, M., Sladky, T.J. and Kang, W. (2004) 'Census of juveniles in residential placement databook'. Available online at: http://www.ojjdp.ncjrs.org/ojstatbb/cjrp/

Sim, J., Ruggiero, V. and Ryan, M. (1995) 'Punishment in Europe: perceptions and commonalities', in Ruggiero et al. (1995), pp. 1–23.

Simmons, J. and Dodd, T. (eds) (2003) *Crime in England and Wales 2002/2003*, Home Office Statistical Bulletin 07/03. London: Home Office.

Simon, J. (1993) *Poor Discipline: Parole and the Social Control of the Underclass, 1890–1990*. Chicago: University of Chicago Press.

Simon, J. and Feeley, M. (1995) 'True Crime: The New Penology and Public Discourse on Crime', in T. Blomberg and S. Cohen (eds), *Punishment and Social Control: Essays in Honour of Sheldon Messinger*. New York: Aldine De Gruyter, pp. 147–80.

Sloth-Nielsen, J. (2001) 'Minimum sentences for juveniles cut down to size', Available online at: http://www.sn.apc.org/users/clc/children/minimum%20sentences2.doc

Sloth-Nielsen, J. (2003) 'Statistics on children under 14 years of age in prison', *Article 40: the Dynamics of Youth Justice and the Convention on the Rights of the Child in South Africa*. Vol. 5 (no. 1) March, 2003.

Sloth-Nielsen, J. and Muntingh, L.M. (2001) *Juvenile Justice Review 1999–2000*. Available online at: http://www.sn.apc.org/users/clc/children/jjreview9900.doc

Snyder, H.N. and Sickmund, M. (1999) *Juvenile Offenders and Victims: A National Report*. Washington DC: Office of Juvenile Justice and Delinquency Prevention.

Socialstyrelsen (National Board of Health and Welfare) (2000) *Social Services in Sweden 1999: Needs, Interventions, Development*. Stockholm: SOS.

Sonnen, B.-R. (2002) 'Juristiche Voraussetzungen des Umgangs mit Kinderdelinquenz' *DVJJ-Journal*, vol. 13: 326–31.

South African Law Commission (1997) *Juvenile Justice*. Issue Paper 9, Project 106. Pretoria: South African Law Commission.

South African Law Commission (2000) *Report on Juvenile Justice*, Project 106. Pretoria: South African Law Commission. Also available online at: http://wwwserver.law.wits.ac.za/salc/report/project106.html

South African Truth and Reconciliation Commission (1998) *The Report of the Truth and Reconciliation Commission*. Available online at: http://www.truth.org.za/final/execsum.html.

Spier, P. and Norris, M. (1993) *Conviction and Sentencing of Offenders in New Zealand, 1983–92*. Wellington, New Zealand: Ministry of Justice.

Spohn, C., Gruhl, J. and Welch, S. (1981–2) 'The effect of race on sentencing: a re-examination of an unsettled question', *Law and Society Review*, 16: 71–88.

Sridharan, S., Greenfield, L. and Blakley, B. (2004) 'A study of prosecutorial certification practice in Virginia'. *Criminology and Public Policy*, 3(4): 605–32.

Stang Dahl, T. (1985) *Child Welfare and Social Defence*. Oslo: Norwegian University Press.

Steele, J. (1997) 'South African white whine leaves sour taste', *The Guardian*, 29 March 1997.

Steering Committee for the Review of Commonwealth State Services (1997) *Reforms in Government Services 1997*. Melbourne: Steering Committee for the Review of Commonwealth/State Service Provision/Productivity Commission. Also available online at: http://www.pc.gov.au/gsp/studies/case/case.pdf (Accessed 23 September 2003).

Stephan, J. (1989) *Prison Rule Violators*, BJS Special Report. Washington, DC: US Department of Justice.

Stern, V. (1987) *Bricks of Shame: Britain's Prisons*. London: Penguin.

Stern, V. (1998) *A Sin Against the Future: Imprisonment in the World*. London: Penguin.

Stolzenberg, L. and D'Alessio, S.J. (1997) '"Three strikes and you're out". The impact of California's new mandatory sentencing law on serious crime rates', *Crime and Delinquency*, 43: 457–69.

Strang, H., Barnes, G., Braithwaite, J. and Sherman, L. (1999) *Experiments in Restorative Policing: A Progress Report on the Canberra Reintegrative Shaming Experiments (RISE)*, Australian Federal Police and Australian National University, Canberra. Also available online at: http://www.aic.gove.au/rjustice/rise/progress/1999.html

Strategos Consulting Limited (1989) *Department of Justice Management Review*. Wellington, New Zealand: Strategos Consulting Limited.

Streib, V.L. (1987) *Death Penalty for Juveniles*. Bloomington and Indianapolis, IN: Indiana University Press.

Supreme Court of Japan (2000) *Annual Report of Judicial Statistics, Criminal Cases*. Available online at: http://www.stat.go.jp/english/data/nenkan/zuhyou/b2313000.xls

Sutton, J.R. (1980) *Stubborn Children: Controlling Delinquents in the United States*. Berkeley: University of California Press.

Swedish Committee on Juvenile Delinquency (Ungdomsbrottskommitten) (1993) *Betänkande angående Reaktion mot ungdomsbrottskommitten* (Sanctions against juvenile crime), Report 1993: 35. Malmö: SOU.

Swedish National Council for Crime Prevention (BRÅ) (2000) *The Sanction System for Young Offenders (English summary)*. Stockholm: Swedish National Council for Crime Prevention. Also available online at: http://www.bra.se/dynamaster/publication/pdf_archive/00062217714.pdf

Swedish Prison Administration (2004) *Kriminalvård och Statistik 2003*. Swedish Prison Administration: Stockholm.

Tabata, H. (1990) *The Japanese Welfare State: Its Structure and Transformation*. Tokyo: University of Tokyo, Institute of Social Science.

Tak, P.J.P. (1998) 'Changes in sentencing in the Netherlands 1970–1995'. Paper presented to conference at University of Minnesota Law School, May 1–3, 1998. Nijmegen: Katholieke Universiteit Nijmegen.

Tak, P.J.P. and van Kalmthout, A.M. (1998) 'Prison population growing faster in the Netherlands than in US', *Overcrowded Times*, (9) 3: 1, 12–16.

Tanenhaus, D.S. (2002) 'The evolution of juvenile courts in the early twentieth century: beyond the myth of immaculate construction', in M.K. Rosenheim, F.E. Zimring, D.S. Tanenhaus and B. Dohrn (eds), *A Century of Juvenile Justice*. Chicago: University of Chicago Press, Chapter 2.

Tanenhaus, D.S. (2004) *Juvenile Justice in the Making*. New York: Oxford University Press.

Tavuchis, N. (1991) *Mea Culpa: a Sociology of Apology and Reconciliation*. Stanford, CA: Stanford U.P.

Terblanche, S. (1998) 'Sentencing in South Africa', in Tonry and Hatlestad (1998), pp. 172–7.

Terrill, R.J. (1992) *World Criminal Justice Systems: A Survey*, 2nd edn. Cincinnati, OH: Anderson Publishing Co.

Terrill, R.J. (1999) *World Criminal Justice Systems*, 4th edn. Cincinnati, OH: Anderson Publishing Co.

Tham, H. (1995) 'From treatment to just deserts in a changing welfare state', in A. Snare (ed.), *Beware of Punishment*, Scandinavian Studies in Criminology vol. 14. Oslo: Pax Forlag, pp. 89–122.

Tham, H. (1996) 'On the background and causes of juvenile criminality in Sweden'. Lecture given at the ELSA Workshop, Lund, April 1996.

Tham, H. (1998) 'Crime and the welfare state: the case of the United Kingdom and Sweden', in V. Ruggiero, N. South and I. Taylor (eds), *New European Criminology: Crime and Social Order in Europe*, London: Routledge, pp. 368–94.

Thomas, C. and Logan, C. (1993) 'The development, present status and future potential of correctional privatization in America', in G.W. Bowman, S. Hakim and P. Seidenstat (eds), *Privatizing Correctional Institutions*. New Brunswick: Transaction Publishers, pp. 213–40.

Thomas, C.W., Bolinger, D. and Badalmenti, J. (1997) *Private Adult Correctional Facility Census*, 10th edn. Gainesville, FL: University of Florida, Center for Studies in Criminology and Law, Private Corrections Project.

Thorp, T.M. (1997) 'Sentencing and punishment in New Zealand, 1981–1993', in Tonry and Hatlestad (1997), pp. 163–8.

Thorpe, D.H., Smith, D., Green, C.J. and Paley, J.H. (1980) *Out of Care: The Community Support of Juvenile Offenders*. London: Allen and Unwin.

Tonry, M. (2004) *Thinking About Crime: Sense and Sensibility in American Penal Culture*. Oxford: Oxford University Press.

Tonry, M. and Frase, R.S. (eds) (2001) *Sentencing and Sanctions in Western Countries*. Oxford: Oxford University Press.

Tonry, M. and Hatlestad, K. (eds) (1997) *Sentencing Reform in Overcrowded Times: A Comparative Perspective*. Oxford: Oxford University Press.

Torbet, P. and Szymanski, L. (1998) *State Legislative Responses to Violent Juvenile Crime: 1996–97 Update*. Washington DC: Office of Juvenile Justice and Delinquency Prevention.

Torbet, P., Gable, R., Hurst IV, H., Montgomery, I., Szymanski, L. and Thomas, D. (1996) *State Responses to Serious and Violent Juvenile Crime: Research Report*. Washington DC: Office of Juvenile Justice and Delinquency Prevention, National Centre for Juvenile Justice.

Törnudd, P. (1993) *Fifteen Years of Decreasing Prisoner Rates in Finland*. Helsinki: Oikeuspolittinen Tutkimuslaitos.

Törnudd, P. (1997) '15 years of decreasing prisoner rates in Finland', in HEUNI (1997) *Prison Population in Europe and in North America: Problems and Solutions*. Helsinki: Ministry of Justice, pp. 245–68.

Umbreit, M. and Greenwood, J. (1998) *National Survey of Victim Offender Mediation Programs in the US*. University of Minnesota: Center for Restorative Justice and Peacemaking.

UNAFEI (2000) *Criminal Justice in Japan*. Available online at: http://www.unafei.or.jp/english/publications/criminal_justice.html

United Nations General Assembly (1985) *United Nations Standard Minimum Rules for the Administration of Juvenile Justice ('The Beijing Rules')*. Adopted by General Assembly resolution 40/33 of 29 November 1985. Also available online at: http://www.unhchr.ch/html/menu3/b/h_comp48.htm

United Nations General Assembly (1989) *Convention on the Rights of the Child*. Document A/RES/44/25 (12 December 1989). Also available online at: http://www.cirp.org/library/ethics/UN-convention/

United Nations Human Rights Committee (2002) *Concluding Observations on New Zealand*. CCPR/CO/75/NZL. 7 August 2002. Also available online at: http://www.hri.ca/forthere-cord2002/documentation/tbodies/ccpr-co-75-nzl.htm (Accessed 2 October 2003).

United Nations Office on Drugs and Crime (2004) *The Seventh United Nations Survey on Crime Trends and the Operations of Criminal Justice Systems (1998–2000)*. Available online at: http://www.unodc.org/unodc/crime_cicp_survey_seventh.html

USA Today (2003) 'Growing prison populations challenge already cash-strapped states', *USA Today*, 27 July 2003.

US Bureau of Justice (2003) *Statistics Bulletin*, April 2003. NCJ 1988877.

US Bureau of Justice (2004) *Prison and Jail Inmates at Midyear 2003*, Bureau of Justice Statistics Bulletin, US. Also available online at: http://www.ojp.usdoj.gov

USDOJ (2002) *United States Department of Justice Performance Report 2002*. Available online at: http://www.usdoj.gov/ag/annualreports/pr2000/NEWSG5.htm (Accessed 13 November 2003).

Vagg, J. (1994) *Prison Systems: A Comparative Study of Accountability in England, France, Germany and the Netherlands*. Oxford: Clarendon Press.

van der Laan, P.H. (1988) 'Innovations in the Dutch juvenile justice system: alternative sanctions', in J. Junger-Tas and R.L. Block, *Juvenile Delinquency in the Netherlands*. Amsterdam: Kugler Publications, pp. 203-39.

von der Laan, P.H. (2003a) 'Police and judicial reactions to youth crime – the situation in the Netherlands', in F. Dünkel (ed.), *Youth Violence: New Patterns and Local Responses – Experiences in East and West*, Mönchengladbach: Forum Verlag Godesberg, pp. 78-85.

van der Veen, R. and Trommel, W. (1998) *The Dutch Miracle: Managed Liberalisation of the Dutch Welfare State: A Review and Analysis of the the Reform of the Dutch Social Security System 1985-97*. London: IPPR Publications.

van Dijk, J.J.M. and Mayhew, P. (1992) *Criminal Victimization in the Industrialized World: Key Findings of the 1989 and 1992 International Crime Surveys*. The Hague: Directorate for Crime Prevention, Ministry of Justice.

van Heerden, J. (1996) *Prison Health Care in South Africa*. Cape Town: University of Cape Town.

van Kalmthout, A. and Tak, P. (1988) *Sanctions-Systems in the Member States of the Council of Europe*. Deventer: Kluwer.

van Swaaningen, R. and de Jonge, G. (1995) 'The Dutch prison system and penal policy in the 1990s: from humanitarian paternalism to penal business management', in Ruggiero et al. (1995), pp. 24-45.

van Zyl Smit, D. (1996) 'Some features of correctional reform in South Africa'. Unpublished paper.

van Zyl Smit, D. (1998) 'Change and continuity in South African prisons', in Weiss and South (1998), pp. 401-26.

van Zyl Smit, D. (1999) 'Criminological ideas and the South African transition', *British Journal of Criminology*, 39: 198-215.

van Zyl Smit, D. (2000) 'Mandatory sentences: a conundrum for the New South Africa?', *Punishment & Society*, 2: 197-212.

van Zyl Smit, D. (2001a) 'South Africa', in van Zyl Smit. and Dünkel (2001), pp. 589-608.

van Zyl Smit, D. (2001b) 'Tough justice: South African style?', in E. Fattah and S. Parmentier (2001), *Victim Policies and Criminal Justice on the Road to Restorative Justice: Essays in Honour of Tony Peters*. Leuven: Leuven University Press.

van Zyl Smit, D. (2004) 'Swimming against the tide', in B. Dixon and E. van der Spuy (eds), *Justice Gained? Crime and Crime Control in South Africa's Transition*. Cullompton: Willan, pp. 227-58.

van Zyl Smit, D. and Dünkel, F. (eds) (1991) *Imprisonment Today and Tomorrow: International Perspectives on Prisoners' Rights and Prison Conditions*, 1st edn. Deventer: Kluwer Law International.

van Zyl Smit, D. and Dünkel, F. (eds) (2001) *Imprisonment Today and Tomorrow: International Perspectives on Prisoners' Rights and Prison Conditions*, 2nd edn. The Hague: Kluwer Law International.

van Zyl Smit, D. and van der Spuy, E. (2004) '"Importing criminological ideas in a new democracy: recent South African experiences"', in T. Newburn and R. Sparks (eds), *Criminal Justice and Political Cultures*. Cullompton: Willan, pp. 184-233.

Vasseur, V. (2000) *Médecin-chef à la Prison de la Santé*. Paris: La Cherche Midi.

Victorian Sentencing Committee (Starke Committee) (1989) *Sentencing: Report of the Victorian Sentencing Committee*. Melbourne: Attorney-General's Department.

von Hirsch, A. (1976) *Doing Justice: The Choice of Punishments* (Report of the Committee for the Study of Incarceration). New York: Hill and Wang.

von Hirsch, A. (1993) *Censure and Sanctions*. Oxford: Clarendon Press.

von Hofer, H. (2000) 'Electronic monitoring of offenders in Sweden'. Unpublished paper.

von Hofer, H. (2001) 'Crime and punishment in Scandinavia: an overview', in Scandinavian Research Council for Criminology, *Social Change and Crime in Scandinavian and Baltic Region*. Copenhagen: Scandinavian Research Council for Criminology, pp. 35–49.

von Hofer, H. (2002) 'Prison population and prison policy in Holland'. Unpublished paper.

van Hofer, H. (2003a) 'Entwicklunstendenzen und Reformstrategien im Schwedischen Jugendstrafrecht'. Available online at: http://www.crim.su.se/downloads/SCHWED2.PDF

von Hofer, H. (2003b) 'Prison populations as political constructs: the case of Finland, Holland and Sweden', *Journal of Scandinavian Studies in Criminology and Crime Prevention*, 4: 21–38.

von Hofer, H. (2004) '"Die dummen Schweden" oder Warum steigen die Gefangenenzahlen in Schweden?'. Unpublished paper.

von Hofer, H. and Marvin, R. (2001) 'Swedish prisons', in van Zyl Smit and Dünkel (2001), pp. 653–75.

von Hofer, H., Sarnecki, J. and Tham, H. (1997) 'Minorities, crime, and criminal justice in Sweden', in I.H. Marshall (ed.), *Minorities, Migrants and Crime: Diversity and Similarity Across Europe and the United States*, Thousand Oaks: Sage, pp. 62–85.

Wagatsuma, H. and Rosett, A. (1986) 'The implications of apology: law and culture in Japan and the United States'. *Law and Society Review*, 20: 461–98.

Walgrave, L. (2004) 'Restoration in Youth Justice', in M. Tonry and A. N. Doob (eds), *Youth Crime and Youth Justice: Comparative and Cross-National Perspectives*. Crime and Justice: A Review of Research, Vol. 31. Chicago and London: University of Chicago Press, pp. 543–97.

Walker, J. (1994) 'User-friendly prisoner forecasting', *Criminology Australia*, Jan/Feb., 21.

Walker, J., Collier, P. and Tarling, R. (1990) 'Why are prison rates in England and Wales higher than in Australia?', *British Journal of Criminology*, 30: 24–35.

Walmsley, R. (1997) *Prison Populations in Europe and North America: Some Background Information*, HEUNI Paper no. 10. Helsinki: HEUNI.

Walmsley, R. (1999) *World Prison Population List*. Research, Development and Statistics Directorate Research Findings no. 88. London: HMSO. Also available online at: http://www.homeoffice.gov.uk/rds/rfpubs1.html

Walmsley, R. (2000) *World Prison Population List*, 2nd edn. Home Office Walmsley, R. (2001) 'World prison populations: an attempt at a complete list', in van Zyl Smit and Dünkel (2001), pp. 775–95.

Walmsley, R. (2002) *World Prison Population List*, 3rd edn. Home Office Research Findings 166. London: Home Office. Also available online at: http://www.homeoffice.gov.uk/rds/rfpubs1.html

Walmsley, R. (2003a) *World Prison Population List*, 4th edn. Home Office Research Findings 188. London: Home Office. Also available online at: http://www.homeoffice.gov.uk/rds/rfpubs1.html

Walmsley, R. (2003b) *World Prison Population List*, 5th edn. Home Office Research Findings 234. London: Home Office. Also available online at: http://www.homeoffice.gov.uk/rds/rfpubs1.html

Watt, E. (2003) *A History of Youth Justice in New Zealand*. Available online at: http:// www.justice.govt.nz/youth/history/

Weber, M. (1968) *Economy and Society: An Outline of Interpretive Sociology*. New York: Bedminster Press.

Weigend, T. (1997) 'Germany reduces use of prison sentences', in Tonry and Hatlestad (1997), pp. 177–81.

Weijers, I. (2002) 'The youth court: its justification and its requirements'. Conference paper presented at the second international conference on Sentencing and Society, Glasgow, June 2002.

Weiss, R.P. and South, N. (eds) (1998) *Comparing Prison Systems: Toward a Comparative and International Penology*. Amsterdam: Gordon and Breach.

Weitekamp, E.G.M., Kerner, H.-J. and Herberger, S.M. (1998) 'Germany', in Mehlbye and L. Walgrave (eds), *Confronting Youth in Europe: Juvenile Crime and Juvenile Justice*. Copenhagen: AFK Forlaget, Chapter 7.

West, D.J. (1982) *Delinquency: Its Roots, Careers and Prospects*. London: Heinemann.

Western, B. and Beckett, K. (1999) 'How unregulated is the US labor market? The penal system as labor market institution', *American Journal of Sociology*, 104: 1030–60.

White, P. and Powar, I. (1998) *Revised Predictions of Long Term Trends in the Prison Population to 2005*, Home Office Statistical Bulletin 2/98. London: Home Office.

White, P., Woodbridge, J. and Flack, K. (1999) *Projections of Long Term Trends in the Prison Population to 2006*, Home Office Statistical Bulletin 1/99. London: Home Office.

Wilbanks, W. (1987) *The Myth of a Racist Criminal Justice System*. Monterey: Brooks/Cole Publishing.

Wilkins, L.T. and Pease, K. (1987) 'Public demand for punishment', *International Journal of Sociology and Social Policy*, 7: 16–29.

Wood, F. (1996) 'Cost-Effective Ideas in Penology: The Minnesota Approach', *Corrections Today*, 58: 52–6.

Wood, P.J. (2003) 'The rise of the prison industrial complex in the United States', Chapter 1 in Coyle et al. (2003).

Woolf, H. and Tumim, S. (1991) *Prison Disturbances April 1990*, Cm. 1456. London: HMSO.

Wundersitz, J. (1994) 'Family conferencing and juvenile justice reform in South Australia', in C. Alder and J. Wundersitz (eds), *Family Conferencing and Juvenile Justice: The Way Forward or Misplaced Confidence?* Canberra: Australian Institute of Criminology, Chapter 4.

Wundersitz, J. (1996) *The South Australian Juvenile Justice System: A Review of its Operation*. Adelaide, South Australia: Office of Criminal Statistics.

Yamasaki, Y. and Hosaka, T. (1995) *Social Security in Japan*. Tokyo: Foreign Press Centre.

Yoshida, T. (2000) 'Confession, apology, repentance and settlement out-of-court in the Japanese criminal justice system: is Japan a model of "restorative justice"'? Paper presented at the 4th International Conference on Restorative Justice for Juveniles, Tübingen, Germany, 1–4 October 2000.

Yoshida, T. (2001) 'The future of the Japanese criminal justice system: from retributive-deterrent-oriented criminal justice towards restorative justice'. Paper presented at the fifth International Conference on Restorative Justice for Juveniles, Leuven, Belgium, 16–19 September 2001.

Young, W. (1986) 'Influences upon the use of imprisonment: a review of the literature', *Howard Journal of Criminal Justice*, 25: 125–36.

Young, W. and Brown, M. (1993) 'Cross-national comparisons of imprisonment', in M. Tonry (ed.), *Crime and Justice: A Review of Research*, 17: 1–49. Chicago: University of Chicago Press.

Younge, G. (1998) 'Mandela's OK, but he's no John Pilger', *The Guardian*, 22 April 1998.

Youth Justice Board (2001) 'Curb short term custody – end justice by geography'. Press release, 9 October, 2001. Youth Justice Board.

Youth Justice Board (2004) *Youth Justice Annual Statistics 2003/2004*. London: Youth Justice Board. Also available online at: http:www/youth-justice-board.gov.uk/Publications/Downloads/Annual%20Statistics%200304%20Full.pdf

Zaal, F.N. and Matthias, C.R. (1996) 'Journeys to nowhere: moving children from juvenile courts to children's courts' in J. Sloth-Nielsen (ed.), *South African Juvenile Justice: Law Practice and Policy*. Unpublished. Cape Town: Community Law Centre, University of Western Cape.

Zimring, F. and Hawkins, G. (1991) *The Scale of Imprisonment*. Chicago: University of Chicago Press.

Zimring, F.E., Hawkins, G. and Kamin, S. (2001) *Punishment and Democracy: Three Strikes and You're Out in California*. Oxford: Oxford University Press.

Index